THIRD CANADIAN EDITION
BUSINESS COMMUNICATION
BUILDING CRITICAL SKILLS

Kitty O. Locker
The Ohio State University

Stephen Kyo Kaczmarek
Columbus State Community College

Kathryn Braun
Sheridan Institute of Technology and Advanced Learning

McGraw-Hill Ryerson

Toronto   Montréal   Boston   Burr Ridge, IL   Dubuque, IA   Madison, WI   New York   San Francisco   St. Louis   Bangkok
Bogotá   Caracas   Kuala Lumpur   Lisbon   London   Madrid   Mexico City   Milan   New Delhi   Santiago Seoul
Singapore   Sydney   Taipei

McGraw-Hill Ryerson

Business Communication
Third Edition

Statistics Canada information is used with the permission of the Minister of Industry, as Minister responsible for Statistics Canada. Information on the availability of the wide range of data from Statistics Canada can be obtained from Statistics Canada's Regional Offices, its World Wide Web site at http://www.statcan.ca, and its toll-free access number 1-800-263-1136.

ISBN-13: 978-0-07-095826-5
ISBN-10: 0-07-095826-2

2 3 4 5 6 7 8 9 10 QPV 0 9 8 7

Printed and bound in the United States

The Conference Board of Canada
Insights You Can Count On

The Conference Board of Canada's Employability Skills 2000+ are used with the permission of The Conference Board of Canada. Information about The Conference Board of Canada is available at http://www.conferenceboard.ca.

Sponsoring Editor: Lisa Rahn
Marketing Manager: Marc Trudel
Developmental Editor: Christine Gilbert
Editorial Associate: Christine Lomas
Supervising Editor: Elizabeth Priest
Copy Editor: Gillian Scobie
Production Coordinator: Zonia Strynatka

Cover and Interior Design: Greg Devitt
Cover Image: Baker, Ryan McVay/Getty Images;
couple, Stockbyte/PunchStock;
Interview, Digital Vision/Getty Images;
meeting, StockBytePlatinum/Getty Images.
Page Layout: S R Nova Pvt Ltd., Bangalore, India
Printer: Quebecor Printing Versailles (U.S.)

Library and Archives Canada Cataloguing in Publication

Locker, Kitty O
    Business communication: building critical skills / Kitty O. Locker,
Stephen Kyo Kaczmarek, Kathryn Braun. – 3rd Canadian ed.

Includes bibliographical references and index.

ISBN-13: 978-0-07-095826-5
ISBN-10: 0-07-095826-2

1. Business communication–Textbooks. 2. Business writing–Textbooks. 3. Communication in organizations–Textbooks. I. Kaczmarek, Stephen Kyo II. Hughes, Kathryn, 1945– III. Title.

HF5718.L63   2007   658.4'5   C2006-904145-8

Brief Contents

■ Unit One
Building Effective Messages 2

MODULE 1   Introduction to Business Communication   4

MODULE 2   Adapting Your Message to Your Audience   24

MODULE 3   Communicating across Cultures   46

MODULE 4   Planning, Writing, and Revising   70

MODULE 5   Designing Documents, Slides, and Screens   86

■ Unit Two
Creating Goodwill   104

MODULE 6   You-Attitude   106

MODULE 7   Positive Emphasis   120

MODULE 8   Reader Benefits   134

■ Unit Three
Letters, Memos, and Email Messages   148

MODULE 9   Formats for Hard-Copy Letters and Memos   150

MODULE 10   Email Messages   168

MODULE 11   Informative and Positive Messages   182

MODULE 12   Negative Messages   204

MODULE 13   Persuasive Messages   226

■ Unit Four
Polishing Your Writing   256

MODULE 14   Revising Sentences and Paragraphs   258

MODULE 15   Choosing the Right Word   278

MODULE 16   Editing for Grammar and Punctuation   296

■ Unit Five
Interpersonal Communication   320

MODULE 17   Listening   322

MODULE 18   Working and Writing in Teams   332

MODULE 19   Planning, Managing, and Recording Meetings   350

MODULE 20   Making Oral Presentations   364

■ Unit Six
Research, Reports, and Visuals   382

MODULE 21   Finding, Analyzing, and Documenting Information   384

MODULE 22   Proposals and Progress Reports   404

MODULE 23   More Short Reports   424

MODULE 24   Formal Reports   440

MODULE 25   Using Visuals   466

■ Unit Seven
Job Hunting   486

MODULE 26   Researching Jobs   488

MODULE 27   Creating Persuasive Résumés   502

MODULE 28   Job Application Letters   528

MODULE 29   Preparing for Job Interviews   544

MODULE 30   Following the Interview: Follow-up Letters and Emails, and Job Offers   560

Contents

About the Authors   xiv

Preface   xv

Acknowledgements   xxiii

Walkthrough   xxiv

■ Unit One
Building Effective Messages   2

OPENING VIGNETTE   3

■ **MODULE 1**   Introduction to Business Communication   4

How is business communication different?   5

What does business communication accomplish?   7

What communications skills are integral to business success?   8

Will I really have to write?   9

How much does correspondence cost?   10

What makes a message effective?   11

The Benefits of Becoming a Better Writer   11

How do I begin to analyze business communication situations?   11

Expanding a Critical Skill: Thinking Creatively   12

Employability Skills 2000+   15

Review of Key Points   17

Assignments for Module 1   17

■ *Polishing Your Prose: Sentence Fragments   21*

Online Learning Centre   22

■ **MODULE 2**   Adapting Your Message to Your Audience   24

Who is my audience?   25

Why is audience so important?   25

Audience and the Communication Process   25

Audience and Business Messages   28

What do I need to know about my audience?   29

Analyzing Individuals and Members of Groups   29

Expanding a Critical Skill: Understanding What Your Organization Wants   31

Analyzing People in Organizations   34

How do I use audience analysis to reach my audience?   36

What if my audiences have different needs?   37

How do I reach my audience?   38

Employability Skills 2000+   40

Review of Key Points   40

Assignments for Module 2   40

■ *Polishing Your Prose: Comma Splices   44*

Online Learning Centre   45

■ **MODULE 3**   Communicating across Cultures   46

What is culture?   47

What is Canadian culture?   47

How does culture impact business communication?   48

Values, Beliefs, and Practices   49

Expanding a Critical Skill: Dealing with Discrimination   50

Non-verbal Communication   51

Body Language   52

Time   54

Other Non-verbal Symbols   55

Oral Communication   55

Writing to International Audiences   57

With so many different cultures, how can I know enough to communicate?   58

How can I make my documents bias free?   59

Making Language Non-sexist   59

Making Language Non-racist and Non-agist   61

Talking about People with Disabilities and Diseases   62

Choosing Bias-Free Photos and Illustrations   63

Employability Skills 2000+   64

Review of Key Points   64

Assignments for Module 3   64

■ *Polishing Your Prose: Using Idioms* 68
Online Learning Centre 69

MODULE 4 Planning, Writing, and Revising 70

What is the writing process? 71
Does it matter what process I use? 72
How should I approach business writing? 73
I don't have much time. How should I use it? 73
What planning should I do before I begin writing or speaking? 74
What is revision? How do I do it? 77
Can a grammar checker edit for me? 79
I use a spell checker. Do I still need to proofread? 79
How can I get better feedback? 80
Expanding a Critical Skill: Revising after Feedback 81
Can I use form letters? 81
How can I overcome writer's block? 82
Employability Skills 2000+ 83
Review of Key Points 83
Assignments for Module 4 83
■ *Polishing Your Prose: Commas in Lists* 85
Online Learning Centre 85

MODULE 5 Designing Documents, Slides, and Screens 86

Why is design important? 87
When should I think about design? 87
How should I design paper pages? 87
  Use White Space 87
  Use Headings 88
  Limit the Use of Words Set in All Capital Letters 89
  Use No More Than Two Fonts in a Single Document 91
  Decide Whether to Justify Margins Based on the Situation and the Audience 92
How should I design presentation slides? 92
How should I design Web pages? 93
Expanding a Critical Skill: Using Computer Software to Create Good Design 94
How do I know whether my design works? 95
Employability Skills 2000+ 96

Review of Key Points 96
Assignments for Module 5 96
■ *Polishing Your Prose: Active and Passive Voice 101*
Online Learning Centre 102
CBC Video Case 102
Cases for Communicators 102

■ Unit Two
Creating Goodwill 104
OPENING VIGNETTE 105

MODULE 6 You-Attitude 106
What is you-attitude in writing? 107
How do I create you-attitude? 107
  1. Talk about the Reader, not about Yourself 109
  2. Avoid Talking about Feelings, Except to Congratulate or Offer Sympathy 109
  3. Use *You* More Often Than *I* in Positive Situations. Use *We* When it Includes the Reader 110
  4. Avoid *You* in Negative Situations 110
Expanding a Critical Skill: Seeing Another Point of View 111
Does you-attitude mean using the word *you*? 112
I've revised my sentences. Do I need to do anything else? 112
Employability Skills 2000+ 116
Review of Key Points 116
Assignments for Module 6 116
■ *Polishing Your Prose: It's/Its 118*
Online Learning Centre 118

MODULE 7 Positive Emphasis 120
What's the point of positive emphasis? 121
What should I do if my message is bad news? 121
How do I create positive emphasis? 122
  Negative Words and Words with Negative Connotations 122
Expanding a Critical Skill: Using Positive Emphasis Ethically 125
  Focus on What the Reader Can Do Rather Than on Limitations 125

Justify Negative Information by Giving a
Reason or Linking It to a Reader Benefit   126
Omit the Negative If It Is Truly Unimportant   126
Bury the Negative Information and Present It
Compactly   126

Why do I need to think about tone, politeness,
and power?   127

What's the best way to apologize?   129

Employability Skills 2000+   130

Review of Key Points   130

Assignments for Module 7   130

■ *Polishing Your Prose: Singular and Plural
Possessives   133*

Online Learning Centre   133

MODULE 8   Reader Benefits   134

Why do reader benefits work?   135

How do I identify reader benefits?   135

1. Think of Feelings, Fears, and Needs That May
Motivate Your Reader   135

2. Identify the Objective Features of Your
Product or Policy, Then Think How These
Features Could Benefit the Audience   137

How detailed should each benefit be?   138

How do I decide which benefits to use?   140

1. Use at Least One Benefit for Each Subgroup
in Your Audience   140

2. Use Intrinsic Benefits   140

Expanding a Critical Skill: Matching the Benefit to
the Audience   141

3. Use the Benefits You Can Develop Most
Fully   142

What else do reader benefits need?   143

Employability Skills 2000+   144

Review of Key Points   144

Assignments for Module 8   144

■ *Polishing Your Prose: Plurals and
Possessives   146*

Online Learning Centre   146

CBC Video Case   146

Case for Communicators   146

Unit Three
Letters, Memos, and Email
Messages   148

OPENING VIGNETTE   149

**MODULE 9   Formats for Hard-Copy
Letters and Memos   150**

What are the standard formats for letters?   151

Expanding a Critical Skill: Creating a Business
Image   155

What courtesy titles should I use?   158

When You Know the Reader's Name but Not the
Gender   160

When You Know Neither the Reader's Name nor
Gender   160

How should I set up hard-copy memos?   161

Employability Skills 2000+   165

Review of Key Points   165

Assignments for Module 9   165

■ *Polishing Your Prose: Making Subjects and
Verbs Agree   166*

Online Learning Centre   167

MODULE 10 Email Messages   168

What do I need to know about email
messages?   169

How should I set up email messages?   170

What should I know about content and tone?   172

Do I write email messages the same way I write
paper messages?   173

Writing Positive and Informative Email
Messages   173

Writing Negative Email Messages   173

Writing Persuasive Email Messages   174

What kinds of subject lines should I use for email
messages?   174

Subject Lines for Informative and Positive Email
Messages   174

Subject Lines for Negative Email Messages   175

Subject Lines for Persuasive Email
Messages   175

What "netiquette" rules should I follow?   175

Expanding a Critical Skill: Managing Your
Time   176

How and when should I use attachments?   177

Employability Skills 2000+   178

Review of Key Points   178

Assignments for Module 10   178

■ *Polishing Your Prose: Making Nouns and
Pronouns Agree   181*

Online Learning Centre   181

MODULE 11 Informative and Positive Messages 182

How should I organize informative and positive messages? 183

When should I use reader benefits in informative and positive messages? 186

What kinds of informative and positive messages am I likely to write? 186

Instructions 187

Transmittals 188

Confirmations 188

Summaries 188

Adjustments and Responses to Complaints 189

Thank-You and Congratulatory Notes 189

What's the best subject line for an informative or positive message? 190

Making Subject Lines Specific 190

Making Subject Lines Concise 190

Making Subject Lines Appropriate for the Pattern of Organization 190

How can the PAIBOC formula help me write informative and positive messages? 192

Problem 192

Analysis of the Problem 192

Discussion of the Sample Solutions 193

Expanding a Critical Skill: Writing a Goodwill Ending 194

Employability Skills 2000+ 196

Review of Key Points 196

Assignments for Module 11 196

■ *Polishing Your Prose: Dangling Modifiers 203*

Online Learning Centre 203

MODULE 12 Negative Messages 204

How should I organize negative messages? 205

Giving Bad News to Customers and Other People Outside Your Organization 205

The Buffer 208

Explanation 209

Expanding a Critical Skill: Thinking about the Legal and Ethical Implications of What You Say 210

Refusals 210

Alternatives 211

Endings 211

Giving Bad News to Superiors 212

Giving Bad News to Peers and Subordinates 212

What are the most common kinds of negative messages? 214

Rejections and Refusals 214

Disciplinary Notices and Negative Performance Appraisals 214

Layoffs and Firings 215

What's the best subject line for a negative message? 215

How can PAIBOC help me write negative messages? 215

Problem 216

Analysis of the Problem 216

Discussion of the Sample Solutions 217

Employability Skills 2000+ 221

Review of Key Points 221

Assignments for Module 12 221

■ *Polishing Your Prose: Parallel Structure 224*

Online Learning Centre 225

MODULE 13 Persuasive Messages 226

What are persuasive appeals? 227

What is the best persuasive strategy? 228

How should I organize persuasive messages? 229

Writing Direct Requests 229

Organizing Problem-Solving Messages 230

How do I identify and overcome objections? 231

What other techniques make my messages more persuasive? 234

Build Credibility 234

Build Rational Appeal 234

Build Emotional Appeal 234

Use the Right Tone 235

Offer a Reason for the Reader to Act Promptly 235

Expanding a Critical Skill: Preparing for a Performance Appraisal 236

What are the most common kinds of persuasive messages? 237

Orders 237

Collection Letters 237

Performance Appraisals 238

Letters of Recommendation 239

What's the best subject line for a persuasive message? 241

How can PAIBOC help me write persuasive messages? 242

  Problem 242

  Analysis of the Problem 242

  Discussion of the Sample Solutions 243

Employability Skills 2000+ 247

Review of Key Points 247

Assignments for Module 13 247

■ *Polishing Your Prose: Narrative Voice 254*

Online Learning Centre 255

■ Unit Four
Polishing Your Writing 256

OPENING VIGNETTE 257

MODULE 14 Revising Sentences and Paragraphs 258

What is good business writing style? 259

Expanding a Critical Skill: Using the Right Tone 260

Are there rules I should follow? 261

What should I look for when I revise sentences? 261

  1. Use Active Verbs Whenever Possible 262

  2. Use Strong Action Verbs to Carry the Weight of Your Sentence 263

  3. Make Your Writing Concise 265

  4. Vary Sentence Length and Sentence Structure 268

  5. Use Parallel Structure 270

  6. Put Your Readers in Your Sentences 271

What should I look for when I revise paragraphs? 271

  1. Begin Most Paragraphs with Topic Sentences 271

  2. Use Transitions to Link Ideas 272

How does corporate culture affect style? 272

Employability Skills 2000+ 274

Review of Key Points 274

Assignments for Module 14 274

■ *Polishing Your Prose: End Punctuation 277*

Online Learning Centre 277

MODULE 15 Choosing the Right Word 278

Why does using the right word matter? 279

  Getting Your Meaning Across 279

  Getting the Response You Want 279

Expanding a Critical Skill: Thinking Critically 281

How do words derive their meanings? 282

When is it appropriate to use jargon? 283

What words confuse some writers? 284

Employability Skills 2000+ 291

Review of Key Points 291

Assignments for Module 15 291

■ *Polishing Your Prose: Run-on Sentences 294*

Online Learning Centre 295

MODULE 16 Editing for Grammar and Punctuation 296

What grammatical errors should I focus on? 297

  Agreement 297

Expanding a Critical Skill: Building a Professional Image 298

  Case 299

  Dangling Modifier (DM) 300

  Misplaced Modifier (MM) 301

  Parallelism 301

  Predication Errors 301

How can I fix sentence errors? 302

  Comma Splices (CS) 302

  Run-on Sentences (RO) 303

  Sentence Fragments (Frag) 303

When should I use commas? 304

What punctuation should I use inside sentences? 304

  Apostrophes 304

  Colons 305

  Commas 306

  Dashes 307

  Hyphens 307

  Parentheses 307

  Periods 308

  Semicolons 308

What do I use when I quote sources? 309

  Quotation Marks 309

  Square Brackets 309

  Ellipses 309

Italics versus Underlining   310

How should I write numbers and dates?   310

How do I mark errors I find when proofreading?   311

Employability Skills 2000+   313

Review of Key Points   313

Assignments for Module 16   313

■ *Polishing Your Prose: Using Spell Checkers and Grammar Checkers   317*

Online Learning Centre   317

CBC Video Cases   317

Cases for Communicators   318

Unit Five

Interpersonal Communication   320

OPENING VIGNETTE   321

MODULE 17 Listening   322

What do good listeners do?   323

  1. Pay Attention   323

  2. Focus on the Other Speaker(s) in a Generous Way   323

  3. Avoid Making Assumptions   324

  4. Listen for Feelings as Well as Facts   324

What is active listening?   325

How do I show people that I'm listening to them?   326

Can I use these techniques if I really disagree with someone?   326

Expanding a Critical Skill: Leading by Listening   327

Employability Skills 2000+   328

Review of Key Points   328

Assignments for Module 17   328

■ *Polishing Your Prose: Combining Sentences   330*

Online Learning Centre   331

MODULE 18 Working and Writing in Teams   332

What kinds of communication happen in groups?   333

What roles do people play in groups?   334

  Leadership in Groups   335

  Characteristics of Successful Student Groups   335

Expanding a Critical Skill: Leading With Integrity   336

  Peer Pressure and Groupthink   337

How should we handle conflict?   337

  Steps in Conflict Resolution   339

  Responding to Criticism   340

  You-Attitude in Conflict Resolution   341

How can we create the best co-authored documents?   341

  Discussing Drafts and Revisions   341

  Planning the Work and the Document   342

  Composing the Drafts   343

  Revising the Document   343

  Editing and Proofreading the Document   343

  Making the Group Process Work   343

Employability Skills 2000+   345

Review of Key Points   345

Assignments for Module 18   345

■ *Polishing Your Prose: Delivering Criticism   349*

Online Learning Centre   349

MODULE 19 Planning, Managing, and Recording Meetings   350

What planning should precede a meeting?   352

When I'm in charge, how do I keep the meeting on track?   354

Expanding a Critical Skill: Networking   355

What decision-making strategies work well in meetings?   356

How can I be an effective meeting participant?   357

What should be in meeting minutes?   358

How can I use informal meetings with my boss to advance my career?   358

Do virtual meetings require special consideration?   359

Employability Skills 2000+   360

Review of Key Points   360

Assignments for Module 19   360

■ *Polishing Your Prose: Hyphens and Dashes   361*

Online Learning Centre   363

MODULE 20 Making Oral Presentations   364

What decisions do I need to make as I plan a presentation?   365

  Choosing the Kind of Presentation   366

How should I organize a presentation?   367

How Can I Adapt My Ideas to the Audience?   368

How can I create a strong opening and close?   369

Expanding a Critical Skill: Finding Your Best Voice   371

How should I use visuals?   371

What are the keys to delivering an effective presentation?   374

Using Fear   374

Using Eye Contact   375

Standing and Gesturing   375

Using Notes and Visuals   375

How should I handle questions from the audience?   376

What are the guidelines for group presentations?   376

Employability Skills 2000+   378

Review of Key Points   378

Assignments for Module 20   378

■ Polishing Your Prose: Choosing Levels of Formality   379

Online Learning Centre   380

CBC Video Case   380

Cases for Communicators   380

Unit Six
Research, Reports, and Visuals   382

OPENING VIGNETTE   383

MODULE 21 Finding, Analyzing, and Documenting Information   384

How do I begin my research?   385

How can I find information online and in print?   385

How do I write questions for surveys and interviews?   388

Expanding a Critical Skill: Using the Internet for Research   391

How do I decide whom to survey or interview?   392

How should I analyze the information I've collected?   393

Understanding the Source of the Data   393

Analyzing Quantitative Data   393

Analyzing Qualitative Data   394

Checking Your Logic   394

How should I document sources?   395

Why should I document my sources?   395

Employability Skills 2000+   399

Review of Key Points   399

Assignments for Module 21   399

■ Polishing Your Prose: Using MLA and APA Style   401

Online Learning Centre   403

MODULE 22 Proposals and Progress Reports   404

What is a "report"?   405

How do I identify a problem or situation to study?   405

What should go into a proposal?   408

Proposals for Class Research Projects   408

Sales Proposals   411

Expanding a Critical Skill: Identifying "Hot Buttons"   416

Proposals for Funding   416

Figuring the Budget   417

What should go into a progress report?   417

Chronological Progress Reports   418

Task Progress Reports   420

Recommendation Progress Reports   420

Employability Skills 2000+   421

Review of Key Points   421

Assignments for Module 22   421

■ Polishing Your Prose: Who/Whom and I/Me   422

Online Learning Centre   423

MODULE 23 More Short Reports   424

How should I organize my report?   425

Informative and Closure Reports   425

Feasibility Reports   425

Justification or Analytical Reports   427

What are the basic strategies for organizing information?   428

1. General to Particular or Particular to General   428

2. Comparison or Contrast   429

3. Problem-Solution   429

4. Elimination of Alternatives   429

5. Geographic or Spatial   430

6. Functional   430

7. Chronological   430

Should I use the same style for reports as for other business documents?   430

1. Say What You Mean   431

2. Keep Your Writing Concise   431

3. Use Blueprints, Transitions, Topic Sentences, and Headings   431

Expanding a Critical Skill: Asking Specific and Polite Questions   433

Employability Skills 2000+   435

Review of Key Points   435

Assignments for Module 23   435

■ *Polishing Your Prose: Being Concise   437*

Online Learning Centre   439

MODULE 24 Formal Reports   440

What does a formal report look like?   441

I've never written a long document. How should I organize my time?   441

How do I create each part of a formal report?   442

Title Page   442

Letter or Memo of Transmittal   442

Table of Contents   443

List of Illustrations   443

Executive Summary   443

Expanding a Critical Skill: Projecting Professional Attitude   444

Introduction   444

Background or History   445

Conclusions and Recommendations   445

Employability Skills 2000+   462

Review of Key Points   462

Assignments for Module 24   462

■ *Polishing Your Prose: Improving Paragraphs   464*

Online Learning Centre   465

MODULE 25 Using Visuals   466

Why should I use visuals?   467

What are stories, and how do I find them?   467

Does it matter what kind of visual I use?   470

What design conventions should I follow?   471

Tables   471

Pie Graphs   471

Bar Graphs   472

Line Graphs   472

Can I use colour and clip art?   473

Expanding a Critical Skill: Integrating Visuals into Your Text   474

What else do I need to check for?   475

Can I use the same visual in my document and in my presentation?   476

Employability Skills 2000+   477

Review of Key Points   477

Assignments for Module 25   477

■ *Polishing Your Prose: Writing Subject Lines and Headings   483*

Online Learning Centre   484

CBC Video Case   484

Cases for Communicators   484

■ **Unit Seven**
Job Hunting   486

OPENING VIGNETTE   487

MODULE 26 Researching Jobs   488

What do I need to know about myself to job hunt?   489

What do I need to know about companies that might hire me?   490

What is the information interview?   491

Expanding a Critical Skill: Selling Yourself in the New Work World   492

What is the "hidden job market"? How do I tap into it?   493

How do I present my non-traditional experiences?   495

"All My Experience Is in My Family's Business"   495

"I've Been out of the Job Market for a While"   496

"I Want to Change Fields"   496
"I Was Fired"   496
"I Don't Have Any Experience"   497
"I'm a Lot Older Than They Want"   497
Employability Skills 2000+   498
Review of Key Points   498
Assignments for Module 26   498
■ *Polishing Your Prose: Using Details   500*
Online Learning Centre   501

MODULE 27 Creating Persuasive Résumés   502

How can I encourage the employer to pay attention to my résumé?   503
Expanding a Critical Skill: Use the KISS Checklist to Create Attention-Getting Résumés   504
What kind of résumé should I use?   505
How do résumé formats differ?   505
Chronological Résumés   511
Functional or Combination Résumés   514
Skills Résumés   514
What parts of résumé formats are the same?   517
Career Objective   517
Interpersonal Profile/Communications Skills, Career Achievements   517
Education   518
Honours and Awards   519
References   520
What should I do if the standard categories don't fit?   520
When should I limit my résumé to just one page?   520
How do I create a scannable résumé?   521
Employability Skills 2000+   524
Review of Key Points   524
Assignments for Module 27   524
■ *Polishing Your Prose: Proofreading   526*
Online Learning Centre   527

MODULE 28 Job Application Letters   528

What kind of letter should I use?   529
How are the two letters different?   530
The First Paragraph of a Solicited Letter   533
First Paragraphs of Prospecting Letters   533
Last Paragraphs   535

What parts of the two letters are the same?   535
Showing a Knowledge of the Position and the Company   536
Separating Yourself from Other Applicants   536
How long should my letter be?   536
Expanding a Critical Skill: Targeting a Specific Company in Your Letter   537
How do I create the right tone?   537
You-Attitude   538
Positive Emphasis   538
The company wants an email application. What should I do?   538
Employability Skills 2000+   540
Review of Key Points   540
Assignments for Module 28   540
■ *Polishing Your Prose: Using You and I   542*
Online Learning Centre   543

MODULE 29 Preparing for Job Interviews   544

Why do I need an interview strategy?   545
What details should I think about?   546
What to Wear   546
What to Bring to the Interview   547
Note-Taking   547
How to Get There   547
Should I practise before the interview?   548
How to Act   548
Parts of the Interview   548
How should I answer traditional interview questions?   549
How can I prepare for behavioural, situational, and stress interviews?   553
Stress Interviews   554
Expanding a Critical Skill: Negotiating Salary and Benefits   555
How can I prepare for phone or video interviews?   555
Employability Skills 2000+   557
Review of Key Points   557
Assignments for Module 29   557
■ *Polishing Your Prose: Matters on Which Experts Disagree   559*
Online Learning Centre   559

MODULE 30 Following the Interview: Follow-up Letters and Emails, and Job Offers 560

What should I say in a follow-up email or letter? 561

What do I do if my first offer isn't for the job I most want? 562

Employability Skills 2000+ 565

Review of Key Points 565

Assignments for Module 30 565

Polishing Your Prose: Using Standard English 566

Online Learning Centre 566

CBC Video Case 566

Cases for Communicators 567

CREDITS 569

POLISHING YOUR PROSE ANSWERS 571

NOTES 575

INDEX 582

About the Authors

Kitty O. Locker was an Associate Professor of English at The Ohio State University, where she taught courses in workplace discourse and research methods. She received her B.A. from DePauw University and her M.A. and Ph.D. from the University of Illinois at Urbana. She also wrote *Business and Administrative Communication* (6th ed., Irwin/McGraw-Hill, 2003), *The Irwin Business Communication Handbook: Writing and Speaking in Business Classes* (1993), and co-edited *Conducting Research in Business Communication* (1988). Her consulting clients included URS Greiner, Abbott Laboratories, the Ohio Civil Service Employees Association, AT&T, and the American Medical Association. In 1994–95, she served as President of the Association for Business Communication (ABC). From 1997 to 2000, she edited ABC's *Journal of Business Communication*. She received ABC's Outstanding Researcher Award in 1992 and ABC's Meada Gibbs Outstanding Teacher Award in 1998. Kitty Locker recently passed away. Without her vision, this book would not exist. For that we are forever indebted.

Stephen Kyo Kaczmarek is an Assistant Professor at Columbus State Community College. He teaches business and technical communication, composition, creative writing, journalism, public relations, freshman experience, and courses in film and literature he has designed. Steve received an M.A. in English and B.A.s in journalism and English from Ohio State. His consulting clients have included Nationwide Insurance, The Ohio Historical Society, The Ohio Association of Historical Societies and Museums, The Ohio Museums Association, United Energy Systems, The Thomas Moyer for Chief Justice of Ohio Campaign, and Van Meter and Associates. Prior to joining Columbus State, Steve managed staff development and information for the Franklin County, Ohio, Commissioners. He received an Award of Excellence from the National Association of County Information Officers. A movie buff, Steve has also appeared in educational videos and television commercials.

Kathryn Braun taught rhetoric and composition at Sheridan Institute of Technology and Advanced Learning for 31 years. Kathryn also taught business and interpersonal communications to postsecondary students in every discipline, including the arts, business, community and health services, computer studies, journalism, and public relations. She received her Honours B.A. from McMaster University and her Masters degree from the University of Toronto. Kathryn has published articles on communications and the media, authored a variety of multi-media education and distance education texts, and is the co-author of *The Report Writer's Manual*. Through her consulting business, communicore inc., Kathryn facilitates customized training in contemporary business communications for corporate and small business clients. Her areas of expertise include business language and culture, communication formats, international and nonverbal communications, negotiating and presentation skills. For more information, visit the communicore Web site at http://www.communicore.on.ca.

Preface

Wherever students' careers take them—working for a large corporation, small firm, non-profit, the government, or themselves—selecting the best communication model will be critical to their success. *Business Communication: Building Critical Skills* offers practical advice and approaches for achieving success in all forms of workplace communication.

The third Canadian edition builds on the outstanding features from the previous two editions:

- The **PAIBOC model** (pronounced "payback") provides definitive strategies for selecting communication modes and composing messages. Prompting readers to consider Purpose, Audiences, Information, Benefits, Objections, and Context, this innovative acronym helps students analyze and craft messages from the recipient's viewpoint. By applying the PAIBOC model, students learn to listen, speak, and write for results.
- Based on an extensive body of scholarship, the book's connection of theory to real-life experiences makes the material accessible.
- The **Conference Board of Canada's Employability Skills** fosters an understanding of how the learning materials relate to achieving career goals.
- The **modular format** offers unlimited flexibility. Easily tailored to any course length or organization, the modules can be taught in any order.

Our Audience

Context is vital to understanding. Students respond to material that is relevant to their own experiences. This edition provides illustrations, references, examples, and stories to which Canadian students can relate. The young Canadians whose profiles begin each unit represent the working-life realities of their communities. Seven engaging CBC video segments, such as "Schmoozing to Create Goodwill," relate business communication skills to real-world examples.

Responding to Instructor Needs

The third Canadian edition of *Business Communication: Building Critical Skills* went through an extensive development and rigorous revision process with the help of instructors across Canada. I am indebted to the reviewers, whose constructive comments resulted in an improved text.

Many changes were implemented as a result of this extensive feedback. You will notice that the text's pages have been completely re-designed. The new sleek and attractive interior makes reading the module material easier.

The third edition is more interactive than ever. Module review questions instead of summaries challenge students to think critically about their reading.

Please see page xvi of the preface for more changes in the third edition.

Topical Coverage that Builds Critical Skills

Module 1 introduces the **Conference Board of Canada's Employability Skills 2000+**, describing the attitudes and skills today's knowledge workers must be able to demonstrate and build upon. For each subsequent module, students can use the **Conference Board of Canada's Employability Skills 2000+ checklist** posted online as a focus for their learning reflection.

Module 1 also introduces the innovative PAIBOC (pronounced "payback") model for analyzing communication context. This model reappears in the marginalia of every module to reinforce the critical thinking skills communicators use to achieve intended results. Indeed, the attention to audience-centred communication is the textbook's central theme and most important message.

Module 2 presents a primer on audience analysis, introducing learners to demographic, geographic, and psychographic assessments and to the concept of discourse communities. Module 2's table on **Myers-Briggs personality preferences in communications** is an invaluable tool for instructors and students alike.

Module 3 provides the latest research advantages of Canada's richest resource—our cultural diversity. Reflecting this nation's multicultural experiences through a wealth of verbal and non-verbal examples and numerous exercises helps students appreciate the importance of intercultural communication.

Modules 5 and 25 describe effective visual design and application. Samples, examples, and illustrations provide pointers on **how to create effective documents, Web pages, and slides. Module 20** expands on how to prepare professional visuals, offering a step-by-step approach to planning and delivering powerful presentations. Again, readers learn how to **reframe their ideas, and to use visuals to engage their audience.**

Modules 4, 14, 15, and 16 provide **practical tips on revising, editing, and proofreading.** Specific, student-relevant examples demonstrate that **writing is rewriting.**

Modules 6, 7, and 8 (Unit 2) offer in-depth coverage of how to create reader goodwill, an essential element of writing for results. In **Module 8**, students review audience focus through Maslow's **needs analysis,** a universal, cross-disciplinary model.

Units 3 and 6 provide a plethora of sample documents on both **the form and content of business writing.** As a professional writer, I find format models save time for more essential writing tasks— like research, revision, and editing. As a teacher of business writing, I find format and product models allow students the freedom to focus on writing processes.

Building interpersonal communication skills (Unit 5) is vital. Emphasizing the relational nature of communication, students learn that communication is something that they do *with* others, not *to* them. **Working and Writing in Teams** (Module 18) appears immediately after **Listening** (Module 17) because the best teams have members who actively listen to one another, and the text offers ample research to support this truism. True to the central theme of the book, Unit 5 emphasizes the importance of audience.

Unit 7's **Job Hunting** information begins with a unique profile of a young Canadian who has been both a job seeker and recruiter. Sample documents—resumes, application letters, and interview guides—will be invaluable when students begin their job search.

What's New in the Third Canadian Edition

Here are a few of the many changes in the third Canadian edition of *Business Communication: Building Critical Skills.*

Module 1: Introduction to Business Communication

- Demonstrates the power of the word to transform people's lives
- Quotes Canadian communications expert Helen Wilkie on how much writing costs

- Proves that competent writers are very well paid
- Reinforces more clearly the distinction between letters as external documents and memos as internal documents

Module 2: Adapting Your Message to Your Audience

- Provides Canadian examples of businesses adapting to their audience
- Offers a constructivist analysis of the communication process
- Discusses features of geodemographic audience analysis
- Further elaborates on how discourse communities are important cultural influences

Module 3: Communicating across Cultures

- Explains both culture and cultural relativism
- Includes updated statistics on Canada's cultural diversity
- Describes recent Canadian research on learned cultural norms
- Asks students to apply their learning by reflecting on their own experiences with discrimination in the context of recent, well-publicized events

Module 4: Planning, Writing, and Revising

- Increases clarity and reduces wordiness by using a chart to illustrate the writing process
- Describes the specific processes of two Canadian writers
- Challenges students to identify and articulate their own writing protocols

Module 5: Designing Documents, Slides, and Screens

- Explains the rhetorical purposes of design choices
- Provides new Canadian design examples
- Uses bullet lists to increase clarity and reduce wordiness

Module 6: You-Attitude

- Updates Canadian examples and writing models
- Provides a you-attitude checklist for writers of all abilities
- Asks students to apply their learning by considering the ethics of writing choices

Module 7: Positive Emphasis

- Emphasizes the psychological, physiological, and economic benefits of positive communication
- Provides examples of Canadian organizations and entrepreneurs who prosper through positive emphasis
- Asks students to apply their learning by analyzing the dynamics of tone, courtesy, and power in their choice of discourse community

Module 8: Reader Benefits

- Illustrates how to use reader benefits with three Canadian examples
- Details the benefits that evoke positive reader responses

- Uses examples of contemporary technology to prove the psychological allure of intrinsic benefits

Module 9: Formats for Hard-copy Letters and Memos

- Adds five writing models to demonstrate current letter and memo formats
- Further clarifies the differences in purpose and layout between memos and letters
- Asks students to apply their learning by analyzing letter and memo examples

Module 10: Email Messages

- Moves current information on email after formats for letters and memos
- Emphasizes ethical and legal repercussions of email messages
- Provides expert tips on formats, emoticons, and email etiquette

Module 11: Informative and Positive Messages

- Demonstrates informative message organization in two sample documents, a memo, and an email
- Uses current Canadian examples to illustrate the rhetorical purposes of organizing informative messages

Module 12: Negative Messages

- Focuses on ethical considerations in organizing negative messages
- Provides a new model negative letter

Module 13: Persuasive Messages

- Introduces the elements of persuasion
- Provides tips on dressing for success
- Illustrates the persuasive appeal of the young Canadian entrepreneur who founded 1-800-GOT-JUNK
- Asks students to apply their learning by analyzing the ethics of persuasive appeals

Module 14: Revising Sentences and Paragraphs

- Focuses on the revision part of the writing process
- Provides specific tips on practising reader-friendly writing style
- Uses a Quebec company's innovative design to illustrate the power of revision

Module 15: Choosing the Right Word

- Uses Canadian examples and illustrations to challenge readers' assumptions about language
- Uses Canadian entrepreneurs, writers, and heroes to challenge readers' assumptions about diversity and adversity
- Asks students to apply their learning by analyzing the ethics of word choice

Module 16: Editing for Grammar and Punctuation

- Introduces tips on editing for the Web

Module 17: Listening

- Asks students to reflect on the cultural influences of their own listening habits
- Asks students to apply their learning by observing and analyzing the listening behaviours of four other cultures

Module 18: Working and Writing in Teams

- Introduces Dr. Bruce Tuckman's "Forming, Storming, Norming, Performing" model of group dynamics
- Describes Harvard Business School professor Amy Edmondson's ten tips for integrity in interpersonal leadership
- Asks students to apply their learning by identifying and analyzing the specific dynamics of their group

Module 19: Planning, Managing, and Recording Meetings

- Uses bullet lists to increase clarity and reduce wordiness
- Introduces blogging as a new meeting forum
- Asks students to apply their learning by identifying how they can increase their networking activities

Module 20: Making Oral Presentations

- Reorders information to increase clarity, unity, and coherence
- Provides experts' presentations tips and techniques
- Asks students to apply their learning by creating a presentation skills evaluation rubric

Module 21: Finding, Analyzing, and Documenting Information

- Illustrates examples of online university and college research resources
- Provides a wealth of current print and electronic resources
- Asks students to apply their learning by analyzing and reporting on their own primary research findings

Module 22: Proposals and Progress Reports

- Provides a model of a real business proposal
- Illustrates successful audience appeals with contemporary Canadian examples

Module 23: More Short Reports

- Directs students to online resources for writing proposals, short reports and business plans
- Illustrates the importance of writing good proposals for successful Canadian grant applications

Module 24: Formal Reports

- Adds more Canadian examples
- Asks students to apply their learning by analyzing a feasibility study
- Asks students to apply their learning by writing sections of their reports, and using peers to provide feedback

Module 25: Using Visuals

- Clarifies why and how writers use visuals effectively and ethically
- Uses the PAIBOC model to help students choose and use visuals
- Asks students to apply their learning by analyzing the cultural impact of visuals

Module 26: Researching Jobs

- Updates information on the realities of the new world of work
- Provides practical, expert tips on beginning the job search, researching prospective employers, and preparing for interviews

Module 27: Creating Persuasive Résumés

- Provides a checklist for creating résumés that work
- Uses Canadian examples to illustrate experts' tips

Module 28: Job Application Letters

- Revises model letter to reflect you-attitude
- Refers students to online career and job-hunting guides

Module 29: Preparing for Job Interviews

- Identifies current hot jobs and industry sectors
- Describes the industries where Canadians are in demand globally
- Provides expert tips on overseas self-recruitment

Module 30: Following the Interview: Follow-up Letters and Emails, and Job Offers

- Illustrates the multiple attractions of jobs in the skilled trades
- Gives hourly wages for employment sectors

Instructor Resources

i-Learning Sales Specialist

Your **Integrated Learning Sales Specialist** is a McGraw-Hill Ryerson representative who has the experience, product knowledge, training, and support to help you assess and integrate any of the below-noted products, technology, and services into your course for optimum teaching and learning performance. Whether it's using our test bank software, helping your students improve their grades, or putting your entire course online, your *i*-Learning Sales Specialist can help you do it. Contact your local *i*-Learning Sales Specialist today to learn how to maximize all McGraw-Hill Ryerson's resources!

i-Learning Services Program

McGraw-Hill Ryerson offers a unique *i*-Services package designed for Canadian faculty. Our mission is to equip providers of higher education with the superior tools and resources required for excellence in teaching. For additional information, visit http://www.mcgrawhill.ca/highereducation/iservices/.

Instructor's Resource CD-ROM

This CD-ROM contains complete instructor supplements, fully adapted to accord with the third Canadian edition of *Business Communication: Building Critical Skills*: Instructor's Manual, Test Bank, Computerized Test Bank, and Transparency Masters. These supplements can be customized to help you plan classes and create presentations.

- The **Instructor's Manual** includes overviews of each module, key lecture points supported by teaching tips, in-class exercises, answers to textbook assignments, and answers to the even-numbered Polishing Your Prose exercises.
- The **Computerized Test Bank** provides all the Test Bank questions in the powerful and accessible Brownstone test-generating program for Macintosh and Windows systems. Instructors can easily select questions and print tests and answer keys. Instructors can also customize questions, headings, and instructions; add or import their own questions; and print tests in a choice of printer-supported fonts.
- A set of **Transparency Masters** with key points from each module are available for printing and duplication.

CBC Video Cases

Visit the Online Learning Centre at http://www.mcgrawhill.ca/olc/locker to view seven brief CBC video segments, such as "Schmoozing to Create Goodwill" and "The Trouble with Teams," that relate to critical skills in business communication. Students can watch the videos and answer associated questions on the Student Edition of the Online Learning Centre. Full video notes are available on the Instructor Edition of the Online Learning Centre.

Online Learning Centre

The Online Learning Centre for *Business Communication*, third Canadian edition, at http://www.mcgrawhill.ca/olc/locker features a variety of instructor resources, including CBC video cases, web links, and Microsoft® PowerPoint® slides, in a passcode-protected environment.

PageOut™

Create a custom course Website with **PageOut**, free with every McGraw-Hill Ryerson textbook.

To learn more, contact your McGraw-Hill Ryerson publisher's representative or visit www.mhhe.com/solutions

Build your own course Web site in less than an hour. You don't have to be a computer whiz to create a Web site, especially with an exclusive McGraw-Hill product called PageOut. It requires no prior knowledge of HTML, no long hours of coding, and no design skills on your part. With PageOut, even the most inexperienced computer user can quickly and easily create a professional-looking course Web site. Simply fill in templates with your information and with content provided by McGraw-Hill, choose a design, and you've got a Web site specifically designed for your course. Visit us at www.mhhe.com/pageout to find out more.

Student Resources

Online Learning Centre

The Online Learning Centre for *Business Communication: Building Critical Skills*, third Canadian edition at http://www.mcgrawhill.ca/olc/locker features learning and study tools such as module quizzes, CBC video cases, Sites to See, letter and résumé templates, and additional student writing samples.

Acknowledgements

This third Canadian edition is the result of my ongoing collaboration with the McGraw-Hill Ryerson team: Lisa Rahn, Sponsoring Editor; Marc Trudel, Marketing Manager; Elizabeth Priest, Supervising Editor; Gillian Scobie, Copy Editor; Zonia Strynatka, Production Coordinator; Denise Foote, Senior Developmental Editor, and Christine Gilbert, my most patient Developmental Editor.

The constructive comments of reviewers, who generously provided their expertise, also contributed to the creation of this edition. I offer them sincere thanks:

La Royce Batchelor, Red River College
Kathryn Brillinger, Conestoga College
Vicky Day, Northern Alberta Institute of Technology (NAIT)
Rachel Howison, Mohawk College
Shannon MacRae, Mohawk College
Joanne E. Marshall, St. Clair College of Applied Arts and Technology
Kathryn Pallister, Red Deer College
Linda Schofield, Ryerson University
Heather Skanes, Memorial University
Dena Tooma, Mohawk College
Joan Vinall-Cox, Sheridan College Institute of Technology and Advanced Learning
Kathy Voltan, Ryerson University
Wendy Wilson, Fanshawe College

For ideas, inspiration, and innovation I am particularly indebted to editor Gillian Scobie, and to all the students, colleagues, and aspiring writers who continue to teach me so much, so generously.

Kathryn Braun

Please take a moment to page through the highlights of the third Canadian edition to learn how its pedagogical features reinforce its flexible, audience-focused approach.

Unit-Opening Vignettes

Seven vignettes profile Canadians, describing how they use business communication skills in their jobs. These vignettes reinforce the relevance of effective communication to students' future careers.

One of Toyota Canada's top salespeople originally studied to become a nurse. However, completing the hospital practicum part of his course meant that Burt Townsend would have to quit the night security job he worked at to pay for his education. Burt had to leave college.

When he spied an automotive industry recruitment ad, he was intrigued by the promise of further education. A week's intensive training and scrutiny were required for both the career in the automotive industry and post-secondary education. "I've always been a car buff, and the opportunity appealed to me." Of the 1,000 applicants who showed up that first morning, Burt was one of only 10 graduates five days later. Toyota hired him within a week of interviewing him.

Ten years later, Burt is not only his dealership's most successful salesperson, he is also the youngest, and the most accredited. Toyota University's awards of achievement adorn his office wall, testament to his commitment to Toyota, and to himself. "You always have to be willing to learn, and to upgrade your skills."

Clients' letters and emails, unanimous in their praise, crowd his bulletin board. Customers want Burt, and Burt's boss, to know how well he treated them; how personable and personal, honest and knowledgeable he is; how they will buy or lease their next car nowhere

else but this Toyota dealership, because of Burt Townsend.

"Toyota believes that quality sells, so my university courses focus on knowing the product. I learn everything I can about the vehicles, their engineering, technical, and functional operations, ... about the competition ... I even learn about Toyota quality anecdotally, by listening to suppliers' stories. Toyota makes a quality product. That's why it's forecasted to lead car sales in 2006.

"I couldn't sell the product if I didn't believe in it, and I've had plenty of other offers. So believing in what I'm selling, and having the product knowledge are big advantages. But that's not the whole story.

"Anyone can sell that first car. What about the second, and the third? My focus is on building the relationship. People don't want to buy the car and know that's the end of the transaction. What about after the sale? What if they need information or advice? What if they have an accident? My clients continue to depend, and to call on me, five, six years after the initial sale. People want to know that someone they trust will be there to take care of them, long after the sale.

"It's not about the sale. It's about the relationship after the sale. At the end of the day, did I do my best for my clients? Then I've done the job."

P A I B O C

Analysis

1. In what two ways does Burt create goodwill with clients?

2. What methods does Toyota Canada use to communicate goodwill?

3. According to Burt, who are Toyota's customers?

FYI

FYI sidebars provide fun facts to illustrate how business communication affects everyday life.

Sincerely and *Cordially* are standard **complimentary closes**. When you are writing to people in special groups or to someone who is a friend as well as a business acquaintance, you may want to use a less formal close. Depending on the circumstances, the following informal closes might be acceptable: *Yours for a better environment*, or even *Ciao*.

In **two-point** or **mixed punctuation**, a colon follows the salutation and a comma follows the close. Today, many people use a comma after the salutation to make the letter look like a personal letter rather than a business letter. In **open punctuation**, omit all punctuation after the salutation and the close. Mixed punctuation is traditional. Open punctuation is faster to type.

FYI

A University of British Columbia long-term study validates the direct correlation between communications skills and salary. For each additional year of education, Canadians earn an additional 8.3 percent, or $2490 in salary, of which $772 is attributed to literacy.

Sources: Statistics Canada, *The Daily*, http://www.statcan.ca/Daily/English/010319/d010319a.htm, retrieved June 27, 2001; *Toronto Star*, Monday, March 19, 2001, A11.

Set side margins of 2.5 cm to 3.5 cm (1" to 1.5") on the left and 1.5 cm to 2.5 cm (0.75" to 1") on the right. If your letterhead extends all the way across the top of the page, set your margins even with the ends of the letterhead for the most visually pleasing page. The top margin should be three to six lines under the letterhead, or 5 cm (2") down from the top of the page if you aren't using letterhead. If your letter is very short, you may want to use bigger side and top margins so that the letter is centred on the page.

Many letters are accompanied by other documents. Whatever these documents may be—a multi-page report or a two-line note—they are called **enclosures**, since they are enclosed in the envelope. The writer should refer to the enclosures in the body of the letter: "As you can see from my résumé, ..." The enclosure line is usually abbreviated: Encl. (see Figure 9.4 on page 154). The abbreviation reminds the person who seals the letter to include the enclosure(s).

Sometimes you write to one person but send copies of your letter to other people. If you want the reader to know that other people are getting copies, list their names on the last page. The abbreviation *cc* originally meant *carbon copy* but now means *computer copy*. Other acceptable abbreviations include *pc* for *photocopy* or simply *c* for *copy*. You can also send copies to other people without telling the reader. Such copies are called **blind copies**. Blind copies are not mentioned on the original; they are listed on the copy saved for the file with the abbreviation *bc* preceding the names of people getting these copies.

You do not need to indicate that you have shown a letter to your superior or that you are saving a copy of the letter for your own files. These are standard practices.

Use two capital letters with no punctuation to abbreviate province and state names in letters and memos. See Table 9.2 for a list of **postal service abbreviations**.

What courtesy titles should I use?

Research your reader's preference.

Today, most salutations use "Dear *first name last name*." However, some people and many cultures prefer their professional titles: Director Chadraba, President Mauricio. Use *Ms., Mr.,* or *Mrs.* when your audience has signed their correspondence that way.

1. Use professional titles when they're relevant.

> Dr. Kristen Sorenson is our new company physician.
> The Rev. Robert Townsley gave the invocation.

2. If a woman prefers to be addressed as *Mrs.* or *Miss*, rather than *Ms.*, use the title she prefers. (You-attitude ◄ Module 6 takes precedence over non-sexist language:

Sites to See

Marginal icons and topic headings lead students to the Online Learning Centre at http://www.mcgrawhill. ca/olc/locker to explore Web sites related to text content.

SEE THE OLC!

View Sample Geodemographic Clusters

SEE THE OLC!

What Psychographic Group Do You Belong To?

Table 2.2 suggests how you can use this information to adapt a message to your audience.

You'll be most persuasive if you play to your audience's strengths. Indeed, many of the general principles of business communications reflect the types most common among managers. Putting the main point up front satisfies the needs of judging types, and some 75 percent of managers are judging. Giving logical reasons satisfies the needs of the nearly 80 percent of managers who are thinking types.[4]

Values and Beliefs

Psychographic characteristics are qualitative rather than quantitative and include values, beliefs, goals, and lifestyles. Knowing what your audience finds important allows you to organize information in a way that seems natural to your audience and to choose appeals that audience members will find persuasive.

Looking at values enables a company to identify customer segments. The Canadian-born Tim Hortons chain introduced a more diverse menu (croissants, muffins, soup, and sandwiches) to attract new fast-food clients and to appeal to its original, increasingly weight-conscious customers. Ranked as Canada's "best-managed brand," based on customer service, Tim Hortons continues to expand in Canada and internationally.[5]

Eresearcher Mary Modahl's survey of 250 000 households found that online buying depends on psychographics: the consumer's attitude toward technology along a continuum from "profoundly suspicious" to "eagerly accepting."

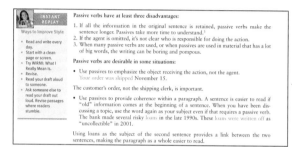

INSTANT REPLAY

Ways to Improve Style

- Read and write every day.
- Start with a clean page or screen.
- Try WIRMI: What I Really Mean Is.
- Read your draft aloud to someone.
- Revise.
- Ask someone else to read your draft out loud. Revise passages where readers stumble.

Passive verbs have at least three disadvantages:

1. If all the information in the original sentence is retained, passive verbs make the sentence longer. Passives take more time to understand.[3]
2. If the agent is omitted, it's not clear who is responsible for doing the action.
3. When many passive verbs are used, or when passives are used in material that has a lot of big words, the writing can be boring and pompous.

Passive verbs are desirable in some situations:

- Use passives to emphasize the object receiving the action, not the agent.
  Your order was shipped November 15.

The customer's order, not the shipping clerk, is important.

- Use passives to provide coherence within a paragraph. A sentence is easier to read if "old" information comes at the beginning of a sentence. When you have been discussing a topic, use the word again as your subject even if that requires a passive verb. The bank made several risky loans in the late 1990s. These loans were written off as "uncollectible" in 2001.

Using loans as the subject of the second sentence provides a link between the two sentences, making the paragraph as a whole easier to read.

Instant Replays

Instant Replay sidebars reinforce key concepts presented earlier in the module. The third Canadian edition's Instant Replays review those concepts students need to understand.

Sample Documents

More than fifty sample documents provide examples for students. Green annotations indicate exemplary documents, while red annotations point out areas for improvement.

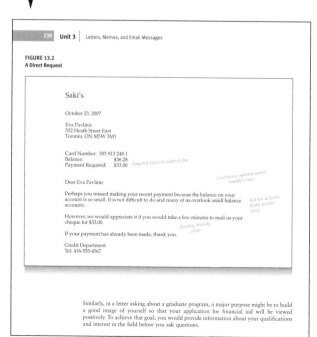

230 **Unit 3** | Letters, Memos, and Email Messages

FIGURE 13.2
A Direct Request

Saki's

October 23, 2007

Eva Pavlinic
532 Heath Street East
Toronto, ON M5W 3M1

Card Number: 503 913 248 1
Balance: $36.28
Payment Required: $33.00 *Request topic in subject line*

Dear Eva Pavlinic *Courteous opening saves reader's face*

Perhaps you missed making your recent payment because the balance on your account is so small. It is not difficult to do and many of us overlook small balance accounts. *Ask for actions. Make action easy*

However, we would appreciate it if you would take a few minutes to mail us your cheque for $33.00. *Positive, friendly close*

If your payment has already been made, thank you.

Credit Department
Tel: 416-555-4567

Similarly, in a letter asking about a graduate program, a major purpose might be to build a good image of yourself so that your application for financial aid will be viewed positively. To achieve that goal, you would provide information about your qualifications and interest in the field before you ask questions.

Fast-Forward/Rewind Icons

These icons cross-reference topics in the text to help students make connections among concepts in different modules.

1. Adapt the message to the specific audience.
2. Show the audience members how they benefit from the idea, policy, service, or product (◀▮▶ Module 8).
3. Overcome any objections the audience may have.
4. Use a good attitude and positive emphasis (◀▮▶ Modules 6 and 7).
5. Use visuals to clarify or emphasize material (◀▮▶ Module 25).
6. Specify exactly what the audience should do.

Expanding a Critical Skill

In each module these boxes focus on how a particular skill works in organizations and suggest ways students can develop these skills. Topics include dealing with discrimination and creating a professional image.

EXPANDING A CRITICAL SKILL

Creating a Business Image

The way you and your documents look affects the way people respond to you and to them. Every organization has a dress code. One young man was upset when an older man told him he should wear wing-tip shoes. He was wearing leather shoes but not the kind that said "I'm promotable" in that workplace. Dress codes are rarely spelled out; the older worker was doing the young man a favour by being direct. If you have a mentor in the organization, ask him or her if there are other ways you can make your appearance even more professional. If you don't have a mentor, look at the people who rank above you. Notice clothing, jewellery, and hairstyles. If you're on a budget, go to stores that sell expensive clothing to check the kind of buttons, the texture and colours of fabric, the width of lapels and belts. Then go to stores in your price range and choose garments that imitate the details of expensive clothing.

Documents need to look professional, too. Now that most documents are keyed on computers and printed with laser printers, we don't need to worry about whited-out errors or uneven key strokes. We do need to make sure that the ink or toner is printing evenly and that the document uses a standard format.

Some organizations prescribe a standard format for documents. If your organization does, follow it. If you have your choice, use one of the formats in this book. They're widely used in businesses, so they communicate a message of competence.

Conference Board of Canada's Employability Skills 2000+

A complete list of applicable skills from the Conference Board of Canada's Employability Skills 2000+ appears in Module 1. The list of skills for each module can be found on the Online Learning Centre at www.mcgrawhill.ca/olc/locker. These ensure that students understand how the module content relates to achieving their employment goals.

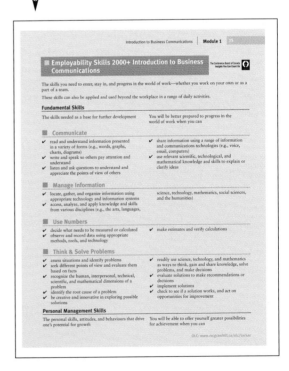

Introduction to Business Communications | **Module 1**

■ Employability Skills 2000+ Introduction to Business Communications The Conference Board of Canada Insights You Can Count On

The skills you need to enter, stay in, and progress in the world of work—whether you work on your own or as a part of a team.

These skills can also be applied and used beyond the workplace in a range of daily activities.

Fundamental Skills

The skills needed as a base for further development	You will be better prepared to progress in the world of work when you can

■ Communicate

✔ read and understand information presented in a variety of forms (e.g., words, graphs, charts, diagrams)
✔ write and speak so others pay attention and understand
✔ listen and ask questions to understand and appreciate the points of view of others

✔ share information using a range of information and communications technologies (e.g., voice, email, computers)
✔ use relevant scientific, technological, and mathematical knowledge and skills to explain or clarify ideas

■ Manage Information

✔ locate, gather, and organize information using appropriate technology and information systems
✔ access, analyze, and apply knowledge and skills from various disciplines (e.g., the arts, languages,

science, technology, mathematics, social sciences, and the humanities)

■ Use Numbers

✔ decide what needs to be measured or calculated
✔ observe and record data using appropriate methods, tools, and technology

✔ make estimates and verify calculations

■ Think & Solve Problems

✔ assess situations and identify problems
✔ seek different points of view and evaluate them based on facts
✔ recognize the human, interpersonal, technical, scientific, and mathematical dimensions of a problem
✔ identify the root cause of a problem
✔ be creative and innovative in exploring possible solutions

✔ readily use science, technology, and mathematics as ways to think, gain and share knowledge, solve problems, and make decisions
✔ evaluate solutions to make recommendations or decisions
✔ implement solutions
✔ check to see if a solution works, and act on opportunities for improvement

Personal Management Skills

The personal skills, attitudes, and behaviours that drive one's potential for growth	You will be able to offer yourself greater possibilities for achievement when you can

OLC www.mcgrawhill.ca/olc/locker

Assignments

Each module contains a variety of problems and exercises for in-class activities or homework.

Assignments for Module 10

Questions for Critical Thinking

10.1 Why are spelling and punctuation still important in email?

10.2 Why should you compose important email messages offline?

10.3 When should writers avoid humour, sarcasm, and emoticons in their email content?

10.4 Why is it OK for your boss to send you a message with the subject line "To Do," even though that wouldn't work when you need to ask a colleague to do something?

Polishing Your Prose

These exercises, at the end of each module, provide a review of grammar, style, and usage. Answers to the odd-numbered exercises are found at the back of the book to help students check their progress. Answers to even-numbered exercises, which can be assigned for homework or used for quizzes, are included in the Instructor's Manual.

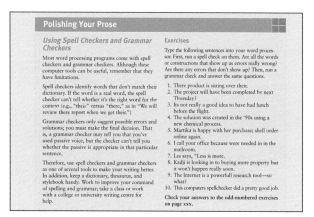

Polishing Your Prose

Using Spell Checkers and Grammar Checkers

Most word processing programs come with spell checkers and grammar checkers. Although these computer tools can be useful, remember that they have limitations.

Spell checkers identify words that don't match their dictionary. If the word is a real word, the spell checker can't tell whether it's the right word for the context (e.g., "their" versus "there," as in "We will review there report when we get their.")

Grammar checkers only suggest possible errors and solutions; you must make the final decision. That is, a grammar checker may tell you that you've used passive voice, but the checker can't tell you whether the passive is appropriate in that particular sentence.

Therefore, use spell checkers and grammar checkers as one of several tools to make your writing better. In addition, keep a dictionary, thesaurus, and stylebook handy. Work to improve your command of spelling and grammar; take a class or work with a college or university writing centre for help.

Exercises

Type the following sentences into your word processor. First, run a spell check on them. Are all the words or constructions that show up as errors really wrong? Are there any errors that don't show up? Then, run a grammar check and answer the same questions.

1. There product is sitting over their.
2. The project will have been completed by next Thursday?
3. Its not really a good idea to have had lunch before the flight.
4. The solution was created in the '90s using a new chemical process.
5. Martika is happy with her purchase; shell order online again.
6. I call your office because were needed in the mailroom.
7. Les says, "Less is more.
8. Kadji is looking in to buying more property but it won't happen really soon.
9. The Internet is a powerfull research tool—so what?
10. This computers spellchecker did a pretty good job.

Check your answers to the odd-numbered exercises on page xxx.

Cases for Communicators

Seven unit-ending cases provide both individual and team activities to solve communication challenges faced by real-life companies and organizations.

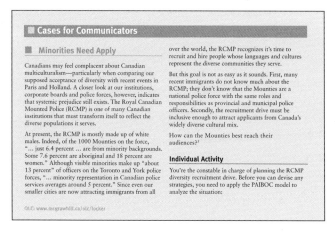

Cases for Communicators

Minorities Need Apply

Canadians may feel complacent about Canadian multiculturalism—particularly when comparing our supposed acceptance of diversity with recent events in Paris and Holland. A closer look at our institutions, corporate boards and police forces, however, indicates that systemic prejudice still exists. The Royal Canadian Mounted Police (RCMP) is one of many Canadian institutions that must transform itself to reflect the diverse populations it serves.

At present, the RCMP is mostly made up of white males. Indeed, of the 1000 Mounties on the force, "... just 6.4 percent ... are from minority backgrounds. Some 7.6 percent are aboriginal and 18 percent are women." Although visible minorities make up "about 13 percent" of officers on the Toronto and York police forces, "... minority representation in Canadian police services averages around 5 percent." Since even our smaller cities are now attracting immigrants from all

over the world, the RCMP recognizes it's time to recruit and hire people whose languages and cultures represent the diverse communities they serve.

But this goal is not as easy as it sounds. First, many recent immigrants do not know much about the RCMP; they don't know that the Mounties are a national police force with the same roles and responsibilities as provincial and municipal police officers. Secondly, the recruitment drive must be inclusive enough to attract applicants from Canada's widely diverse cultural mix.

How can the Mounties best reach their audiences?[5]

Individual Activity

You're the constable in charge of planning the RCMP diversity recruitment drive. Before you can devise any strategies, you need to apply the PAIBOC model to analyze the situation:

CBC Video Cases

A CBC icon at the end of units 2, 4, 5, and 7 prompts students to visit the Online Learning Centre at http://www.mcgrawhill.ca/olc/locker to view a CBC video clip and answer related questions. Topics include résumés and teamwork.

■ **CBC Video Case**

CBC ● Visit the Online Learning Centre at www.mcgrawhill.ca/olc/locker to view "Résumés," an online CBC Video Case featuring advice from experts on how to put your résumé together. What comes first? What do you include? These questions and more are answered.

Unit 1

Building Effective Messages

Teenager Skawenniio Barnes wrote the letter that built a library.

The thirteen year old couldn't research her high school assignment because there was no library in the Mohawk community of Kahnawake, Québec. Her letter to the community chief and the Mohawk council, asking for a library on the reserve, emphasized the many benefits of access to a variety of current reading materials. Barnes wrote passionately about the rewards of reading, such as increased knowledge and vocabulary, and enhanced imagination. She also mentioned that the parents of children in the English-immersion classes, who helped teach their children to read and write, needed contemporary resources.

When her words got no immediate action, Barnes sent her letter on to the *Eastern Door*, a community newspaper. People responded positively. Then the Montréal media and Global Television focused on the story. Momentum grew, and Barnes became a member of the new library committee.

Meanwhile, Barnes had entered and won the CosmoGirl! of the Year contest. In her essay to *Cosmopolitan* magazine, Barnes told her story of trying to establish a community library. The resulting increased media attention garnered national awareness, and boxes of donated books arrived from across the country and around the world.

Retired McGill professor Ian McLachlin heard a CBC interview with Barnes and decided to help. When he discovered that the library needed a feasibility plan, he offered his MBA students the project for an independent study credit. Four students—Erika Rodrigues, Laird McLean, Juan Quiceno, and Rozel Gonzales—took on the project during spring break. McLachlin believed the students were motivated by "…the opportunity to work with First Nations people, and…the chance to…do something meaningful with their skills, in an unconventional way."

Through discussions and collaboration with the entire Mohawk community, the MBA student consultants created a detailed feasibility plan. In 2003, two years after Barnes wrote her letter, the Kahnawake Public Library was built and filled with books from enthusiastic donors.

Nominated by the people in her community, Barnes received the Peter Gzowski Literacy Award for her accomplishment.

Skawenniio means "one beautiful word." Barnes' words prove the power of one, and of one's beautiful words.

P A I B O C
Analysis

1. For what **purposes** did Barnes write?
2. How did Barnes reach multiple **audiences**?
3. What **audience** benefits did Barnes emphasize?

1

Introduction to Business Communication

Module Outline

- Why do we communicate?
- How is business communication different?
- What communications skills are integral to business success?
- Will I really have to write?
- How much does correspondence cost?
- What makes a message effective?
- How do I begin to analyze communications situations?

Review of Key Points

Assignments for Module 1

Polishing Your Prose: Sentence Fragments

LEARNING OBJECTIVES

After reading and applying the information in Module 1, you will be able to demonstrate

Knowledge of

- Why we communicate
- What business communication accomplishes
- How to begin to analyze communication situations
- What communication and interpersonal skills employers seek

Skills to

- Identify the characteristics of effective business messages
- Begin to analyze communication situations

The Conference Board of Canada
Insights You Can Count On

See pages 15 to 17 to preview the key skills from the Conference Board of Canada's Employability Skills 2000+.

We communicate to plan, change, and reflect on our lives. We communicate to imagine alternatives, to strategize and solve problems, to build models, to organize ourselves, to persuade others, to assess new situations, to reassess and change behaviours, to think critically and reflectively, and to establish and develop meaningful relationships. We communicate to express ourselves, to get work done, to gain recognition, and to make our lives meaningful.

From the moment we are born, our primary motivation is to connect—to make meaning—by communicating.

Working people communicate to develop, improve, and expand products, services and access to information; to make and maintain positive work relationships; to hire, orient, train, and motivate others; to produce, manufacture, and deliver products; to persuade customers to buy, and to bill them for their purchases. Business communication makes everything happen: communication creates, promotes, sells, and delivers products, services, and information.

We communicate most successfully when we 1) take the time to consider consciously what outcomes we want, and 2) adapt our message content, tone and style to meet the needs of our audience, so we can achieve those outcomes. In other words, successful communication usually includes elements of persuasion: we cannot get what we want, unless and until we identify and satisfy the other person's needs and wants.

How is business communication different?

Business communication focuses on getting the job done.

Business relies on clear, concise meaning exchange to get the job done. Because in business "time is money," your audience's primary need is to understand the message, clearly and completely, the first time. Therefore, business communication must meet your audience's needs, and achieve your purpose(s), as efficiently as possible.

While this task may sound easy, it is remarkably complicated. Because of the transformation wrought by technology, we now live and work in a post-industrial, knowledge-based, global workplace. Most of our messages have multiple purposes, and our audiences a variety of needs. Furthermore, technological innovation has trained us to

FIGURE 1.1

Example of Typical Business Communication

Date: September 28, 2007

To: Lindsay Marshall

From: Brandon Schraff

Subject: Health and Safety Seminar

Thank you for arranging last week's health and safety seminar for plant personnel. You did a great job; the feedback was impressive and I've noticed that staff are applying what they learned.

Lunch and Learn Ideas

For next month's lunch and learn, people suggested the following topics:

- Tips for time management

- Best management practices

- Email etiquette

- Negotiating strategies

Let me know your ideas, and let's talk after the management meeting next Thursday to choose a topic.

expect easy, immediate message transfer while simultaneously increasing the complexity of our communication exchanges.

As a result, workers today must communicate more often, using more media, and with more sophistication and finesse than ever before.

Both the Conference Board of Canada and the U.S. Secretary's Commission on Achieving Necessary Skills (SCANS) identify sophisticated communications skills as one of the keys to careers in the twenty-first century. (See page 15 for the complete text of the Conference Board of Canada's Employability Skills 2000+. The skills that are pertinent to each module of this book are included on the OLC.)

In his study *Education and Technological Revolution: The Role of the Social Sciences and the Humanities in the Knowledge-based Economy*, University of British Columbia economics professor Robert Allen finds that communications skills are the most sought after in today's knowledge-based economy. "Demand is increasing for those workers who can... understand the information generated by computer systems, apply models to problems, deal effectively with customers and other members of a team, speak and write clearly, and make informed and independent judgments."[1]

Thus, today's university and college graduates are discovering that abilities like speaking persuasively with clients, working productively in teams, and managing projects are critical for finding employment.[2]

SEE THE OLC!

Conference Board of Canada's Employability Skills 2000+ Report

Documents' Purposes

Business documents have three purposes: to inform, to request or persuade, and to build goodwill. Most documents have more than one purpose.

◼ What does business communication accomplish?

Communication makes everything happen.

According to Canadian management guru Dr. Henry Mintzberg, managers have three jobs: to collect and convey information, to make decisions, and to promote interpersonal unity—that is, to make people want to work together to achieve organizational goals.[3] All these jobs require communication. Effective knowledge workers are able to use a wide variety of media and strategies to communicate. They know how to interpret comments from informal channels such as the company grapevine; they can speak effectively in small groups and in formal presentations; and they write well.

Business communications—oral, non-verbal, and written—go to both internal and external audiences. **Internal audiences** (Figure 1.2) are other people in the same organization: subordinates, superiors, peers. **External audiences** (Figure 1.3) are people outside the organization: customers, suppliers, unions, stockholders, potential employees, government agencies, the press, and the public.

Internal and External Audiences

Internal audiences are other people in the same organization: subordinates, peers, superiors and **External audiences** are the people outside the organization: customers, suppliers, unions, stockholders, potential employees, government agencies, the press, and the public.

FIGURE 1.2

The Internal Audiences of the Sales Manager, West

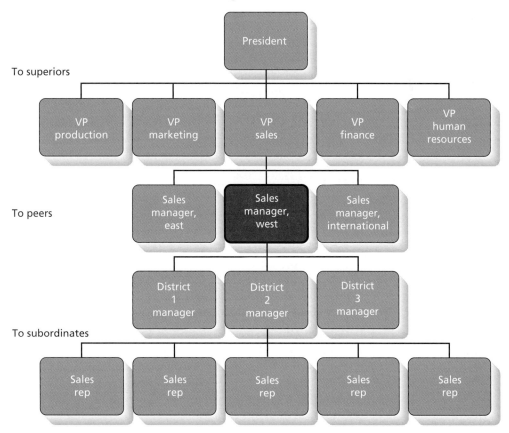

FIGURE 1.3
The Organization's External Audiences

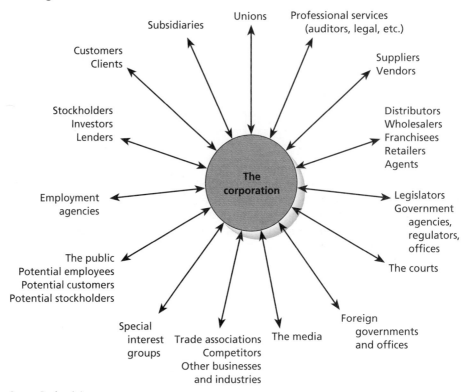

Source: Daphne A. Jameson.

■ What communications skills are integral to business success?

Knowledge workers rely on their listening, speaking, interpersonal, and writing skills to get the job done.

Listening, speaking, and working in groups are integral to doing business successfully. In every job, you need to listen to others to find out what you are supposed to do, to learn about the organization's culture and values, and to establish and maintain work relationships. Your interpersonal communications skills connect you to the **grapevine**, an informal source of organizational information. Moreover, networking and working with others—inside and outside your workplace—are crucial to developing positive relationships, and to your personal and professional growth.

Business, government, and not-for-profit organizations—in fact, every organization—also depend on written messages. People in organizations produce written documents for the record, to inform, request, or persuade. When you write to inform, you tell or explain something to your readers. When you write to request or persuade, you want readers to do something. However, the primary purpose of business messages is to build goodwill with the reader: to create a positive image of yourself, and your organization, so readers will want to do business with you.

■ Will I really have to write?

Yes, You will have to write—a lot.

People's claims that they can get by without writing are false.

Claim 1: Assistants will do all my writing.

Reality: Technology has transformed organizational structures and reduced the need for support staff. Of the assistants who remain, 71 percent are executive assistants whose duties are managerial, not clerical.[4]

Technological innovation requires workers to exhibit increasingly sophisticated listening, critical and creative thinking, writing, reading, and speaking skills.

Today, for example, businesses expect their junior engineers to manage projects and write reports. In response to industry complaints about graduates' poor communications skills, universities across Canada now emphasize writing and leadership courses in their undergraduate engineering faculties. According to Gabriel Desjardins, a Queen's University computer engineering graduate working in California's Silicon Valley, "Engineers with excellent writing skills are often promoted over people with superior technical skills."[5]

Claim 2: I'll use form letters or templates when I need to write.

Reality: A **form letter** is a prewritten fill-in-the-blank letter designed to fit standard situations. But form letters cover only routine situations. The higher you rise, the more frequently you'll face situations that aren't routine and that demand creative thinking and written solutions.

Claim 3: I'm being hired as an accountant, not as a writer.

Reality: Almost every entry-level professional or managerial job requires you to write memos and email messages, and to work productively in small groups. People who do these things well are more likely to be promoted beyond the entry level. Furthermore, advances in technology have transformed knowledge workers' roles and responsibilities. Because of Simply Accounting software, for example, people can do their own low-level accounting tasks. Today, accountants earning between $40 000 and $45 000 annually must have more specialized knowledge, and "be analytical with good communication and interpersonal skills."[6] Finally, since writing is such a high-level cognitive skill, people who have developed good writing abilities also tend to demonstrate superior reading and thinking skills. Superior communicators achieve more recognition and make more money.

Claim 4: I'll just pick up the phone.

Reality: Important phone calls require follow-up letters, memos, or email messages. People in organizations put things in writing to create a record, to make themselves visible, to convey complex data, to make things convenient for the reader, to save money, and to convey their own messages more effectively. "If it isn't in writing," says a manager at one company, "it didn't happen." Writing well is an essential way to make yourself visible and convey a favourable impression of you and your organization.

FYI

Recent surveys of the accountancy, aerospace, automotive, and engineering sectors identified a direct link between essential soft skills abilities and employee productivity.

To remain competitive in the global market, according to employers, Canadian professionals need business basics that include "communications, team building, report writing and preparing presentations."

Source: Terrence Belford, "Engineers Need 'Soft' Skills," *The Globe and Mail*, January 13, 2003, B10.

How much does correspondence cost?

Business correspondence is very expensive, and even more costly when it doesn't work.

Writing costs money. Canadian communications expert and professional speaker Helen Wilkie maintains that written correspondence—emails, letters, reports, memos—is an "integral part of doing business. If a $40 000-a-year employee spends just two hours a day reading, writing and managing e-mail, that's a $9 000 annual cost." Moreover, as Wilkie and other experts point out, two hours a day is a very conservative estimate of the amount of time employees spend composing, revising, and reading written documents.[7]

In many organizations, all external documents must be approved before they go out. A document may cycle from writer to superior to writer to another superior to writer again three, four, or even 11 times before it is finally approved. The **cycling** process increases the cost of correspondence.

Longer documents can involve large teams of people and take months to write. An engineering firm that relies on military contracts for its business calculates that it spends $500 000 to put together an average proposal and $1 million to write a large proposal.[8]

Poor correspondence costs even more. When writing isn't clear, complete, and correct, you and your organization pay in wasted time, wasted effort, and lost goodwill.

Sometimes the cost is incalculable; poor writers imperil their futures, as Unit Four's Case for Communicators: "A Hard Lesson in Grammar" demonstrates (see page 269).

FYI

Scholars believe that writing was invented to record inventories of livestock and grain and to calculate taxes.

Source: Denise Schmandt-Besserat, "The Earliest Precursor of Writing," *Scientific American*, 238, no. 6 (1978): 50–59.

POOR WRITING

- Poor writing takes more time to read and interpret.
- It requires more time for revisions.
- It confuses and irritates the reader.
- It delays action while the reader requests more information, or tries to figure out the meaning.

Quite simply, ineffective messages get negative results. A reader who has to guess what the writer means may guess wrong. A reader who finds a letter or memo unconvincing or insulting won't do what the message asks.

Whatever the literal content of the words, every letter, memo, and report serves either to enhance or to damage the image the reader has of the writer. Poor messages damage business relationships. Good communication is worth every minute it takes and every penny it costs. In fact, in a survey conducted by the International Association of Business Communicators, CEOs said that communication yielded a 235 per-cent return on investment.[9]

People communicate to plan products and services; to hire, train, and motivate workers; to coordinate manufacturing and delivery; to persuade customers to buy; and to bill them for the sale.

What makes a message effective?

Successful business correspondence builds goodwill by focusing on the reader.

SEE THE OLC!

Grammar Resources

An effective, reader-centred message meets five criteria:

1. The message is **clear**: the writer chooses the facts—and the organization and language to convey those facts—that enable the reader to get the meaning that the writer intended.
2. The message is **concise**: the writer conveys maximum meaning using as few words as possible.
3. The message is **comprehensive**: the style, organization, and visual impact of the message help the reader to read, understand, and act.
4. The message is **complete**: the reader has enough information to evaluate the message and act on it.
5. The message is **correct**: the information in the message is accurate and is free of errors in punctuation, spelling, grammar, word order, and sentence structure.

An effective message initiates or cements a positive relationship between the writer and the reader (◀▮▶ Modules 6–8).

The Benefits of Becoming a Better Writer

Good business writers are more productive and make more money!

- **Good writing saves time,** because well-written correspondence is easy to read and respond to.
- **It saves money,** because effective writing increases the number of requests that are answered positively and promptly the first time, and presents your point of view—to other people in your organization; to clients, customers, and suppliers; to government agencies; and to the public—more persuasively.
- **Good writing saves energy,** because effective messages reduce the misunderstandings that occur when the reader has to supply missing or unclear information, and because good writing clarifies the issues so that disagreements can surface and be resolved more quickly.
- **It builds goodwill,** because it projects a positive image of your organization and an image of the writer as a knowledgeable, intelligent, capable person.

INSTANT REPLAY

Criteria for Effective Messages

Effective business and administrative writing is clear, concise, comprehensive, complete, and correct. The best messages save the reader time and build goodwill. Whether a message meets these criteria depends on the *interactions among the writer, the audience, the purposes of the message, and the situation.* No single set of words will work in all situations.

How do I begin to analyze business communication situations?

Consider the context!

Before you write—or listen, speak, or read—you need to analyze and understand the situation. What do you really want to happen as a result of your communication? How can you get the results you want?

Communication has consequences. To get the results you want, consider these questions:

- **What's the point?** What information am I reading, imparting, or listening to, and why is it relevant?

EXPANDING A CRITICAL SKILL

Timberjack Corporation's "VP of Fun": Toronto comic Ted Bisaillion uses his creative talent to earn a good living by doing what he loves. Bisaillion, who provides a repertoire of customized performance theatre for companies such as Dell, Levi Strauss, and Shoppers Drug Mart, claims that employees who laugh are healthier and more productive. His corporate clients clearly agree: Bisaillion's latest ventures include corporate humour lectures and a video series (with New Horizons) to promote organizations' sales incentives programs.

Thinking Creatively

Creative thinkers perceive the world imaginatively. Because change is the only constant in today's workplace, the ability to bring a fresh perspective to situations is essential for success. For example,

- Author Gordon MacKenzie's job as "creative paradox" for Hallmark Cards was to encourage workplace creativity. To stimulate his own thinking, he used fantasy

and visualization techniques: "Think in metaphors, fantasize, anything that might bring a broader perspective. I used to fantasize that I was the founder of the company.... [B]y secretly pretending that I was Mr. Hallmark, I assumed responsibility for seeing what most needed tending to, and I attended to it."

- In 1991, Finnish student Linus Torvolds developed a computer operating system and posted the code online as an innovative alternative to the Microsoft monopoly. Today, corporations including Corel, IBM, Dell Computer, and Red Hat Inc. are pursuing software applications initiatives based on the free Linux open-source code.

Innovative solutions come out of preparedness: you can generate insights only by immersing yourself in the situation. But creative, right-brain, or lateral thinking can be learned, like any skill, with practice. Improve your flexible thinking by approaching even mundane tasks in new ways: brush your teeth with your non-dominant hand, for example. In writing, assess problems creatively using brainstorming and mind-mapping techniques.

IBM's tips for creativity are even more diverse:

- Have an argument.
- Brainstorm with someone 10 years older and someone 10 years younger.
- Clean your desk.
- Come in early and enjoy the quiet.
- Leave the office. Sit with a pencil and a pad of paper. See what happens.

Sources: "Bob Rosner, "How Do You Think Outside of the Box? One Expert Weighs In," http://www.reddingemployment.com/redding—employment/stories/20030520hold076.shtml; retrieved September 28, 2006; "Destroying More Creatively," *Report on Business Magazine*, August 2000, http://globeandmail.workopolis.com/servlet/News/robmag/20010126/RO02BES6, retrieved June 28, 2001; Liz Zack, "How IBM Gets Unstuck," *Fast Company*, October 1999, 104. New Horizons Productions, http://www.newhorizonmedia.com/folio00.html, retrieved September 28, 2006.

- **What's my purpose?** What is the intended result? What do I want to have happen as a result of this communication? Do I want to inform or to confirm plans? Do I want to change attitudes and behaviours? Do I want to make a favourable impression? What do I really want as a result?
- **Who's my audience?** What are their wants and needs? What do they already know? What do they need to know to make a decision? What's in it for them?

FIGURE 1.4

P A I B O C

Questions for Analysis

Use the PAIBOC (pronounced "payback") questions to analyze business communication problems:

P What are your **purposes** in writing?

A Who is your **audience?** How do members of your audience differ? What audience characteristics are relevant to this particular message?

I What **information** must your message include?

B What reasons or reader **benefits** can you use to support your position?

O What **objections** can you expect your readers to have? What negative elements of your message must you de-emphasize or overcome?

C How will the **context** affect the reader's response? Think about your relationship to the reader, the morale in the organization, the economy, the time of year, and any special circumstances.

- **Where will the communication happen?** Is the environment conducive to my intention? If I'm reading complicated material, where's the quietest place for me to be? If my message is confidential, how can I ensure maximum privacy?
- **When will the communication happen?** What time of day and what length of time have I chosen to deliver the message? When will the audience really be able to pay attention to my message? If I am reading difficult material, when am I most alert to absorb it? What is the best time of day for my team to meet for highest productivity?
- **What's the best way?** Formal channels—paper documents and presentations—require the most preparation but give you considerable control over the message. Email, phone calls, and office visits are considered less formal. Face-to-face conversations—informal and the most personal—often work best for group decision making, negotiating, and conflict resolution, but they may require a written record for reference. Sometimes you may need more than one message, over more than one channel.

In every communication situation, your success depends on your critical thinking strategies. Use the PAIBOC questions (Figure 1.4) to analyze the communication context and to brainstorm solutions that resolve the problem and meet the psychological needs of the people involved:

P What are your purposes in writing or speaking?

What must this message do to solve the problem? What must it do to meet your own needs? What do you want your audience to do, to think, or to feel? List all your purposes, major and minor. Specify exactly what you want your reader to know or think or do. Specify exactly what kind of image of you and of your organization you want to project. Answer, "What do I want to happen as a result of this message?"

Even a simple message may have several related purposes: to announce a new policy, to make readers aware of the policy's provisions and requirements, to convince readers that the policy is a good one, to tell readers that the organization cares about its employees, and to show readers that you are a competent writer and manager.

A Who is your audience? How are readers going to feel about your message? What do they care about? What do they value? What's in the message that will appeal to them?

How much does your audience know about your topic? How will audience members respond to your message? Some characteristics of your readers will be irrelevant; focus on ones that matter for this message. Whenever you write to several people or to a group (like a memo to all employees), try to identify the economic, cultural, or situational differences that may affect how various subgroups respond to what you have to say.

I What information must your message include?

Make a list of the points that must be included; check your draft to make sure you include them all. If you're not sure whether a particular fact must be included, ask your instructor or your boss.

To include information without emphasizing it, put it in the middle of a paragraph or document and present it as briefly as possible.

B What reasons or reader benefits can you use to support your position?

Brainstorm to develop reasons for your decision, the logic behind your argument, and possible benefits to readers if they do as you ask. Reasons and reader benefits do not have to be monetary. Making the reader's job easier or more pleasant is a good reader benefit. In an informative or persuasive message, identify at least five reader benefits. In your message, use those that you can develop most easily and most effectively.

Be sure that the benefits are adapted to your reader. Many people do not identify closely with their companies; the fact that the company benefits from a policy will help the reader only if the saving or profit is passed directly on to the employees. That is rarely the case: savings and profits are often eaten up by returns to stockholders, bonuses to executives, and investments in plants and equipment or in research and development.

O What objections can you expect your reader(s) to have? What negative elements of your message must you de-emphasize or overcome?

Some negative elements can only be de-emphasized. Others can be overcome. Be creative: is there any advantage associated with (even though not caused by) the negative? Can you rephrase or redefine the negative to make the reader see it differently?

C How will the **context** affect the reader's response? Think about your relationship to the reader, the morale in the organization, the economy, the time of year, and any special circumstances.

Readers may like you or resent you. You may be younger or older than the people you're writing to. The organization may be prosperous or going through hard times; it may have just been reorganized or it may be stable. All these different situations will affect what you say and how you say it.

Consider the news, interest rates, the economy, and the weather. Think about the general business and regulatory climates, especially as they affect the organization specified in the problem. Use the real world as much as possible. Is the industry in which the problem is set doing well? Is the government agency in which the problem is set enjoying general support? Think about the time of year. If it's fall when you write, is your business in a seasonal slowdown after a busy summer? gearing up for the holiday shopping rush? or going along at a steady pace unaffected by seasons?

To answer these questions, draw on your experience, your courses, and your research. Talk to other students, read newspapers and magazines, search the Internet, and look at a company's annual report. You may want to phone a local businessperson to get information. For instance, if you need more information on reader benefits for a problem set in a bank, call a local bank representative to research services and loan rates.

The remaining modules in this book will show you how to use the PAIBOC ("Payback") analysis to create business messages that meet your needs, the needs of the audience, and the needs of the organization.

■ Employability Skills 2000+ Introduction to Business Communications

The Conference Board of Canada
Insights You Can Count On

The skills you need to enter, stay in, and progress in the world of work—whether you work on your own or as a part of a team.

These skills can also be applied and used beyond the workplace in a range of daily activities.

Fundamental Skills

The skills needed as a base for further development

You will be better prepared to progress in the world of work when you can

■ Communicate

✔ read and understand information presented in a variety of forms (e.g., words, graphs, charts, diagrams)
✔ write and speak so others pay attention and understand
✔ listen and ask questions to understand and appreciate the points of view of others

✔ share information using a range of information and communications technologies (e.g., voice, email, computers)
✔ use relevant scientific, technological, and mathematical knowledge and skills to explain or clarify ideas

■ Manage Information

✔ locate, gather, and organize information using appropriate technology and information systems
✔ access, analyze, and apply knowledge and skills from various disciplines (e.g., the arts, languages,

science, technology, mathematics, social sciences, and the humanities)

■ Use Numbers

✔ decide what needs to be measured or calculated
✔ observe and record data using appropriate methods, tools, and technology

✔ make estimates and verify calculations

■ Think & Solve Problems

✔ assess situations and identify problems
✔ seek different points of view and evaluate them based on facts
✔ recognize the human, interpersonal, technical, scientific, and mathematical dimensions of a problem
✔ identify the root cause of a problem
✔ be creative and innovative in exploring possible solutions

✔ readily use science, technology, and mathematics as ways to think, gain and share knowledge, solve problems, and make decisions
✔ evaluate solutions to make recommendations or decisions
✔ implement solutions
✔ check to see if a solution works, and act on opportunities for improvement

Personal Management Skills

The personal skills, attitudes, and behaviours that drive one's potential for growth

You will be able to offer yourself greater possibilities for achievement when you can

■ Demonstrate Positive Attitudes & Behaviours

✔ feel good about yourself and be confident
✔ deal with people, problems, and situations with honesty, integrity, and personal ethics
✔ recognize your own and other people's good efforts

✔ take care of your personal health
✔ show interest, initiative, and effort

■ Be Responsible

✔ set goals and priorities balancing work and personal life
✔ plan and manage time, money, and other resources to achieve goals
✔ assess, weigh, and manage risk

✔ be accountable for your actions and the actions of your group
✔ be socially responsible and contribute to your community

■ Be Adaptable

✔ work independently or as a part of a team
✔ carry out multiple tasks or projects
✔ be innovative and resourceful: identify and suggest alternative ways to achieve goals and get the job done

✔ be open and respond constructively to change
✔ learn from your mistakes and accept feedback
✔ cope with uncertainty

■ Learn Continuously

✔ be willing to continuously learn and grow
✔ assess personal strengths and areas for development
✔ set your own learning goals

✔ identify and access learning sources and opportunities
✔ plan for and achieve your learning goals

■ Work Safely

✔ be aware of personal and group health and safety practices and procedures, and act in accordance with these

Teamwork Skills

The skills and attributes needed to contribute productively

You will be better prepared to add value to the outcomes of a task, project, or team when you can

■ Work with Others

✔ understand and work within the dynamics of a group
✔ ensure that a team's purpose and objectives are clear
✔ be flexible: respect, be open to, and be supportive of the thoughts, opinions, and contributions of others in a group
✔ recognize and respect people's diversity, individual differences, and perspectives

✔ accept and provide feedback in a constructive and considerate manner
✔ contribute to a team by sharing information and expertise
✔ lead or support when appropriate, motivating a group for high performance
✔ understand the role of conflict in a group to reach solutions
✔ manage and resolve conflict when appropriate

■ Participate in Projects & Tasks

✔ plan, design, or carry out a project or task from start to finish with well-defined objectives and outcomes

✔ develop a plan, seek feedback, test, revise, and implement

✔ work to agreed quality standards and specifications

✔ select and use appropriate tools and technology for a task or project

✔ adapt to changing requirements and information

✔ continuously monitor the success of a project or task and identify ways to improve

■ Review of Key Points

1. Why do we communicate?
2. What does business communication accomplish?
3. Why do people write?
4. Who are an organization's internal audiences? Who are its external audiences?
5. What are the characteristics of effective business writing?
6. What are the PAIBOC (Payback) questions?
7. Why analyze the communication situation?

■ Assignments for Module 1

■ Questions for Critical Thinking

1.1 Why do you need to understand the purposes, audience, and context for a message to know whether a specific set of words will work?

1.2 Why do writing and speaking become even more important as people rise in the organization?

1.3 If you're just looking for an entry-level job, why is it still useful to be able to write and speak well?

1.4 Is the writing you've done for other classes more like "school" writing or business writing?

■ Exercises and Problems

1.5   Business Communications Analysis

How do business messages differ from the communication methods you have learned in school? Together with three of your classmates, analyze a minimum of four business messages (memos, letters, slide shows, advertisements, proposals, flyers, brochures), using the following criteria:

• Purposes
• Audiences

• Information (Content and length)
• Organization
• Style (wording, sentence length, paragraph length)
• Layout
• Visuals

Create a table comparing academic writing with the business messages you have chosen. Be prepared to present and explain your results.

1.6   Letters for Discussion—Landscape Plants

Your nursery sells plants, not only in your store but also by mail order. Today you've received a letter from Pat Sykes, complaining that the plants (in a $572 order) did not arrive in satisfactory condition. "All of them were dry and wilted. One came out by the roots when I took it out of the box. Please send me a replacement shipment immediately."

The following letters are possible approaches to answering this complaint. How well does each message meet the needs of the reader, the writer, and the organization? Is the message clear, complete, and correct? Does it save the reader time? Does it build goodwill?

1.   Dear Sir:

I checked to see what could have caused the defective shipment you received. After ruling out problems in transit, I discovered that your order was packed by a new worker who didn't understand the need to water plants thoroughly before they are shipped. We have fired the worker, so you can be assured that this will not happen again.

Although it will cost our company several hundred dollars, we will send you a replacement shipment.

Let me know if the new shipment arrives safely. We trust that you will not complain again.

2.   Dear Pat:

Sorry we messed up that order. Sending plants across country is a risky business. Some of them just can't take the strain. (Some days I can't take the strain myself!) We'll credit your account for $572.

3.   Dear Mr. Smith:

I'm sorry you aren't happy with your plants, but it isn't our fault. The box clearly says "Open and water immediately." If you had done that, the plants would have been fine. And anybody who is going to buy plants should know that a little care is needed. If you pull by the leaves, you will pull the roots out. Always lift by the stem! Since you don't know how to handle plants, I'm sending you a copy of our brochure, "How to Care for Your Plants." Please read it carefully so that you will know how to avoid disappointment in the future.

We look forward to your future orders.

4.   Dear Ms. Sikes:

Your letter of the 5th has come to the attention of the undersigned.

According to your letter, your invoice #47420 arrived in an unsatisfactory condition. Please be advised that it is our policy to make adjustments as per the Terms and Conditions listed on the reverse side of our Acknowledgment of Order. If you will read that document, you will find the following:

"...if you intend to assert any claim against us on this account, you shall make an exception on your receipt to the carrier and shall, within 30 days after the receipt of any such goods, furnish us detailed written information as to any damage."

Your letter of the 5th does not describe the alleged damage in sufficient detail. Furthermore, the delivery receipt contains no indication of any exception. If you expect to receive an adjustment, you must comply with our terms and see that the necessary documents reach the undersigned by the close of the business day on the 20th of the month.

5.   Dear Pat Sykes:

Next week you'll receive a replacement shipment of the perennials you ordered.

Your plants were watered carefully before shipment and packed in specially designed cardboard containers. But if the weather is unusually warm, or if the truck is delayed, small root balls may dry out. Perhaps this happened with your plants. Plants with small root balls are easier to transplant, so they do better in your yard.

The violas, digitalis, aquilegias, and hostas you ordered are long-blooming perennials that will get even prettier each year. Enjoy your garden!

1.7   Memos for Discussion—Announcing a Web Page

The Acme Corporation has just posted its first Web page. Ed Zeplin in Management Information Systems (MIS) created the page and wants employees to know about it.

The following memos are possible approaches. How well does each message meet the needs of the reader, the writer, and the organization? Is the message clear, complete, and correct? Does it save the reader time? Does it build goodwill?

1.   Subject: It's Ready!

I am happy to tell you that my work is done. Two months ago the CEO finally agreed to fund a Web page for Acme, and now the work of designing and coding is done.

I wanted all of you to know about Acme's page. (Actually it's more than 40 pages.) Now maybe the computerphobes out there will realize that you really do need to learn how to use this stuff. Sign up for the next training session! The job you save may be my own.

If you have questions, please do not hesitate to contact me.

L. Ed Zeplin, MIS

2.   Subject: Web Page

Check out the company Web page at

www.server.acme.com/homepage.html

3.   Subject: Visit Our Web Page

Our Web pages are finally operational. The 43 pages take 460 MB on the server and were created using Hot Metal, a program designed to support HTML creation. Though the graphics are sizable and complex, interlacing and code specifying the pixel size serve to minimize download time. Standard HTML coding is enhanced with forms, Java animation, automatic counters, and tracking packages to ascertain who visits our site.

The site content was determined by conducting a survey of other corporate Web sites to become cognizant of the pages made available by our competitors and other companies. The address of our Web page is www.server.acme.com/homepage.html. It is believed that this site will support and enhance our marketing and advertising efforts, improving our outreach to desirable demographic and psychographic marketing groups.

L. Ed Zeplin, MIS

Voice: 713-555-2879; Fax: 713-555-2880; Email: zeplin.1@acme.com

"Only the wired life is worth living."—Anonymous

4.   Subject: Web Page Shows Acme Products to the World, Offers Tips to Consumers, and Tells Prospective Employees
        about Job Possibilities

Since last Friday, Acme's been on the World Wide Web. Check out the page at www.server.acme.com/homepage.html. You can't view the page if you don't have a computer.

I have included pages on our products, tips for consumers, and job openings at Acme in the hope of making our page useful and interesting. Content is the number one thing that brings people back, but I've included some snazzy graphics, too.

When I asked people for ideas for the company pages, almost nobody responded. But if seeing the page inspires you, let me know what else you'd like. I'll try to fit it into my busy schedule.

So check it out. But don't spend too much time on the Web: you need to get your work done, too!

L. Ed Zeplin, MIS

zeplin.1@acme.com

Today's Joke

Fun Links

5.   Subject: How to Access Acme's Web Page

Tell your customers that Acme is now on the Web:

www.server.acme.com/homepage.html

Web pages offer another way for us to bring our story to the public. Our major competitors have Web pages; now we do, too. Our advertisements and packaging will feature our Web address. And people who check out our Web page can learn even more about our commitment to selling quality products, protecting the environment, and meeting customer needs.

If you'd like to learn more about how to use the Web or how to create Web pages for your unit, sign up for one of our workshops. For details and online registration, see www.server.acme.com/training.

If you have comments on Acme's Web pages or suggestions for making them even better, just let me know.

L. Ed Zeplin

zeplin.1@acme.com

1.8   Discussing Strengths

Introduce yourself to a small group of students. Identify three of your strengths that might interest an employer. These can be experience, knowledge, or personality traits (like enthusiasm).

1.9   Introducing Yourself to Your Instructor

Write a memo (at least 1.5 pages long) introducing yourself to your instructor. Include the following topics:

- Background: Where did you grow up? What have you done in terms of school, extracurricular activities, jobs, and family life?
- Interests: What are you interested in? What do you like to do? What do you like to think about and talk about?
- Achievements: What achievements have given you the greatest personal satisfaction? List at least five. Include achievements that gave you a real sense of accomplishment and pride, whether or not you'd list them on a résumé.

- Goals: What do you hope to accomplish this term? Where would you like to be professionally and personally five years from now?

Use a memo format with appropriate headings. Your teacher will provide you with an overview of the memo format. (◀▶ Module 9 for examples of memo format.) Use a conversational writing style; check your draft to polish the style and edit for mechanical and grammatical correctness. A good memo will enable your instructor to see you as an individual. Use specific details to make your memo vivid and interesting. Remember that one of your purposes is to interest your reader!

1.10 Describing Your Experiences in and Goals for Writing

Write a memo (at least 1.5 pages long) to your instructor describing the experiences you've had writing and what you'd like to learn about writing during this course. Use any of the following questions to prompt you:

- What would you most like to learn in a writing course? What topics would motivate your interest in writing?
- What memories do you have of writing? What made writing fun or miserable in the past?
- What have you been taught about writing? List the topics, rules, and advice you remember.
- What kinds of writing have you done in school? How long have the papers been?
- How has your school writing been evaluated?
- Did the instructor mark or comment on mechanics and grammar? style? organization? logic? content? audience analysis and adaptation? Have you received extended comments on your papers? Have instructors in different classes had the same standards, or have you changed aspects of your writing for different classes?
- What voluntary writing have you done—journals, poems, stories, essays? Has this writing been just for you, or has some of it been shared or published?
- Have you ever written on a job or in a student or volunteer organization? Have you ever typed other people's writing? What have these experiences led you to think about real-world writing?
- What do you see as your current strengths and weaknesses in writing skills? What skills do you think you'll need in the future? What kinds of writing do you expect to do after you graduate?

Use a complete memo format with appropriate headings. Your instructor will provide you with an overview of the memo format. (◄|► Module 9 for examples of memo format.) Use a conventional writing style; edit your final draft for mechanical and grammatical correctness.

Polishing Your Prose

Sentence Fragments

A complete sentence has a subject and a verb. If either the subject or the verb is missing, the result is a sentence fragment.

The job candidates.

Passed seven rounds of interviews.

And have taken three tests.

To fix the fragment, add a subject or a verb to make a complete sentence.

The job candidates passed seven rounds of interviews and have taken three tests.

Sentence fragments also occur when a clause has both a subject and a verb but is unable to stand by itself as a complete sentence.

Although I read my email

Because she had saved her work

If he upgrades his computer

The words *although, because,* and *if* make the clause subordinate, which means the clause cannot stand alone. It must be joined to a main clause.

Although I read my email, I did not respond to the draft of the proposal.

Because she had saved her work, Paula was able to restore it after the crash.

If he upgrades his computer, he will be able to use the new software.

Words that make clauses subordinate include

after	if
although, though	when, whenever
because, since	while, as
before, until	

Sometimes fragments are OK. For instance, fragments are used in résumés, advertisements, and some sales and fundraising letters. However, fragments are inappropriate for most business documents. Because they are incomplete, they can confuse or mislead readers.

The biggest problem with grammatical errors like sentence fragments is that readers sometimes assume that people who make errors are unprofessional or illiterate (◀▶ Module 16). Of course, using "incorrect" grammar has nothing to do with intelligence, but many people nevertheless use grammar as a yardstick. People who cannot measure up to that yardstick may be stuck in low-level jobs.

Exercises

Make the following sentence fragments into complete sentences.

1. Our retail sales division.
2. Faxed the contract to the Legal Department for review.
3. Ms. Singh began the meeting a few minutes late. Because the computer crashed.
4. Making our profit margin higher.
5. Although the car ran fine. We were late to the meeting because of traffic.
6. Our first attempt to make the document more readable.
7. Terrell announced a plan to introduce our latest computer model. To retail electronics stores.
8. But instead completed the report.
9. The Accounting Department.
10. Works well into the night.

Check your answers to the odd-numbered exercises on page 571.

▧ Online Learning Centre

Visit the Online Learning Centre at www.mcgrawhill.ca/olc/locker to access module quizzes, a searchable glossary, résumé and letter templates, additional business writing samples, CBC videos, and other learning and study tools.

2

Adapting Your Message to Your Audience

Module Outline

- Who is my audience?
- Why is audience so important?
- What do I need to know about my audience?
- How do I use audience analysis to reach my audience?
- What if my audiences have different needs?
- How do I reach my audience?

Review of Key Points

Assignments for Module 2

Polishing Your Prose: Comma Splices

LEARNING OBJECTIVES

After reading and applying the information in Module 2, you'll be able to demonstrate

Knowledge of

- The variables of the communication process
- The audiences who may evaluate your business messages
- The importance of adapting your message to your audience
- Audience analysis

Skills to

- Analyze your audience when composing messages
- Adapt the content, organization, and form of your messages to meet audience needs

The Conference Board of Canada
Insights You Can Count On

Please see the OLC to preview the key skills from the Conference Board of Canada's Employability Skills 2000+ covered in this module.

Five Kinds of Audiences

Initial: Is first to receive the message; may assign message
Gatekeeper: Has the power to stop the message before it gets to primary audience
Primary: Decides whether to accept recommendations; acts on message
Secondary: Comments on message or implements recommendations
Watchdog: Has political, social, or economic power; may base future actions on evaluation of message

Audience analysis is fundamental to the success of any message: to capture and hold an audience's attention and to motivate readers and listeners, you must shape your message to meet the audience's goals, interests, and needs.

■ Who is my audience?

Your audience may include more people than you might think.

In an organizational setting, a message may have five audiences.[1]

1. The **initial audience** receives the message first and routes it to other audiences. Sometimes the initial audience also tells you to write the message.
2. The **primary audience** will make the decision to act on your message.
3. The **secondary audience** may be asked to comment on your message or to implement your ideas after they've been approved. Secondary audiences can also include lawyers who may use your message—perhaps years later—as evidence of your organization's culture and practices.
4. A **gatekeeper** has the power to stop your message before it gets to the primary audience. The executive assistant who decides which personnel get to speak to the boss is a gate-keeper. Sometimes the supervisor who assigns the message is also the gatekeeper; however, sometimes the gatekeeper is higher in the organization. Occasionally, gatekeepers exist outside the organization. For example, regulatory boards are gatekeepers.
5. A **watchdog audience**, though it does not have the power to stop the message and will not act directly on it, has political, social, or economic power. The watchdog pays close attention to the transaction between you and the primary audience and may base future actions on its evaluation of your message. The media, boards of directors, and members of program advisory committees can all be watchdogs.

As Figures 2.1 and 2.2 on the next page show, one person or group can be part of two audiences. Frequently, a supervisor is both the initial audience and the gatekeeper. The initial audience can also be the primary audience who will act on the message.

■ Why is audience so important?

Successful messages anticipate and meet the audience's needs.

Audience focus is central to both the communication process and message analysis (PAIBOC).

■ Audience and the Communication Process

Understanding what your audience needs and expects, and adapting your messages accordingly, greatly enhances your chances of communicating successfully.

The communication process is the most complex of human activities, and the audience is central to that process. We communicate unceasingly. Our audiences interpret our communication symbols unceasingly. Our words, tonal quality, volume and rate of speech, our posture, stance and gait, our height and weight, our hair style and hair colour, our choice of clothing styles and colours—all the thousands of symbols that we use, intentionally and unintentionally—are perceived and translated according to our audience's perceptions, shaped by age, gender, culture, intelligence, and the experiences unique to every individual.

INSTANT REPLAY

The Communication Process

Stimulus or sender: People, animals, traffic lights, colours: every aspect of our environment can be a stimulus

Message: The meaning we make: meaning is encoded in symbols, including words, gestures, colours, apparel, people's use of space

Channel or method of message transmission: The two primary channels are light waves and airwaves; we humans rely on our five senses to transmit communication stimuli

Receiver: The audience for the message

Feedback: The response, verbal or non-verbal, to the message; feedback may be direct or indirect, immediate or delayed

Noise: The physical, emotional, or psychological static that affects every part of the communication process

FIGURE 2.1
The Audiences for a Marketing Plan

Dawn is an account executive in an ad agency.

Her boss asks her to write a proposal for a marketing plan for a new product the agency's client is introducing. Her boss, who must approve the plan before it is submitted to the client, is both the **initial audience and the gatekeeper.**

Her **primary audience** is the executive committee of the client company, who will decide whether to adopt the plan.

The **secondary audience** includes the marketing staff of the client company, who will be asked for comments on the plan, as well as the artists, writers, and media buyers who will carry out details of the plan if it is adopted.

FIGURE 2.2
The Audiences for a Consulting Report

Jim and Hiro work for a consulting think-tank.

Their company has been hired by a consortium of manufacturers of a consumer product to investigate how proposed federal regulations would affect manufacturing, safety, and cost. The consortium is both the consultants' **initial audience and a gatekeeper.** If the consortium doesn't like the report, it won't send the report to the federal government.

The federal government agency that regulates this consumer product is the **primary audience.** It will set new regulations, based in part (the manufacturers hope) on Jim and Hiro's report. Within this audience are economists, engineers, and policymakers.

Secondary audiences include the public, other manufacturers of the product, and competitors and potential clients of the consulting company.

During the revision process, industry reviewers emerge as a **watchdog audience.** They read drafts of the report and comment on it. Although they have no direct power over this report, their goodwill is important for the consulting company's image—and its future contracts. Their comments are the ones that the authors take most seriously as they revise their drafts.

Source: Based on Vincent J. Brown, "Facing Multiple Audiences in Engineering and R&D Writing: The Social Context of a Technical Report," *Journal of Technical Writing and Communication* 24, no. 1 (1994): 67–75.

Throughout the process, both sender and receiver construct meaning together. Genuine communication occurs when both parties agree on the meaning and significance of the symbols they are exchanging.

Suppose you and your friend Mediha are having a cup of coffee together, and you realize that you need help studying for the upcoming economics exam. You decide to ask Mediha for her help. You choose to **encode** your request in words. Words, of course, are not the only symbols we use to convey ideas. Thousands and thousands of other messages are embedded in our nonverbal symbols — our surroundings, and our own personal style, for example.

FIGURE 2.3
Two-Person Communication

Misunderstandings can occur in any part of the communication process.

Once you have chosen your words, you must **transmit** your **message** to Mediha via a **channel**. Channels include face-to-face, memos, Blackberries, iPods, billboards, telephones, television, and radio, just to name a few.

Mediha must **perceive** the message in order to **receive** it. That is, Mediha must have the physical ability to hear your request. Then she **decodes** your words: she makes meaning from your symbols. Then Mediha interprets the message, chooses a response, and encodes it. Her response is **feedback**. Feedback may be direct and immediate, or indirect and delayed; feedback also consists of both verbal and nonverbal symbols.

Meanwhile, **noise** influences every part of the process. Noise can be physical or psychological. While you're talking to Mediha, the noise in the cafeteria could drown out your words. Or someone could start talking to Mediha just as you make your request. That noise could distort your message to Mediha just as the noise of lawnmowers in spring could interfere with your classroom concentration.

Psychological noise includes emotional, intellectual, or psychological dissonance: it could include disliking a speaker, being concerned about something other than the message, having preconceived notions about an issue, or harbouring prejudices about the message or the messenger.

For example, Mediha has already studied extensively for the exam, and feels that you have not worked hard enough; Mediha feels overwhelmed by her part-time job; Mediha is worried about her uncle, who is ill; Mediha herself is not feeling well. In any of these possibilities, psychological noise will influence her decision, and her message back to you.

Channel overload occurs when the channel cannot handle all the messages that are being sent. Two people may be speaking to you simultaneously, or a small business may have only two phone lines so no one else can get through when both lines are in use.

Information overload occurs when more messages are transmitted than the human receiver can handle. Because of technology, information overload seems to be a constant modern complaint. Some receivers process information on a "first-come, first-served" basis. Some may try to select the most important messages and ignore others. A third way is to depend on abstracts or summaries prepared by other people. None of these ways is completely satisfactory.

At every stage, both Mediha and you can misperceive, misinterpret, choose badly, encode poorly, or choose inappropriate channels. Miscommunication also frequently occurs because every individual makes meaning using **different frames of reference**. We always interpret messages in light of our personal experiences, our cultures and subcultures, and the time in which we live.

Successful communication depends on identifying and establishing common ground between you and your audience. Choose information that your audience needs and will find interesting. Encode your message in words and other symbols the audience will understand. Transmit the message along channels that your audience pays attention to.

Correctly identifying your audience and then choosing audience-appropriate symbols (words, gestures, illustrations) guarantees a more accurate meaning transfer.

Walking coach Lee Scott, president of WOW Company, uses newspaper ads, email newsletters, her company Web site, and word of mouth to attract clients from all over Ontario. WOW's walkers—men and women of all cultures, ages, and incomes—have finished first in charity events around the world.

■ Audience and Business Messages

Consider the PAIBOC questions introduced in Module 1. Five of the six questions relate to audience:

P What are your purposes in communicating?

Your purposes come from you and your organization. Your audience determines how you achieve those purposes.

A Who is your audience? What audience characteristics are relevant to this particular message?

These questions ask directly about your audience.

I What **information** must your message include?

The information you need to give depends on your audience. You need to add relevant facts when the topic is new to your audience. If your audience has heard something but may have forgotten it, protect readers' egos by saying "As you know," or putting the information in a subordinate clause: "Because we had delivery problems last quarter,..." If your audience is familiar with specific facts, concentrate more on clarifying new information.

B What reasons or reader benefits can you use to support your position?

Regardless of your own needs, a good reason or benefit depends on your audience's perception. For some audiences, personal experience counts as a good reason. Other audiences are more persuaded by scientific studies or by experts. For some people, saving money is a good benefit of growing vegetables. Other people may care more about avoiding chemicals, growing varieties that aren't available in grocery stores, or working outside in the fresh air than about costs or convenience. Module 8 ◄│► gives more information on developing reader benefits.

FYI

Audience analysis helps writers avoid adding to the information overload we struggle with daily:

- Every issue of *The New York Times* contains more information than someone in the 17th century would have read in a lifetime.
- There is enough scientific information written every year to keep a person busy reading day and night for 460 years.
- In the past 30 years we have produced more information than in the previous 5000.
- The amount of recorded scientific knowledge is doubling approximately every 15 to 20 years.
- More than 1000 books are published around the world every day.
- Every day seven million new documents are published on the Web, where there are already more than 550 billion.
- The world produces between one and two exabytes of unique content per year, which is roughly 250 megabytes for every man, woman, and child on earth.

Source: Gerry McGovern and Rob Norton, *Content Critical*, (Great Britain; FT Prentice Hall, 2002), pp. 4 & 5.

O What objections can you expect your readers to have? What elements of your message will your audience perceive as negative? How can you arrange the message to overcome audience objections or de-emphasize negative elements?

Different audiences have different attitudes. One audience may object to a price increase. Another audience may see price changes as routine but be bothered by time constraints. Module 13 ◀▶ on persuasion gives more information on overcoming objections.

C How will the **context** affect reader response? Consider your relationship to the reader, the reader's values and expectations, recent organizational history and current morale, the economy, the time of year, the place and time of day, and any special circumstances surrounding the message exchange.

People, information, and organizations exist in a context. How well your audience knows you, how they feel about you and your organization, how well the economy is doing, even what's been in the news recently: all influence their response to your message.

What do I need to know about my audience?

You need to know everything that's relevant to what you're writing or talking about.

Almost everything about your audience is relevant to some message, but for any particular message, only a few facts about your audience will be relevant. These facts will vary depending on each communication situation (see Table 2.1).

In general, you need to use empathy and critical-thinking tools. **Empathy** is the ability to put yourself in someone else's shoes, to feel with that person. Empathy requires being audience-centred because the audience is not just like you.

Critical thinking involves gathering as much information as you can about someone or something and then making decisions based on that information.

You need to use your research and your knowledge about people and about organizations to predict likely responses.

Analyzing Individuals and Members of Groups

When you write or speak to people in your own organization, and in other organizations you work with, you may be able to analyze your audience as individuals. You may already know your audience; it will usually be easy to get additional information by talking to members of your audience, talking to people who know your audience, and observing your audience.

In other organizational situations, however, you'll analyze your audience as members of a group: "taxpayers who must be notified that they owe more income tax," "customers living in the northeast end of the city," or "employees with small children."

FYI

North American Boomers (people born between 1946 and 1957) represent the most significant demographic in history. Because of their numbers (and expectations), Boomers will continue to wield enormous economic clout. By 2012, when Canadian Boomers start to turn 65, these 14 million seniors will influence every aspect of the market, from financial services, real estate, and retail, to health care and funeral industries.

Source: Charles Davies, "The New Golden Age," *National Post Business*, January 2003, 45–51.

TABLE 2.1
Identifying Key Audience Characteristics for Messages

Message or Purpose	Audience	Relevant factors
Memo announcing that the company will reimburse employees for tuition if they take work-related college or university courses	All employees	1. Attitudes toward education (some people find courses enjoyable; others may be intimidated) 2. Time available (some may be too busy) 3. Interest in being promoted or in receiving cross-training 4. Attitude toward company (those committed to its success will be more interested in the program)
Letter offering special financing on a new or used car	Post-secondary students	1. Income 2. Expectations of future income (and ability to repay loan) 3. Interest in having a new car 4. Attitude toward cars offered by that dealership 5. Knowledge of interest rates 6. Access to other kinds of financing
Letter containing a meeting agenda and saying that you can bring your child along	Client	1. How well the client knows you 2. How much the client likes you 3. How important the agenda items are to the client 4. How the client feels about children 5. Physical space for meeting (room for the child to play)

SEE THE OLC!

Strategis: Canada's Business and Consumer Site

Since audience analysis is central to the success of your message, you'll need to consider the following pertinent information about your audience:

- Their knowledge about your topic
- Their demographic factors, such as age, gender, education, income, class, marital status, number of children, home ownership, location
- Their attitudes, values, and beliefs
- Their personality
- Their past behaviour

Prior Knowledge

Even people in your own organization won't share all your knowledge. Salespeople in the automotive industry, for example, don't know the technical language of their service mechanics.

Most of the time, you won't know exactly what your audience knows. Moreover, even if you've told readers before, they may not remember the old information when they read the new message. In any case, avoid mind-numbing details. If, however, you want to remind readers of *relevant facts* tactfully,

- Preface statements with "As you know," "As you may know," "As we've discussed," or a similar phrase.

EXPANDING A CRITICAL SKILL

Understanding What Your Organization Wants

Michelle wondered whether her boss was sexist. Everyone else who had joined the organization when she did had been promoted. Her boss never seemed to have anything good to say about her or her work.

Michelle didn't realize that, in her boss's eyes, she wasn't doing good work. Michelle was proud of her reports; she thought she was the best writer in the office. But her boss valued punctuality, and Michelle's reports were always late.

Just as every sport has rules about scoring, so too do workplaces have rules about what "counts." Even in the same industry, different organizations and different supervisors may care about different things. One boss circles misspelled words and posts the offending message on a bulletin board for everyone to see. Other people are more tolerant of errors. One company values original ideas, while

another workplace tells employees just to do what they're told. One supervisor likes technology and always buys the latest hardware and software; another is technophobic and has to be persuaded to get needed upgrades.

Succeeding in an organization depends first on understanding what "counts" at your organization. To find out what counts in your organization,

- Ask your boss, "What parts of my job are most important? What's the biggest thing I could do to improve my work?"
- Listen to the stories colleagues tell about people who have succeeded and those who have failed. When you see patterns, check for confirmation: "So his real problem was that he didn't socialize with co-workers?" This gives your colleagues a chance to provide feedback: "Well, it was more than never coming to happy hour. He didn't really seem to care about the company."
- Observe. See who is praised, who is promoted.

- Always spell out acronyms the first time you use them: "Employee Stock Ownership Plan (ESOP)."
- Provide brief definitions in the text: "the principal (the money you have invested)."
- Put information readers should know in a subordinate clause: "Because the renovation is behind schedule,…"

Demographic Factors

Demographic characteristics can be objectively quantified, or measured, and include age, gender, religion, education level, income, location, and so on.

Sometimes demographic information is irrelevant; sometimes it's important. Does age matter? Almost always, since people's perspectives and priorities change as they grow older. For example, if you were explaining a change in your company's pension plan, you would expect older workers to pay much closer attention than younger workers. And you would need to shape your explanation to appeal to that older audience.

Demographic data has certainly determined the sharp increase in small business start-ups devoted to personal services. For example, the North American concierge industry—providing services from housesitting to running errands—is thriving because it offers time to busy Boomers.

SEE THE OLC!

Statistics Canada

Business and non-profit organizations get demographic data by surveying their customers, clients, and donors; by using Statistics Canada data; or by purchasing demographic data from marketing companies. For many messages, simply identifying subsets of your audience is enough. For example, a school board trying to win support for a tax increase knows that not everyone living in the district will have children in school. It isn't necessary to know the exact percentages to realize that successful messages need to contain appeals not only to parents but also to voters who won't directly benefit from the improvements that the tax increase will fund.

Personality

SEE THE OLC!

Identify Your Myers-Briggs Type

Understanding and adapting to your primary audience's personality can also help make your message more effective.

Personality and learning style assessment instruments can provide you with useful insights into your own and others' behaviours. In his bestsellers *Secrets of Powerful Presentations* and *Leadership from Within*, business consultant Peter Urs Bender says that knowing your audience is key to communication success. Bender describes four personality types, and offers a free online assessment for readers to identify their type.[2] Another popular assessment tool, the Myers-Briggs Type Indicator, uses four dimensions (introvert–extrovert, sensing–intuitive, thinking–feeling, judging–perceiving) to identify personality preferences[3]:

1. **Introvert–extrovert:** the source of one's energy. Introverts get their energy from within; extroverts are energized by interacting with other people.
2. **Sensing–intuitive:** how someone gathers information. Sensing types gather information step by step through their senses. Intuitive types see relationships among ideas.
3. **Thinking–feeling:** how someone makes decisions. Thinking types use objective logic to reach decisions. Feeling types make decisions that feel "right."
4. **Judging–perceiving:** the degree of certainty someone needs. Judging types like closure. Perceptive types like possibilities.

SEE THE OLC!

View Sample Geodemographic Clusters

Table 2.2 suggests how you can use this information to adapt a message to your audience.

You'll be most persuasive if you play to your audience's strengths. Indeed, many of the general principles of business communications reflect the types most common among managers. Putting the main point up front satisfies the needs of judging types, and some 75 percent of managers are judging. Giving logical reasons satisfies the needs of the nearly 80 percent of managers who are thinking types.[4]

Values and Beliefs

SEE THE OLC!

What Psychographic Group Do You Belong To?

Psychographic characteristics are qualitative rather than quantitative and include values, beliefs, goals, and lifestyles. Knowing what your audience finds important allows you to organize information in a way that seems natural to your audience and to choose appeals that audience members will find persuasive.

Looking at values enables a company to identify customer segments. The Canadian-born Tim Hortons chain introduced a more diverse menu (croissants, muffins, soup, and sandwiches) to attract new fast-food clients and to appeal to its original, increasingly weight-conscious customers. Ranked as Canada's "best-managed brand," based on customer service, Tim Hortons continues to expand in Canada and internationally.[5]

Eresearcher Mary Modahl's survey of 250 000 households found that online buying depends on psychographics: the consumer's attitude toward technology along a continuum from "profoundly suspicious" to "eagerly accepting."

TABLE 2.2
Using Myers-Briggs Types in Persuasive Messages

If your audience is	Use this strategy	For this reason
An introvert	Write a memo and let the reader think about your proposal before responding.	Introverts prefer to think before they speak. Written documents give them the time they need to think through a proposal carefully.
An extrovert	Try out your idea orally, in an informal setting.	Extroverts like to think on their feet. They are energized by people; they'd rather talk than write.
A sensing type	Present your reasoning step by step. Get all your facts exactly right.	Sensing types usually reach conclusions step by step. They want to know why something is important, but they trust their own experience more than someone else's say-so. They're good at facts and expect others to be, too.
An intuitive type	Present the big picture first. Stress the innovative, creative aspects of your proposal.	Intuitive types like solving problems and being creative. They can be impatient with details.
A thinking type	Use logic, not emotion, to persuade. Show that your proposal is fair, even if some people may be hurt by it.	Thinking types make decisions based on logic and abstract principles. They are often uncomfortable with emotion.
A feeling type	Show that your proposal meets the emotional needs of people as well as the dollars-and-cents needs of the organization.	Feeling types are very aware of other people and their feelings. They are sympathetic and like harmony.
A perceiving type	Show that you've considered all the alternatives. Ask for a decision by a specific date.	Perceiving types want to be sure they've considered all the options. They may postpone coming to closure.
A judging type	Present your request quickly.	Judging types are comfortable making quick decisions. They like to come to closure so they can move on to something else.

Source: Based on Isabel Briggs Myers, "Effects of Each Preference in Work Situations," *Introduction to Type* (Palo Alto, CA: Consulting Psychologists Press, 1962, 1980).

Ford Motor Company's ebusiness transformation strategy depends on direct contact with consumers. Ford has partnered with Teletech, the consumer-marketing firm, to identify consumer preferences and trends as part of its business-to-consumer brand value enhancement. The company also sponsors interactive automotive sections on teen Web sites to cultivate and build relationships with future car buyers.[6]

Geodemographic data analyze audiences according to their location and spending habits. Postal code clusters identify current and potential customers based on two truisms: 1) people are what they buy, and 2) birds of a feather flock together: "…our shopping habits are shaped by environment and our desire to belong."

Every time we use credit cards or give our postal codes at the checkout, we provide data miners like Tony Lea, vice-president of Environics Analytics, with a snapshot of ourselves and our values. Lea uses that information to tell businesses how to find and reach their target markets. "He advises banks where to locate new branches, he knows which grocery stores should stock thin-crust pizza and he can design direct mail to [consumers'] tastes." Lea has even successfully advised a federal political party on how to appeal to undecided voters in specific neighbourhoods.

Matching consumers' buying habits with their environment demonstrates that culture influences shopping attitudes and choices: "When Environics ran its numbers, it produced 15 clusters that were distinctly Québecois ... Quebeckers shop differently than English-speaking Canada. Québec cities appear as almost uniform groupings, keen on good wine, fine restaurants, and high fashion. One study found that Quebéckers and New Yorkers together outclassed the rest of the continent in fashion-consciousness."

Analyzing Canadians' shopping habits is "... a $550 million industry," and technological innovation continues to refine research methods. *Neuromarketing* uses MRI scans to "chart how the emotional side of the brain reacts ..." in consumer product testing and purchasing decisions. *Commercial ethnography* films consumers as they shop, to "brainstorm new products and test designs." International marketing firms use

Home Depot store.

"global ethnography" to study the impact of culture on consumerism. And researchers increasingly take advantage of the speed and convenience of the Internet to analyze audiences through online surveys and focus groups.[7]

Past Behaviour

Human resource managers maintain that you can analyze and predict people's future actions based on their past behaviours; the more recent the behaviour, the more accurate the prediction.

■ Analyzing People in Organizations

Audience reaction is also strongly influenced by the perceptions and expectations of the groups to which they belong. These groups, or **discourse communities**, include family, peers, professional associations, clubs, and the workplace—all communities with which your audience identifies. Discourse communities are groups whose members create the affiliation, the rules and the norms, through discourse, or dialogue. Members communicate through symbols (language, nonverbals) that may or may not be exclusive to their group, but which identify them as members of that group.

Therefore, a discourse community is a group of people who share assumptions about their particular culture and values: what to wear; how to behave; what topics to discuss and how to discuss them; what channels; formats, and styles to use; and what constitutes evidence. Each person is part of several discourse communities, which may or may not overlap.

Consider your own discourse communities: perhaps you wear jeans to signify your membership in the student community; your hairstyle or piercing indicates your membership in a sub-culture; your iPod holds music that reflects your affiliation to another group. When you go for a job interview, you might cut your hair and put on more formal clothes to display the norms of the organizational culture you want to join.

INSTANT REPLAY

Discourse Community

A **discourse community** is a group of people who share assumptions about what channels, formats, and styles to use, what topics to discuss and how to discuss them, and what constitutes evidence.

When analyzing an organization's discourse community, consider both non-verbal and verbal clues:

- What does the physical environment say about who and what are valued? What departments and services are front and centre? Where is the reception area located? What messages do the furnishings and decor send? How are visitors welcomed? Is the company mission statement prominent? What does the office space layout indicate about the organization's values? Where are the library, training rooms, gymnasium, and cafeteria located? How well are they resourced?
- Where do the managers work? Do bosses dress differently from other employees?
- How are employees treated? How are new hires oriented? How is employee performance recognized? What's featured in the company newsletter? How do people in the organization get important information?
- How do people in the organization communicate? What channels, formats, and styles are preferred for communication? Do they write a paper memo, send an email, or walk down the hall to talk to someone? How formal or informal are people expected to be—in their dress, on the telephone, in meetings?
- What do people talk about? What is not discussed?
- What kind of and how much evidence is needed to be convincing? Is personal evidence convincing? Do people need to supply statistics and formal research to be convincing?

Some symbols may no longer serve an obvious purpose as in this photo of children dressed up for Halloween.

An organization's **culture** is expressed through its values, attitudes, and philosophies. **Organizational** or **corporate** culture reveals itself verbally in the organization's myths, stories, and heroes, and non-verbally in the allocation of space, money, and power (◀|▶ Module 3).

The following questions will help you analyze an organization's culture:

- What are the organization's goals? making money? serving customers and clients? advancing knowledge? contributing to the community?
- What does the organization value? diversity or homogeneity? independence or being a team player? creativity or following orders?
- How do people get ahead? Are rewards based on seniority, education, being well-liked, making technical discoveries, or serving customers? Are rewards available to only a few top people, or is everyone expected to succeed?
- How formal are behaviour, language, and dress?
- What behavioural expectations predominate? How do employees treat one another? Do employees speak in "I," "we," or "them and us" language? How do employees get organizational information?

Two companies in the same business may express very different cultures. Their company Web sites can offer some clues to those cultures. Royal Bank's standing as Canada's oldest bank is reflected in its corporate Web site: conservative dark-blue and gold colours and a few, metaphoric pictures. TD-Canada Trust's green and white Web site—implying a fresh approach—offers photos of young, happy people, apparently delighted by the products and services the bank provides.[8]

INSTANT REPLAY

Organizational Culture

An organization's **culture** is its values, attitudes, and philosophies. **Organizational culture** (or **corporate culture**, as it is also called) is revealed verbally in the organization's myths, stories, and heroes, and non-verbally in the allocation of space, money, and power.

Many companies describe their cultures as part of the section on employment. Job candidates who research the corporate culture to identify how their skills match with the company have a significant advantage in an interview. Researcher Jennifer Chatman found that new hires who "fit" a company's culture were more likely to stay with the job, be more productive, and be more satisfied than those who did not fit the culture.[9]

Organizations also contain several subcultures. For example, manufacturing and marketing may represent different subcultures in the same organization: workers may dress differently and espouse different values. In a union environment, management and union representatives traditionally employ adversarial language to advance their own sub-culture's perspective while undermining the other's point of view.

You can learn about organizational culture by paying attention to communication clues and cues. For example, observe people and listen to their stories. Every discourse community and every culture creates and perpetuates meaning and membership through the stories their members share. The Sleeman's Brewery story, for example, is that the quality of its beer is the result of family recipes handed down through five generations. And McCain Foods continues to present itself as a "family business" culture, despite its 20 000 employees and multinational, global presence.

Conscious awareness of an organization's spoken and unspoken messages can provide you with important information on its values and norms.

How do I use audience analysis to reach my audience?

SEE THE OLC!

Analyze the Corporate Cultures of Grocery Gateway and the Royal Bank

Use it to plan strategy, organization, style, document design, and visuals.

Take the time to analyze your audience; then adapt your strategy, style, and organizational pattern to your audience's needs. For paper or electronic documents, you can also adapt the document's design and the photos or illustrations you choose. For the best results, revise your message with your audience in mind.

Strategy

- Choose appeals and reader benefits that work for the specific audience (◀▶ Module 8).
- Use details and language that reflect your knowledge of, and respect for, the specific audience, the organizational culture, and the discourse community.
- Make it easy for the audience to respond positively.
- Include only necessary information.
- Anticipate and overcome objections (◀▶ Modules 7, 10, and 12 show you how to emphasize positive aspects, decide how much information to include, and overcome obstacles).

Organization

- It's usually better to get to the point right away. The major exceptions are
  - When you must persuade a reluctant reader
  - When your audience would see the message as bad news and you want to break the news gradually

- Anticipate and meet the audience's expectations of format: make the organizational pattern clear to the audience. (◀▶ Modules 9, 23, and 24 show you how to use headings and overviews. Module 20 shows how to use overviews and signposts in oral presentations.)

Style

**Canadian and American
Niche Groups**

- Strive for clarity and accessibility: use simple words, a mixture of sentence lengths, and short paragraphs with topic sentences (◀▶ Modules 14 and 15).
- Use natural, conversational, personable, tactful language: avoid negative, defensive, arrogant, and "red-flag" words—*unfortunately, fundamentalist, liberal, crazy, incompetent, dishonest*—that may generate a negative reaction.
- Use the language that appeals to your audience. In parts of Canada, including Québec and some areas of Manitoba and New Brunswick, bilingual messages in English and in French, with French first, are the norm.
- Use conversational language.

Document Design

- Use telegraphing: bulleted lists, headings, and a mix of paragraph lengths create white space.
- Choose the format, footnotes, and visuals expected by the organizational culture or the discourse community. (◀▶ Module 5 discusses effective document design.)

Photographs and Visuals

- Photos and visuals can make a document look more informal or more formal. Carefully consider the difference between cartoons and photos of "high art."
- Use bias-free photographs. Unintentional cultural, gender, religious, and economic assumptions can offend readers and lose business.
- Choose photographs and illustrations that project positive cultural meanings for your audience. Middle-Eastern readers, for example, find pictures of barelegged and bare-armed women offensive and may also object to pictures of clean-shaven men.
- Do your research and audience analysis: some cultures (e.g., France and Japan) use evocative photographs that bear little direct relationship to the text. North American audiences expect photos to relate to the text.

▪ What if my audiences have different needs?

Focus on gatekeepers and decision makers.

When the members of your audience share the same interests and the same level of knowledge, you can use these principles for individual readers or for members of homogenous groups. But sometimes, different members of the audience have different needs.

When you are writing or speaking to pluralistic audiences, meet the needs of gatekeepers and primary audiences first.

Content and Choice of Details

- Always provide an overview—the introductory or topic sentence—for reader orientation.
- In the body of the document, provide enough evidence to prove your point.

Best Buy and Future Shop share the same parent company and offer similar products. Their customer demographic, however, differs. Future Shop is designed to attract a more up-scale customer.

Organization

- Organize your message based on the primary audience's attitudes toward it: give good news up front; provide the explanation before you deliver the bad news.
- Organize documents to make reading easy: provide a table of contents for documents more than five pages long so that your readers can turn to the portions that interest them.
- Use headings as signposts: use headings to tell readers what they're about to read and to connect ideas throughout your document. This strategy reinforces your credibility through unity and coherence. If the primary audience doesn't need details that other audiences will want, provide those details in attachments or appendices.

Level of Language

- Contemporary business communication uses conversational, semi-formal language. Use "I" and "you," and address your reader by name. Do research, however, to discover your reader's title preference (for example, Mr., Ms.).
- When both internal and external audiences will read the document, use a slightly more formal style and the third person; avoid "I."
- Use a more formal style when you write to international audiences.

Technical Terms and Theory

- Know what your reader knows; then provide only the necessary information. Use technical terms only if these will increase reader comprehension (◀▶ Module 15).
- Put background information and theory under separate headings. Readers can use the headings to read or skip these sections, as their knowledge dictates.
- If primary audiences will have more knowledge than other audiences, provide a glossary of terms. Early in the document, let readers know that the glossary exists.

▮ How do I reach my audience?

Effective messages make use of multiple channels.

Communication channels vary in
- transmission speed
- transmission accuracy

FYI

Be prudent when you publish: your audience could be anyone because your every e-mail leaves a retrievable record.

An employee types an e-mail and hits send. A copy is often maintained on the employee's desktop computer.

The message travels to the company's e-mail server before it is sent on. A copy is cached—possibly for many months—as set by corporate policy.

The server's cached files are backed up, usually on tape, where a copy of the e-mail is preserved. Although tape archives are more difficult to search, they are also never completely over-written or deleted.

The e-mail is sent from the company server to the Internet, and directed to the recipient. Along the way, the e-mail may go through ISP servers where there's a small risk that a footprint or copy of the e-mail may remain, thanks to anti-spam or anti-virus programs' queues.

The e-mail arrives at the recipient's e-mail server; a copy is kept according to IT policy.

Again, a copy of the e-mail is backed up, either on tape, or possibly by an automated archiving system on a separate in-house server. It could also be outsourced to a third-party server to be stored for up to seven years.

The e-mail is delivered to the recipient. Unlimited copies may be saved or forwarded elsewhere.

Source: Andrew Wahl, "How to Track an Email," *Canadian Business*, June 20–July 17, 2005, http://www.canadian business.com/managing/career/article.isp?content= 20060111_123404_4184, retrieved October 23, 2006.

- cost
- efficiency
- audience impact

Your purpose, the audience, and the situation—*known as the communication context*—will all determine which and how many channels you choose (refer to the PAIBOC questions on page 13):

A written message makes it easier to do several things:

- Present many specific details of a law, policy, or procedure
- Present extensive or complex financial data
- Minimize undesirable emotions

Writing, however, often requires more time than speaking face-to-face. Furthermore, once you mail the letter, or hit Send, writing is "for the record." Your documents, including your e-mail messages, are permanent and potentially available to everyone.

When you do decide to write, use the channel that best meets the expectations of your audience. Email messages are appropriate for routine messages to people you already know. Paper is usually better for someone to whom you're writing for the first time.

Speaking is easier and more efficient when you need to do any of the following:

- Answer questions, resolve conflicts, and build consensus
- Use emotion to help persuade the audience
- Provoke an immediate action or response
- Focus the audience's attention on specific points
- Modify a proposal that may not be acceptable in its original form

Scheduled meetings and oral presentations are more formal than phone calls or stopping someone in the hall. Important messages should use more formal channels, whether they're oral or written.

Oral and written messages have many similarities. In both, you should do six things:

1. Adapt the message to the specific audience.
2. Show the audience members how they benefit from the idea, policy, service, or product (◀▶ Module 8).
3. Overcome any objections the audience may have.
4. Use a good attitude and positive emphasis (◀▶ Modules 6 and 7).
5. Use visuals to clarify or emphasize material (◀▶ Module 25).
6. Specify exactly what the audience should do.

Even when everyone in an organization has access to the same channels, different discourse communities often prefer different channels. When a university updated its employee benefits manual, the computer scientists and librarians wanted the information online. Faculty wanted to be able to read the information on paper. Maintenance workers and carpenters wanted to get answers on voicemail.[10]

The bigger your audience, the more complicated channel choice becomes, because few channels reach everyone. When possible, use multiple channels. Also use multiple channels for very important messages. For example, talk to key players about a written document before the meeting where the document will be discussed.

Employability Skills 2000+

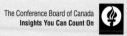

The Conference Board of Canada
Insights You Can Count On

Please see the OLC to preview the key skills from the Conference Board of Canada's Employability Skills 2000+ covered in this module.

Review of Key Points

1. What five audiences may your message reach? Give a specific example of each.
2. Describe the communication process. Explain why even simple communications can fail.
3. What is a discourse community? Identify three separate discourse communities you belong to. Identify two symbols (verbal or nonverbal) that differentiate each of your discourse communities.
4. What is organizational culture? Identify three symbols (verbal or nonverbal) that your college/university uses to reflect its culture.
5. What are three ways you can analyze your audience?
6. What is a channel?
7. What are three ways you can adapt your messages to your audience?

Assignments for Module 2

Questions for Critical Thinking

2.1 What are your options if your boss' criteria for a document are different from those of the primary audience?
2.2 Emphasizing the importance of audience, salespeople often say, "The customer is king," or "The customer is always right," or "The customer is in control." To what extent do you feel in control as a customer, a citizen, or a student? What could you do to increase your feelings of control?
2.3 If you are employed, which aspects of your organization's culture match your own values? Describe the culture you would most like to work in.

Exercises and Problems

2.4   Identifying Audiences

In each of the following situations, label the audiences as initial, gatekeeper, primary, secondary, or watchdog.

1. Russell is seeking venture capital so that he can expand his business of offering soccer camps to youngsters. He's met an investment banker whose clients regularly hear presentations from businesspeople seeking capital. The investment banker decides who will get a slot on the program, based on a comprehensive audit of each company's records and business plan.
2. Maria is marketing auto loans. She knows that many car buyers choose one of the financing options presented by the car dealership, so she wants to persuade dealers to include her financial institution in the options they offer.
3. Paul works for the mayor's office in a big city. As part of a citywide cost-cutting measure, a panel has recommended requiring employees who work more than 40 hours in a week to take compensatory time off rather than be paid overtime. The only exceptions will be the police and fire departments. The mayor asks Paul to prepare a proposal for the city council, which will vote on whether to implement the change. Before they vote, council members will hear from (1) citizens, who will have

an opportunity to read the proposal and communicate their opinions to the city council; (2) mayors' offices in other cities, who may be asked about their experiences; (3) union representatives, who may be concerned about the reduction in income that will result if the proposal is implemented; (4) department heads, whose ability to schedule work might be limited if the proposal passes; and (5) panel members and government lobbying groups. Council members come up for re-election in six months.

2.5   Choosing a Channel to Reach a Specific Audience

Suppose that your business, government agency, or non-profit group has a product, service, or program targeted for each of the following audiences. What would be the best channel(s) to reach people in that group in your city? Would that channel reach all group members?

1. Renters
2. Sikh owners of small businesses
3. People who use wheelchairs
4. Teenagers who work part-time while attending school
5. Competitive athletes
6. Parents whose children play soccer
7. People willing to work part-time
8. Financial planners
9. Hunters
10. New immigrants

2.6   Introducing a Wellness Program

Assume your organization has decided to implement a wellness program that will give modest rebates to employees who adopt healthful practices (see Problem 11.11 on page 198). As director of human resources, you explain the program and build support for it. Pick a specific organization that you know something about and answer the following questions about it.

1. What percentage of employees currently (a) smoke? (b) drink heavily? (c) are overweight? (d) don't exercise? (e) have high blood pressure? (f) have high cholesterol?
2. Why don't people already follow healthful lifestyles?
3. Do company vending machines, cafeteria, or other facilities make it easy for employees to get low-fat snacks and meals?
4. How much exercise do people get on the job? What work-related injuries are most common?
5. What exactly do people do on the job? Will being healthier help them work more efficiently? deal better with stress? have more confidence interacting with clients and customers?
6. What aspects of health and fitness would employees like to know more about? What topics might seem boring or stale?

2.7   Persuading an Organization to Adopt Flextime

Flextime is a system that allows employees to set their own starting and stopping times.

Flextime is especially appealing to organizations that have a hard time keeping good employees or that cannot easily raise salaries. It is also appealing to companies with the philosophy of giving workers as much independence as possible. Most employees prefer flextime. However, in some organizations, flextime creates conflicts between workers who get the schedules they want and those who have to work traditional hours to cover the phones. Some firms are afraid that the quality of work may suffer if employees and supervisors aren't on the job at the same time. Record keeping may be more complicated.

Identify the major argument that you could use to persuade each of the following organizations to use flextime and the major objection you anticipate. Which of the organizations would be fairly easy to convince? Which would be harder to persuade?

1. A large, successful insurance company
2. A branch bank
3. A small catering service
4. The admissions office on your campus
5. A church, synagogue, temple, or mosque with a staff of two clergy, a director of music, two secretaries, and a custodian
6. A government agency

2.8 Analyzing the Other Students in Your College or University

Analyze the students in your college or university. (If your college or university is large, analyze the students in your program of study.) Is there a "typical" student? If all students are quite different, how are they different? Consider the following kinds of information in your analysis:

Demographic Data

Age (Average; high and low)

Gender (What proportion are men? What proportion are women?)

Ethnic background (What groups are represented? How many of each?)

Languages

Marital status

Number of children

Parents' income/personal or family income

Going to school full- or part-time

Outside jobs (What kinds? How many hours a week?)

Membership in campus organizations

Religious affiliations

Political preferences

Proportion going on for further education after graduation

Psychographics

What values, beliefs, goals, and lifestyles do students have? Which are common? Which are less common?

What's the relationship between the students' values and their choice of major or program?

What do students hope to gain from the classes they're taking? What motivates them to do their best work in class?

Additional Information

What are students' attitudes toward current campus problems? current political problems?

What is the job market like for students in your school or major? Will students find it easy to get jobs after graduation? How much will they be making? Where will they be working?

After you answer these questions, identify the factors that would be most relevant in each of the following situations:

1. You want to persuade students to participate in an internship program.
2. You want to persuade students to join a campus organization.
3. You want to find out whether there are enough parking spaces on campus.
4. You want to know whether the campus placement office is providing adequate services to students.
5. You want to hire students to staff a business that you're starting.

2.9 Analyzing People in Your Organization

1. Analyze your supervisor:
   - Does he or she like short or long explanations?
   - Does he or she want to hear about all the problems in a unit or only the major ones?
   - How important are punctuality and deadlines?
   - How well informed about a project does he or she want to be?
   - Is he or she more approachable in the morning or the afternoon?
   - What are your supervisor's major hassles?

2. Analyze other workers in your organization:

- Is work "just a job" or do most people really care about the organization's goals?
- How do workers feel about clients or customers?
- What are your co-workers' major hassles?

3. Analyze your customers or clients:
- What attitudes do they have toward the organization and its products or services?
- How is the way they read affected by education, age, or other factors?
- What are their major hassles?

As your instructor directs,

a. Write a memo to your instructor summarizing your analysis.
b. Discuss your analysis with a small group of students.
c. Present your analysis orally to the class.
d. Combine your information with classmates' information to present a collaborative report comparing and contrasting your audiences at work.

2.10   Analyzing a Discourse Community

Analyze the way one of your discourse communities uses language. Possible groups include

- Family
- Peers
- Work teams
- Sports teams
- Associations, organizations, and other service or social groups
- Churches, synagogues, temples, and mosques
- Geographic or ethnic group

Questions to ask include the following:

- What specialized terms might not be known to outsiders?
- What topics do members talk or write about? What topics are considered unimportant or improper?
- What channels do members use to convey messages?

- What forms of language do members use to build goodwill? to demonstrate competence or superiority?
- What strategies or kinds of proof are convincing to members?
- What formats, conventions, or rules do members expect messages to follow?

As your instructor directs,

a. Share your results orally with a small group of students.
b. Present your results in an oral presentation to the class.
c. Present your results in a memo to your instructor.
d. Share your results in an email message to the class.
e. Share your results with a small group of students and write a joint memo reporting the similarities and differences you found.

2.11   Analyzing Corporate Culture on the Web

Analyze three organizations' Web descriptions of their corporate cultures.

1. Do all three discuss the same aspects of corporate culture?
2. Are the statements about each organization's culture consistent with the rest of its Web pages? with what you know about each organization?
3. What aspects of each culture do you like best? What, if anything, do you not like? What questions do you have about the organizations' culture that the Web pages don't answer?

As your instructor directs,

a. Share your results orally with a small group of students.
b. Present your results in an oral presentation to the class.
c. Present your results in a memo to your instructor.
d. Share your results in an email message to the class.
e. Share your results with a small group of students and write a joint memo reporting the similarities and differences you found.

2.12 Analyzing an Organization's Culture

Interview several people about the culture of their organization. Possible organizations include

- Work teams
- Sports teams
- Associations, organizations, and other service or social groups
- Churches, synagogues, temples, and mosques
- Geographic or ethnic group
- Groups of friends

Questions to ask include those in this module and the following:

1. Tell me about someone in this organization you admire. Why is he or she successful?
2. Tell me about someone who failed in this organization. What did he or she do wrong?

3. What ceremonies and rituals does this organization have? Why are they important?
4. Why would someone join this group rather than joining a competitor?

As your instructor directs,

a. Share your results orally with a small group of students.
b. Present your results in an oral presentation to the class.
c. Present your results in a memo to your instructor.
d. Share your results in an email message to the class.
e. Share your results with a small group of students and write a joint memo reporting the similarities and differences you found.

Polishing Your Prose

Comma Splices

In filmmaking, editors splice, or connect, two segments of film to create one segment. A comma splice occurs when writers try to create one sentence by connecting two sentences with only a comma.

Correct: We shipped the order on Tuesday. It arrived on Wednesday.

Incorrect: We shipped the order on Tuesday, it arrived on Wednesday. (comma splice)

Comma splices are almost always inappropriate in business communication. (Poetry and fiction sometimes use comma splices to speed up action or simulate dialect; some sales letters and advertisements use comma splices for the same effect, though not always successfully.)

You can fix a comma splice in four ways:

1. If the ideas in the sentences are closely related, use a semicolon:
   We shipped the order on Tuesday; it arrived on Wednesday.

2. Add a coordinating conjunction (*and, yet, but, or, for, nor*):
   We shipped the order on Tuesday, and it arrived on Wednesday.
3. Make the incorrect sentence into two correct ones:
   We shipped the order on Tuesday. It arrived on Wednesday.
4. Subordinate one of the clauses:
   Because we shipped the order on Tuesday, it arrived on Wednesday.

Exercises

Fix the comma splices in the following sentences.

1. The conference call came at 1 P.M., we took it immediately.
2. We interviewed two people for the accounting position, we made a job offer to one.
3. Janelle drafted her problem-solving report, she sent a copy to each committee member for review.
4. The director of purchasing went to our Main Street warehouse to inspect the inventory, Chuck called him later to ask how things had gone.

5. Katya called the hotel in Montreal for a reservation, the desk staff booked a room for her immediately.
6. Mr. Margulies gave an audiovisual presentation at our September sales meeting in Whistler, it went very well.
7. I'll have Tina call the main office, you ask Brian to set up an appointment for the four of us tomorrow.

8. Working weekends is tough, it's part of life in the business world today.
9. I like to make oral presentations, they're fun.
10. Sunil is our most experienced employee, he joined the department in 1992.

Check your answers to the odd-numbered exercises on page 571.

Online Learning Centre

Visit the Online Learning Centre at www.mcgrawhill.ca/olc/locker to access module quizzes, a searchable glossary, résumé and letter templates, additional business writing samples, CBC videos, and other learning and study tools.

3 Communicating across Cultures

Module Outline

- What is culture?
- What is Canadian culture?
- How does culture affect business communication?
- With so many different cultures, how can I know enough to communicate?
- How can I make my documents bias free?

Review of Key Points

Assignments for Module 3

Polishing Your Prose: Using Idioms

LEARNING OBJECTIVES

After reading and applying the information in Module 3, you'll be able to demonstrate

Knowledge of

- The components of culture
- Workplace diversity
- The importance and variety of non-verbal communication symbols
- Bias-free language

Skills to

- Consider diversity as part of your audience analysis
- Apply your awareness of others' values to your spoken and written messages
- Use bias-free language and photos

The Conference Board of Canada
Insights You Can Count On

Please see the OLC to preview the key skills from the Conference Board of Canada's Employability Skills 2000+ covered in this module.

FYI

Many experts consider "race" a socio-cultural construct. Because of the Human Genome Project, we know that all humans are 99 percent genetically matched, and our closest genetic relative is the chimpanzee. Thus, the concept of "race" may have neither genetic nor biological validity.

Source: Nicholas, Wade. "Articles Highlight Different Views on Genetic Basis of Race", *The New York Times* (online), October 27, 2004, p.1. http://www.howard.edu/newsevents/announcements/1-10-27/genetics.htm, retrieved October 23, 2006.

FYI

Exchanging business cards with people from Asia is an important cultural ritual. Chinese and Japanese businesspeople expect your card to be written in their language on one side and English on the other. Hold your card with two hands, the English print facing your recipient, and hand it over with a slight bow. When you receive the other person's card, study it carefully before putting it away.

SEE THE OLC!

Asian Business Etiquette

All human beings conform to a culturally determined reality. Our culture shapes the way we "see" reality. Often we are unaware of our cultural assumptions until we come into contact with people whose cultural biases differ from ours. If we come from a culture where cows and pigs are raised to be food, for example, that may seem normal until we meet people whose cultures consider these animals sacred, or unclean, or people who consider raising any animal for consumption to be cruel and barbaric. Regardless of our cultural convictions, our ability to communicate flexibly and sensitively with others is a standard for success. Moreover, multicultural acuity makes sound economic, ethical, and legal sense.

What is culture?

*Our **culture** is a learned set of assumptions that shape our perceptions of the world, and of appropriate values, norms, attitudes, and behaviours.*

We learn our culture. Perceptions about gender, age, and social class are culturally based, as are our ideas about

- race
- ethnicity
- religious practices
- sexual orientation
- physical appearance and ability, and
- regional and national characteristics.

No culture is monolithic. Nor is cultural diversity restricted to ethnicity. (◀▶ Module 2, discourse communities) Linguistics professor and gender communications expert Deborah Tannen maintains that women and men often communicate according to very different cultural norms. A study of work team behaviours validates this hypothesis. Professors Jennifer Berdahl, University of Toronto, and Cameron Anderson, University of California, Berkeley, studied the teamwork and leadership behaviours of students enrolled in a course in organizational behaviour. Students were divided into teams. "The researchers found that all the teams [whether] predominantly male or female[,] started off with leadership concentrated in one person." However, the teams made up mostly of women evolved into shared leadership; "those with mostly men continued taking direction from one person." The teams with shared leadership performed better and received higher grades.[1]

What is Canadian culture?

Canada is a cultural polyglot.

Our cultural diversity is now very much a part of the Canadian identity. Canada, home to "… more than 200 different ethnic groups, and a foreign-born population second only to Australia's …" is becoming the most culturally diverse country in the world. Almost a quarter of a million people from all over the world choose to immigrate to Canada every year.

Because two out of three of these immigrants settle in our largest cities, Toronto is the most "… ethnically diverse city in North America and probably the world," with Vancouver close behind. Indeed, by 2016, "… visible minorities will account for one-fifth of Canada's citizens."[2]

SEE THE OLC!

Statistics Canada: 2001 Census

FYI

Extensive studies prove that cultivating fluency in two languages contributes to reading and learning success.

Source: James Crawford, "A Nation Divided by One Language," in Learning English, *The Guardian Weekly*, February 2001, 3.

FYI

Statistics Canada's ethnic diversity survey found that " ... almost one-quarter (23 percent) of Canada's population aged 15 and over, or 5.3 million people, were first generation [immigrants born outside Canada]. Not since 1931 has the proportion of people born outside the country been this high." The survey also found that recent immigrants felt stronger ties with their ethnic groups than "those who were two or more generations in Canada." However, loyalty to their ethnic origins also varied within groups of people. People from countries with a longer history of immigration to Canada were more likely to view themselves as Canadian first.

Source: Adapted from Statistics Canada (2002), Ethnic Diversity Survey, *The Daily*, September 29, 2003; retrieved November 20, 2005, from http://www.statcan.da/Daily/English/030929/d030929a.htm; And, Omar El Akkad, "Canadians in Poll Value Diversity, but Demand Loyalty above All," *The Globe and Mail*, October 13, 2005, p. A3.

Besides contributing to our architecture, visual and performing arts, fashion, festivals, festivities and food, literature, medicine, music, and science—among others—immigrants to Canada are essential for business productivity. Without our immigrant population, Canada would not have had the labour force necessary to prosper during the boom times of the late 1990s: "skilled immigrants who arrived in the past ten years accounted for 70 percent of the growth in Canada's labour force during the same period."[3] Moreover, as the workforce continues to age (half of North America's Boomers will be 55 or older by 2011), skilled worker shortages will be filled by new Canadians.[4]

Recognition of, and respect for the diverse views of others is also legally responsible behaviour. Legal support for the heterogeneous population in Canadian workplaces is articulated in the *Canadian Charter of Rights and Freedoms* (1982), the *Canadian Human Rights Act* (1985), the *Multiculturalism Act* (1985), the *Official Languages Act* (1988), the *Pay Equity Act* (1990), and the *Employment Equity Act* (1995). "Provinces and territories also have laws, human rights commissions and programs that promote diversity."[5]

Globalization demands effective intercultural communication. Foreign trade is essential to the growth of both individual businesses and Canada's economy. Although the United States remains our primary trading partner, the North American Free Trade Agreement (NAFTA) and the economic interests of countries worldwide, like China and India, represent opportunities for Canadian businesses.

How does culture impact business communication?

Cultural assumptions and expectations determine both the form and the content of every business interaction.

Cultural anthropologist E. T. Hall theorized that people's cultural values and beliefs determine their communication style. Hall characterized these communication behaviours as high context and low context.

- In **high-context cultures**, most of the information is inferred from the context of a message; little is "spelled out." Chinese, Japanese, Arabic, and Latin American cultures could be considered high context.
- In **low-context cultures**, context is less important; most information is explicitly spelled out. German, Scandinavian, and the dominant North American cultures could be considered low context.

As David Victor points out in Table 3.1, high-context and low-context cultures value different kinds of communication and have different attitudes toward oral and written channels.[6] As Table 3.1 shows, low-context cultures favour direct approaches and perceive indirectness as dishonest or manipulative. The written word is seen as more important than spoken agreements, so contracts are binding but promises may be broken. Details, logic, and time constraints matter. North American communication practices reflect these low-context preferences.

Thus, culture influences every single aspect of business communication: how to show politeness and respect, how much information to give; how to motivate people; when, how much, and how loudly to talk and laugh; how to organize a letter; even what size paper to use.

TABLE 3.1
Views of Communication in High-Context and Low-Context Cultures

	High Context	Low Context
	(Examples: Japan, United Arab Emirates)	(Examples: Germany, Canada, the United States)
Preferred communication strategy	Indirectness, politeness, ambiguity	Directness, confrontation, clarity
Reliance on words to communicate	Low	High
Reliance on non-verbal signs to communicate	High	Low
Importance of written word	Low	High
Agreements made in writing	Not binding	Binding
Agreements made orally	Binding	Not binding
Attention to detail	Low	High

Source: Adapted from David A. Victor, *International Business Communication* (New York: HarperCollins, 1992), Table 5.1, p. 148. Reprinted by permission of Addison-Wesley Educational Publishers, Inc.

FIGURE 3.1
National Culture, Organizational Culture, and Personal Culture Overlap

Communication is also influenced by the organizational culture and by personal culture, such as gender, race and ethnicity, social class, and so forth. As Figure 3.1 suggests, these cultures intersect to determine the communication needed in a given situation. Sometimes one kind of culture may dominate another culture. For example, in a study of aerospace engineers in Europe, Asia, and the United States, researchers John Webb and Michael Keene found that the similarities of the professional discourse community (one kind of culture) outweighed differences in national cultures.[7]

■ Values, Beliefs, and Practices

Values and beliefs, often unconscious, affect our response to people and situations. Most Canadians, for example, value "fairness." "You're not playing fair" is a sharp criticism calling for changed behaviour. In some countries, however, people expect certain groups to receive preferential treatment. Most North Americans accept competition and believe that it produces better performance. The Japanese, however, believe that competition leads to disharmony. U.S. businesspeople believe that success is based on individual achievement and is open to anyone who excels. Canadians prefer co-operation to blatant competition. In England and in France, success is more obviously linked to social class. And in some countries, the law prohibits people of some castes or races from participating fully in society.

Many North Americans value individualism. Other countries rely on group consensus for decision making. In traditional classrooms, North American students are expected to complete assignments alone; if they receive too much help from anyone else, they're "cheating." In Japan, however, groups routinely work together to solve problems. In the dominant North American culture, quiet is a sign that people are working. In Latin American, Mediterranean, Middle Eastern, and Asian countries, people talk to get the work done.[8] Conversely, the extroverted behaviours rewarded in the classrooms and boardrooms of North America are considered rude and crazy in Japanese culture.

Dealing with Discrimination

Although two-thirds of us believe that our treatment of visible minorities is better today than in 1975, many Canadians deal with discrimination daily. Aboriginal peoples and Canadians of East Asian, Middle Eastern, and Asian background often face prejudice. In the Greater Toronto Area, where visible minorities compose more than 50 percent of the population, black people in particular have real concerns. And no ethnic group is more stigmatized than the Jamaican community. Three-quarters of Jamaicans polled believe that the media misrepresents the black community and that the police treat them unfairly. And two-thirds believe that Canada Customs and the courts treat them inequitably.

Media Misrepresentation

Anthropology professor and Caribbean community and anti-racism expert Frances Henry agrees. Her study of racist discourse in the media demonstrated that one-third of the Toronto newspaper articles featuring Jamaicans focused on "... crime, justice, deportation, immigration and social programs. Another 38.3 percent of articles ... involved sports and entertainment." when reporting about Jamaica, the stories are about crime in Jamaica, political tension, or police brutality," Henry says. "Where are the stories about the general vibrancy of Jamaican culture, the superb accomplishments of its people, its serious musicians, its excellent literature and poetry?" Henry found racism "... rampant in schools.... There have been a lot of good education initiatives, but they don't touch down into the day-to-day experiences in the classroom." According to Henry, only Vietnamese Canadians come close to receiving similarly negative media coverage.

Race, Class, or Cultural Discrimination?

Other black Canadians speak of different experiences. According to Ilias Abdurhman, who immigrated to Toronto from Ethiopia a decade ago, "Everything is 100 percent better here. I don't have any fear of being discriminated against. I'm not saying everything is perfect here, but overall, Toronto is a wonderful place." Barbadian-born business analyst David Grant offers a similar perspective, "I'm sure there are stereotypes but I don't let it be a problem.... My attitude is 'That's

their problem.' I go about my business and try to be respectful of other people.... I believe in trying to get along with people without giving up your identity. I like my culture, but I truly believe in the corporate world, there are no differences.... I love Toronto...." Moreover, Grant suggests that discrimination may be class- rather than race-based, "I think if you survey professional blacks and non-professionals, the answers would be dramatically different. It all depends on the people you associate with." Although Ontario provincial Parliament member Alvin Curling, who was born in Jamaica, agrees that the media foster discriminatory attitudes, he believes that ignorance of cultural character contributes to racist stereotypes, "It comes from a positive assertiveness of Jamaicans. If it's discrimination or a job opportunity, they will go after it in a very aggressive and assertive way."

Positive Cultural Identity Promotes Success

Many community leaders feel that increasing awareness of ethnic Canadians' cultural identities—and of their contribution to Canadians' pride in their pluralistic society—will change attitudes. Worrick Russell, head of the Caribbean and African Canadian Chamber of Commerce, asserts that this awareness is reflected in our education, legal, and social systems. Political involvement, he believes, will create the greatest attitudinal change, as such involvement did for waves of other immigrants.

Meanwhile, school systems across the country are experimenting with educational choices that provide young people with a positive sense of their cultural identity. Edmonton's Amiskwaciy Academy public school, which opened in the fall of 2000, follows the provincial curriculum within the context of significant aboriginal cultural norms: "elders provide guidance through storytelling, sweat lodges, ghost dances, and other ceremonies." Amiskwaciy Academy is one of many alternative education choices— including parent-run charter schools, home schools, and private schools—that not only address a growing aboriginal student population, but also meet a specific "customer" need within the Edmonton public school system. Similarly, the Toronto school board's parents, teachers, and trustees have fought successfully to retain its programs in international languages and black culture at 17 schools across the city. While students' continuity in their mother tongue is preserved, they learn about their cultural heritage and heroes. Language learning facilitates all learning, according to Jack Jedwab, executive director of the Association for Canadian Studies at the University of Quebec, Montreal. Equally important, the success of these students will transform the Canadian cultural landscape.

Sources: Brian Bergman, "Edmonton Experiments with a Diversity of Choice," *Maclean's*, May 14, 2001, 25; Catherine Dunphy, "'My Boys have Done Well,'" *Toronto Star*, May 27, 2001, A7; Elaine Carey, "Black Pride, City Prejudice: Discrimination Lingers on—Racism Remains a Concern for 71% of Those Polled," http://www.geocities.com/CapitolHill/2381/tobeblack1.html, retrieved October 18, 2006; and Ashante Infantry, "You Don't Have to be Black to Suffer Prejudice. You Just Have to Sound Black," http://www.geocities.com/obarri.geo/tobeblack.html, retrieved October 18, 2006.

SEE THE OLC!

Media Coverage of Minority Groups: Ryerson University

Values and beliefs are often influenced by religion. Christianity coexists with a view of the individual as proactive. In some Muslim and Asian countries, however, it is seen as presumptuous to predict the future by promising action by a certain date. Some Amish and Jewish communities live and work in strict adherence to traditional customs. The Puritan work ethic, embraced as a cultural value throughout the northeastern United States regardless of race or religion, legitimizes wealth by seeing it as a sign of divine favour. In other Christian cultures, a simpler lifestyle is considered to be closer to God.

These differences in values, beliefs, and practices lead to differences in the kinds of appeals that motivate people, as Table 3.2 below illustrates.

◼ Non-verbal Communication

Non-verbal communication—communication that makes meaning without words—permeates every part of our lives. Facial expressions, gestures, our use of time and space—even our pauses and vocal intonations—all communicate pleasure or anger, friendliness or distance, power, and status.

SEE THE OLC!

Test Your Intercultural IQ with "Culture Connect"

Non-verbal communication is older and more powerful than spoken language. And its symbols can be misinterpreted just as easily as can verbal symbols (words). For example, a woman brought a new idea to her boss, who glared at her, brows together in a frown, as she explained her proposal. The stare and lowered brows symbolized anger to her, and she assumed that he was rejecting her idea. Several months later, she learned that her boss

TABLE 3.2
Cultural Contrasts in Motivation

	North American	**Japan**	**Arab Countries**
Emotional appeal	Opportunity	Group participation; company success	Religion; nationalism; admiration
Recognition based on	Individual achievement	Group achievement	Individual status; status of class or society
Material rewards	Salary; bonus; profit sharing	Annual bonus; social services; fringe benefits	Gifts for self or family; salary
Threats	Loss of job	Loss of group membership	Demotion, loss of reputation
Values	Competition; risk taking; freedom	Group harmony; belonging	Reputation; family security; religion

Source: Adapted from Farid Elashmawi and Philip R. Harris, *Multicultural Management 2000: Essential Cultural Insights for Global Business Success* (Houston: Gulf, 1998), 169.

British language expert and researcher David Graddol claims that we will all attempt to learn at least a smattering of other languages, as a result of living in the global village. English will no longer dominate, and over the next ten years Mandarin will become the most popular second-language choice.

Source: David Graddol, "English Won't Dominate as World Language," *Science* 27 February 2004: Vol. 303. no. 5662, http://www. sciencemag.org/cgi/content/ abstract/303/5662/1329? rbfvrToken=E1e6644aa44ad ba34388a5b25475a0eeeb8 5a9e98 and http://msnbc. msn.com/id/4387421/, retrieved October 18, 2006.

always "frowned" when he was concentrating. The facial expression she had interpreted as anger had been intended to convey thinking.

Misunderstandings are even more common in communication across cultures, since non-verbal signals are culturally defined. An Arab student assumed that his North American roommate disliked him intensely because the roommate sat around the room with his feet up on the furniture, soles toward the Arab roommate. Arab culture sees the foot in general and the sole in particular as unclean; showing the sole of the foot is an insult.[9]

As is true of any aspect of communication, knowledge is power: learning about non-verbal symbols gives you the information you need to project the image you want and makes you more conscious of the signals you are interpreting. Since experts claim that 93 percent of all our communication is based on non-verbal symbols, your awareness and correct interpretation of non-verbal communication is vital to your personal and professional development. Remember, however, always to check your perceptions before making assumptions about others' non-verbal signals.

■ Body Language

Posture and **body language** connote self-concept, energy, and openness. North American **open body positions** include leaning forward with uncrossed arms and legs, with the arms away from the body. **Closed or defensive body positions** include leaning back, arms and legs crossed or close together, or hands in pockets. As the labels imply, open positions suggest that people are accepting and open to new ideas. Closed positions suggest that people are physically or psychologically uncomfortable, that they are defending themselves and shutting other people out.

People who cross their arms or legs claim that they do so only because the position is more comfortable. Certainly crossing one's legs is one way to be more comfortable in a chair that is the wrong height. Canadian women used to be taught to adopt a "ladylike" posture: arms close to their bodies and knees and ankles together. But notice your own body the next time you're in a perfectly comfortable discussion with a good friend. You'll probably find that you naturally assume open body positions. The fact that so many people in organizational settings adopt closed positions may indicate that many people feel at least slightly uncomfortable in school and on the job.

People of eastern cultures value the ability to sit quietly. They may see the North American tendency to fidget and shift as an indication of a lack of mental or spiritual balance. Even Canadian interviewers and audiences usually respond negatively to nervous gestures such as fidgeting with a tie or hair or jewellery, tapping a pencil, or swinging a foot.

INSTANT REPLAY

Culture is a learned set of assumptions about the norms and values that we internalize and accept as true. Our culture shapes our perceptions of the world around us and influences our communication styles and content.

Eye Contact

Canadians of European background see eye contact as a sign of honesty. But in many cultures, dropped eyes are a sign of appropriate deference to a superior. Puerto Rican children are taught not to meet the eyes of adults.[10] The Japanese are taught to look at the neck.[11] In Korea, prolonged eye contact is considered rude. The lower-ranking person is expected to look down first.[12] In Muslim countries, women and men are not supposed to make eye contact.

These differences can lead to miscommunication in the multicultural workplace. Supervisors may infer from their eye contact that employees are being disrespectful, when, in fact, the employee is behaving appropriately according to the norms of his or her culture.

Gestures

Canadians sometimes assume that, if language fails, they can depend on gestures to communicate with non-English-speaking people. But Birdwhistell reported that "although we have been searching for 15 years [1950–65], we have found no gesture or body motion which has the same meaning in all societies."[13]

Gestures that mean approval in Canada may have very different meanings in other countries. The "thumbs up" sign that means "good work" or "go ahead" in Canada, the United States, and most of Western Europe is a vulgar insult in Greece. The circle formed with the thumb and first finger that means OK in Canada is obscene in Southern Italy and Brazil, and it can mean "you're worth nothing" in France and Belgium.[14]

In the question period after a lecture, a man asked the speaker, a Puerto Rican professor, if shaking the hands up and down in front of the chest, as though shaking off water, was "a sign of mental retardation." The professor was horrified: in her culture, the gesture meant "excitement, intense thrill."[15]

Space

Concepts of space are also culturally understood. **Personal space** is the distance someone wants between himself/herself and other people in ordinary, non-intimate interchanges. Observation and limited experimentation show that most North Americans, North Europeans, and Asians want a bigger personal space than do Latin Americans, French, Italians, and Arabs. People who are accustomed to lots of personal space and are forced to accept close contact on a crowded elevator or subway react in predictable and ritualistic ways: they stand stiffly and avoid eye contact with others.

Even within a culture, some people like more personal space than do others. One study found that men took up more personal space than women did. In many cultures, people who are of the same age and sex take less personal space than do mixed-age or mixed-sex groups. Latin Americans stand closer to people of the same sex than North Americans do, but North Americans stand closer to people of the opposite sex.

Concepts of space are culturally understood.

Touch

Repeated studies prove that babies need to be touched to grow and thrive, and that older people are healthier both mentally and physically if they are touched. But some people are more comfortable with touch than others. Some people shake hands in greeting but otherwise don't like to be touched at all, except by family members or lovers. Other people, having grown up in families that touch a lot, hug as part of a greeting and touch even casual friends. Each kind of person may misinterpret the other. A person who dislikes touch may seem unfriendly to someone who's used to touching. A toucher may seem overly familiar to someone who dislikes touch.

Studies indicate that in North American culture, touch is interpreted as power: more powerful people touch less powerful people. When the toucher has higher status than the recipient, both men and women liked being touched.[16]

Most parts of North America allow opposite-sex couples to hold hands or walk arm in arm in public but frown on the same behaviour in same-sex couples. People in Asia, the Middle East, and South America have the opposite expectation: male friends or female friends can hold hands or walk arm in arm, but it is slightly shocking for an opposite-sex couple to touch in public. In Iran and Iraq, handshakes between men and women are seen as improper.[17]

Spatial Arrangements

In North America, the size, placement, and privacy of a person's office connote status. Large corner offices have the highest status. An individual office with a door that closes suggests more status than a desk in a common area.

SEE THE OLC!

Tips for Doing Business Internationally

People who don't know each other well may feel more comfortable with each other if a piece of furniture separates them. For example, in most Canadian interviews, a desk, which both people perceive as part of the interviewer's space, separates the interviewer and the applicant. It's considered inappropriate for the applicant to place his or her property (notebook, purse) on a desk or to lean on the desk. In some situations, a group may work better sitting around a table than just sitting in a circle. In North America, a person sitting at the head of a table

In low-context cultural settings, the size, placement, and privacy of a person's office connote status.

is generally assumed to be the group's leader. However, one experiment showed that when a woman sat at the head of a mixed-sex group, observers assumed that one of the men in the group was the leader.[18]

■ Time

SEE THE OLC!

A Beginner's Guide to Culture and Communication

Canadian organizations—businesses, government, and schools—keep time by the calendar and the clock. Being "on time" is seen as a sign of dependability. Other cultures may keep time by the seasons and the moon, the sun, internal "body clocks," or a personal feeling that "the time is right."

Canadians who believe that "time is money" are often frustrated in negotiations with people who take a much more leisurely approach. Part of the miscommunication stems from a major perception difference: people in many other cultures want to take the time to establish a personal relationship before they decide whether to do business with each other.

Miscommunication occurs because various cultures perceive time differently. Many Canadians measure time in five-minute blocks. Someone who is five minutes late to an appointment or a job interview feels compelled to apologize. If the executive or interviewer is running half an hour late, the caller expects to be told about the likely delay when he or she arrives. Some people won't be able to wait that long and will need to reschedule their appointments. But in Latin American and other cultures, 15 minutes or half an hour may be the smallest block of time. To someone who mentally measures time in 15-minute blocks, being 45 minutes late is no worse than being 15 minutes late to someone who is conscious of smaller units.

Edward T. Hall distinguishes between **monochronic cultures**, where people do only one important activity at a time, and **polychronic cultures**, where people do several things at once. Researchers see the United States as monochronic. When U.S. managers feel offended because a Latin American manager also sees other people during "their" appointments, the two kinds of time are in conflict. However, people who eat breakfast while they drive are doing more than one thing at a time. In a few organizations, it is even acceptable to do other work during a meeting. Such "multi-tasking" may indicate that some North American companies are evolving from a monochronic culture to a somewhat polychronic culture.

According to some scholars, Europeans schedule fewer events in a comparable period than North Americans. Perhaps as a result, Germans and German Swiss see North Americans as too time-conscious.[19]

Other Non-verbal Symbols

Many other symbols can carry non-verbal meanings: clothing, colours, age, and height, to name a few.

In Canada, certain styles and colours of clothing are considered more "professional" and more "credible." Certain cloths and fabrics—silk and linen, for example—carry non-verbal messages of success, prestige, and competence. In Japan, clothing denotes not only status but also occupational group. Private-school students wear uniforms. Company badges indicate rank within the organization. Workers wear different clothes when they are on strike than they do when they are working.[20]

Colours can also carry cultural meanings in a culture. In Canada, mourners wear black to funerals, while brides wear white at their wedding. In pre-Communist China and in some South American tribes, white is the colour of mourning. Purple flowers are given to the dead in Mexico.[21] In Korea, red ink is used to record deaths but never to write about living people.[22]

North American culture values youth. More and more individuals choose to colour their hair and have surgery to look as youthful as possible. In Japan, younger people defer to older people. North Americans attempting to negotiate in Japan are usually taken more seriously if at least one member of the team is noticeably grey-haired.

Height connotes status in many parts of the world. Executive offices are usually on the top floors; the underlings work below. Even being tall can help a person succeed. Studies have shown that employers are more willing to hire men more than 1.85m tall than shorter men with the same credentials. Studies of real-world executives and graduates have shown that taller men make more money. In one study, every extra inch of height brought in an extra $600 a year.[23] But being too big can be a disadvantage. A tall, brawny football player complained that people found him intimidating off the field and assumed that he "had the brains of a Twinkie."

Oral Communication

Effective oral communication also requires cultural understanding. As Table 3.3 shows, both purpose and content of business introductions differ across cultures.

TABLE 3.3

Cultural Contrasts in Business Introductions

	North America	**Japan**	**Arab Countries**
Purpose of introduction	Establish status and job identity; network	Establish position in group, build harmony	Establish personal rapport
Image of individual	Independent	Member of group	Part of rich culture
Information	Related to business	Related to company	Personal
Use of language	Informal, friendly; use first name	Little talking	Formal; expression of admiration
Values	Openness, directness, action	Harmony, respect, listening	Religious harmony, hospitality, emotional support

Source: Adapted from Farid Elashmawi and Philip R. Harris, *Multicultural Management 2000: Essential Cultural Insights for Global Business Success* (Houston: Gulf, 1998), 113.

SEE THE OLC!

Deborah Tannen

Deborah Tannen uses the term conversational style to denote our conversational patterns and the meanings we give to them: the way we show interest, courtesy, social decorum.[24] Your answers to the following questions reveal your own conversational style:

- How long a pause tells you that it's your turn to speak?
- Do you see interruption as rude? Or do you say things while other people are still talking to show that you're interested and to encourage them to say more?
- Do you show interest by asking lots of questions? Or do you see questions as intrusive and wait for people to volunteer whatever they have to say?

One conversational style is not better or worse than another, but people with different conversational styles may feel uncomfortable without knowing why. A boss who speaks slowly may frustrate a subordinate who talks quickly. People who talk more slowly may feel shut out of a conversation with people who talk more quickly. Someone who has learned to make requests directly ("Please pass the salt") may be annoyed by someone who uses indirect requests ("This casserole needs some salt").

In the workplace, conflicts may arise because of differences in conversational style. Generation Xers often use a rising inflection on statements as well as questions. Xers see this style as gentler and more polite. But Boomer bosses may see this speech pattern as hesitant, as if the speaker wants advice—which they then proceed to deliver.[25]

Daniel N. Maltz and Ruth A. Borker believe that differences in conversational style may be responsible for the miscommunication that sometimes occurs in male–female conversations. For example, researchers have found that women are much more likely to nod and to say yes or say *mm hmm* than men are. Maltz and Borker hypothesize that to women, these symbols mean simply, "I'm listening; go on." Men, on the other hand, may decode these symbols as "I agree" or at least "I follow what you're saying so far." A man who receives nods and *mms* from a woman may feel that she is inconsistent and unpredictable if she then disagrees with him. A woman may feel that a man who doesn't provide any feedback isn't listening to her.[26]

Understatement and Exaggeration

Closely related to conversational style is the issue of understatement and overstatement. The British have a reputation for understatement. Someone good enough to play at Wimbledon may say he or she "plays a little tennis." Or ask a Canadian how the meeting yesterday or last night's game went, and the answer will be "Not bad!" even if the event was a roaring success. On the other hand, many people in the United States exaggerate. A U.S. businessman negotiating with a German said, "I know it's impossible, but can we do it?" The German saw the statement as nonsensical: by definition, something that is impossible cannot be done at all. The American saw "impossible" as merely a strong way of saying "difficult" and assumed that with enough resources and commitment, the job could, in fact, be done.[27]

Compliments

The kinds of statements that people interpret as compliments and the socially correct way to respond to compliments also vary among cultures. The statement "You must be really tired" is a compliment in Japan since it recognizes the other person has worked hard. The correct response is "Thank you, but I'm OK." A Canadian who is complimented on giving a good oral presentation will probably say "Thank you." A Chinese or Japanese person, in contrast, will apologize: "No, it wasn't very good."[28]

Statements that seem complimentary in one context may be inappropriate in another. For example, businesswomen may feel uncomfortable if male colleagues or superiors compliment them on their appearance: the comments suggest that the women are being treated as visual decoration rather than as contributing workers.

Successful intercultural communicators attempt to understand the communication style the other group prefers.

Source: The Far Side © 1985 Earworks, Inc. Used by permission.

Silence

Silence also has different meanings in different cultures and subcultures. North Americans have difficulty doing business in Japan because they do not realize that silence almost always means that the Japanese do not like the ideas.

Different understandings of silence can prolong problems with sexual harassment in the workplace. Women sometimes use silence to respond to comments they find offensive, hoping that silence will signal their lack of appreciation. But some men may think that silence means appreciation or at least neutrality.

■ Writing to International Audiences

Most cultures are more formal than ours. When you write to international audiences, use titles, not first names. Avoid contractions, slang, and sports metaphors.

TABLE 3.4
Cultural Contrasts in Written Persuasive Documents

	North America	Japan	Arab Countries
Opening	Request action or get reader's attention	Offer thanks; apologize	Offer personal greetings
Way to persuade	Immediate gain or loss of opportunity	Waiting	Personal connections; future opportunity
Style	Short sentences	Modesty, minimize own standing	Elaborate expressions; many signatures
Closing	Specific request	Desire to maintain harmony	Future relationship, personal greeting
Values	Efficiency; directness, action	Politeness; indirectness; relationship	Status; continuation

Source: Adapted from Farid Elashmawi and Philip P. Harris, *Multicultural Management 2000: Essential Cultural Insights for Global Business Success* (Houston: Gulf, 1998), 139.

P A I B O C

Questions for Analysis

Use the PAIBOC questions to prepare to communicate interculturally

P What are your **purposes** in communicating?

A Who is your **audience**? What are their values and expectations? How will they react to the content of your message? What form will make your message accessible to your audience? How should you frame your message to your audience's expectations?

I What **information** will meet the needs of your audience and your purposes?

(continued)

The patterns of organization that work for Canadian audiences may need to be modified for international correspondence beyond the United States. For most cultures, buffer negative messages (◀I▶ Module 12) and make requests (◀I▶ Module 13) more indirect. As Table 3.4 suggests, you may need to modify style, structure, and strategy when writing to international readers. Make a special effort to avoid phrases that your audience could interpret as arrogant or uncaring. Cultural mistakes made orally may float away on the air; those made in writing are permanently recorded.

With so many different cultures, how can I know enough to communicate?

Focus on being sensitive and flexible.

The first step in understanding people of another culture is to realize that they may do things very differently and that they value their way as much as you do yours. Moreover, people within a single culture differ. The kinds of differences summarized in this module can turn into stereotypes, which can be just as damaging as ignorance. Don't try to memorize the material here as a rigid set of rules. Instead, use the examples to get a sense for the kinds of things that differ from one culture to another. Test these generalizations against your experience. When in doubt, ask.

If you work with people from other cultures or if you plan to travel to a specific country, read about that country or culture and learn a little of the language. Also talk to people. That's really the only way to learn whether someone is wearing black as a sign of mourning, as a fashion statement, or as a colour that slenderizes and doesn't show dirt.

As Brenda Arbeláez suggests, the successful international communicator is

- Aware that his or her preferred values and behaviours are influenced by culture and are not necessarily "right"
- Flexible and open to change
- Sensitive to verbal and non-verbal behaviour

B What reasons or audience benefits can you use to support your position?

O What objections can you expect from your audience? What negative content must you de-emphasize or overcome?

C What is the **context** of the message, and how will the context affect your audience's response? What is your relationship with your audience? What time of day are you delivering your message? What cultural differences should you be sensitive to? What special circumstances should shape the form and content of your message?

INSTANT REPLAY

The successful international communicator is

- Aware that his or her preferred values and behaviours are influenced by culture and are not necessarily "right"
- Flexible and open to change
- Sensitive to verbal and non-verbal behaviour
- Aware of the values, beliefs, and practices in other cultures
- Sensitive to differences among individuals within a culture

- Aware of the values, beliefs, and practices in other cultures
- Sensitive to differences among individuals within a culture.[29]

How can I make my documents bias free?

Start by using non-sexist, non-racist, and non-agist language.

Bias-free language is language that does not discriminate against people on the basis of sex, physical condition, race, age, or any other category. Bias-free language is fair and friendly; it complies with the law. It includes all readers; it helps to sustain goodwill. When you produce newsletters or other documents with photos and illustrations, choose a sampling of the whole population, not just part of it.

Making Language Non-sexist

Non-sexist language treats both sexes neutrally. Check to be sure that your writing is free from sexism in four areas: words and phrases, job titles, pronouns, and courtesy titles. Courtesy titles are discussed in ◀|▶ Module 9 on format. Words and phrases, job titles, and pronouns are discussed in this module.

Words and Phrases

If you find any of the terms in the first column in Table 3.5 in your writing or your company's documents, replace them with terms from the second column.

Not every word containing *man* is sexist. For example, *manager* is not sexist. The word comes from the Latin *manus*, meaning *hand*; it has nothing to do with maleness.

Avoid terms that assume that everyone is married or is heterosexual.

Biased:	You and your husband or wife are cordially invited to the dinner.
Better:	You and your guest are cordially invited to the dinner.

Job Titles

Use neutral titles that imply that a person of either gender could hold the job. Many job titles are already neutral: *accountant, banker, doctor, engineer, inspector, manager, nurse, pilot, secretary, technician*, to name a few. Other titles reflect gender stereotypes and need to be changed. (See Table 3.5 for specific examples.)

Pronouns

When you write about a specific person, use the appropriate gender pronouns:

In his speech, John Jones said that...
In her speech, Judy Jones said that...

Some developing countries have gone straight to cell phones, skipping the expensive step of laying cables. Many owners of cellphones have become entrepreneurs, making calls on their phones for a small fee. Now farmers can call to find out what prices are in the cities, so they aren't at the mercy of brokers' claims.

TABLE 3.5
Eliminating Sexist Terms and Phrases

Instead of	Use	For this reason
The girl at the front desk	The woman's name or job title: "Ms. Browning," "Rosa," "the receptionist"	Call female employees women just as you call male employees men. When you talk about a specific woman, use her name, just as you use a man's name to talk about a specific man.
The ladies on our staff	The women on our staff	Use parallel terms for males and females. Therefore, use ladies only if you refer to the males on your staff as gentlemen. Few businesses do, since social distinctions are rarely at issue.
Manpower Manhours Manning	Personnel Hours or worker hours Staffing	The power in business today comes from both women and men. Use non-sexist alternatives.
Managers and their wives	Managers and their guests	Managers may be female; not everyone is married.
Businessman	A specific title: executive, accountant, department head, owner of a small business, men and women in business, businessperson	Gender-neutral title
Chairman	Chair, chairperson, moderator	Gender-neutral title
Foreman	Supervisor	Gender-neutral title
Salesman	Salesperson, sales representative	Gender-neutral title
Waitress	Server	Gender-neutral title
Woman lawyer	Lawyer	Gender-neutral title. You would not describe a man as a "male lawyer."
Workman	Worker, employee, or use a specific title: crane operator, bricklayer, etc.	Gender-neutral title

When you are not writing about a specific person, but about anyone who may be in a given job or position, avoid using traditional gender pronouns.

Sexist: a. Each supervisor must certify that the time sheet for his department is correct.

Sexist: b. When the nurse fills out the accident report form, she should send one copy to the Central Division Office.

Business writing uses four ways to eliminate sexist generic pronouns: use plurals, use second person (you), revise the sentence to omit the pronoun, and use pronoun pairs. Whenever you have a choice of two or more ways to make a phrase or sentence non-sexist, choose the alternative that is the smoothest and least conspicuous.

The following examples use these methods to revise sentences *a* and *b* above.

1. Use plural nouns and pronouns.

Non-sexist: a. Supervisors must certify that the time sheets for their departments are correct.

Note: When you use plural nouns and pronouns, other words in the sentence may need to be made plural too. In the example above, plural supervisors have plural time sheets and departments.

Avoid mixing singular nouns and plural pronouns.

Non-sexist: but a. Each supervisor must certify that the time sheet for their
lacks agreement: department is correct.

Since *supervisor* is singular, it is incorrect to use the plural *they* to refer to it. The resulting lack of agreement is acceptable orally but is not yet acceptable to many readers in writing. Instead, use one of the four grammatically correct ways to make the sentence non-sexist.

2. Use *you*.

Non-sexist: a. You must certify that the time sheet for your department is correct.

Non-sexist: b. When you fill out an accident report form, send one copy to the Central Division Office.

You is particularly good for instructions and statements of the responsibilities of someone in a given position. Using *you* frequently shortens sentences, because you write "Send one copy" instead of "You should send one copy." It also makes your writing more direct.

3. Substitute an article (a, an, or the) for the pronoun, or revise the sentence so that the pronoun is unnecessary.

Non-sexist: a. The supervisor must certify that the time sheet for
the department is correct.

Non-sexist: b. The nurse will

1. Fill out the accident report form.

2. Send one copy of the form to the Central Division Office.

4. When you must focus on the action of an individual, use pronoun pairs.

Non-sexist: a. The supervisor must certify that the time sheet for his or her department is correct.

Non-sexist: b. When the nurse fills out the accident report form, he or she should send one copy to the Central Division Office.

■ Making Language Non-racist and Non-agist

Language is **non-racist** and **non-agist** when it treats all races and ages fairly, avoiding negative stereotypes of any group. Use these guidelines to check for bias in documents you write or edit:

- **Give someone's race or age only if it is relevant to your story.** When you do mention these characteristics, give them for everyone in your story—not just the non-Caucasian, non-young-to-middle-aged adults you mention.

- **Refer to a group by the term it prefers. As preferences change, change your usage.** Sixty years ago, *Negro* was preferred as a more dignified term than *coloured* for North Americans of African origin. As times changed, *black person* and *African American* replaced it in the United States. In Canada, *black person* is generally preferred to *African Canadian*, which is more often used for recent immigrants from Africa and thus might not include, for example, black Canadians from Caribbean nations, or black Canadians who came to Nova Scotia as Loyalists in the late eighteenth century.

  Asian is preferred to *Oriental*, which may be considered offensive.

  East Indian is frequently misused to include people of non-Indian origin, such as new Canadians from Pakistan, Sri Lanka, and Bangladesh. *South Asian* is more accurate, and *Pakistani, Sri Lankan*, and *Bangladeshi* are preferred.

  Eskimo is a negative label. A better term is *Inuit*, which means *the people*.

  Aboriginal peoples is generally used to refer to Canada's indigenous peoples: First Nations, Inuit, and Métis. But usage will vary depending on the preference of the individual or group referred to. For example, most Aboriginal peoples consider *Indian* offensive or at least a source of confusion with people from India. Where possible, consider referring to the specific band or nation of the individual (for example, Métis, Mohawk, Cree, Haida).

  Older people and *mature customers* are more generally accepted terms than *senior citizens* or *golden agers*.

- **Avoid terms that suggest that competent people are unusual.** The statement "She is an intelligent Métis woman" suggests that the writer expects most Métis women to be stupid. "He is an asset to his race" suggests that excellence in the "race" is rare. "He is a spry 70-year-old" suggests that the writer is amazed that anyone that old can still move.

◼ Talking about People with Disabilities and Diseases

A disability is a physical, mental, sensory, or emotional impairment that interferes with the major tasks of daily living. A March 2000 study identified 14.5 percent of the working-age Canadian population as having a disability. The number of people with disabilities will rise as the population ages.[30]

- **People-first language** focuses on the person, not the condition. Use it instead of outdated adjectives used as nouns that imply that the condition defines the person.

- **Avoid negative terms, unless the audience prefers them.** Preference takes precedence over positive emphasis: use the term a group prefers. People who lost their hearing as infants, children, or young adults often prefer to be called *deaf*. But people who lose their hearing as older adults often prefer to be called *hard of hearing*, even when their hearing loss is just as great as someone who identifies as part of deaf culture.

Just as people in a single ethnic group may prefer different labels based on generational or cultural divides, so differences exist within the disability community (see Table 3.6). Using the right term requires keeping up with changing preferences. If your target audience is smaller than the whole group, use the term preferred by that audience, even if the group as a whole prefers another term.

Some negative terms, however, are never appropriate. Negative terms such as *afflicted, suffering from, the victim of, and struck down by* also suggest an outdated view of illness.

TABLE 3.6
Eliminating Terms and Phrases That Discriminate against People with Disabilities

Instead of	Use	For this reason
The mentally retarded	Developmentally delayed	The condition does not define the person or his or her potential
The blind	People with vision impairments	
Cancer patients	People being treated for cancer	

■ Choosing Bias-Free Photos and Illustrations

When you produce a document with photographs or illustrations, check the visuals for possible bias. Do they show people of both sexes and all races? Is there a sprinkling of various kinds of people (younger and older, people using wheelchairs, etc.)? It's OK to have individual pictures that have just one sex or one race; the photos as a whole do not need to show exactly 50 percent men and 50 percent women. But the general impression should suggest that diversity is welcome and normal.

Check relationships and authority figures as well as numbers. If all the men appear in business suits and the women in maids' uniforms, the pictures are sexist even if an equal number of men and women are pictured. If the only black people and Filipinos pictured are factory workers, the photos support racism even when equal numbers of people from each race are shown.

Don't use biased clip art or stock photos: look for alternatives to the kind of clip art shown at left, or create your own bias-free illustrations.

Employability Skills 2000+

Please see the OLC to preview the key skills from the Conference Board of Canada's Employability Skills 2000+ covered in this module.

Review of Key Points

1. Define culture. Give five examples of your cultural norms.
2. What five behaviours do successful intercultural communicators adopt?
3. What four methods can you use to make a sentence non-sexist?
4. What policies and laws recognize diversity in the workplace?
5. What is bias-free language?
6. Identify and explain six nonverbal symbols that differ among cultures.

Assignments for Module 3

Questions for Critical Thinking

3.1 It's sexist to always put the male pronoun first in pronoun pairs (e.g., he or she rather than she or he or s/he). Why do the authors of this book recommend that method? Which method do you prefer?

3.2 Suppose you know your audience is sexist, agist, racist, or otherwise prejudiced. How should you adapt your message to your audience? What are the ethical implications of your adapting?

3.3 You can't possibly learn what every symbol means in every culture. How can you avoid offending the people you work with?

3.4 What other cultures are you most likely to work with? How could you learn about those cultures?

Exercises and Problems

3.5   Revising Sexist Job Titles

Suggest non-sexist alternatives for each of the following:

cleaning lady   mailman
alderman   night watchman

garbage man   repairman
male nurse   salesman
mail boy   waitress
actress   stewardess

3.6   Eliminating Biased Language

Explain the source of bias in each of the following and revise to remove the bias.

1. We recommend hiring Jim Renker and Elizabeth Shuman. Both were very successful summer interns. Jim drafted the report on using rap music in ads, and Elizabeth really improved the look of the office.

2. All sales associates and their wives are invited to the picnic.

3. Although he is blind, Mr. Morin is an excellent group leader.

4. Unlike many Caribbean Canadians, Yvonne has extensive experience designing Web pages.

5. Chris Gottlieb
   Pacific Perspectives
   6300 West 12th Avenue
   Vancouver, BC
   Gentlemen:
6. Enrique Torres is very intuitive for a man.
7. Twenty-First-Century Parenting shows you how to persuade your husband to do his share of child-care chores.
8. Mr. Paez, Mr. O'Connor, and Tonya will represent our office at the convention.
9. Sue Corcoran celebrates her 50th birthday today. Stop by her cubicle at noon to get a piece of cake and to help us sing "The Old Grey Mare Just Ain't What She Used to Be."
10. Because older customers tend to be really picky, we will need to give a lot of details in our ads.

3.7   Dealing with Discrimination

Despite Canada's reputation for tolerance, courtesy, and fair play, many of its citizens frequently experience discriminatory behaviour. Some believe that prejudice is systemic—that bias against visible minorities, women, people with disabilities, and seniors is built into our legal and judicial systems and demonstrated daily in our assumptions and attitudes.

Recent media attention has focused on such culturally sensitive issues as racism among members of the police force and discriminatory hiring and promotion practices in Canadian post-secondary institutions.

Find a specific, relevant news story of cultural bias or discrimination. Or use your own experience to identify a serious miscommunication based on cultural assumptions. Write a summary of the news story or of your experience. Using what you have learned in Modules 1 and 2, write a memo to your classmates and your professor, providing specific ideas about how to deal positively with such a situation.

3.8   Identifying Sources of Miscommunication

In each of the following situations, identify one or more ways that cultural differences may be leading to miscommunication.

a.   Alan is a Canadian sales representative in Mexico. He makes appointments and is careful to be on time. But the person he's calling on is frequently late. To save time, Alan tries to get right to business. But his hosts want to talk about sightseeing and his family. Even worse, his appointments are interrupted constantly, not only by business phone calls, but also by long conversations with other people and even the customers' children who come into the office. Alan's first progress report is very negative. He hasn't yet made a sale. Perhaps Mexico just isn't the right place to sell his company's products.

b.   To help her company establish a presence in Japan, Susan wants to hire a local interpreter who can advise her on business customs. Kana Tomari has superb qualifications on paper. But when Susan tries to probe about her experience, Kana just says, "I will do my best. I will try very hard." She never gives details about any of the previous positions she's held. Susan begins to wonder whether the résumé is inflated.

c.   Stan wants to negotiate a joint venture with a Chinese company. He asks Tung-Sen Lee if the Chinese people have enough discretionary income to afford his product. Mr. Lee is silent for a time, and then says, "Your product is good. People in the West must like it." Stan smiles, pleased that Mr. Lee recognizes the quality of his product, and he gives Mr. Lee a contract to sign. Weeks later, Stan still hasn't heard anything. If China is going to be so inefficient, he wonders if he really should try to do business there.

d.   Elspeth is very proud of her participatory management style. On assignment in India, she is careful not to give orders but to ask for suggestions. But people rarely suggest anything. Even a formal suggestion system doesn't work. And to make matters worse, she doesn't sense the respect and camaraderie of the plant she managed in Canada. Perhaps, she decides gloomily, people in India just aren't ready for a female boss.

3.9 Advising a Hasty Subordinate

Three days ago, one of your subordinates forwarded to everyone in the office a bit of email humour he'd received from a friend. Titled "You know you're a Newfie when..." the message poked fun at Newfoundland and Labrador speech, attitudes, and lifestyles. Today you get this message from your subordinate:

Subject: Should I Apologize?

I'm getting flamed left and right because of the Newfoundland message. I thought it was funny, but some people just can't take a joke. So far I've tried not to respond to the flames, figuring that would just make things worse. But now I'm wondering if I should apologize. What do you think?

Answer the message.

3.10 Responding to a Complaint

You're the director of corporate communications; your office produces the employee newsletter.

Today you get this email message from Caroline Huber:

Subject: Complaint about Sexist Language

The article about the "Help Desk" says that Martina Luna and I "are the key customer service representatives 'manning' the desk." I don't MAN anything! I WORK.

Respond to Caroline, and send a message to your staff, reminding them to edit newsletter stories as well as external documents to replace biased language.

3.11 Asking about Travel Arrangements

The CEO is planning a trip to visit colleagues in another country (you pick the country). As executive assistant to the CEO of your organization, it's your job to make travel plans. At this stage, you don't know anything except dates and flights. (The CEO will arrive in the country at 7 A.M. local time on the 28th of next month, and stay for three days.) It's your job to find out what the plans are and communicate any of the CEO's requirements.

Write an email message to your contact.

Hints:

- Pick a business, non-profit organization, or government agency you know something about, making assumptions about the kinds of things its executive would want to do during an international visit.
- How much international travelling does your CEO do? Has he or she ever been to this country before? What questions will he or she want answered?

3.12 Sending a Draft to Japan

You've drafted instructions for a product that will be sold in Japan. Before the text is translated, you want to find out whether the pictures will be clear. So you send an email to your Japanese counterpart, Takashi Haneda, asking for a response within a week.

Write an email message; assume that you will send the pictures as an attachment.

3.13 Creating a Web Page

Create a Web page for managers who must communicate across cultures.

Assume that this page can be accessed from the organization's intranet. Offer at least seven links. (More links are better.) You may offer information as well as links to other pages with information. At the top of the page, offer an overview of what the page covers. At the bottom of the page, put the creation and update date and your name and email address.

As your instructor directs,

a. Turn in two printed copies of your page(s). On another page, give the URLs for each link.
b. Turn in one printed copy of your page(s) and a disk with the HTML code and .gif files.
c. Write a memo to your instructor identifying the audience for whom the page is designed and explaining (1) the search strategies you used to find material on this topic, (2) why you chose the pages and information you've included, and (3) why you chose the layout and graphics you've used.
d. Post your memo in an email message to the class.
e. Present your page orally to the class.

Hints:

• Limit your page to just one culture or country.
• Try to cover as many topics as possible: history, politics, notable people, arts, conversational style, customs, and so forth. For a culture in another country, also include money, living accommodations, geography, transport, weather, business practices, and so forth.
• Chunk your links into small groups under headings.
• See ◁▷ Module 5 on Web page design.

3.14 Requesting Information about a Country

Use one or more of the following ways to get information about a country. Information you might focus on could include

• Business opportunities
• History and geography
• Principal exports and imports
• Dominant religions
• Holidays
• School system
• Political system

1. Visit Industry Canada's Strategis Web site for International Market Research and Country Commercial Guides at http://strategis.ic.gc.ca/epic/internet/inibi-iai.nsf/vwGeneratedInterE/Home and click Country/Region Information.
2. Check the country's trade office, if there is one in your city.
3. Interview someone from that country or someone who has lived there.
4. Read published materials about the country.

As your instructor directs,

a. Share your findings orally with a small group of students.
b. Summarize your findings in a memo to your instructor.
c. Present your findings to the class.
d. Email your findings to the class.
e. Join with a group of classmates to write a group report on the country.

3.15 Answering an Inquiry about Photos

You've just been named vice president for diversity, the first person in your organization to hold this position.

Today, you receive the following memo from Sheila Lathan, who edits the employee newsletter:

Subject: Photos in the Employee Newsletter

Please tell me what to do about photos in the monthly employee newsletter. I'm concerned that almost no single issue represents the diversity of employees we have here.

As you know, our layout allows two visuals each month. One of those is always the employee of the month (EM). In the last year, most of those have been male and all but two have been white. What makes it worse is that people want photos that make them look good. You may remember that Ron Olmos was the EM two months ago; in the photo he wanted me to use, you can't tell that he's in a wheelchair. Often the EM is the only photo; the other visual is a graph of sales or something relating to quality.

Even if the second visual is another photo, it may not look balanced in terms of gender and race. After all, 62 percent of our employees are women, and 70 percent are non-white. Should the pictures try to represent those percentages? The leadership positions (both in management and in the union) are heavily male and white. Should we run pictures of people doing important things and risk continuing the imbalance?

I guess I could use more visuals, but then there wouldn't be room for as many stories—and people really like to see their names in print. Plus, giving people information about company activities and sales is important to maintaining goodwill. A bigger newsletter would be one way to have more visuals and keep the content, but with the cost-cutting measures we're under, that doesn't look likely.

What should I do?

As your instructor directs,

a. Work in a small group with students to come up with a recommendation for Sheila.

b. Write a memo responding to Sheila.

c. Write an article for the employee newsletter about the photo policy you recommend and how it relates to the company's concern for diversity.

Polishing Your Prose

Using Idioms

Idioms are phrases that have specific meanings different from the meanings for each individual word.

Idiom	Meaning
Cut to the chase	Express your main point immediately
Read between the lines	Look for a hidden message

Like idioms, slang changes the definitions of words. *Bad*, a word that is negative, becomes positive when used in slang to denote something good or desirable. Dictionaries often are slow to adapt to slang, which changes constantly.

You need to understand a culture to make sense of its idioms. Because idioms usually violate the rules of standard edited English, they are particularly troublesome for people new to the language.

To learn idioms,

1. Study native speakers in person and on television. When possible, ask native speakers what unfamiliar words and phrases mean.

2. Underline unfamiliar passages in newspapers and magazines. Ask a friend or your instructor to explain their meaning.

3. Practise what you learn with a conversation partner.

Exercises

Explain what these 10 common idiomatic phrases mean in business.

1. Race the clock
2. From A to Z
3. Juggle a schedule
4. Catch a plane (or cab)
5. Punch the clock
6. Sign on the dotted line
7. Cold call a customer
8. In the black/in the red
9. Open up new markets
10. Slamdunk the competition

Check your answers to the odd-numbered exercises on page 571.

Online Learning Centre

Visit the Online Learning Centre at www.mcgrawhill.ca/olc/locker to access module quizzes, a searchable glossary, résumé and letter templates, additional business writing samples, CBC videos, and other learning and study tools.

Module Outline

- What is the writing process?
- Does it matter which process I use?
- How should I approach business writing?
- I don't have much time. How should I use it?
- What planning should I do before I begin writing or speaking?
- What is revision? How do I do it?
- Can a grammar checker edit for me?
- How can I get better feedback?
- Can I use form letters?
- How can I overcome writer's block?

Review of Key Points

Assignments for Module 4

Polishing Your Prose: Commas in Lists

LEARNING OBJECTIVES

After reading and applying the information in Module 4, you'll be able to demonstrate

Knowledge of

- The activities in the writing process
- How professional writers apply the process

Skills to

- Begin to apply the activities in the writing process
- Begin to identify and analyze your own strategies
- Begin to use revision and editing techniques
- Begin to practise overcoming writer's block

The Conference Board of Canada
Insights You Can Count On

Skilled performances look easy and effortless. In reality, as every dancer, musician, and athlete knows, they're the product of hard work, hours of practice, attention to detail, and intense concentration. Like all skilled performances, writing rests on a base of work. Writers themselves agree that writing is like communicating in another language, with its own set of rules and requirements.

Writing is rewriting.

The payoff, however, is enormous: being able to write well is a powerful skill. It's powerful, first of all, because writing is a transferable skill. Good writers write well in every situation, whether crafting a proposal to sell clients on a new product, or sending a letter to their child's hockey coach to protest a practice time.

Furthermore, the writing process demands the highest-level thinking skills, including analysis, problem solving, organization, critical thinking, and synthesis, among others. Therefore, the more you practise the process, the better you develop these skills.

What is the writing process?

The process can include eight activities: planning, gathering information, writing, assessing, getting feedback, revising, editing, and proofreading, as described in Table 4.1

No wonder writing is so difficult and takes so much time.

Note, however, that writers do not necessarily follow these activities in order. For example, some writers compose completely in their heads, write a first draft, and then use a reader, revise, edit, and proofread. Other writers constantly interrupt the composition process to revise and edit. Despite experts' claims, there is no one right way to write.

In her book *Writing on Both Sides of the Brain*, Henriette Anne Klauser argues that the revising, editing, and proofreading activities of the writing process are left-brain, or logical. Composing comes from the right brain: our intuitive, creative side. Our critical, logical side can interrupt our creative side, causing anxiety and writer's block. Therefore, according to Peter Elbow, writer and expert in teaching students to write, we should get the words down—any words, and as many words as possible—before applying any revising or editing strategies.[1]

Liz Braun revises and edits her writing as she composes.

Freelancer Leslie Butler agrees … in theory. However Butler "can't go forward unless [I] go backward: I may write two paragraphs; then I have to go back and reread what I've written, over and over again. Sometimes I read and revise and edit the first paragraph twelve to thirty times."[2]

Liz Braun, *Toronto Sun* entertainment columnist, also revises and edits as she composes. Braun reads her writing aloud

TABLE 4.1
Activities in the Writing Process

Planning	Apply PAIBOC: Identify & analyze the situation; define purpose; identify and analyze audience; consider necessary information, audience objections & benefits, and context; outline; choose a pattern of development, or organization.
Gathering/researching	Get the information: from the initial message; from the client (teacher); from conversations with colleagues; from the Internet; from interviews, surveys or focus groups; from print sources.
Composing/writing	Create: get words down; make lists; free write; mind-map; make drafts.
Assessing	Read and reread: how does it sound? Is it audience-centred? Does it meet the audience's needs? Will they understand it? Will it achieve intended results? Is it courteous, friendly, and complete?
Getting Feedback	Use a reader and ask for comments: writers who want to achieve intended results get a colleague, friend, spouse, parent, or sibling—an interested party—to read and react to the form and content of their documents. Whether beginners or proficient writers, people who want their writing to succeed ask others for feedback, and **apply useful advice in their revision and editing activities.**
Revising	Adapt, change, and rewrite: **writing is rewriting.** Revising is rewriting and reworking the document to reflect your own assessment and helpful feedback from others. Revising could mean changing a few sentences, or writing headings; it could mean deleting whole paragraphs, or moving whole sections. Although technology has increased the amount and complexity of writing, software programs like Microsoft® Word have simplified the revision part of the process.
Editing	Focus on the surface of the writing, ensuring appropriate word choice and correct format, spelling, grammar, usage, and punctuation.
Proofreading	Check the final copy to ensure it's free from typographical errors.

while she writes. When a word doesn't "sound right," she stops and looks it up in the dictionary. "I never use spell-check. I think it's sloppy; I need to look up the word as a form of discipline; if I look it up enough times, I may learn how to spell the word correctly." Braun also interrupts her composing activity to read, revise, and edit what she has written so far, even though her writing will be read, vetted, and edited by at least three other people, including a lawyer.[3]

Whatever strategies they use, however, writers always consider the writing process to be a **work in progress.** They understand that they may well have to repeat part or all of the process over and over again. They write, read, and assess what they have written, revise, edit, and then write some more. They know they can change anything right up until the document is published.

■ Does it matter what process I use?

The more you write—and read—the more you'll become aware of what processes work best for you and the more your writing will improve.

Just as athletes can improve their game by studying videotapes and focusing on exactly how they kick a ball or spin during a jump, so writers improve their writing by studying their own processes. No single writing process works for all writers all the time. However, expert writers seem to use different processes than novice writers.[4] Expert writers are more likely to do these things:

- Understand that the first draft will be revised
- Have clear goals focusing on purpose and audience
- Read daily
- Write regularly
- Have a large vocabulary
- Break big writing jobs into a series of steps
- Choose and use several different strategies
- Use rules flexibly

Research shows that experts differ from novices in identifying and analyzing the initial problem more effectively, understanding the task more broadly and deeply, drawing from a wider repertoire of strategies, and seeing patterns more clearly. Experts actually compose more slowly than novices, perhaps because they rarely settle for work that is just "passable." Finally, experts are better at evaluating their own work.[5]

Thinking about the processes you currently use, and trying out experts' strategies, can help you to become a better writer.

How should I approach business writing?

Think KISS. Plan how to make it easy for the reader.

Writing for business means concentrating on your readers' needs for clarity and completion. In contrast to academic writing (◀▮▶ Module 1), the best business writing **keeps it short and simple (KISS)**. The best-written documents are those the audience can easily read and understand. These messages are productive because 1) readers do not have to spend time asking for clarification, and 2) the writer doesn't have to spend time doing it right the second time.

Therefore, when business writing (whether emails, memos, letters, proposals, and/or reports) compose documents that make it easy for your reader to read, understand, and respond to.

I don't have much time. How should I use it?

Swiss-cheese the process. Use every opportunity to make notes on your research and thinking. Save plenty of time for rewriting.

Professional writers, those who write for a living, concur on one aspect of the writing process: it takes a lot of time. Writing professionals Braun and Butler, both of whom have been writing for over 20 years, budget hours and sometimes days for their writing tasks. Braun's weekly 600-word film review can take between one and three hours. A profile or feature story, which involves primary research, can take her up to four eight-hour days (32 hours).

The writing process can include many critical thinking strategies.

Recently, Butler spent 40 hours on a story about school board politics: her research (interviews) took 10 hours; composing, revising, and editing took another 30 hours. Different projects have different lead times, as Figure 4.1 shows.

Writing is time-consuming. However, the task becomes easier when you become conscious of what strategies work for you. Whether beginner, second-language, proficient, or expert, however, writers agree that the best strategy is talking about the task with someone who is interested. At every stage of the process, from planning through composition to proofreading, writers claim they benefit most from discussions with other writers about their work.

◼ What planning should I do before I begin writing or speaking?

Do as much planning as you can ahead of time.

Spend at least one-third of your time planning and organizing before you begin to write. The better your ideas are when you start, the fewer drafts you'll need to produce a good document. Start by using the analysis questions from ◀|▷ Module 1 to identify purpose and audience. Use the strategies described in ◀|▷ Module 2 to analyze audience and in ◀|▷ Module 8 to develop reader benefits. Gather information you can use for your document.

If ideas won't come, try the following techniques:

- **Brainstorming.** Write down all your ideas without judging them. Consciously try to get at least a dozen different ideas before you stop.
- **Freewriting.**[6] Make yourself write, without stopping, for 10 minutes or so, even if you have to write "I will think of something soon." At the end of 10 minutes, read what you've written and identify the best point in the draft. Get a clean paper or screen and write for another 10 uninterrupted minutes. Read this draft, marking anything that's good and should be kept, and then write again for another 10 minutes. By the third session, you will probably produce several sections that are worth keeping—maybe even a complete draft that's ready to be revised.
- **Clustering.**[7] Write your topic in the middle of the page and circle it. Write down the ideas the topic suggests, circling them, too. (The circles are designed to tap into the non-linear half of your brain.) When you've filled the page, look for patterns or repeated ideas. Use different-coloured pens to group related ideas. Then use these ideas to develop reader benefits in a memo, questions for a survey, or content for the body of a report. Figure 4.3 presents the clusters that one writer created about business communication in Canada and France.
- **Talk to your audiences.** As communications analyst Rachel Spilka's research shows, talking to internal and external audiences helped writers involve readers in the planning process, understand the social and political relationships among readers, and negotiate conflicts orally rather than depending solely on the document. These writers were then able to think about content as well as about organization and style, appeal to common ground (such as reducing waste or increasing productivity) that several readers shared, and reduce the number of revisions needed before documents were approved.[8]

SEE THE OLC!

Cluster Ideas On-Screen

FIGURE 4.1

Time Lines for Various Documents (your actual times may vary)

Email message answering a simple question. Total time: 15 minutes

5 minutes	5 minutes	5 minutes
Read the question	Draft the message	Reread the message
Gather any information		Run the message
necessary for reply		through a spell checker
Plan the message		Make small changes
		Send the message

Email message answering a question that requires simple research. Total time: 2 hours

1 hour	30 minutes	30 minutes
Read the question	Draft the message	Reread the message
Think about what	and any attachments	Revise the message
is needed to reply		and attachments
Do research (on the		Run the message
Web, ask people, etc.)		through a spell checker
Analyze the information		Send the message
Plan the message		

Memo explaining a new policy. Total time: 6 hours

90 minutes	60 minutes	90 minutes	30 minutes	90 minutes
Understand the policy	Draft	Reread draft	Ask for feedback	Revise draft based on feedback
Answer the PAIBOC questions		Measure draft against PAIBOC questions and principles of business communication		Run a spell check
(◀▶ Module 1)				Proof by eye
Think about document design		Revise draft		Initial memo
Organize the message				Duplicate and distribute document

Report recommending ways to improve customer service. Total time: 30 business days

6 days	1 day	2 days	9 days
Collect information about weaknesses in service	Ask for feedback on proposal, research plan	Revise proposal	Conduct research
Plan research to gather more information			Analyze data
Get library sources; check the Web; plan survey or interview questions			Create visuals for report
Write proposal to do research to find solution			Prepare appendices

5 days	1 day	5 days	1 day
Draft report	Ask for feedback on recommendations, report design, and visuals	Revise report	Submit report
Evaluate draft against proposal and principles of business communication		Revise visuals	Present results orally
		Plan oral presentation	
		Edit document and visuals	
		Run a spell check	
		Proof by eye	
		Duplicate document	

FIGURE 4.2

P A I B O C

Questions for Analysis

Use the PAIBOC questions to analyze business communication problems:

P What are your **purposes** in writing?

A Who is your **audience**? How do members of your audience differ? What audience characteristics are relevant to this particular message?

I What **information** must your message include?

B What reasons or reader **benefits** can you use to support your position?

O What **objections** can you expect your readers to have? What negative elements of your message must you de-emphasize or overcome?

C How will the **context** affect reader response? Think about your relationship to the reader, the morale in the organization, the economy, the time of year, and any special circumstances.

FIGURE 4.3
Clustering Helps Generate Ideas

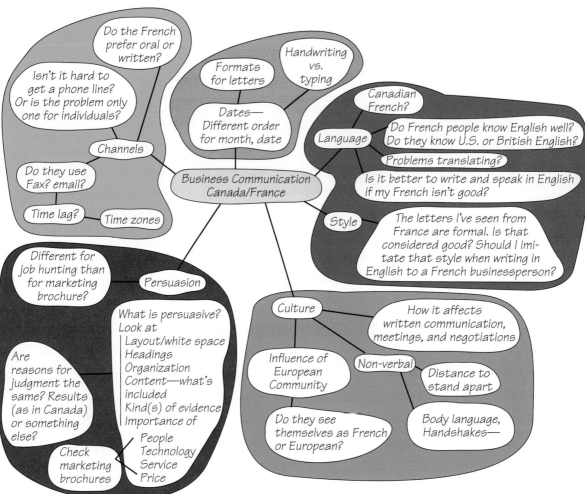

Thinking and talking to others about the content, layout, or structure of your document can also give you ideas. For long documents, *write out the headings you'll use*. For anything that's shorter than five pages, less formal notes will probably work. You may want to jot down ideas that you can use as the basis for a draft. For an oral presentation, a meeting, or a document with lots of visuals, use your presentation software to create a **storyboard**, or make your own paper storyboard with a rectangle representing each page or unit. Draw a box with a visual for each main point. Below the box, write a short caption or label.

Letters and memos will go faster if you choose a basic organizational pattern before you start. ◁▷ Modules 10, 12, and 13 give detailed patterns of organization for the most common kinds of letters and memos. You may want to customize those patterns with a **planning guide**[9] to help you keep the big picture in mind as you write. Figure 4.4 shows planning guides developed for specific kinds of documents.

FIGURE 4.4
Customized Planning Guides for Specific Documents

Planning guide for a trip report
- The Big Picture from the Company's Point of View: We Can Go Forward on the Project
- Criteria/Goals
- What We Did
- Why We Know Enough to Go Forward

Planning guide for a proposal
- Customer's Concern #1 Our Proposal or Answer
- Customer's Concern #2 Our Proposal or Answer
- Customer's Concern #3 Our Proposal or Answer

Planning guide for an email message
- My Purpose
- Points I Want to Make
- Document(s) to Attach
- Next Steps

Planning guide for a credit rejection
- Reason
- Refusal
- Alternative (Layaway/ Co-signer/Provide more information)
- Goodwill Ending

Source: Email and proposal guides based on Fred Reynolds, "What Adult Work-World Writers Have Taught Me About Adult Work-World Writing," *Professional Writing in Context: Lessons from Teaching and Consulting in Worlds of Work* (Hillsdale, NJ: Lawrence Erlbaum Associates, 1995), 18, 20.

What is revision? How do I do it?

Revision means "re-seeing" the document from the reader's point of view.

Good writers make their drafts better by revising, editing, and proofreading from the reader's point of view.

- *Revising* means making changes that will better satisfy your purposes and your audience.
- *Editing* means making surface-level changes that make the document grammatically correct.
- *Proofreading* means checking to be sure the document is free from typographical errors.

When you're writing to a new audience or solving a particularly difficult problem, plan to revise the draft at least three times. The first time, look for content and clarity. The second time, check the organization and layout. Finally, check style and tone, using the information in ◀▶ Modules 14 and 15. Figure 4.5 summarizes the questions you could ask.

Often you'll get the best revision by setting aside your draft, getting a blank page or screen, and redrafting. This strategy takes advantage of the thinking you did on your first draft without locking you into the sentences in it.

FIGURE 4.5

Checklist for Thorough Revision

Content and Clarity

❑ Does your document meet the needs of the organization and of the reader—and make you look good?

❑ Have you given readers all the information they need to understand and act on your message?

❑ Have you organized your message for optimal positive audience impact? (◀▶ Modules 2 and 11)

❑ Is all the information accurate?

❑ Is each sentence clear? Is the message free from apparently contradictory statements?

❑ Are generalizations and benefits backed up with adequate supporting detail?

Organization and Layout

❑ Does the design of the document make it easy for readers to find the information they need? Is the document visually inviting?

❑ Are transitions between ideas smooth? Do ideas within paragraphs flow smoothly?

❑ Are the most important points emphasized?

❑ Are the first and last paragraphs effective?

Style and Tone

❑ Does the message build goodwill?

❑ Is the message easy to read?

❑ Is the message friendly and free from biased language?

FIGURE 4.6

Checklist for Light Revision

❑ Are the first and last paragraphs effective?

❑ Does the design of the document make it easy for readers to find the information they need?

❑ Have I told the reader what to do?

As you revise, be sure to read the document through from start to finish. This is particularly important if you've composed it in several sittings or if you've used text from other documents. Researchers have found that such documents tend to be well organized but don't flow well.[10] You may need to add transitions (◀▶ Module 14), cut repetitive parts, or change words to create a uniform level of formality throughout the document.

If you're really short on time, do a light revision (see Figure 4.6). The quality of the final document may not be as high as with a thorough revision, but even a light revision is better than skipping revision.

Can a grammar checker edit for me?

No. You have to decide whether to make each change.

Grammar checkers are good at finding missing halves. For example, if you open a parenthesis and never close it, a grammar checker will note that a second one is needed. Of course, you have to decide where it goes. In terms of other errors, all a grammar checker can do is to ask you about what you have done. A grammar checker can tell you that you've used a passive verb (◀▶ Module 14) and ask whether you want to change it. But you have to decide whether the passive is justified. If it finds the word *well*, the grammar checker can tell you that *good* and *well* are sometimes confused. But you have to decide which word fits your meaning (◀▶ Module 15). You still need to know the rules so that you can decide which changes to make.

Check to be sure that the following are accurate:

- Sentence structure
- Subject-verb and noun-pronoun agreement
- Punctuation
- Word usage
- Spelling—including spelling of names
- Numbers

You need to know the rules of grammar and punctuation to edit. Most writers make a small number of errors repeatedly. If you know that you have trouble with dangling modifiers or subject-verb agreement, for example, specifically look for them in your draft. Also look for any errors that especially bother your boss and correct them.

Grammar checkers frequently include an option for checking the **readability** of a selected passage. Microsoft Word's grammar checker will indicate readability based on the Flesch-Kincaid Grade Level (corresponding to years of education required to comprehend the material) and a Flesch Reading Ease score (assessing the difficulty level based on the average number of words per sentence and the average number of syllables per word). Table 4.2 sets out guidelines for interpreting these results.

Measure Your Writing's "Fogginess"

Try to edit *after* you revise. There's no point in taking time to fix a grammatical error in a sentence that may be cut when you clarify your meaning or tighten your style. Some writers edit more accurately when they print out a copy of a document and edit the hard copy. But beware: laser printing makes a page look good but does nothing to correct errors.

I use a spell checker. Do I still need to proofread?

Yes.

Proofread every document both with a spell checker and by eye to catch the errors a spell checker can't find.

Proofreading is hard because writers tend to see what they know should be there rather than what really is there. Since it's always easier to proof something you haven't written, you may want to swap papers with a proofing buddy. (Be sure the person looks for typos, not for content.)

TABLE 4.2
Interpreting Flesch Readability Scores

Flesch Reading Ease	Difficulty	Flesch-Kincaid Grade Level	Example
0–29	Very difficult	Post-graduate	
30–49	Difficult	College	32: Harvard Law Review 40–50: standard score for insurance documents required by law in several U.S. states
50–59	Fairly difficult	High school	52: Time
60–69	Standard	Grade 8 to 9	60: "plain English" (20 words per sentence, 1.5 syllables per word) 65: Reader's Digest
70–79	Fairly easy	Grade 7	
80–89	Easy	Grade 5 to 6	
90–100	Very easy	Grade 4 to 5	

Source: Tom McArthur, ed., *The Oxford Companion to the English Language* (Oxford: Oxford University Press, 1992), 407.

INSTANT REPLAY

Writing is a complex, time-consuming process that includes **planning, researching, composing, assessing, getting feedback, revising, editing,** and **proofreading**. Writers do not follow these activities in order, although the most successful writers focus their time on **planning, researching, revising,** and **proofreading**.

To proofread, follow these steps:

- Read once quickly for meaning to see that nothing has been left out.
- Read a second time, slowly. When you find an error, correct it and then *reread that line*. Readers tend to become less attentive after they find one error and may miss other errors close to the one they've spotted.
- To proofread a document you know well, read the lines backward or the pages out of order.

Always triple-check numbers, headings, first and last paragraphs, and the reader's name.

■ How can I get better feedback?

Ask for the kind of feedback you need.

Revising documents is a fact of life in business, government, and non-profit organizations.

To improve the quality of the feedback you get, and of your revisions, tell people which aspects you'd especially like comments about. For example, when you give a reader the outline or planning draft,[11] you might want to know whether the general approach is appropriate. After your second draft, you might want to know whether reader benefits are well developed. When you reach the polishing draft, you'll be ready for feedback on style and grammar. Figure 4.7 lists questions to ask.

It's easy to feel defensive when someone criticizes your work. If the feedback stings, put it aside until you can read it without feeling defensive. Even if you think that the reader has misunderstood what you were trying to say, the fact that the reader complained means the section could be improved. If the reader says "This isn't true" and you know that the statement is true, rephrasing the statement, giving more information or examples, or documenting the source might make the truth clear to the reader.

EXPANDING A CRITICAL SKILL

Revising after Feedback

When you get feedback that you understand and agree with, make the change.

If you get feedback you don't understand, ask for clarification.

- Paraphrase: "So you're asking me to give more information?"
- Ask for more information: "Can you suggest a way to do that?"
- Test your inference: "Would it help if I did this?"

Sometimes you may get feedback you don't agree with.

- If it's an issue of grammatical correctness, check this book (sometimes even smart people get things wrong).
- If it's a matter of content, recognize that something about the draft isn't as good as it could be: something is leading the reader to respond negatively.

- If the reader thinks a fact is wrong (and you know it's right), show where the fact came from "According to...."
- If the reader suggests a change in wording you don't like, try another option.
- If the reader seems to have misunderstood or misread, think about ways to make the meaning clearer.

Your supervisor's comments on a draft can help you improve that document, help you write better drafts the next time, and teach you about the culture of your organization. Look for patterns in the feedback you receive. Are you asked to use more formal language, or to make the document more conversational? Does your boss want to see an overview before details? Does your company prefer information presented in bulleted lists rather than in paragraphs?

▦ Can I use form letters?

Yes, but make sure they're good.

A **form letter** is a pre-written, fill-in-the blank letter designed for routine situations. Some form letters have different paragraphs that can be inserted, depending on the situation.

FIGURE 4.7

Questions to Ask Readers
Outline or Planning Draft
❏ Does the plan seem to be on the right track?
❏ What topics should be added? Should any be cut?
❏ Do you have any other general suggestions?
Revised Draft
❏ Does the message satisfy all its purposes?
❏ Is the message adapted to the audience(s)?
❏ Is the organization effective?
❏ Are any parts unclear?
❏ What ideas need further development?
❏ Do you have any other suggestions?
Polished Draft
❏ Are there any problems with word choice or sentence structure?
❏ Did you find any inconsistencies?
❏ Did you find any typos?
❏ Is the document's design effective?

For example, a form letter admitting students to university might add additional paragraphs for students receiving financial aid.

Boilerplate is language—sentences, paragraphs, even pages—from a previous document that a writer includes in a new document. In academic papers, material written by others must be quoted and documented. However, because businesses own the documents their employees write, text from those documents may be included without attribution.

In some cases, boilerplate may have been written years ago. For example, many legal documents, including apartment leases and sales contracts, are almost completely boilerplated. In other cases, writers may use boilerplate they themselves have written. For example, a section from a proposal describing the background of the problem could also be used in the final report after the proposed work was completed. A section from a progress report describing what the writer has done could be used with only a few changes in the methods section of the final report.

Writers use form letters and boilerplate to save time and energy and to use language that has already been approved by the organization's legal staff. However, reusing old text creates two problems:[12]

- Using unrevised boilerplate can create a document with incompatible styles and tones.
- Form letters and boilerplate can encourage writers to see situations and audiences as identical when, in fact, they differ.

Before you use a form letter, make sure that it is well written and that it applies to the situation in which you are thinking of using it.

Before you incorporate old language in a new document,

- Check to see that the old section is well written.
- Consciously look for differences between the two situations, audiences, or purposes that may require different content, organization, or wording.
- Read through the whole document at a single sitting to be sure that style, tone, and level of detail are consistent.

■ How can I overcome writer's block?

Talk and practise.

Whether learners or professionals, writers claim that talking about the task facilitates it. During the planning and composition stages, talking with interested colleagues helps people get ideas, find sources, and identify reader benefits and organizational patterns.[13]

Writing teachers and experts like Peter Elbow suggest that writers can reduce anxiety and overcome writer's block by

- freewriting
- writing daily
- writing as if you were speaking to your audience
- focusing first on creative or composing processes
- applying the critical or revising processes only after you have written
- using others as readers.

Remember that writing becomes easier the more you do it. And it helps to talk to other people about your writing.

Employability Skills 2000+

The Conference Board of Canada
Insights You Can Count On

Please see the OLC to preview the key skills from the Conference Board of Canada's Employability Skills 2000+ covered in this module.

Review of Key Points

1. What eight activities are involved in the writing process?
2. What is different about business writing?
3. What strategies do expert writers use?
4. Why do some writers finish composing before using revising and editing strategies?
5. What kind of feedback should you ask for? When?
6. What are four strategies you can use to overcome writer's block?

Assignments for Module 4

Questions for Critical Thinking

4.1 Of the processes that expert writers use, which do you already use? How could you modify your process to incorporate at least one more on the list?

4.2 Of the people who have seen your writing, which one(s) have given you the most useful feedback? What makes it useful?

4.3 In which areas are you best at giving feedback to other people? How could you make your feedback even better?

4.4 Think about the form letters you have received. How do they make you feel? If they have flaws, how could they be improved?

Exercises and Problems

4.5   Interviewing Writers About Their Composing Processes

Interview someone who writes for a living about the composing process(es) he or she uses. Questions you could ask include the following:

- What kind of planning do you do before you write? Do you make lists? formal or informal outlines?
- When you need more information, where do you get it?
- How do you compose your drafts? Do you dictate? draft with pen and paper? compose on screen? How do you find uninterrupted time to compose?
- When you want advice about style, grammar, and spelling, what sources do you consult?
- Does your supervisor ever read your drafts and make suggestions?
- Do you ever work with other writers to produce a single document? Describe the process you use.

- Describe the process of creating a document that you felt reflected your best work.
- Describe the process of creating a document that you found difficult or frustrating. What sorts of things make writing easier or harder for you?

As your instructor directs,

a. Share your results orally with a small group of students.
b. Present your results in an oral presentation to the class.
c. Present your results in a memo to your instructor.
d. Post an email message to the class discussing your results.
e. Share your results with a small group of students and write a joint memo reporting the similarities and differences you found.

4.6 Applying Your Revision and Editing Strategies

Apply your revision and editing strategies to the following memo. As you read the memo 1) write down your reactions as they occur to you; 2) write down your reasons as you revise; 3) identify whether you are revising or editing as you make changes. Be prepared to present your results, including the notes on your own processes, to your teacher in a memo.

November 10, 2005

Memo to: Bartenders, wait servers and busing staff
Memo From: Omar
Re: Christmas

While we're planning our Christmas party we should also be thinking about what we're going to do about who's going to be responsible for cleaning up and locking up after the party. If we start partying after closing time at 1 A.M. on the 21st, and we party until 3 or 4, that's fine with the managers, but we need people to stay to clean up and set up for the next day's lunch crowd. Also, somebody has to take the day's receipts and money for safekeeping, and bank it the next day.

Can you let me know who will volunteer to do that?

4.7 Analyzing Your Own Writing Processes

Save your notes and drafts from several assignments so that you can answer the following questions:

- Which of the eight activities in the writing process discussed in Module 4 do you use?
- How much time do you spend on each of the eight activities?
- What kinds of revisions do you make most often?
- Do you use different processes for different documents, or do you have one process that you use most of the time?
- Which practices of good writers do you follow?
- What parts of your process seem most successful? Are there any places in the process that could be improved? How?

- What relation do you see between the process(es) you use and the quality of the final document?

As your instructor directs,

a. Discuss your process with a small group of students.

b. Write a memo to your instructor analyzing in detail your process for composing one of the papers for this class.

c. Write a memo to your instructor analyzing your process during the term. What parts of your process(es) have stayed the same throughout the term? What parts have changed?

4.8 Checking Spell Checkers and Grammar Checkers

Each of the following paragraphs contains errors in grammar, spelling, and punctuation. Which errors does your spelling or grammar checker catch? Which errors does it miss? Does it flag as errors any words that are correct?

1. Answer to an Inquiry
   Enclosed are the tow copies you requested of our pamphlet, "Using the Internet to market Your products. The pamphlet walks you through the steps of planning the Home Page (The first page of the web cite, shows examples of other Web pages we have designed, and provide a questionnaire that you can use to analyze audience the audience and purposes).

2. Performance Appraisal
   Most staff accountants complete three audits a month. Ellen has completed 21 audits in this past six months she is our most productive staff accountant. Her technical skills our very good however some clients feel that she could be more tactful in suggesting ways that the clients accounting practices could be improved.

3. Brochure
   Are you finding that being your own boss crates it's own problems? Take the hassle out of working at home with a VoiceMail Answering System. Its almost as good as having your own secretary.

4. Presentation Slides

How to Create a Web Résumé

- Omit home address and phone number
- Use other links only if they help an employer evaluate you
- Be professional

- Carefully craft and proof-read the phrase on the index apage

How to Create a Scannable Résumé

- Create a "plain vanilla" document
- Use a "Keywords" section. Include personality traits as well as accomplishments
- Be specific and quantifiable

Polishing Your Prose

Commas in Lists

Use commas in lists to separate items:

> At the office supply store, I bought pens, stationery, and three-ring binders.

Commas show distinctions between items in a list. Technically, the comma before the coordinating conjunction *and* is optional, but the additional comma always adds clarity. Use commas consistently throughout your document. Missing or improperly placed commas confuse readers:

> We bought the following items for the staff lounge: television cabinet computer desk refrigerator and microwave oven.

Does television describe cabinet or is it a separate item? Is computer desk one item? Or are computer and desk two separate things? Inserting commas makes the distinction clear:

> We bought the following items for the staff kitchen: television, cabinet, computer, desk, refrigerator, and microwave oven.

Semicolons replace commas in lists where the items themselves contain commas:

> Our company has plants in Moncton, New Brunswick; Flin Flon, Manitoba; and Lethbridge, Alberta.

Exercises

Use commas to make these lists clearer.

1. Please send the "fruit of the month" in April May June and July.
2. At the weekly staff meeting we will be joined by Mr. Loomis Ms. Handelman Ms. Lang and Mr. Kim.
3. The special parts division is opening offices in Brampton Ontario Fredericton New Brunswick and Big Salmon Yukon.
4. Buy small medium and large paper clips at the office supply store.
5. I need to telephone Mary Frank and Paul to finish my report and mail copies of it to Ted Sam and Latanya.
6. Applicants should send copies of their résumés to Mr. Arthur Bramberger human resource director Ms. Tina Ramos vice president of marketing and Ms. Ellen Choi administrative assistant in marketing.
7. The weather affects our offices in Montreal New York City and Philadelphia.
8. Interns will be rotated through the receiving claims adjustment customer service and shipping departments.
9. Elizabeth Tyrone Mark and Sara presented the team's recommendations.
10. We are open until 9 P.M. on Mondays Wednesdays Fridays and Saturdays.

Check your answers to the odd-numbered exercises on page 571.

Online Learning Centre

Visit the Online Learning Centre at www.mcgrawhill.ca/olc/locker to access module quizzes, a searchable glossary, résumé and letter templates, additional business writing samples, CBC videos, and other learning and study tools.

Designing Documents, Slides, and Screens

Module Outline

- Why is design important?
- When should I think about design?
- How should I design paper pages?
- How should I design presentation slides?
- How should I design Web pages?
- How do I know whether my design works?

Review of Key Points

Assignments for Module 5

Polishing Your Prose: Active and Passive Voice

LEARNING OBJECTIVES

After reading and applying the information in Module 5, you'll be able to demonstrate

Knowledge of

- The importance of document appearance, layout, and design
- Essential design principles
- The relationship between readability and your credibility

Skills to

- Apply design principles to paper pages, presentation slides, and Web pages
- Use computer software to increase document readability

The Conference Board of Canada
Insights You Can Count On

Please see the OLC to preview the key skills from the Conference Board of Canada's Employability Skills 2000+ covered in this module.

FYI

FedEx saved $400 000 a year by redesigning its ground-operations manuals. Before, employees could find the right answer only 53 percent of the time. Afterward, their success rate was 80 percent, and they found answers 25 percent faster.

Source: Joseph Kimble, "Writing for Dollars, Writing to Please," *The Scribes Journal of Legal Writing*, 6 (1996–1997): 14–15.

A well-designed document looks inviting, friendly, and accessible. Good document design saves time and money, builds goodwill, and reduces legal problems. Effective design also groups ideas visually, making the structure of the document more obvious and easier to read. Research shows that easy-to-read documents enhance your credibility and build an image of you as a professional, competent person.[1]

Why is design important?

Design is essential to meaning making.

Your audience brings expectations to and constructs meaning from the design of your message. Business audiences expect document and slide design to make it easy for them to read and understand the content.

When should I think about design?

Think about design at each stage of the writing process.

Because layout and design make the first impression on readers, document design is a vital component of persuasion. Indeed, you create the best documents when you think about design at each stage of your writing process:

- As you plan, think about your audience. Are they skilled readers? Are they busy? Will they read the document straight through or skip around in it? Design the document to meet readers' needs and expectations.
- As you write, incorporate lists and headings. Use visuals to convey numerical data clearly and forcefully.
- Get feedback from people who will be using your document. What parts of the document do they find hard to understand? What additional information do they need?
- As you revise, check your draft against the guidelines in this module.

How should I design paper pages?

Follow the design principles of contrast, repetition, alignment, and proximity to meet audience expectations.[2]

Use the following guidelines to create visually attractive documents:

- Use white space to separate and emphasize points.
- Use headings to group points.
- Limit the use of words set in all capital letters.
- Use no more than two typefaces in a single document.
- Decide whether to justify margins based on the situation and the audience.

Use White Space

White space—the empty space on the page—emphasizes the material that it separates from the rest of the text. This emphasis makes the material easier to read. Creating white space is also known as "menu writing," because the visual design principle—brief text highlighted by space—is the same as you find on restaurant menus.

You can create white space in several ways:

- Use headings.
- Use a mix of paragraph lengths (maximum six to seven typed lines).
- Use lists.
- Use tabs or indents—not spacing—to align items vertically.
- Use numbered lists when the number or sequence of items is exact.
- Use **bullets** (large dots or squares like those in this list) when the number and sequence are equal.

When you create a list, use parallelism: begin each item on the list with the same part of speech. If you begin your list with a verb, for example, begin every following item on the list with a verb. This parallel structure meets the reader's subconscious expectation. *And meeting reader expectation is the most important aspect of business writing.*

Not parallel: The following suggestions can help employers avoid bias in job interviews:
1. Base questions on the job description
2. Questioning techniques
3. Selection and training of interviewers

Parallel: The following suggestions can help employers avoid bias in job interviews:
1. Base questions on the job description
2. Ask the same questions of all applicants
3. Select and train interviewers carefully

Also parallel: Employers can avoid bias in job interviews by
1. Basing questions on the job description
2. Asking the same questions of all applicants
3. Selecting and training interviewers carefully

Figure 5.1 shows an original typed document. In Figure 5.2 the same document is improved by using shorter paragraphs, lists, and headings. These devices take space. When saving space is essential, it's better to cut the text and keep white space and headings.

Use Headings

Headings are words or short phrases that identify a complete idea and divide your letter, memo, or report into sections. Headings increase readability because they summarize what the reader is about to read and increase white space.

- Make headings specific.
- Make each heading cover all the material until the next heading.
- Keep headings at any one level parallel: all nouns, all complete sentences, or all questions.

In a letter or memo, type main headings flush with the left-hand margin in bold. Capitalize the first letters of the first word and of other major words; use lowercase for all other letters. (See Figure 5.2 on page 90 for an example.) In single-spaced text, triple space between the previous text and the heading; double space between the heading and the text that follows.

FIGURE 5.1
A Document with Poor Visual Impact

Full capital letters make title hard to read

MONEY DEDUCTED FROM YOUR WAGES TO PAY CREDITORS

When you buy goods on credit, the store will sometimes ask you to sign a Wage Assignment form allowing it to deduct money from your wages if you do not pay your bill. When you buy on credit, you sign a contract agreeing to pay a certain amount each week or month until you have paid all you owe. The Wage Assignment Form is separate. It must contain the name of your present employer, your social insurance number, the amount of money loaned, the rate of interest, the date when payments are due, and your signature. The words "Wage Assignment" must be printed at the top of the form and also near the line for your signature. Even if you have signed a Wage Assignment agreement, Roysner will not withhold part of your wages unless all of the following conditions are met: 1. You have to be more than forty days late in payment of what you owe; 2. Roysner has to receive a correct statement of the amount you are in default and a copy of the Wage Assignment form; and 3. You and Roysner must receive a notice from the creditor at least twenty days in advance stating that the creditor plans to make a demand on your wages. This twenty-day notice gives you a chance to correct the problems yourself. If these conditions are all met, Roysner must withhold 15 percent of each paycheque until your bill is paid and give this money to your creditor.

Long para- graph is visually uninviting

If you think you are not late or that you do not owe the amount stated, you can argue against it by filing a legal document called a "defence." Once you file a defence, Roysner will not withhold any money from you. However, be sure you are right before you file a defence. If you are wrong, you have to pay not only what you owe but also all legal costs for both yourself and the creditor. If you are right, the creditor has to pay all these costs.

Important information is hard to find

In a report, you may need more levels of headings. ◄► Module 15 shows how to set up five levels of headings for reports.

■ Limit the Use of Words Set in All Capital Letters

We recognize words by their shapes.[3] (For example, try reading each line in Figure 5.3) Using capital letters, all words are rectangular; letters lose the descenders and ascenders that make reading easier and faster. Use full capitals sparingly. Instead, bold text to emphasize it.

FIGURE 5.2
A Document Revised to Improve Visual Impact

Money Deducted from Your Wages to Pay Creditors

First letter of each main word capitalized— Title split onto two lines

When you buy goods on credit, the store will sometimes ask you to sign a Wage Assignment form allowing it to deduct money from your wages if you do not pay your bill.

Have You Signed a Wage Assignment Form?

Headings divide document into chunks

When you buy on credit, you sign a contract agreeing to pay a certain amount each week or month until you have paid all you owe. The Wage Assignment Form is separate. It must contain the following:

- The name of your present employer
- Your social insurance number
- The amount of insurance
- The rate of interest
- The date when payments are due
- Your signature

List with bullets where order of items doesn't matter

The words "Wage Assignment" must be printed at the top of the form and also near the line for your signature.

When Would Money Be Deducted from Your Wages to Pay a Creditor?

Headings must be parallel. Here, all are questions.

Even if you have signed a Wage Assignment agreement, Roysner will not withhold part of your wages unless all of the following conditions are met:

1. You have to be more than 40 days late in payment of what you owe.
2. Roysner has to receive a correct statement of the amount you are in default and a copy of the Wage Assignment form.
3. You and Roysner must receive a notice from the creditor at least 20 days in advance stating that the creditor plans to make a demand on your wages. This 20-day notice gives you a chance to correct the problem yourself.

Numbered list where number, order of items matter

White space between items emphasizes them

If these conditions are all met, Roysner must withhold fifteen percent (15 percent) of each paycheque and give this money to your creditor until your bill is paid.

What Should You Do If You Think the Wage Assignment Is Incorrect?

If you think you are not late or that you do not owe the amount stated, you can argue against it by filing a legal document called a "defence." Once you file a defence, Roysner will not withhold any money from you. However, be sure you are right before you file a defence. If you are wrong, you have to pay not only what you owe but also all legal costs for both yourself and the creditor. If you are right, the creditor has to pay these costs.

FIGURE 5.3
Full Capitals Hide the Shape of a Word

Full capitals hide the shape of a word and slow reading 19% .

FULL CAPITALS HIDE THE SHAPE OF A WORD AND SLOW READING 19% .

◾ Use No More Than Two Fonts in a Single Document

Each font comes in several sizes and usually in several styles (bold, italic, etc.). Most computer fonts are **proportional**: wider letters (like *w*) take more space than narrow letters (like *i*). Times Roman, Palatino, Helvetica, Geneva, and Arial are proportional fonts. Fonts such as Courier and Prestige Elite, which were designed for typewriters and are still offered as computer fonts, are **fixed**. Every letter takes the same space, so that an *i* takes the same space as a *w*.

Serif fonts have little extensions, called serifs, from the main strokes. (In Figure 5.4, look at the feet on the *t* in Times Roman and the little flicks on the ends of the top bar of the *t*.) Courier, Times Roman, Palatino, and Lucinda Calligraphy are serif fonts. *Serif fonts are easier to read* because the serifs help the eyes move from letter to letter. Helvetica, Geneva, and Arial are called **sans serif** fonts because they lack serifs (*sans* is French for *without*). Sans serif fonts are good for titles, tables, and narrow columns.

In magnified text, sans serif fonts are easier to read; therefore, use sans serif fonts for your PowerPoint™ presentations.

Most business documents use just one font—usually Times Roman, Palatino, Helvetica, or Arial in 11-point or 12-point. In a complex document, use bigger type for main headings and slightly smaller type for subheadings and text. If you combine two fonts in one document, choose one serif and one sans serif typeface.

FIGURE 5.4
Examples of Different Fonts

> This sentence is set in 12-point Times Roman.
>
> This sentence is set in 12-point Arial.
>
> This sentence is set in 12-point New Courier.
>
> *This sentence is set in 12-point Lucinda Calligraphy.*
>
> **This sentence is set in 12-point Broadway.**
>
> This sentence is set in 12-point Technical.

The visual design of a message can support or undercut the impact of the words.

Decide Whether to Justify Margins Based on the Situation and the Audience

Margins that are justified on the left are sometimes called **ragged right margins**. Lines end in different places because words are of different lengths. The FYI boxes use ragged right margins, which are most common in current business usage. However, computers allow you to use **full justification**, so that type on the both sides of the page is evenly lined up. Books, like this one, usually use full justification.

Use ragged right margins in these cases:

• You do not have proportional typefaces.
• You want a less formal look.
• You want to be able to revise an individual page without reprinting the whole document.

Use justified margins in these cases:

• You can use proportional typefaces.
• You want a more formal look.
• You use very short line lengths.

How should I design presentation slides?

Keep slides simple, relevant, and interesting.

SEE THE OLC!

Web Page and Power Point™ Design Tips

As you design slides for PowerPoint™ and other presentation programs, keep these guidelines in mind:

• Create slides that emphasize your key ideas.
• Emphasize visuals. Pictures, charts, and graphs have much greater impact: they appeal to the right, or creative, side of the brain; they are more easily accessible than text; and they are more memorable.
• Use audience-relevant photos or metaphoric illustrations to keep memorable images in your listeners' minds.
• Keep the text to an absolute minimum; give your audience slide handouts on which they can write notes.
• Use bullet-point phrases with concrete words.

- Contrast background and text: the rule is light on dark or dark on light.
- Use a big font: 44-point or 50-point for titles, 32-point for subheads, and 28-point for examples.
- Customize your slides with the company logo, charts, and scanned-in photos and drawings.
- Place illustrations at the top right of the slide for a stronger and longer impression.

Avoid death by PowerPoint™: never, ever read text to your audience. Presenters who put plenty of text on their slides, and then *read* the text, only exasperate their audiences. People do not want presenters to read to them; they can read for themselves. The last thing they want to read is an uninterrupted block of text.

Use clip art only if the art is really appropriate to your points and only if you are able to find non-sexist and non-racist images.

Choose a consistent template, or background design, for the entire presentation. Make sure that the template is appropriate for your subject matter. For example, use a globe only if your topic is international business and palm trees only if you're talking about tropical vacations. PowerPoint's™ basic templates may seem repetitive to people who see lots of presentations. Whenever possible, customize the basic template.

Choose a light background if the lights are off during the presentation and a dark background if the lights are on. Slides will be easier to read if you use high contrast between the words and background. See Figure 5.5 for examples of effective and ineffective colour combinations.

How should I design Web pages?

Pay attention to content, navigation, and the first page.

Good Web pages have both good content and an interesting design.

Your home page is crucial. Jakob Nielsen claims that only 10 percent of users scroll beyond the first page.[4] To make it more likely that visitors will scroll down, do the

FIGURE 5.5
Effective and Ineffective Colours for Presentation Slides

Effective

Ineffective

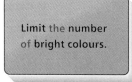

EXPANDING A CRITICAL SKILL

Using Computer Software to Create Good Design

Standard word-processing programs such as WordPerfect and Word help you create well-designed documents.

Different versions of each program handle commands differently. Look up the bolded terms below in a manual, a book about the program, or the online Help menu of your computer program to find out how to use each feature.

Letters and Memos

Choose a businesslike **font** in 11-point or 12-point type. Times Roman, Palatino, Helvetica, and Arial are the most commonly used business fonts.

Use **bold** headings. Avoid having a heading all by itself at the bottom of the page. If you can't have at least one line of text under it, move the heading to the next page. You can check this by eye or set your program to avoid **widows** and **orphans**.

Use **tabs** or **indents** to line up the return address and signature blocks in modified block format (◁ | ▷ Module 9), the To/From/Subject line section of a memo, or the items in a list.

Change your **tab settings** to create good visual impact. A setting at 0.6" (1.5 cm) works well for the Date/To/From/Subject line section of memos. Use 0.4" (1 cm) for paragraphs and 0.6" (1.5 cm) for the start of bulleted lists. For lists with 10 or more items, the setting will need to be a bit further to the right—about 0.65" (1.65 cm).

Choose the design for **bullets** under **Insert** or **Format**. Both WordPerfect and Word will create bulleted or numbered lists automatically. If you have lists with paragraphs, turn off the automatic bullets and create them with the bullets in Symbols. Use indent (not tab) to move the whole list in, not just a single line of it.

Use a **header** (in the **Insert** or **View** menu) with automatic **page numbering** (pull down **Format** to **Page**) for second and subsequent pages. That way, when you delete a paragraph or expand your reader benefits, you don't have to move the header manually. You can either delay the header till page 2 or create it on page 2. For best visual impact, make your header one point size smaller than the body type.

For a two-page document, change the top **margin** of the second page to 0.5" (1.25 cm) so the header is close to the top of the page.

Use the same side margins as your letterhead. If you aren't using letterhead, use 1" (2.5 cm) side margins.

On a two-page document, make sure the second page has at least four to six lines of text for letters and at least 10 lines of text for memos. If you have less, either (1) add details, (2) start the message further down on page 1 so that there is more text on page 2, or (3) make the text fit on just one page by (a) tightening your prose, (b) using full justification to save space, or (c) using less white space.

Word processing programs have a **quick correct** or **auto correct** feature that changes *hte* to *the*, (c) to ©, and so forth. Go into the **Tools** or **Format** menus to find these features and edit them so they make only the changes you want.

Hyphenation may be under **Format** or **Language** in **Tools**.

Before you print, centre your document on the page like a picture in a frame. Go to **file, page setup, layout, vertical alignment, centre**.

Printing

To save paper, check **print preview** on the **File** menu. You'll be able to see how your document will look on the page and make minor layout changes before you print.

If you prepare your document on one computer and print it from another, be sure to open the document and check all of it before you print. Different printers may change margins slightly. Even the same size font may differ from printer to printer: a document that fits on one page in 11-point on one computer may take up more room on a different one.

following on the first page:

- Provide an introductory statement orienting the reader to the organization.
- Offer an overview of the content of your page, with links to take readers to the parts that interest them.
- Include information that will be the most interesting and useful to the most readers.

The rest of the page can contain information that only a limited number of readers will want. When a document reaches four pages or more, think about dividing it into several documents. Specialized information can go on another page, which readers can click on if they want it.

Make it clear what readers will get if they click on a link.

Ineffective phrasing: **Employment.** <u>Openings and skills levels are determined by each office.</u>

Better phrasing: Employment. Openings listed by <u>skills level</u> and by <u>location.</u>

Minimize the number of links readers have to click through to get to the information they want.

Keep these points in mind as you design the pages:

- Use small graphics; keep animation to a minimum. Both graphics and animation take time to load, especially with a slow modem.
- Provide visual variety. Use indentations, bulleted or numbered lists, and headings.
- Unify multiple pages with a small banner, graphic, or label so surfers know whom the pages belong to.
- On each page, provide a link to the home page, the name and email address of the person who maintains the page, and the date when the page was last revised.

■ How do I know whether my design works?

Test it.

A design that looks pretty may or may not work for the audience. To know whether your design is functional, test it with your audience:

- Watch someone as he or she uses the document to do a task. Where does the reader pause, reread, or seem confused? How long does it take? Does the document enable the reader to complete the task accurately?
- Ask the reader to "think aloud" while completing the task, interrupt the reader at key points to ask what he or she is thinking, or ask the reader to describe his or her thought processes after completing the document and the task. Exploring the reader's thought processes is important, since a reader may get the right answer for the wrong reasons. You can thus identify where and how the design needs work.
- Test the document with the people who are most likely to have trouble with it: very young readers, people with little education, people who read English as a second language, and people who have little experience with Web pages.

■ Employability Skills 2000+

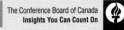

The Conference Board of Canada
Insights You Can Count On

Please see the OLC to preview the key skills from the Conference Board of Canada's Employability Skills 2000+ covered in this module.

■ Review of Key Points

1. Why is document design important?
2. What are the four basic principles of document design?
3. Identify four strategies writers can use to create attractive documents.
4. What should presenters remember when creating slides?

5. What are the key characteristics of well-designed Web pages?
6. What criteria can you use to assess your document design choices?

■ Assignments for Module 5

■ Questions for Critical Thinking

5.1 "Closed captions" for people with hearing impairments are almost always typed in full capital letters. Why is that a bad idea? Are there any advantages to using full capitals? What arguments could you use for changing the practice?

5.2 Suppose that, in one company, a worker says, "We don't need to worry about design. People pay a toll charge to call us, and we make a slight profit on each call. So if they have questions about the product, that's OK. If better design reduced the number of calls, we might actually lose money!" How would you persuade such a person that good document design is worth doing?

5.3 Royal College is preparing a brochure to persuade prospective students to consider taking classes. The school doesn't want to invest a lot of money in full-scale document testing. What free or almost-free things could it do to make the document as effective as possible?

5.4 Design choices have ethical implications. Indicate whether you consider each of the following actions ethical, unethical, or a grey area. Which of the actions would you do? Which would you feel uncomfortable doing? Which would you refuse to do? Why?

1. Putting the advantages of a proposal in a bulleted list, while discussing the disadvantages in a paragraph
2. Using a bigger type size so that a résumé fills a whole page
3. Putting the services that are not covered by your health plan in full caps to make it less likely that people will read the page

■ **Exercises and Problems**

5.5 Evaluating Page Designs

Use the guidelines in Module 5 to evaluate each of the following page designs. What are their strong points? What could be improved?

A Special Report: Living Healthy

Lorem ipsum dolor sit amet, con secteuer adipiscing elit, sed diam nonnumy nibh euismod tempor inci dunt ut labore et dolore magna ali quam erat volupat. Ut wisi enim as minim veniam, quis nostrud exerci tation ullamcorper suscipit laboris nisl ut aliquip ex ea commodo con sequat. Duis autem vel eum irure dolor in henderit in vulputate velit esse consequat. Lorem ipsum dolor sit amet, con secteuer adipiscing elit, sed diam nonnumy nibh euismod tempor inci dunt ut labore et dolore magna ali quam erat volupat. Ut wisi enim as minim veniam, quis nostrud exerci tation ullamcorper suscipit laboris nisl ut aliquip ex ea commodo con sequat. Duis autem vel eum irure dolor in henderit in vulputate velit esse consequat.

Sit amet, con secteuer adipi-

cising elit, sed diam nonnumy nibh euismod tempor inci dunt ut labore et dolore magna ali quam erat volupat. Ut wisi enim as minim veniam, quis nostrud exerci tation ullamcorper suscipit laboris nisl ut aliquip ex ea commodo con sequat. Duis autem vel eum irure dolor in henderit in vulpu tate velit esse consequat.

Dolor sit amet, con secteuer adipiscing elit, sed diam nonnumy nibh euismod tempor inci dunt ut labore et dolore magna ali quam erat volupat.Duis autem vel eum irure dolor in henderit in vulpu tate velit esse consequat.

Ipsum dolor sit amet, con secteuer adipiscing elit, sed diam nonnumy nibh euismod tempor inci dunt ut labore et dolore magna ali quam erat volupat. Ut wisi enim as minim veniam, quis nostrud exerci

tation ullamcorper suscipit laboris nisl ut aliquip ex ea commodo con sequat. Lorem ipsum dolor sit amet, con secteuer adipi-cising elit, sed diam nonnumy nibh euismod tempor inci dunt ut labore et dolore magna ali quam erat volupat. Ut wisi enim as minim veniam, quis nostrud exerci tation ullamcor-per suscipit laboris nisl ut aliquip ex ea commodo con sequat. Duis autem vel eum irure dolor in henderit in vulpu tate velit esse consequat.

Lorem ipsum dolor sit amet, con secteuer adipiscing elit, sed diam nonnumy nibh euis-mod tempor inci dunt ut labore et dolore magna ali quam erat volupat. Ut wisi enim as minim

Sit amet, con secteuer adipiscing elit, sed diam nonnumy nibh euismod tempor inci duni ut labore et dolore

Sit amet, con secteuer adipiscing elit, sed diam nonnumy nibh euismod tempor inci duni ut labore et dolore

A Special Report: Living Healthy

Lorem ipsum dolor sit amet, con secteuer adipiscing elit, sed diam nonnumy nibh euis-mod tempor inci dunt ut labore et dolore magna ali quam erat volupat. Ut wisi enim as minim veniam, quis nostrud exerci tation ullamcorper suscipit laboris nisl ut aliquip ex ea commodo con sequat. Duis autem vel eum irure dolor in henderit in vulputate velit esse consequat. Lorem ipsum dolor sit amet, con secteuer adipi-cising elit, sed diam nonnumy nibh euismod tempor inci dunt ut labore et dolore magna ali quam erat volupat. Ut wisi enim as minim veniam, quis nostrud exerci tation ullamcorper suscipit laboris nisl ut aliquip ex ea commodo con sequat. Duis autem vel eum irure dolor in henderit in vulpu tate velit esse consequat.

Sit amet, con secteuer adi-cising elit, sed diam nonnumy

nibh euismod tempor inci dunt ut labore et dolore magna ali quam erat volupat. Ut wisi enim as minim veniam, quis nostrud exerci tation ullamcor-per suscipit laboris nisl ut aliquip ex ea commodo con sequat. Duis autem vel eum irure dolor in henderit in vulpu tate velit esse consequat.

Dolor sit amet, con secteuer adipiscing elit, sed diam nonnumy nibh euismod tempor inci dunt ut labore et dolore magna ali quam erat volupat.Duis autem vel eum irure dolor in henderit in vulpu tate velit esse consequat.

Ipsum dolor sit amet, con secteuer adipiscing elit, sed diam nonnumy

laboris nisl ut aliquip ex ea commodo con sequat. Duis autem vel eum irure dolor in henderit in vulpuate velit esse consequat. Lorem ipsum dolor sit amet, con secteuer adipi-cising elit, sed diam nonnumy nibh euismod tempor inci dunt ut labore et dolore magna ali quam erat volupat. Ut wisi enim as minim veniam, quis nostrud exerci tation ullamcor-per suscipit laboris nisl ut aliquip ex ea commodo con sequat. Duis autem vel eum irure dolor in henderit in vulpu tate velit esse consequat.

Lorem ipsum dolor sit amet, con secteuer adipiscing elit, sed diam nonnumy nibh euis-mod tempor inci dunt ut labore et dolore magna ali quam erat volupat. Ut wisi enim as minim veniam, quis nostrud exerci tation ullamcorper suscipit

Sit amet, con secteuer adipiscing elit, sed diam nonnumy nibh euismod tempor inci dunt ut labore et dolore

A Special Bulletin: Living Healthy

Counting Calories and Watching Cholesterol

Lorem ipsum dolor sit amet, con secteuer adipiscing elit, sed diam nonnumy nibh euismod tempor inci dunt ut labore et dolore magna ali quam erat volupat. Ut wisi enim as minim veniam, quis nostrud exerci tation ullamcorper suscipit laboris nisl ut aliquip ex ea commodo con sequat. Duis autem vel eum irure dolor in henderit in vulputate velit esse consequat. Lorem ipsum dolor sit amet, con secteuer adipiscing elit, sed diam nonnumy nibh euismod tempor inci dunt ut labore et dolore magna ali quam erat volupat. Ut wisi enim as minim veniam, quis nostrud exerci tation ullamcorper suscipit laboris nisl ut aliquip ex ea commodo con sequat. Duis autem vel eum irure dolor in henderit in vulputate velit esse consequat.

Sit amet, con secteuer adipi-cising elit, sed diam nonnumy nibh euismod tempor inci dunt ut labore et dolore magna ali quam erat volupat. Ut wisi enim as minim veniam, quis nostrud exerci tation ullamcorper suscipit laboris nisl ut aliquip ex ea commodo con sequat. Duis autem vel eum irure dolor in henderit in vulputate velit esse consequat.

Dolor sit amet, con secteuer adipiscing elit, sed diam non-numy nibh euismod tempor inci dunt ut labore et dolore magna ali quam erat volu pat Duis autem vel eum irure dolor in henderit in vulputate velit esse

Exercising and Eating Healthy in a Busy Lifestyle

Ipsum dolor sit amet, con secteuer adipiscing elit, sed diam nonnumy nibh euismod tempor inci dunt ut labore et dolore magna ali quam erat volupat. Ut wisi enim as minim veniam, quis nostrud exerci tation ullamcorper suscipit laboris nisl ut aliquip ex ea commodo con sequat. Duis autem vel eum irure dolor in henderit in vulputate velit esse consequat. Lorem ipsum dolor sit amet, con secteuer adipiscing elit, sed diam nonnumy nibh euismod tempor inci dunt ut labore et dolore magna ali quam erat volupat. Ut wisi

Company Briefs

nim as minim veniam, quis nostrud exerci tation ullamcorper suscipit laboris nisl ut aliquip ex ea commodo con sequat. Duis autem vel eum irure dolor in henderit in vulputate velit esse con-sequat.

Lorem ipsum dolor sit amet, con secteuer adipi-cising elit, sed diam nonnumy nibh euismod ...tempor inci dunt ut labore et dolore magna ali

Managing Your Sleep

quam erat volupat. Ut wisi enim as minim veniam, quis nostrud exerci tation ullamcor-per suscipit laboris nisl ut aliquip ex ea commodo con sequat. Duis autem vel eum irure dolor in henderit in vulputate velit esse consequat. Lorem ipsum dolor sit amet, con secteuer adipiscing elit, sed diam nonnumy nibh euis-mod tempor inci dunt ut labore et dolore magna ali quam erat volupat. Ut wisi enim as minim veniam, quis nostrud exerci tation ullamcorper suscipit laboris nisl ut aliquip ex ea com-modo con sequat. Duis au-tem vel eum irure dolor in henderit in vulpu-tate velit esse consequat.

Sit amet, con secteuer adipi-cising elit, sed diam nonnumy nibh euismod tempor inci dunt ut labore et dolore magna ali quam erat volupat. Ut wisi enim as minim veniam, quis nostrud exerci tation ullamcor-

 finis

A Special Bulletin: Living Healthy

Counting Calories and Watching Cholesterol

Lorem ipsum dolor sit amet, sed diam nonnumy nibh euismod tempor inci dunt ut labore et dolore magna ali quam erat volupat. Ut wisi enim as minim veniam, quis nostrud exerci tation ul-lamcorper suscipit laboris nisl ut aliquip ex ea commodo con sequat. Duis autem vel eum irure dolor in henderit in vulputate velit esse consequat. Lorem ipsum dolor sit amet, sed diam nonnumy nibh

euismod tempor inci dunt ut labore et dolore magna ali quam erat volupat. Ut wisi enim as minim veniam, quis nostrud exerci tation ul-lamcorper suscipit laboris nisl ut aliquip ex ea commodo con sequat. Duis autem vel eum irure dolor in henderit in vulputate velit esse consequat. Lorem ipsum dolor sit amet, con secteuer adipiscing elit, sed diam nonnumy nibh

Exercising and Eating Healthy in a Busy Lifestyle

Lorem ipsum dolor sit amet, con secteuer adipiscing elit, sed diam nonnumy nibh euismod tempor inci dunt ut labore et dolore magna ali quam erat volupat. Ut wisi enim as minim veniam, quis nostrud exerci tation ul-lamcorper suscipit laboris nisl ut aliquip ex ea commodo con sequat. Duis autem vel eum irure dolor in henderit in vulputate velit esse consequat. Lorem ipsum dolor sit amet, sed diam nonnumy nibh

euismod tempor inci dunt ut labore et dolore magna ali quam erat volupat. Ut wisi enim as minim veniam, quis

The group will visit many lovely areas

Managing Your Sleep

Lorem ipsum dolor sit amet, con secteuer adipiscing elit, sed diam nonnumy nibh euismod tempor inci dunt ut labore et dolore magna ali quam erat volupat. Ut wisi enim as minim veniam, quis nostrud exerci tation ul-lamcorper suscipit laboris nisl ut aliquip ex ea commodo con sequat. Duis autem vel eum irure dolor in henderit in vulputate velit esse consequat. Lorem ipsum dolor sit amet, con secteuer adipiscing elit, sed diam nonnumy nibh euismod tempor inci dunt ut labore et dolore magna ali quam erat volupat. Ut wisi enim as minim veniam, quis nostrud exerci tation ul-lamcorper suscipit laboris nisl ut aliquip ex ea commodo con sequat. Duis autem vel eum irure dolor in henderit in vulputate velit esse consequat.

Sit amet, con secteuer adipi-cising elit, sed diam nonnumy nibh euismod tempor inci dunt ut labore et dolore magna ali quam erat volupat. Ut wisi

Source: Diane Burns and S. Venit, "What's Wrong with This Paper?" *PC Magazine* no. 17 (October 13, 1987) pp. 174–75.

5.6   Evaluating PowerPoint Slides

Evaluate the following drafts of PowerPoint™ slides.

- Is the background appropriate for the topic?
- Do the slides use words or phrases rather than complete sentences?

- Is the font big enough to read from a distance?
- Is the art relevant and appropriate?
- Is each slide free from errors?

a.
  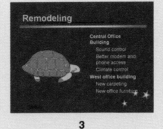 

1   2   3   4

b.
  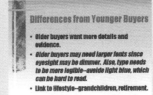 

1   2   3   4

c.
 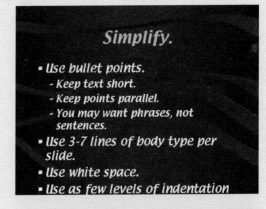

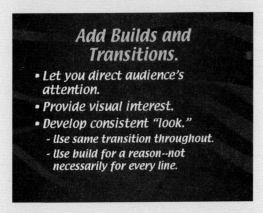 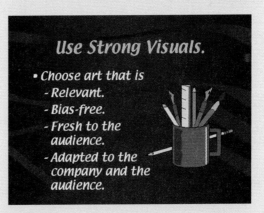

5.7 Using Headings

Reorganize the items in each of the following lists, using appropriate headings. Use bulleted or numbered lists as appropriate.

a. Rules and Procedures for a Tuition Reimbursement Plan

1. You are eligible to be reimbursed if you have been a full-time employee for at least three months.
2. You must apply before the first class meeting.
3. You must earn a "C" or better in the course.
4. You must submit a copy of the approved application, an official grade report, and a receipt for tuition paid to be reimbursed.
5. You can be reimbursed for courses related to your current position or another position in the company, or for courses that are part of a degree related to a current or possible job.
6. Your supervisor must sign the application form.
7. Courses may be at any appropriate level (high school, college or university, or graduate school).

b. Activities in Starting a New Business
   - Getting a loan or venture capital
   - Getting any necessary city or provincial licences
   - Determining what you will make, do, or sell
   - Identifying the market for your products or services
   - Pricing your products or services
   - Choosing a location
   - Checking zoning laws that may affect the location
   - Identifying government and university programs for small business development
   - Figuring cash flow
   - Ordering equipment and supplies
   - Selling
   - Advertising and marketing

5.8 Analyzing Documents

Collect several documents available to you as a worker, student, or consumer: letters and memos, newsletters, ads and flyers, reports. Use the guidelines in Module 5 to evaluate each of them.

As your instructor directs,

a. Discuss the documents with a small group of classmates.
b. Write a memo to your instructor evaluating three or more of the documents. Include originals or photocopies of the documents you discuss as an appendix to your memo.
c. Write a memo to your supervisor recommending ways the organization can improve its documents.
d. In an oral presentation to the class, explain what makes one document good and another one weak. If possible, use transparencies so classmates can see the documents as you evaluate them.

5.9 Evaluating Web Pages

Compare three Web pages in the same category (for example, non-profit organizations, car companies, university departments, sports information). Which pages are most effective? Why? What would you change? Why?

As your instructor directs,

a. Discuss the pages with a small group of classmates.
b. Write a memo to your instructor evaluating the pages. Include the URLs of the pages in your memo.
c. In an oral presentation to the class, explain what makes one page good and another one weak. If possible, put the pages onscreen so classmates can see the pages as you evaluate them.
d. Post your evaluation of the pages in an email message to the class. Include hot links to the pages you evaluate.

5.10   Analyzing a Document

Your municipal and provincial governments may offer internships and cooperative placements to postsecondary students. Research (visit, telephone, email, find someone who knows someone) the placement possibilities through your college/university co-op placement office, or contact the government department directly. Request a copy of the application or information documents for these positions. Write an analysis of the document's layout and page design.

5.11   Revising a Financial Aid Form

You've just joined the Financial Aid office at your school. The director gives you the accompanying form and asks you to redesign it.

"We need this form to see whether parents have other students in college or university besides the one requesting aid. Parents are supposed to list all family members that the parents support—themselves, the person here, any other kids in college or university, and any younger dependent kids.

"Half of these forms are filled out incorrectly. Most people just list the student going here; they leave out everyone else.

"If something is missing, the computer sends out a letter and a second copy of this form. The whole process starts over. Sometimes we send this form back two or three times before it's right. In the meantime, students' financial aid is delayed—maybe for months. Sometimes things are so late that they can't register for classes, or they have to pay tuition themselves and get reimbursed later.

"If so many people are filling out the form wrong, the form itself must be the problem. See what you can do with it. But keep it to a page."

As your instructor directs,

a. Analyze the current form and identify its problems.
b. Revise the form. Add necessary information; reorder information; change the chart to make it easier to fill out.

Hints:

*   Where are people supposed to send the form? What is the phone number of the financial aid office? Should they need to call the office if the form is clear?
*   Does the definition of *half-time* apply to all students or just those taking courses beyond high school?
*   Should capital or lowercase letters be used?
*   Are the lines big enough to write in?
*   What headings or subdivisions within the form would remind people to list all family members whom they support?
*   How can you encourage people to return the form promptly?

Please complete the chart below by listing all family members for whom you (the parents) will provide more than half support during the academic year (July 1 through June 30). Include yourselves (the parents), the student, and your dependent children, even if they are not attending college or university.

EDUCATIONAL INFORMATION, 2006–2007						
FULL NAME OF FAMILY MEMBER	AGE	RELATIONSHIP OF FAMILY MEMBERS TO STUDENT	NAME OF SCHOOL, COLLEGE, OR UNIVERSITY SCHOOL YEAR	FULL TIME	HALF-TIME* OR MORE	LESS THAN HALF-TIME
STUDENT APPLICANT						

*Half-time is defined as 6 credit hours or 12 clock hours a term.

When the information requested is received by our office, processing of your financial aid application will resume.

Please sign and mail this form to the above address as soon as possible. Your signature certifies that this information and the information on the FAF is true and complete to the best of your knowledge. If you have any questions, please contact a member of the needs analysis staff.

_____   _____
Signature of Parent(s)   Data

Polishing Your Prose

Active and Passive Voice

Because it depicts the action, the verb is the most important word in the sentence. Verbs indicate who or what is doing the action through "voice." When whoever is acting is also the subject of the sentence, the verb is active; in the passive voice, the subject is acted on by someone or something else.

Contemporary communication prefers verbs in the active voice, because the resulting sentence is clearer and shorter. When writers want to avoid or downplay delegating responsibility, they use the passive voice.

Active: The man bought grapes at the store.

Passive: The grapes were bought by the man at the store.

In the active voice, the subject—the man—is doing the action—bought. In the passive version, "The grapes" is the subject, yet it is the man, not the grapes, that is actually doing the action. It is harder for the reader to follow who or what did the action. In addition, it takes more words to convey the same idea.

To change a passive voice construction into the active voice, start by identifying who or what is doing the action. If no agent ("by _____") is present in the sentence, you will need to supply it. A passive verb is usually accompanied by a copula verb, such as *is*, *are*, or *were*. Rewrite the sentence by putting the actor in the role of subject and dropping the helping verb:

Passive: The plan was approved by our clients.

Active: Our clients approved the plan.

Passive: PowerPoint™ slides have been created.

Active: Susan created the PowerPoint™ slides.

Passive: It is desired that you back up your work daily.

Active: Back up your work daily.

In business communication, active voice is usually better. However, passives are better in three situations:

1. Use passives to emphasize the object receiving the action, not the agent.

   Your order was shipped November 15. The customer's order, not the shipping clerk, is important.

2. Use passives to provide coherence within a paragraph. A sentence is easier to read if "old" information comes at the beginning of a sentence. When you have been discussing a topic, use the word again as your subject even if that requires a passive verb.

   The bank made several risky loans in the late 1990s. These loans were written off as "uncollectible" in 2003.

   Using loans as the subject of the second sentence provides a link between the two sentences, making the paragraph as a whole easier to read.

3. Use passives to avoid assigning blame.

   The order was damaged during shipment.

   An active verb would require the writer to specify who damaged the order. The passive here is more tactful.

Exercises

Identify whether the passives in the following sentences are acceptable, or whether the verb should be changed to active.

1. The contract was signed by the vice president of finance.
2. New employees Ms. Taleroski, Mr. Franklin, and Ms. Holbreck were introduced at last week's staff meeting.
3. Two visitors are expected to arrive at headquarters tomorrow.
4. Outgoing correspondence was collected by the mailroom staff.
5. The proposal was turned in late.

Turn these passive voice constructions into active voice:

6. Correspondence was collected by the mailroom staff.
7. Phone calls were returned by the human resources administrator.
8. In April, budgets were amortized and files created for the project.
9. Phone calls need to be returned within 24 hours.
10. Packages are to be sent to the mailroom for delivery.

Check your answers to the odd-numbered exercises on page 571.

Online Learning Centre

Visit the Online Learning Centre at www.mcgrawhill.ca/olc/locker to access module quizzes, a searchable glossary, résumé and letter templates, additional business writing samples, CBC videos, and other learning and study tools.

CBC Video Case

Visit the Online Learning Centre at www.mcgrawhill.ca/olc/locker to view "Free Cycle," an online CBC Video Case for Unit 1 that explores how environmental awareness influences your communication.

Cases for Communicators

Minorities Need Apply

Canadians may feel complacent about Canadian multiculturalism—particularly when comparing our supposed acceptance of diversity with recent events in Paris and Holland. A closer look at our institutions, corporate boards and police forces, however, indicates that systemic prejudice still exists. The Royal Canadian Mounted Police (RCMP) is one of many Canadian institutions that must transform itself to reflect the diverse populations it serves.

At present, the RCMP is mostly made up of white males. Indeed, of the 1000 Mounties on the force, "… just 6.4 percent … are from minority backgrounds. Some 7.6 percent are aboriginal and 18 percent are women." Although visible minorities make up "about 13 percent" of officers on the Toronto and York police forces, "… minority representation in Canadian police services averages around 5 percent." Since even our smaller cities are now attracting immigrants from all over the world, the RCMP recognizes it's time to recruit and hire people whose languages and cultures represent the diverse communities they serve.

But this goal is not as easy as it sounds. First, many recent immigrants do not know much about the RCMP; they don't know that the Mounties are a national police force with the same roles and responsibilities as provincial and municipal police officers. Secondly, the recruitment drive must be inclusive enough to attract applicants from Canada's widely diverse cultural mix.

How can the Mounties best reach their audiences?[5]

Individual Activity

You're the constable in charge of planning the RCMP diversity recruitment drive. Before you can devise any strategies, you need to apply the PAIBOC model to analyze the situation:

Purpose(s): Why are we recruiting? What results do we want from our recruiting drive? How can we best attract the positive attention of our audiences?

Audiences(s): Who are our target audiences? What groups are considered "diverse"? What do these groups know about the RCMP force? What do they need to know to be attracted to the force? How homogeneous are these target groups? What values of these disparate groups can we appeal to?

Information: What information must our recruitment strategies convey? Why?

Benefits: What are the many benefits, tangible and intangible, of joining the Mounties? What benefits would specifically attract our target groups?

Objections: What objections about joining the RCMP might I expect? How can I best eliminate, overcome, or respond to those objections?

Context: How do my target audiences feel about the RCMP? About policing in general? What current economic, political, legal and/or social events can I use to my advantage? What current events might deter members of my target audiences from joining the RCMP?

Write down your thoughts for future reference. Be as thorough as possible in your analysis.

Next, visit and tour the RCMP Web site at **http:///www.rcmp-grc.gc.ca**.

How many of the groups identified as diverse do you see represented in the photos on the site? What is your opinion of the current recruitment drive strategies identified on the site? Jot down your impressions.

Group Activity

Form a recruitment drive committee with three other classmates. Compare notes on your PAIBOC analyses, and your analyses of the RCMP Web site. Together with your committee members, identify four recruitment strategies that will attract any/all of your four target groups.

Write a letter from your committee to Geoff Gruson, executive director of the Police Sector Council, in Ottawa, describing your recruitment drive strategies in detail.

Unit 2

Creating Goodwill

One of Toyota Canada's top salespeople originally studied to become a nurse. However, completing the hospital practicum part of his course meant that Burt Townsend would have to quit the night security job he worked at to pay for his education. Burt had to leave college.

When he spied an automotive industry recruitment ad, he was intrigued by the promise of further education. A week's intensive training and scrutiny were required for both the career in the automotive industry and post-secondary education. "I've always been a car buff, and the opportunity appealed to me." Of the 1,000 applicants who showed up that first morning, Burt was one of only 10 graduates five days later. Toyota hired him within a week of interviewing him.

Ten years later, Burt is not only his dealership's most successful salesperson, he is also the youngest, and the most accredited. Toyota University's awards of achievement adorn his office wall, testament to his commitment to Toyota, and to himself. "You always have to be willing to learn, and to upgrade your skills."

Clients' letters and emails, unanimous in their praise, crowd his bulletin board. Customers want Burt, and Burt's boss, to know how well he treated them; how personable and personal, honest and knowledgeable he is; how they will buy or lease their next car nowhere else but this Toyota dealership, because of Burt Townsend.

"Toyota believes that quality sells, so my university courses focus on knowing the product. I learn everything I can about the vehicles, their engineering, technical, and functional operations, ... about the competition ... I even learn about Toyota quality anecdotally, by listening to suppliers' stories. Toyota makes a quality product. That's why it's forecasted to lead car sales in 2006.

"I couldn't sell the product if I didn't believe in it, and I've had plenty of other offers. So believing in what I'm selling, and having the product knowledge are big advantages. But that's not the whole story.

"Anyone can sell that first car. What about the second, and the third? My focus is on building the relationship. People don't want to buy the car and know that's the end of the transaction. What about after the sale? What if they need information or advice? What if they have an accident? My clients continue to depend, and to call on me, five, six years after the initial sale. People want to know that someone they trust will be there to take care of them, long after the sale.

"It's not about the sale. It's about the relationship after the sale. At the end of the day, did I do my best for my clients? Then I've done the job."

PAIBOC

Analysis

1. In what two ways does Burt create goodwill with clients?

2. What methods does Toyota Canada use to communicate goodwill?

3. According to Burt, who are Toyota's customers?

6

You-Attitude

Module Outline

- What is you-attitude in writing?
- How do I create you-attitude?
- Does you-attitude mean using the word *you*?
- I've revised my sentences. Do I need to do anything else?

Review of Key Points

Assignments for Module 6

Polishing Your Prose: It's/Its

LEARNING OBJECTIVES

After reading and applying the information in Module 6, you'll be able to demonstrate

Knowledge of
- The differences between writer-centred and reader-centred messages

Skills to
- Begin building goodwill
- Adapt your message to the audience
- Emphasize what the reader wants to know
- Assess your messages for you-attitude

The Conference Board of Canada
Insights You Can Count On

Please see the OLC to preview the key skills from the Conference Board of Canada's Employability Skills 2000+ covered in this module.

FYI

Does rudeness cost? Absolutely: 80 percent of people polled by North American etiquette companies felt that incivility in business had increased, and 58 percent claimed that, as a result, they'd take their business elsewhere, no matter the cost or inconvenience to do so.

Source: Eileen Brill Wagner, "Good Manners are Good for Business," *The Business Journal of Phoenix*, http://phoenix.bizjournals. com/phoenix/stories/2001/ 01/29/smallb3.html, retrieved October 18, 2006.

You-attitude means understanding and meeting the needs of the audience. Effective communicators know that they can get what they want only when they recognize and attempt to provide what their audience wants.

You-attitude is a way of thinking that

- Looks at the situation from the audience's point of view
- Respects the audience's intelligence
- Protects the audience's ego
- Emphasizes what the audience wants to know.

Kirk Layton

You-attitude also means making it easy for your audience to do what you want. For example, entrepreneur Kirk Layton, founder and president of Eservus.com Online Services Ltd., has made his online concierge services accessible and easy to use. His audience—property managers and building tenants across Canada—get exclusive access to "… discounted sports, theatre and movie tickets, flower … [and] travel services and a variety of other things usually associated with traditional in-house concierges at high-end properties." Layton markets his services by getting clients to register online; registrants' "… weekly permission-based email newsletter" generates services sales and builds Eservus' client base. Layton has translated his you-attitude focus into a $3-million-dollar enterprise.[1]

What is you-attitude in writing?

You-attitude messages are reader-centred.

Writers create you-attitude through their rhetorical choices (◀▷ Module 5). Appearance, layout, visuals, content, and language all contribute to reader-centred documents, as Figure 6.1 demonstrates.[2]

Compare the authorial choices in Figure 6.1 with those of the writer in Figure 6.2:

This writer-centred memo refers to the author throughout, and the last paragraph sounds condescending: no colleague or supervisor would appreciate being spoken to this way.

How do I create you-attitude?

Talk about the reader—except in negative situations.

To create you-attitude,

1. Talk about the reader, not about yourself.
2. Avoid talking about feelings, except to congratulate or offer sympathy.
3. Use *you* more often than *I* in positive situations. Use *we* when it includes the reader.
4. Avoid *you* in negative situations.

FIGURE 6.1

Christmas appeal from the Salvation Army demonstrates you-attitude through visuals, layout, and language choices[2]

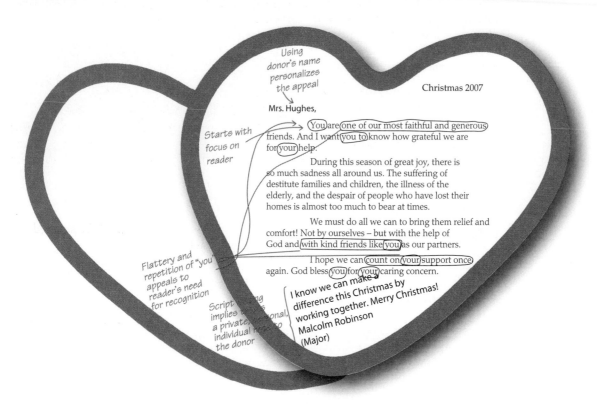

FIGURE 6.2

Writer-centred memo does not demonstrate you-attitude

Date: April 3, 2007

To: Li Zhou

From: Adrian Trin

Subject: Guest Speaker

I would like to take the opportunity to thank you for arranging to have Chris Bosh come to speak to my Grade 8 students. I have greatly admired Bosh's prowess on the court, so I was truly thrilled when I heard he was coming to our school.

I was amazed to hear how young Bosh was when he came to Canada to play for the Raptors, and I was also surprised to find out how far-reaching his foundation is. I was most gratified, however, by the opportunity to speak with Bosh after his presentation.

I want to say thanks again, and keep up the great work!

■ 1. Talk about the reader, not about yourself.

Readers want to know how they benefit or are affected. When you provide this information, you make your message more complete and more interesting.

Lacks you-attitude: I have negotiated an agreement with Apex Rent-a-Car that gives you a discount on rental cars.

You-attitude: As a Sun Life employee, you can now get a 20 percent discount when you rent a car from Apex.

Any sentence that focuses on the writer's work or generosity lacks you-attitude, even if the sentence contains the word *you*. Instead of focusing on what you are doing for the reader, it's important to stress how the reader will benefit. To change the emphasis, you may need to change the structure of the sentence.

Lacks you-attitude: We are shipping your order of September 21 this afternoon.

You-attitude: The two dozen print cartridges you ordered will be shipped this afternoon and should reach you by September 28.

Emphasize what the reader wants to know. The reader is less interested in when you shipped the order than in when it will arrive. Note that the phrase "should reach you by" leaves room for variations in delivery schedules. If you can't be exact, give your reader the information you do have: "UPS shipment from Burnaby to Regina normally takes three days." If you have absolutely no idea, give the reader the name of the carrier, so the reader knows whom to contact if the order doesn't arrive promptly.

SEE THE OLC!

Customer Relations Management (CRM) Emphasizes You-Attitude

INSTANT REPLAY

Definition of You-Attitude

You-attitude is a style of writing that

- Looks at things from the reader's point of view
- Respects the reader's Intelligence
- Protects the reader's ego
- Emphasizes what the reader wants to know

■ 2. Avoid talking about feelings, except to congratulate or offer sympathy.

Lacks you-attitude: We are happy to extend you a credit line of $5000.

You-attitude: You can now charge up to $5000 on your Bank of Montreal card.

In most business situations, your feelings are irrelevant. The reader doesn't care whether you're happy, bored stiff at granting a routine application, or worried about granting so much to someone who barely qualifies. *All the reader cares about is the situation from his or her point of view.*

It is appropriate to talk about your own emotions in a message of congratulation or condolence.

You-attitude: Congratulations on your promotion to district manager! I was really pleased to read about it.

You-attitude: I was sorry to hear that your father died.

In internal memos, it may be appropriate to comment that a project has been gratifying or frustrating. In the letter of transmittal that accompanies a report, it is permissible to talk about your feelings about doing the work. But other readers in your own organization are primarily interested in their own concerns, not in your feelings.

Don't talk about the reader's feelings, either. It can be offensive to have someone else tell us how we feel—especially if the writer is wrong.

Lacks you-attitude:	You'll be happy to hear that Open Grip Walkway Channels meet Occupational Health and Safety requirements.
You-attitude:	Open Grip Walkway Channels meet Occupational Health and Safety requirements.

Maybe the reader expects that anything you sell meets government regulations (Occupational Health and Safety, Canada's national centre for workplace safety, is a federal government agency). The reader may even be disappointed if he or she expected higher standards. Simply explain the situation or describe a product's features; don't predict the reader's response.

When you have good news for the reader, simply give the good news.

Lacks you-attitude:	You'll be happy to hear that your scholarship has been renewed.
You-attitude:	Congratulations! Your scholarship has been renewed.

■ 3. Use *you* more often than *I* in positive situations. Use *we* when it includes the reader.

Talk about the reader, not you or your company.

Lacks you-attitude:	We provide dental coverage to all employees.
You-attitude:	You receive dental coverage as a full-time BCE employee.

Most readers are tolerant of the word *I* in email messages and memos. Edit external messages to ensure *I* is used rarely. *I* suggests that you're concerned about personal issues, not about the organization's problems, needs, and opportunities. *We* works well when it includes the reader. Avoid *we* if it excludes the reader (as it would in a letter to a customer or supplier, or as it might in a memo about what *we* in management want *you* to do).

■ 4. Avoid *you* in negative situations.

To avoid blaming the reader, use an impersonal expression or a passive verb. Talk about the group to which the reader belongs so readers don't feel that they're being singled out for bad news.

Lacks you-attitude:	You failed to sign your cheque.
You-attitude (impersonal):	Your cheque arrived without a signature.
You-attitude (passive)	Your cheque was not signed.

Impersonal constructions omit people and talk only about things.

Passive verbs describe the action performed on something, without necessarily saying who did it. (◀▶ Module 5 for active and passive voice. ◀▶ Module 14 for a full discussion of passive verbs.)

In most cases, active verbs are better. But when your reader is at fault, passive verbs may be useful to avoid assigning blame.

Normally, writing is most lively when it's about people—and most interesting to readers when it's about them. When you have to report a mistake or bad news, however, you can protect the reader's ego by using an impersonal construction, one in which things, not people, do the acting.

INSTANT REPLAY

Four Ways to Create You-Attitude

1. Talk about the reader, not about yourself.
2. Avoid talking about feelings, except to congratulate or offer sympathy.
3. In positive situations, use *you* more often than *I*. Use *we* when it includes the reader.
4. Avoid *you* in negative situations.

EXPANDING A CRITICAL SKILL

Seeing Another Point of View

John Hall attributes the success of his joint venture with Chinese entrepreneurs to his interest in and respect for the Chinese way of doing business. Hall, owner of Ontario's Kittling Ridge Estate Wines and Spirits distillery, began doing business in Taiwan in 1992. He entered the Chinese market in 1998 when a group of Chinese businessmen asked him to make a green tea whiskey. Dragon's Well Tea Whiskey sold well in mainland China until the Asian economic crisis. Although product sales never recovered, Hall forged important interpersonal relationships and gained invaluable knowledge about doing business in China.

As a result of Hall's "corporate citizen" approach, in February 2000, the Chinese government, Chinese entrepreneurs, and Hall launched the Holiturn Winery and Distillery Corporation, a Sino-Canadian joint venture. One of the few vodka-producing facilities in China, the distillery, which employs 100 people and uses domestic products, also produces, markets, and distributes a wide range of international products, all affordable, made in China, and immune from import tariffs.

"I think Canada has established a very good rapport with China and tries to establish and nurture relationships. ... The key is that, when you go into a different country, especially a developing country, you have to be a corporate citizen and invest in that community. That's why we have a plant in China, where we employ educated, university graduates who are seeking a sense of personal satisfaction in creating a quality product. ... It's a misplaced idea that people in China want to become Western," says Hall. "They don't. They want to become modern."

Solutions come from the flexibility to see another point of view. Listening to understand another person's perspective allows you to identify commonalities for compromise. Being open to another point of view builds successful business relationships.

Source: Kathryn Korchok, "Building a Market, One Drink at a Time," World & Business," *Toronto Star*, May 27, 2001 B1–8.

http://www.kittlingridge.com
Kittling Ridge Estate Wines and Spirits

Lacks you-attitude:	You made no allowance for inflation in your estimate.
You-attitude (passive):	No allowance for inflation has been made in this estimate.
You-attitude (impersonal):	This estimate does not allow for inflation.

A purist might say that impersonal constructions are illogical. An estimate, for example, is inanimate and can't "allow" anything. In the pragmatic world of business writing, however, impersonal constructions often help you convey criticism tactfully.

When you restrict the reader's freedom, talk about the group to which the reader belongs rather than about the reader as an individual.

| **Lacks you-attitude:** | You must get approval from the director before you publish any articles or memoirs based on your work in the agency. |
| **You-attitude:** | Agency personnel must get approval from the director to publish any articles or memoirs based on their work at the agency. |

When you have negatives, third person is better you-attitude than second person because third person shows that everyone is being treated the same way.

Does you-attitude mean using the word *you*?

No.

FYI

The word *company* has the same root as the word *companion*: both come from the Latin words for eating bread together.

All messages should use you-attitude, but the words to achieve it will change depending on the situation.

- In a positive message, focus on what the reader can do. "We give you" lacks you-attitude because the sentence focuses on what *we* are doing.
- Avoid *you* when it criticizes the reader or limits the reader's freedom.
- In a job application letter, create you-attitude by showing how you can help meet the reader's needs, but keep the word *I* to a minimum (◀|▶ Module 28).

I've revised my sentences. Do I need to do anything else?

Emphasize what the reader wants to know.

Good messages apply you-attitude beyond the sentence level by using *content and organization* as well as style to build goodwill.

Consider the letter in Figure 6.3. As the red marginal notes indicate, many individual sentences in this letter lack you-attitude. The last sentence in paragraph one sounds both harsh and defensive; the close is selfish. The language is stiff and filled with outdated jargon. Perhaps the most serious problem is that the fact most interesting to the reader is buried in the middle of the first paragraph. Since we have good news for the reader, we should put that information first. (See ◀|▶ Module 11).

Fixing individual sentences could improve the letter. However, it really needs to be rewritten. Figure 6.4 shows a possible revision. The revision is clearer, easier to read, and friendlier.

To create goodwill with *content*,

- Be concise and complete: give the reader the necessary information and *only* the necessary information to get the results you want.
- Consider using an appendix for information that the reader may want to see but that does not directly support your purpose.
- Anticipate and answer questions or objections the reader is likely to have.
- Show why information that the reader did not ask for, but that you've included, is important.
- Explain to readers how the subject of your message affects them.

To build goodwill with *organization*,

- Put the information that readers are most interested in first.
- Arrange the information to meet your reader's needs, not yours.
- Use headings and lists so that the reader can find key points quickly.

FIGURE 6.3
A Letter Lacking You-Attitude

SIMMONS STRUCTURAL STEEL

700 Upper Ottawa Street Hamilton ON L8T 3T6 (905) 555-4670 FAX: (905) 555-4672

December 11, 2007

Ms. Carol McFarland
Rollins Equipment Corporation
3105 Unity Drive
Mississauga, ON L5L 4L1

Dear Ms. McFarland:

Not you-attitude *Legalistic*

We are now ready to issue a cheque to Rollins Equipment in the amount of $14 207.02. To receive said cheque, you will deliver to me a release of the mechanic's liens in the amount of $14 207.02.

Sounds dictatorial

Focuses on negative *Lacks you-attitude*

Before we can release the cheque, we must be satisfied that the release is in the proper form. We must insist that we be provided with a stamped original of the lien indicating the document number in the appropriate court where it is filed. Also, either the release must be executed by an officer of Rollins Equipment, or we must be provided with a letter from an officer of Rollins Equipment authorizing another individual to execute the release.

Hard to read, remember

Please contact the undersigned so that an appointment can be scheduled for this transaction.

Jargon

Sincerely,

Lucy Gervasi

Lucy Gervasi

FIGURE 6.4
A Letter Revised to Improve You-Attitude

700 Upper Ottawa Street Hamilton ON L8T 3T6 (905) 555-4670 FAX: (905) 555-4672

December 11, 2007

Ms. Carol McFarland
Rollins Equipment Corporation
3105 Unity Drive
Mississauga, ON L5L 4L1

Dear Ms. McFarland:

Emphasizes cooperation

Together we can clear up the lien in the Allen contract.

Starts with main point from the reader's point of view

courteous (add to notes)

Focuses on what reader gets

Your company will receive a cheque for $14 207.02 as soon as you give us a release for the mechanic's lien of $14 207.02. To assure that the release is in the proper form, please

1. Give us a stamped original of the lien indicating the document's court number, and

2. Either
    a. Have an officer of Rollins Equipment sign the release
        or
    b. Give us a letter from a Rollins officer authorizing someone else to sign the release.

List makes it easy to see that reader needs to do two things—and that the second can be done in two ways.

Please call to tell me which way works best for you.

Emphasizes reader's choice

Sincerely,

Lucy Gervasi

Extension number makes it easy for reader to phone.

Lucy Gervasi
Extension 5318

Use the following checklist to assess your messages for the you-attitude that builds goodwill.

FIGURE 6.5

You-Attitude Checklist

1. **The message is clear:**
   - ❏ signals to the reader that it's a business message
   - ❏ defines the purpose of the message
   - ❏ organized so that form follows function
   - ❏ uses business language
   - ❏ provides specific details in concrete language

2. **The message is concise:**
   - ❏ provides all relevant information using the fewest possible words

3. **The message is comprehensive:**
   - ❏ uses a format appropriate to the purpose, the audience, and the situation
   - ❏ has a beginning, middle, and end
   - ❏ uses a thesis to establish unity and coherence
   - ❏ establishes rapport; is reader-centred
   - ❏ demonstrates that the writer knows, understands, and respects the audience
   - ❏ uses transitional words and phrases to lead the reader from one idea to the next
   - ❏ tells the audience what's in it for them

4. **The message is complete:**
   - ❏ gives all necessary proof, explanations, and examples
   - ❏ anticipates the audience's questions, concerns, and objections
   - ❏ tells the audience what to do next or what's going to happen next

5. **The message is correct:**
   - ❏ is error-free
   - ❏ demonstrates revision, editing, and proofreading

Employability Skills 2000+

The Conference Board of Canada
Insights You Can Count On
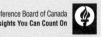

Please see the OLC to preview the key skills from the Conference Board of Canada's Employability Skills 2000+ covered in this module.

Review of Key Points

1. What is you-attitude?
2. What are four characteristics of you-attitude?
3. What four strategies can you use to create reader-centred documents?
4. What design principles create you-attitude?
5. Does using the word "you" always create you-attitude? Why or why not?

Assignments for Module 6

Questions for Critical Thinking

6.1 Why do sentences starting with "We give you" lack you-attitude?

6.2 Think of a time when you felt that a business cared about you. What words or actions made you feel that way?

6.3 Can you think of situations in which the four strategies would *not* create you-attitude? If so, how would you create you-attitude in those situations?

Exercises and Problems

6.4 The Ethical Consideration of You-Attitude

In what situation(s) might you consider audience-focused messages unethical? Consider, for example, print and Internet advertising, and the persuasive tactics of telemarketers, or people selling energy savings door-to-door. When have you felt uncomfortable, or exploited, by you-attitude messages?

6.5 Using Passives and Impersonal Constructions to Improve You-Attitude

Revise each of these sentences to improve you-attitude, first using a passive verb, then using an impersonal construction (one in which things, not people, do the action). Are both revisions equally good? Why or why not?

1. You did not send us your cheque.
2. You did not include all the necessary information in your letter.
3. By failing to build a fence around your pool, you have created a health hazard.

6.6 Improving You-Attitude

Revise these sentences to improve you-attitude. Eliminate any awkward phrasing. In some cases, you may need to add information to revise the sentence effectively.

1. We are pleased to offer you the ability to sign up for dental coverage online on our intranet.
2. You will be happy to know that you can use your new cellphone number anywhere in Canada.
3. After hours of hard work, I have negotiated a new employee benefit for you.
4. I urge you to attend a meeting about the new benefits package so that we can inform you about your rights and responsibilities.
5. You will be happy to learn that additional cards for your spouse or child are free.

6. We have added another employee benefit for you.
7. Today, we shipped the book you ordered.
8. In your report, you forgot to tell how many people you surveyed.

9. I hope that it is obvious to you that we want to give you the very best prices on furniture.
10. You didn't order enough doughnuts for the meeting.

6.7 Improving You-Attitude

Revise these sentences to improve you-attitude. Eliminate any awkward phrasing. In some cases, you may need to add information to revise the sentence effectively.

1. Starting next month, the company will offer you a choice of three different health plans.
2. We provide dental coverage to all full-time employees.
3. At the meeting, we'll explain to you how the new prescription drug plan will work.
4. I have ordered a new computer for you. I expect it to arrive by the 15th, and I'll get it ready for you to use as soon as my schedule permits.
5. We are happy to enrol you in our stock-purchase plan.

6. You will be happy to learn that you can transfer credits from our business diploma programs to a university commerce degree.
7. We give you the following benefits when you join our "Frequent Flier" program.
8. We are pleased to send you a copy of "Investing in Stocks," which you requested.
9. Your audit papers did not convert U.S. revenue into Canadian dollars.
10. Of course we want to give you every possible service that you might need or want.

6.8 Revising a Form Letter for You-Attitude

You've taken a part-time job at a store that sells fine jewellery. In orientation, the manager tells you that the store photographs the jewellery it sells or appraises and mails the photo as a goodwill gesture after the transaction. However, when you see the form letter, you know that it doesn't build much goodwill—and you say so.

The manager says, "Well, you're in university. Suppose you rewrite it."

Rewrite the letter. Use square brackets for material (like the customer's name) that would have to be inserted in the form letter to vary it for a specific customer. Add information that would help build goodwill.

> Dear Customer:
>
> We are most happy to enclose a photo of the jewellery that we recently sold you or appraised for you. We feel that this added service, which we are happy to extend to our fine customers, will be useful should you want to insure your jewellery.
>
> We trust you will enjoy this additional service. We thank you for the confidence you have shown by coming to our store.
>
> Sincerely,
>
> Your Sales Associate

6.9   Evaluating You-Attitude in Documents That Cross Your Desk

Identify three sentences that use (or should use) you-attitude in documents you see as a student, consumer, or worker. If the sentences are good, write them down or attach a copy of the document(s) marking the sentence(s) in the margin. If the sentences need work, provide both the original sentence and a possible revision.

As your instructor directs,

a.   Share your examples with a small group of students.

b.   Write a memo to your instructor discussing your examples.

c.   Post an email message to the class discussing your examples.

d.   Present two or three of your examples to the class in a short presentation.

e.   With your small group, write a collaborative short report to your instructor about the patterns you see.

Polishing Your Prose

It's/Its

With an apostrophe, *it's* is a contraction meaning *it is*. Without an apostrophe, *its* is a possessive pronoun meaning *belonging to it*.

Contractions always use apostrophes:

> It is → it's
>
> I have → I've
>
> You will → you'll
>
> They are → they're

Possessive pronouns (unlike possessive nouns) do not use apostrophes:

> His/hers/its
>
> My/mine/our/ours
>
> Your/yours
>
> Their/theirs

Since both *it's* and *its* sound the same, you have to look at the logic of your sentence to choose the right word. If you could substitute *it is*, use *it's*.

Exercises

Choose the right word in the set of parentheses.

1. (It's/its) too bad that the team hasn't finished (it's/its) presentation.
2. The company projected that (it's/its) profits would rise during the next quarter.
3. (It's/its) going to require overtime because the data centre needs (it's/its) reports quickly.
4. I don't want responsibility for the project unless (it's/its) important.
5. The company will announce (it's/its) new name at a press conference.
6. I'm not sure whether (it's/its) a good idea to offer a conference.
7. (It's/its) a good idea to keep your travel receipts in a separate file.
8. (It's/its) good that our computer automatically backs up (it's/its) files.
9. The Saskatoon office will share (it's/its) findings with the other branch offices.
10. (It's/its) cash reserves protected the company from a hostile takeover.

Check your answers to the odd-numbered exercises on page 571.

Online Learning Centre

Visit the Online Learning Centre at www.mcgrawhill.ca/olc/locker to access module quizzes, a searchable glossary, résumé and letter templates, additional business writing samples, CBC videos, and other learning and study tools.

Positive Emphasis

Module Outline

- What's the point of positive emphasis?

- What should I do if my message is bad news?

- How do I create positive emphasis?

- Why do I need to think about tone, politeness, and power?

- What's the best way to apologize?

Review of Key Points

Assignments for Module 7

Polishing Your Prose: Singular and Plural Possessives

LEARNING OBJECTIVES

After reading and applying the information in Module 7, you'll be able to demonstrate

Knowledge of
- The impact of negative information on your reader
- The legal and practical advantages of doing business ethically
- Techniques to convey appropriate tone in your messages

Skills to
- Continue building goodwill
- Emphasize the positive
- Use positive emphasis ethically
- Choose an appropriate tone

The Conference Board of Canada
Insights You Can Count On

Please see the OLC to preview the key skills from the Conference Board of Canada's Employability Skills 2000+ covered in this module.

Positive emphasis is a way of perceiving a situation. Although you may not be optimistic by nature, you can choose to create positive messages through your words, content, organization, and layout (◄|► Module 5).

What's the point of positive emphasis?

Positive emphasis is part of creating goodwill.

FYI

A study of national personalities recently published in *Science* demonstrated that cultural self-perceptions are often self-serving and perpetuate stereotypes. Canadians perceive themselves to be "... polite, modest and somewhat introverted ... extremely agreeable ... very calm and not irritable, very even-tempered." Americans believe themselves to be "... very disagreeable ... anxious and hostile." However, researchers found that Canadians and Americans share most personality traits, along with "... cultures around the globe." Why do Canadians want to see themselves as nicer than Americans? According to the researchers, Canadians embrace this stereotype to "... assert a national identity ..." and to differentiate us from Americans.

Source: Sheryl Ulebacker, "Eh? Study of Stereotypes Show Canadians, Americans Not So Different After All," http://www.recorder.ca/CP/National/051007/n100769A.html, retrieved October 19, 2006.

Positive emphasis works. A positive work environment is essential to recruit, retain, and motivate employees.[1] And, according to Vancity Credit Union CEO Dave Mowatt, a positive workplace is more productive: "... '[Y]ou can draw a direct, straight-line relationship to the financial success of your company. It is just a fact that the higher the morale of your organization, the more money you make.'"[2]

Furthermore, people who choose to communicate positively tend to live longer and more healthily.[3] Positive emphasis is part of successful communication.

Indeed, positive emphasis is characteristic of successful entrepreneurs, since they perceive opportunities and are undaunted by failure.[4] CV Technologies' CEO and Chief Scientific Officer (CSO) Jacqueline Shan couldn't speak English when she emigrated from China "... to pursue a PhD in physiology at the University of Alberta." Shan concentrated her research on the potential for scientifically validating herbal medicines. Together with partner

Dr. Shan

Peter Pang, Shan developed Cold-fX "... a ginseng-derived cold-and-flu preventative ..." that is now "... the top-selling cold remedy in Canada." Before Cold-fX attracted media attention and investors, CV Technologies floundered financially. Shan never gave up. She began managing CV's business and marketing operations, and sales grew. In the first half of 2005, CV Technologies' "... net income [went] from a loss of $58,569 to a profit of $6.8 million." And Cold-fX's potential is such that "[a]n Edmonton-based study is ... examining whether it could become a 'standard of care' for the prevention of upper respiratory infections in Canadian nursing homes."[5]

What should I do if my message is bad news?

Deliver the news responsibly: be clear, sensitive, and ethical.

- Straightforward negatives build credibility when you have bad news to give the reader, such as announcements of layoffs, product defects and recalls, or price increases. Being honest about the drawbacks of a job situation increases motivation, morale, and the likelihood that employees will stay.
- Negatives may help people take a problem seriously. Wall Data improved the reliability of its computer programs when it eliminated the term *bugs* and used the term *failures* instead.

Even in a rejection letter, good writers avoid negative words that insult or attack the reader.

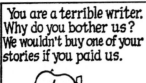

- There are legal, ethical, and practical reasons to deliver negative information sensitively. In some messages, such as negative performance appraisals, your purpose is to deliver a rebuke with no alternative. In these situations, you are legally responsible for ensuring that your language conforms to organizational and governmental regulations (in a union environment, to the rules in the collective agreement; in every workplace situation, to the province's Employment Standards Act/Code and to the Human Rights Commission mandates concerning issues of harassment and discrimination).

In most situations, however, it's better to be positive. People respond more favourably to positive than to negative language and are more likely to act on a positively worded request.[6]

How do I create positive emphasis?

De-emphasize or omit negative words and information.

The following five techniques de-emphasize negative information:

1. Avoid negative words and words with negative connotations.
2. Focus on what the reader can do rather than on limitations.
3. Justify negative information by giving a reason or linking it to a reader benefit.
4. Omit the negative if it is unimportant.
5. Put the negative information in the middle and present it compactly.

In some messages, especially negative ones (◀▮▶ Module 12), you won't use all five techniques. Practise each of these techniques so that you can use them when they're appropriate to your purpose and the needs of your audience.

Negative Words and Words with Negative Connotations

Table 7.1 lists some common negative words. If you find one of these words in a draft, substitute a more positive word. When you must use a negative, use the *least negative* term that will convey your meaning.

The following examples show how to replace negative words with positive words.

Negative: We have failed to finish taking inventory.

Better: We haven't finished taking inventory.

Still better: We will be finished taking inventory Friday.

TABLE 7.1
Negative Words to Avoid

Negative words			Some *dis*-words:	Some *mis*-words:
afraid	except	not	disapprove	misfortune
anxious	fail	objection	dishonest	missing
avoid	fault	problem	dissatisfied	mistake
bad	fear	reject		
careless	hesitate	reluctant	**Many *in*-words:**	**Many *un*-words:**
damage	ignorant	sorry	inadequate	unclear
delay	ignore	terrible	incomplete	unfair
delinquent	impossible	trivial	inconvenient	unfortunate
deny	lacking	trouble	injury	unfortunately
difficulty	loss	wait	insincere	unpleasant
eliminate	neglect	weakness		unreasonable
error	never	worry		unreliable
	no	wrong		unsure

Negative: If you can't understand this explanation, feel free to call me.

Better: If you have further questions, please call me.

Still better: Omit the sentence.

If a sentence has two negatives, substitute one positive term.

Negative: Do not forget to back up your disks.

Better: Always back up your disks.

When you must use a negative term, use the least negative word that is accurate.

Negative: Your balance of $835 is delinquent.

Better: Your balance of $835 is past due.

Getting rid of negatives has the added benefit of making what you write easier to understand. Sentences with three or more negatives are very hard to understand.[7]

Hospitals and people with cancer worldwide will benefit from the passionate positive emphasis of angel investor Milton Wong. For three years, Wong poured his energy and millions of dollars into Vancouver's ATI Technologies—even as the small company floundered. Wong's faith in the ATI team, backed by his personal finances, gave ATI the resources to produce innovative medical imaging technology that will revolutionize health care. A member of the Order of Canada, Wong believes that capital is a tool for creative, socially responsible solutions.

Beware of **hidden negatives**: words that are not negative in themselves but become negative in context. *But* and *however* indicate a shift, so, after a positive statement, they are negative. I *hope* and I *trust that* suggest that you aren't sure. *Patience* may sound like a virtue, but it is a necessary virtue only when things are slow. Even positives about a service or product may backfire if they suggest that in the past the service or product was bad.

Negative: I hope this is the information you wanted.
[Implication: I'm not sure.]

Better: Enclosed is a brochure about road repairs scheduled for 2007–08.

Still better: The brochure contains a list of all roads and bridges scheduled for repair during 2007–08. Call Gwen Wong at 604-555-3245 for specific dates when work will start and stop, and for alternate routes.

Negative: Please be patient as we switch to the automated system.
[Implication: you can expect problems.]

Better: If you have questions during our transition to the automated system, call Melissa Morgan.

Still better: You'll be able to get information instantly about any house on the market when the automated system is in place. If you have questions during the transition, call Melissa Morgan.

Negative: Now Crispy Krisp tastes better.
[Implication: it used to taste terrible.]

Better: Now Crispy Krisp tastes even better.

Removing negatives does not mean being arrogant or pushy.

Negative: I hope that you are satisfied enough to place future orders.

Arrogant: I look forward to receiving all of your future business.

Better: Call Mercury whenever you need transistors.

When you eliminate negative words, be sure to maintain accuracy. Words that are exact opposites will usually not be accurate. Instead, use specifics to be both positive and accurate.

Negative: The exercycle is not guaranteed for life.

Not true: The exercycle is guaranteed for life.

True: The exercycle is guaranteed for 10 years.

Negative: Customers under 60 are not eligible for the Prime Time discount.

Not true: You must be over 60 to be eligible for the Prime Time discount.

True: If you're 60 or older, you can save 10 percent on all your purchases with RightWay's Prime Time discount.

Legal phrases also have negative connotations for most readers and should be avoided whenever possible. The idea will sound more positive if you use everyday English.

Negative: If your account is still delinquent, a second, legal notice will be sent to you informing you that cancellation of your policy will occur 30 days after the date of the legal notice if we do not receive your cheque.

Better: Even if your cheque is lost in the mail and never reaches us, you still have a 30-day grace period. If you do get a second notice, you will know that your payment hasn't reached us. To keep your account in good standing, stop payment on the first cheque and send a second one.

EXPANDING A CRITICAL SKILL

Using Positive Emphasis Ethically

Several of the methods to achieve positive emphasis can be misused. Consider omission.

A bank notified customers that chequing account fees were being "revised" but omitted the amounts. Customers had to go into the bank and copy down the new (higher) fees themselves.

In another case, a condominium resort offered an "all-terrain vehicle" as a prize for visiting. (Winners had to pay $29.95 for "handling, processing, and insurance.") The actual "prize" was a lawn chair with four wheels that converted into a wheeled cart. The company claims it told the truth: "It is a vehicle. It's a four-wheel cart you can take anywhere—to the beach, to the pool. It may not be motorized, but [we] didn't say it was motorized."

In both cases, full disclosure might have affected decisions: some customers might have chosen to change banks; some customers would have declined the condominium visit. It isn't ethical to omit information that people need to make decisions.

Presenting information compactly can also go too far. A credit card company mailed out a letter with the good news that the minimum monthly payment was going down. But a separate small flyer explained that interest rates (on the charges not repaid) were going up. The print was far too small to read: 67 lines of type were crowded into five vertical inches of text.

Ethicist Chris MacDonald suggests that making ethical choices, regardless of our motivation, leads to positive results. Even when businesses act ethically because doing so "... is good for the bottom line," everyone benefits. An organization that treats its employees, clients, and share-holders ethically enhances its reputation and builds its business. Furthermore, even when it originates out of self-interest, ethical behaviour can be habit-forming.

Source: Chris MacDonald, "Why Act Ethically? And Does the Answer a Company Gives Matter?" August 4, 2004, http://www.ethicsweb.ca/be-pubs.html, retrieved August 8, 2006.

Sources: Carmella M. Padilla, "It's a ... a ... a ... All-Terrain Vehicle, Yeah, That's It, That's the Ticket," *The Wall Street Journal*, July 17, 1987, 17; and Donna S. Kienzler, "Visual Ethics," *Journal of Business Communication* 34 (1997): 175–76.

SEE THE OLC!

More about business ethics

■ Focus on What the Reader Can Do Rather Than on Limitations

Sometimes, positive emphasis is a matter of the way you present something: is the glass half empty or half full? Sometimes it's a matter of eliminating double negatives. When there are limits, or some options are closed, focus on the alternatives that remain.

Negative: We will not allow you to charge more than $1500 on your VISA account.

Better: You can charge $1500 on your new VISA card.

Or: Your new VISA card gives you $1500 in credit that you can use at thousands of stores nationwide.

As you focus on what will happen, check for you-attitude (◀▶ Module 6). In the last example, "We will allow you to charge $1500" is positive, but it lacks you-attitude.

When you have a benefit, and a requirement the reader must meet to get the benefit, the sentence is usually more positive if you put the benefit first.

Negative: You will not qualify for the student membership rate of $25 a year unless you are enrolled for at least 10 hours.

Better: You get all the benefits of membership for only $25 a year if you're enrolled for 10 hours or more.

Justify Negative Information by Giving a Reason or Linking It to a Reader Benefit

A reason can help your reader see that the information is necessary; a benefit can suggest that the negative aspect is outweighed by positive factors. Be careful, however, to make the logic behind your reason clear and to leave no loopholes.

Negative: We cannot sell computer disks in lots of fewer than 10.

Loophole: To keep down packaging costs and to help you save on shipping and handling costs, we sell computer disks in lots of 10 or more.

Suppose the customer says, "I'll pay the extra shipping and handling. Send me seven." If you can't or won't sell in lots of fewer than 10, you need to write:

Better: To keep down packaging costs and to help customers save on shipping and handling costs, we sell computer disks only in lots of 10 or more.

If you link the negative element to a benefit, be sure that it is an audience-based benefit. Avoid telling people that you're doing things "for their own good." They may have a different notion of what their own good is. You may think you're doing customers a favour by limiting their credit so they don't get in over their heads and go bankrupt. They may feel they'd be better off with more credit so they could expand in hopes of making more sales and more profits.

Omit the Negative If It Is Truly Unimportant

Omit negatives entirely only in three instances:

- The reader does not need the information to make a decision.
- You have already given the reader the information, and he or she has access to the previous communication.
- The information is trivial.

The following examples suggest the kind of negatives you can omit:

Negative: A one-year subscription to *Canada Business* is $49.97. That rate is not as low as the rates charged for some magazines.

Better: A One-year subscription to *Canada Business* is $49.97.

Still better: A one-year subscription to *Canada Business* is $49.97. You save 43 percent off the newsstand price of $87.78.

Negative: If you are unsatisfied with Sun Life Insurance, do not renew your policy.

Better: Omit the sentence.

Bury the Negative Information and Present It Compactly

The beginning and end of a message are always positions of emphasis. Put negatives there only if you want to emphasize the negative, as you may in a negative message (◀▶ Module 12). To de-emphasize a negative, put it in the middle of a paragraph rather than in the first or last sentence, or in the middle of the message rather than in the first or last paragraphs.

When a letter or memo runs several pages, remember that the bottom of the first page is also a position of emphasis, even if it is in the middle of a paragraph, because of the extra white space of the bottom margin. (The first page gets more attention since it is on top, and the reader's eye may catch some lines of the message even when he or she isn't consciously reading it; the tops and bottoms of subsequent pages don't get this extra attention.) If possible, avoid placing negative information at the bottom of the first page.

Giving a topic plenty of space emphasizes it. You can de-emphasize negative information by giving it as little space as possible. Give negative information only once in your message. Don't list negatives vertically on the page, since lists take space and emphasize material.

Why do I need to think about tone, politeness, and power?

Think about these factors so that you don't offend people by mistake.

No one likes to deal with people who seem condescending or rude. Poorly chosen words can create that sense, whether the sender "meant" to be rude or not. Tone is the implied attitude of the writer toward the reader. Tone is tricky because it interacts with power: the words that might seem friendly from a superior to a subordinate may seem uppity if used by the subordinate to the superior. Norms for politeness are cultural and generational. Language that is acceptable within one group may be unacceptable if used by someone outside the group (◀|▶ Module 3).

Cultures that value group cohesiveness place a much greater emphasis on courtesy than the dominant North American culture does. Politeness spares others' feelings, and "saves face" for both message sender and receiver. A direct "No" response is rude in Pakistani and Chinese culture, for example, and such discourtesy could lose a deal.

The desirable tone for business writing is businesslike but not stiff, friendly but not phony, confident but not arrogant, polite but not grovelling. The following guidelines will help you achieve the tone you want:

- **Use courtesy titles for people outside your organization whom you don't know well.** Canadian organizations use first names for everyone, whatever their age or rank. But many people don't like being called by their first names by people they don't know or by someone much younger. When you talk or write to people outside your organization, use first names only if you've established a personal relationship. If you don't know someone well, use a courtesy title (◀|▶ Module 9):

  Dear Mr. Reynolds:
  Dear Ms. Lee:

- **Be aware of the power implications of the words you use.** "Thank you for your co-operation" is generous coming from a superior to a subordinate; it's not appropriate in a message to your superior.

Different ways of asking for action carry different levels of politeness, as Table 7.2 shows.[8]

You need to be more polite if you're asking for something that will inconvenience the reader and help you more than the person who does the action. Generally, you need to be less polite when you're asking for something small, routine, or to the reader's benefit. Most readers and some discourse communities, however, prefer that even small requests be made politely.

TABLE 7.2

Forms of Request and Their Levels of Politeness

Form of request	Level of politeness	Example
Order	Lowest politeness	Turn in your time card by Monday.
Polite order	Mid-level politeness	Please turn in your time card by Monday.
Indirect request	Higher politeness	Time cards should be turned in by Monday.
Question	Highest politeness	Would you be able to turn in your time card by Monday?

Lower politeness: To start the scheduling process, please describe your availability for meetings during the second week of the month.

Higher politeness: Could you let me know what times you'd be free for a meeting the second week of the month?

Higher levels of politeness may be unclear. In some cases, a question may seem like a request for information to which it's acceptable to answer, "No, I can't." In other cases, it will be an order, simply phrased in polite terms.

Generally, requests sound friendliest when they use conversational language.

Poor tone: Return the draft with any changes by next Tuesday.

Better tone: Let me know by Tuesday whether you'd like any changes in the draft.

When the stakes are low, be straightforward. Messages that "beat around the bush" sound pompous and defensive.

Poor tone: Distribution of the low-fat plain granola may be limited in your area. May we suggest that you discuss this matter with your store manager.

Better tone: Our low-fat granola is so popular that there isn't enough to go around. We're expanding production to meet the demand. Ask your store manager to keep putting in orders, so that your grocery is on the list of stores that will get supplies when they become available.

Or: Store managers decide what to stock. If your store has stopped carrying our low-fat granola, the store manager has stopped ordering it. Talk to the manager. Managers try to meet customer needs, so if you say something you're more likely to get what you want.

When you must give bad news, consider hedging your statement. Linguistic experts John Hagge and Charles Kostelnick have shown that auditors' suggestion letters rarely say directly that firms are using unacceptable accounting practices. Instead, they use three strategies to be more diplomatic: specifying the time ("currently, the records are quite informal"), limiting statements ("it appears," "it seems"), and using impersonal statements that do not specify who caused a problem or who will perform an action.[9]

■ What's the best way to apologize?

Apologize early, briefly, and sincerely.

FYI

People who "put on a happy face," or behave cheerfully even when they don't particularly feel that way can actually cause their mood to become more positive.

Source: Don Oldenburg, "Act Optimistic to Turn Frown Upside Down, Researcher Says," *Columbus Dispatch*, August 12, 1999, E1.

When you are at fault, you build goodwill by admitting that fact promptly. However, apologies may have legal implications, so some organizations prefer that their employees not offer apologies to customers.

When you have done everything you can for your customer, and when a delay or problem is due to circumstances beyond your control, you aren't at fault and don't need to apologize. It may be appropriate to include an explanation so the reader knows you weren't negligent. If the news is bad, put the explanation first. If you have good news for the reader, put it before your explanation.

Negative: I'm sorry that I could not answer your question sooner. I had to wait until the sales figures for the second quarter were in.

Better (neutral or bad news):   We needed the sales figures for the second quarter to answer your question. Now that they're in, I can tell you that …

Better (good news):   The new advertising campaign is a success. The sales figures for the second quarter are finally in, and they show that …

If the delay or problem is long or large, it is good you-attitude to ask the reader whether he or she wants to confirm the original plan or make different arrangements.

Negative: I'm sorry that the chairs will not be ready by August 25 as promised.

Better: Because of a strike against the manufacturer, the desk chairs you ordered will not be ready until November. Do you want to keep that order, or would you like to look at the models available from other suppliers?

When an apology is appropriate, do so early, briefly, and sincerely.

Apologize only once, early in the message. Let the reader move on to other, more positive information.

Even if major trouble or inconvenience has resulted from your error, you don't need to go on about all the horrible things that happened. The reader already knows this negative information, and you can omit it. Instead, focus on what you have done to correct the situation.

If you don't know whether any inconvenience has resulted, don't raise the issue at all. Why draw attention to a negative your reader may not have considered?

Negative: I'm sorry I didn't answer your letter sooner. I hope that my delay has not inconvenienced you.

Better: I'm sorry I didn't answer your letter sooner.

Employability Skills 2000+

The Conference Board of Canada
Insights You Can Count On

Please see the OLC to preview the key skills from the Conference Board of Canada's Employability Skills 2000+ covered in this module.

Review of Key Points

1. Why is it important to use positive emphasis?
2. Identify five strategies for emphasizing information positively.
3. When and how should you apologize? Why do you have to be careful when you apologize to customers?
4. Why is it important to use positive emphasis ethically?
5. What is business tone? How can you achieve the tone you want?
6. Why should you avoid using negative words? Give examples.

Assignments for Module 7

Questions for Critical Thinking

7.1 Some negative phrases (such as "please do not hesitate") are business clichés. Why is it better to avoid them?

7.2 Think of a situation when an apology was appropriate. What strategy was actually used? Would another strategy have been better?

7.3 If you work for a company that claims to be egalitarian, do you still need to attend to tone, power, and politeness?

7.4 Can you think of situations in which positive emphasis might backfire or be inappropriate? What strategies would be most likely to meet the audience's needs in those situations?

Exercises and Problems

7.5   Analyzing Your Discourse Community for Tone, Courtesy, and Power

Analyze the cultural norms for tone, levels of courtesy, and use of power in your organization. Choose a discourse community of which you are a member—you can use a club, social, ethnic, religious or academic organization, or your place of work.

Identify a minimum of three oral and three written messages that exemplify the norms and attitudes toward power in the organization. Write a memo to your instructor and classmates about your findings.

7.6   Evaluating the Ethics of Positive Emphasis

The first word in each line at the right is negative; the second is a positive term that is sometimes substituted for it. Which of the positive terms seem ethical? Which seem unethical? Briefly explain your choices.

junk bonds	high-yield bonds	nervousness	adrenaline
second mortgage	home-equity loan	problem	challenge
tax	user fee	price increase	price change
tax increase	revenue enhancement		

7.7 Focusing on the Positive

Revise each of the following sentences to focus on the options that remain, not those that are closed off.

1. As a first-year employee, you are not eligible for dental insurance.
2. I will be out of the country October 25 until November 10 and will not be able to meet with you until I return.
3. You will not get your first magazine for at least four weeks.
4. I'm sorry I'm away from my desk and cannot answer your call.

7.8 Identifying Hidden Negatives

Identify the hidden negatives in the following sentences and revise to eliminate them. In some cases, you may need to add information to revise the sentence effectively.

1. This publication is designed to explain how your company can start a recycling program.
2. I hope you find the information in this brochure beneficial to you and a valuable reference as you plan your move.
3. In thinking about your role in our group, I remember two occasions where you contributed something.

7.9 Revising Sentences to Improve Positive Emphasis

Revise the following sentences to improve positive emphasis. In some cases, you may need to add or omit information to revise effectively.

1. It will be necessary for you to submit Form PR-47 before you can be reimbursed for your travel expenses.
2. If you have further questions, please do not hesitate to contact me.
3. I'm sorry you were worried about your health insurance. It is not too late to sign up for a flexible spending account.
4. You cannot return this item for a full refund if you keep it more than 30 days.
5. When you write a report, do not make claims that you cannot support with evidence.
6. Although I was only an intern and didn't actually make presentations to major clients, I was required to prepare PowerPoint™ slides for the meetings and to answer some of the clients' questions.
7. You will pay $30 more if you wait till after October 1 to register for the conference.
8. To reduce unnecessary delays in processing your order, please check the form at the end of this letter to see that nothing is omitted or incorrect before you sign the form and return it.
9. The figures for budget changes made at the meeting may be wrong, as I got lost during John's presentation. Please check the figures and let me know if they need correction.
10. We cannot process your application to graduate because you did not supply all of the necessary information.

7.10 Revising Sentences to Improve Positive Emphasis

Revise the following sentences to improve positive emphasis. In some cases, you may need to add or omit information to revise effectively.

1. No subcontractor shall be employed without the previous consent of the director.
2. To avoid unnecessary delays, call for an appointment before coming in to the office.
3. I realize that Wednesday at 10 A.M. is not a convenient time for everyone, but I was unable to arrange a time that is good for everyone.

4. I'm sorry you were worried about the résumé you emailed us. We did not have any problems scanning it into our system.

5. I am anxious to talk with you about the job.

6. People who come to work late may be perceived as unreliable.

7. I hope that you receive the April spreadsheet (three pages) that follows and that the fax quality isn't too poor.

8. I was treasurer of the accounting club. Of course, we didn't have much money so I didn't have much responsibility, but I was able to put into practice principles I learned in the classroom.

9. If you have any problems using your email account, I will try to explain it so that you can understand.

10. If you submitted a travel request, as you claim, we have failed to receive it.

7.11 Revising a Memo to Improve Positive Emphasis

Revise the following memo to improve the you-attitude and positive emphasis.

Subject: Status of Building Renovations

The renovation of the lobby is not behind schedule. By Monday, October 9, we hope to be ready to open the west end of the lobby to limited traffic.

The final phase of the renovation will be placing a new marble floor in front of the elevators. This work will not be finished until the end of the month.

Insofar as is possible, the crew will attempt to schedule most of the work during the evenings so that normal business is not disrupted.

Please exercise caution when moving through the construction area. The floor will be uneven and steps will be at unusual heights. Watch your step to avoid accidentally tripping or falling.

7.12 Identifying Positive Emphasis in Ads and Documents

Look at print advertisements and at documents you receive from your college or university, from your workplace, and from organizations to which you belong. Identify five sentences that either (a) use positive emphasis or (b) should be revised to be more positive.

As your instructor directs,

a. Share your examples with a small group of students.

b. Write a memo to your instructor discussing your examples.

c. Post an email message to the class discussing your examples.

d. Present two or three of your examples to the class in a short presentation.

e. With your small group, write a collaborative short report to your instructor about the patterns you see.

Polishing Your Prose

Singular and Plural Possessives

With an apostrophe, *it's* is a contraction meaning *it is*. Without an apostrophe, *its* is a possessive pronoun meaning *belonging to it*.

To show possession when a noun is singular, put the apostrophe right after the word; then add *s*:

> Allen's
> The manager's
> The company's

If the possessing noun is plural, put the apostrophe right after the word:

> Customers'
> Employees'
> Companies'

In names that end with *s* or an *s* sound, style books permit either form:

> Thomas'
> Thomas's
> Linux'
> Linux's

Often, the location of the apostrophe tells the reader whether the noun is singular or plural.

Singular Possessive	Plural Possessive
The employee's Product's	The employees' Products'

Because the singular and plural possessives sound the same, look at the logic of your sentence to choose the right word. Also note that when you have plural possessive nouns, other words in the sentence will also become plural.

Plural employees have plural opinions. Plural products have plural prices.

We listen to our employees' opinions.

You can find all of our products' prices on our Web site.

Exercises

Choose the correct word in each set of parentheses.

1. We design products based on our (customer's/customers') needs.
2. The winter holiday season can account for one-quarter to one-half of a (store's/stores') annual profits.
3. (Canadian's/Canadians') views of the economy reflect their confidence in the stock market.
4. To sell in another country, you need to understand its (people's/peoples') culture.
5. We meet the local, provincial, and federal (government's/governments') standards for quality control.
6. Two of our (computer's/computers') monitors need to be repaired.
7. The (committee's/committees') duties will be completed after it announces its decision.
8. Employees who have worked as Big Sisters have enjoyed seeing the (girl's/girls') progress.
9. We'll decide whether to have more computer training sessions based on (employee's/employees') feedback.
10. The (company's/companies') benefit plan is excellent.

Check your answers to the odd-numbered exercises on page 571.

■ Online Learning Centre

Visit the Online Learning Centre at www.mcgrawhill.ca/olc/locker to access module quizzes, a searchable glossary, résumé and letter templates, additional business writing samples, CBC videos, and other learning and study tools.

8 Reader Benefits

Module Outline

- Why do reader benefits work?
- How do I identify reader benefits?
- How detailed should each benefit be?
- How do I decide which benefits to use?
- What else do reader benefits need?

Review of Key Points

Assignments for Module 8

Polishing Your Prose: Plurals and Possessives

LEARNING OBJECTIVES

After reading and applying the information in Module 8, you'll be able to demonstrate

Knowledge of
- Maslow's Hierarchy of Needs
- Elements of reader-centred messages
- The importance of identifying audience benefits

Skills to
- Use audience analysis to identify and choose reader benefits
- Develop reader benefits with logic and detail
- Match the benefit to the audience

The Conference Board of Canada
Insights You Can Count On

Please see the OLC to preview the key skills from the Conference Board of Canada's Employability Skills 2000+ covered in this module.

Reader benefits sell ideas, products, and services.

In informative messages, reader benefits give reasons to comply with the policies you announce and suggest how and why the policies are good ones. In persuasive messages, reader benefits provide reasons to act, in order to reduce reader resistance. Negative messages (◀▶ Module 12) may not give reader benefits; however, negative messages are organized to provide maximum reader appeal (◀▶ Modules 5, 7, 12).

The best reader benefits are

- Adapted specifically to the audience
- Based on intrinsic advantages
- Supported clearly and comprehensively
- Phrased in you-attitude

■ Why do reader benefits work?

Reader benefits appeal to the audience's attitudes and actions.

Reader benefits appeal to both the attitudes and the behaviour of your audience. When you provide benefits that focus on readers' needs and wants, people feel more positive about you and your request. Providing reader benefits makes it easier for you to accomplish your goals.

Expectancy theory says most people try to do their best only when they believe that they can succeed and when they want the rewards that success brings. Reader benefits tell readers that they can do the job successfully and that they will be rewarded.[1] Reader benefits help overcome two problems that reduce motivation: people may not think of all the possible benefits, and they may not understand the relationships among efforts, performance, and rewards.[2]

■ How do I identify reader benefits?

Know your reader and brainstorm!

Sometimes reader benefits are obvious and easy to describe. When they are harder to identify, brainstorm:

1. Think of the feelings, values, fears, and needs that may motivate your reader. Then identify features of your product or policy that meet those values or needs.
2. Identify the objective features of your product or policy. Then think how these features could benefit the audience.

Try to brainstorm at least three to five possible benefits for every informative message, and five to seven benefits for every persuasive message. The more benefits you think of, the easier it will be to choose ones that will appeal directly to your reader.

■ 1. Think of Feelings, Fears, and Needs That May Motivate Your Reader

One of the best-known analyses of needs is Abraham H. Maslow's **hierarchy of needs**.[3] Physical needs are the most basic, followed by needs for safety and security, for love and a sense of belonging, for esteem and recognition, and finally for self-actualization or self-fulfillment. We move back and forth between higher-level and lower-level needs. Whenever lower-level needs make themselves felt, they take priority.

Maslow's model is a good starting place to identify the feelings, fears, and needs that may motivate your audience. Figure 8.1 shows organizational motivators for each of the levels in Maslow's hierarchy.

Compare the PAIBOC model with Maslow's hierarchy in Figure 8.1. Notice that your message **purpose(s)**, **information**, **anticipated objections**, and **context** must all be defined and refined according to the needs of your audience.

Often a product or idea can meet needs on several levels. Focus on the ones that your audience analysis suggests are most relevant for your audience. But remember: even the best analysis may not reveal all of a reader's needs. For example, a well-paid manager may still be worried about security needs if her spouse has lost his job or if the couple is supporting children in university, or a parent at home.

P A I B O C

Questions for Analysis

Use the PAIBOC questions to analyze business communication problems:

P What are your purposes in writing?

A Who is your audience?

I What information must your message include?

B What reasons or reader benefits can you use to support your position?

O What objections can you expect from your readers?

C How will the context affect reader response?

FIGURE 8.1
Organizational Motivations for Maslow's Hierarchy of Needs

Self-actualization
- Using your talents and abilities
- Finding solutions to problems
- Serving humanity
- Feeling self-respect and pride
- Being the best you can be

Esteem, recognition
- Being publicly recognized for achievements
- Being promoted or gaining authority
- Having status symbols
- Having a good personal reputation
- Having a good corporate reputation

Love, belonging
- Having friends, working with people you like
- Cooperating with other people on a project
- Conforming to a group's norms
- Feeling needed
- Being loyal or patriotic
- Promoting the welfare of a group you identify with or care about

Safety, security
- Earning enough to afford a comfortable standard of living
- Having pleasant working conditions
- Having good health insurance and pension plans
- Understanding the reasons for actions by supervisors
- Being treated fairly
- Saving time and money
- Conserving human and environmental resources

Physical
- Earning enough to pay for basic food, clothing, shelter, and medical care
- Having safe working conditions
- Being free from physical pain or suffering

The reader benefits of this ad are both intrinsic and extrinsic.

■ 2. Identify the Objective Features of Your Product or Policy, Then Think How These Features Could Benefit the Audience

A feature by itself is not a benefit. Often, a feature has several possible benefits.

Feature: Bottled water

Benefits: Is free from chemicals, pollutants
Tastes good
Has no calories
Is easy to carry to class; can be used while biking, driving, hiking

Feature: Closed captions on TV shows and movies

Benefits: Enables hard-of-hearing and deaf viewers to follow dialogue
Helps speakers of English as a second language learn phrases and idioms
Helps small children learn to read

Feature: Flextime

Benefits: Enables workers to accommodate personal needs
Helps organizations recruit, retain workers
Makes more workers available in early morning and in evening
Enables office to stay open longer—more service to clients, customers
Enables workers to communicate with colleagues in different time zones more easily

Different features may benefit different subgroups in your audience. Depending on the features a restaurant offers, you could appeal to one or more of the subgroups shown in Table 8.1.

To develop your benefits, think about the details of each one. If your selling point is your relaxing atmosphere, think about the specific details that make the restaurant relaxing.

TABLE 8.1
Audience Subgroups

Subgroup	Features to meet the subgroup's needs
People who work outside the home	A quick lunch; a relaxing place to take clients or colleagues
Parents with small children	High chairs, child-sized portions, and activities to keep the kids entertained while they wait for their order
People who eat out a lot	Variety both in food and in decor
People on tight budgets	Economical food; a place where they don't need to tip (cafeteria or fast food)
People on special diets	Low-sodium and low-calorie dishes; vegetarian food; kosher food
People to whom eating out is part of an evening's entertainment	Music or a floor show; elegant surroundings; reservations so they can get to a show or event after dinner; late hours so they can come to dinner after a show or game

If your strong point is elegant dining, consider all the details that contribute to that elegance. Sometimes you may offer features that do not meet any particular need but are still good benefits. In a sales letter for a restaurant, you might also want to mention your free coatroom, your convenient location, free parking or a drive-up window, and speedy service.

Whenever you're writing to customers or clients about features that are not unique to your organization, it's wise to present both the benefits of the features themselves and the benefits of dealing with your company. If you talk about the benefits of dining in a relaxed atmosphere but don't mention your own restaurant, people may go somewhere else!

How detailed should each benefit be?

Use strong, vivid details. Paint a mental picture.

You'll usually need at least three to five sentences to give enough details about a reader benefit. If you develop two or three reader benefits fully, you can use just a sentence or two for less important benefits. Develop reader benefits by linking each feature to the readers' needs—and provide details to make the benefit vivid!

Weak: We have placemats with riddles.

Better: Answering all the riddles on Caesar's special placemats will keep the kids happy till your pizza comes. If they don't have time to finish (and they may not, since your pizza is ready so quickly), just take the riddles home—or answer them on your next visit.

Make your reader benefits specific.

Weak: You get quick service.

Better: If you only have an hour for lunch, try our Business Buffet. Within minutes, you can choose from a variety of main dishes, vegetables, and a make-your-own-sandwich-and-salad bar. You can put together a lunch that's as light or filling as you want, with time to enjoy it—and still be back to the office on time.

Psychological description is a technique you can use to develop vivid, specific reader benefits. **Psychological description** means creating a scenario rich with sense impressions—what the reader sees, hears, smells, tastes, feels—so readers can picture themselves using your product or service and enjoying its benefits. You can also use psychological description to describe the problem your product will solve. Psychological description works best early in the message to catch readers' attention.

Feature:	Snooze alarm
Benefit:	When you press the snooze button, the alarm goes off and comes on again nine minutes later.
Psychological description:	Some mornings, you really want to stay in bed just a few more minutes. With the Sleepytime Snooze Alarm, you can snuggle under the covers for a few extra winks, secure in the knowledge that the alarm will come on again to get you up for that breakfast meeting with an important client. If you want to sleep in, you can keep hitting the snooze alarm for up to an additional 63 minutes of sleep. With Sleepytime, you're in control of your mornings.
Feature:	Tilt windows
Benefit:	Easier to clean
Psychological description:	It's no wonder so many cleaners "don't do windows." Balancing precariously on a rickety ladder to clean upper-story windows … shivering outside in the winter winds and broiling in the summer sun as you scrub away … running inside, then outside, then inside again to try to get the spot that always seems to be on the other side. Cleaning traditional windows really is a chore.
	You'll find cleaning a breeze with Tilt-in Windows. Just pull the inner window down and pull the bottom toward you. The whole window lifts out! Repeat for the outer window. Clean inside in comfort (sitting down or even watching TV if you choose). Then replace the top of the outer window in its track, slide up, and repeat with the inner window. Presto! Clean windows!
Feature:	Prearranged, timed, prerecorded telephone calls
Benefit:	High-tech way to exit unpleasant/uncomfortable social situations
Psychological description:	We've all done it: told a friend to call our cell phone during a first date to give us an emergency out if needed. Now, this modern ritual has gone high-tech. With the "Saved by the call!" service, Fido cell phone subscribers can arrange to have the phone ring at a prearranged time with a prerecorded message urging them to drop everything. There is also a "panic button" option: press #22 and a call is made within seconds.[4]

In psychological description, you're putting your reader in a picture. If the reader doesn't feel that the picture fits, the technique backfires. To prevent this, psychological description often uses subjunctive verbs ("if you like …" "if you were …") or the words *maybe* and *perhaps*.

You're hungry but you don't want to bother with cooking. Perhaps you have guests to take to dinner. Or it's 12 noon and you only have an hour for lunch. Whatever the situation, the Illini Union has a food service to fit your needs. If you want convenience, we have it. If it's atmosphere you're seeking, it's here too. And if you're concerned about the price, don't be. When you're looking for a great meal, the Illini Union is the place to find it.

—*Illini Union brochure*

How do I decide which benefits to use?

Use the following three principles to decide.

Three principles guide your choice of reader benefits:

1. Use at least one benefit for each subgroup in your audience.
2. Use intrinsic benefits.
3. Use the benefits you can develop most fully.

1. Use at Least One Benefit for Each Subgroup in Your Audience

FYI

People are more motivated by the promise of rewards than they are de-motivated by threats of punishment. Consider the ubiquitous cell phone: despite research suggesting a link between cell-phone use and brain and organ damage, and proof that cell-chatting drivers have more accidents, Canadians continue to be among the world's most voracious cell-phone users.

Sources: 8 A.M. News, 96.3AM, July 12, 2005, and http://www.statcan.ca/Daily/English/041213/d041213b.htm, December 13, 2004, retrieved August 8, 2006.

Most messages go to multiple audiences. In a memo announcing a company-subsidized day-care program, you want to describe benefits not only for parents who might use the service but also for people who don't have children or whose children are older. Reader benefits for these last two audiences help convince them that spending money on day care is a good use of scarce funds.

In a letter to "consumers" or "voters," different people will have different concerns. The more of these concerns you speak to, the more persuasive you'll be.

2. Use Intrinsic Benefits

Intrinsic benefits come automatically from using a product or doing something. **Extrinsic benefits** are "added on." Someone in power decides to give them; they do not necessarily come from using the product or doing the action. Table 8.2 on page 141 gives examples of extrinsic and intrinsic rewards for four activities.

Intrinsic rewards or benefits are better than extrinsic benefits for two reasons:

1. There just aren't enough extrinsic rewards for everything you want people to do. You can't give a prize to every customer every time he or she places an order or to every subordinate who does what he or she is supposed to do.
2. Research suggests that you'll motivate people more effectively by stressing the intrinsic benefits of following policies and adopting proposals.

In a groundbreaking study of professional employees, Frederick Herzberg found that the things people said they liked about their jobs were all intrinsic rewards—pride in achievement, an enjoyment of the work itself, responsibility. Extrinsic features—pay, company policy—were sometimes mentioned as things people disliked, but they were never cited as things that motivated or satisfied them. People who made a lot of money still did not mention salary as a good point about the job or the organization.[5]

EXPANDING A CRITICAL SKILL

Matching the Benefit to the Audience

Suppose that you manufacture a product and want to persuade dealers to carry it. The features you may cite in ads directed toward customers—stylish colours, sleek lines, convenience, durability, good price—won't convince dealers. Shelf space is at a premium, and no dealer carries all the models of all the brands available for any given product. Why should the dealer stock your product? To be persuasive, talk about the features that are benefits from the dealer's point of view: turnover, profit margin, a national advertising campaign to build customer awareness and interest, special store displays that will draw attention to the product.

Depending on their demographic and cultural circumstances (◀ ▶ Modules 2 and 3), consumers value different benefits. The Hudson's Bay Company, for example, targets its Bay and Zellers department stores' features to different shoppers. Zellers promises "budget-minded" Canadians low prices and rewards customer loyalty with its Club Z program. Savings realized through self-service and central check-outs are passed on to consumers. The more upscale Bay stores across Canada offer in-store events customized to their specific communities: the Calgary and Edmonton stores promote monthly events different from those in Ottawa and Toronto, which are different again from those held in stores in Montreal and Vancouver.

In every organization, different audiences care about different "benefits." Workplace flexibility, for example, is a major enticement for recruiting and retaining top performers, according to the Conference Board of Canada's research.

Michael Turczyniak, president of Mico Systems Inc., focuses on the benefits of his hardware and software solutions to his target market: accounting professionals.

Talented female executives in particular are attracted by organizations that help them balance their family and work responsibilities. To retain "rising star" Debbie Landers, IBM Canada offered her a full-time work-at-home job. Landers manages her global responsibilities, and her staff, from her home office 400 km from IBM's corporate headquarters.

To find the benefits that will have the most appeal, begin by identifying your audience: who will be reading or listening to your message? Then brainstorm to decide what's in it for them: what intrinsic and extrinsic rewards can your message offer that match your audience's needs?

Sources: Mike Duff, "A Seasoned Helmsman From A to Club Z," *Discount Store News*, May 24, 1999, http://www.findarticles.com/p/articles/mi_3092/is_10_38/ai_54737802, retrieved October 13, 2006; "Shopping is Good With a Brand New Bay Destination," Hudson's Bay Press Release, www.newswire.ca/releases/November2000/22/c7073.html, retrieved July 28, 2001; Katherine Harding, "Work-At-Home Bosses? Why Not?" *The Globe and Mail*, May 28, 2003, C3.

TABLE 8.2
Extrinsic and Intrinsic Rewards

Activity	Extrinsic Reward	Intrinsic Reward
Making a sale	Getting a commission	Pleasure in convincing someone; pride in using your talents to create a strategy and execute it
Turning in a suggestion to a company suggestion system	Getting a monetary reward when the suggestion is implemented	Solving a problem at work; making the work environment a little pleasanter; feeling of pride for a job well done
Writing a report that solves an organizational problem	Getting praise; a good performance appraisal, and maybe a raise	Pleasure in having an effect on an organization; pride in using your skills to solve problems; pleasure in solving the problem itself

SEE THE OLC!

Intrinsic Rewards

Many family-friendly companies have discovered that a culture of care keeps turnover low. The higher salary that a competitor might pay just doesn't overcome the advantage of working at a supportive, flexible company that values its employees.[6] In the current competitive job market, different candidates want different things. But many accept lower salaries to get flextime, stock options, interesting work, or people they want to work with.[7]

Since money is not a motivator, choose reader benefits that identify intrinsic as well as extrinsic motivators for following policies and adopting ideas.

For example, the Sleep Country Web site on page 137 appeals to readers' needs for

- conserving human and environmental resources (safety, security)
- conforming to group norms (love, belonging)
- promoting others' welfare (love, belonging)
- having a good personal reputation (esteem, recognition)
- finding solutions to problems (self-actualization)
- serving humanity (self-actualization)
- feeling self-respect (self-actualization)

Through these intrinsic benefits, the Web site acknowledges the values of Sleep Country's target customers.

3. Use the Benefits You Can Develop Most Fully

One-sentence benefits don't do much. Use benefits that you can develop in three to five sentences or more.

A reader benefit is a claim or assertion that the reader will benefit if he or she does something. Convincing the reader, therefore, requires two steps: ensuring that the benefit appeals to your reader and really will happen, and explaining it to the reader.

If the logic behind a claimed reader benefit is faulty or inaccurate, there's no way to make that particular reader benefit convincing. Revise the benefit to make it logical.

Faulty logic: Using a computer will enable you to write letters, memos, and reports much more quickly.

Analysis: If you've never used a computer, in the short run it will take you *longer* to create a document using a computer than it would to type it. Even after you know how to use a computer and its software, the real time savings come when a document incorporates parts of previous documents or goes through several revisions. Creating a first draft from scratch still takes planning and careful composing; the time savings may or may not be significant.

Revised reader benefit: Using a computer allows you to revise and edit a document more easily. It eliminates retyping as a separate step and reduces the time needed to proofread revisions. It allows you to move the text around on the page to create the best layout.

If the logic is sound, making that logic evident to the reader is a matter of providing enough evidence and showing how the evidence proves the claim that there will be a benefit. Always provide enough detail to be vivid and concrete. You'll need more detail in the following situations:

- The reader has not thought of the benefit before.
- The benefit depends on the difference between the long run and the short run.

- The reader will be hard to persuade, and you need detail to make the benefit vivid and emotionally convincing.

Does the following statement have enough detail?

> You'll save money by using our shop-at-home service.

Readers always believe their own experience. Readers who have never used a shop-at-home service may think, "If somebody else does my shopping for me, I'll have to pay that person. I'll save money by doing it myself." They may not think of the savings in gas and parking, in travel time, and in less car wear and tear. Readers who already use shop-at-home services may believe you if they compare your items and services with another company's to see that your cost is lower. Even then, you could make saving money seem more forceful and more vivid by telling readers how much they could save and mentioning some of the ways they could use your service.

What else do reader benefits need?

Check for you-attitude.

If reader benefits aren't in you-attitude (◀|▶ Module 6), they'll sound selfish and won't be as effective as they could be. A Xerox letter selling copiers with strong you-attitude as well as reader benefits got a far bigger response than an alternative version with reader benefits but no you-attitude.[8] It doesn't matter how you phrase reader benefits while you're brainstorming and developing them, but in your final draft, edit for you-attitude.

Lacks you-attitude: We have the lowest prices in town.

You-attitude: At Abbotsford Toyota, you get the best deal in town.

Employability Skills 2000+

The Conference Board of Canada
Insights You Can Count On

Please see the OLC to preview the key skills from the Conference Board of Canada's Employability Skills 2000+ covered in this module.

Review of Key Points

1. What are three characteristics of effective reader benefits?
2. Why use reader benefits?
3. How can writers and presenters create reader benefits?
4. What is psychological description?
5. What are intrinsic benefits?
6. How are intrinsic benefits related to the theory of Maslow's hierarchy of needs?
7. What are the ethical considerations of using reader benefits?

Assignments for Module 8

Questions for Critical Thinking

8.1 If you are writing to multiple audiences with different needs, should you include all the reader benefits you can think of in the message?

8.2 Why do reader benefits need to be phrased using you-attitude?

8.3 How do reader benefits help you achieve your goals?

Exercises and Problems

8.4   Identifying and Developing Reader Benefits

Listed here are five things an organization might like its employees to do:

1. Use less paper.
2. Attend a brown bag lunch to discuss ways to improve products or services.
3. Become more physically fit.
4. Volunteer for community organizations.
5. Ease a new hire's transition into the unit.

As your instructor directs,

a. Identify the motives or needs that might be met by each of the activities.
b. Develop each need or motive as a reader benefit in a full paragraph. Use additional paragraphs for the other needs met by the activity. Remember to use you-attitude!

8.5   Identifying Objections and Reader Benefits

Think of an organization you know something about, and answer the following questions for it.

1. Your organization is thinking of creating a training video. What objections might people have? What benefits could videos offer your organization? Which people would be easiest to convince?
2. The advisory council of Nunavut Arctic College recommends that business faculty have three-month internships with local organizations to learn material. What objections might people in your organization have to bringing in faculty interns? What benefits might your organization receive? Which people would be easiest to convince?

3. Your organization is thinking of buying laptop computers for all employees who travel. What fears or objections might people have? What benefits might your organization receive? Which people would be easiest to convince?

As your instructor directs,

a. Share your answers orally with a small group of students.
b. Present your answers in an oral presentation to the class.
c. Email your answers to class members.
d. Write a paragraph developing the best reader benefit you identified. Remember to use you-attitude.

8.6   Identifying and Developing Reader Benefits for Different Audiences

Assume that you want to encourage people to do one of the activities listed below.

1. Hire a personal trainer

   Audiences: Professional athletes
   Busy managers
   Someone trying to lose weight
   Someone making a major lifestyle change after a heart attack

2. Buy a cell phone

   Audiences: People who do a lot of driving
   Older people
   People who do a lot of driving in rural areas
   People who do a lot of flying

3. Get advice about interior decorating

   Audiences: Young people with little money to spend
   Parents with small children
   People upgrading or adding to their furnishings
   Older people moving from single-family homes into smaller apartments or condominiums
   Builders furnishing model homes

4. Get advice on investment strategies

   Audiences: New college or university graduates
   People earning more than $100 000 annually
   People responsible for investing funds for a church, synagogue, or temple
   Parents with small children
   People within 10 years of retirement

5. Garden

   Audiences: People with small children
   People in apartments
   People concerned about reducing pesticides
   People on tight budgets
   Retirees
   Teenagers

6. Buy a laptop computer

   Audiences: College and university students
   Financial planners who visit clients at home
   Sales representatives who travel constantly

People who make PowerPoint™ presentations
Older people

7. Teach adults to read

   Audiences: Retired workers
   Businesspeople
   Students who want to become teachers
   High school, college, and university students
   People concerned about poverty

8. Vacation at a luxury hotel

   Audiences: Stressed-out people who want to relax
   Tourists who like to sightsee and absorb the local culture
   Businesspeople who want to stay in touch with the office even on vacation
   Parents with small children
   Weekend athletes who want to have fun

9. Attend a fantasy sports camp (you pick the sport), playing with and against retired players who provide coaching and advice

10. Attend a health spa where clients get low-fat and low-calorie meals, massages, beauty treatments, and guidance in nutrition and exercise

As your instructor directs,

a. Identify needs that you could meet for the audiences listed here. In addition to needs that several audiences share, identify at least one need that would be particularly important to each group.

b. Identify a product or service that could meet each need.

c. Write a paragraph or two of reader benefits for each product or service. Remember to use you-attitude.

d. Develop one or more of the benefits using psychological description.

Hints:

- For this assignment, you can combine benefits or programs as if a single source offered them all.
- Add specific details about particular sports, cities, tourist attractions, activities, and so on, as material for your description.
- Be sure to move beyond reader benefits to vivid details and sense impressions.
- Phrase your benefits using you-attitude.

Polishing Your Prose

Plurals and Possessives

Singular possessives and plurals sound the same but are spelled differently. A possessive noun will always have an apostrophe. Most possessives of singular nouns are formed by adding's to the word.

Singular Possessive	Plural
company's	companies
computer's	computers
family's	families
job's	jobs
manager's	managers
team's	teams

Since singular possessive nouns and plurals sound the same, you will have to look at the logic of your sentence to choose the right word.

Exercises

Choose the right word in each set of parentheses.

1. Canadian (companies, company's) are competing effectively in the global market.
2. We can move your (families, family's) furniture safely and efficiently.
3. The (managers, manager's) ability to listen is just as important as his or her technical knowledge.
4. A (memos, memo's) style can build goodwill.
5. (Social workers, social worker's) should tell clients about services available in the community.
6. The (companies, company's) benefits plan should be checked periodically to make sure it continues to serve the needs of employees.
7. Information about the new community makes the (families, family's) move easier.
8. The (managers, manager's) all have open-door policies.
9. (Memos, memo's) are sent to other workers in the same organization.
10. Burnout affects a (social workers, social worker's) productivity as well as his or her morale.

Check your answers to the odd-numbered exercises on page 571.

Online Learning Centre

Visit the Online Learning Centre at www.mcgrawhill.ca/olc/locker to access module quizzes, a searchable glossary, résumé and letter templates, additional business writing samples, CBC videos, and other learning and study tools.

CBC Video Case

Visit the Online Learning Centre at www.mcgrawhill.ca/olc/locker to view "Schmoozing," an online CBC Video Case for Unit 2 that discusses the increasing importance of proper professional etiquette.

Case for Communicators

Web-Cast, Get Your Web-Cast Here!

When companies first began establishing themselves on the Internet, online advertising was viewed as a veritable gold mine, an endless source of revenues.

Today, Internet advertising is no longer viewed as a prime revenue generator. As a result, many online businesses have begun charging fees for their products and services. For example, many online newspapers now charge customers a monthly access fee, and even some employment search engines require an upfront payment from job seekers. This has not been an easy pill for online consumers to swallow, however, as they were accustomed to receiving these same benefits and services at no cost.

ABC News finds itself in this new, revenue-starved online environment. ABC News provides high-quality, detailed coverage of national and international news <http://www.abcnews.com>. Its news stories, including numerous video clips, had been available free, but the company has now launched a new online video subscription service, News On Demand, for paying consumers. News On Demand, promoted as "Video news on your schedule," includes audiocasts; video clips from special news segments, such as Exclusives, In the News, and Today's Features; and broadcasts of popular ABC News programs, including *20/20*, *Nightline*, and *World News Tonight*.

One of ABC's primary competitors, CNN, already charges a fee for its video offerings. Will online users be willing to pay the $4.95 subscription fee, particularly when television broadcasts and the text versions of news stories are still available to them free?

Source: Daniel Sorid, "Livewire: Will Consumers Pay for News Web-Casts?" Reuters, August 2, 2002, http://www.freerepublic.com/focus/f-news/726728/posts, retrieved October 19, 2006.

Individual Activity

You work in the marketing department at ABC News and have been selected to work on the advertising campaign being developed to promote News On Demand. ABC News knows that its products are perceived as being high quality, but this will likely not be enough to convince consumers that they should subscribe to the new video service. To achieve this goal, the marketing department has developed a plan to email informational advertisements to prospective subscribers.

The company has gathered email addresses from users who have signed up for News Alerts and other special services. To reach new audiences, the company plans to purchase specialized email databases of potential customers.

Subscribers will receive the following new benefits:

- Personalization tools that will allow customers to create a unique "video experience"
- An increased number of available video clips

- Versions of the video product that would be accessible via hand-held units such as PDAs and cellphones (the company already provides its news stories via these devices)
- Improved video quality and content

Identify the audiences who might respond to these benefits. Consider the following questions:

- What other benefits are inherent to the News On Demand product?
- Who is likely to access these Web-casts and why?
- Why would customers pay for News On Demand rather than a similar product that costs less or is free?
- What types of customers might gain from the product's benefits?
- What feelings or fears might be motivating these users, particularly those who are used to getting this product at no cost?
- What needs may motivate these users?

Identify as many different potential customer groups, or audiences, as you can think of, noting at least one benefit that each group can expect to gain from the News On Demand product.

Give enough detail in your customer descriptions so that the marketing department can use your information to guide its purchase of the email databases.

Group Activity

Plan the email that will be sent out to these potential News On Demand customers. How can you convince ABC News users that they should subscribe to this new offering, in effect paying for a product that they used to receive free?

Combine the results of your list with those of your classmates to generate a comprehensive list of user benefits and potential audiences. Then, as a group, discuss these audiences and the corresponding benefits, and select the best five on which to focus. Together, develop benefits that can be part of the letter to these potential News On Demand subscribers:

- Use you-attitude.
- Include a benefit for each audience.
- Justify negative information, focusing on what the reader can do rather than on limitations.
- Omit unnecessary negative information.
- Talk about the reader, not the company.

Unit 3

Letters, Memos, and Email Messages

"I was hired to say no," says writer/publicist Liza Drozdov, assistant to Mike Holmes, renowned renovation expert and host of *Holmes on Homes*.™ Liza's ability to field the thousands of requests for Mike Holmes' time, and decline most with grace and tact, are part of the creativity she brings to her multifaceted workday.

Liza must say no to over thirty requests a day. People write to request Mike's appearance at their school assembly or their community decorating show. Others write to solicit Mike's endorsement of their products or services. The media want Mike to appear on a television special or to speak on a radio spot. Others write to complain about Home Depot or about Mike's business relationship with Home Depot.

As part of his commitment to getting things done right the first time, Holmes has signed a three-year agreement with Home Depot Canada. Holmes' role is to improve and promote Home Depot Canada's home-install services. His responsibilities include visiting on-site installations across Canada to view work-in-progress, chat with Home Depot customers, listen to complaints, and fix problems. Since Holmes' hands-on involvement, Home Depot Canada claims a 40 percent improvement in home installation orders.

Because of his reputation for integrity, Holmes is very much in demand: people want him associated with their products or services. Liza receives all these requests, identifies those consistent with Holmes' vision and values, and declines the rest. Liza may say no because of time constraints, because the product or service is inappropriate, or because Holmes would not use or endorse the product.

Liza follows the bad news format when responding with no. She thanks writers for their request(s) in the first paragraph of her message. In the second paragraph, she explains how busy Mike Holmes is, and provides specific examples of his current projects. After courteously declining the request, Liza ends positively: "Please try again next year, and thank you for your request."

Liza always wanted to be a writer, and has complemented her B.A. in English with a college course in screenwriting. Her writing credits include two novels, a screenplay, television and radio scripts, and numerous newspaper and magazine articles.

"I always find writing challenging. But my creative writing experience contributes to my critical thinking and flexibility, no question. And working with Mike in an environment of mutual trust means I can write honestly and positively."

PAIBOC

Analysis

1. What are three **purposes** for Liza's writing?

2. What **audience** characteristics are relevant to Liza's choice of message organization?

3. How does Liza de-emphasize the negative in her messages? What **information** is vital in Liza's *no* messages?

MODULE

9 Formats for Hard-copy Letters and Memos

Module Outline

- What are the standard formats for letters?
- What courtesy titles should I use?
- How should I set up memos?

Review of Key Points

Assignments for Module 9

Polishing Your Prose: Making Subjects and Verbs Agree

LEARNING OBJECTIVES

After reading and applying the information in Module 9, you'll be able to demonstrate

Knowledge of

- How purpose and audience determine format
- Basic business formats

Skills to

- Choose and use standard formats
- Use non-sexist courtesy titles
- Create a business image

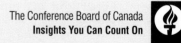

The Conference Board of Canada
Insights You Can Count On

Please see the OLC to preview the key skills from the Conference Board of Canada's Employability Skills 2000+ covered in this module.

When deciding *how* to deliver your message, remember the principle of all good design: *form follows function*. This design principle is essential to communication success: you achieve intended results when you shape your message (form) to meet the needs of your audience and your purpose (function)—(see Figure 9.1, PAIBOC Questions for Analysis).

When you write, the format of your document is as important as the wording. Format—the parts of the document and the way these parts are arranged on the page—provides a **context** for the reader, signalling *what kind* of message the audience is reading. Because text layout and organization establish reader expectation, the way you format your document is an integral part of establishing your credibility as a writer.

Business communication—letters, memos, and reports—conforms to very specific formats.

Letters and memos are both brief business messages, similar in formality, length, style, and organization. **Letters**, however, go to people outside the organization, whereas **memos** are internal messages sent to people within your organization. Because they have a different *audience*, letters and memos differ in format.

What are the standard formats for letters?

Letters are written in block and modified block.

The two most common letter formats are block, sometimes called full block (see Figure 9.2 on page 152), and modified block (see Figure 9.3 on page 153). **Block format** is the format most frequently used for business letters; readers expect it; it can be typed quickly, since everything lines up at the left margin. Speed-readers say that it is easier to read. **Modified block format** creates a visually attractive page by moving the date and signature block into what would otherwise be empty white space. Modified block is a more traditional format, so some readers feel comfortable with it. (See Table 9.1 for a summary of the two formats.)

TABLE 9.1
Differences between Letter Formats

	Block	**Modified Block**
Date and signature block	Lined up at left margin	Lined up 1/2 or 2/3 over to the right
Paragraph indentation	None	Optional
Subject line	Optional	Rare

Block and modified block business letters share many elements:

- Organizations include their return address in their letterhead.
- Written documentation is for the record, so the date is essential.
- Readers are addressed by name in the salutation.
- Subject and reference lines direct readers' attention to your purpose.
- A standard complimentary close comes before your signature.
- Correct punctuation is essential for credibility.
- Continuation pages maintain coherence.
- "Enclosure" tells the reader that you have included additional material, like a duplicated document or a résumé.

The examples of the formats in Figures 9.2 and 9.3 show one-page letters on company letterhead. **Letterhead** is preprinted stationery with the organization's name, logo, address,

FIGURE 9.2
Block Format on Letterhead (mixed punctuation; collection letter)

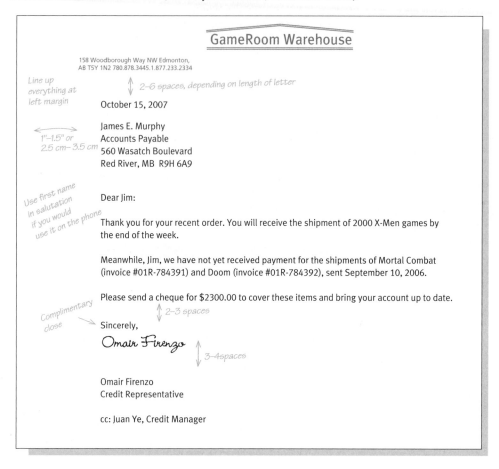

and phone number. Figure 9.4 on page 154 shows how to set up modified block form at when you do not have letterhead. (It is also acceptable to use block format without letterhead.)

When your letter runs two or more pages, use a **continuation heading** on the second page to identify it. Putting the reader's name helps the writer, who may be printing out many letters at a time, to make sure the right second page gets in the envelope. Note that even when the signature block is on the second page, it is still lined up with the date.

Reader's Name
Date
Page Number

or

| Reader's Name | Page Number | Date |

FIGURE 9.3
Indented Format on Letterhead (mixed punctuation; employee evaluation letter)

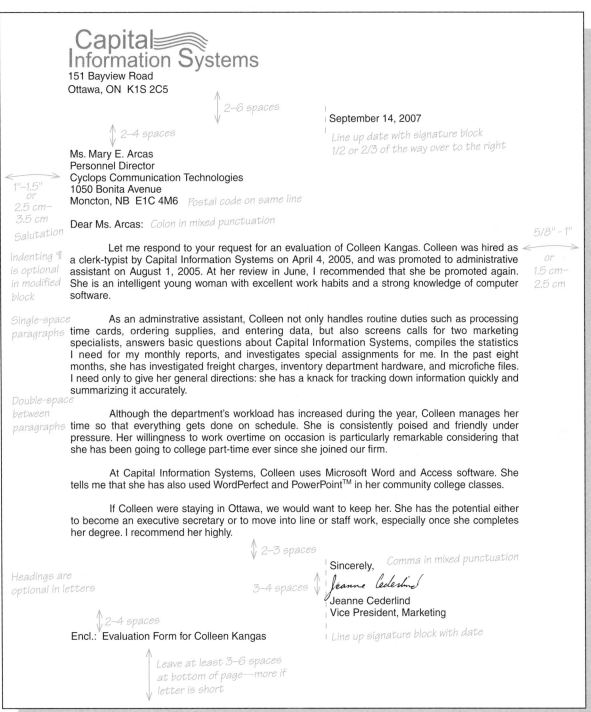

Capital Information Systems
151 Bayview Road
Ottawa, ON K1S 2C5

2–6 spaces

2–4 spaces

September 14, 2007
Line up date with signature block
1/2 or 2/3 of the way over to the right

Ms. Mary E. Arcas
Personnel Director
Cyclops Communication Technologies
1050 Bonita Avenue
Moncton, NB E1C 4M6   *Postal code on same line*

1"–1.5" or 2.5 cm– 3.5 cm

Salutation

Dear Ms. Arcas: *Colon in mixed punctuation*

Indenting ¶ is optional in modified block

5/8" - 1" or 1.5 cm– 2.5 cm

    Let me respond to your request for an evaluation of Colleen Kangas. Colleen was hired as a clerk-typist by Capital Information Systems on April 4, 2005, and was promoted to administrative assistant on August 1, 2005. At her review in June, I recommended that she be promoted again. She is an intelligent young woman with excellent work habits and a strong knowledge of computer software.

Single-space paragraphs

    As an adminstrative assistant, Colleen not only handles routine duties such as processing time cards, ordering supplies, and entering data, but also screens calls for two marketing specialists, answers basic questions about Capital Information Systems, compiles the statistics I need for my monthly reports, and investigates special assignments for me. In the past eight months, she has investigated freight charges, inventory department hardware, and microfiche files. I need only to give her general directions: she has a knack for tracking down information quickly and summarizing it accurately.

Double-space between paragraphs

    Although the department's workload has increased during the year, Colleen manages her time so that everything gets done on schedule. She is consistently poised and friendly under pressure. Her willingness to work overtime on occasion is particularly remarkable considering that she has been going to college part-time ever since she joined our firm.

    At Capital Information Systems, Colleen uses Microsoft Word and Access software. She tells me that she has also used WordPerfect and PowerPoint™ in her community college classes.

    If Colleen were staying in Ottawa, we would want to keep her. She has the potential either to become an executive secretary or to move into line or staff work, especially once she completes her degree. I recommend her highly.

2–3 spaces

Sincerely,   *Comma in mixed punctuation*

Headings are optional in letters

3–4 spaces

Jeanne Cederlind
Jeanne Cederlind
Vice President, Marketing

Line up signature block with date

2–4 spaces

Encl.: Evaluation Form for Colleen Kangas

Leave at least 3–6 spaces at bottom of page—more if letter is short

FIGURE 9.4
Modified Block Format without Letterhead (open punctuation; claim letter)

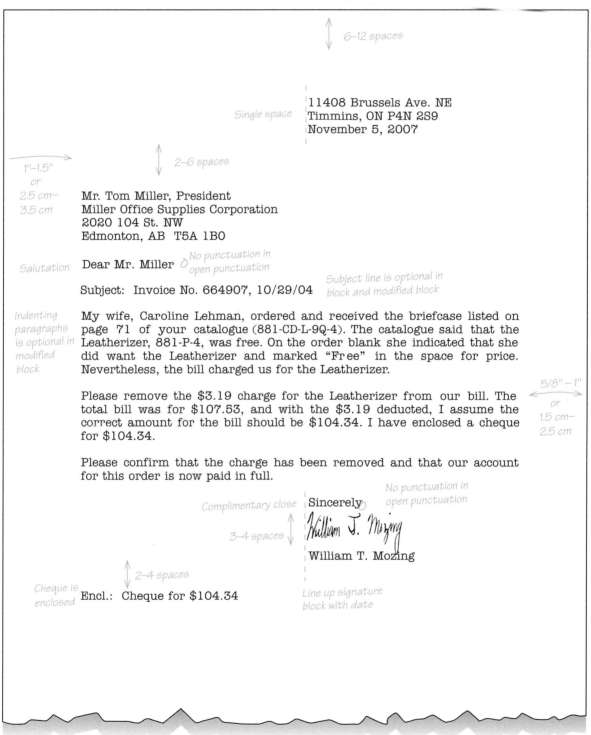

6–12 spaces

Single space

11408 Brussels Ave. NE
Timmins, ON P4N 2S9
November 5, 2007

1"–1.5"
or
2.5 cm–
3.5 cm

2–6 spaces

Mr. Tom Miller, President
Miller Office Supplies Corporation
2020 104 St. NW
Edmonton, AB T5A 1B0

Salutation   Dear Mr. Miller   No punctuation in
open punctuation

Subject: Invoice No. 664907, 10/29/04   Subject line is optional in
block and modified block

Indenting
paragraphs
is optional in
modified
block

My wife, Caroline Lehman, ordered and received the briefcase listed on page 71 of your catalogue (881-CD-L-9Q-4). The catalogue said that the Leatherizer, 881-P-4, was free. On the order blank she indicated that she did want the Leatherizer and marked "Free" in the space for price. Nevertheless, the bill charged us for the Leatherizer.

Please remove the $3.19 charge for the Leatherizer from our bill. The total bill was for $107.53, and with the $3.19 deducted, I assume the correct amount for the bill should be $104.34. I have enclosed a cheque for $104.34.

5/8" – 1"
or
1.5 cm–
2.5 cm

Please confirm that the charge has been removed and that our account for this order is now paid in full.

Complimentary close   Sincerely   No punctuation in
open punctuation

3–4 spaces

William T. Mozing

2–4 spaces

Cheque is
enclosed   Encl.: Cheque for $104.34   Line up signature
block with date

EXPANDING A CRITICAL SKILL

Creating a Business Image

The way you and your documents look affects the way people respond to you and to them. Every organization has a dress code. One young man was upset when an older man told him he should wear wing-tip shoes. He was wearing leather shoes but not the kind that said "I'm promotable" in that workplace. Dress codes are rarely spelled out; the older worker was doing the young man a favour by being direct. If you have a mentor in the organization, ask him or her if there are other ways you can make your appearance even more professional. If you don't have a mentor, look at the people who rank above you. Notice clothing, jewellery, and hairstyles. If you're on a budget, go to stores that sell expensive clothing to check the kind of buttons, the texture

and colours of fabric, the width of lapels and belts. Then go to stores in your price range and choose garments that imitate the details of expensive clothing.

Documents need to look professional, too. Now that most documents are keyed on computers and printed with laser printers, we don't need to worry about whited-out errors or uneven key strokes. We do need to make sure that the ink or toner is printing evenly and that the document uses a standard format.

Some organizations prescribe a standard format for documents. If your organization does, follow it. If you have your choice, use one of the formats in this book. They're widely used in businesses, so they communicate a message of competence.

When a letter runs two or more pages, use letterhead only for page 1. (See Figures 9.5 and 9.6 on pages 156 and 157.) For the remaining pages, use plain paper that matches the letterhead in weight, texture, and colour.

Use the same level of formality in the **salutation**, or greeting, as you would use in talking to that person on the phone: *Dear Ahmed* if you're on a first-name basis, and *Dear Mr. Guten* if you don't know the reader well enough to use a first name.

A **subject line** tells what the letter is about. Subject lines are required in memos; they are optional in letters. If you do use a subject line in your letter, place it after the salutation. Good subject lines are specific, concise, and appropriate for your purposes and the response you expect from your reader.

- When you have good news, put it in the subject line.
- When your information is neutral, summarize it concisely in the subject line.
- When your information is negative, use a negative subject line if the reader may not read the message or needs the information to act, or if the negative is your error.
- When you have a request that will be easy for the reader to grant, put either the subject of the request or a direct question in the subject line.
- When you must persuade a reluctant reader, use a common ground, a reader benefit, or a directed subject line (◀▮▶ Module 13) that makes your stance on the issue clear.

For examples of subject lines in each of these situations, ◀▮▶ Modules 11, 12, and 13.

A **reference line** refers the reader to the number used on previous correspondence, or the order or invoice number that this letter is about. Government organizations, such as the Canada Customs and Revenue Agency, use numbers on every piece of correspondence they send out to quickly find the earlier document to which an incoming letter refers.

Although not every example uses the same devices to provide visual impact, both block and modified block formats use headings, lists, and indented sections (known as telegraphing, highlighting, bulleting or dot-jotting) for emphasis.

SEE THE OLC!

Canada Post: Find Postal Codes and Postal Outlets

FIGURE 9.5

Second Page of a Two-Page Letter, Block Format (mixed or two-point punctuation; informative letter)

45226 Bernard Avenue
Chilliwack, BC V2P 1H1
Adrienne@hotmail.ca

May 4, 2007

2–6 spaces

1" – 1.5"
or
2.5 cm–3.5 cm

Stephanie Voight
Director
Corporate Communications
Spincity Incorporated
715 2nd Avenue East
Moose Jaw, SK S9X 1G9

2–3 spaces

Indenting paragraphs is optional in modified block.

Dear Stephanie Voight: *Colon in mixed punctuation*

Thank you for your prompt response to my inquiry about cooperative opportunities at
Spincity. My academic qualifications and previous work experience meet the criteria you
designated in your letter.

5/8" – 1"
or
1.5 cm–2.5 cm

Academic Qualifications

I have only one semester remaining in the Honours Media and Communications program
at Simon Fraser University. Our rigorous curriculum includes Writing for Publication,

---

Plain paper for page 2

*1/2" – 1" or
1.25 cm–2.5 cm*

Centre

Stephanie Voigt   2   May 4, 2007

Reader's name

*Also OK to line up page number
date at left under reader's name*

My B.A., Journalism from the University of Western Ontario allowed me direct entry into
the fourth year of the program.

Triple space before each new heading

Work Experience   *Bold headings*

Use same margins as p 1.

For the past three summers I have worked in the public relations department of Chang
Design Solutions, writing ad copy and creating media relations kits for this design firm.
As special events coordinator I was responsible for the company's grand opening,
attended by 300 retail managers from Canada, the Northwestern United States and Hong
Kong. I have additional, related experience that I would be happy to discuss with you in
person.

Enclosed you will find my most recent grades transcript and press clippings from the
Chang Design Solutions opening gala.

Please call me at (604) 555-5445, to arrange a meeting time at your convenience.

Sincerely,   *Comma in mixed punctuation*

3–4 spaces

Cedrienne Lee

Headings are optional in letters

Adrienne Lee

2–4 spaces

Encl.: Transcript, press releases

FIGURE 9.6

Second Page of a Two-Page Letter, Modified Block Format (mixed or two-point punctuation; informative and goodwill letter)

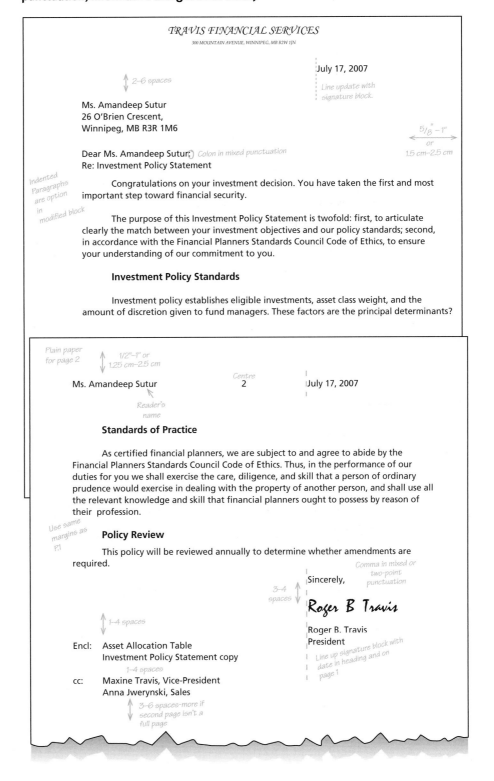

TRAVIS FINANCIAL SERVICES
300 MOUNTAIN AVENUE, WINNIPEG, MB R2W 1JN

July 17, 2007

↕ *2–6 spaces*

Line update with signature block.

Ms. Amandeep Sutur
26 O'Brien Crescent,
Winnipeg, MB R3R 1M6

*5/8" – 1"
or
1.5 cm–2.5 cm*

Dear Ms. Amandeep Sutur: *Colon in mixed punctuation*
Re: Investment Policy Statement

Indented Paragraphs are option in modified block

Congratulations on your investment decision. You have taken the first and most important step toward financial security.

The purpose of this Investment Policy Statement is twofold: first, to articulate clearly the match between your investment objectives and our policy standards; second, in accordance with the Financial Planners Standards Council Code of Ethics, to ensure your understanding of our commitment to you.

Investment Policy Standards

Investment policy establishes eligible investments, asset class weight, and the amount of discretion given to fund managers. These factors are the principal determinants?

Plain paper for page 2

↕ *1/2"–1" or 1.25 cm–2.5 cm*

Ms. Amandeep Sutur   *Centre* 2   July 17, 2007

Reader's name

Standards of Practice

As certified financial planners, we are subject to and agree to abide by the Financial Planners Standards Council Code of Ethics. Thus, in the performance of our duties for you we shall exercise the care, diligence, and skill that a person of ordinary prudence would exercise in dealing with the property of another person, and shall use all the relevant knowledge and skill that financial planners ought to possess by reason of their profession.

Use same margins as P.1

Policy Review

This policy will be reviewed annually to determine whether amendments are required.

Comma in mixed or two-point punctuation

Sincerely,

3–4 spaces

Roger B Travis

Roger B. Travis
President

Line up signature block with date in heading and on page 1

↕ *1–4 spaces*

Encl: Asset Allocation Table
        Investment Policy Statement copy

1–4 spaces

cc: Maxine Travis, Vice-President
        Anna Jwerynski, Sales

↕ *3–6 spaces-more if second page isn't a full page*

Sincerely and *Cordially* are standard **complimentary closes**. When you are writing to people in special groups or to someone who is a friend as well as a business acquaintance, you may want to use a less formal close. Depending on the circumstances, the following informal closes might be acceptable: *Yours for a better environment*, or even *Ciao*.

In **two-point** or **mixed punctuation**, a colon follows the salutation and a comma follows the close. Today, many people use a comma after the salutation to make the letter look like a personal letter rather than a business letter. In **open punctuation**, omit all punctuation after the salutation and the close. Mixed punctuation is traditional. Open punctuation is faster to type.

Set side margins of 2.5 cm to 3.5 cm (1" to 1.5") on the left and 1.5 cm to 2.5 cm (0.75" to 1") on the right. If your letterhead extends all the way across the top of the page, set your margins even with the ends of the letterhead for the most visually pleasing page. The top margin should be three to six lines under the letterhead, or 5 cm (2") down from the top of the page if you aren't using letterhead. If your letter is very short, you may want to use bigger side and top margins so that the letter is centred on the page.

Many letters are accompanied by other documents. Whatever these documents may be—a multi-page report or a two-line note—they are called **enclosures**, since they are enclosed in the envelope. The writer should refer to the enclosures in the body of the letter: "As you can see from my résumé, …" The enclosure line is usually abbreviated: *Encl.* (see Figure 9.4 on page 154). The abbreviation reminds the person who seals the letter to include the enclosure(s).

Sometimes you write to one person but send copies of your letter to other people. If you want the reader to know that other people are getting copies, list their names on the last page. The abbreviation *cc* originally meant *carbon copy* but now means *computer copy*. Other acceptable abbreviations include *pc* for *photocopy* or simply *c* for *copy*. You can also send copies to other people without telling the reader. Such copies are called **blind copies**. Blind copies are not mentioned on the original; they are listed on the copy saved for the file with the abbreviation *bc* preceding the names of people getting these copies.

You do not need to indicate that you have shown a letter to your superior or that you are saving a copy of the letter for your own files. These are standard practices.

Use two capital letters with no punctuation to abbreviate province and state names in letters and memos. See Table 9.2 for a list of **postal service abbreviations**.

■ What courtesy titles should I use?

Research your reader's preference.

Today, most salutations use "Dear *first name last name*." However, some people and many cultures prefer their professional titles: Director Chadraba, President Mauricio. Use *Ms.*, *Mr.*, or *Mrs.* when your audience has signed their correspondence that way.

1. Use professional titles when they're relevant.

> Dr. Kristen Sorenson is our new company physician.
> The Rev. Robert Townsley gave the invocation.

2. If a woman prefers to be addressed as *Mrs.* or *Miss*, rather than *Ms.*, use the title she prefers. (You-attitude ◀▮▶ Module 6 takes precedence over non-sexist language:

FYI

A University of British Columbia long-term study validates the direct correlation between communications skills and salary. For each additional year of education, Canadians earn an additional 8.3 percent, or $2490 in salary, of which $772 is attributed to literacy.

Sources: Statistics Canada, *The Daily*, http://www.statcan.ca/Daily/English/010319/d010319a.htm, retrieved June 27, 2001; *Toronto Star*, Monday, March 19, 2001, A11.

TABLE 9.2
Postal Service Abbreviations for Canadian Provinces, Territories, and U.S. States

Province/Territory Name	Postal Service Abbreviation	State/Territory Name	Postal Service Abbreviation
Alberta	AB	New Jersey	NJ
British Columbia	BC	New Mexico	NM
Manitoba	MB	New York	NY
New Brunswick	NB	North Carolina	NC
Newfoundland and		North Dakota	ND
Labrador	NL	Ohio	OH
Northwest Territories	NT	Oklahoma	OK
Nunavut	NU	Oregon	OR
Nova Scotia	NS	Pennsylvania	PA
Ontario	ON	Rhode Island	RI
Prince Edward Island	PE	South Carolina	SC
Quebec	QC	South Dakota	SD
Saskatchewan	SK	Tennessee	TN
Yukon Territory	YT	Texas	TX
		Utah	UT
		Vermont	VT
		Virginia	VA
State/Territory Name	**Postal Service Abbreviation**	Washington	WA
		West Virginia	WV
Alabama	AL	Wisconsin	WI
Alaska	AK	Wyoming	WY
Arizona	AZ	Guam	GU
Arkansas	AR	Puerto Rico	PR
California	CA	Virgin Islands	VI
Colorado	CO		
Connecticut	CT		
Delaware	DE		
District of Columbia	DC		
Florida	FL		
Georgia	GA		
Hawaii	HI		
Idaho	ID		
Illinois	IL		
Indiana	IN		
Iowa	IA		
Kansas	KS		
Kentucky	KY		
Louisiana	LA		
Maine	ME		
Maryland	MD		
Massachusetts	MA		
Michigan	MI		
Minnesota	MN		
Mississippi	MS		
Missouri	MO		
Montana	MT		
Nebraska	NE		
Nevada	NV		
New Hampshire	NH		

TABLE 9.3
Use Parallel Forms for Names

Not Parallel	Parallel
Members of the committee will be Mr. Jones, Mr. Yacone, and Lisa	Members of the committee will be Mr. Jones, Mr. Yacone, and Ms. Melton or Members of the committee will be Irving, Ted, and Lisa

address the reader as she—or he—prefers to be addressed.) To find out whether a woman prefers a traditional title:

a. Check the signature block in previous correspondence. If a woman types her name as *(Miss) Elaine Anderson* or *(Mrs.) Kay Royster*, use the title she designates.
b. Notice the title a woman uses in introducing herself on the phone. If she says, "This is Robin Stine," use *Dear Robin Stine* when you write to her. If she says, "I'm Mrs. Stine," use the title she specifies.
c. Check your company directory. In some organizations, women who prefer traditional titles list them with their names.
d. When you're writing job letters or other crucial correspondence, call the company and ask the receptionist which title your reader prefers.

Ms. is particularly useful when you do not know a woman's marital status. However, when you know that a woman is married or single, **use courtesy titles only when your audience requests them.**

In addition to using parallel courtesy titles, use parallel forms for names. See Table 9.3.

When You Know the Reader's Name but Not the Gender

When you know your reader's name but not the gender, you can do two things:

1. Call the company and ask the receptionist.
2. Use the reader's full name in the salutation.

Dear Chris Crowell:
Dear J. C. Meath:

When You Know Neither the Reader's Name Nor Gender

When you know neither the reader's name nor gender, you have four options:

1. Use an attention line:

Attention: Customer Service
Attention: Human Resources
Attention: Office of the Registrar

FYI

The word "dear" in the salutation of a letter or email reflects the sender's knowledge of standard business convention rather than the writer's relationship to the reader. "The word *deore* or *diore* in Old English meant glorious, honourable, noble, worthy. Initially an adjective, it was used throughout the thirteenth, fourteenth, and fifteenth centuries when addressing somebody … . Since the seventeenth century, 'dear' has been used as a polite term of addressing an equal when writing to them."

Source: Laurence Urdang, editor, *Verbatim*, quoted in *The Daily Mail*, cited by Michael Kesterton, "Social Studies," *The Globe and Mail*, August 28, 2001, p. A22.

2. Use the reader's position or job title:

> Dear Loan Officer:
> Attention: Registrar

3. Use a general group to which your reader belongs:

> Dear Investor:
> Attention: Admissions Committee

4. Omit the salutation and use a subject line in its place:

> Subject: Recommendation for Ben Wandell

Using **bolded** attention and subject lines is acceptable.

◼ How should I set up hard-copy memos?

The standard memo uses block format but has no salutation, close, or signature.

Memos are written messages sent within an organization; they are formatted differently from letters, which are messages sent to audiences outside the company. Memos omit both the salutation and the close. Memos never indent paragraphs. Subject lines are required; headings are optional. Each heading must cover all the information until the next heading. Never use a separate heading for the first paragraph.

Figures 9.7 and 9.8 illustrate the standard memo format typed on a plain sheet of paper. Note that the first letters of the reader's name, the writer's name, and the subject phrase are lined up vertically. Note also that memos are usually initialled beside the To/From block. Initialling tells the reader that the memo's writer takes responsibility for the document.

Some organizations have special letterhead for memos. When *Date/To/From/Subject* are already printed on the form, the date, writer's and reader's names, and subject may be set at the main margin to save typing time. (See Figure 9.8 on page 163.)

Some organizations alter the order of items in the *Date/To/From/Subject* block. Some organizations ask employees to sign memos rather than simply initialling them. The signature goes below the last line of the memo, starting halfway over on the page, and prevents anyone adding unauthorized information.

If the memo runs two pages or more, use a heading at the top of the second and subsequent pages (see Figure 9.9 on page 164). Since many of your memos go to the same people, putting a brief version of the subject line will be more helpful than just using "All Employees."

> Brief Subject Line
> Date
> Page Number

or

> Brief Subject Line   Page Number   Date

FIGURE 9.7
Memo Format (on plain paper; analytical proposal/short report)

Everything lined up at left

2–4 spaces

Double space

1" – 1.5"

or

2.5 cm–3.5 cm

No heading for ¶ 1

October 8, 2007   *Plain paper*

Line up

To: Annette T. Califero

From: Kyle B. Abrams **KBA**   *Writer's initials added in ink*

Subject: A Low-Cost Way to Reduce Energy Use   *Capitalize first letter of each major word in subject line*

As you requested, I've investigated low-cost ways to reduce our energy use. Reducing the building temperature on weekends is a change that we could make immediately, that would cost nothing, and that would cut our energy use by about 6 percent.

5/8" – 1"

or

1.5 cm–2.5 cm

Triple space before each new heading

The Energy Savings from a Lower Weekend Temperature   *Bold headings*

Single-space paragraphs; double-space between paragraphs

Lowering the temperature from 20° C to 15.5° C from 8 p.m. Friday evening to 4 a.m. Monday morning could cut our total consumption by 6 percent. It is not feasible to lower the temperature on weeknights because many staff members work late; the cleaning crew is also on duty from 6 p.m. to midnight. Turning the temperature down for only four hours would not result in a significant heat saving.

Turning the heat back up at 4 a.m. on Mondays will allow the building temperature to be back to 20° C by 9 a.m. Our furnace already has computerized controls which can be set to automatically lower and raise the temperature.

Triple space

How a Lower Temperature Would Affect Employees   *Capitalize first letter of each major word of heading*

A survey of employees shows that only seven people use the building every weekend or almost every weekend. Eighteen percent of our staff have worked at least one weekend day in the last two months; 52 percent say they "occasionally" come in on weekends.

Do not indent paragraphs

People who come in for an hour or less on weekends could cope with the lower temperature just by wearing warm clothes. However, most people would find 15.5° C too cool for extended work. Employees who work regularly on weekends might want to install space heaters.

Action Needed to Implement the Change

Would you also like me to check into the cost of buying a dozen portable space heaters? Providing them would allow us to choose units that our wiring can handle and would be a nice gesture toward employees who give up their weekends to work. I could have a report to you in two weeks.

We can begin saving energy immediately. Just authorize the lower temperature, and I'll see that the controls are reset for this weekend.

Memos are initialled by To/From/Subject block—no signature   *Headings are optional in memos*

FIGURE 9.8
Memo Format (on memo letterhead; good news)

Kimball,
Walls, and
Morganstern

Date: March 15, 2007   *Line up horizontally with printed Date/To/From/Subject*

To: Annette T. Califero

From: Kyle B. Abrams *KBA*   *Writer's initials added in ink*

Capitalize first letter of each major word in subject line

Subject: The Effectiveness of Reducing Building Temperatures on Weekends

Triple space

Margin lined up with items in To/From/Subject block to save typing time

Reducing the building temperature to 20° C on weekends has cut energy use by 4 percent compared to last year's use from December to February and has saved our firm $22 000.

This savings is particularly remarkable when you consider that this winter has been colder than last year's, so more heat would have been needed to maintain the same temperature.

5/8" – 1" or 1.6 cm–2.5 cm

Fewer people have worked weekends during the past three months than during the preceding three months, but snow and bad driving conditions may have had more to do with keeping people home than the fear of being cold. Five of the 12 space heaters we bought have been checked out on an average weekend. On one weekend, all 12 were in use and some people shared their offices so that everyone could be in a room with a space heater.

Fully 92 percent of our employees support the lower temperature. I recommend that we continue turning down the heat on weekends through the remainder of the heating season and that we resume the practice when the heat is turned on next fall.

Headings are optional in memos

FIGURE 9.9
Option 2 for Page 2 of a Memo (analytical proposal/short report)

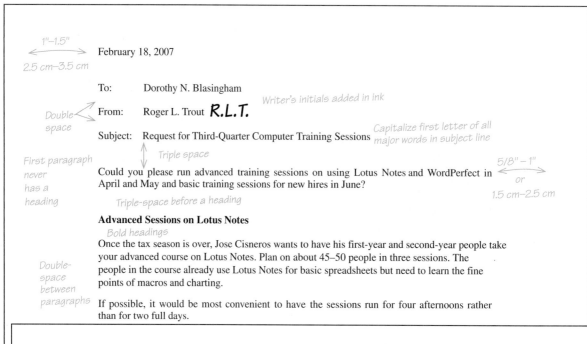

February 18, 2007

1"–1.5"
2.5 cm–3.5 cm

To: Dorothy N. Blasingham

Double space

From: Roger L. Trout **R.L.T.**

Writer's initials added in ink

Subject: Request for Third-Quarter Computer Training Sessions

Capitalize first letter of all major words in subject line

First paragraph never has a heading

Triple space

Could you please run advanced training sessions on using Lotus Notes and WordPerfect in April and May and basic training sessions for new hires in June?

5/8" – 1"
or
1.5 cm–2.5 cm

Triple-space before a heading

Advanced Sessions on Lotus Notes

Bold headings

Once the tax season is over, Jose Cisneros wants to have his first-year and second-year people take your advanced course on Lotus Notes. Plan on about 45–50 people in three sessions. The people in the course already use Lotus Notes for basic spreadsheets but need to learn the fine points of macros and charting.

Double-space between paragraphs

If possible, it would be most convenient to have the sessions run for four afternoons rather than for two full days.

Plain paper for page 2

1/2"–1"
or
1.25 cm–2.5 cm

Dorothy N. Blasingham

Brief subject line or reader's name

2

Page number

February 18, 2007

Also OK to line up page number, date at left under reader's name

Same margins as p 1.

before the summer vacation season begins.

Orientation for New Hires

Capitalize first letter of all major words in heading

With a total of 16 full-time and 34 part-time people being hired either for summer or permanent work, we'll need at least two and perhaps three orientation sessions. We'd like to hold these the first, second, and third weeks in June. By May 1, we should know how many people will be in each training session.

Would you be free to conduct training sessions on how to use our computers on June 8, June 15, and June 22? If we need only two dates, we'll use June 8 and June 15, but please block off the 22nd too, in case we need a third session.

Triple-space before a heading

Request for Confirmation

Let me know whether you're free on these dates in June, and which dates you'd prefer for the sessions on Lotus Notes and WordPerfect. If you'll let me know by February 25, we can get information out to participants in plenty of time for the sessions.

Thanks!

Memos are initialed by To/From/Subject block

Headings are optional in memos

Employability Skills 2000+

The Conference Board of Canada
Insights You Can Count On

Please see the OLC to preview the key skills from the Conference Board of Canada's Employability Skills 2000+ covered in this module.

Review of Key Points

1. How can PAIBOC analysis help you decide whether to send a letter or a memo?
2. What are the two standard letter formats?
3. What are the differences between the two letter formats?

4. How do you decide whether or not to use courtesy titles?
5. What is the standard memo format?
6. Where do you sign a memo?

Assignments for Module 9

Questions for Critical Thinking

9.1 Which letter format do you prefer? Why?
9.2 What are the advantages in telling your reader who is getting copies of your message?

9.3 Does following a standard format show a lack of originality and creativity?

Exercises and Problems

9.4 Formatting a Message

Correct the format errors in the following message.

March 3, 2007

To: Professor Hughes
From: Adele Cameron
Subject: My Writing Progress

Overview

Thank you for the opportunity to review my writing progress so far. Because I have been using a reader to provide specific feedback, my writing has improved since the beginning of the semester.

Writing Strategies

When you encouraged us to find someone to read and respond to our writing, I asked my older brother, a recent university graduate, to do so. He and I sit together while he reads the first drafts of my writing assignments. He gives me specific feedback on my organization, content, word choice and transitions.

Initially I felt very awkward and defensive when Daniel was reading my papers. He often stopped reading to ask me to clarify an argument, or to explain the meaning of a sentence that seemed pretty obvious to me. After a few such meetings, however, I found that my brother's feedback was forcing me to examine my writing in a new way. I was learning to move from the role of writer to the role of reader, in order to assess whether what I was trying to say made sense from the reader's point of view. Now I reread my papers from the reader's perspective.

Editing Strategies

Daniel also critiqued my grammar and punctuation, which have never been strong. After watching and listening to him, I was able to make some of these corrections myself. Although by no means an expert, I am learning how to edit and proof read my own work.

Thank you very much for the suggestion about using a reader. This practice, and my patient brother's assistance, has helped me to improve my writing skills.

Sincerely,

Adele Cameron

9.5   Analyzing and Revising Message Formats

As consumers, employees and/or students, we all receive hard-copy letters and memos regularly. Bring in two letters and two memos you have received recently.

As your instructor directs,

a. Share your examples with a small group of students.

b. Identify the formats the writers are using.
c. Identify any format errors.
d. Be prepared to present your results to the rest of the class.

Polishing Your Prose

Making Subjects and Verbs Agree

Make sure the subjects and verbs in your sentences agree. Subjects and verbs agree when they are both singular or both plural:

Correct: The laser printer no longer works.

Correct: The broken laser printers are in the storeroom.

Often, subject-verb errors occur when other words come between the subject and verb. Learn to correct errors by looking for the subject—who or what is doing the principal action—and the verb—the action itself:

Correct: A team of marketing researchers is reviewing our promotional campaign.

Correct: The four-colour brochures, which cost about $1000 to print and ship, were sent to our Vancouver affiliate.

Canadian and American usage treats company names and the words *company* and *government* as singular nouns. In England and countries adopting the British system, these nouns are plural:

Correct: Clarica is headquartered in Water-
(Canada)   loo, Ontario.

Correct: National Insurance is head-
(U.S.)   quartered in Columbus, Ohio.

Correct: Loyds of London are headquartered
(U.K.)   in London.

Use a plural verb when two or more singular subjects are joined by *and*.

Correct: Mr. Simmens, Ms. Lopez, and Mr. Yee were in Seoul for a meeting last week.

Use a singular verb when two or more singular subjects are joined by *or, nor,* or *but*.

Correct: Neither Dr. Hroscoe nor Mr. Jamieson is in today.

When the sentence begins with *There* or *Here*, make the verb agree with the subject that follows the verb:

Correct: There were blank pages in the fax we received.

Correct: Here is the information on the job candidate you requested.

Some words that end in *s* are considered singular and require singular verbs:

Correct: The World Series features advertisements of our product in the stadium.

When you encounter situations that don't seem to fit the rule, or when following the rules produces an awkward sentence, rewrite the sentence to avoid the problem:

Problematic: The grant coordinator in addition to the awarding agency (is, are?) happy with the latest proposal we submitted.

Better: The grant coordinator and the awarding agency are happy with the latest proposal we submitted.

Exercises

Choose the correct verb or rewrite the sentence.

1. Each of us (is, are) entitled to company health care benefits.
2. KPMG, a leading management consulting firm, (operate, operates) in nine Canadian provinces.
3. The price of our stocks (is, are) increasing.
4. Every project team (train, trains) for at least 90 days before projects (is, are) started.
5. We (order, orders) a dozen new toner cartridges each month.
6. A series of meetings (is, are) planned for February.
7. Ms. Schiff and her assistant (is, are) attending the conference in Halifax.
8. Make it a point to (has, have) your report ready by Monday.
9. Professor Beauparlant, Mr. Kincaid, and Ms. Carolla (is, are) on the guest list and (plan, plans) to sit at the same table.
10. The offices in Buenos Aries (report, reports) a 19 percent increase in employee turnover for the past year.

Check your answers to the odd-numbered exercises on page 572.

Online Learning Centre

Visit the Online Learning Centre at www.mcgrawhill.ca/olc/locker to access module quizzes, a searchable glossary, résumé and letter templates, additional business writing samples, CBC videos, and other learning and study tools.

10 Email Messages

Module Outline

- What do I need to know about email messages?
- How should I set up email messages?
- What should I know about content and tone?
- Do I write email messages the same way I write paper messages?
- What kinds of subject lines should I use?
- What netiquette rules should I follow?
- How and when should I use attachments?

Review of Key Points

Assignments for Module 10

Polishing Your Prose: Making Nouns and Pronouns Agree

LEARNING OBJECTIVES

After reading and applying the information in Module 10, you'll be able to demonstrate

Knowledge of
- Current formats for business email
- SMART goals

Skills to
- Write effective business emails
- Apply proven time management techniques

The Conference Board of Canada
Insights You Can Count On

Please see the OLC to preview the key skills from the Conference Board of Canada's Employability Skills 2000+ covered in this module.

In 1971, computer engineer Ray Tomlinson sent messages between computers as part of his research on computer networking.[1]

Over the next 15 years, the applications of Tomlinson's research would transform communications. Today, the ubiquitous email has influenced even business discourse, that most conservative of human expression.

What do I need to know about email messages?

While formats and language continue to evolve, one reality is constant: electronic privacy does not exist.

York University professor Heather Lotherington, a multitechnological literacy expert, claims that as soon as people could chat in real time (what Lotherington calls "synchronous messages"), they developed a code to convey meaning instantaneously. This systematic email code includes such symbols as sound-based abbreviations (c u ltr), emoticons, sentence fragments, full-caps (for shouting) and cyber names.[2]

Despite the online language evolution, however, writing business email memos and letters is as labour-intensive as every composition, and a perilous activity for the uninformed.

FIGURE 10.2
Email Message with Hyperlink and Emoticon

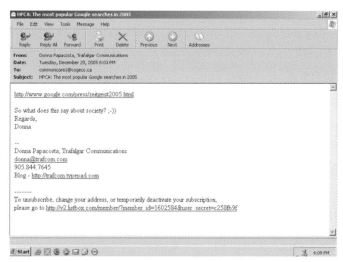

You need to know that

- Grammar, spelling, punctuation, and usage matter unless your emails are to family or friends
- Abbreviations (e.g., lol) are inappropriate in business communications
- Organizations can trace and monitor all employee electronic communications—from email messages to online searches and surfing
- Your emails have the same legal and ethical accountability as hard-copy documents do
- When you hit SEND, you publish, and your message can be sent to anyone, anywhere, in seconds

Even personal BlackBerry conversations are in the public domain, as the recent court case between CIBC and Genuity Capital Markets Technology demonstrated. CIBC was able to trace the BlackBerry users' private, PIN-to-PIN messages to use as evidence.[3]

FIGURE 10.3
Microsoft Word Letter and Memo Templates

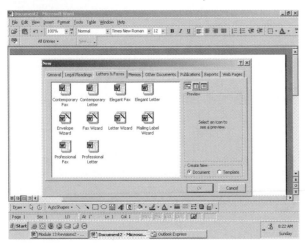

How should I set up email messages?

Follow organizational formats, or use a software template.

Many organizations use boilerplate formats for their electronic and hard-copy documents. If you are unsure about how to format a document, research the expectations of your discourse community (◀️▶️ Module 2).

Other resources include software and email programs that provide formats you can customize.

FIGURE 10.4
Outlook Express Email Memo Template

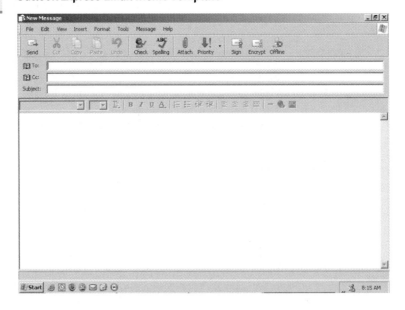

FIGURE 10.5
A Basic Email Message in Eudora (direct request)

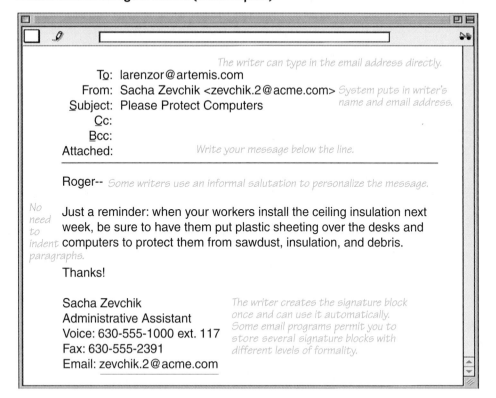

Although the email screen has a "To" line (as do memos), some writers still use an informal salutation, as in Figure 10.5. The writer in Figure 10.5 ends the message with a signature block. These conventions depend on context: your relations to the reader and the assumptions and expectations of your company's culture. (See Figure 10.1, PAIBOC analysis.)

You can store a signature block in the email program and set the program to insert the signature block automatically. In contrast, the writer in Figure 10.6 omits both the salutation and his name. When you send a message to an individual or a group you have set up, the "From:" line will have your name and email address. If you post a message to an email group someone else has set up, be sure to give at least your name and email address at the end of your message, as some programs strip out identifying information when they process messages.

When you hit "reply," the email program automatically uses "Re:" (Latin for *about*) and the previous subject. You may want to change the subject line to make it more appropriate for your message. If you do change the subject line, include the original one in parentheses in case the reader sorts messages by thread. If you create a new subject line, delete the word "Re:"

If you prepare your document in a word processor, use 5 ml (2ʺ) side margins to create short line lengths. If the line lengths are too long, they'll produce awkward line breaks. Use two- or three-space tab settings to minimize the wasted space on the screen.

FIGURE 10.6

An Email Message with an Attachment (direct request)

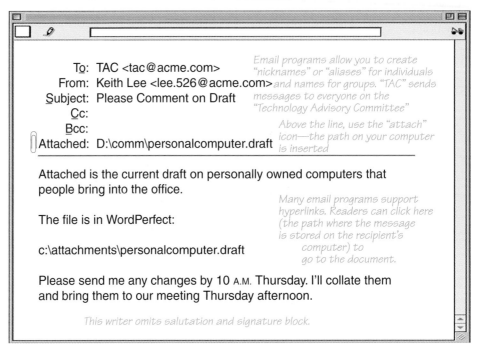

To: TAC <tac@acme.com>
From: Keith Lee <lee.526@acme.com>
Subject: Please Comment on Draft
Cc:
Bcc:
Attached: D:\comm\personalcomputer.draft

Email programs allow you to create "nicknames" or "aliases" for individuals and names for groups. "TAC" sends messages to everyone on the "Technology Advisory Committee"

Above the line, use the "attach" icon—the path on your computer is inserted

Attached is the current draft on personally owned computers that people bring into the office.

The file is in WordPerfect:

Many email programs support hyperlinks. Readers can click here (the path where the message is stored on the recipient's computer) to go to the document.

c:\attachments\personalcomputer.draft

Please send me any changes by 10 A.M. Thursday. I'll collate them and bring them to our meeting Thursday afternoon.

This writer omits salutation and signature block.

What should I know about content and tone?

Use PAIBOC analysis, and act ethically.

FYI

Professor William Haskell of Stanford University calculates that workers who spend 2.5 minutes an hour each day sending email to co-workers instead of walking over to talk with them will gain 1.1 lb. (0.5 kg) of body fat a year.

Source: "Raw Data," Wired, May 1999, 21, http://www.wired.com/wired/archive/7.05/mustread.html?pg=21, retrieved October 19, 2006.

While experts like Heather Lotherington agree that technology will continue to change how, what, and when we communicate, standards for business messages remain relatively rigid. When composing email messages, consider your audience carefully. Humour, sarcasm, jokes, and chain letters do not travel well: some recipients find them a waste of time and resources. Indeed, many employees feel overwhelmed by the amount of email they receive daily.[4]

Remember to

- **Format attachments appropriately:** attached documents (letter, resumes, reports, invoices, etc.) should follow standard paper formats.
- **Compose and copy with discretion:** in email memos, **cc** denotes computer copies; your recipient can see the names of other people getting the message. **Bcc** denotes blind computer copies; the recipient does not see the names of these people. Copying your supervisor and/or other people unnecessarily is inflammatory and unethical.
- **Count to ten before you SEND:** when you write, you are on the record. Emails sent in anger, to the wrong person, or to everyone on a list can damage your relationships, your reputation, or your future.

Do I write email messages the same way I write paper messages?

Because of the limitations of the medium, deliver sensitive messages in person whenever possible.

Negative and persuasive messages are more efficiently delivered face to face, because the important nuances added through non-verbal communication speak volumes and can save time and energy. If, however, you must deliver negative information electronically, write so that it's easy for readers to understand and act on the information quickly.

Writing Positive and Informative Email Messages

Email is especially appropriate for positive and informative messages. Figures 10.5 and 10.6 are examples of an informative message and a request for feedback on a document, respectively.

Writing Negative Email Messages

Major negatives, such as firing someone, must be delivered in person, not by email. But email is appropriate for many less serious negatives.

Never send email messages when you're angry. If a message infuriates you, wait till you're calmer before you reply—even then, reply only if you must. Writers using email are much less inhibited than they would be on paper or in person, sending insults, swearing, name-calling, and making hostile statements.[5] **Flaming** is the name given to this behaviour. Flaming reflects badly on the sender: it does not make you look like a mature, level-headed candidate for bigger things. And since employers have the right to read all email, flaming—particularly if directed at co-workers, regulators, suppliers, or customers—could cause an employee to be fired.

In the body of the email message, give a reason only if it is watertight and reflects well on the organization. Give an alternative, if one exists.

Edit and proofread your message carefully. An easy way for an angry reader to strike back is to attack typos or other errors.

Remember that email messages, like any written text, can become relevant documents in lawsuits. When a negative email is hard to write, you may want to compose it offline so that you can revise and even get feedback before you send the message.

Technology has so expanded working hours that people need personal service experts to manage everything from their in-boxes to their clutter. Home and office professional organizer Maxine Henry (www.maxinehenry.com) earns $60 hourly helping people get organized so they can increase their productivity.[6]

■ Writing Persuasive Email Messages

When you ask for something small or for something that it is part of the reader's job duties to provide, your request can be straightforward. (See Figure 10.5.)

- In the body of the message, give people all the information they need to act.
- At the end of the message, ask for the action you want. Make the action as easy as possible, and specify when you need a response. You may want an immediate response now ("Let me know asap whether you can write a story for the newsletter so that I can save the space") and a fuller one later ("we'll need the text by March 4").

When you ask for something big or something that is not a regular part of that person's duties, the first paragraph must not only specify the request but also make the reader view it positively. Use the second paragraph to provide an overview of the evidence that the rest of the message will provide: "Here's why we should do this. Let me describe the project. Then, if you're willing to be part of it, I'll send you a copy of the proposal." Use audience analysis (◀▶ Module 2 pp. 29–38) to find a reason to do as you ask that the reader will find convincing. Everyone is busy, so you need to make the reader want to do as you ask. Be sure to provide complete information that the reader will need to act on your request. Ask for the action you want.

Major requests that require changes in values, culture, or lifestyles should not be made in email messages.

■ What kinds of subject lines should I use for email messages?

Use subject lines that are specific, concise, and catchy.

Subject lines in email are even more important than those in letters and memos because it's so easy for the recipient to hit the delete key. Subject lines must be specific, concise, and catchy. Many email users get so many messages that they don't bother reading messages if they don't recognize the sender or if the subject doesn't catch their interest.

Try to keep the subject line short. If that's difficult, put the most important part into the first few words because some email programs only show the first 28 characters of the subject line.

If your message is very short, you may be able to put it in the subject line. "EOM" (end of message) tells your reader there is no additional information in the body of the message.

> Subject: Will Attend 3:00 P.M. Meeting EOM

■ Subject Lines for Informative and Positive Email Messages

If you have good news to convey, be sure it's in the subject line. Be as brief as you can.

The following subject lines would be acceptable for informative and good news email messages:

> Subject: Travel Plans for Sales Meeting
> Subject: Your Proposal Accepted
> Subject: Reduced Prices During February

SEE THE OLC!

Finding Email Addresses

When you reply to a message, the email system automatically creates a subject line "Re: [subject line of message to which you are responding]." If the subject line is appropriate, that's fine. If it isn't appropriate, create a new subject line with the old one in parentheses. And if a series of messages arises, create a new subject line with the old one in parentheses. "Re: Re: Re: Re: Question" is not an effective subject line.

FYI

Email Acronyms

AFAIK	As far as I know
ASAP	As soon as possible
BTW	By the way
EOM	End of message
FAQ	Frequently asked questions
FYI	For your information
IMHO	In my humble opinion
TMOT	Trust me on this

■ Subject Lines for Negative Email Messages

When you say "no" to an email request, just hit "Reply" and use "Re:" plus whatever the original subject line was for your response. When you write a new message, you will have to decide whether to use the negative in the subject line. The subject line should contain the negative in three situations:

* The negative is serious. Many people do not read all their email messages. A neutral subject line may lead the reader to ignore the message.
* The reader needs the information to make a decision or act.
* You report your own errors (as opposed to the reader's).

The following would be acceptable subject lines in email messages:

> Subject: We Lost Lick's Account
> Subject: Power to Be Out Sunday, March 12
> Subject: Error in Survey Data Summary

In other situations, a neutral subject line is appropriate.

> Subject: Results of 360° Performance Appraisals

INSTANT REPLAY

Keep Subject Lines Short

Try to keep the subject line short. If that's difficult, put the most important part into the first few words because some email programs only show the first 28 characters of the subject line.

■ Subject Lines for Persuasive Email Messages

The subject line of a persuasive email message should make it clear that you're asking for something. If you're sure that the reader will read the message, something as vague as "Request" may work. Most of the time, it's better to be more specific.

> Subject: Move Meeting to Tuesday?
> Subject: Need an Extension
> Subject: Want You for United Way Campaign

INSTANT REPLAY

Subject Lines for Persuasive Emails

The subject line of a persuasive email message should make it clear that you're asking for something.

■ What "netiquette" rules should I follow?

Follow these guidelines to be a good netizen.

* Use audience-appropriate language, structure, and organization: once you hit "Send," you are published, potentially worldwide.
* Avoid using full caps; use mixed case in subject lines and use full caps only if you must emphasize a single word or two. Putting the whole message in full caps is considered shouting.
* Never send angry messages by email. If you have a conflict with someone, work it out face to face, not electronically.

EXPANDING A CRITICAL SKILL

Managing Your Time

Do you need more time? Welcome to the club! Although researchers claim that we have more leisure hours than we did 20 years ago, most of us feel more overworked than ever. And the number of things you'll need to do will only increase as you assume more job responsibilities.

The secret is to manage yourself, so that you feel more in control.

The first step in managing your time is to establish short- and long-term **SMART** goals, goals that describe your Specific, Measurable, Achievable, Realistic "to do's" in a definite Timeframe. "Starting today, I'm going to reserve a half-hour a day to read the paper, every day," is an example of a SMART goal. Identify your immediate and long-term SMART goals, write them down, and cross your daily SMART goals off as you achieve them. Following this process keeps you focused and positive.

As an immediate SMART time management goal, divide projects or incoming mail into three piles (real or imaginary). Put urgent items in the A pile, important items in the B pile, and other items in the C pile. Do the A items first. Most people find that they never get to their C piles.

At the end of the day, make a list of the two most important things you need to do the next day—this list is your SMART goal record—and leave the paper where you'll see it when you start work the next morning.

Initiate a systematic problem-solving approach to understanding how you currently manage yourself:

1. For at least a week, log how you spend your time. Record what you're doing in 15-minute intervals.

2. Analyze your log to identify patterns, time obligations, time wasters, and frustrations. You may be surprised to find how much time you spend playing computer games. Or you may discover that answering email takes an hour every morning—not the five minutes or so that you'd estimated.

3. Clarify your SMART goals. What do you want to accomplish on the job and in your personal life? What strategies or steps (for example, taking a course, learning a new skill, or sending out job applications) will you need to do to reach your goals?

4. Set short-term SMART priorities. For the next month, what do you need to accomplish? In addition to goals for school and work, think also about building relationships, meeting personal obligations, and finding time to plan, to relax, and to think.

5. Ask for help or negotiate compromises. Maybe you and another parent can share baby-sitting so that you each have some time to yourselves. If your responsibilities at work are impossible, talk to your supervisor to see whether some of your duties can be transferred to someone else or whether you should stop trying to be excellent and settle for "good enough." You won't be willing or able to eliminate all your obligations, but sometimes dropping just one or two responsibilities can really help.

6. Schedule your day to reflect your priorities. You don't necessarily have to work on every goal every day, but each goal should appear on your schedule at least three times a week. Schedule some time for yourself, too.

7. Evaluate your new use of time. Are you meeting more of your goals? Are you feeling less stressed? If not, go back to step 1 and analyze more patterns, obligations, time wasters, and frustrations to see how you can make the best use of the time you have.

- Send people only messages they need. Send copies to your boss or CEO only if he or she has asked you to.
- Find out how your recipient's system works and adapt your messages to it. Most people would rather get a separate short message on each of several topics, so that the messages can be stored in different mailboxes. But people who pay a fee to download each message may prefer longer messages that deal with several topics.
- When you respond to a message, include only the part of the original message that is essential to your reply so that the reader understands your posting. Delete the rest. If the quoted material is lengthy, put your response first, then the original material.

SEE THE OLC!

Netiquette Tips

When you send emails just for information, put "FYI" at the end of the subject line.

- When you compose a message in your word processor and call it up in email, use short line lengths (set the right margin at two inches or five centimetres). That way you'll avoid awkward line breaks.

How and when should I use attachments?

Send attachments only when the reader expects and needs them.

Any text document can be copied and pasted into the body of your email message. Sending attachments makes most sense when you send any of these:

- A business letter
- A long text document
- A text document with extensive formatting
- A non-text file (e.g., PowerPoint™ slides, html file, spreadsheet)

When you send an attachment, tell the reader what program it's in (see Figure 10.6). Word-processing programs can generally open documents in earlier programs but not later ones. Thus, WordPerfect 2003 can open documents in Word 98 but not in Word XP.

A computer **virus** is a script that harms your computer or erases your data. You can't get a virus through email, but viruses can infect files that are "attached" to email messages or that you download. You can do several things to stay virus-free:[7]

- Install an anti-virus program on your computer, and keep it up to date.
- Ask people who send you attachments to include their names in the document titles. Virus titles aren't that specific.
- If you're in doubt about an attachment, don't open it.
- Forward email messages only when you're sure of the source and contents.

SEE THE OLC!

Virus Netiquette

Employability Skills 2000+

The Conference Board of Canada
Insights You Can Count On

Please see the OLC to preview the key skills from the Conference Board of Canada's Employability Skills 2000+ covered in this module.

Review of Key Points

1. Why take the trouble to compose email messages offline?
2. When is it appropriate to send your supervisor a copy of your emails?
3. How do subject lines in email messages differ from those of paper messages?
4. When should you be concerned about your email grammar, spelling, punctuation, and usage?
5. When is it appropriate to forward chain letters and jokes to others?
6. How do you decide on the format for an email letter?

Assignments for Module 10

Questions for Critical Thinking

10.1 Why are spelling and punctuation still important in email?
10.2 Why should you compose important email messages offline?
10.3 When should writers avoid humour, sarcasm, and emoticons in their email content?
10.4 Why is it OK for your boss to send you a message with the subject line "To Do," even though that wouldn't work when you need to ask a colleague to do something?

Exercises and Problems

10.5   Telling an Employee That a Workshop Is Full

As director of human resources, you sponsor a variety of workshops for employees. You received this email message today:

> Subject: Re: Oral Presentations Workshops
>
> Please register me for the workshop on giving oral presentations next week. My supervisor has told me I should attend this.

The workshop is full, however, and you already have three people on a waiting list to fill vacancies if anyone should cancel.

You will repeat the workshop only if you have guarantees for at least 15 participants.

Write the message.

10.6   Saying No to the Boss

Today, you received this email from your boss.

> Subject: Oversee United Way
>
> I'm appointing you to be the company representative to oversee United Way. You've done a good job the last three years, so this year should be a piece of cake.

It's true that you know exactly what to do. The job wouldn't be hard for you. But that's just the problem. You wouldn't learn anything, either. You'd rather have an assignment that would stretch you, teach you new skills, or enable you to interact with new people. Continuing to grow is your insurance of continued employability and mobility. Three upcoming projects in your division might offer growth: creating DVDs for a "town meeting" for all employees to be held at the beginning of next quarter, creating an intranet for the company, or serving on the diversity committee. Any of these would be time-consuming, but no more time-consuming than running the United Way campaign.

Write to your boss, asking for something more challenging to do.

10.7   Persuading the CEO to Attend Orientation

As the director of education and training of your organization, you run orientation sessions for new hires. You're planning next quarter's session (new quarters start in January, April, July, and October) for a big group of new college graduates. You'd really like the organization's president and CEO to come in and talk to the group for at least 15 minutes. Probably most of the employees have seen the CEO, but they haven't had any direct contact. The CEO could come any time during the three-day session. Speaking just before or after lunch would be ideal, because then the CEO could also come to lunch and talk informally with at least a few people. Next best would be speaking just before or after the midmorning or midafternoon breaks. But the CEO is busy, and you'll take what you can get.

As your instructor directs,

a.   Assume that your instructor is your CEO, and send an email message persuading him or her to come to orientation.

b.   Send an email message to your instructor, asking him or her to address new members of a campus organization.

c.   Address the CEO of your university, college or workplace, asking him or her to speak to new employees.

10.8   Asking for More Time or Resources

Today, this message shows up in your email inbox from your boss:

Subject: Re: Want Culture Report

This request has come down from the CEO. I'm delegating it to you. See me a couple of days before the board meeting—the first Monday of next month—so we can go over your presentation.

I want a report on the culture for underrepresented groups in our organization. A presentation at the last board of directors' meeting showed that although we do a good job of hiring women and minorities, few of them rise to the top. The directors suspect that our culture may not be supportive and want information on it. Please prepare a presentation for the next meeting. You'll have 15 minutes to speak.

Making a presentation to the company's board of directors could really help your career. But preparing a good presentation and report will take time. You can look at exit reports filed by Human Resources when people leave the company, but you'll also need to interview people—lots of people. And you're already working 60 hours a week on three major projects, one of which is behind schedule. Can one of the projects wait? Can someone else take one of the projects? Can you get some help? Should you do just enough to get by? Ask your boss for advice—in a way that makes you look like a committed employee, not a slacker.

10.9 Asking for Volunteers

You have an executive position with one of the major employers in town. (Pick a business, non-profit organization, or government office you know something about.) Two years ago, your company "adopted" a local school. You've provided computers and paid for Internet access; a small number of workers have signed up to be mentors. Today you get a call from the school's principal, a friend of yours. "I'd like to talk to you about the mentoring program. You're providing some mentors, and we're grateful for them, but we need 10 times that number."

(You wince. This program has not been one of your successes.) "I know that part of the program hasn't worked out as well as we hoped it would. But people are really busy here. Not all that many people have two or three hours a week to spend with a kid."

"So you think the time it takes is really the problem."

(Maybe your friend will appreciate that you can't force people to do this.) "Pretty much."

"Do you think people would be willing to be mentors if we could find a way for it to take less time?"

"Maybe." (You sense that a hook is coming, and you're wary.)

"Your people spend a lot of time on email, don't they?"

"Yes. Two to three hours a day, for most of them."

"What if we created a new mentoring structure where people just emailed their mentees instead of meeting with them? That way they could still provide advice and support, but they could do it at any time of the day. And it wouldn't have to take long."

(This sounds interesting.) "So people would just have email conversations. That would be a lot easier, and we'd get more people. But can they really have a relationship if they don't meet the kids?"

"Maybe we could have a picnic or go to a game a couple of times a year so people could meet face to face."

"And all the kids have computers?"

"Not necessarily at home. But they all have access to email at school. Writing email to professionals will also give them more practice and more confidence. People like to get email."

"Not when they get 200 messages a day, they don't."

"Well, our kids aren't in that category. What do you say?"

"I think it will work. Let's try it."

"Great. Just send me a list of the people who are willing to do this, and we'll match them up with the kids. We'd like to get this started as soon as possible."

Write an email message to all employees asking them to volunteer.

10.10 Asking for Something Different for Administrative Professionals' Week

Your clerical job gives you the flexibility you need while you're in school. Administrative Professionals' (formerly Secretaries') Week is approaching, and you really don't want flowers or a free lunch. You'd much rather have a bonus or at least time off to attend an educational seminar (resourced by the company). You're interested in learning advanced features of a computer program or assertive behaviour techniques.

Write an email to the person who supervises clerical workers in your unit, asking that Administrative Professionals' Week give you something useful.

Hints:
- Assume that you work in an organization you know something about.
- Specify one or more seminars you'd like to attend.
- Some seminars may cost a lot more than flowers or lunch; some may cost less. How much financial flexibility does the organization have?
- Are there other clerical workers? Would they also like bonuses or seminars, or do some prefer flowers or lunch?
- How well does the person who will make the decision know you? How positively does he or she view you and any other clerical workers?

Polishing Your Prose

Making Nouns and Pronouns Agree

Pronouns must agree with the nouns to which they refer in two ways: (1) person and (2) number—singular or plural.

	Singular	Plural
First person	I, my, mine, me, myself	we, our, us, ourselves
Second person	you, your, yourself	you, your, our, ours, yourselves
Third person	he, she, it, him, her, his, hers	they, their, them, themselves

Incorrect: In my internship, I learned that you have to manage your time wisely.

Correct: In my internship, I learned to manage my time wisely.

Incorrect: The sales team reached their goal.

Correct: The sales team reached its goal.

Canadian and U.S. usage treats company names and the words *company* and *government* as singular nouns. In Great Britain, these nouns are plural and require plural pronouns:

Correct (Canadian): Clarica trains its agents well.

Correct (U.S.): Nationwide Insurance trains its agents well.

Correct (U.K.): Lloyd's of London train their agents well.

Exercises

Identify and correct any errors. Note that some sentences do not contain errors.

1. An administrative assistant should help his or her boss work efficiently.
2. The mayor should give themselves credit for doing a good job.
3. The company announces their quarterly profits today.
4. Most new employees find that they need to learn a new culture.
5. A CEO's pay is often based on the performance of their company.
6. The union votes today on whether they will go on strike.
7. In my first month of work, I learned that you need to check email at least three times a day.
8. One of the features of my corporate culture is a willingness to share ideas.
9. The team will present its recommendations to the Executive Committee.
10. Every employee is interested in improving their technical skills.

Check your answers to the odd-numbered exercises on page 572.

■ Online Learning Centre

Visit the Online Learning Centre at www.mcgrawhill.ca/olc/locker to access module quizzes, a searchable glossary, résumé and letter templates, additional business writing samples, CBC videos, and other learning and study tools.

11 Informative and Positive Messages

Module Outline

- How should I organize informative and positive messages?

- What's the best subject line for an informative or positive message?

- When should I use reader benefits in informative and positive messages?

- What kinds of informative and positive messages am I likely to write?

- How can the PAIBOC formula help me write informative and positive messages?

Review of Key Points

Assignments for Module 11

Polishing Your Prose: Dangling Modifiers

LEARNING OBJECTIVES

After reading and applying the information in Module 11, you'll be able to demonstrate

Knowledge of

- The criteria that define positive messages
- The "good news" message structure
- The persuasive component of all effective messages

Skills to

- Further analyze business communication situations
- Organize and write positive messages
- Write informative and positive messages

The Conference Board of Canada
Insights You Can Count On

Please see the OLC to preview the key skills from the Conference Board of Canada's Employability Skills 2000+ covered in this module.

Competent communicators classify messages as neutral, positive, or negative, depending on the audience's anticipated reaction. When we convey information that the reader will receive neutrally, the message is informative. If we anticipate that the reader will respond positively to our information, the message is a **positive** or **good news message**.

Positive and informative messages make no demands on the reader's time or wallet, although the writer may want the reader to save the information and act on it later. Regardless of your purpose, in every writing situation you want to build positive attitudes about yourself and the information you are presenting **to get the results you want and to keep the reader's goodwill**. Informative and positive messages, therefore, contain persuasive elements.

Examples of informative and positive messages include

- Acceptances
- Announcements of changes that the reader will see as positive or neutral
- Information about procedures, products, services, or options
- Positive answers to reader requests
- News that benefits the reader

Informative or good news messages usually have several purposes.

Primary purposes

- To give information or good news to the reader, or to reassure the reader
- To have the reader read the message, understand it, and view the information positively
- To de-emphasize any negative elements

Underlying purposes

- To reduce or eliminate future correspondence on the same subject
- To build a good image of the writer
- To build a good image of the writer's organization
- To initiate or build a good relationship between the writer and reader

INSTANT REPLAY

Primary and Secondary Purposes

You want to build positive attitudes toward the information you are presenting, so in that sense, even an informative message has a persuasive element.

How should I organize informative and positive messages?

Consider your audience's needs: put the good news and a summary of the information first.

Using the appropriate pattern can help you compose more quickly and create a more effective final product. The patterns of organization described in this module and the modules that follow will work for 70 percent to 90 percent of business writing situations.

- Be sure you understand the rationale behind each pattern so that you can modify the pattern if necessary. (For example, when you write instructions, any warnings should go up front, not in the middle of the message.) (◀▶ p. 187 Figure 11.4)
- Sometimes you can present several elements in one paragraph. Sometimes you'll need several paragraphs for just one element.

Present informative and positive messages in the following order:

1. **Give any good news and summarize the main points.** Share good news immediately. Include details such as the date that policies begin and the percent of a discount. If the reader has already raised the issue, make it clear that you're responding.

FIGURE 11.1

An Informative Email

Dear Dennis Baronski,

Thank you for shopping at 23books.ca. We are pleased to confirm that the item(s)
listed below has shipped from your order, OR141133149. Any item(s) remaining in your
order will ship as they become available. If you paid for your order by credit card, we are
now processing a charge to your card for the shipped item(s).

To check your order's status, sign-in to your Online Account and reference your Order
History.

ITEM(S) SHIPPED
1. Bob Dylan: In His Own Words – 1 @ 29.88
2. Down the Highway: The Life of Bob Dylan – 1 @ 49.35

Item(s) Subtotal: $79.23
Shipping: $0.00
GST: $5.55

———————————
———————————

TOTAL: $ 84.78

FIGURE 11.2

How to Organize an Informative or Positive Message

Main Point
Details
Negatives
Reader Benefits
Goodwill Ending

2. **Give details, clarification, and background.** Don't repeat information from the first paragraph. Do answer all the questions your reader is likely to have; provide all the information necessary to achieve your purposes. Present details in **the order of importance to the reader.**

3. **Present any negative elements as positively as possible.** A policy may have limits; information may be incomplete; or the reader may have to satisfy requirements to get a discount or benefit. Make these negatives clear, but present them as positively as possible.

4. **Explain any reader benefits.** Most informative memos need reader benefits. Show that the policy or procedure helps readers, not just the company. Give enough detail to make the benefits clear and convincing. In letters, you may want to give the benefits of dealing with your company as well as the benefits of the product or policy (◀▶ Module 8). In a good news message, it's often possible to combine a short reader benefit with a goodwill ending in the last paragraph.

5. **Use a goodwill ending: positive, personal, and forward-looking.** Shifting your emphasis away from the message to the specific reader suggests that serving the reader is your real concern.

Figure 11.2 summarizes the pattern. Figures 11.1 and 11.3 illustrate two ways to apply the pattern.

FIGURE 11.3
A Positive Memo

Memo

Date: December 15, 2007
To: All Family Centre Therapy Employees
From: Sundra Owusu SO
Subject: New Tuition Reimbursement Program

Good news in subject line and first paragraph

Starting February 1, full-time employees with more than three months of service can be reimbursed up to $2500 a year for tuition and fees for career-related courses.

These include

- courses related to your current position, including licence currency
- courses to prepare you for advancement at Family Therapy Centre
- courses required for a job-related degree program

You may take the courses at any level, from high school to graduate school.

Reimbursement   *Headings prepare the reader and provide good visual impact*

You'll receive reimbursement if you earn a C grade or better. If you are eligible for other financial aid (scholarships, grants) you will be reimbursed up to $2500 per calendar year for tuition and fees not covered by that aid.

Negatives presented as positively as possible

Program Application

Please pick up an application form in the Human Resources office, fill it out, and have it signed by your supervisor. Return it to Human Resources at least two weeks before your classes start. Your application must be approved as part of the program requirements.

Details about the program and necessary documentation for reimbursement are attached to the program application.

Please note that the courses you choose do not have to relate to counselling and psychology. Management, interpersonal, teamwork, advanced computer courses: any of these would contribute to our collective productivity.

Benefit for people not yet eligible to participate

This program gives us the opportunity to build on our strengths as we help people face the challenges in their lives.

When should I use reader benefits in informative and positive messages?

Use reader benefits when you want readers to view your policies and your organization positively.

Not all informative and positive messages need reader benefits (◄▮► Module 8).

You don't need reader benefits when

- You're presenting factual information only
- The reader's attitude toward the information doesn't matter
- Stressing benefits may make the reader sound selfish
- The benefits are so obvious that to restate them insults the reader's intelligence

You do need reader benefits when

- You are presenting policies
- You want to shape readers' attitudes toward the information or toward your organization
- Stressing benefits presents readers' motives positively
- Some of the benefits may not be obvious to readers

INSTANT REPLAY

Use reader benefits when

- Presenting policies
- Shaping readers' attitudes toward the information or toward your organization
- Stressing benefits to present readers' motives positively
- Describing benefits that may not be obvious to readers

Messages to customers or potential customers sometimes include a sales paragraph promoting products or services you offer in addition to the product or service that the reader has asked about. Sales promotion in an informative or positive message should be low-key, not "hard sell."

Reader benefits are hardest to develop when you are announcing policies. The organization has probably decided to adopt the policy because it appears to help the organization; the people who made the decision may not have thought about whether it would help or hurt employees. Yet reader benefits are most essential in this kind of message so readers see the reason for the change and support it.

When you present reader benefits, be sure to present the advantages **for the reader**. Most new policies help the organization in some way, but few workers will see their own interests as identical with those of the organization. Even if the organization saves money or increases its profits, workers will benefit directly only if they own stock in the company, if they are to receive bonuses, if the savings enables a failing company to avoid layoffs, or if all the savings goes directly to employee benefits. In many companies, any money saved will go to executive bonuses, shareholder profits, or research and development.

To develop reader benefits for informative and positive messages, use the steps suggested in Module 8. Be sure to think about the intrinsic benefits (◄▮► p. 140) of your policy: what benefits come from the activity or policy itself, apart from any financial benefits? How does a policy improve the hours people spend at work?

What kinds of informative and positive messages am I likely to write?

You will likely write instructions, transmittals, confirmations, summaries, adjustments, and thank-you notes.

Messages are informative, negative, or persuasive depending on how the reader perceives what you have to say. Readers may feel neutral about assembly, safety, and fire drill instructions (unless, of course, these are badly written and therefore hard to understand

and follow; then readers may feel irritation or frustration). A transmittal can be positive when you're sending glowing sales figures or persuasive when you want the reader to act on the information. A performance appraisal is positive when you evaluate someone who's doing superbly, negative when you want to compile a record to justify firing someone, and persuasive when you want to motivate a satisfactory worker to continue to improve. A collection letter is persuasive; it becomes negative in the last stage when you threaten legal action. Each of these messages is discussed in this module for the pattern it uses most frequently. However, in some cases you will need to use a pattern from a different module.

Instructions

Information on new procedures may generate hostility, since most of us are reluctant to change. You can use placement, language, and font size for effective emphasis. Instructions for complicated procedures (electronic application, machine assembly) require diagrams right beside the text.

FIGURE 11.4
A Safety Procedures Memo

Date: May 11, 2007
Memo to: All chefs, sous-chefs, wait staff, staff
From: Franco
Re: Procedures for Spills

To comply with Health and Safety legislation, and to protect your own safety, and the safety of all employees and patrons, please ensure that you read, understand, and comply with the following instructions for dealing with spills:

1. STOP! Whatever you are doing immediately

2. Alert the person closest to you.
   Indicate to that person
   a. The exact location of the spill
   b. The nature of the spill (e.g., grease, juice, water, gravy, sauce, etc.)

3. WHILE THAT PERSON WAITS IN PLACE, get the yellow warning sign, and a pail and mop from cupboard #3

4. Place the sign and clean the spill immediately

5. Ensure floor/area is completely clean

6. Ensure the floor/area is completely dry

7. Return the sign, mop and pail to cupboard #3

Your cooperation is essential for the safety, security, and comfort of us all.

■ Transmittals

When you send someone in an organization something, attach a memo or letter of transmittal explaining what you're sending. A transmittal can be as simple as a small yellow Post-it™ note with "FYI" ("For Your Information") written on it or it can be a separate typed document, especially when it transmits a formal document such as a report (◀▶ Module 24).

Organize a memo or letter of transmittal in this order:

1. Tell the reader what you're sending.
2. Summarize the main point(s) of the document.
3. Indicate any special circumstances or information that would help the reader understand the document. Is it a draft? Is it a partial document that will be completed later?
4. Tell the reader what will happen next. Will you do something? Do you want a response? If you do want the reader to act, specify exactly what you want the reader to do and give a deadline.

Frequently, transmittals have important secondary purposes, such as building goodwill and showing readers that you're working on projects they value.

■ Confirmations

Many informative messages record oral conversations. These messages are generally short and give only the information shared orally; they go to the other party in the conversation. Start the message by indicating that it is a confirmation, not a new message:

As we discussed on the phone today, …

As I told you yesterday, …

Attached is the meeting schedule we discussed earlier today.

■ Summaries

You may be asked to summarize a conversation, document, or an outside meeting for colleagues or superiors. (Minutes of an internal meeting are usually more detailed. See ◀▶ Module 18 for advice on writing minutes of meetings.)

In a summary of a conversation for internal use, identify

- Who was present
- What was discussed
- What was decided
- Who does what next

To summarize a document,

1. Start with the main point.
2. Give supporting evidence and details.
3. Evaluate the document, if your audience asks for evaluation.

Identify the actions that your organization should take based on the document. Should others in the company read this book? Should someone in the company write a letter to the editor responding to this newspaper article? Should your company try to meet with someone in the organization that the story is about?

Sean Lerner left his corporate job as a computer systems designer to work for himself. Lerner's first design creation—the TTC Subway Rider Efficiency Guide—shows passengers where to sit to access their exits most quickly. Get your guide free at www.ttcrider.ca.

Source: Kevin McGran, "For TTC Riders in a Rush," *Toronto Star*, June 11, 2005. B3.

■ Adjustments and Responses to Complaints

A study showed that when people had gripes but didn't complain, only 9 percent would buy from the company again. But when people did complain—and their problems were resolved quickly—82 percent would buy again.[2]

When you grant a customer's request for an adjusted price, discount, replacement, or other benefit to resolve a complaint, do so in the very first sentence.

> Your VISA bill for a night's lodging has been adjusted to $63. Next month a credit of $37 will appear on your bill to reimburse you for the extra amount you were originally asked to pay.

Don't talk about your own process in making the decision. Don't say anything that sounds grudging. Give the reason for the original mistake only if it reflects credit on the company. (In most cases, it doesn't, so the reason should be omitted.)

■ Thank-You and Congratulatory Notes

Sending a **thank-you note** recognizes and acknowledges a person's contribution and is invaluable in fostering goodwill. Furthermore, your recognition of others will make people more willing to help you again in the future. Thank-you letters are short and prompt. They need to be specific to sound sincere.

Congratulating someone can build good feelings between you and the reader and enhance your own visibility.

Avoid language that seems condescending or patronizing. A journalism professor was offended when a former student wrote to congratulate her for a feature article that had appeared in a major newspaper. As the professor pointed out, the letter's language implied that the writer had more status than the professor herself. The former student was "quite impressed," congratulated the professor on reaching a conclusion that the writer had already reached, and assumed

Sample Thank You Letter

Electronic Greeting Cards

that the professor would have wanted to discuss matters with the writer. To the reader, "Keep up the good work!" implied that the former student cheering her on had superior status.[3]

What's the best subject line for an informative or positive message?

The best subject line contains the basic information or good news.

A subject line is the title of a document. It aids in filing and retrieving the document, tells readers why they need to read the document, and provides a framework or context in which to set what you're about to say.

Subject lines are standard in memos. Letters are not required to have subject lines (◀▮▶ Module 9). However, since a subject line saves the reader's time (and builds the writer's credibility), most businesspeople consider a subject line in a letter to be very important. A good subject line meets three criteria: it is specific, concise, and appropriate to the kind of message (positive, negative, persuasive).

Making Subject Lines Specific

The subject line needs to be specific enough to differentiate that message from others on the same subject, but broad enough to cover everything in the message.

Too general: Training Sessions
Better: Technical Training Sessions Dates
or: Evaluation of Training Sessions on Conducting Interviews
or: Should We Schedule a Short Course on Proposal Writing?

Making Subject Lines Concise

Most subject lines are relatively short—usually no more than 10 words, often only three to seven words.[1]

Wordy: Survey of Student Preferences in Regards to Various Pizza Factors
Better: Students' Pizza Preferences
or: The Feasibility of a Pizza Pizza Branch on Campus
or: What Students Like and Dislike about Pizza Pizza

If you can't make the subject both specific and short, be specific.

Making Subject Lines Appropriate for the Pattern of Organization

In general, do the same thing in your subject line that you would do in the first paragraph.

When you have good news for the reader, build goodwill by **highlighting** it in the subject line. When your information is neutral, summarize it concisely for the subject line.

Subject: Discount on Rental Cars Effective January 2

Starting January 2, as an employee of Amalgamated Industries you can get a
15 percent discount on cars you rent for business or personal use from Roadway
Rent-a-Car.

Subject: Update on Arrangements for Videoconference with Montreal.

In the last month, we have chosen the participants and developed a tentative agenda for the videoconference with our Montreal office scheduled for March 21.

The checklist in Figure 11.5 summarizes the points to remember when writing informative and positive messages.

Sharing information is crucial to business success. To drive home that point, Siemens sent 60 managers from around the world to the shores of a lake south of Munich, Germany, and told them to build rafts. They weren't allowed to talk: They had to write messages and diagrams on flip charts. Back in the office, ShareNet lets employees around the world ask questions and share answers.

FIGURE 11.5

Checklist for Informative and Positive Messages

- ❏ In positive messages, does the subject line give the good news? In either message, is the subject line specific enough to differentiate this message from others on the same subject?
- ❏ Does the first paragraph summarize the information or good news? If the information is too complex to fit into a single paragraph, does the paragraph list the basic parts of the policy or information in the order in which the memo discusses them?
- ❏ Is all the information given in the message? (The information needed will vary depending on the message, but information about dates, places, times, and anything related to money usually needs to be included. When in doubt, ask!)
- ❏ In messages announcing policies, is there at least one reader benefit for each segment of the audience? Do all reader benefits seem likely to occur in this organization?
- ❏ Is each reader benefit developed, showing that the benefit will come from the policy and why the benefit matters to this organization? Do the benefits build on the job duties of people in this organization and on the specific circumstances of the organization?
- ❏ Does the message end with a positive paragraph—preferably one that is specific to the readers, not a general one that could fit any organization or policy?

Originality in a positive or informative message may come from

- ❏ Creating good headings, lists, and visual impact
- ❏ Developing reader benefits
- ❏ Thinking about readers and giving details that answer their questions and make it easier for them to understand and follow the policy

And, for all messages, not just informative and positive ones,

- ❏ Does the message use you-attitude and positive emphasis?
- ❏ Is the style easy to read and friendly?
- ❏ Is the visual design of the message inviting?
- ❏ Is the format correct?
- ❏ Does the message use standard grammar? Is it free from typos?

How can the PAIBOC formula help me write informative and positive messages?

The PAIBOC questions help you examine the points your message should include.

Before you tackle the assignments for this module, examine the following problem. See how the PAIBOC questions in Figure 11.6 probe the basic points required for a solution. Study the two sample solutions to see what makes one unacceptable and the other one good. Note the recommendations for revision that could make the good solution excellent.[4] The checklist in Figure 11.5 can help you evaluate a draft.

Problem

Canwest Insurance uses computers to handle its payments and billings. There is often a time lag between receiving a payment from a customer and recording it on the computer. Sometimes, while the payment is in line to be processed, the computer sends out additional notices: past due notices, collection letters, even threats to sue. Customers are frightened or angry and write asking for an explanation. In most cases, if customers just waited a little longer, the situation would be straightened out. But policyholders are afraid that they'll be without insurance because the company thinks the bill has not been paid.

Canwest doesn't have the time to check each individual situation to see whether the cheque did arrive and has been processed. It wants you to write a letter that will persuade customers to wait. If something is wrong and the payment never reaches Canwest, the company sends a legal notice to that effect, saying that the policy will be cancelled by a certain date (which the notice would specify) at least 30 days after the date on the original premium bill. Continuing customers always get this legal notice as a third chance (after the original bill and the past-due notice).

Prepare a form letter that can go out to every policyholder who claims to have paid a premium for automobile insurance and resents getting a past-due notice. The letter should reassure readers and build goodwill for Canwest.

Analysis of the Problem

P What are your **purposes** in writing or speaking?

To reassure readers: they're covered for 30 days; to inform them they can assume everything is OK unless they receive a second notice; to avoid further correspondence on this subject; to build goodwill for Canwest: (a) we don't want to suggest Canwest is error-prone or too cheap to hire enough people to do the necessary work; (b) we don't want readers to switch companies; (c) we do want readers to buy from Canwest when they're ready for more insurance.

A Who is your **audience**? How do the members of your audience differ from one another? What audience characteristics are relevant to this particular message?

The audience is automobile insurance customers who say they've paid but have still received a past-due notice. They're afraid they're no longer insured. Since it's a form letter, different readers will have different situations: in some cases payment did arrive late, in some cases the company made a mistake, in some the reader never paid (cheque lost in mail, unsigned, bounced, etc.)

I What **information** must your message include?

Readers are still insured. We cannot say whether their cheques have now been processed (company doesn't want to check individual accounts). Their insurance will be cancelled only if they do not pay after receiving the second past-due notice (the legal notice).

B What reasons or reader **benefits** can you use to support your position?

Computers help us provide personal service to policyholders. We offer policies to meet all their needs. Both of these points would need specifics to be interesting and convincing.

O What **objections** can you expect your readers to have? What negative elements of your message must you de-emphasize or overcome?

Computers appear to cause errors. We don't know whether the cheques have been processed. We will cancel policies if their cheques don't arrive.

C How will the **context** affect the reader's response? Think about your relationship to the reader, the morale in the organization, the economy, the time of year, and any special circumstances.

The insurance business is highly competitive—other companies offer similar rates and policies. The customer could get a similar policy for about the same money from someone else. Most people find that money is tight, so they'll want to keep insurance costs low. On the other hand, the fact that prices are steady or rising means that the value of what they own is higher—they need insurance more than ever.

Many insurance companies are refusing to renew policies (car, liability, malpractice insurance). These refusals to renew have received lots of publicity, and many people have heard horror stories about companies and individuals whose insurance has been cancelled or not renewed after a small number of claims. Readers don't feel very kindly toward insurance companies.

In Canada, drivers are legally required to have car insurance. If their insurance policies are cancelled because of a computer error, drivers have a legitimate worry.

◼ Discussion of the Sample Solutions

The solution in Figure 11.7 is unacceptable. The red marginal comments show problem spots. Since this is a form letter, we cannot tell customers we have their cheques; in some

FIGURE 11.7

An Unacceptable Solution to the Sample Problem

> *Need date*
> *Not personalized: not you-focussed*
>
> Dear Customer:
>
> *Not necessarily true.*
> *Reread problem.*
>
> Relax. We got your cheque.
>
> *This explanation makes company look bad.*
> There is always a time lag between the time payments come in and the time they are processed. While payments are waiting to be processed, the computer with super-human quickness is sending out past-due notices and threats of cancellation.
>
> *Too negative*
> Cancellation is not something you should worry about. No policy would be cancelled without a legal notice to that effect giving a specific date for cancellation which would be at least 30 days after the date on the original premium notice.
>
> *Need to present this positively*
> If you want to buy more insurance, just contact your local Canwest Life Insurance agent. We will be happy to help you.
>
> *This paragraph isn't specific enough to work as a reader benefit. It lacks you-attitude and positive emphasis.*
> Sincerely,

EXPANDING A CRITICAL SKILL

Writing a Goodwill Ending

Goodwill endings focus on the business relationship you share with your reader. When you write to one person, tailor the last paragraph to that person specifically. When you write to someone who represents an organization, the last paragraph can refer to your company's relationship with the reader's organization. When you write to a group (for example, to "All Employees") your ending should apply to the whole group.

Possibilities include complimenting the reader for a job well done, describing a reader benefit, or looking forward to something positive that relates to the subject of the message.

For example, consider possible endings for responding to an information query about tours of Wikwemikong Indian reserve on Manitoulin Island. The People of the Three Fires community offer group tours for special interest groups.

Weak closing paragraph: Should you have any questions regarding this matter, please feel free to call me.

Goodwill ending: Upon request, the People of the Three Fires Tours can develop custom tours for educational institutions and corporate retreats. Please contact us for further information.

Some writers end every message with a standard invitation:

If you have questions, please do not hesitate to ask.

That sentence lacks positive emphasis (◄|► Module 7). But saying "feel free to call"—though more positive—is rarely a good idea. Most of the time, the writer should omit the sentence. Don't make more work for yourself by inviting calls to clarify simple messages. And avoid clichés.

One of the reasons you write is to save the time needed to tell everyone individually. People in business aren't shrinking violets; they will call if they need help. Do make sure your phone number is in the letterhead or is typed below your name. You can also add your email address below your name.

cases, we may not. The letter is far too negative. The explanation in paragraph 2 makes Canwest look irresponsible and uncaring. Paragraph 3 is far too negative. Paragraph 4 is too vague; there are no reader benefits; the ending sounds selfish.

A major weakness with the solution is that it lifts phrases straight out of the problem; the writer does not seem to have thought about the problem or about the words he or she is using. Measuring the draft against the answers to the questions for analysis suggests that this writer should start over.

The solution in Figure 11.8 is much better. The green marginal comments show the letter's strong points. The message opens with the good news that is true for all readers. (Whenever possible, one should use the good news pattern of organization.) Paragraph 2 explains Canwest's policy. It avoids assigning blame and ends on a positive note. The negative information is buried in paragraph 3 and is presented positively: The notice is information, not a threat; the 30-day extension is a grace period. Telling the reader what to do if a second notice arrives eliminates the need for a second exchange of letters. Paragraph 4 offers benefits for using computers, since some readers may blame the notice on computers, and offers benefits for being insured by Canwest. Paragraph 5 promotes other policies the company sells and prepares for the last paragraph.

FIGURE 11.8
A Good Solution to the Sample Problem

Need date

Use computer to personalize. Put in name and address of a specific reader.

Dear Amjit Sunder:

Your auto insurance is still in effect. *Good paragraph #1: True for all readers*

Good to treat notice as information, tell reader what to do if it arrives

Past-due notices are mailed out if the payment has not been processed within three days after the due date. This may happen if a cheque is delayed in the mail or arrives without a signature or account number. When your cheque arrives with all the necessary information, it is promptly credited to your account. *Good you-attitude*

Even if a cheque is lost in the mail and never reaches us, you still have a 30-day grace period. If you do get a second notice, you'll know that we still have not received your cheque. To keep your insurance in force, just stop payment on the first cheque and send a second one.

Benefits of using computers

Computer processing of your account guarantees that you get any discounts you're eligible for: multicar, accident-free record, good student. If you have a claim, your agent uses computer tracking to find matching parts quickly, no matter what kind of car you drive. You get a cheque quickly—usually within three working days—without having to visit dealer after dealer for time-consuming estimates.

Today, your home and possessions are worth more than ever. You can protect them with Canwest Insurance's homeowners' and renters' policies. Let your local agent show you how easy it is to give yourself full protection. If you need a special rider to insure a personal computer, a coin, or stamp collection, or a fine antique, you can get that from Canwest, too. *Good specifics*

Whatever your insurance needs—auto, home, life, or health—one call to Canwest can do it all. *Acceptable ending*

Sincerely,

As the red comments indicate, this good solution could be improved by including the name and number of the local agent. Computers could make both of those insertions easily. This good letter could become an excellent letter by revising paragraph 4 to include more reader benefits. For instance, do computers help agents advise clients of the best policies for them? Does Canwest offer good service—quick, friendly, non-pressured—that could be stressed? Are agents well trained? All of these might yield ideas for additional reader benefits.

Employability Skills 2000+

The Conference Board of Canada
Insights You Can Count On

Please see the OLC to preview the key skills from the Conference Board of Canada's Employability Skills 2000+ covered in this module.

Review of Key Points

1. Describe the pattern of organization for informative/positive messages.
2. What four secondary purposes might motivate people to write informative/positive messages?
3. In what four circumstances would your informative/positive messages contain reader benefits?
4. What three criteria should you use when writing any subject line?
5. What should the informative/persuasive message subject line contain?

Assignments For Module 11

Questions for Critical Thinking

11.1 What's wrong with the subject line "New Policy"?
11.2 Is it unethical to "bury" any negative elements in an otherwise positive or informative message?
11.3 Why is it important to recognize the secondary as well as the primary purposes of your message?
11.4 Are you more likely to need reader benefits in informative letters or memos? Why?

Exercises and Problems

11.5 Revising a Letter

Your assistant gives you the following letter to sign:

> Dear Ms. Hebbar:
>
> I received your request to send a speaker to participate in "Career Day" at King Elementary School next month. I am pleased to be able to send Audrey Lindstrom to speak at your school about her job at the child-care centre.
>
> Audrey has been working in the child-care centre for over five years. She trains contracted centre personnel on policies and procedures of the department.
>
> Another commitment later that day will make it impossible for her to spend the whole day at your school. She will be happy to spend two hours with your class participating in the event.
>
> Call Audrey to coordinate the time of the program, the expected content, and the age group of the audience.
>
> Your students will see the importance of trained day-care providers in our neighbourhoods.
>
> Thank you for asking our agency to be part of your school's special event. Our future lies in the hands of today's students.
>
> Sincerely,

This draft definitely needs some work. It lacks you-attitude and positive emphasis, it isn't well organized, and it doesn't have enough details. "Ms. Lindstrom" would be more professional than "Audrey." And more information is needed. Exactly when should she show up? Will she be giving a speech (how long?), speaking as a member of a panel, or sitting at a table to answer questions? Will all grade levels be together, or will she be speaking to specific grades? Will all students hear each speaker, or will there be several concurrent speakers from which to choose?

As your instructor directs,

a. Write a memo to your subordinate, explaining what revisions are necessary.
b. Revise the letter.

11.6 Responding to a Supervisor's Request

You've received this email message from your supervisor:

Answer the message, describing something that you or others in your unit do well.

Subject: Need "Best Practices"

Our organization is putting together something on "Best Practices" so that good ideas can be shared as widely as possible. Please describe something our unit does well—ideally something that could be copied by or at least applied to other units.

Be specific. For example, don't just say "serve customers"—explain exactly what you do and how you do it to be effective. Anecdotes and examples would be helpful.

Also indicate whether a document, a videotape, or some other format would be the best way to share your practice. We may use more than one format, depending on the response.

I need your answer asap so that I can send it on to my boss.

11.7 Accepting Suggestions

Your municipal government encourages money-saving suggestions to help balance the city budget. The suggestion committee, which you chair, has voted to adopt five suggestions:

1. Direct deposit paycheques to save distribution and printing costs. Suggested by Poh-Kim Lee, in Recreation and Parks.
2. Buy supplies in bulk. Suggested by Jolene Zigmund, in Maintenance.
3. Charge nearby towns and suburbs a fee for sending their firefighters through the city fire academy. Suggested by Charles Boxell, in Fire Safety.
4. Set up an honour system for employees to reimburse the city for personal photocopies or phone calls. Suggested by Maria Echeverria, in Police.
5. Install lock boxes so meter readers don't have to turn off water valves when people move. This causes wear and tear, and broken valves must be dug up and replaced. Suggested by Travis Gratton, in Water Line Maintenance.

Each suggester gets $100. The Accounting Department will cut cheques the first of next month; cheques should reach people in interoffice mail a few days later.

As your instructor directs,

a. Write to one of the suggesters, giving the good news.
b. Write to all employees, announcing the award winners.

11.8 Giving Good News

Write to a customer or client, to a vendor or supplier, or to your boss announcing good news. Possibilities include a product improvement, a price cut or special, an addition to your management team, a new contract.

11.9 Easing New Hires' Transition into Your Unit

Prepare a document to help new hires adjust quickly to your unit. You may want to focus solely on work procedures; you may also want to discuss aspects of the corporate culture.

11.10 Announcing a Change in Group Life Insurance Rates

Your organization provides group life insurance to your salaried employees, worth 2.5 times the employee's annual salary. Hourly employees who worked 30 hours or more a week in the last year receive life insurance equal to what the person was paid in the last year. The premium that the organization pays has been considered taxable income. The exact value is listed on the pay stub in the box labelled "Employer-Paid Benefits." Now, the Ministry of Finance has announced a reduction in the rates used to calculate the taxable value of this employer-provided life insurance. As a result, the value of the insurance will be slightly lower, and all the taxes based on pay will be slightly lower: federal, provincial, city, provincial hospitalization insurance, and school district taxes. These changes will be effective in the paycheque issued at the end of this month for employees paid monthly and in the paycheque issued 10 days from now for employees paid biweekly.

Write a memo to all employees, explaining the change.

11.11 Introducing a Wellness Program

Your company has decided to launch a wellness program in an effort to get employees to adopt healthier lifestyles. Studies show that people who smoke, who are moderate or heavy drinkers, who are overweight, and who do not exercise regularly have higher rates of absence due to illness. They visit doctors more often, need more prescription drugs, and are hospitalized more often and for longer periods of time.

You'll give a $100 rebate (annually) to each employee who doesn't smoke or use chewing tobacco. Employees who don't drink to excess (more than an average of 170 mL of beer or 85 mL of wine or 42 mL of hard liquor a day) and who don't use illegal drugs can also get $100, as can those whose cholesterol isn't over 150. Employees who exercise at least 30 minutes a day, three times a week, will get rebates of $50. Exercise doesn't have to be difficult: walking and gardening count. Another rebate of $50 is available for a waist-to-hip ratio under 0.8 for women or 0.95 for men.

As part of the wellness program, the company cafeteria will focus on serving healthier foods and the company will offer twice-yearly health fairs with free routine immunizations and flu shots for employees and dependants. These parts of the program will begin next month.

Write a memo to all employees informing them about the wellness program.

Hints:
- Choose an organization you know something about to use for this message.
- If the organization saves money through reduced absenteeism, will employees benefit?
- Why don't people already follow healthy practices? What can you do to overcome these objections?
- Saving money may not motivate everyone. Offer intrinsic benefits as well.
- Use the analysis that you developed for exercise 2.6 in Module 2.

11.12 Explaining Packing Material

Your organization ships thousands of boxes to fill orders from catalogues and from your Web site. To cushion items, you fill the empty spaces around the items with plastic "popcorn." Some customers have written to complain about the plastic, which is not biodegradable. Some have asked you to use real popcorn, paper, or starch (which will degrade when wet). However, these materials do not cushion as well as plastic does (so that more items are damaged during shipment) and weigh more (so that shipping costs are higher). In addition, popcorn is subject to Canadian Food Inspection Agency regulations, which you do not want to monitor; paper fill creates dust and thus is a health hazard for packers; and starch doesn't work in very humid or very dry climates. You want to use one packing material for all boxes, wherever they are going.

Customers could save and reuse the plastic packaging material. If they can't reuse it, they may be able to recycle it. They can call their local solid waste department to find out. Or they could check The Internet Consumer Recycling Guide, an online guide for Canadian and U.S. consumers, at http://www.obviously.com/recycle/guides/hard.html

As your instructor directs,

a. Write a letter to one customer who has complained, showing why you are continuing to use plastic fill.

b. Prepare a one-page insert to be included in every package, explaining your decision about packaging.

11.13 Reminding Guests about the Time Change

Twice a year the switch to and from daylight-saving time affects people in Canada. The time change can be disruptive for hotel guests, who may lose track of the date, forget to change the clocks in their rooms, and miss appointments as a result.

Prepare a form letter to leave in each hotel room reminding guests of the impending time change. What should guests do?

Write the letter.

Hints:

- Use an attention-getting page layout so readers don't ignore the message.
- Pick a specific hotel or motel chain you know something about.
- Use the letter to build goodwill for your hotel or motel chain. Use specific references to services or features the hotel offers, focusing not on what the hotel does for the reader, but on what the reader can do at the hotel.

11.14 Confirming a Reservation

You work in reservations at Basin Hot Springs Lodge in Banff National Park. Most travellers phone 13 months in advance to reserve a room and once you process the credit card payment for the first night, you then write to them to confirm the reservation.

The confirmation contains the amount charged to the credit card, the date on which the reservation was made, the confirmation number, the kind of room (Lakefront Retreat or Mountainview Retreat), and the dates the guest will be arriving and leaving.

In addition, the letter needs to give several pieces of general information. The amount of the deposit and the amount quoted per night are the rates for the current calendar year. However, the guest will be charged the rate for the calendar year of the stay, and that amount is likely to increase by about 4 percent to 5 percent. In addition to paying the new rate for each additional night, the guest will need to pay the difference between the amount of the deposit and the new rate for the first night.

Anyone who wants a refund must cancel the reservation in writing four days before the scheduled arrival date.

Cancellations may be faxed: the fax number is on the letterhead the letter will be printed on.

Parking is limited. People who bring big motorhomes, boats, or camp trailers may have to park in the main parking area rather than right by their cabins.

All the rooms are cabin style with three to four rooms in each building. There are no rooms in a main lodge. People will need to walk from their cabins to the restaurants, unless they do their own cooking.

Both Lakefront and Mountainview Retreats have kitchenettes with microwaves, but guests must bring their own cooking utensils, dishes, supplies, and food. The bedroom area (with a king-size bed in the Lakefront Retreats and a queen-size bed in the Mountainview Retreats) has a sliding divider that can separate it from the sitting area, which has a sofa bed.

Since the deposit pays for the first night (less any increase in room rate), the room will be held regardless of the time of arrival. Check-in time is 3 P.M.; earlier room availability cannot be guaranteed. Check-out time is 11 A.M.

All cabins are non-smoking. Smoking is permitted on the decks of the Lakefront Retreats or the porches of the Mountainview Retreats.

The guest should present the confirmation letter when checking in.

As your instructor directs,

a. Write a form letter that can be used for one type of room (either Lakefront or Mountainview Retreat). Indicate with square brackets material that would need to be filled in for each guest: for instance, arriving [date of arrival] and departing [date of departure].

b. Write a letter to Stephanie Lafleur, who has reserved a Lakefront Retreat room arriving September 18 and departing September 20. Her credit card is being billed for $187.25 ($175 plus GST—the current rate). Her address is 3122 Rue Laurier, Québec City, QC, G1R 3M7.

11.15 Lining up a Consultant to Teach Short Courses in Presentations

As director of education and training, you oversee all in-house training programs. Five weeks ago, Runata Hartley, vice president for human resources, asked you to set up a training course on oral presentations. After making some phone calls, you tracked down Brian Barreau, a professor of communications at a nearby college.

"Yes, I do short courses on oral presentations," he told you on the phone. "I would want at least a day and a half with participants—two full days would be better. They need time to practise the skills they'll be learning. I'm free Thursdays and Fridays.

"I'm willing to work with up to 20 people at a time. Tell me what kind of presentations they make, whether they know how to use PowerPoint™, and what kinds of things you want me to emphasize. I'll need a digital videocamera to record each participant's presentations and a DVD for each person. My fee is $2000 a day."

You told him you thought a two-day session would be feasible, but you'd have to get back to him after you got budget approval. You wrote a quick memo to Runata explaining the situation and asking about what the session should cover.

Two weeks ago, you received this memo.

I've asked for budget approval of $4000 for a two-day session plus no more than $500 for all expenses. I don't think there will be a problem.

We need some of the basics: how to plan a presentation, how to deal with nervousness. Adapting to the audience is a big issue: our people give presentations to varied audiences with very different levels of technical knowledge and interest. Most of our people have PowerPoint™ on their computers, but the slide shows I've seen have been pretty amateurish.

I don't want someone to lecture. We need practical exercises that can help us practise skills that we can put into effect immediately.

Attached is a list of 18 people who can attend a session Thursday and Friday of the second week of next month. Note that we've got a good mix of people. If the session goes well, I may want you to schedule additional sessions.

Today, you got approval from the vice president to schedule the session, pay Professor Barreau's fee, and reimburse him for expenses to a maximum of $500. He will have to keep all receipts and turn in an itemized list of expenses to be reimbursed; you cannot reimburse him if he does not have receipts.

You also need to explain the mechanics of the session. You'll meet in the Conference Room, which has a screen and flip charts. You have an overhead projector, a laptop, a digital videocamera, and a monitor, but you need to reserve these if he wants to use them. Will he bring his own laptop computer, or does he want you to provide the computer?

Write to Professor Barreau. You don't have to persuade him to come since he's already informally agreed, but you do want him to look forward to the job and to do his best work.

Hints:
- Choose an organization you know something about.
- What audiences do people speak to? How formal are these talks? What are their purposes?

- Is this session designed to hone the skills of people who are competent, or is it designed to help people who are very weak, perhaps even paralyzed by fright?

- What role do presentations play in the success of the organization and of individuals in it?
- Check the calendar to get the dates. If there's any ambiguity about what "the second week of next month" is, call Runata to check.

11.16 Answering an International Inquiry

Your business, government, or non-profit organization has received the following inquiries from international correspondents. (You choose the country the inquiry originated from.)

1. Please tell us about a new product, service, or trend so that we can decide whether we want to buy, licence, or imitate it in our country.
2. We have heard about a problem [technical, social, political, or ethical] that occurred in your organization. Could you please tell us what really happened and estimate how it is likely to affect the long-term success of the organization?
3. Please tell us about college or university programs in this field. We are interested in sending some of our managers to your country to complete a degree.
4. We are considering setting up a plant in your city. We have already received adequate business information. However, we would also like to know how comfortable our nationals would feel. Do people in your city speak our language? How many? What opportunities exist for our nationals

to improve their English? Does your town already have people from a wide mix of nations? Which are the largest groups?

5. Our organization would like to subscribe to an English-language trade journal. Which one would you recommend? Why? How much does it cost? How can we order it?

As your instructor directs,

a. Answer one or more of the inquiries. Assume that your reader either reads English or can have your message translated.
b. Write a memo to your instructor explaining how you've adapted the message for your audience.

Hints:

- Even though you can write in English, English may not be your reader's native language. Write a letter that can be translated easily.
- In some cases, you may need to spell out background information that might not be clear to someone from another country.

11.17 Writing a Thank-You Letter

Write a thank-you letter to someone who has helped you achieve your goals.

As your instructor directs,

a. Turn in a copy of the letter.

b. Mail the letter to the person who helped you.
c. Write a memo to your instructor explaining the choices you made in writing the thank-you letter.

11.18 Evaluating Web Pages

Today you received this email from your boss:

Subject: Evaluating Our Web Page

Our CEO wants to know how our Web page compares to those of our competitors. I'd like you to do this in two steps. First, send me a list of your criteria. Then give me an evaluation of two of our competitors' pages and of our own pages. I'll combine your memo with others on other Web pages to put together a comprehensive evaluation for the next executive meeting.

As your instructor directs,

a. List the generic criteria for evaluating a Web page. Think about the various audiences for the page and the content that will keep them coming back, page organization and navigation, the visual design, and the details, such as a creation or update date.

b. List criteria for pages of specific kinds of organizations. For example, a non-profit organization might want information for potential and current donors, volunteers, and clients. A financial institution might want to project an image both of trustworthiness and optimism.

c. Evaluate three Web pages of similar organizations. Which is best? Why?

Hint:

Review the information on Web page design in ◄▐▷ Module 5.

11.19 Creating a Human Resources Web Page

As firms attempt to help employees balance work and family life (and as employers become aware that personal and family stresses affect performance at work), human resource departments sponsor an array of programs and provide information on myriad subjects. However, some people might be uncomfortable asking for help, either because the problem is embarrassing (who wants to admit needing help to deal with drug or spousal abuse or addiction to gambling?) or because they feel that focusing on non-work issues (e.g., child care) might lead others to think they aren't serious about their jobs. The World Wide Web allows organizations to post information that employees can access privately—even from home.

Create a Web page that could be posted by human resources to help employees with one of the challenges they face. Possible topics include

- Appreciating an ethnic heritage
- Buying a house
- Caring for dependants: child care, helping a child learn to read, living with teenagers, elder care, and so forth
- Dealing with a health issue: exercising, having a healthy diet, and so on
- Dealing with a health problem: alcoholism, cancer, diabetes, heart disease, obesity, and so on
- Dressing for success or dressing for casual days
- Managing finances: basic budgeting, deciding how much to save, choosing investments, and so on
- Nourishing the spirit: meditation, religion, mindfulness
- Planning for retirement
- Planning vacations
- Reducing stress
- Resolving conflicts on the job or in families

Assume that this page can be accessed from another of the organization's pages. Offer at least seven links. (More links are better.) You may offer information as well as links to other pages with information. At the top of the page, offer an overview of what the page covers. At the bottom of the page, put the creation and update date and your name and email address.

As your instructor directs,

a. Turn in two printed copies of your page(s). On another page, give the URLs for each link.

b. Turn in one printed copy of your page(s) and a disk with the HTML code and .gif files.

c. Write a memo to your instructor identifying the audience for which the page is designed and explaining (1) the search strategies you used to find material on this topic, (2) why you chose the pages and information you've included, and (3) why you chose the layout and graphics you've used.

d. Present your page orally to the class.

Hints:

- Pick a topic you know something about.
- Realize that audience members will have different needs. You could explain the basics of choosing day care or stocks, but don't recommend a specific day-care centre or a specific stock.
- If you have more than nine links, chunk them in small groups under headings.
- Create a good image of the organization.
- Review the information on Web page design in Module 5.

Polishing Your Prose

Dangling Modifiers

Modifiers are words or phrases that give more information about parts of a sentence. For instance, an adjective is a modifier that usually describes a noun. **Dangling modifiers** make no sense to readers because the word they modify is not in the sentence. If you diagrammed the sentence, the modifier would not be attached to anything; it would dangle.

Dangling: Confirming our conversation, your Hot Springs Hot Tub Spa is scheduled for delivery April 12.

(This sentence says that the spa is doing the confirming.)

Correct a dangling modifier in either of these ways:

1. Rewrite the modifier as a subordinate clause.

Correct: As I told you yesterday, your Hot Springs Hot Tub Spa is scheduled for delivery April 12.

2. Rewrite the main clause so its subject or object can be modified correctly.

Correct: Talking on the phone, we confirmed that your Hot Springs Hot Tub Spa is scheduled for delivery April 12.

Exercises

Correct the dangling modifiers in these sentences.

1. After working a year, dental insurance covers you.
2. Using the fax machine, new orders are processed quickly.
3. At the age of 10, I bought my daughter her first share of stock.
4. Working in teams, projects can be completed quickly.
5. Calling ahead of time, the reservations can be made efficiently.
6. Before joining our company, your résumé shows a good deal of experience with computer software.
7. Confirming our telephone call, your order was shipped on April 1.
8. A simple notebook filled with thoughts and ideas, you can keep a journal of your business experiences.
9. Sharing files with our legal department, our attorneys can work better with you.
10. As a new employee, your supervisor can answer your questions.

Check your answers to the odd-numbered exercises on page 572.

■ Online Learning Centre

Visit the Online Learning Centre at www.mcgrawhill.ca/olc/locker to access module quizzes, a searchable glossary, résumé and letter templates, additional business writing samples, CBC videos, and other learning and study tools.

MODULE

12 Negative Messages

Module Outline

- How should I organize negative messages?

- What are the most common kinds of negative messages?

- What's the best subject line for a negative message?

- How can PAIBOC help me write negative messages?

Review of Key Points

Assignments for Module 12

Polishing Your Prose: Parallel Structure

LEARNING OBJECTIVES

After reading and applying the information in Module 12, you'll be able to demonstrate

Knowledge of

- The criteria that define negative messages
- The bad news message structure
- The legal and ethical implications of your messages

Skills to

- Organize negative messages
- Give bad news while retaining goodwill
- Write common kinds of negative messages
- Further analyze business communication situations

The Conference Board of Canada
Insights You Can Count On

Please see the OLC to preview the key skills from the Conference Board of Canada's Employability Skills 2000+ covered in this module.

FYI

Recent studies indicate that work-life balance has become the dominant concern for Canadian employees. Employees' hierarchy of needs follows Maslow's model: if people do not feel physically and emotionally secure, the organization's investment in compensation and professional development programs is wasted. In fact, people's commitment to their work is directly related to their perception of how committed their company is to them.

Sources: "Companies Slow To Make Employees' Work/Life Harmony a Priority," *the training report*, Jan/Feb 2001, p. 12; Patricia Chisholm, "Redesigning Work," *Maclean's*, March 5, 2001, 34–38.

Messages are positive or negative based on audience impact. Negative messages contain information that will cost the reader comfort, time, money, esteem, or resources. When we expect the reader to be disappointed or angry at the information, we are composing a negative message.

Negative messages include the following:

- Rejections and refusals
- Announcements of policy changes that do not benefit customers or consumers
- Requests the reader will see as bothersome, insulting, or intrusive
- Negative performance appraisals and disciplinary notices
- Product recalls or notices of defects

A negative message always has several purposes:

Primary purposes

- To give the reader the bad news
- To have the reader read, understand, and accept the message
- To maintain as much goodwill as possible

Secondary purposes

- To build a good image of the writer
- To build a good image of the writer's organization
- To reduce or eliminate future correspondence on the same subject so the message doesn't create more work for the writer

Although readers may not be happy with the news we must convey, we still want readers to feel several positive things:

- They have been taken seriously.
- Your decision is fair and reasonable.
- If they were in your shoes, they would make the same decision.

How should I organize negative messages?

It depends on your purposes and audiences. However, for optimum meaning exchange, follow the indirect, inductive, or bad news pattern.

"Meaning" resides in people, not words. Whatever your purpose—compliance, agreement, action—your audience's emotional, or affective response is vital to getting the results you want. Whether notifying a client about a price increase, or emailing colleagues about extra work they must complete, you want to convey information and maintain goodwill. Otherwise, you'll waste time and money in lost customers and disruptive work relationships.

Giving Bad News to Customers and Other People Outside Your Organization

The following pattern helps writers maintain goodwill:

1. **Start with a neutral statement, or buffer.** These openings are meant to orient readers and psychologically prepare them for news that they are not going to like. Whether writing or speaking, the best buffers begin with areas that both you and your audience

can agree on. Buffer statements such as "Thank you for your letter," in response to a complaint or query, acknowledge that you have read, understood, and are responding to your reader's concern.

2. **Explain.** A good reason prepares the reader to expect the refusal.

3. **Give the negative just once, clearly.** Inconspicuous refusals can be missed, making it necessary to say *no* a second time.

4. **Always present an alternative or compromise, if one is available.** An alternative not only gives readers another way to get what they want but also suggests that you care about the readers and want to help them solve their problems.

5. **End with a positive, forward-looking statement.**

Figure 12.1 summarizes the pattern. Figure 12.2 uses the basic pattern.

FIGURE 12.1
A Negative Letter

Nature's Lifesource Incorporated
111 Pleasant Street
Stephen, NB E3L 1B4
506-555-1376
www.naturlif@origin.ca

August 20, 2004

Alyssa Scarangella
72 Rue Windermere
Montreal, PQ H9A 2C4

Dear Alyssa Scarangella:

Subject: **Shipments # 3101-3105 inclusive**

Buffer: neutral statement
Thank you for the information you provided yesterday.

Explanation: reasons
As we discussed during our telephone conversation, the last three shipments have arrived with product damage. Both our transportation service suppliers and our warehouse personnel have expressed concerns about the security of the loading. The quality of pallets supporting the products and the equipment fastenings could lead to load shifts, creating dangerous highway conditions.

Explanation: proof
As you requested, I have enclosed photographs of the damages to shipments # 3103, 3104, and 3105. These photographs demonstrate the condition of the pallets and the manner in which the load was secured. Since our research indicates that these two factors led to the damage, I would appreciate your help in recouping our costs for the damaged products.

Negative: reader is expected to pay for the damaged shipments and ensure adherence to safety standards

Positive ending
Thank you for your assurance that the quality of pallets and the fastenings of all future shipments will provide a safe, secure load.

When you have reviewed the photographs, please let me know what additional information you will need.

Sincerely,

Leovee Yang

Leovee Yang

Enclosure

FIGURE 12.2
A Refusal with an Alternative

AlbertaFilmInstitute

8th Floor Commerce Place 10155 102 Street Edmonton AB T5J 4L6
T: 780.415.0293 F: 780.422.8582 E: stephan.blackbird@gov.ab.ca

November 22, 2007

Mr. Marco Novelli
319 Sweetwater Bay
Winnipeg, MB R2J 3G4

Dear Mr. Novelli:

Subject: Original Script *Doubtful*

Thank you for your recent submission.

Although *Doubtful* is a highly original, well-crafted script, we have found that film noir themes do not attract a large box office. Therefore, we cannot use your story at this time.

With your permission, however, we'd like to send your treatment on to Jessie Prynne, chair of the Alberta Arts Foundation. The Foundation is always looking for original works to stage.

If this is agreeable to you, please let me know via email, letter or telephone.

Meanwhile, please keep writing, and please continue to send us your work.

Sincerely,

Stephan Blackbird

Script Supervisor

■ The Buffer

A buffer is a neutral or positive statement that allows you to delay the negative. You'll want to begin messages with a neutral statement or buffer when the reader (individually or culturally) values harmony or when the buffer serves another purpose. For example, when you must thank the reader somewhere in the letter, putting the "thank you" in the first paragraph allows you to start on a positive note.

To be effective, a buffer must put the reader in a good frame of mind—not give the bad news but not imply a positive answer either—and provide a natural transition to the body of the letter. The kinds of statements most often used as buffers are good news, facts and chronologies of events, references to enclosures, thanks, and statements of principle, as the examples below illustrate.

1. Start with any good news or positive elements the letter contains.

> Starting Thursday, June 26, you'll have access to your money 24 hours a day at TD Canada Trust.

Letter announcing that the drive-up windows will be closed for two days while automatic teller machines are installed

2. State a fact or provide a chronology of events.

> As a result of the new graduated dues schedule—determined by vote of the delegate assembly last December and subsequently endorsed by the executive council—members are now asked to establish their own dues rate and to calculate the total amount of their remittance.

Announcement of a new dues structure that will raise most members' dues

3. Refer to enclosures in the letter.

> Enclosed is a new sticker for your car. You may pick up additional ones in the office if needed. Please destroy old stickers bearing the signature of "L.S. LaVoie."

Letter announcing an increase in parking rental rates

4. Thank the reader for something he or she has done.

> Thank you for scheduling appointments for me with so many senior people at the Bank of Montreal. My visit there March 14 was very informative.

Letter refusing a job offer

5. State a general principle.

> Good drivers should pay substantially less for their auto insurance. The Good Driver Plan was created to reward good drivers (those with five-year accident-free records) with our lowest available rates. A change in the plan, effective January 1, will help keep those rates low.

Letter announcing that the company will now count traffic tickets, not just accidents, in calculating insurance rates—a change that will raise many people's premiums

Buffers are hard to write. Even if you think the reader would prefer to be let down easily, use a buffer only when you can write a good one.

INSTANT REPLAY

Effective Buffers

To be effective, a **buffer** must put the reader in a good frame of mind, not give the bad news but not imply a positive answer either, and provide a natural transition to the body of the letter.

It's better *not* to use a buffer (1) if the reader might ignore a letter with a bland first paragraph, (2) if the reader or the organization prefers "bottom-line-first messages," (3) if the reader is suspicious of the writer, or (4) if the reader "won't take *no* for an answer."

■ Explanation

Make the reason for the refusal clear and convincing in terms of the audience's needs and wants. Your readers would find the following reason emotionally unconvincing:

Weak reason: The goal of the ValuDrug CHARGE-ALL Centre is to provide our customers with faster, more personalized service. Since you now live outside the Halifax ValuDrug CHARGE-ALL service area, we can no longer offer you the advantages of a local CHARGE-ALL Centre.

If the reader says, "I don't care if my bills are slow and impersonal," will the company let the reader keep the card? No. The real reason for the negative is that the drugstore's franchise allows it to have cardholders only in a given geographical region.

Better reason: Each local CHARGE-ALL Centre offers accounts to customers in a specific regional area. The Nova Scotia ValuDrug CHARGE-ALL Centre serves customers east of Quebec. You can continue to use your current card until it expires. When that happens, you'll need to open an account with a CHARGE-ALL Centre that serves Quebec.

Don't hide behind "company policy": readers will assume the policy is designed to benefit you at their expense. If possible, show how the readers benefit from the policy. If they do not benefit, don't mention policy.

Weak reason: I cannot write an insurance policy for you because company policy does not allow me to do so.

Better reason: General Insurance insures cars only when they are normally garaged at night. Standard insurance policies cover a wider variety of risks and charge higher fees. Limiting the policies we write gives General's customers the lowest possible rates for auto insurance.

Avoid saying that you *cannot* do something. Most negative messages exist because the writer or company has chosen certain policies or cutoff points. In the example above, the company could choose to insure a wider variety of customers if it wanted to do so.

Often you will enforce policies that you did not design. Don't pass the buck by saying, "This is a terrible policy." Carelessly criticizing your superiors is never a good idea. If you really think a policy is bad, try to persuade your superiors to change it. If you can't think of convincing reasons to change the policy, maybe it isn't so bad after all.

If you have several reasons for saying no, use only those that are strong and watertight. If you give five reasons and readers dismiss two of them, readers may feel that they've won and should get the request.

Weak reason: You cannot store large bulky items in the dormitory over the summer because moving them into and out of storage would tie up the stairs and the elevators right at the busiest times when people are moving in and out.

Way to dismiss the reason: We'll move large items before or after the two days when most people are moving in or out.

INSTANT REPLAY

Organizing Negative Letters to Customers

1. Provide a buffer, if possible.
2. Give the reason for the refusal before the refusal itself when you have a reason that readers will understand and accept.
3. Give the negative just once, clearly.
4. Present an alternative or compromise, if one is available.
5. End with a positive, forward-looking statement.

EXPANDING A CRITICAL SKILL

Thinking about the Legal and Ethical Implications of What You Say

Any message that is recorded—on paper (even a napkin), on a disk or hard drive, on voicemail—can be subpoenaed in a legal case, as former CIBC employees who used their BlackBerrys, assuming total confidentiality, found to their chagrin. Even an electronic message that has been erased can be reconstituted by experts. In any message you write, however informal or hurried, you need to be sure to say exactly what you mean. The Supreme Court of Canada and provincial defamation legislation protect individuals' dignity, right to privacy, and reputation. Libel and slander liability can include everyone who participates in disseminating injurious material.

Thinking about the legal implications of what you say is particularly important in negative messages. In an effort to cushion bad news, writers sometimes give reasons that create legal liabilities. For example, as Elizabeth McCord has shown, the statement that a plant is "too noisy and dangerous" for a group tour could be used as evidence against the company in a worker's compensation claim. In another case, a writer telling a job candidate that the firm had hired someone else said that he thought she was the best candidate. She sued and won.

Although you may choose the direct or indirect bad news pattern organization—depending on your audience's expectations—you also need to think about the ethical implications of your messages. People prefer to do business with someone they trust; therefore, it's good business to deliver negative message honestly and sensitively.

Acting ethically means acting out of enlightened self-interest: treating others as you want to be treated. You need to assume your audience's point of view to figure out what to say—or not to say. Think about how a reasonable person might interpret your words. If that interpretation isn't what you mean, revise the passage so that it says what you mean, in a way that you would find acceptable.

Sources: Sinclair Stewart and Richard Bloom, "BlackBerry Battle Chills Bay St. Gossips," July 7, 2005, http://www.theglobeandmail.com/servlet/ArticleNews/TPStory/LAC/20050107/BLACKBERRY07/TPNational/TopStories, retrieved August 8, 2006; and Javad Heydary (May 26, 2005), "Is Your Boss Monitoring Your BlackBerry?" *E-Commerce Times*, May 26, 2005, http://www.ecommercetimes.com/story/43376.html, retrieved August 8, 2006; Elizabeth A. McCord, "The Business Writer, the Law, and Routine Business Communication: A Legal and Rhetorical Analysis," *Journal of Business and Technical Communication* 5, no. 2 (1991): 173–99.

If you do not have a good reason, omit the reason rather than use a weak one. Even if you have a strong reason, omit it if it reflects poorly on your organization.

Reason that reflects poorly on company:	Our company is not hiring at the present time because profits are down. In fact, the downturn has prompted top management to reduce the salaried staff by 5 percent just this month, with perhaps more reductions to come.
Better:	Our company does not have any openings now.

■ Refusals

De-emphasize the refusal by putting it in the same paragraph as the reason, rather than in a paragraph by itself.

Sometimes you may be able to imply the refusal rather than stating it directly.

Direct refusal:	You cannot get insurance for just one month.
Implied refusal:	The shortest term for an insurance policy is six months.

Be sure that the implication is clear. Any message can be misunderstood, but an optimistic or desperate reader is particularly likely to misunderstand a negative message. One of your purposes in a negative message is to close the door on the subject. You do not want to have to write a second letter saying that the real answer is *no*.

■ Alternatives

Giving the reader an alternative or a compromise, if one is available, does several things:

- It offers the reader another way to get what he or she wants.
- It suggests that you really care about the reader and about meeting his or her needs.
- It enables the reader to reestablish the psychological freedom you limited when you said no.
- It allows you to end on a positive note and to present yourself and your organization as positive, friendly, and helpful.

When you give an alternative, give readers all the information they need to act on it, but let readers decide whether to try the alternative.

Brehm's Theory

Negative messages limit the reader's freedom. People may respond to a limitation of freedom by asserting their freedom in some other arena. University of Kansas psychology professor Jack W. Brehm calls this phenomenon **psychological reactance**.[1] Psychological reactance is at work when a customer who has been denied credit no longer buys even on a cash basis, or a subordinate who has been passed over for a promotion gets back at the company by deliberately doing a poor job.

Psychological reactance in action.

Source: NON SEQUITUR © 1997 Wiley. Distributed by Universal Press Syndicate. Reprinted with permission. All rights reserved.

An alternative allows the reader to react in a way that doesn't hurt you. By letting readers decide for themselves whether they want the alternative, you allow them to reestablish their sense of psychological freedom.

The specific alternative will vary depending on the circumstances. In Figure 12.2, the script supervisor of the Alberta Film Institute refuses to accept *Doubtful*, but tells the filmmaker he is sending his film on to someone who might use it.

■ Endings

If you have a good alternative, refer to it in your ending: "If you can use A515 grade 70, let me know."

The best endings look to the future, as in this example of refusing to continue a charge account for a customer who has moved:

> Wherever you have your account, you'll continue to get all the service you've learned to expect from CHARGE-ALL and the convenience of charging items at more than a thousand ValuDrugs stores in Canada—and in Halifax, too, whenever you come back to visit!

FIGURE 12.3
How to Organize a Negative Letter

- Buffer
- Explanation
- Negative
- Alternative
- Goodwill Ending

To maintain goodwill and retain a positive business relationship, end sincerely:

> Please call me at 403-555-7700 if you need further clarification.

Avoid endings that seem insincere or clichéd:

> We are happy to have been of service, and should we be able to assist you in the future, please do not hesitate to contact us.

This ending lacks you-attitude and would not be good even in a positive message. In a situation where the company has just refused to help, it's likely to sound sarcastic.

Giving Bad News to Superiors

Your superior expects you to solve minor problems by yourself. But sometimes, solving a problem requires more authority or resources than you have. When you give bad news to a superior, recommend a way to deal with the problem. Turn the negative message into a persuasive one.

FIGURE 12.4
How to Organize a Negative Memo to Your Superior

1. **Describe the problem.** Say what's wrong, clearly and unemotionally.
2. **Tell how it happened.** Provide the background. What underlying factors led to this specific problem?
3. **Describe the options for fixing it.** If one option is clearly best, you may need to discuss only one. But if the reader will think of other options, or if different people will judge the options differently, describe all the options, giving their advantages and disadvantages.
4. **Recommend a solution and ask for action.** Ask for approval so that you can go ahead to make the necessary changes to fix the problem.

Figure 12.4 summarizes the pattern.

Giving Bad News to Peers and Subordinates

When giving serious bad news to peers and subordinates, use a variation of the pattern to superiors:

1. **Describe the problem.** Say what's wrong, clearly and unemotionally.
2. **Present an alternative or compromise, if one is available.** An alternative gives readers another way to get what they want and also suggests that you care about the readers and want to help them meet their needs.
3. **If possible, ask for input or action.** People in the audience may be able to suggest solutions. And workers who help make a decision are far more likely to accept the consequences.

FIGURE 12.5
How to Organize a Negative Memo to Peers or Subordinates

Figure 12.5 summarizes this pattern.

No serious negative (such as being downsized or laid off) should come as a complete surprise. Managers can prepare for possible negatives by giving full information as it becomes available. It is also possible to let the people who will be affected by a decision participate in setting the criteria. Someone who has bought into the criteria for awarding cash for

INSTANT
REPLAY

**Organizing Bad News
to Superiors**

1. Describe the problem.
2. Tell how it happened.
3. Describe the options
   for fixing it.
4. Recommend a
   solution and ask for
   action.

suggestions or retaining workers is more likely to accept decisions using such criteria. And in some cases, the synergy of groups may make possible ideas that management didn't think of or rejected as unacceptable. Some workplaces, for example, might decide to reduce everyone's pay slightly rather than laying off some individuals.

When the bad news is less serious, as in Figure 12.6, use the bad news organizational pattern (buffer, explanation, bad news, positive ending) unless your knowledge of the reader suggests that another pattern will be more effective.

Whatever the medium, the context of communication is crucial. The reader's reaction is influenced by the answers to these questions:

FIGURE 12.6
A Negative Memo to Subordinates

Memo

**Brampton Corporate Trade
Peel County, Brampton, ON**

Date: January 10, 2007

To: All Employees

From: Floyd E. Loer, Dorothy A. Walters, and Stewart Mattson

Subject: Accounting for Work Missed Because of Bad Weather

Reason

Our office is always open for our customers, whatever the weather. Employees who missed work during the snowstorm last week may count the absence as vacation, sick day(s), or personal day(s).

Refusal, stated as positively as possible

Hourly workers who missed less than a day have the option of taking the missed time as vacation, sick, or personal hours or of being paid only for the hours they worked.

One small positive

Approval of vacation or personal days will be automatic; the normal requirement of giving at least 24 hours' notice is waived.

Goodwill ending

Thanks for all the efforts you have made to continue giving our customers the best possible service during one of the snowiest winters on record.

- Do you and the reader have a good relationship?
- Does the organization treat people well?
- Have readers been warned of possible negatives?
- Have readers "bought into" the criteria for the decision?
- Do communications after the negative build goodwill?

What are the most common kinds of negative messages?

INSTANT REPLAY

Organizing Bad News to Peers and Subordinates

1. Describe the problem.
2. Present an alternative or compromise, if one is available.
3. If possible, ask for input or action.

Rejections and refusals, disciplinary notices, negative perform-ance appraisals, and layoffs and firings are common negative messages.

Three of the most difficult kinds of negative messages to write are rejections and refusals, disciplinary notices and negative performance appraisals, and layoffs and firings.

Rejections and Refusals

When you refuse requests, try to use a buffer. Give an alternative if one is available. For example, if you are denying credit, it may still be possible for the reader to put an expensive item on layaway.

Politeness and length help. An experiment using a denial of additional insurance found that subjects preferred a rejection letter that was longer, more tactful, and more personal. The preferred letter started with a buffer, used a good reason for the refusal, and offered sales promotion in the last paragraph.[2]

Since English-speaking Canadians and Canadian immigrants from high-context cultures (Chinese, Japanese, Indian, Pakistani) value courtesy, they would prefer this organizational structure.[3]

SEE THE OLC!

The Business Writer's Free Library

When you refuse requests within your organization, use your knowledge of the organization's culture and of the specific individual to craft your message. In some organizations, it may be appropriate to use company slogans, offer whatever help already established departments can give, and refer to the individual's good work. In less personal organizations, a simple negative without embellishment may be more appropriate.

Disciplinary Notices and Negative Performance Appraisals

Present disciplinary notices and negative performance appraisals directly, with no buffer. A buffer might encourage the recipient to minimize the message's importance—and might even become evidence in a court case that the employee had not been told to shape up "or else." Cite quantifiable observations of the employee's behaviour, rather than generalizations or inferences based on it. If an employee is disciplined by being laid off without pay, specify when the employee is to return.

Performance appraisals are discussed in detail in ◄|► Module 13 on persuasive messages. Performance appraisals will be positive when they are designed to help a good employee improve. But when an employee violates a company rule or fails to improve after repeated appraisals, the company may discipline the employee or build a dossier to support firing him or her.

■ Layoffs and Firings

Information about layoffs and firings is normally delivered orally but accompanied by a written statement explaining severance pay or unemployment benefits that may be available. The written statement should start either with the reason or with the decision itself. A buffer would not be appropriate.

If a company is in financial trouble, management needs to communicate the problem clearly long before it is necessary to lay anyone off. Sharing information and enlisting everyone's help in finding solutions may make it possible to save jobs. Sharing information also means that layoff notices, if they become necessary, will be a formality; they should not be new information to employees.

Before you fire someone, double-check the facts. Make sure that the employee has been told about the problem and that he or she will be fired if the problem is not corrected. Give the employee the real reason for the firing. Offering a face-saving reason unrelated to poor performance can create legal liabilities. But avoid broadcasting the reason to other people: doing so can leave the company liable to a defamation suit.[4]

■ What's the best subject line for a negative message?

Only use negative subject lines if you think the reader may otherwise ignore the message.

Letters don't require subject lines (◀▶ Module 9, p. 155). Omit a subject line in negative letters unless you think readers may ignore what they think is a routine message. (See, for example, Figure 12.1 on 206 of this module.)

When you give bad news, use a subject line that focuses on solutions, not problems:

> Subject: Improving Our Subscription Letter

Or, you can put the topic (but not your action on it) in the subject line:

> Subject: Status of Conversion Table Program
>
> Because of heavy demands on our time, we have not yet been able to write programs for the conversion tables you asked for.

■ How can PAIBOC help me write negative messages?

The PAIBOC questions help you examine the points your message should include.

Before you tackle the assignments for this module, examine the following problem. As in Module 10, the PAIBOC questions probe the basic points required for a solution. Study the two sample solutions to see what makes one unacceptable and the other one good.[5] The checklist in Figure 12.10 on page 220 can help you evaluate a draft.

FIGURE 12.7

P A I B O C

Questions for Analysis

Use the PAIBOC questions to analyze business communication problems:

P What are your **purposes** in writing?

A Who is your **audience?** How do members of your audience differ? What audience characteristics are relevant to this particular message?

I What **information** must your message include?

B What reasons or reader **benefits** can you use to support your position?

O What **objections** can you expect your readers to have? What negative elements of your message must you de-emphasize or overcome?

C How will the **context** affect reader response? Think about your relationship to the reader, the morale in the organization, the economy, the time of year, and any special circumstances.

■ Problem

You're director of employee benefits for a Fortune 500 company. Today, you received the following memo:

> From: Michelle Jagtiani
>
> Subject: Getting My Retirement Benefits
>
> Next Friday will be my last day here. I am leaving [name of company] to take a position at another firm.
>
> Please process a cheque for my retirement benefits, including both the deductions from my salary and the company's contributions for the last three and a half years. I would like to receive the cheque by next Friday if possible.

You have bad news for Michelle. Although the company does contribute an amount to the retirement fund equal to the amount deducted for retirement from the employee's paycheque, employees who leave with fewer than five years of employment get only their own contributions. Michelle will get back only the money that has been deducted from her own pay, plus 4 percent interest compounded quarterly. Her payments and interest come to just over $17 200; the amount could be higher depending on the amount of her last paycheque, which will include compensation for any unused vacation days and sick leave. Furthermore, since the amounts deducted were not considered taxable income, she will have to pay income tax on the money she receives.

You cannot process the cheque until after her resignation is effective, so you will mail it to her. You have her home address on file; if she's moving, she needs to let you know where to send the cheque. Processing the cheque may take two to three weeks.

Write a memo to Michelle. Use the PAIBOC questions in Figure 12.7.

■ Analysis of the Problem

P What are your **purposes** in writing or speaking?

- To tell Michelle that she will get only her own contributions, plus 4 percent interest compounded quarterly; that the cheque will be mailed to her home address two to three weeks after her last day on the job; and that the money will be taxable as income
- To build goodwill so that she feels that she has been treated fairly and consistently; to minimize negative feelings she may have
- To close the door on this subject

A Who is your **audience?** How do the members of your audience differ from each other? What audience characteristics are relevant to this particular message?

The audience is Michelle Jagtiani. Unless she's a personal friend, you probably wouldn't know why she's leaving and where she's going.

There's a lot you don't know. She may or may not know much about taxes; she may or may not be able to take advantage of tax-reduction strategies. You can't assume the answers because you wouldn't have them in real life.

I What **information** must your message include?

Your message must tell Michelle when the cheque will arrive; the facts that the cheque will be based on her contributions, not her employer's, and that the money will be taxable income; how lump-sum retirement benefits are calculated; and the fact that you have her current address on file but need a new address if she's moving.

B What reasons or reader **benefits** can you use to support your position?

Stating the amount currently in her account may make Michelle feel that she is getting a significant sum of money. Suggesting someone who can give free tax advice (if the company offers this as a fringe benefit) reminds her of the benefits of working with the company. Wishing her luck with her new job is a nice touch.

O What **objections** can you expect your readers to have? What negative elements of your message must you de-emphasize or overcome?

Michelle is getting about half the amount she expected, since she won't receive any matching funds.

She might have been able to earn more than 4 percent interest if she had invested the money herself. Depending on her personal tax situation, she may pay more tax on the money as a lump sum than would have been due had she paid it each year as she earned the money.

C How will the **context** affect the reader's response? Think about your relationship to the reader, the morale in the organization, the economy, the time of year, and any special circumstances.

The stock market has not been doing well; 4 percent interest is looking good.

◼ Discussion of the Sample Solutions

The solution in Figure 12.8 on page 218 is not acceptable. The subject line gives a negative with no reason or alternative. The first sentence has a condescending tone that is particularly offensive in negative messages. The last sentence focuses on what is being taken away rather than what remains. Paragraph 2 lacks you-attitude and is vague. The memo ends with a negative. There is nothing anywhere in the memo to build goodwill.

The solution in Figure 12.9 on page 219, in contrast, is very good. The policy serves as a buffer and explanation. The negative is stated clearly but is buried in the paragraph to avoid overemphasizing it. The paragraph ends on a positive note by specifying the amount in the account and the fact that the sum might be even higher.

Paragraph 3 contains the additional negative information that the amount will be taxable but offers the alternative that it may be possible to reduce taxes. The writer builds goodwill by suggesting a specific person the reader could contact.

Paragraph 4 tells the reader what address is in the company files (Michelle may not know whether the files are up to date), asks that she update it if necessary, and ends with the reader's concern: getting her cheque promptly.

The final paragraph ends on a positive note. This generalized goodwill is appropriate when the writer does not know the reader well.

FIGURE 12.8

An Unacceptable Solution to the Sample Problem

April 20, 2007

To: Michelle Jagtiani

From   Lisa Niaz *LN*

Negative!

Subject   Denial of Matching Funds

Give reason before refusal

You cannot receive a cheque the last day of work and you will get only your own contributions, not a matching sum from the company, because you have not worked for the company for at least five full years.

Better to be specific

This is lifted straight from the problem. The language in problems is often negative and stuffy; information is disorganized.

Your payments and interest come to just over $17 200; the amount could be higher depending on the amount of your last paycheque, which will include compensation for any unused vacation days and sick leave. Furthermore, since the amounts deducted were not considered taxable income, you will have to pay income tax on the money you receive.

The cheque will be sent to your home address. If the address we have on file is incorrect, please correct it so that your cheque is not delayed. *— Negative —*

Think about the situation and use your own words to create a satisfactory message.

How will reader know what you have on file? Better to give current address as you have it.

FIGURE 12.9
A Good Solution to the Sample Problem

April 20, 2007

To: Michelle Jagtiani

From: Lisa Niaz *LN*

Subject: Receiving Employee Contributions from Retirement Accounts   *Neutral*

Good to state reason in third person to de-emphasize negative
Employees who leave the company with at least five full years of employment are entitled both to the company contributions and to the retirement benefit paycheque deductions contributed to retirement accounts. Those employees who leave the company with fewer than five years of employment will receive the employee paycheque contributions made to their retirement accounts.

Good to be specific
You now have $17 240.62 in your account, which includes 4% interest compounded quarterly. The amount you receive could be even higher since you will also receive payment for any unused sick leave and vacation days.

Good to show how company can help
Because you now have access to the account, the amount you receive will be considered taxable income. Beth Jordan in Employee Financial Services can give you information about possible tax deductions and financial investments that can reduce your income taxes.

Good to be specific
The cheque will be sent to your home address on May 16. The address we have on file is 2724 Merriman Road, Kingston, ON K7L 3N7. If your address changes, please let us know so you can receive your cheque promptly. *Positive*

Good luck with your new job!
Forward-looking

FIGURE 12.10

Checklist for Negative Messages

❏ Is the subject line appropriate?
❏ If a buffer is used, does it avoid suggesting either a positive or a negative response?
❏ Is the reason presented before the refusal? Is the reason relevant to the reader?
❏ Is the negative information clear?
❏ Is an alternative given, if a good one is available? Does the message provide all the information needed to act on the alternative but leave the choice up to the reader?
❏ Does the last paragraph avoid repeating the negative information?
❏ Is the tone acceptable—not defensive, cold, preachy, or arrogant?

Checklist for All Messages, Not Just Negative Ones

❏ Does the message use you-attitude and positive emphasis?
❏ Is the style easy to read and friendly?
❏ Is the visual design of the message inviting?
❏ Is the format correct?
❏ Does the message use standard grammar? Is it free from typos?

Add Originality in a Negative Message

❏ Use an effective buffer, if one is appropriate.
❏ Include a clear, complete statement of the reason for the refusal.
❏ Offer a good alternative, clearly presented, that shows that you're thinking about what the reader really needs.
❏ Add details that show you're thinking about a specific organization and the specific people in that organization.

Employability Skills 2000+

The Conference Board of Canada
Insights You Can Count On

Please see the OLC to preview the key skills from the Conference Board of Canada's Employability Skills 2000+ covered in this module.

Review of Key Points

1. How should writers organize negative letters?
2. How should writers organize negative messages to supervisors?
3. How should writers organize negative messages to peers and subordinates?
4. What are the most common types of buffers?
5. What are four good reasons for offering alternatives or compromises when refusing requests?
6. What are three good reasons to consider the ethical implications of what you say?

Assignments for Module 12

Questions for Critical Thinking

12.1 How do specific varieties of negative messages adapt the basic pattern?

12.2 How do you use positive emphasis in a negative message?

12.3 How do you decide whether to give the negative directly or to buffer it?

Exercises and Problems

12.4 Rejecting Employees' Suggestions

For years, businesses have had suggestion programs, rewarding employees for money-saving ideas. Now your city government has adopted such a program, but not all the suggestions are adopted. Today, you need to send messages to the following people.

Because their suggestions are being rejected, they will not get any cash award.

1. Diane Hilgers, secretary, Mayor's office. Suggestion: Charge for 911 calls. Reason for rejection: "This would be a public relations disaster. People call because they have emergencies. We already charge for ambulance or paramedic trips; to charge just for the call will offend people. And it might not save money. It's a lot cheaper to prevent a burglary or murder than to track down

the person afterward—to say nothing of the trauma of the loss or death. Bad idea."

2. Steve Rieneke, building and grounds supervisor. Suggestion: Fire the city's public relations specialists. Reason for rejection: "Positive attitudes toward city workers and policies make the public more willing to support public programs and taxes. In the long run, we think this is money well spent."

3. Jose Rivera, Accountant I. Suggestion: Schedule city council meetings during the day to save on light bills and staff overtime. Reason for rejection: "Having the meetings in the evening enables more citizens to attend. People have to be able to comment. Open meetings are essential so that citizens don't feel that policies and taxes are being railroaded through."

Write the messages.

12.5 Telling the Boss about a Problem

In any organization, things sometimes go wrong. Tell your supervisor about a problem in your unit and recommend what should be done.

As your instructor directs,

a. Prepare notes for a meeting with your supervisor.

b. Write an email message to your supervisor.
c. Write a memo to your supervisor.
d. Give an oral presentation on the problem.
e. Write a memo to your instructor explaining the problem, the corporate culture, and the reasons for your solution.

12.6 Telling Customers That Prices Are Going Up

Periodically, organizations raise prices or impose separate fees for services that were previously free. Think of an increase in the prices your customers pay.

As your instructor directs,

a. Write a letter to customers, telling them about the new fees or higher prices.

b. Examine your organization's files for messages sent out the last time prices were raised. Are the messages effective?

Why or why not? Include copies of the messages with your analysis of them.

12.7 Refusing a Gift

As the head of a charitable organization, you spend a lot of your time asking for money. But today, you're turning down a gift: a time-share condominium in Florida. Time-shares are so difficult to sell that regular real-estate agents do not list them. Places that list time-shares frequently charge an upfront fee (not just a commission, which is paid if and when the unit sells). If you accepted the gift, your organization would have to pay maintenance fees charged by the homeowners' association and taxes until the unit sold (if it sold). And you'd probably have to hire someone to check on the property occasionally, since the maintenance fee covers general building maintenance, not repairs for a specific unit. You don't want the expense and hassle of something that may or may not ever yield funds for your organization, so you're going to refuse the gift.

Write a letter to the would-be donors, Benjamin and Sarah Mellon, refusing the gift.

As your instructor directs,

Write letters for one or more of the following situations.

a. Yours is a well-known national charity. You have never met the Mellons, but your records show that they have given small gifts (under $100) in three of the last five years.

b. Yours is a local religious organization; the Mellons are prominent members. They don't give much money, but they're active and faithful.

c. Yours is a local charitable organization that struggles to stay open. The Mellons are major contributors. Sarah Mellon served on your board of directors, in a term ending three years ago.

d. Yours is a national charity. No one in the office has ever heard of the Mellons. They haven't contributed in the last three years—your records don't go back further.

Hints:
- Choose a charitable organization you know something about.
- Give the real reason for the refusal. You would accept real estate that seemed easy to sell.
- In situations (a) to (c) above, thank the Mellons for their past support. Be specific about what they've done.
- Use a salutation and complimentary close that are appropriate to the situation.
- In all the situations, encourage the donor to give other (more liquid) gifts to you in the future. Tell about upcoming opportunities for giving.

12.8 Refusing to Participate on a Panel

As a prominent speaker, you get many requests to appear before various groups. Today, you've received a request to participate in a panel of three to five professionals who will talk about "Succeeding in the Real World." The session will run from 2:00 to 5:00 P.M. on the second Sunday of next month.

You're trying to cut back on outside commitments. Work continues to take much of your time; you have major obligations in a volunteer organization; and you want some time for yourself and your family. This request does not fit your priorities.

Decline the invitation.

As your instructor directs,

Assume that the request is from one of the following:

a. A university business honour society that expects 250 students at the session
b. The youth group at the church, synagogue, temple, or mosque you attend
c. The Chinese Student Association at the local college or university

12.9 Announcing Cost-Savings Measures

Your company has to cut costs but would prefer to avoid laying off workers. Therefore, you have adopted the following money-saving ideas. Some can be implemented immediately; some will be implemented at renewal dates. The company will no longer pay for

* Flowers at the receptionist's desk and in executive offices
* Skyboxes for professional sporting events
* Employees' dues for professional and trade organizations
* Liquor at business meals

Only essential business travel will be approved. The company will pay only for the lowest cost of air travel (coach, reservation 7 to 14 days in advance, stay over Saturday night).

The company will no longer buy tables or blocks of tickets for charitable events and will not make any cash donations to charity until money is less tight.

Counters will be put on the photocopiers. People must have access numbers to make photocopies; personal photocopies will cost $0.10 a page.

As the chief financial officer, write a memo to all employees, explaining the changes.

12.10 Closing Bill-Payment Offices

For many years, Chilliwack Public Utilities Commission had five office locations where people could take their payments. On the first of the month following next month, you're closing these offices. On that date, 100 local merchants, such as grocers, will begin to accept utility payments. Closing the freestanding offices will save your municipality almost $1 million a year. Customers will still be able to mail in payments or have them deducted automatically from their bank accounts.

Write a notice that can be inserted in utility bills this month and next month.

12.11 Giving a Customer Less Credit Than She Wants

Yang-Ming Lee applied for your VISA card, asking for a credit limit of $15 000 and a separate card for her husband, Chad Hoang. You've checked the credit references, and they're good enough to merit granting a credit card. But you generally give new customers only a $7500 limit, even when the family income is very high, as it is in this case. You might make an exception if your bank had a previous relationship with the client, but no such relationship exists here. Although you have no set policy for reviewing and raising credit limits, normally you would expect at least six months of paying the minimum amount promptly.

Write a letter to Ms. Lee, granting her a credit card with a $7500 limit.

12.12 Rejecting a Member's Request

All non-supervisory public service workers in your province are union members. As a paid staff person for the union, you spend about a third of your time writing and editing the monthly magazine, *Public [Your Province] Employee*. You receive this letter:

Dear Editor:

Every month, we get two copies of the union magazine—one addressed to me, one to my husband. We have different last names, so your computer may not realize that we're connected, but we are, and we don't need two copies. Sending just one copy will save printing and postage costs and reduce environmental waste. My name is Dorothy Livingston; my husband is Eric Beamer. Please combine our listings to send just one copy.

Sincerely,

Dorothy Livingston

As it happens, a couple of years ago you investigated possible savings of sending just one mailing to couples who both work for the province. Sophisticated computerized merge/purge programs to eliminate duplicates are far too expensive for the union's tight budget. And going through the mailing list manually to locate and change duplications would cost more than would be saved in postage. Printing costs wouldn't necessarily drop either, since it actually costs less for each copy to print big runs.

But you want to build goodwill—both with this writer and for the union in general. Extra copies of the magazine (whether a double mailing or simply a copy someone is finished with) could be given to a non-member or taken to a doctor's or dentist's waiting room or a barber or beauty shop. Such sharing would help spread public support for the union and provincial government workers.

Write a letter to Ms. Livingston, explaining why you can't combine mailings.

Polishing Your Prose

Parallel Structure

Use parallel structure in lists, headings, and subheadings in documents by using the same grammatical form for ideas that have the same relationship in your sentence.

Not parallel: Good reports are factual, logical, and demonstrate clarity.

It may be easier to see faulty parallelism by listing parts that need to be parallel. Check to make sure each component fits with the words that introduce the list.

Not parallel: Good reports are
Factual
Logical
Demonstrate clarity

Parallel: Good reports are
Factual
Logical
Clear

Make sure all of the list is horizontal or vertical. Don't start a list horizontally and finish it vertically.

Incorrect: As department manager,
I supervised eight employees.
- Wrote the department budget
- Presented our sales strategy to the board of directors

Correct: As department manager, I supervised eight employees, wrote the department budget, and presented our sales strategy to the board of directors.

Also correct: As department manager, I
- Supervised eight employees.
- Wrote the department budget.
- Presented our sales strategy to the board of directors.

Headings must be parallel throughout the document, but subheads need only be parallel to other subheads in the same section.

Not parallel: Should Ogden Industries Purchase Blue Chip International in 2002?
- Short-Term Costs
- What Are the Long-Term Gains?

Parallel: Should Ogden Industries Purchase Blue Chip International in 2002?
- Short-Term Costs
- Long-Term Gains

In addition to grammatical parallelism, also check your sentences for logical parallelism.

Incorrect: The group ranges from males and females to people in their 20s, 30s, and 40s.

Better: We interviewed men and women ranging in age from 20 to 50.

Gender is one category; age is another.

Exercises

Rewrite the following sentences or headings to make them parallel.

1. Last week, Alain and Rochelle flew to Toronto, Montreal, Québec City, and the capital of the state of Michigan.
2. Ask Ms. Liken, Mr. Fitzgerald, Bill Anderson, and Professor Timmons to join us for the meeting.
3. To ship a package
   1. Fill out an address form.
   2. Specify on the form how the package should be sent.
3. If you want to send a package by overnight mail, your supervisor must initial the appropriate box on the address form.
4. Make sure benefits announcements get routed to managers, supervisors, and the folks in the Human Resources Department.
5. Appointments can be scheduled in 5-minute, 10-minute, quarter-hour, or 20-minute intervals.
6. The project's fixed costs include material, salaries, advertising, bonus packages for anyone who goes above and beyond the call of duty, and the cost of travel to different cities.
7. This report discusses
   Why We Should Upgrade Capital Equipment
   Why We Should Increase Staff by 25 percent
   The Benefits of Decreasing Employee Turnover
   The Importance of Identifying New Product Markets
8. The selection committee reviews each job applicant based on education, experience, extracurricular activities, the awards the employee has received, and the strength of the applicant's personal statement.
9. Use the telephone to answer customer questions, email to send order confirmations, and take orders using our Web page.
10. Each agency should estimate
    Annual Costs
    Costs per Month
      Salaries
      New Equipment Costs
      How Much You Need in a Reserve Fund for Unexpected Expenses

Check your answers to the odd-numbered exercises on page 572.

Online Learning Centre

Visit the Online Learning Centre at www.mcgrawhill.ca/olc/locker to access module quizzes, a searchable glossary, résumé and letter templates, additional business writing samples, CBC videos, and other learning and study tools.

MODULE

13

Persuasive Messages

Module Outline

- What are persuasive appeals?
- What is the best persuasive strategy?
- How should I organize persuasive messages?
- How do I identify and overcome objections?
- What other techniques make my messages more persuasive?
- What are the most common kinds of persuasive messages?
- What's the best subject line for a persuasive message?
- How can PAIBOC help me write persuasive messages?

Review of Key Points

Assignments for Module 13

Polishing Your Prose: Narrative Voice

LEARNING OBJECTIVES

After reading and applying the information in Module 13, you'll be able to demonstrate

Knowledge of
- Persuasive appeals
- Persuasive organization patterns

Skills to
- Choose and use persuasive strategies
- Organize persuasive messages
- Identify and overcome objections
- Write common kinds of persuasive messages
- Write effective subject lines for persuasive messages
- Further analyze business communication situations

The Conference Board of Canada
Insights You Can Count On

Please see the OLC to preview the key skills from the Conference Board of Canada's Employability Skills 2000+ covered in this module.

FYI

We are more readily persuaded by what is familiar. Because of our cultural affinity with Americans, for example, Canada is not only a prime tourist location, but also a prime provider of outsourcing services for U.S. companies.

Source: Virginia Galt, "Canada a Comfort Zone for Distant Firms," *The Globe and Mail*, November 15, 2004. B1.

FYI

Smart retailers target women shoppers, since women in North America make the majority of purchases. And many more of these purchases are being made online. Initially, Canadians purchased the safe and familiar—books, music, electronics. Now Canadian women spend more than $3 billion annually shopping online for "... home/family, health and beauty ..." products and services.

Source: Deborah Fulsang, "Shopping Canada On-line," *The Globe and Mail*, June 25, 2005. L7.

In our knowledge-based economy, where brains are capital, businesses depend on persuasion and buy-in to get quality work done. You can command people to make widgets. You can't command knowledge workers to be creative. And even if you're making widgets, just going through the motions isn't enough. You want people to make high-quality widgets while reducing scrap and other costs. Internal commitment is needed to make that happen.

External motivation doesn't last. Some people may buy a certain brand of pizza if they have a coupon. But when the coupon expires, or if another company offers the same deal, customers may leave. In contrast, if customers like your pizza better—in other words, if they are motivated internally to choose it—then you may keep your customers even if another company comes in with a lower price.

In general, people are internally motivated when they believe both the message and the messenger.

What are persuasive appeals?

People are persuaded by their perceptions of 1) the trustworthiness of the messenger, and 2) the emotional and logical resonances of the message.

Your audience will attend to your message if they perceive you to be a trustworthy or credible person; they will act on your message if the *facts and the way you present* those facts appeal to their *deepest values and beliefs*. Aristotle identified these rhetorical (persuasive) elements as *ethos* (the audience's perception of the speaker or writer's trustworthiness), *nomos* (the messenger's appeal to beliefs or values he or she shares with the audience), *pathos* (the message's appeal to the audience's emotions), and *logos* (the message's appeal to the audience's logic).

Because all successful communication contains a persuasive element, the ability to persuade others is a fundamental interpersonal leadership skill. Knowing the elements of persuasion and your audience's needs enables you to convince others effectively.

Persuasive messages include the following:

- Orders and requests
- Proposals and recommendations
- Sales and fundraising letters
- Job application letters
- Reports, if they recommend action
- Efforts to change people's behaviour, such as collection letters, criticisms or performance appraisals where you want the subordinate to improve behaviour, and public-service ads designed to reduce drunk driving, drug use, and so on

All persuasive messages have several purposes.

Primary purposes

- To have the reader act
- To provide enough information so that the reader knows exactly what to do
- To overcome any objections that might prevent or delay action

Secondary purposes

- To establish a good impression of the writer
- To build a good image of the writer's organization
- To build a good relationship between the writer and reader
- To reduce or eliminate future correspondence on the same subject

What is the best persuasive strategy?

It depends on how much and what kinds of resistance you expect.

FYI

The best persuasive strategy of all is making a good first impression. First impressions do count—a lot! In fact, we make our minds up about others almost immediately, and become so attached to that first impression that little can convince us to alter our initial judgment. Context contributes to forming first impressions. That's why, for example, we might not recognize our teachers at the mall: they're out of context. To make that vital first impression, dress for the occasion. Similarly, make that vital first impression with your documents' appearance and design: use format, white space, font type and size, sentence and paragraph length to meet readers' expectations in context.

Four basic short-term strategies exist: direct request, problem-solving persuasion, sales,[1] and reward and punishment. This book will focus on the first two strategies. Rewards and punishment have limited use, in part because they don't produce permanent change and because they produce psychological reactance (◀▶ Module 12, p. 210). To effect a major change, no single message will work, as anti-smoking lobbyists are well aware. To change attitudes and behaviours, you will need a campaign with a series of messages, preferably from a variety of sources.

Your organizational pattern is part of your message's persuasive element, because specific patterns meet the audience's expectations and are, therefore, logically and emotionally appealing.

Use the **direct (deductive or good news) request pattern** in these instances:

- The audience will do as you ask without any resistance.
- You need a response only from the people who are willing to act.
- The audience is busy and may not read all the messages received.
- Your organization's culture prefers direct requests.

Use the **indirect (problem-solving, inductive, bad news) pattern** in the following cases:

- The audience is likely to object to doing as you ask.
- You need action from everyone.
- You trust the audience to read the entire message.

To choose the best persuasive content, analyze your audience. The most persuasive argument is the one that best meets your audience's needs. (◀▶ Module 8, Maslow's Hierarchy of Needs)

Your message strategy must also conform to the values and norms of your corporate culture. A persuasive strategy that works in one organization may be unacceptable elsewhere.

Corporate culture (◀▶ Module 2, p. 35), conveyed through multiple spoken and unspoken messages, is learned by imitation and observation. Observe the style of powerful people in your organization: when you show a draft to your boss, are you told to tone down your statements or to make them stronger? Role models and advice are two ways that organizations communicate their cultures to newcomers.

Different ethnic and national cultures also have different preferences for gaining compliance. Canada's international reputation as a welcoming nation of courteous peacekeepers is reflected in English Canadians' cultural preference for indirect requests, even though Canada is a low-context culture. Canadian newcomers emigrating from Southeast Asia, India, Pakistan, and the Philippines also communicate using indirect requests; high-context cultures see direct requests as rude and aggressive.

How should I organize persuasive messages?

In direct requests, start with the request. In a problem-solving message, start with the problem you share.

Start with the request only when you anticipate ready agreement, when you fear that a busy reader may not read a message whose relevance isn't clear, or when your organization's culture prefers direct requests.

Writing Direct Requests

When you expect quick agreement, save the reader's time by presenting the request directly.

1. **Consider asking immediately for the information or service you want.** Delay the request if it seems too abrupt or if you have several purposes in the message.
2. **Give readers all the information and details they will need to act on your request.** Number your questions or set them off with bullets so the reader can check to see that all of them have been answered.

In a claim (where a product is under warranty or a shipment was defective), explain the circumstances so that the reader knows what happened. Be sure to include all the relevant details: date of purchase, model or invoice number, and so on.

In more complicated direct requests, anticipate possible responses. Suppose you're asking for information about equipment meeting certain specifications. Explain which criteria are most important so that the reader can recommend an alternative if no single product meets all your needs. You may also want to tell the reader what your price constraints are and ask whether the item is in stock or must be special ordered.

3. **Ask for the action you want.** Do you want a cheque? a replacement? a catalogue? answers to your questions? If you need an answer by a certain time, say so. If possible, show the reader why the time limit is necessary.

Figure 13.1 summarizes this pattern. Figure 13.2 illustrates the pattern. Note that direct requests do not contain reader benefits and do not need to overcome objections: they simply ask for what is needed.

Direct requests should be direct. Don't make the reader guess what you want.

Indirect request: Is there a newer version of the 2001 *Accounting Reference Manual*?

Direct request: If there is a newer version of the 2001 *Accounting Reference Manual*, please send it to me.

In some direct requests, your combination of purposes may suggest a different organization. For example, in a letter asking a prospective employer to reimburse you for expenses after a job interview, you'd want to thank your hosts for their hospitality and reinforce the good impression you made at the interview. To do that, you'd spend the first two paragraphs talking about the trip and the interview. Only in the last third of the letter (or even in the postscript) would you make your request for reimbursement.

INSTANT REPLAY

Use the direct request pattern in these instances:

- The audience will do as you ask without any resistance.
- You need a response only from the people who are willing to act.
- The audience is busy and may not read all the messages received.
- Your organization's culture prefers direct requests.

Use the problem-solving pattern in these cases:

- The audience is likely to object to doing as you ask.
- You need action from everyone.
- You trust the audience to read the entire message.
- You expect logic to be more important than emotion in the decision.

FIGURE 13.1
How to Organize a Direct Request

> Request for Action

> Details

> Request for Action

FIGURE 13.2
A Direct Request

Saki's

October 23, 2007

Eva Pavlinic
532 Heath Street East
Toronto, ON M5W 3M1

Card Number: 503 913 248 1
Balance: $36.28
Payment Required: $33.00   *Request topic in subject line*

Courteous opening saves reader's face

Dear Eva Pavlinic

Perhaps you missed making your recent payment because the balance on your account is so small. It is not difficult to do and many of us overlook small balance accounts.   *Ask for actions. Make action easy.*

However, we would appreciate it if you would take a few minutes to mail us your cheque for $33.00.

Positive, friendly close

If your payment has already been made, thank you.

Credit Department
Tel: 416-555-4567

Similarly, in a letter asking about a graduate program, a major purpose might be to build a good image of yourself so that your application for financial aid will be viewed positively. To achieve that goal, you would provide information about your qualifications and interest in the field before you ask questions.

■ Organizing Problem-Solving Messages

Use an indirect (inductive or bad news) approach and the problem-solving pattern or organization when you expect resistance from the reader but you can show that doing what you suggest will solve the problem. This pattern allows you to disarm opposition by showing all the reasons in favour of your position before you give your readers a chance to say *no*.

1. **Mention the problem you share (which your request will solve).** Because you're interested in solving the problem, mention the problem objectively: it's a waste of time and ink to assign blame or mention personalities.

2. **Detail the results of the problem** *as they affect your reader.* Be specific about the cost in money, time, lost goodwill, inconvenience, and so on. Persuade your readers that *something* has to be done before you convince them that your solution is the best one.

3. **Explain the solution to the problem.** If you know that the reader will favour another solution, start with that solution and show why it won't work before you present your solution.

   Present your solution, focusing on practicality, workability, and desirability without using the words *I* or *my.* Appeal to the reader's wallet or sense of enlightened self-interest.

4. **Prove that any negative elements (cost, time, etc.) are outweighed by the advantages.**

5. **Summarize any additional benefits of the solution.** The main benefit—solving the problem—can be presented briefly since you described the problem in detail. However, if there are any additional benefits, mention them.

6. **Ask for the action you want.** Often your reader will authorize or approve something; other people will implement the action. Give your reader a reason to act promptly, perhaps offering a new reader benefit. ("By buying now, we can avoid the next quarter's price hikes.")

FIGURE 13.3
How to Organize a Problem-Solving Persuasive Message

Shared Problem

Details

Solution

Negatives

Reader Benefits

Request for Action

Figure 13.3 summarizes the pattern. Figure 13.4 implements the pattern. Reader benefits can be brief in this kind of message since the biggest benefit comes from solving the problem.

■ How do I identify and overcome objections?

Know your audience. Talk to your audience. Then try these strategies.

FYI

Because the most persuasive messages make it easy for the audience to comply, effective communicators try to express themselves as clearly as possible. You can find audience-focused communication resources on the Plain Language Association International website: http://www.plainlanguagenetwork.org/

The easiest way to learn about objections your audience may have is to ask knowledgeable people in your organization or your network.

• **Use open questions and phrase your questions neutrally,** so that people feel encouraged to express their opinions openly: "What concerns would you have about a proposal to do *x*?" "Who makes a decision about *y*?" "What do you like best about [the supplier or practice you want to change]?"

• **Ask follow-up questions** to be sure you understand: "Would you be likely to stay with your current supplier if you could get a lower price from someone else? Why?"

People are most aware of and willing to share objective constraints such as time and money. We are all less willing to disclose emotional anxieties. We all have a vested interest in something when we benefit directly from keeping things as they are. For example, those in power have a vested interest in retaining the system that gives them their power. Someone who designed a system has a vested interest in protecting that system from criticism. To admit that the system has faults is to admit that the designer made mistakes. In such cases, you'll need to probe to find out what the real reasons are.

The best way to deal with an objection is to eliminate it. To sell Jeep Cherokees in Japan, Mitsuru Sato convinced Chrysler to put the driver's seat on the right side, to make an extra preshipment quality check, and to rewrite the instruction booklet in Japanese style, with big diagrams and cartoons.[2]

If an objection is false, based on misinformation, give the response to the objection without naming the objection. In a brochure, you can present responses in a "question/answer" format. When objections have already been voiced, you may want to name the objection so that your audience realizes that you are responding to that specific objection. However, to

FIGURE 13.4
A Problem-Solving Persuasive Message

Memorandum

Date:　　February 15, 2007
To:　　　All Staff Members
From:　　Melissa J. Gutridge　*MJG*
Subject:　Why We Are Implementing a New Sign-out System

Directed subject line indicates writer's position

Shared problem

Successfully mainstreaming our clients into the community is very important, and daily interaction with the public is necessary. Our clients enjoy the times they get to go to the mall or out to lunch instead of remaining here all day. Recently, however, clients have been taken out on activities without staff members knowing where the client is and whom the client is with.

Specific example of problem

We need to know where all clients are at all times because social workers, psychologists, and relatives constantly stop by unannounced. Last week Janet's father stopped by to pick her up for a doctor's appointment and she was not here. No one knew where she was or whom she was with. Naturally her father was very upset and wanted to know what kind of program we were running. Staff members not knowing where our clients are and whom they are with is damaging to the good reputation of our staff and program.

Solution presented impersonally

Starting Monday, February 25, a sign-out board will be located by Betty's desk. Please write down where you and the client are going and when you expect to be back. When signing out, help clients sign themselves out. We can turn this into a learning experience for our clients. Then when a social worker stops by to see someone who isn't here, we can simply look at the sign-out board to tell where the client is and when he or she will return.

Additional reader benefit

Ask for action

Please help keep up the superb reputation you have helped us earn as a quality centre for adults with disabilities. Sign you and clients out at all times.

avoid solidifying the opposition, don't attribute the objection to your audience. Instead, use a less personal attribution and neutral language: "Some people wonder…"; "Some citizens are concerned that…"

If real objections remain, try one or more of the following strategies to counter objections:

1. Specify how much time or money is required—it may not be as much as the reader fears.

   Distributing flyers to each house or apartment in your neighbourhood will probably take two afternoons.

2. Put the time or money in the context of the benefits they bring.

   The additional $152 500 will (1) allow the Open Shelter to remain open 24 rather than 16 hours a day, (2) pay for three social workers to help men find work and homes, and (3) keep the neighbourhood bank open, so that men don't have to cash welfare cheques in bars, and so that they can save the $800 they need to have upfront to rent an apartment.

Toyota responded to North American brand loyalty by customizing its automotive products, promotions, and services to the Canadian market. Besides the products developed specifically for Canadian winters, the company's Canadian investments include financial support for local community organizations and Canada's Special Olympics, and partnerships with the Evergreen Learning Grounds Program and community colleges' technical training programs.

3. Show that money spent now will save money in the long run.

   By replacing the boiler now, we'll no longer have to release steam that the overflow tank can't hold. Depending on how severe the winter is, we will save $100 to $750 a year in energy costs. If energy costs rise, we'll save even more.

4. Show that doing as you ask will benefit a group or a cause the reader supports, although the action may not help the reader directly.

   By being a Big Brother or a Big Sister, you'll give a child the attention he or she needs to become a well-adjusted, productive adult.

5. Show the reader that the sacrifice is necessary to achieve a larger, more important goal to which he or she is committed.

   These changes will mean more work for all of us. But we've got to cut our costs 25 percent to keep the plant open and to keep our jobs.

6. Show that the advantages as a group outnumber or outweigh the disadvantages as a group.

> None of the locations is perfect. But the Québec City location gives us the most advantages and the fewest disadvantages.

7. Turn a disadvantage into an opportunity.

> With the hiring freeze, every department will need more lead time to complete its own work. By hiring a freelance worker, the Planning Department could provide that lead time.

What other techniques make my messages more persuasive?

Build credibility and emotional appeal. Use the right tone, and offer a reason to act promptly.

Persuasive messages—whether short term or long term—will be more effective if you build credibility and emotional appeal, use the right tone, and offer a reason to act promptly.

Build Credibility

Credibility is the audience's response to the source of the message. People are more easily persuaded by someone they see as expert, powerful, attractive, or trustworthy. We are also more easily persuaded by people whom we perceive to be like us (similar in class, values, and age) and by those who are articulate, confident, and likeable.

Build Rational Appeal

When you don't yet have the credibility that comes from being an expert or being powerful, build credibility by the language and strategy you use:

- **Be factual.** Use concrete language, supportive statistics, and exact dollar or time requirements. Don't exaggerate.

- **Be specific.** If you say "X is better," show in detail how it is better. Show the reader exactly where the savings or other benefits come from so that it's clear that the proposal really is as good as you say it is.

- **Be reliable.** If you suspect that a project will take longer to complete, cost more money, or be less effective than you originally thought, tell your audience *immediately*. Negotiate a new schedule that you can meet.

Build Emotional Appeal

Emotional appeal means making the reader want to do what you ask. People make decisions—even business decisions—logically and emotionally.[3]

For example, during his summer job, an engineering student saw how his company's waste treatment system could be redesigned to save the company more than $200 000 a year. He wrote a report recommending the change and gave it to his boss. Nothing happened. Why not? His supervisor wasn't about to send up a report that would require him to explain why he'd been wasting more than $200 000 a year of the company's money.[4]

Stories and psychological description (◀▶ p. 139) are effective ways to build emotional appeal. Emotional appeal works best when people want to be persuaded. Even when you need to provide statistics or numbers to convince the careful reader that your anecdote is a representative example, telling a story first makes your message more persuasive. Recent research suggests that stories are more persuasive because people remember them.[5]

Use the Right Tone

When you ask for action from people who report directly to you, you have several choices. Although orders ("Get me the Ervin file") and questions ("Do we have the third-quarter numbers yet?") might work, you'll get greater compliance with courtesy. When you need action from co-workers, superiors, or people outside the organization, you may need to be firm but you must always be polite.

Avoiding messages that sound parental or preachy is often a matter of tone. Saying "please" is important, especially to people on your level or outside the organization. Tone works better when you give reasons for your request.

Parental: Everyone is expected to comply with these regulations. I'm sure you can see that they are common-sense rules needed for our business.

Better: Even on casual days, visitors expect us to be professional. So please let's leave the gym clothes at home!

When you write to people you know well, humour can work. Just make sure that the message isn't insulting to anyone who doesn't find the humour funny.

Writing to superiors is trickier. You may want to tone down your request by using subjunctive verbs and explicit disclaimers that show you aren't taking a *yes* for granted.

Arrogant: Based on this evidence, I expect you to give me a new computer.

Better: If department funds permit, I would like a new computer.

Passive verbs and jargon sound stuffy. Use active imperatives—perhaps with "Please" to create a friendlier tone.

Stuffy: It is requested that you approve the above-mentioned action.

Better: Please authorize us to create a new subscription letter.

Offer a Reason for the Reader to Act Promptly

The longer people delay, the less likely they are to carry through with the action they had decided to take. In addition, you want a fast response so you can go ahead with your own plans.

Request action by a specific date. Always give people at least a week or two: they have other things to do besides respond to your requests. Set deadlines in the middle of the month, if possible. If you say, "Please return this by March 1," people will think, "I don't need to do this until March." Ask for the response by February 28 instead. If you can use a response even after the deadline, say so. Otherwise, people who can't make the deadline may not respond at all.

EXPANDING A CRITICAL SKILL

Preparing for a Performance Appraisal

Your performance appraisal constitutes a persuasive message for both you and the savvy supervisor: formative evaluation is a key retention technique. People crave performance feedback; indeed, top performers are primarily motivated by the recognition inherent in the performance appraisal. If your organization does not appraise or evaluate your performance at least once a year, ask for this feedback.

Use the occasion to accomplish three goals:

- Identify your boss's specific opinions about your performance.
- Communicate your ambitions.
- Ask for the training and experience you want.

Some supervisors don't know how to talk about subordinates' performance strengths and the skills they need to improve. If your supervisor doesn't specify them, ask, "What am I doing well?" and "Specifically, what are the two or three things I could do that would most improve my performance?"

In the twenty-first century, most of us will change employers a minimum of seven times. Even supposedly staid accountants will job-hop an average of five times during their careers. "Employers are impressed by people who make strategic career moves at various stages of their careers to improve or broaden their skills," according to Kathryn Bolt, district president of the Canadian division responsible for recruiting and placing accountants at Robert Half International Inc. To remain employable, therefore, you need to add to your current skill set and get new experiences (not just keep doing the same old thing). Be ready to name one or two training programs you'd like to take in the next six months. Indicate the kinds of projects you'd like a chance to try.

Let your boss know that you want to contribute even more to the organization; make it clear that you're interested in lateral or vertical moves. Ask, "What kinds of things should I do now so that I'm promotable a year (or two) from now?"

Having frequent discussions about work is a sign that your supervisor sees you as promotable. If your supervisor just asks you "yes/no" questions, he or she may not think of you as someone who has the ability or desire to advance. Use the performance appraisal to change the way your supervisor sees you and to prepare for the job you really want.

Source: Virginia Galt, "Job-hopping Now an Accepted Principle," *The Globe and Mail*, May 29, 2001, B15.

Show why you need a quick response:

- **Show that the time limit is real.** Perhaps you need information quickly to use it in a report that has a due date. Perhaps a decision must be made by a certain date to catch the start of the school year, the holiday selling season, or an election campaign. Perhaps you need to be ready for a visit from out-of-town or international colleagues.
- **Show that acting now will save time or money.** If business is slow and your industry isn't doing well, then your company needs to act now (to economize, to better serve customers) in order to be competitive. If business is booming and everyone is making a profit, then your company needs to act now to get its fair share of the available profits.
- **Show the cost of delaying action.** Will labour or material costs be higher in the future? Will delay mean more money spent on repairing something that will still need to be replaced?

An arresting image and concise text make this marketing postcard memorable.

What are the most common kinds of persuasive messages?

Orders, collection letters, performance appraisals, and letters of recommendation are the most common persuasive messages.

Orders

Orders may be written on forms, phoned in, or made by clicking boxes on the Web. When you write an order, be sure to do three things:

- Be specific. Give model or page numbers, colours, finishes, and so forth.
- Tell the company what you want if that model number is no longer available.
- Double-check your arithmetic, and add sales tax and shipping charges.

Collection Letters

Most businesses find that phoning rather than writing results in faster payment. But as more and more companies install voicemail systems, you may sometimes need to write a collection series of letters when leaving messages doesn't work.

Collection letters ask customers to pay (as they have already agreed to do) for the goods and services they have already received. Good credit departments send a series of letters. Letters in the series should be only a week or two apart. Waiting a month between letters implies that you're prepared to wait a long time—and the reader will be happy to oblige you.

Early letters are gentle, assuming that the reader intends to pay but has met with temporary problems or has forgotten. However, the request should assume that the cheque has been mailed but did not arrive. A student who had not yet been reimbursed by a company for a visit to the company's office put the second request in the P.S. of a letter refusing a job offer:

> P.S. The cheque to cover my expenses when I visited your office in March hasn't come yet. Could you check to see whether you can find a record of it? The amount was $490 (airfare, $290; hotel room, $185; taxi, $15).

FYI

Canada's aging population will result in a skilled labour shortage and a profound shift in the balance of power between workers and employers. Organizations will soon have to sell themselves to prospective employees, says Roger Martin, dean of the Joseph L. Rotman School of Management, University of Toronto.

Source: Andrea Gordon, "The Thirty-Five Best Companies to Work for," Report on *Business Magazine*, http://www.robmagazine.com/archive/2000ROBfebruary/html/cover35_best. html, retrieved July 9, 2001.

If one or two early letters don't result in payment, call the customer to ask whether your company has created a problem. It's possible that you shipped something the customer didn't want or sent the wrong quantity. It's possible that the invoice arrived before the product and was filed and forgotten. It's possible that the invoice document is poorly designed, so customers set it aside until they can figure it out. If any of these situations apply, you'll build goodwill by solving the problem rather than arrogantly asking for payment.[6]

Middle letters are more assertive in asking for payment. Figure 9.2 (◀|▶ p. 152) gives an example of a middle letter. Middle letters offer to negotiate a schedule for repayment if the reader is not able to pay the whole bill immediately, remind the reader of the importance of a good credit rating (which will be endangered if the bill remains unpaid), educate the reader about credit, and explain why the creditor must have prompt payment.

Unless you have firm evidence to the contrary, assume that readers have some legitimate reason for not yet paying. Even people who do not have enough money to pay all their bills, or people who put payment off as long as possible will respond more quickly if you do not accuse them. If a reader is offended by your assumption that he or she is dishonest, that anger can become an excuse to continue delaying payment.

Late letters threaten legal action if the bill is not paid. *Under federal law,* the writer can not threaten legal action unless he or she actually intends to sue. Other regulations also spell out what a writer may and may not do in a late letter.

Many small businesses find that establishing personal relationships with customers is the best way to speed payment.

■ Performance Appraisals

At regular intervals, supervisors evaluate or appraise the performance of their subordinates. In most organizations, employees have access to their files; sometimes they must sign the appraisal to show that they've read it. The supervisor normally meets with the subordinate to discuss the appraisal.

As a subordinate, you should prepare for the appraisal interview by listing your achievements and goals. Where do you want to be in one year? Five years? What training and experience do you need to reach your goals? Also think about any skills you'd like to improve. If you need training, advice, or support from the organization to build on your strengths, the appraisal interview is a good time to ask for this help.

Appraisals both motivate the employee and protect the organization. But these two purposes may conflict. People, particularly top performers, need praise and reassurance to believe that they're valued and can do better. But the praise that motivates someone to improve can come back to haunt the company if the person does not eventually do acceptable work. An organization is in trouble if it tries to fire someone whose evaluations never mention mistakes.

Avoid labels (*wrong, bad*) and inferences. Instead, cite specific observations that describe behaviour.

Inference: Sam is an alcoholic.

Vague observation: Sam calls in sick a lot. Subordinates complain about his behaviour.

Specific observation:	Sam called in sick 12 days in the past two months. After a business lunch with a customer last week, Sam was walking unsteadily. Two of his subordinates have said that they would prefer not to make sales trips with him because they find his behaviour embarrassing.

Sam might be an alcoholic. He might also be having a reaction to a physician-prescribed drug; he might have a mental illness; he might be showing symptoms of a physical illness other than alcoholism. A supervisor who jumps to conclusions creates ill will, closes the door to solving the problem, and may provide grounds for legal action against the organization.

Be specific in an appraisal.

Too vague:	Sue does not manage her time as well as she could.
Specific:	Sue's first three weekly sales reports have been three, two, and four days late, respectively; the last weekly sales report for the month is not yet in.

Without specifics, Sue won't know that her boss objects to late reports. She may think that she is being criticized for spending too much time on sales calls or for not working 80 hours a week. Without specifics, she might change the wrong behaviours in a futile effort to please her boss.

Good managers try not only to identify the specific problems in subordinates' behaviour but also to discover the causes of the problem and to provide resources for change. Does the employee need more training? Perhaps a training course or a mentor will help. Does he or she need to work more effectively? Perhaps this is a time-management, organization, or motivation problem.

Performance appraisals are motivational and therefore useful when they occur frequently and regularly, when managers' behaviours are consistent with organizational values and when employees feel engaged in the process. Persuasive performance appraisals focus on specific attitudes and behaviours relevant to department and company goals. When evaluating others' performances, it's vital to clarify the most important areas and to elicit specific recommendations for improvement from the employee. No one can improve 17 weaknesses at once. Which two should the employee work on this month? Is getting reports in on time more important than increasing sales? Supervisors should explicitly identify these priorities during the appraisal interview.

Identify goals and benchmarks in specific, measurable, achievable, relevant, and time-lined terms. Achieving "considerable progress toward completing" a report could mean anything when the manager thinks that "considerable progress" means 50 percent or 85 percent of the total work. When the manager and employee articulate and agree on concrete goals, both the employee and the organization benefit. (See Figure 13.5.)

■ Letters of Recommendation

In an effort to protect themselves against lawsuits, some companies state only how long they employed someone and the position that person held. Such bare-bones letters have themselves been the target of lawsuits when employers did not reveal relevant negatives. Whatever the legal climate, there may be times when you want to recommend someone for an award or for a job.

Letters of recommendation must be specific. General positives that are not backed up with specific examples and evidence are seen as weak recommendations. Letters of recommendation that focus on minor points also suggest that the person is weak.

FIGURE 13.5

A Performance Appraisal

Date: February 13, 2007

To: Barbara Buchanan

From: Brittany Papper *BAP*

Subject: Your Performance Thus Far in Our Collaborative Group   *Subject line indicates that memo is a performance appraisal*

Overall evaluation You are a strong contributor to our group's success. Overall, our business communication group has been one of the best groups I have ever worked with, and I think that only minor improvements are needed to make our group even better.

What You're Doing Well

Specific observations provide dates, details of performance You demonstrated flexibility and compatibility at our last meeting, before we turned in our proposal on February 12, by offering to type the proposal since I had to study for an exam in one of my other classes. I really appreciated this because I really did not have the time to do it. I will remember this if you are ever too busy with your other classes and cannot type the final report.

Another positive critical incident occurred February 5. We had discussed researching the topic of sexual discrimination in hiring and promotion at Northern Insurance. As we read more about what we had to do, we became uneasy about reporting the information from our source who works at Northern. I called you later that evening to talk about changing our topic to a less personal one. You were very understanding and said that you agreed that the original topic was a touchy one. You offered suggestions for other topics and had a positive attitude about the adjustment. Your suggestions ended my worries and made me realize that you are a positive and supportive person.

Other strengths Your ideas definitely contribute to our group. You're good at brainstorming ideas, yet you're willing to go with whatever the group decides. That's a nice combination of creativity and flexibility.

Areas for Improvement

Two minor improvements could make you an even better member.

Specific recommendations for improvement The first improvement is to be more punctual to meetings. On February 5 and February 8 you were about 10 minutes late. This makes the meetings last longer. Your ideas are valuable to the group, and the sooner you arrive the sooner we can share in your suggestions.

Specific behaviour to be changed The second suggestion is one we all need to work on. We need to keep our meetings positive and productive. I think that our negative attitudes were worst at our first group meeting February 5. We spent about half an hour complaining about all the work we had to do and about our busy schedules in other classes. In the future if this happens, maybe you could offer some positives about the assignment to get the group motivated again.

Overall Compatibility

Positive, forward-looking ending I feel that this group works very well together. You have been very flexible in finding times to meet and have always been willing to do your share of the work. I have never had this kind of luck with a group in the past and I hope you'll consider me for future group projects.

Either in the first or the last paragraph, summarize your overall evaluation of the person. To establish your credibility, show early in the letter how well and how long you've known the person, perhaps in the first paragraph. In the middle of the letter, offer specific details about the person's performance. At the end of the letter, indicate whether you would be willing to rehire the person and repeat your overall evaluation. See Figure 9.3 (◀▶ p. 153).

Experts are divided on whether you should include negatives. Some people feel that any negative weakens the letter. Other people feel that presenting but not emphasizing honest negatives makes the letter more convincing.

To help pay his way through the University of British Columbia, Brian Scudamore "... started a junk removal service with the slogan 'We'll Stash Your Trash in a Flash!'" Today the CEO and founder of 1-800-GOT-JUNK runs an international franchise business boasting sales over $36 million.

Source: Advancing Canadian Entrepreneurship Inc., Alumni Profiles, http://www.acecanada.ca/alumni/default.asp. (2004), retrieved August 8, 2006.

SEE THE OLC!

Find out how to join Advancing Canadian Entrepreneurship Inc. (ACE).

What's the best subject line for a persuasive message?

For direct requests, use the request, the topic, or a question. For problem-solving messages, use a directed subject line or a reader benefit.

In a direct request, put the request, the topic of the request, or a question in the subject line.

Direct request subject line

> Subject: Request for Updated Software
> My copy of HomeNet does not accept the aliases for Magnus accounts.

Direct request subject line

> Subject: Status of Account #3548-003
> Please send me the following information about account #3548-003.

Direct request subject line

> Subject: Do We Need an Additional Training Session in October?
> The two training sessions scheduled for October will accommodate 40 people. Last month, you said that 57 new staff accountants had been hired. Should we schedule an additional training session in October? Or can the new hires wait until the next regularly scheduled session in February?

When you have a reluctant reader, putting the request in the subject line just gets a quick no before you've had a chance to give all your arguments. One option is to use a **directed subject line** that makes your stance on the issue clear. In the following examples, the first is the most neutral. The remaining two increasingly reveal the writer's preference.

Directed subject line

> Subject: A Proposal to Change the Formula for Calculating Retirees' Benefits

Directed subject line

> Subject: Arguments for Expanding the Bramalea Plant

Directed subject line

> Subject: Why Cassano's Should Close Its West-Side Store

Another option is to use common ground (*nomos*) (◀|▶ p. 227) or a reader benefit—something that shows readers that this message will help them.

FIGURE 13.6

P A I B O C

Questions for Analysis

Use the PAIBOC questions to analyze business communication problems:

P What are your **purposes** in writing?

A Who is your **audience?** How do members of your audience differ? What audience characteristics are relevant to this particular message?

I What **information** must your message include?

B What reasons or reader **benefits** can you use to support your position?

O What **objections** can you expect your readers to have? What negative elements of your message must you de-emphasize or overcome?

C How will the **context** affect reader response? Think about your relationship to the reader, the morale in the organization, the economy, the time of year, and any special circumstances.

> Subject: Reducing Energy Costs in the Office
> Energy costs in our office have risen 12 percent in the last three years, although the cost of gas has risen only 8 percent and the cost of electricity has risen only 5 percent.

Although your first paragraph may be negative in a problem-solving message, your subject line should be neutral or positive, to show that you are solving a problem, not just reporting one.

Both directed subject lines and benefit subject lines can also be used as report titles.

How can PAIBOC help me write persuasive messages?

The PAIBOC questions help you examine the points your message should include.

Before you tackle the assignments for this module, examine the following problem. As in Modules 11 and 12, the PAIBOC questions in Figure 13.6 probe the basic points required for a solution. Study the two sample solutions to see what makes one unacceptable and the other one good.[7] The checklists in Figures 13.9 and 13.10 can help you evaluate your draft.

Problem

In one room in the production department of Golden Electronics Company, employees work on computer monitors in conditions that are scarcely bearable because of the heat. Even when the temperature outside is only 23°C, it is more than 30°C in the monitor room. In June, July, and August, 24 out of 36 workers quit because they couldn't stand the heat. This turnover happens every summer.

In a far corner of the room sits a quality control inspector in front of a small fan (the only one in the room). The production workers, in contrast, are carrying 10kg monitors. As production supervisor, you tried to get air conditioning two years ago, before Golden acquired the company, but management was horrified at the idea of spending $500 000 to insulate and air condition the warehouse (it is impractical to air condition the monitor room alone).

You're losing money every summer. Write a memo to Jennifer M. Kirkland, operations vice president, renewing your request.

Analysis of the Problem

P What are your **purposes** in writing or speaking?

You need to persuade Kirkland to authorize insulation and air-conditioning, and you want to build a good image.

A Who is your **audience?** How do members of your audience differ? What audience characteristics are relevant to this particular message?

The operations vice president will be concerned about keeping costs low and keeping production running smoothly. Kirkland may know that the request was denied two years ago, but another person was vice president then; Kirkland wasn't the one who said no.

I What **information** must your message include?

You need to include the cost of the proposal and the effects of the present situation.

B What reasons or reader **benefits** can you use to support your position?

Cutting turnover may save money and keep the assembly line running smoothly. Experienced employees may produce higher-quality parts. Putting in air conditioning would relieve one of the workers' main complaints; it might make the union happier.

O What **objections** can you expect your readers to have? What negative elements of your message must you de-emphasize or overcome?

The cost, including the cost of the time that operations will be shut down while installation is taking place will be the main objection.

C How will the **context** affect reader response? Think about your relationship to the reader, the morale in the organization, the economy, the time of year, and any special circumstances.

Prices on computer components are falling; interest rates are low. Nonetheless, the company will be reluctant to make a major expenditure. Unemployment is low, and filling vacancies in the monitor room is hard—we are getting a reputation as a bad place to work. Summer is over, but the problem will reoccur next year.

■ Discussion of the Sample Solutions

Solution 1, shown in Figure 13.7 is unacceptable. By making the request in the subject line and the first paragraph, the writer invites a *no* before giving all the arguments.

FIGURE 13.7

An Unacceptable Solution to the Sample Problem

Date: October 12, 2007

To: Jennifer M. Kirkland, Operations Vice President

From: Arnold M. Morgan, Production Supervisor AMM

Subject: Request for Air Conditioning in the Monitor Room

Request in subject line stiffens resistance when reader is reluctant

Please put air conditioning in the monitor room. This past summer, 2/3 of our employees quit because it was so hot. It's not fair that they should work in unbearable temperatures when management sits in air-conditioned comfort.

Inappropriate emphasis on writer

I propose that we solve this problem by air conditioning the monitor room to bring down the temperature to 26 °C.

attacks reader

Insulating and air conditioning the monitor room would cost $500 000.

Please approve this request promptly.

Cost sounds enormous without a context

Memo sounds arrogant. Logic isn't developed. This attacks reader instead of enlisting reader's support.

FIGURE 13.8
A Good Solution to the Sample Problem

Date: October 12, 2007

To: Jennifer M. Kirkland, Operations Vice President

From: Arnold M. Morgan, Production Supervisor   *AMM*

Subject: Improving Summer Productivity

Reader benefit in subject line

Shared problem

Golden forfeited a possible $186 000 in profits last summer because of a 17 percent drop in productivity. That's not unusual: Golden has a history of low summer productivity. We can, however, reverse the trend and bring summer productivity in line with the rest of the year's.

Good to show problem can be resolved

Cause of problem

The problem starts in the monitor room. Because of high turnover and reduced efficiency from workers who are on the job, we just don't make as many monitors as we do during the rest of the year.

Additional reason to solve problem

Both the high turnover and reduced efficiency are due to the unbearable heat in the monitor room. Temperatures in the monitor room average 20 °C higher than the outside temperature. During the summer, when work starts at 8:00 A.M., it's already 29 °C in the tube room. By 11:30 A.M., it's at least 30 °C. On six days last summer, it hit 35 °C. When the temperatures are that high, we may be violating Occupational Health and Safety regulations.

Production workers are always standing, moving, or carrying 10 kg monitors. When temperatures hit 30 °C, they slow down. When no relief is in sight, many of them take sick days or quit.

We replaced 24 of the 36 employees in the monitor room this summer. When someone quits, it takes an average of five days to find and train a replacement; during that time, the trainee produces nothing. For another five days, the new person can work at only half speed. And "full speed" in the summer is only 90 percent of what we expect the rest of the year.

More details about problem

Here's where our losses come from:

Normal production = 50 units a person each day (upd)

Loss due to turnover:
loss of 24 workers for 5 days =   6 000 units
24 at ½ pace for 5 days =   3 000 units
Total loss due to turnover =   9 000 units

Shows detail—Set up like an arithmetic problem

Loss due to reduced efficiency:
loss of 5 upd × 12 workers × 10 days =   600 units
loss of 5 upd × 36 × 50 days =   9 000 units
Total loss due to reduced efficiency =   9 600 units

Total loss =   18 600 units

FIGURE 13.8
A Good Solution to the Sample Problem (continued)

Jennifer M. Kirkland　　　　2　　　　October 12, 2007

Shows where numbers in paragraph 1 come from

According to the accounting department, Golden makes a net profit of $10 on every monitor we sell. And, as you know, we sell every monitor we make. Those 18 600 units we don't produce are costing us $186 000 a year.

Additional benefit

Bringing down the temperature to 25 °C (the minimum allowed under provincial guidelines) from the present summer average of 30 °C will require an investment of $500 000 to insulate and air condition the warehouse. Extra energy costs for the air-conditioning will run about $30 000 a year. We'll get our investment back in less than three years. Once the investment is recouped, we'll be making an additional $150 000 a year—all without buying additional equipment or hiring additional workers.

Tells reader what to do

By installing the insulation and air conditioning this fall, we can take advantage of lower off-season rates. Please authorize the Purchasing Department to request bids for the system. Then, next summer, our productivity can be at an all-time high. *Reason to act promptly*

Ends on positive note of problem solved, reader enjoying benefit

The writer does nothing to counter the objections that any manager will have to spend a great deal of money. By presenting the issue in terms of fairness, the writer creates defensiveness rather than finding a common ground. The writer doesn't use details or emotional appeal to show that the problem is indeed serious. The writer asks for fast action but doesn't show why the reader should act now to solve a problem that won't occur again for eight months.

Solution 2, shown in Figure 13.8, is an effective persuasive message. The writer chooses a positive subject line. The opening sentence is negative, catching the reader's attention by focusing on a problem the reader and writer share. However, the paragraph makes it clear that the memo offers a solution to the problem. The problem is spelled out in detail. Emotional impact is created by taking the reader through the day as the temperature rises. The solution is presented impersonally. There are no *I*'s in the memo.

The memo stresses reader benefits: the savings that will result once the investment is recovered. The last paragraph tells the reader exactly what to do and links prompt action to a reader benefit. The memo ends with a positive picture of the problem solved.

Figures 13.9 and 13.10 provide checklists for direct requests and problem-solving persuasive messages.

FIGURE 13.9

Checklist for Direct Requests

❏ If the message is a memo, does the subject line indicate the request? Is the subject line specific enough to differentiate this message from others on the same subject?
❏ Does the first paragraph summarize the request or the specific topic of the message?
❏ Does the message give all the relevant information? Is there enough detail?
❏ Does the message answer questions or overcome objections that readers may have without introducing unnecessary negatives?
❏ Does the last paragraph ask for action? Does it give a deadline if one exists and a reason for acting promptly?

Checklist for All Messages, Not Just Direct Requests

❏ Does the message use you-attitude and positive emphasis?
❏ Is the style easy to read and friendly?
❏ Is the visual design of the message inviting?
❏ Is the format correct?
❏ Does the message use standard grammar? Is it free from typos?

Add Originality to a Direct Request

❏ Provide good lists and visual impact.
❏ Think about readers and give details that answer their questions, overcome any objections, and make it easier for them to do as you ask.
❏ Add details that show you're thinking about a specific organization and the specific people in that organization.

FIGURE 13.10

Checklist for Problem-Solving Persuasive Messages

❏ If the message is a memo, does the subject line indicate the writer's purpose or offer a reader benefit? Does the subject line avoid making the request?
❏ Is the problem presented as a joint problem both writer and reader have an interest in solving, rather than as something the reader is being asked to do for the writer?
❏ Does the message give all the relevant information? Is there enough detail?
❏ Does the message overcome objections that readers may have?
❏ Does the message avoid phrases that sound dictatorial, condescending, or arrogant?
❏ Does the last paragraph ask for action? Does it give a deadline if one exists and a reason for acting promptly?

Checklist for All Messages, Not Just Persuasive Ones

❏ Does the message use you-attitude and positive emphasis?
❏ Is the style easy to read and friendly?
❏ Is the visual design of the message inviting?
❏ Is the format correct?
❏ Does the message use standard grammar? Is it free from typos?

Add Originality to a Problem-Solving Persuasive Message

❏ Use a good subject line and common ground.
❏ Include a clear and convincing description of the problem.
❏ Be sure the content reflects readers' interests, gives details that answer their questions, overcomes objections, and makes it easier for them to do as you ask.
❏ Include details that show you're thinking about a specific organization and the specific people in that organization.

Employability Skills 2000+

The Conference Board of Canada
Insights You Can Count On

Please see the OLC to preview the key skills from the Conference Board of Canada's Employability Skills 2000+ covered in this module.

Review of Key Points

1. When would you choose to communicate with the direct request pattern?
2. When would you choose to communicate with the problem-solving pattern?
3. How is the problem-solving persuasive message organized?
4. What criteria would you use when developing your persuasive content?
5. Identify seven strategies for overcoming objections.
6. Is it ethical to appeal to people's feelings, needs, and fears to get them to do what you want? Why or why not?

Assignments for Module 13

Questions for Critical Thinking

13.1 What do you see as the advantages of positive and negative appeals? Illustrate your answer with specific messages, advertisements, or posters.

13.2 Is it dishonest to "sneak up on the reader" by delaying the request in a problem-solving persuasive message?

13.3 Think of a persuasive message (or a commercial) that did not convince you to act. Could a different message have convinced you? How?

Exercises and Problems

13.4 Revising a Form Memo

You've been hired as a staff accountant; one of your major duties will be processing expense reimbursements. Going through the files, you find this form memo:

> Subject: Reimbursements
>
> Enclosed are either receipts that we could not match with the items in your request for reimbursement, or a list of items for which we found no receipts, or both. Please be advised that the Accounting Department issues reimbursement cheques only with full documentation. You cannot be reimbursed until you give us a receipt for each item for which you desire reimbursement. We must ask that you provide this information. This process may be easier if you use the Expense Report Form, available in your department.
>
> Thank you for your attention to this matter. Please do not hesitate to contact us with questions.

You know this is not a persuasive memo. In addition to wordiness, a total lack of positive emphasis and you-attitude, and a vague subject line, the document design and organization of information bury the request.

Create a new memo that could be sent to people who do not provide all the documentation necessary to be reimbursed.

13.5   Recommending a Co-worker for a Bonus or an Award

Recommend someone at your workplace for a bonus or an award. The award can be something bestowed by the organization itself (Employee of the Month, Dealership of the Year, and so forth), or it can be a community or campus award (Business Person of the Year, Volunteer of the Year, an honorary degree, and so forth).

As your instructor directs,

a.   Create a document or presentation to achieve the goal.

b.   Write a memo to your instructor describing the situation at your workplace and explaining your rhetorical choices (medium, strategy, tone, wording, graphics or document design, and so forth).

13.6   Asking for a Raise or Reclassification

Do you deserve a raise? Should your job be reclassified to reflect your increased responsibilities (with more pay, of course!)? If so, write a memo to the person with the authority to determine pay and job titles, arguing for what you want.

As your instructor directs,

a.   Create a document or presentation to achieve the goal.

b.   Write a memo to your instructor describing the situation at your workplace and explaining your rhetorical choices (medium, strategy, tone, wording, graphics or document design, and so forth).

13.7   Persuading Guests to Allow Extra Time for Check-Out

Your hotel has been the headquarters for a convention, and on Sunday morning you're expecting 1000 people to check out before noon. You're staffing the check-out desk to capacity, but if everyone waits till 11:30 A.M. to check out, things will be a disaster.

So you want to encourage people to allow extra time. And they don't have to stand in line at all: by 4:00 A.M., you'll put a statement of current charges under each guest's door. If that statement is correct and the guest is leaving the bill on the credit card used at check-in, the guest can just leave the key in the room and go. You'll mail a copy of the final bill together with any morning charges by the end of the week.

Write a one-page message that can be put on pillows when the rooms are made up Friday and Saturday night.

13.8   Persuading an Organization to Expand Flextime

Municipal government offices are open from 9:00 A.M. to 5:00 P.M. Employees have limited flextime: they can come in and leave half an hour early or half an hour late. But employees want much more flexible hours. Some people want to start at 6:00 A.M. so they can leave at 2:00 P.M.; others want to work from 11:00 A.M. to 7:00 P.M.

When the idea has been proposed, supervisors have been very negative. "How will we hold staff meetings? How can we supervise people if everyone works different hours? We have to be here for the public, and we won't be if people work whatever hours they please."

But conversations with co-workers and a bit of research show that there are solutions. Many firms that use flextime require everyone to be at work (or at lunch) between 10:00 A.M. and 2:00 P.M. or 11:00 A.M. and 2:00 P.M., so that staff meetings can be scheduled. Right now, when clients call, a representative is frequently on the phone and has to call back. Voicemail and better message forms could solve the problem. And flextime might actually let offices stay open longer hours—say 8:00 A.M. to 6:00 P.M., which would be helpful for taxpayers who themselves work 9:00 A.M. to 5:00 P.M. and now can come in only on their own lunch hours. Write a memo to the mayor and municipal council, persuading them to approve a change in work hours.

Hints:

- Assume that this situation is happening in your own municipal government. What services does the municipality offer?
- Use any facts about your municipality that are helpful (for example, being especially busy right now, having high turnover, dealing with tax issues).
- Use what you know about managing to allay managers' fears.
- Use the analysis that you developed for exercise 2.7 in Module 2 on page 41.

13.9 Persuading Disability Services to Increase the Handivan's Hours

The local community college has a "Handivan" that takes students who use wheelchairs from their residences or apartments to campus locations and back again. But the van stops at 6:00 P.M. (even though there are evening classes, lectures, and events). And it doesn't take people to off-campus restaurants, movies, grocery stores, or shopping centres. Write to the director of disability services, urging that the Handivan's services be increased.

13.10 Handling a Sticky Recommendation

As a supervisor in a not-for-profit provincial agency, you have a dilemma. You received this email message today:

From: John Inoye, Director of Personnel, Communications

Subject: Need Recommendation for Peggy Chafez

Peggy Chafez has applied for a position in the Communications Department. On the basis of her application and interview, she is the leading candidate. However, before I offer the job to her, I need a letter of recommendation from her current supervisor.

Could you please let me have your evaluation within a week? We want to fill the position as quickly as possible

Peggy has worked in your office for 10 years. She designs, writes, and edits your office's monthly newsletter; she designed and maintains the department Web site. Her designs are creative; she's a very hard worker; she seems to know a lot about computers.

However, Peggy is in many ways an unsatisfactory staff member. Her standards are so high that most people find her intimidating. Some find her abrasive. People have complained to you that she's only interested in her own work; she seems to resent requests to help other people with projects. And yet both the newsletter and the Web page are projects that need frequent interaction. She's out of the office a lot. Some of that is required by her job (she takes the newsletters to the post office, for example), but some people don't like the fact that she's out of the office so much. They also complain that she doesn't return voicemail and email messages.

You think managing your office would be a lot smoother if Peggy weren't there. You can't fire her: employees' jobs are secure once they get past the initial six-month probationary period. Because of budget constraints, you can hire new employees only if vacancies are created by resignations. You feel that it would be easy to find someone better.

If you recommended that John Inoye hire Peggy, you would be able to hire someone you want. If you recommended that John hire someone else, you may be stuck with Peggy for a long time.

As your instructor directs,

a. Write an email message to John Inoye.
b. Write a memo to your instructor listing the choices you've made and justifying your approach.

Hints:

- What are your options? Consciously look for more than two.

- Is it possible to select facts or to use connotations so that you are truthful but still encourage John to hire Peggy? Is it ethical? Is it certain that John would find Peggy's work as unsatisfactory as you do? If you write a strong recommendation and Peggy doesn't do well at the new job, will your credibility suffer? Why is your credibility important?

13.11 Writing Collection Letters

You have a small desktop publishing firm. Today, you've set aside some time to work on overdue bills.

As your instructor directs,

Write letters for one or more of the following situations.

a. A $750 bill for producing three monthly newsletters for a veterinarian to mail to her clients. The agreement was that you'd bill her $250 each month. But somehow you haven't sent out bills for the last two months, so they'll go on this month's bill. You'd like payment for the whole bill, and you want to continue this predictable income of $250 a month.
b. A $200 bill for creating flyers for a local rock band to post. You've called twice and left messages on an answering machine, but nothing has happened. The bill is only three weeks

overdue, but the band doesn't seem very stable. You want to be paid now.

c. A $3750 bill, three weeks past due, for designing and printing a series of brochures for Creative Interiors, a local interior decorating shop. When you billed Creative Interiors, you got a note saying that the design was not acceptable and that you would not be paid until you redesigned it (at no extra charge) to the owner's satisfaction. The owner had approved the preliminary design on which the brochures were based; he did not explain in the note what was wrong with the final product. He's never free when you are; indeed, when you call to try to schedule an appointment, you're told the owner will call you back—but he never does. At this point, the delay is not your fault; you want to be paid.

13.12 Getting Permission from Parents for a School Project

As part of a community cleanup program, all public school students will spend the afternoon of the second Friday of April picking up trash. Younger students will pick up trash on school grounds, in parks, and in parking lots; older students will pick up trash downtown. Teachers will supervise the students; where necessary, school buses will transport them. After students are finished, they'll return to their school's playground, where they'll be supervised until the end of the school day. Each school will maintain a study hall for any students whose parents do not give them permission to participate. Trash bags and snacks have been donated by local merchants.

Write a one-page cover letter that students can take home to their parents telling them about the project

and persuading them to sign the necessary permission form. You do not need to create the permission form but do refer to it in your letter.

Hints:

- What objections may parents have? How can you overcome these?
- Where should parents who drive their kids to school pick them up?
- Should students wear their normal school clothing?
- When must the form be returned? Who gets it? Whom can parents call if they have questions before they sign the form?

13.13 Asking an Instructor for a Letter of Recommendation

You're ready for the job market or for transfer to a college or university, and you need letters of recommendation.

As your instructor directs,

a. Assume that you've orally asked an instructor for a recommendation, and he or she has agreed to write one. "Why don't you write up something to remind me of what you've done in the class? Tell me what else you've done, too. And tell me what they're looking for. Be sure to tell me when the letter needs to be in and whom it goes to."

b. Assume that you've been unable to talk with the instructor whose recommendation you want. When you call, no one answers the phone; you stopped by once and no one was in. Write asking for a letter of recommendation.

c. Assume that the instructor is no longer on campus. Write him or her a letter asking for a recommendation.

Hints:

• Detail the points you'd like the instructor to mention.

• How well will this instructor remember you? How much detail about your performance in his or her class do you need to provide?

• Specify the name and address of the person to whom the letter should be written; specify when the letter is due. If there's an intermediate due date (for example, if you must sign the outside of the envelope to submit the recommendation), say so.

13.14 Recommending Investments*

Recommend whether your instructor should invest in a specific stock, piece of real estate, or other investment. As your instructor directs, assume that your instructor has $1000, $10 000, or $100 000 to invest.

Hints:

• Pick a stock, property, or other investment you can research easily.

• What are your instructor's goals? Is he or she saving for a house? for retirement? for the kids'

postsecondary education expenses? to pay off his or her own student loans? When will the money from the investment be needed?

• How much risk is your instructor comfortable with?

• Is your instructor willing to put time into the investment (as managing a rental house would require)?

*Based on an assignment created by Cathy Ryan, The Ohio State University

13.15 Retrieving Your Image

As director of business communication, you get this letter from Sharon Davis, a member of your college advisory board and a major donor:

My bank received this letter from one of your soon-to-be graduates. It seems as though a closer look at writing skills is warranted.

To Whom It May Concern:

This is in reference to the loan soliciation that I received in the mail. This is the second offer that I am now inquiring about. The first offer sent to my previous address I did not respond. But aftersome careful thought and consideration I think it wise to consolidate my bills. Therefore I hope the information provided is sufficient to complete a successful application. I think the main purpose of this loan is to enable me to repair my credit history. I have had problems in the past because of job status as part-time and being a student. I will be graduating in June and now I do have a full-time job. I think I just need a chance to mend the past credit problems that I have had.

(The next two inches of the letter are blocked out, and both the signature and typed name are crossed out so that they cannot be read.)

As your instructor directs,

Write to

a. The faculty who teach business communications, reminding them that the quality of student writing may affect fundraising efforts.

b. Ms. Davis, convincing her that indeed your school does make every effort to graduate students who can write.

13.16 Persuading Employees to Join the Company Volleyball Team

Your company has decided to start a company volleyball team to play in the city recreation league. Now, you need to get people to sign up for the team. Ideally, you'd like to have several teams to involve as many people as possible and build company loyalty. If you have enough teams, they can play each other once a week in a round-robin company tournament.

Write a memo to all employees persuading them to sign up.

Hints:

- How young and how athletic are your employees? How busy are they? Will this be an easy or a difficult thing to persuade them to do?
- Some people may be reluctant to join because their skills are rusty. How can you persuade people that you want everyone to participate even if they're not athletic?
- Will the people who sign up have to pay anything or buy uniforms?
- How do people sign up? Is there a deadline?
- What other perks or positives might team members enjoy?

13.17 Persuading Tenants to Pay the Rent

As the new manager of an apartment complex, you find this message in the files:

ATTENTION!

DERELICTS

If you are a rent derelict (and you know if you are) this communiqué is directed to you!

RENT IS DUE THE 5TH OF EACH MONTH AT THE LATEST!

LEASE HAS A 5-DAY GRACE PERIOD UNTIL THE 5TH OF THE MONTH NOT THE 15TH.

If rent is not paid <u>in total</u> by the 5th, you will pay the $25 late charge. You will pay the $25 late charge when you pay your late rent or your rent will not be accepted.

Half of you people don't even know how much you pay a month. Please read your lease instead of calling up to waste our time finding out what you owe per month! Let's get with the program so I can spend my time streamlining and organizing maintenance requests. My job is maintenance only.

RENT PAYMENT IS YOUR JOB!

If you can show up for a test on time, why can't you make it to the rental office on time or just mail it?

P.S. We don't take cash any longer due to a major theft.

This message is terrible. It lacks you-attitude and may even encourage people who are now paying on the first to wait until the 5th.

Write a message to go to people who have been slow to pay in the past.

13.18 Writing a Performance Appraisal for a Member of a Collaborative Group

During your collaborative writing group meetings, keep a log of events. Record specific observations of both effective and ineffective behaviours of group members. Then evaluate the performance of the other members in your group. (If there are two or more other people, write a separate appraisal for each of them.)

In your first paragraph, summarize your evaluation. Then, in the body of your memo, give the specific details that lead to your evaluation by answering the following questions:

• What specifically did the person do in terms of the task? brainstorm ideas? analyze the information? draft the text? suggest revisions in parts drafted by others? format the document or create visuals? revise? edit? proofread? (In most cases, several people will have done each of these activities together. Don't overstate what any one person did.) What was the quality of the person's work?

• What did the person contribute to the group process? Did he or she help schedule the work?

raise or resolve conflicts? make other group members feel valued and included? promote group cohesion? What roles (◀▮▶ pp. 326–329) did the person play in the group?

Support your generalizations with specific observations. The more observations you have and the more detailed they are, the better your appraisal will be.

As your instructor directs,

a. Write a midterm performance appraisal for one or more members of your collaborative group. In each appraisal, identify the two or three things the person should try to improve during the second half of the term.

b. Write a performance appraisal for one or more members of your collaborative group at the end of the term. Identify and justify the grade you think each person should receive for the portion of the grade-based group process.

c. Give a copy of your appraisal to the person about whom it is written.

Polishing Your Prose

Narrative Voice

Narrative voice refers to the "personality" of the writer. Words, phrases, expressions, and tone convey narrative voice. Just as fiction and composition do, business communication uses narrative voice. The "voice" in memos, letters, and reports can be friendly, assertive, bureaucratic, threatening, or confident, to name just a few possibilities. You'll get the results you want, however, if you "speak" to your reader the way you would want to be spoken to.

Consider the following email message from a student to his instructor: If you were the instructor, how persuasive would you judge this memo?

To: Kathryn

From: Dave

Subject: report

i am sending my final report. i cant remember when its do but here it is.iknow ive missed alot of classes but i have to work. im going to keep on sending this message until you tell me you got it. Whats my final grade.

Narrative voice is as individual as personality. However, we have control over narrative voice because we can choose the language with which we communicate. Knowing your own voice can help you to understand the "personality" it demonstrates.

Exercises

Read the following passages. How would you characterize the narrative voice in each? Which voices seem appropriate for good business communication? Try using your own words to communicate the same basic message.

1. Employees will clock in at their designated hour. Employees will follow their assigned schedules to the letter. There will be NO EXCEPTION to these rules.

2. Hi, Mr. Mills! Just stop in to pick up your order when you get a chance. Give us a ring if you want delivery. Thanks!

3. Please find enclosed my résumé, which speaks to my superlative and most relevant qualities as candidate for the advertised position of account executive with your illustrious organization.

4. Get your act together or you're fired. Got it?

5. It's, like, one of the biggest, like, ideas our department has ever had, you know? It's totally cool.

6. Pertaining to the party of the first part, hereafter called "party first," and excepting any and all objections from the party of the second part, hereafter called "party second," this amendment shall be considered null and void with proper written notice three (3) days prior to the execution of the original agreement.

7. Congratulations on your recent promotion to district manager, Rita. All of us in accounting look forward to working with you.

8. I QUIT.

9. In the event of catastrophic LAN failure, users will

   1. Perform SYS/MD-3 shutdown for affected systems.
   2. Engage standard recovery matrix (SRM), per #4105.1 in SYS/MD Manual (2000: H3-H12).
   3. Record time and date, RE: LAN Failure, in compliance log, cc. MEISNER.
   4. Notify Data Services at ext. 5547, ATTN: J.J. MEISNER.

10. Nope. This idea won't work. It's not very good. I'm not sure the project is even worth our time anymore. I'm definitely not interested in having a meeting to discuss it. Don't call me unless you eggheads hatch something better.

Check your answers to the odd-numbered exercises on page 572.

Online Learning Centre

Visit the Online Learning Centre at www.mcgrawhill.ca/olc/locker to access module quizzes, a searchable glossary, résumé and letter templates, additional business writing samples, CBC videos, and other learning and study tools.

CBC Video Case

Visit the Online Learning Centre at www.mcgrawhill.ca/olc/locker to view "How to Complain," an online CBC Video Case for Unit 3 that discusses effective negative messages.

Unit 4

Polishing Your Writing

Preeti Kanwal is definite about the importance of writing to her job: "I compose more than 50 emails and 5 to 10 incident reports a day. I also write letters, business proposals, learning and professional development plans, even the tests and interview questions for employment interviews," says Preeti. "Requests, trouble-shooting reports, disciplinary action: everything is in writing, because there must be a record. This accountability saves time and resources."

Preeti works for the federal government as a LAN administrator, part of a 15-member IT team supporting almost 1000 employees. "'Put it in writing'—that's the cultural mantra here," says Preeti.

"Without careful documentation, we would spend all our time resolving the same problems. Because we record everything, however, we can resolve most situations immediately. For example, I might get the call and begin an incident report that someone else, at another location, has to read, act on, and finish writing. My email has to be clear and succinct; otherwise my colleague has to start all over." And Preeti's department keeps a database of every question, problem, and resolution, thereby saving time and energy: if the problem or question has come up before, there's a record of action and resolution.

Employees also have to write business plans for all requests that require resources. Preeti says that she has learned to make the request persuasive by appealing to the reader's interests and by stressing the organizational benefits. "I revise and revise, I get other people to read and reread it, and then I edit and proofread it. Writing is rewriting."

"My writing, not my technical skills, got me the job. The written test [to get an interview] included the essay question 'How would you deal with a difficult client?' My answer got me the interview, and the interview got me the job."

Preeti has a B.Sc. in biology and psychology from the University of Toronto, and a diploma in Information Technology Support Services from Sheridan Institute.

How did her education help her to become a good writer?

"Certainly writing a mountain of essays helped," Preeti says. "But I write well because I read all the time. I've always been a reader. Reading teaches vocabulary, sentence structure, style, and syntax. And I was lucky: I had a Grade 7 teacher who really cared about her students. She emphasized language skills and grammar.

"I remember how frustrating it was, all through school, handing in a paper and then getting it back to revise, and resubmitting and getting it back to redo, over and over. But there's no other way to learn to write."

"Now I use that same process every day: I think about the audience's needs and expectations, and I shape the writing accordingly. I read my writing over and over; I revise; I read it aloud and revise; I give it to others to read for their comments; I revise again. That feedback process is vital."

"Writing is integral to everything you do and to how you think, so you have to learn the craft."

P A I B O C

Analysis

1. Why does Preeti write?

2. Who is/are her **audience(s)**?

3. What cultural **context** shapes her writing?

14 Revising Sentences and Paragraphs

Module Outline

- What is "good" style?
- Are there rules I should follow?
- What should I look for when I revise sentences?
- What should I look for when I revise paragraphs?
- How does corporate culture affect style?

Review of Key Points

Assignments for Module 14

Polishing Your Prose: End Punctuation

LEARNING OBJECTIVES

After reading and applying the information in Module 14, you'll be able to demonstrate

Knowledge of
- The elements of style
- Specific revision strategies

Skills to
- Develop your writing style
- Use revision strategies

The Conference Board of Canada
Insights You Can Count On

Please see the OLC to preview the key skills from the Conference Board of Canada's Employability Skills 2000+ covered in this module.

Writing *style* is the result of the conscious choices that writers make to convey meaning. Style elements include every symbol—from page layout, white space, format and organization, to paragraph size, sentence length, and word choice. Style is the way writers use these elements.

Good business style creates messages that are easy for your audience to read and understand. Practiced writers continuously hone their individual style, and adapt their style to their purpose and audience (PAIBOC). Then they revise and edit repeatedly. (Rewind ◀▶ Module 4).

▒ What is good business writing style?

Good business style is polite, friendly, and natural.

Good business writing sounds like one person talking to another. Although academic writing is traditionally more formal than business writing (See Table 14.1), professors also like essays that are written in a lively, engaging style that is grammatically correct.

Most people have several styles of talking, which they vary depending on their audience. Good writers have several styles, too. A memo to your boss complaining about the delays from a supplier will be informal, perhaps even chatty; a letter to the supplier demanding better service will be more formal.

TABLE 14.1
Different Types of Style

	Conversational Style	Good Business Style	Traditional Term-Paper Style
Formality	Highly informal	Conversational; sounds like a real person talking	More formal than conversation would be but retains a human voice
Use of contractions	Many contractions	OK to use occasional contractions	Few contractions, if any
Pronouns	Uses *I*, first- and second-person pronouns	Uses *I*, first- and second-person pronouns	First- and second-person pronouns kept to a minimum
Level of friendliness	Friendly	Friendly	No effort to make style friendly
Personal	Personal; refers to specific circumstances of conversation	Personal; may refer to reader by name; refers to specific circumstances of readers	Impersonal; may generally refer to *readers* but does not name them or refer to their circumstances
Word choice	Short, simple words; slang	Short, simple words but avoids slang	Many abstract words; scholarly, technical terms
Sentence and paragraph length	Incomplete sentences; no paragraphs	Short sentences and paragraphs	Sentences and paragraphs usually long
Grammar	Can be ungrammatical	Uses standard edited English	Uses standard edited English
Visual impact	Not applicable	Attention to visual impact of document	No particular attention to visual impact

EXPANDING A CRITICAL SKILL

Using the Right Tone

The tone of business writing should be businesslike and friendly. But what exactly does "friendly" mean? Well, it depends. It depends on the norms and expectations of your audience, the culture of your workplace, even the part of the country where you work.

Over the past 50 years, Canadian social distance has decreased. In many workplaces, people call each other by their first names, whatever their age or rank. But even in cultures that pride themselves on their egalitarianism, differences in status do exist. When you're a newcomer in an organization, when you're a younger person speaking to someone older, or when you're a subordinate speaking to a superior, you're wise to show your awareness of status in the tone you use.

If you're the boss, it may be appropriate to email your subordinates, "Let me know when you're free next week for a meeting." But if you're a subordinate trying to line up people on your own level or higher up, respect and courtesy pay: "Would you be able to meet next week? Could you let me know what times you have free?"

The difficulty, of course, is that norms for politeness, like those for friendliness, can differ from organization to organization, from group to group, and even in different parts of the country and the world (◀|▶ Modules 2 and 3). Furthermore, the same words that seem polite and friendly coming from a superior to a subordinate can seem pushy or arrogant coming from a subordinate to a superior. "Keep up the good work!" is fine coming from your boss. It isn't, however, something you would say to your boss.

As in other communication situations, you have to analyze the situation. Who are your audiences (◀|▶ Module 2)? What are your purposes? How do other people in the organization talk and write? What kind of response do you get? If a customer winces when you return her credit card and say, "Have a nice day, Mary," maybe she doesn't appreciate hearing a cliché or being called by her first name. Talk to your peers in the organization about communication. What seems to work? What doesn't? Talk to a superior you trust. How do you come across? If you're creating the image you want to create, good. But if people think that you're rude, stuck-up, or arrogant, they may be reacting to your tone. A tone that worked for you in some situations in the past may need to be changed if you're to be effective in a new workplace or a new organization.

Keep the following points in mind when you choose a level of formality for a specific document:

- Use a friendly, informal style for someone you've talked with.
- Avoid contractions, slang, and even minor grammatical lapses in paper documents written to people you don't know. Abbreviations are acceptable in email messages if they're part of the group's culture.
- Pay particular attention to your style when you have to write uncomfortable messages, such as when you write to people in power or when you must give bad news.

When people feel insecure or under stress, their writing style shows it: they rely on nouns rather than verbs; they use longer sentences and paragraphs, and they use more multi-syllabic words.[1] Confident people are more direct. Edit your writing so that you sound confident, whether or not you feel that way.

Good business style allows for individual variation. Your writing style contributes to your narrative voice (◀|▶ p. 254) and expresses how you feel about both your audience and your topic.

Are there rules I should follow?

Keep it short and specific.

Some rules are grammatical conventions. For example, standard edited English requires that each sentence has a subject and verb and that they agree. Business writing normally demands standard grammar, but exceptions exist. Promotional materials such as brochures, advertisements, and sales and fundraising letters may use sentence fragments to gain the effect of speech.

Other rules may be conventions adopted by an organization so that its documents will are consistent. For example, a company might decide to capitalize job titles (e.g., Production Manager), although grammar doesn't require the capitals, or to use a comma before "and" in a series, though a sentence can be grammatical without the comma. A different company might make different choices.

Still other rules are attempts to codify "what sounds good." "Never use *I*" and "use big words" are examples of this kind of rule. These rules must be applied selectively, if at all. Think about your audience (◀▶ p. 25), the discourse community (◀▶ p. 34), your purposes, and the situation. If you want the effect produced by an impersonal style and big words, use them. But use them only when you want the distancing they produce.

Professor Daniel Oppenheimer's research demonstrates that people think authors who use long words and complex fonts to impress readers are less intelligent than those who write simply.

In fact, readers rate writers who use clear, simple language and easy-to-read fonts as more intelligent than those who choose to express themselves in a more complicated style.

You can do several things to improve your style:

- Read and write everyday.
- Start with a clean page or screen, so that you aren't locked into old sentence structures.
- Try WIRMI: What *I* Really Mean Is.[2] Then revise accordingly.
- Try reading your draft aloud to someone sitting nearby. If the words sound stiff, they'll seem stiff to a reader, too.
- Ask someone else to read your draft out loud. Readers stumble if the words on the page aren't what they expect to see. Revise for clarity in the places readers stumble.

What should I look for when I revise sentences?

Try these six techniques to make your writing readable.

1. Use active verbs whenever possible.
2. Use strong action verbs to carry the weight of your sentences.
3. Make your writing concise.
4. Vary sentence length and sentence structure.
5. Use parallel structure.
6. Put your readers in your sentences.

Strong Verbs

1. Use Active Verbs Whenever Possible

"Who does what" sentences that accentuate the action make your writing clearer and more interesting.

A verb is **active** if the subject of the sentence does the action the verb describes. Contemporary business communications favour the use of active verbs. A verb is **passive** if the subject is acted on. Passives are usually made up of a form of the verb *to be* plus a past participle. Passive has nothing to do with the past tense. Passives can be past, present, or future:

were received   (past)
is recommended   (present)
will be implemented   (future)

People who want to avoid responsibility while delivering bad news tend to use passive verbs.

To identify a passive verb, find the verb. If the verb describes something that the subject is doing, the verb is active. If the verb describes something that is being done to the subject, the verb is passive.

Active	**Passive**
The customer received 500 widgets.	Five hundred widgets were received by the customer.
I recommend this method.	This method is recommended by me.
The provincial agencies will implement the program.	The program will be implemented by the provincial agencies.

You can change verbs from active to passive by making the direct object (in the oval) the new subject (in the box). To change a passive verb to an active one, you must make the agent ("by ___" in <>.) the new subject. If no agent is specified in the sentence, you must supply one to make the sentence active.

Active	**Passive**
The plant manager approved the request.	The request was approved by the <plant manager>.
The commitee will decide next month.	A decision will be made next month. No agent in sentence.
[You] Send the customer a letter. informing her about the change.	A letter will be sent informing the customer of the change. No agent in sentence.

If the active sentence does not have a direct object, no passive equivalent exists.

Active	**No Passive Exists**
I would like to go to the conference.	
The freight charge will be $1400.	
The phone rang.	

Passive verbs have at least three disadvantages:

1. If all the information in the original sentence is retained, passive verbs make the sentence longer. Passives take more time to understand.[3]
2. If the agent is omitted, it's not clear who is responsible for doing the action.
3. When many passive verbs are used, or when passives are used in material that has a lot of big words, the writing can be boring and pompous.

Passive verbs are desirable in some situations:

- Use passives to emphasize the object receiving the action, not the agent.
  Your order was shipped November 15.

The customer's order, not the shipping clerk, is important.

- Use passives to provide coherence within a paragraph. A sentence is easier to read if "old" information comes at the beginning of a sentence. When you have been discussing a topic, use the word again as your subject even if that requires a passive verb. The bank made several risky loans in the late 1990s. These loans were written off as "uncollectible" in 2001.

Using loans as the subject of the second sentence provides a link between the two sentences, making the paragraph as a whole easier to read.

- Use passives to avoid assigning blame.
  The order was damaged during shipment.

An active verb would require the writer to specify who damaged the order. The passive here is more tactful.

2. Use Strong Action Verbs to Carry the Weight of Your Sentence

Since the verb is the most important word in any sentence, put the weight of your sentence in the verb. When the verb is a form of the verb *to be*, revise the sentence to use a more forceful verb.

Weak: The financial advantage of owning this equipment instead of leasing it is 10 percent after taxes.

Better: Owning this equipment rather than leasing it will save us 10 percent after taxes.

Nouns ending in *-ment*, *-ion*, and *-al* often hide verbs.

make an adjustment	adjust
make a payment	pay
make a decision	decide
reach a conclusion	conclude
take into consideration	consider
make a referral	refer
provide assistance	assist

FIGURE 14.1
A Request Letter using Concrete Action Verbs

Western New York Public Broadcasting Association
PO Box 399 Fort Eerie, Ontario L2A 5N1
www.wned.org

December, 2005

Mrs. Arlene Hughes
310 Water Street
Oshawa, ON
L1H 8V9

If your WNED year-end investment gift is on its way to the station—thanks!

If not, let me remind you how important the Hughes family's gift is this month…

Dear Hughes Family,

Whether your taste runs to history, music, news, drama, children's or "how to" programming, I know you trust WNED to provide fresh, original, intelligent programs.

The Hughes family's trust is very important to WNED and that's the reason for this reminder letter.

Since I wrote a few weeks ago, we have almost finished planning the winter 2006 season—and WNED has almost met its year-end fundraising goal. But help from your family is still needed to go over the top.

Many families have already mailed their special, end of year investment gifts to the station. But I'm writing to you today because WNED is still one family short of its goal…and it will be, until **your** family mails your special investment gift of **$35** or **$50**.

I know you'll enjoy—and want to add extra support for—the WNED 2005-2006 **Great Performances** season, offering you…

• *Renée Fleming*: Sacred Songs and Carols —an evening of devotional and holiday favourites at the historic Mainz Cathedral in Germany

• *The Barbra Streisand Specials*—combining the two historic musical showcases *My Name is Barbra* and *Color Me Barbra*, to shine a spotlight on the many talents that paved the way for a legendary five-decade career.

• *The Nightingale*—Igor Stravinsky's score, inspired by Hans Christian Andersen's tale of a Chinese emperor enraptured with the beautiful singing of his treasured nightingale, comes to life as never before in a vibrant explosion of live performance and computer animation.

• *Michael Bublé*: Caught in the Act—inspired by the swinging big band sound of his grandfather's generation, the 29-year-old Canadian phenomenon invites comparison to a young Sinatra.

Plus with the holidays upon us, you can count on WNED to bring you plenty of specials, including *Christmas with the Mormon Tabernacle Choir*.

If WNED is to keep up this kind of programming, it is clear that the station will need additional support from every family that watches and enjoys our programs—even generous families like yours who are already members of WNED.

Think about it. If every one of the station's current members increased their support by as little as $20—less than 19 cents per day—WNED would have almost $1 million dollars more to invest in your favourite programs and services.

Remember, WNED must depend on the support of members to provide almost half of the station's annual budget. That's why the station needs your family's investment support more than ever.

And remember, your special investment at this time of year is an immediate investment in a full season of fresh programs, so please mail your gift before December 31st or go online to www.wned.org to make a secure year-end donation.

FIGURE 14.1
A Request Letter (continued)

Your membership is (deeply appreciated) and your special investment contribution this month(plays)a genuinely important role in furthering the network's on-going mission of education and learning for a lifetime, as well as (making)possible programs that you and your family enjoy every day.

Thank you for(watching)and(supporting)WNED, and best wishes for the Holiday Season and a Happy New Year! I look forward to hearing from you soon.

Sincerely,

Donald K. Boswell
President & CEO

P.S. Please don't delay and risk forgetting in the busy holiday season. So please reply with your special investment gift before December 31st. As always, **thank you!**

WNED
Buffalo · Toronto

Western New York Public Broadcasting Association
PO Box 399 Fort Eerie, Ontario L2A 5N1
www.wned.org

This letter uses a polite, friendly, natural style, with plenty of details and action verbs to appeal to its audience.

Use verbs to present the information more forcefully.

Weak: We will perform an investigation of the problem.

Better: We will investigate the problem.

Weak: Selection of a program should be based on the client's needs.

Better: Select the program that best fits the client's needs.

INSTANT REPLAY

Active and Passive Verbs

If the verb describes something that the subject is doing, the verb is **active**. If the verb describes something that is being done to the subject, the verb is **passive**.

■ **3. Make Your Writing Concise**

Writing is **wordy** if the same idea can be expressed in fewer words. Unnecessary words increase typing time, bore your reader, and make your meaning more difficult to follow, since the reader must keep all the extra words in mind while trying to understand your meaning.

Good writing is concise. Concise writing may be long because it is packed with ideas. In (◀▷ Modules 6 to 8), you saw that revisions to create you-attitude and positive emphasis, and to develop reader benefits, were frequently longer than the originals because the revision added information not given in the original.

Sometimes you may be able to look at a draft and see immediately how to tighten it. When wordiness isn't obvious, try the following strategies to make your writing more concise.

a. Eliminate words that say nothing.
b. Use gerunds (the -*ing* form of verbs) and infinitives to make sentences shorter and smoother.
c. Combine sentences to eliminate unnecessary words.
d. Put the meaning of your sentence into the subject and verb to use fewer words.

The purpose of eliminating unnecessary words is to save the reader time, not simply to see how few words you can use. You aren't writing a telegram, so keep the little words that make sentences complete. (Incomplete sentences are fine in lists where all the items are incomplete.)

The following examples show how to use these four methods.

a. Eliminate Words That Say Nothing

INSTANT REPLAY

Wordiness

Writing is **wordy** if the same idea can be expressed in fewer words.

Cut words that are already clear from other words in the sentence. Substitute single words for wordy phrases.

Wordy:	Keep this information on file for future reference.
More Concise:	Keep this information for reference.
	File this information.
Wordy:	Ideally, it would be best to put the billing ticket just below the screen and above the keyboard.
More Concise:	If possible, put the billing ticket between the screen and the keyboard.

Phrases beginning with *of*, *which*, and *that* can often be shortened.

Wordy:	the question of most importance
More Concise:	the most important question
Wordy:	the estimate that is enclosed
More Concise:	the enclosed estimate

Sentences beginning with *There is/are* or *It is* delay the information and bore the reader. Tighten these sentences for readability.

Wordy:	There are three reasons for the success of the project.
More Concise:	Three reasons explain the project's success.
Wordy:	It is the case that college and university graduates advance more quickly in the company.
More Concise:	College and university graduates advance more quickly in the company.

Check your draft. If you find these phrases, or any of the unnecessary words shown in ◀▮▷ Table 15.2, eliminate them.

b. Use Gerunds and Infinitives to Make Sentences Shorter and Smoother

A **gerund** is the *-ing* form of a verb; grammatically, it is a verb used as a noun. In the sentence, "Running is my favourite activity," *running* is the subject of the sentence. An **infinitive** is the form of the verb that is preceded by *to*: *to run* is the infinitive.

In the revision below, a gerund (*purchasing*) and an infinitive (to *transmit*) tighten the revision.

Wordy:	A plant suggestion has been made where they would purchase a fax machine for the purpose of transmitting test reports between plants.
More Concise:	The plant suggests purchasing a fax machine to transmit test reports between plants.

Even when gerunds and infinitives do not greatly affect length, they often make sentences smoother and more conversational.

c. Combine Sentences to Eliminate Unnecessary Words

In addition to saving words, combining sentences focuses the reader's attention on key points, makes your writing sound more sophisticated, and sharpens the relationship between ideas, thus making your writing more coherent.

Wordy: I conducted this survey by telephone on Sunday, April 21. I questioned two groups of third-year and fourth-year students—male and male—who, according to the Student Directory, were still living in the dorms. The purpose of this survey was to find out why some third-year and fourth-year students continue to live in the dorms even though they are no longer required by the university to do so. I also wanted to find out if there were any differences between male and female third-year and fourth-year students in their reasons for choosing to remain in the dorms.

The innovative BluePlanetSmart composter illustrates the fundamental design truism: form follows function. Applying this principle to your writing style guarantees success.

Source: Marjorie Harris, "This Fall I'm Ready to Wrap and Roll," *The Globe and Mail*, September 3, 2005. L6.

More Concise: On Sunday, April 21, I phoned male and female third-year and fourth-year students living in the dorms to find out (1) why they continue to live in the dorms even though they are no longer required to do so, and (2) whether men and women had the same reasons for staying in the dorms.

d. Put the Meaning of Your Sentence into the Subject and Verb to Use Fewer Words

Put the core of your meaning into the subject and verb of your main clause. Think about what you mean and try saying the same thing in several different ways. Some alternatives will be more concise than others. Choose the most concise one.

Wordy: The reason we are recommending the computerization of this process is because it will reduce the time required to obtain data and will give us more accurate data.

Better: We are recommending the computerization of this process because it will save time and give us more accurate data.

Concise: Computerizing the process will give us more accurate data faster.

Wordy: The purpose of this letter is to indicate that if we are unable to mutually benefit from our seller-buyer relationship, with satisfactory material and satisfactory payment, then we have no alternative other than to sever the relationship. In other words, unless the account is handled in 45 days, we will have to change our terms to a permanent COD basis.

Better: A good buyer-seller relationship depends on satisfactory material and satisfactory payment. You can continue to charge your purchases from us only if you clear your present balance within 45 days.

SEE THE OLC!

The Elements of Style

4. Vary Sentence Length and Sentence Structure

Readable prose mixes sentence lengths and varies sentence structure. Most sentences should be between 14 and 20 words. A really short sentence (fewer than 10 words) can add punch to your prose. Really long sentences (more than 30 words) are danger signs.

You can vary sentence patterns in several ways. First, you can mix simple, compound, and complex sentences. **Simple sentences** have one main clause:

We will open a new store this month.

Compound sentences have two main clauses joined with *and*, *but*, *or*, or another conjunction. Compound sentences work best when the ideas in the two clauses are closely related.

We have hired staff, and they will complete their training next week.
We wanted to have a local radio station broadcast from the store during its grand opening, but the DJs were already booked.

Complex sentences have one main and one subordinate clause; they are good for showing logical relationships.

When the stores open, we will have balloons and specials in every department.

Because we already have a strong customer base in the north, we expect the new store to be just as successful as the store in the City Centre Mall.

Compound-complex sentences have two main clauses with one or more subordinate clauses; these sentences combine interdependent, complex ideas:

Although we have a strong customer base in the north, we expect the new store to attract younger, urban professionals, and, therefore, we'll be focusing our promotional efforts on this particular demographic.

You can also vary sentences by changing the order of elements. Normally the subject comes first.

We will survey customers later in the year to see whether demand warrants a third store on campus.

To create variety, begin some sentences with a phrase or a dependent clause.

Later in the year, we will survey customers to see whether demand warrants a third store on campus.

To see whether demand warrants a third store on campus, we will survey customers later in the year.

Use these guidelines for sentence length and structure:

- Always edit sentences for conciseness. Even a 15-word sentence can be wordy.
- When your subject matter is complicated or full of numbers, make a special effort to keep sentences short.
- Use long sentences
  - To show how ideas are linked to each other
  - To avoid a series of short, choppy sentences
  - To reduce repetition
- Group the words in long and medium-length sentences into chunks that the reader can process quickly.[4]
- When you use a long sentence, keep the subject and verb close together.

Let's see how to apply the last three principles.

INSTANT REPLAY

Revise for Readability

- Use active verbs.
- Use action verbs.
- Use as few words as possible.
- Vary sentence length and sentence structure.
- Use parallel structure.
- Put your readers in your sentences.

Use Long Sentences to Show How Ideas Are Linked; to Avoid a Series of Short, Choppy Sentences; and to Reduce Repetition

INSTANT REPLAY

Sentence Length and Sentence Structure

Readable prose mixes sentence lengths and varies sentence structure. Sentences should be 20 words or fewer.

The sentence below is hard to read not simply because it is long but also because it is shapeless. Just cutting it into a series of short, choppy sentences doesn't help. The best revision uses medium-length sentences (between 15 and 20 words) to show the relationship between ideas.

Too long: It should also be noted in the historical patterns presented in the summary that though there were delays in January and February, which we realized were occurring, we are now back where we were about a year ago, and although we are not off line in our collect receivables as compared to last year at this time, we do show a considerable over-budget figure because of an ultraconservative goal on the receivable investment.

Choppy: There were delays in January and February. We knew about them at the time. We are now back to where we were about a year ago. The summary shows this. Our present collect receivables are in line with last year's. However, they exceed the budget. The reason they exceed the budget is that our goal for receivable investment was very conservative.

Better: As the summary shows, although there were delays in January and February (of which we were aware), we have now regained our position of a year ago. Our present collect receivables are in line with last year's, but they exceed the budget because our receivable investment goal was very conservative.

Group the Words in Long and Medium-Length Sentences into Chunks

The "better" revision above has seven chunks. In the list below, the chunks starting immediately after the numbers are main clauses. The chunks that are indented are subordinate clauses and parenthetical phrases.

1. As the summary shows,

2. although there were delays in January and February

3. (of which we were aware),

4. we have now regained our position of a year ago.

5. Our present collect receivables are in line with last year's,

6. but they exceed the budget

7. because our receivable investment goal was very conservative.

The first sentence has four chunks: (1) an introductory phrase, (2) a subordinate clause (3) with a parenthetical phrase, followed by (4) the main clause of the first sentence. The second sentence begins with (5) a main clause. The sentence's (6) second main clause is introduced with *but*, showing that it will reverse the first clause. A subordinate clause (7) explaining the reason for the reversal completes the sentence. At 27 and 23 words, respectively, these sentences aren't short, but they're readable because no chunk is longer than 10 words.

Any sentence pattern will become boring if it is repeated sentence after sentence. Use different sentence patterns—different kinds and lengths of chunks—to keep your prose interesting.

Keep the Subject and Verb Close Together

Often you can move the subject and verb closer together if you put the modifying material in a list at the end of the sentence. For maximum readability, present the list vertically.

Hard to read:	Movements resulting from termination, layoffs and leaves, recalls and reinstates, transfers in, transfers out, promotions in, promotions out, and promotions within are presently documented through the Payroll Authorization Form.
Smoother:	The following movements are documented on the Payroll Authorization Form: termination, layoffs and leaves, recalls and reinstates, transfers in and out, and promotions in, out, and within.
Still better:	The following movements are documented on the Payroll Authorization Form:

- Termination
- Layoffs and leaves
- Recalls and reinstates
- Transfers in and out
- Promotions in, out, and within

Sometimes you will need to change the verb and revise the word order to put the modifying material at the end of the sentence.

Hard to read:	The size sequence code, which is currently used for sorting the items in the NOSROP lists and the composite stock list, is not part of the online file.
Smoother:	The online file does not contain the size sequence code, which is currently used for sorting the items in the composite stock lists and the NOSROP lists.

■ 5. Use Parallel Structure

Words or ideas that share the same logical role in your sentence must also be in the same grammatical form. Parallelism is a powerful device for making your writing smoother and more forceful. Note the **parallel structure** in the following examples:

Faulty:	I interviewed first-year and second-year students and athletes.
Parallel:	I interviewed first-year and second-year students. In each year, I interviewed athletes and non-athletes.
Faulty:	Errors can be checked by reviewing the daily exception report or note the number of errors you uncover when you match the lading copy with the file copy of the invoice.
Parallel:	Errors can be checked by reviewing the daily exception report or by noting the number of errors you uncover when you match the lading copy with the file copy of the invoice.
Also Parallel:	To check errors, note 1. The number of items on the daily exception report 2. The number of errors discovered when the lading copy and the file copy are matched

Note that a list in parallel structure must fit grammatically into the umbrella sentence (or stem) that introduces the list. (See Figure 14.2.)

FIGURE 14.2
Use Parallelism to Make Your Writing More Concise

These are the benefits the customer gets.
• Use tracking information.
• Our products let them scale the software to their needs.
• The customer can always rely on us.

Faulty

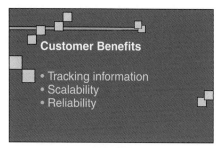

Customer Benefits
• Tracking information
• Scalability
• Reliability

Parallel

6. Put Your Readers in Your Sentences

Use second-person pronouns (*you*) rather than third-person (*he, she, one*) to give your writing more impact. *You* is both singular and plural; it can refer to a single person or to every member of your organization.

Third person: Funds in a participating employee's account at the end of each six months will automatically be used to buy more stock unless a "Notice of Election Not to Exercise Purchase Rights" form is received from the employee.

Second person: Once you begin to participate, funds in your account at the end of each six months will automatically be used to buy more stock unless you submit a "Notice of Election Not to Exercise Purchase Rights" form.

Be careful to use *you* only when it refers to your reader.

Incorrect: My visit with the outside sales rep showed me that your schedule can change quickly.

Correct: My visit with the outside sales rep showed me that schedules can change quickly.

What should I look for when I revise paragraphs?

Check for topic sentences and transitions.

Paragraphs are visual and logical units. Use them to chunk your sentences.

1. Begin Most Paragraphs with Topic Sentences

A good paragraph has **unity**: it is about only one idea, or topic. The **topic sentence** states the main idea and provides a base on which to structure your document. Your writing will be easier to read if you make the topic sentence explicit and put it near the beginning of the paragraph.[5]

Hard to read (no topic sentence): In fiscal 2006, the company filed claims for refund of federal income taxes of $3 199 000 and interest of $969 000 paid as a result of an examination of the company's federal income tax returns by the Canada

Customs and Revenue Agency for the years 2000 through 2005. It is uncertain what amount, if any, may ultimately be recovered.

Better (paragraph starts with topic sentence):   The company and the Canada Customs and Revenue Agency disagree about whether the company is liable for back taxes. In fiscal 2006, the company filed claims for a refund of federal income taxes of $3 199 000 and interest of $969 000 paid as a result of an examination of the company's federal income tax returns by the Canada Customs and Revenue Agency for the years 2000 through 2005. It is uncertain what amount, if any, may ultimately be recovered.

A good topic sentence forecasts the structure and content of the paragraph.

Plan B has economic advantages.

(Prepares the reader for a discussion of B's economic advantages.)

We had several personnel changes in June.
(Prepares the reader for a list of the month's terminations and hires.)

Employees have complained about one part of our new policy on parental leaves.
(Prepares the reader for a discussion of the problem.)

When the first sentence of a paragraph is not the topic sentence, readers who skim may miss the main point. Move the topic sentence to the beginning of the paragraph. If the paragraph does not have a topic sentence, you will need to write one. Without a single sentence that serves as an "umbrella" to cover every sentence, the paragraph lacks unity. To solve the problem, either split the paragraph into two, or eliminate the sentence that digresses from the main point.

◼ 2. Use Transitions to Link Ideas

Transition words and sentences signal the connections between ideas to the reader. Transitions tell whether the next sentence continues the previous thought or starts a new idea; they tell whether the idea that comes next is more or less important than the previous thought. Table 14.2 lists some of the most common transition words and phrases.

◼ How does corporate culture affect style?

Different cultures may prefer different styles.

Different organizations and bosses may legitimately have different ideas about what constitutes good writing. If the style the company prefers seems reasonable, use it. If the style doesn't seem reasonable—if you work for someone who likes flowery language or wordy paragraphs, for example—you have several choices.

- Use the techniques in this chapter. Sometimes seeing good writing changes people's minds about the style they prefer.
- Help your organization learn about writing. Add up-to-date writing reference texts to the company library. (If your company doesn't already offer employees a reference library, start one.)
- Recognize that a style serves many communication purposes. An abstract, hard-to-read style may forge group identity or emphasize exclusivity. For example, government, medical, and legal writing reflect highly specialized knowledge accessible only

TABLE 14.2
Transition Words and Phrases

To Show Addition or Continuation of the Same Idea	To Introduce an Example	To Show That the Contrast Is More Important Than the Previous Idea	To Show Time
and	for example (e.g.)	but	after
also	for instance	however	as
first, second, third	indeed	nevertheless	before
in addition	to illustrate	on the contrary	in the future
likewise	namely		next
similarly	specifically		then
			until
		To Show Cause and Effect	when
To Introduce the Last or Most Important Item	**To Contrast**	as a result	while
		because	
finally	in contrast	consequently	**To Summarize or End**
furthermore	on the other hand	for this reason	
moreover	or	therefore	in conclusion
			in summary
			finally

to the initiated. When big words, jargon, and wordiness are central to a group's self-image, change will be difficult, since changing style will mean changing the corporate culture.

- Ask. Often the documents that end up in files aren't especially good. Later, other workers may find these documents and imitate them, thinking they represent a corporate standard. Bosses may prefer better writing.

Building your own writing style takes energy and effort, but it's well worth the work. Good style makes every document more effective; moreover, developing a good style builds confidence, critical thinking, and competence, and makes you, the writer, valuable to every organization.

Employability Skills 2000+

The Conference Board of Canada
Insights You Can Count On

Please see the OLC to preview the key skills from the Conference Board of Canada's Employability Skills 2000+ covered in this module.

Review of Key Points

1. What is writing style?
2. What are three characteristics of good business writing style?
3. What can you do to build your writing style?
4. Identify and explain six strategies good authors use to write and revise their sentences.

5. What is a passive verb? When can you use passive verbs?
6. What four techniques can make your writing more concise?
7. What is parallel structure? When should writers use parallel structure?

Assignments for Module 14

Questions for Critical Thinking

14.1 Would your other instructors like the style you're learning to use in this class?
14.2 Can a long document be concise?

14.3 Ask a trusted friend or colleague how your tone comes across in classes and at work. What changes in your tone could you make?

Exercises and Problems

14.4 Changing Verbs from Passive to Active

Identify the passive verbs in the following sentences and convert them to active verbs. In some cases, you may need to add information to do so. You may use different words as long as you retain the basic meaning of the sentence. Remember that imperative verbs are active, too.

1. The marketing plan was prepared by Needra Smith.
2. With the assistance of computers, inventory records are updated and invoices are automatically issued when an order is entered by one of our customers.

3. When the Web page is finalized, it is recommended that it be routed to all managers for final approval.
4. As stated in my résumé, Polish is a language I speak fluently.
5. All employees being budgeted should be listed by name and position. Any employee whose name does not appear on the "September Listing of Salaried Employees" must be explained. If this employee is a planned replacement, indicate who will be replaced and when. If it is an addition, the reason must be explained.

14.5 Using Strong Verbs

Revise each of the following sentences to use stronger verbs.

1. The advantage of using colour is that the document is more memorable.

2. Customers who make payments in cash will receive a 1 percent rebate on all purchases.
3. When you make an evaluation of media buys, take into consideration the demographics of the group seeing the ad.

4. We provide assistance to clients who are in the process of reaching a decision about the purchase of hardware and software.

5. We maintain the belief that Web ads are a good investment.

14.6 Reducing Wordiness

1. Eliminate words that say nothing. You may use different words.
   a. It is necessary that we reach a decision about whether or not it is desirable to make a request that the office be allowed the opportunity and option of hiring additional workers.
   b. The purchase of a new computer will allow us to produce form letters quickly. In addition, return-on-investment could be calculated for proposed repairs. Another use is that the computer could check databases to make sure that claims are paid only once.
   c. There are many subjects that interest me.

2. Use gerunds and infinitives to make these sentences shorter and smoother.
   a. The completion of the project requires the collection and analysis of additional data.
   b. The purchase of laser printers will make possible the in-house production of the newsletter.

   c. The treasurer has the authority for the investment of assets for the gain of higher returns.

3. Combine sentences to show how ideas are related and to eliminate unnecessary words.
   a. Some buyers want low prices. Other buyers are willing to pay higher prices for convenience or service.
   b. We projected sales of $34 million in the third quarter. Our actual sales have fallen short of that figure by $2.5 million.
   c. We conducted this survey by handing out questionnaires on January 10, 11, and 12. Our office surveyed 100 customers. We wanted to see whether they would like to be able to leave voicemail messages for their representatives. We also wanted to find out whether our hours are convenient for them. Finally, we asked whether adequate parking was available.

14.7 Improving Parallel Structure

Revise each of the following sentences to create parallelism.

1. Training programs
   - Allow employees to build skills needed for current and future positions
   - Employees enjoy the break from routine work
   - Training programs are a "fringe benefit" that helps to attract and retain good employees
2. Newsletters enhance credibility, four times as many people read them as read standard ad

formats, and allow soft-sell introduction to prospective customers.
3. When you leave a voicemail message,
   - Summarize your main point in a sentence or two.
   - The name and phone number should be given slowly and distinctly.
   - The speaker should give enough information so that the recipient can act on the message.
   - Tell when you'll be available to receive the recipient's return call.

14.8 Editing Sentences to Improve Style

Revise these sentences to make them smoother, less wordy, and easier to read. Eliminate jargon and repetition. Keep the information; you may reword or reorganize it. If the original is not clear, you may need to add information to write a clear revision.

1. The table provided was unclear because of hard-to-understand headings.

2. By working a co-op or intern position, you may have to be in school an additional year to complete the requirements for graduation, but this extra year is paid for by the income you make in the co-op or intern position.
3. There is a seasonality factor in the workload, with the heaviest being immediately prior to quarterly due dates for estimated tax payments.

4. Informational meetings will be held during next month at different dates and times. These meetings will explain the health insurance options. Meeting times are as follows:
    October 17, 12:00 P.M.–1:00 P.M.
    October 20, 4:00 P.M.–5:00 P.M.
    October 23, 2:00 P.M.–3:00 P.M.

5. Listed below are some benefits you get with OHIP:
    1. Routine doctors' visits will be free.
    2. No hassle about where to get your prescriptions filled.
    3. Hospitalization is covered 100 percent.

14.9   Putting Readers in Your Sentences

Revise each of the following sentences to put readers in them. As you revise, use active verbs and simple words.

1. Mutual funds can be purchased from banks, brokers, financial planners, or from the fund itself.

2. Every employee will receive a copy of the new policy within 60 days after the labour agreement is signed.

3. Another aspect of the university is campus life, with an assortment of activities and student groups to participate in and lectures and sports events to attend.

14.10 Using Topic Sentences

Make each of the following paragraphs more readable by opening each paragraph with a topic sentence. You may be able to find a topic sentence in the paragraph and move it to the beginning. In other cases, you'll need to write a new sentence.

1. At Disney World, a lunch put on an expense account is "on the mouse." McDonald's employees "have ketchup in their veins." Business slang flourishes at companies with rich corporate cultures. Memos at Procter & Gamble are called "reco's" because the model P&G memo begins with a recommendation.

2. The first item on the agenda is the hiring for the coming year. Neky has also asked that we review the agency goals for the next fiscal year. We should cover this early in the meeting since it may affect our hiring preferences. Finally, we need to announce the deadlines for grant proposals, decide which grants to apply for, and set up a committee to draft each proposal.

3. Separate materials that can be recycled from your regular trash. Pass along old clothing, toys, or appliances to someone else who can use them. When you purchase products, choose those with minimal packaging. If you have a yard, put your yard waste and kitchen scraps (excluding meat and fat) in a compost pile. You can reduce the amount of solid waste your household produces in four ways

14.11 Writing Paragraphs

Write a paragraph on each of the following topics.

a. Discuss your ideal job.
b. Summarize a recent article from a business magazine or newspaper.
c. Explain how technology is affecting the field you plan to enter.
d. Explain why you have or have not decided to work while you attend college or university.
e. Write a profile of someone who is successful in the field you hope to enter.

As your instructor directs,

a. Label topic sentences, active verbs, and parallel structure.
b. Edit a classmate's paragraphs to make the writing more concise and smoother.

Polishing Your Prose

End Punctuation

Sentences normally end with one of three forms of punctuation: a period, a question mark, or an exclamation point.

Periods end most statements:

The report is on your desk.

Question marks end questions:

Have you read it?

Exclamation marks end statements with strong emphasis or emotion:

The report is on fire!

Overusing exclamation points creates a "gushy" tone instead of a businesslike tone.

Exercises

Use appropriate punctuation at the end of each of the following sentences.

1. Where is the file on the Richman proposal
2. Would you send me a copy of that memo
3. Ms. Amarotti will arrive by plane tomorrow
4. Watch out
5. Take a moment to read the instructions before completing the form
6. Are you sure that the times on this meeting roster are correct
7. Congratulations on your recent promotion to line manager
8. Please fax the invoices to us at 519-555-2222
9. Remember, when we turn on the breakroom lights, everyone is to yell, "Happy Birthday, Susharita"
10. I can never remember what the purpose of making three copies of each purchase order is

Check your answers to the odd-numbered exercises on page 572.

Online Learning Centre

Visit the Online Learning Centre at www.mcgrawhill.ca/olc/locker to access module quizzes, a searchable glossary, résumé and letter templates, additional business writing samples, CBC videos, and other learning and study tools.

Choosing the Right Word

Module Outline

- Why does using the right word matter?

- How do words derive their meanings?

- When is it OK to use jargon?

- What words confuse some writers?

Review of Key Points

Assignments for Module 15

Polishing Your Prose: Run-on Sentences

LEARNING OBJECTIVES

After reading and applying the information in Module 15, you'll be able to demonstrate

Knowledge of
- The power of words

Skills to
- Consider and choose appropriate language

The Conference Board of Canada
Insights You Can Count On

Please see the OLC to preview the key skills from the Conference Board of Canada's Employability Skills 2000+ covered in this module.

Using the "best" words depends on context: the situation, your purposes, your audience, and the words you have already used.

To communicate most effectively, follow two guidelines:

1. Use words that are accurate, appropriate, and familiar. Accurate words mean exactly what you want to say. Appropriate words convey the attitudes you want and fit well with the other words in your document. Familiar words are easy to read and understand.
2. Use technical jargon only when it is essential and known to the reader. Eliminate business jargon.

Why does using the right word matter?

The right word helps you look professional and get the response you want.

SEE THE OLC!

Canadian Business Culture

Using the right word helps to demonstrate that you're part of a discourse community (◀▮▷ p. 34). Using simple words helps to create a friendly image of you and your organization (◀▮▷ Module 14). Using words that are part of standard edited English helps to build credibility and demonstrate professionalism.

Getting Your Meaning Across

(◀▮▷ Module 14) When the words on the page don't say what you mean, the reader has to work harder to figure out your meaning. Sometimes your audience can figure out what you mean. Sometimes, your meaning will be lost. Sometimes the wrong word can result in a lawsuit.

Denotation is a word's literal or dictionary meaning. Most common words in English have more than one denotation. The word *pound*, for example, means or denotes a unit of weight, a place where stray animals are kept, a unit of money in the British system, and the verb to *hit*. The British call the car trunk the *boot*. Americans requesting a pop ask for *soda*.

SEE THE OLC!

A culture-based denotation and connotation quiz

When two people use the same word to mean, or denote, different things, **bypassing** occurs. For example, in Canadian meetings, to table an item means to postpone discussing it; in the United Kingdom, to table an item means to bring it up for immediate discussion. Bypassing happens frequently in our multicultural milieu. The writer is responsible for choosing words that denote the same meaning to both writer and reader.

Getting the Response You Want

Using the right word helps you shape the audience's response to what you say. **Connotation** means the emotional colourings or associations that accompany a word. A great many words carry connotations of approval or disapproval, disgust or delight. In Table 15.1, words in the first column suggest approval; words in the second column suggest criticism.

TABLE 15.1
Words with Positive and Negative Connotations

Positive Word	Negative Word
assume	guess
curious	nosy
negotiate	haggle
cautious	fearful
careful	nit-picking
firm	obstinate
flexible	wishy-washy

INSTANT REPLAY

Denotation, Bypassing, and Connotation

Denotation is a word's literal or dictionary meaning. **Bypassing** occurs when two people use the same word to mean or denote different things. **Connotation** means the emotional colourings or associations that accompany a word.

A supervisor can "tell the truth" about a subordinate's performance and yet write either a positive or a negative performance appraisal, based on the connotations of the words in the appraisal. Consider an employee who pays close attention to details. A positive appraisal might read, "Terry is a meticulous team member who takes care of details that others sometimes ignore." But the same behaviour might be described negatively: "Terry is hung up on trivial details."

Advertisers carefully choose words with positive connotations. Expensive cars are never used; instead, they're *pre-owned, experienced,* or even *preloved.*

Words may also connote status or class distinctions. Both *salesperson* and *sales representative* are non-sexist job titles. But the first sounds like a clerk in a store; the second suggests someone selling important items to corporate customers.

Use familiar words that are in almost everyone's vocabulary. Try to use specific, concrete words. They're easier to understand and remember.[1] Short, common words sound friendlier. Table 15.2 gives a few examples of short, simple alternatives.

TABLE 15.2
Formal Words and Their Simple Alternatives

Formal	Short and Simple
ameliorate	improve
commence	begin
enumerate	list
finalize	finish, complete
initiate	begin
prioritize	rank
utilize	use
viable option	choice

EXPANDING A CRITICAL SKILL

Thinking Critically

Like many terms, critical thinking has more than one meaning.

In its most basic sense, critical thinking means using precise words and asking questions about what you read and hear.

Vague: This *Vancouver Sun* story discusses international business.

Precise: This *Vancouver Sun* story

- tells how Bombardier plans to expand into Europe
- challenges the claim that a Canadian company needs a native partner to succeed in international business
- gives examples of translation problems in international business
- compares and contrasts accounting rules in Europe and in Asia
- tells how three women have succeeded in international business

Questions for thinking critically about a *Vancouver Sun* story might include the following:

- What information is the story based on? Did the reporter interview people on both sides of the issue?

- When was the information collected? Is it still valid?
- Does evidence from other newspapers and magazines and from your own experience tend to confirm or contradict this story?
- How important is this story? Does it call for action on your part?

In a more advanced sense, critical thinking means the ability to analyze and identify problems, gather and evaluate evidence, identify and evaluate alternative solutions, and recommend or act on the best choice—while understanding that information is always incomplete and that new information might change the judgment of the "best" choice.

In its most advanced sense, critical thinking means asking about and challenging fundamental assumptions. For example, stories in business magazines and newspapers like *The Wall Street Journal* and *The Globe and Mail* generally assume that capitalism is good, that a major goal of any business is to make money, and that it's OK for top executives to make much more money than other workers.

Source: Carol Roever and Gerry Hines, "Teaching the Two C's Needed for Business Success: Critical Thinking and Creativity," Conference on Teaching Communication, Ohio State University, July 30–31, 1999.

Formal: Please give immediate attention to ensure that the pages of all reports prepared for distribution are numbered sequentially and in a place of optimum visibility.[2]

Simple: Please put page numbers on all reports in the top right corner.

There are four exceptions to the general rule that "shorter is better."

1. Use a long word if it is the only word that expresses your meaning exactly (◀▶ Module 14).
2. Use a long word if it is more familiar than a short word. *Send out* is better than *emit* and a *word in another language for a geographic place or area* is better than *exonym* because more people understand the first item in each pair.
3. Use a long word if its connotations are more appropriate. *Exfoliate* is better than *scrape off dead skin cells*.
4. Use a long word if the discourse community (◀▶ Module 2) prefers it.

Although connotations rarely appear in a dictionary, they are not individual or idiosyncratic. The associations a word evokes will be consistent in any one culture but may differ among cultures. Even within a culture, connotations may change over time.

Individual exploits can challenge our assumptions and our language. Winnipeg MP Steven Fletcher, MBA, patient advocate, Tory Parliamentary Secretary to the Minister of Health, and award-winning sailor transcends stereotypical assumptions and labels such as *disabled*, *cripple* and *wheelchair victim*. Terry Fox's courage made him immortal while focusing world attention on the need for cancer research.

Source: Christie Blatchford, "The MP Who Is His Own Health Story," *The Globe and Mail*, December 3, 2005, A29.

The word *charity* had acquired such negative connotations by the nineteenth century that people began to use the term *welfare* instead. Now, *welfare* has acquired negative connotations.

How positively can we present something and still be ethical? *Pressure-treated lumber* sounds acceptable. But naming the product by the material injected under pressure—*arsenic-treated lumber*—may lead the customer to make a different decision. We have the right to package our ideas attractively, but we also have the responsibility to give the public or our superiors all the information they need to make decisions.

How do words derive their meanings?

Most meanings depend on usage.

You can find the meaning of standard words in dictionaries. Some dictionaries are *descriptive*: their definitions describe the way people actually use words. In such a dictionary, the word *verbal* might be defined as *spoken, not written*, because many people use the word that way. In a *prescriptive* dictionary, words are defined as they are supposed to be used, according to a panel of experts. In such a dictionary, *verbal* would be defined as *using words*—which of course includes both writing and speaking. The *Oxford Encyclopedic English Dictionary* is an example of a prescriptive dictionary, whereas the

SEE THE OLC!

Word Origins

Canadian Oxford Dictionary is a descriptive one. Check the introduction to your dictionary to find out which kind it is.

When a word has more than one meaning or isn't in the dictionary at all, we learn meanings by context, by being alert and observant. Some terms will have a specialized meaning in a social or work group. We learn some meanings by formal and informal study: "generally accepted accounting principles" is one. What the garbage can on an email screen symbolizes is another. Some meanings are negotiated as we interact one on one with another person, attempting to communicate. Some words persist, even though the reality behind them has changed. In Canada's two largest cities, so-called "visible minorities" are already in the majority. Some people are substituting the term *traditionally underrepresented groups* for *minorities*, but the old term is likely to remain in use for some time.

INSTANT REPLAY

Types of Jargon

Technical jargon includes words that have specific technical meanings. Use this kind of jargon only in job application letters. Avoid other technical jargon unless it's essential.

Business jargon and **businessese** are words that do not have specialized meanings. Avoid these terms.

When is it appropriate to use jargon?

Use language appropriate to your audience and purpose.

Jargon includes technical terminology, slang, and outdated language. *LIFO* and *FIFO* are technical terms in accounting; *byte* and *baud* are computer jargon; *scale-free, pickled,* and *oiled* designate specific characteristics of steel. A job application letter is the one occasion when it's desirable to use technical jargon; using the technical terminology of the reader's field helps suggest that you're a peer who also is competent in that field. In other messages, use technical jargon only when the term is essential. Define the term when you're not sure whether the reader knows it.

If a technical term has a "plain English" equivalent, use the simpler term:

Jargon: Foot the average monthly budget column down to Total Variable Cost, Total Management Fixed Cost, Total Sunk Costs, and Grand Total.

Better: Add the figures in the average monthly budget column for each category to determine the Total Variable Costs, the Total Management Fixed Costs, and the Total Sunk Costs. Then add the totals for each category to arrive at the Grand Total.

The revision here is longer but better because it uses simple words. The original will be meaningless to a reader who does not know what *foot* means.

Business slang includes terms that are borrowed from technical fields but are used in a more general sense: *bottom line, GIGO, blindsiding,* and *downsize.* These terms are appropriate in job application letters and in messages for people in your own organization, who are likely to share the vocabulary.

General slang includes words like *awesome, diss,* and *going postal.* Slang is sometimes used in business conversations and presentations, but it is too casual for business and administrative writing.

Another kind of jargon is the **businessese** or outdated language that some writers still use: *as per your request, enclosed please find, please do not hesitate.* None of the words in this category of jargon is necessary. Indeed, some writers call these terms *deadwood,* since they are no longer living words. Some of these terms, however, seem to float through the air like germs. If any of the terms in the first column of Table 15.3 show up in your writing, replace them with contemporary language.

TABLE 15.3
Eliminating Businessese

Instead of	Use	For This Reason
At your earliest convenience	The date you need a response	If you need it by a deadline, say so. It may never be convenient to respond.
As per your request; 60 km per hour	As you requested; 60 km an hour	*Per* is a Latin word for *by* or *each*. Use *per* only when the meaning is correct; don't mix English and Latin.
Enclosed please find	Enclosed is; Here is	An enclosure isn't a treasure hunt. If you put something in the envelope, the reader will find it.
Forward same to this office	Return it to this office	Omit legal jargon.
Hereto, herewith	Omit	Omit legal jargon.
Please be advised; Please be informed	Omit—simply state your response	You don't need a preface. Go ahead and start.
Please do not hesitate	Omit	Omit negative words.
Pursuant to	According to; or omit	*Pursuant* does not mean *after*. Omit legal jargon.
Said order	Your order	Omit legal jargon.
This will acknowledge receipt of	Omit—start your response.	If you answer a letter, then your letter reader knows you got it.
Trusting this is satisfactory, we remain	Omit	Eliminate *-ing* endings. When you are through, stop.

What words confuse some writers?

Words with similar sounds can have very different meanings.

Here's a list of words that are frequently confused. Master them, and you'll be well on the way to using the right word.

1. accede/exceed
   accede: to yield
   exceed: to go beyond, surpass

   I accede to your demand that we not exceed the budget.

2. accept/except
   accept: to receive
   except: to leave out or exclude; but

   I accept your proposal except for point 3.

3. access/excess
   access: the right to use; admission to
   excess: surplus

   As supply clerk, he had access to any excess materials.

4. adept/adopt
    adept: skilled
    adopt: to take as one's own

    She was adept at getting people to adopt her ideas.

5. advice/advise
    advice: (noun) counsel
    advise: (verb) to give counsel or advice to someone

    I asked him to advise me but I didn't like the advice I got.

6. affect/effect
    affect: (verb) to influence or modify
    effect: (verb) to produce or cause; (noun) result

    He hoped that his argument would affect his boss's decision, but so far as he could see, it had no effect.

    The tax relief effected some improvement for the citizens whose incomes had been affected by inflation.

7. affluent/effluent
    affluent: (adjective) rich, possessing in abundance
    effluent: (noun) something that flows out

    Affluent companies can afford the cost of removing pollutants from the effluents their factories produce.

8. a lot/allot
    a lot: many (informal)
    allot: divide or give to

    A lot of players signed up for this year's draft. We allotted one first-round draft choice to each team.

9. amount/number
    amount: (use with concepts that cannot be counted individually but can only be measured)
    number: (use when items can be counted individually)

    It's a mistake to try to gauge the amount of interest he has by the number of questions he asks.

10. are/our
    are: (plural linking verb)
    our: belonging to us

    Are we ready to go ahead with our proposal?

11. assure/ensure/insure
    assure: to give confidence, to state confidently
    ensure: to make safe (figuratively)
    insure: to make safe, often by paying a fee against possible risk

    I assure you that we ensure employees' safety by hiring bodyguards.

    The pianist insured his fingers against possible damage.

12. attributed/contributed
    attributed: was said to be caused by
    contributed: gave something to

    The rain probably contributed to the accident, but the police officer attributed the accident to driver error.

FYI

Spell checkers won't catch the following:

- Incorrect word usage, such as *anaesthetic* (numbing) for *unaesthetic* (unpleasing)
- Homonymns (e.g., *their* and *there*, *which* and *witch*) and sound-alikes such as plurals and possessives (*companies* or *company's*)
- Legitimate but incorrect words (e.g., when *the* becomes *then* or replacing *not* with *now*)

Source: Geoffrey J. S. Hart, "Spelling and Grammar Checkers," *Intercom*, April 2001, 40.

13. between/among
     between: (use with only two choices)
     among: (use with more than two choices)

     This year the differences between the two candidates for president are unusually clear.

     I don't see any major differences among the candidates for city council.

14. cite/sight/site
     cite: (verb) to quote
     sight: (noun) vision, something to be seen
     site: (noun) real or virtual location

     She cited the old story of the building inspector who was depressed by the very sight of the site for the new factory.

15. complement/compliment
     complement: (verb) to complete, finish; (noun) something that completes
     compliment: (verb) to praise; (noun) praise

     The compliment she gave me complemented my happiness.

16. compose/comprise
     compose: make up, create
     comprise: consist of, be made up of

     Twelve members compose the city council. Each district comprises an area 50 blocks.

17. confuse/complicate/exacerbate
     confuse: to bewilder
     complicate: to make more complex or detailed
     exacerbate: to make worse

     Because I missed the first 20 minutes of the movie, I didn't understand what was going on. The complicated plot exacerbated my confusion.

18. describe/prescribe
     describe: list the features of something, tell what something looks like
     prescribe: specify the features something must contain

     The law prescribes the priorities for making repairs. His report describes our plans to comply with the law.

19. discreet/discrete
     discreet: tactful, careful not to reveal secrets
     discrete: separate, distinct

     I have known him to be discreet on two discrete occasions.

20. do/due
     do: (verb) act or make
     due: (adjective) scheduled, caused by

     The banker said she would do her best to change the due date.

     Due to the computer system, the payroll is produced in only two days for all 453 employees.

21. elicit/illicit
     elicit: (verb) to draw out
     illicit: (adjective) not permitted, unlawful

     The reporter could elicit no information from the Senator about his illicit love affair.

38. quiet/quite

    quiet: not noisy
    quite: very

    It was quite difficult to find a quiet spot anywhere near the floor of the stock exchange.

39. regulate/relegate

    regulate: control
    relegate: put (usually in an inferior position)

    If the federal government regulates the size of lettering on county road signs, we may as well relegate the current signs to the garbage bin.

40. residence/residents

    residence: home
    residents: people who live in a building

    The residents had different reactions when they learned that a shopping mall would be built next to their residence.

41. respectfully/respectively

    respectfully: with respect
    respectively: to each in the order listed

    When I was introduced to the Queen, the prime minister, and the court jester, I bowed respectfully, shook hands politely, and winked, respectively.

42. role/roll

    role: part in a play or script, function (in a group)
    roll: (noun) list of students, voters, or other members; round piece of bread; (verb) move by turning over and over

    While the teacher called the roll, George—in his role as class clown—threw a roll he had saved from lunch.

43. simple/simplistic

    simple: not complicated
    simplistic: watered down, oversimplified

    She was able to explain the proposal in simple terms without making the explanation sound simplistic.

44. stationary/stationery

    stationary: not moving, fixed
    stationery: paper

    During the earthquake, even the stationery was not stationary.

45. their/there/they're

    their: belonging to them
    there: in that place
    they're: they are

    There are plans, designed to their specifications, for the house they're building.

46. to/too/two

    to: (preposition) function word indicating proximity, purpose, time, etc.
    too: (adverb) also, very, excessively
    two: (adjective) the number 2

    The formula is too secret to entrust to two people.

47. unique/unusual
    unique: sole, only, alone
    unusual: not common

    I believed that I was unique in my ability to memorize long strings of numbers until I consulted *Guinness World Records* and found that I was merely unusual: Someone else had equaled my feat in 1997.

48. verbal/oral
    verbal: using words
    oral: spoken, not written

    His verbal skills were uneven: His oral communication was excellent, but he didn't write well. His sensitivity to non-verbal cues was acute: He could tell what kind of day I had just by looking at my face.

    Hint: Oral comes from the Latin word for mouth, *os*. Think of Oral-B Tooth-brushes: For the mouth.

    Verbal comes from the Latin word for word, *verba*. Non-verbal language is language that does not use words (e.g., body language).

49. whether/weather
    whether: (conjunction) used to introduce possible alternatives
    weather: (noun) atmosphere: wet or dry, hot or cold, calm or storm

    We will have to see what the weather is before we decide whether to hold the picnic indoors or out.

50. your/you're
    your: belonging to you
    you're: you are

    You're the top candidate for promotion in your division.

Employability Skills 2000+

The Conference Board of Canada
Insights You Can Count On

Please see the OLC to preview the key skills from the Conference Board of Canada's Employability Skills 2000+ covered in this module.

Review of Key Points

1. What is the difference between denotation and connotation?
2. What is bypassing?
3. Why should writers use short, simple words?

4. When should writers use long words?
5. When is it appropriate to use jargon?
6. Why is choosing the right word ethically important?

Assignments for Module 15

Questions for Critical Thinking

15.1 If you were going to buy a new dictionary, would you want a descriptive or a prescriptive one? Why?

15.2 Why is it desirable to use technical jargon in a job letter and a job interview?

15.3 Is it possible to avoid connotations entirely?

Exercises and Problems

15.4   Identifying Words with Multiple Denotations

a. Each of the following words has several denotations. How many can you list without using a dictionary? How many additional meanings does a good dictionary list?

browser   log
court   table

b. List five words that have multiple denotations.

15.5   Explaining Bypassing

Show how different denotations make bypassing possible in the following examples:

a. France and Associates: Protection from Professionals

b. We were not able to account for the outstanding amount of plastic waste generated each year.

c. I scanned the résumés when I received them.

15.6   Evaluating Connotations

a. Identify the connotations of each of the following metaphors for a multicultural nation:
melting pot   garden salad
mosaic   stew

tapestry   tributaries
crazy quilt

b. Which connotations seem most positive? Why?

15.7   Evaluating the Ethical Implications of Connotations

In each of the following pairs, identify the more favourable term. Is its use justified? Why or why not?

1. wastepaper recovered fibre
2. feedback   criticism
3. deadline   due date

4. scalper   ticket reseller
5. budget   spending plan

15.8   Correcting Errors in Denotation and Connotation

Identify and correct the errors in denotation or connotation in the following sentences.

1. I will take credit for the mistake.
2. The technology for virtual reality looms on the horizon.
3. The three proposals are diametrically opposed to one another.
4. In her search for information, she literally devours *The Globe and Mail* and several business magazines each week.
5. Approximately 489 customers answered our survey.

15.9   Using Connotations to Shape Response

Write two sentences to describe each of the following situations. In one sentence, use words with positive connotations; in the other, use negative words.

1. Lee talks to co-workers about subjects other than work, such as last weekend's ball game.
2. Lee spends a lot of time sending email messages and monitoring email newsgroups.
3. As a supervisor, Lee rarely gives specific instructions to subordinates.

15.10   Choosing Levels of Formality

Identify the more formal word in each pair. Which term is better for most business documents? Why?

1. adapted to   geared to
2. befuddled   confused
3. assistant   helper
4. pilot project   testing the waters
5. cogitate   think

15.11   Identifying Jargon

How many of these business jargon terms do you know? Write a definition for each one.

1. Sticky Web site
2. Alpha geek
3. Road warrior
4. Think outside the box
5. Be on the same page
6. A new paradigm

15.12   Eliminating Jargon and Simplifying Language

Revise these sentences to eliminate jargon and to use short, familiar words. In some sentences, you'll need to reword, reorganize, or add information to produce the best revision.

1. Computers can enumerate pages when the appropriate keystroke is implemented.
2. Any alterations must be approved during the 30-day period commencing 60 days prior to the expiration date of the agreement.
3. As per your request, the undersigned has compiled a report on claims paid in 2005. A copy is attached hereto.
4. Please be advised that this writer is unable to attend the meeting on the fifteenth due to an unavoidable conflict.
5. Enclosed please find the schedule for the training session. In the event that you have alterations that you would like to suggest, forward same to my office at your earliest convenience.

15.13 Choosing the Right Word

Choose the right word for each sentence.

1. Exercise is (good, well) for patients who have had open-heart surgery.
2. This response is atypical, but it is not (unique, unusual).
3. The personnel department continues its (roll, role) of compiling reports for the federal government.
4. The Accounting Club expects (its, it's) members to come to meetings and participate in activities.
5. Part of the fun of any vacation is (cite, sight, site)-seeing.
6. The (lectern, podium) was too high for the short speaker.
7. The (residence, residents) of the complex have asked for more parking spaces.
8. Please order more letterhead (stationary, stationery).
9. The closing of the plant will (affect, effect) housing prices in the area.
10. Better communication (among, between) design and production could enable us to manufacture products more efficiently.'

15.14 Choosing the Right Word

Choose the right word for each sentence.

1. The audit revealed a small (amount, number) of errors.
2. Diet beverages have (fewer, less) calories than regular drinks.
3. In her speech, she (implied, inferred) that the vote would be close.
4. We need to redesign the stand so that the catalogue is at eye-level instead of (laying, lying) on the desk.
5. (Their, There, They're) is some evidence that (their, there, they're) thinking of changing (their, there, they're) policy.
6. The settlement isn't yet in writing; if one side wanted to back out of the (oral, verbal) agreement, it could.
7. In (affect, effect), we're creating a new department.
8. The firm will be hiring new (personal, personnel) in three departments this year.
9. Several customers have asked that we carry more campus merchandise, (i.e., e.g.,) pillows and mugs with the university seal.
10. We have investigated all of the possible solutions (accept, except) adding a turning lane.

15.15 Choosing the Right Word

Choose the right word for each sentence.

1. The author (cites, sights, sites) four reasons for computer phobia.
2. The error was (do, due) to inexperience.
3. (Your, you're) doing a good job motivating (your, you're) subordinates.
4. One of the basic (principals, principles) of business communication is "Consider the reader."
5. I (implied, inferred) from the article that interest rates would go up.
6. Working papers generally (compose, comprise) the working trial balance, assembly sheets, adjusting entries, audit schedules, and audit memos.
7. Eliminating punch clocks will improve employee (moral, morale).
8. The (principal, principle) variable is the trigger price mechanism.
9. (Its, It's) (to, too, two) soon (to, too, two) tell whether the conversion (to, too, two) computerized billing will save time.
10. Formal training programs (complement, compliment) on-the-job opportunities for professional growth.

Polishing Your Prose

Run-on Sentences

A sentence with too many ideas, strung together by coordinating conjunctions that lack the required comma, is a run-on. (Remember that coordinating conjunctions such as *and*, *or*, *for*, *yet*, and *but* need a comma to connect independent clauses.)

Although most run-on sentences are long, length is not the real problem. Don't confuse run-ons with grammatically correct long sentences whose ideas are still clear to readers.

Run-ons confound readers because there are too many ideas competing for attention and because the missing commas make the ideas harder to follow. The effect is similar to listening to a speaker who does not pause between sentences—where does one point begin and another end?

Test for run-ons by looking for more than two main ideas in a sentence and a lack of commas with coordinating conjunctions:

We installed the new computers this morning and they are running fine but there aren't enough computers for everyone so we are going to purchase more on Wednesday and we will install them and then the department will be fully operational.

Count the number of things going on in this sentence. Where are the commas?

Fix a run-on in one of three ways:

1. For short run-ons, add the missing commas:
Incorrect: The purchasing department sent order forms but we received too few so we are requesting more.
Correct: The purchasing department sent order forms, but we received too few, so we are requesting more.
2. Rewrite the sentence using subordination:
Correct: Because we received too few order forms, we are requesting more from the purchasing department.
3. For longer run-ons, break the run-on into two or more sentences, add missing commas, and subordinate where appropriate.

Correct: We installed the new computers this morning. They are running fine, but because there aren't enough computers for everyone, we are going to purchase more on Wednesday. We will install them, and then the department will be fully operational.

Exercises

Fix the following run-on errors.

1. The marketing department ordered new brochures that are really nice and the brochures are in four-colour.
2. All expense accounts should be itemized based on type and cost so remember to include the appropriate shipping confirmation number.
3. Work into your schedule some time to meet next week and we can talk about your promotion so you can transition easily into the new job.
4. We will take a final product inventory on December 1 and managers will report any lost stock so employees should make sure any broken items are reported and managers should record this information in their computer databases.
5. Employees may request benefits changes during the annual enrolment period and supervisors should pass out the required forms and employees should have them completed by the deadline on the form.
6. Ian leaves his computer on overnight but Aaron turns his off and Marilyn leaves hers on, too, and so does Tashi.
7. Mohammed should make sure he specifies 20-lb. rather than 15-lb. paper stock and Jenna should call the print shop and ask them whether they need anything and Bruce needs to tell Ms. Winans we appreciate her letting us know we originally ordered the wrong stock.
8. The Halifax office is planning a new marketing campaign so the St. John's office will help with the promotion but the Fredericton office is coordinating the product show.

9. A few customers are concerned about the shipping date but the mailroom is sure we can ship overnight and I think there's no reason to be concerned.

10. Last week I went to Montreal and Haj went to Miami and this week Tony took a trip too so our travel budget is almost gone.

Check your answers to the odd-numbered exercises on page 572.

Online Learning Centre

Visit the Online Learning Centre at www.mcgrawhill.ca/olc/locker to access module quizzes, a searchable glossary, résumé and letter templates, additional business writing samples, CBC videos, and other learning and study tools.

16 Editing for Grammar and Punctuation

Module Outline

- What grammatical errors should I focus on?

- How can I fix sentence errors?

- When should I use commas?

- What punctuation should I use inside sentences?

- What do I use when I quote sources?

- How should I write numbers and dates?

- How do I mark errors I find when proofreading?

Review of Key Points

Assignments for Module 16

Polishing Your Prose: Using Spell Checkers and Grammar Checkers

LEARNING OBJECTIVES

After reading and applying the information in Module 16, you'll be able to demonstrate

Knowledge of

- The connection between correct prose and credibility
- Contemporary language usage

Skills to

- Use standard edited English
- Correct common grammatical errors
- Use punctuation correctly
- Mark errors as you proofread

The Conference Board of Canada
Insights You Can Count On

Please see the OLC to preview the key skills from the Conference Board of Canada's Employability Skills 2000+ covered in this module.

With the possible exception of spelling, grammar is the aspect of writing that writers seem to find most troublesome. Faulty grammar is often what executives are objecting to when they complain that college and university graduates or M.B.A.s can't write. Indeed, your credibility is on the line whenever you write for an audience. When readers receive your written message, you're not there to explain, "What I really mean is..." Your document represents you and your organization; it's a permanent record of your capability. Letters, memos, emails, and reports with mechanical errors interfere with readability, reflect poorly on the quality of your work, and, ultimately, cost time and money.

What grammatical errors should I focus on?

Learn how to fix these six errors.

SEE THE OLC!

Grammar in Real Language

Good writers edit to achieve **subject-verb agreement** and **noun-pronoun agreement**, to use the right **pronoun case**, to avoid **dangling modifiers** and **misplaced modifiers**, and to correct **predication errors**.

Agreement

SEE THE OLC!

Differences between Canadian and American Spelling

Singular subjects use singular verbs; plural subjects use plural verbs.

Incorrect: The accountants who conducted the audit was recommended highly.

Correct: The accountants who conducted the audit were recommended highly.

Subject-verb agreement errors often occur when other words come between the subject and the verb. Edit your draft by finding the subject and the verb of each sentence.

Canadian and American usage treats company names and the words *company* and *government* as singular nouns. British usage treats them as plural:

Correct (Canada): Clarica Insurance trains its agents well.

Correct (U.S.): Allstate Insurance trains its agents well.

Correct (U.K.): Lloyd's of London train their agents well.

Use a plural verb when two or more singular subjects are joined by *and*.

Correct: Larry McGreevy and I are planning to visit the client.

Use a singular verb when two or more singular subjects are joined by *or*, *nor*, or *but*.

Correct: Either the shipping clerk or the superintendent has to sign the order.

When the sentence begins with *Here* or *There*, make the verb agree with the subject that follows the verb.

Correct: Here is the booklet you asked for.

Correct: There are the blueprints I wanted.

Note that some words that end in s are considered singular and require singular verbs.

Correct: A series of meetings is planned.

When a situation doesn't seem to fit the rules, or when following a rule produces an awkward sentence, revise the sentence to avoid the problem.

EXPANDING A CRITICAL SKILL

Building a Professional Image

Grammar and mechanics present a paradox. On the one hand, grammar and punctuation are the least important part of any message: the clarity and organization of your ideas matter much more.

On the other hand, grammatical "errors" cause the audience to doubt or ignore your ideas. Grammar, like clothing and table manners, is used to estimate social class. Business people expect documents to use standard edited English. Writers and speakers who use other varieties of English may be seen as unpromotable, poorly trained, or even unintelligent. Readers see errors as a sign of carelessness: "If you don't care enough to get your documents right, how do I know you'll care about the quality of the work you do for me?" Because they convey the quality of your ideas, grammar and punctuation can be the most important part of your message.

Occasionally, errors in grammar and punctuation hide the writer's meaning. More often, it's possible to figure out what the writer probably meant, but the mistake still sends the wrong message (and can be an excuse for a hostile reader or an opposing attorney).

Remember, editing for correctness is part of the polishing or editing process, best done on your penultimate draft. The brain can't attend both to big ideas and to sentence-level concerns at the same time, so don't try to fix errors in your first and second drafts. But do save time to check your almost-final draft to eliminate any errors in grammar, punctuation, and word choice.

Most writers make a small number of grammatical errors repeatedly. Most readers care deeply about only a few grammatical points. Keep track of the feedback you get (from your instructors now, from your supervisor later) and put your energy into correcting the errors that bother the people who read what you write. A command of standard grammar will help you build the credible, professional image you want to create with everything you write.

Problematic: The plant manager, in addition to the sales representative, (was, were?) pleased with the new system.

Better: The plant manager and the sales representative were pleased with the new system.

Problematic: None of us (is, are?) perfect.

Better: All of us have faults.

Errors in *noun-pronoun agreement* occur if a pronoun is of a different number (singular or plural) or person than the word it refers to.

Incorrect: All drivers of leased automobiles are billed $100 if damages to his automobile are caused by a collision.

Correct: All drivers of leased automobiles are billed $100 if damages to their automobiles are caused by collisions.

Incorrect: A manager has only yourself to blame if things go wrong.

Correct: As a manager, you have only yourself to blame if things go wrong.

The following words require a singular pronoun:

| anyone | each | everyone | nobody |
| everybody | either | neither | a person |

Correct: Everyone should bring his or her copy of the manual to the next session on changes in the law.

Because pronoun pairs (*his* or *hers*), which are necessary to avoid sexism, seem cumbersome, use words that take plural pronouns (*people, employees, persons*) or use second-person *you*.

Each pronoun must refer to a specific word. If a pronoun does not refer to a specific term, add a word to correct the error.

Incorrect:	We will open three new stores in the suburbs. This will bring us closer to our customers.
Correct:	We will open three new stores in the suburbs. This strategy will bring us closer to our customers.
Hint:	Make sure *this* and *it* refer to a specific noun in the previous sentence. If either refers to an idea, add a noun ("this strategy") to make the sentence grammatically correct.

Use *who* and *whom* to refer to people and *which* to refer to objects. *That* can refer to anything: people, animals, organizations, and objects.

Correct:	The new executive director, who moved here from St. John's, is already making friends.
Correct:	The information that she wants will be available tomorrow.
Correct:	This confirms the price that I quoted you this morning.

■ Case

Case refers to the grammatical role a noun or pronoun plays in a sentence. Table 16.1 identifies the case of each personal pronoun.

SEE THE OLC!

Grammar Review: Who, Whom, Which, and That

Use subjective or **nominative** pronouns for the **subject** of a clause.

Correct:	Shannon Weaver and I talked to the customer, who was interested in learning more about integrated software.

Use **possessive** pronouns to show who or what something belongs to.

Correct:	Microsoft Office 2000 will exactly meet her needs.

Use **objective pronouns** as **objects** of verbs or prepositions.

Correct:	When you send in the quote, thank her for the courtesy she showed Shannon and me.

TABLE 16.1

The Case of the Personal Pronoun

	Nominative (Subject of Clause)	Possessive	Objective	Reflexive/Intensive
Singular				
1st person	I	my, mine	me	myself
2nd person	you	your, yours	you	yourself
3rd person	he/she/it	his/her(s)/its	him/her/it	himself/herself/itself
	one/who	one's/whose	one/whom	oneself/(no form)
Plural				
1st person	we	our, ours	us	ourselves
2nd person	you	your, yours	you	yourselves
3rd person	they	their, theirs	them	themselves

Hint: Use *whom* when *him* or *her* would fit grammatically in the same place in your sentence.

I am writing this letter to (who, whom?) it may concern.

I am writing this letter to him.

Correct: Whom is correct.

Have we decided (who, whom?) will take notes?

Have we decided she will take notes?

Correct: Who is correct.

Reflexive pronouns emphasize a noun or pronoun that has already appeared in the sentence.

Correct: I myself think the call was a very productive one.

Reflexive pronouns are used very infrequently in Canadian business practice, since they emphasize the writer or speaker unnecessarily.

Do not use reflexive pronouns as subjects of clauses, or as objects of verbs or propositions.

Incorrect: Elaine and myself will follow up on this order.

Correct: Elaine and I will follow up on this order.

Incorrect: He gave the order to Dan and myself.

Correct: He gave the order to Dan and me.

Note that the first-person pronoun comes *after* names or pronouns that refer to other people.

▮ Dangling Modifier (DM)

Modifiers are words or phrases that give more information about the subject, verb, or object in a clause. A modifier dangles when the word it modifies is not actually in the sentence. The solution is to reword the modifier so that it is grammatically correct.

INSTANT REPLAY

Dangling Modifiers

A modifier dangles when the word it modifies is not actually in the sentence.

Incorrect: Confirming our conversation, the truck will leave Monday.
[The speaker is doing the confirming. But the speaker isn't in the sentence.]

Incorrect: At the age of eight, I began teaching my children about business.
[This sentence says that the author was eight when he or she had children who could understand business.]

Correct a dangling modifier in one of these ways:

- Recast the modifier as a subordinate clause.

Correct: As I told you, the truck will leave Monday.

Correct: When they were eight, I began teaching my children about business.

- Revise the main clause so its subject or object can be modified by the now-dangling phrase.

Correct: Confirming our conversation, I have scheduled the truck to leave Monday.

Correct: At the age of eight, my children began learning about business.

Hint: Whenever you use a verb or adjective that ends in *-ing*, make sure it modifies the grammatical subject of your sentence. If it doesn't, reword the sentence.

Misplaced Modifier (MM)

A *misplaced modifier* is a word, phrase, or clause that appears beside a different element of the sentence than the writer intended, causing confusion or misinterpretation.

Incorrect: Customers who complain often alert us to changes we need to make. [Does the sentence mean that customers must complain frequently to teach us something? Or is the meaning that frequently we learn from complaints?]

Correct a misplaced modifier by moving it closer to the word it modifies or by adding punctuation to clarify your meaning. If a modifier modifies the whole sentence, use it as an introductory phrase or clause; follow it with a comma.

Correct: Often, customers who complain alert us to changes we need to make.

Parallelism

Items in a series or list must have the same grammatical structure (◀▶ Module 14).

Not parallel: In the second month of your internship, you will

1. Learn how to resolve customers' complaints.
2. Supervision of desk staff.
3. Interns will help plan store displays.

Parallel: In the second month of your internship, you will

1. Learn how to resolve customers' complaints.
2. Supervise desk staff.
3. Plan store displays.

Also parallel: Duties in the second month of your internship include resolving customers' complaints, supervising desk staff, and planning store displays.

Hint: When you have two or three items in a list (whether the list is horizontal or vertical) make sure the items are in the same grammatical form. Write lists vertically to make them easier to see.

Predication Errors

The predicate of a sentence must fit grammatically and logically with the subject to avoid **predication errors**. In sentences using *is* and other linking verbs, the complement must be a noun, an adjective, or a noun clause.

Incorrect: The reason for this change is because the OSC now requires fuller disclosure.

Correct: The reason for this change is that the OSC now requires fuller disclosure.

Make sure that the verb describes the action done by or done to the subject.

Incorrect:	Our goals should begin immediately.
Correct:	Implementing our goals should begin immediately.

How can I fix sentence errors?

Learn to recognize main clauses.

A **sentence** contains at least one main clause. A **main** or **independent clause** is a complete statement, with a subject and a verb. A **subordinate** or **dependent clause** contains both a subject and verb but is not a complete statement and cannot stand by itself; it depends on an independent clause (a sentence or complete thought) for meaning. A phrase is a group of words that does not contain a verb.

MAIN/INDEPENDENT CLAUSES

Your order will arrive Thursday.

He dreaded talking to his supplier.

I plan to enrol in summer-school classes.

SUBORDINATE/DEPENDENT CLAUSES

If you place your order by Monday

Because he was afraid the product would be out of stock

Since I want to graduate next spring

Although I was prepared for the test

PHRASES

With our current schedule

As a result

A clause with one of the following words will be subordinate:

after	if
although, though	since
because	when, whenever
before, until	while, as

Using the correct punctuation will enable you to avoid three major sentence errors: comma splices, run-on sentences, and sentence fragments.

Comma Splices (CS)

A **comma splice** or **comma fault** occurs when two main clauses are joined only by a comma (instead of by a comma and a coordinating conjunction).

Incorrect: The contest will start in June, the date has not been set.

Correct a comma splice in one of the following four ways:

- If the ideas are closely related, use a semicolon rather than a comma.

Correct: The contest will start in June; the exact date has not been set.

FYI

In the most expensive demonstration of the importance of punctuation in Canada to date, Rogers Communications may have to pay an additional $2.13-million to Aliant Inc. to use Maritime utility poles for Rogers' cable lines. Because lawyers misplaced a comma in a new five-year contract, Aliant claims the contract is good for only one year, after which rates are going-up.

Source: Grant Robertson, "Comma Quirk Irks Rogers," *The Globe and Mail*, August 6, 2006, http://www.theglobeandmail.com/servlet/story/RTGAM-20060806.wr-rogers07/BNStory/Business/, retrieved October 24, 2006.

- If they aren't closely related, start a new sentence.

Correct: The contest will start in June. We need to determine the exact date.

- Add a coordinating conjunction (*and, but, or, for, nor, yet*).

Correct: The contest will start in June, but the exact date has not been set.

- Subordinate one of the clauses.

Correct: Although the contest will start in June, the date has not been set.

Remember that you cannot use just a comma with the following transitional words:

however   therefore   nevertheless   moreover

Instead, use a semicolon to separate the clauses or start a new sentence.

Incorrect: Computerized grammar checkers do not catch every error, however, they may be useful as a first check before an editor reads the material.

Correct: Computerized grammar checkers do not catch every error; however, they may be useful as a first check before an editor reads the material.

SEE THE OLC!

Comma Splice Review

Run-on Sentences (RO)

A **run-on sentence** strings together several main clauses using *and, but, or*, so, and *for*. Run-on sentences and comma splices are "mirror faults." A comma splice uses *only* the comma and omits the coordinating conjunction, while a run-on sentence uses *only* the conjunction and omits the comma. Correct a short run-on sentence by adding a comma. Separate a long run-on sentence into two or more sentences. Consider subordinating one or more of the clauses.

Incorrect: We will end up with a much smaller markup but they use a lot of this material so the volume would be high so try to sell them on fast delivery and tell them our quality is very high.

Correct: Although we will end up with a much smaller markup, volume will be high since they use a lot of this material. Try to sell them on fast delivery and high quality.

Sentence Fragments (Frag)

In a **sentence fragment,** a group of words that is not a complete sentence is punctuated as if it were a complete sentence. Sentence fragments often occur when a writer thinks of additional detail that the reader needs. Fragments are acceptable in résumés, advertising, and sales letters, but they're rarely acceptable in other business documents.

Incorrect: Observing these people, I have learned two things about the program. The time it takes. The rewards it brings.

To fix a sentence fragment, either add whatever parts of the sentence are missing or incorporate the fragment into the sentence before it or after it.

Correct: Observing these people, I have learned that the program is time-consuming but rewarding.

INSTANT REPLAY

Sentence Fragments

In a **sentence fragment,** a group of words that is not a complete sentence is punctuated as if it were a complete sentence.

Remember that clauses with the following words are not complete sentences. Join them to a main clause.

after	if
although, though	since
because	when, whenever
before, until	while, as

Incorrect: We need to buy a new computer system. Because our current system is obsolete.

Correct: We need to buy a new computer system because our current system is obsolete.

■ When should I use commas?

Use commas only to signal a pause for the reader.

INSTANT REPLAY

Comma Splices

A **comma splice** or **comma fault** occurs when two main clauses are joined only by a comma (instead of by a comma and a coordinating conjunction).

Commas, like other punctuation marks, are road signs to help readers predict what comes next, thereby contributing to ease and speed of reading, or **readability**. The easier you make it for the reader to scan and understand the text, the more credible you appear, and the more likely it is that the reader will be persuaded to your point of view.

When you move from the subject to the verb, you're going in a straight line; no comma is needed. When you end an introductory phrase or clause, the comma tells readers the introduction is over and you're turning to the main clause. When words interrupt main clause, like this, commas tell the reader when to turn off the main clause for a short side route and when to return.

■ What punctuation should I use inside sentences?

Use punctuation to clarify meaning for your reader.

A good business and administrative writer knows how to use the following punctuation marks: apostrophes, colons, commas, dashes, hyphens, parentheses, periods, and semicolons.

■ Apostrophes

SEE THE OLC!

Apostrophe Rules Made Easy

1. Use an apostrophe in a contraction to indicate that a letter has been omitted or to indicate a number has been omitted.

TABLE 16.2
What Punctuation Tells the Reader

Mark	Tells the Reader
Period	We're stopping.
Semicolon	What comes next is another complete thought, closely related to what I just said.
Colon	What comes next is an illustration, an example, or a qualification of what I just said.
Dash	What comes next is a dramatic example of or a shift from what I just said.
Comma	What comes next is a slight turn, but we're going in the same direction.

FYI

Because Web editing uses the same skills writers bring to paper documents, PAIBOC analysis readily transfers to all media. However, editors need to focus on Web audiences' expectations of accessibility and immediacy. Web readers begin where they choose, not necessarily at the beginning of the text; they read impatiently, looking for instantaneous comprehension of the site's content and easy navigability. To compensate, editors should ensure the site offers clear concise overviews and is easy to navigate.

Source: Sheilagh Simpson, "Editing for the Web, How-to and Hands-on," EAC/ACR *Active Voice*, February 2002, Vol. 22, P. 1.

We're trying to renegotiate the contract.

The '90s were years of restructuring for our company.

2. To indicate possession, add an apostrophe and an *s* to the word.

The corporation's home office is in Vancouver, British Columbia.

Apostrophes to indicate possession are especially important when one noun in a comparison is omitted.

This year's sales will be higher than last year's.

When a word already ends in an *s*, you may add only an apostrophe to make it possessive.

The meeting will be held at St. Johns' convention centre.

Adding an *s* and an apostrophe would not be incorrect, but doing that can make pronunciation difficult.

With many terms, the placement of the apostrophe indicates whether the noun is singular or plural.

Incorrect: The program should increase the participant's knowledge.
[Implies that only one participant is in the program.]

Correct: The program should increase the participants' knowledge.
[Many participants are in the program.]

Hint: Use *of* in the sentence to see where the apostrophe goes.

The figures of last year = last year's figures

The needs of our customers = our customers' needs

Possessive pronouns (e.g., his, ours) do not have apostrophes. The only exception is *one's*.

The company needs the goodwill of its stockholders.

His promotion was announced yesterday.

One's greatest asset is the willingness to work hard.

3. Use an apostrophe to make plurals that could be confused for other words. However, other plurals do not use apostrophes. I earned A's in all my business courses.

Colons

1. Use a colon to separate the main clause (sentence) and a list, explanation, or qualification that explains the last element in the clause. The items in the list are specific examples of the word that appears immediately before the colon.

Please order the following supplies:
printer ribbons
computer paper (20-lb. white bond)
bond paper (25-lb., white, 25% cotton)
company letterhead
company envelopes

Because English is a living language, grammar, punctuation, and usage rules evolve over time; however, current contemporary Canadian usage indicates a preference for lowercase after the colon. Some authorities suggest capitalizing the first letter after the colon only if a complete sentence follows.

Please order the following supplies: printer ribbons, computer paper (20-lb. white bond), bond paper (25-lb., white, 25% cotton), company letterhead, and company envelopes.

Avoid using a colon when the list is grammatically part of the main clause.

Incorrect: The rooms will have coordinated decors in natural colours such as: eggplant, moss, and mushroom.

Correct: The rooms will have coordinated decors in natural colours such as eggplant, moss, and mushroom.

Correct: The rooms will have coordinated decors in a variety of natural colours: eggplant, moss, and mushroom.

Even if the list is presented vertically, there is no need to introduce the list with a colon if the words in the stem are not a complete sentence.

2. Use a colon to join two independent clauses when the second clause explains or restates the first clause.

Selling is simple: Give people the service they need, and they'll come back with more orders.

Commas

1. Use commas to separate the main clause from an introductory clause, the reader's name, or words that interrupt the main clause. Note that commas both precede and follow the interrupting information.

J. Camaya, the new sales manager, comes to us from the Saskatoon office.

A **non-essential clause** gives extra information that is not needed to identify the noun it modifies. Because nonessential clauses give extra information, they need extra commas.

Sue Decker, who wants to advance in the organization, has signed up for the company training program in sales techniques.

Do not use commas to set off information that restricts the meaning of a noun or pronoun. **Essential clauses** give essential, not extra, information.

Anyone □ who wants to advance in the organization □ should take advantage of on-the-job training.

Do not use commas to separate the subject from the verb, even if you would take a breath after a long subject.

Incorrect: Laws regarding anyone collecting $5000 or more on behalf of another person, apply to schools and private individuals as well to charitable groups and professional fundraisers.

Correct: Laws regarding anyone collecting $5000 or more on behalf of another person □ apply to schools and private individuals as well to charitable groups and professional fundraisers.

2. Use a comma after the first clause in a compound sentence if the clauses are very long or if they have different subjects.

This policy eliminates all sick leave credit of the employee at the time of retirement, and payment will be made only once to any individual.

Do not use commas to join independent clauses without a conjunction. Doing so produces comma splices.

3. Use commas to separate items in a series. Using a comma before the *and* or *or* is not required by some authorities, but using a comma always adds clarity. The comma is essential if any of the items in the series themselves contain the word *and*.

The company contributes equally to full hospital coverage for eligible employees, spouses, and unmarried dependent children under age 21.

■ Dashes

Use dashes to emphasize an aside, or break in thought.

Ryertex comes in 30 grades—each with a special use.

To type a dash, use two hyphens with no space before or after.

■ Hyphens

1. Use a hyphen to indicate that a word has been divided between two lines.

Attach the original receipts for lodging, transportation, and registration fees.

Divide words at syllable breaks. If you aren't sure where the syllables divide, look up the word in a dictionary. When a word has several syllables, divide it after a vowel or between two consonants. Don't divide words of one syllable (e.g., *used*); don't divide a two-syllable word if one of the syllables is only one letter long (e.g., *acre*).

2. Use hyphens to join two or more words used as a single adjective.

Order five 10- or 12-m lengths.

It's a 10-year-old plan.

The computer-prepared Income and Expense statements will be ready next Friday.

The hyphen clarifies meaning. In the first example, five lengths are needed, not lengths of 5, 10, or 12 metres. In the third example, without the hyphen, the reader might think that *computer* was the subject and *prepared* was the verb.

■ Parentheses

1. Use parentheses to set off words, phrases, or sentences used to explain or comment on the main idea.

For the thinnest Ryertex (1 mm) only a single layer of the base material may be used, while the thickest (10 cm) may contain more than 600 greatly compressed layers of fabric or paper. By varying the fabric used (cotton, asbestos, glass, or nylon) or the type of paper, and by changing the kind of resin (phenolic, melamine, silicone, or epoxy), we can produce 30 different grades.

Any additional punctuation goes outside the second parenthesis when the punctuation applies to the whole sentence. It goes inside when it applies only to the words in the parentheses.

Please check the invoice to see whether credit should be issued. (A copy of the invoice is attached.)

2. Use parentheses for the second of two numbers presented both in words and in digits.

Construction must be completed within two (2) years of the date of the contract.

Periods

1. Use a period at the end of a sentence. Leave one space before the next sentence.

2. Use a period after some abbreviations. When a period replaces a person's name, leave one space after the period before the next word. In other abbreviations, no space is necessary.

   P. Chow has been named vice president for marketing.

   The B.C. division plans to hire 10 new M.B.A.s in the next year.

The tendency today is to reduce the use of punctuation. It would also be correct to write

   The BC division plans to hire 10 new MBAs in the next year.

Semicolons

1. Use semicolons to join two independent clauses when they are closely related.

   We'll do our best to fill your order promptly; however, we cannot guarantee a delivery date.

Using a semicolon suggests that the two ideas are very closely connected. Using a period and a new sentence is also correct but implies nothing about how closely related the two sentences are.

2. Use semicolons to separate items in a series when the items themselves contain commas.

   The final choices for the new plant are Edmonton, Alberta; Sydney, Nova Scotia; Mississauga, Ontario; Québec City, Quebec; Winnipeg, Manitoba; Yellowknife, Northwest Territories; and Victoria, British Columbia.

   Hospital benefits are also provided for certain specialized care services such as diagnostic admissions directed toward a definite disease or injury; normal maternity delivery, Caesarean-section delivery, or complications of pregnancy; and in-patient admissions for dental procedures necessary to safeguard the patient's life or health.

Hint: A semicolon could be replaced by a period and a capital letter. It has a sentence on both sides.

What do I use when I quote sources?

Use quotation marks, square brackets, and ellipses when quoting sources.

Quotation marks, square brackets, ellipses, and underlining are necessary when you quote material.

Quotation Marks

1. Use quotation marks around the names of brochures, pamphlets, and magazine articles.

   Enclosed are 30 copies of our pamphlet "Saving Energy."

   You'll find articles like "How to Improve Your Golf Game" and "Can You Keep Your Eye on the Ball?" in every issue.

   In Canada and the United States, periods, and commas go inside quotation marks. Colons and semicolons go outside. Question marks go inside if they are part of the material being quoted.

2. Use quotation marks around words to indicate that you think the term is misleading.

   These "pro-business" policies actually increase corporate taxes.

3. Use quotation marks around words that you are discussing as words.

   Forty percent of the respondents answered "yes" to the first question.

   Use "Ms." as a courtesy title for a woman unless you know she prefers another title.

It is also acceptable to use underlining or to italicize words instead of using quotation marks. Choose one method and use it consistently.

4. Use quotation marks around words or sentences that you quote from someone else.

   "The Fog Index," says its inventor, Robert Gunning, is "an effective warning system against drifting into needless complexity."

Square Brackets

Use square brackets to add your own words to or make changes in quoted material.

MPP Smith's statement: "These measures will increase the deficit."

Your use of Smith's statement: According to MPP Smith, "These measures [in the new tax bill] will increase the deficit."

The square brackets show that Smith did not say these words; you add them so that the quotation makes sense in your document.

Ellipses

Ellipses are spaced dots. In typing, use three spaced periods for an ellipsis. In a word processor, use a true ellipsis. When an ellipsis comes at the end of a sentence, use a period immediately after the last letter of the sentence. Then add three spaced dots or a true ellipsis. A space follows the last of the dots.

1. Use ellipses to indicate that one or more words have been omitted in the middle of quoted material. You do not need ellipses at the beginning or end of a quote.

The Wall Street Journal notes that Japanese magazines and newspapers include advertisements for a "$2.1 million home in New York's posh Riverdale section...185 acres of farmland [and]...luxury condos on Manhattan's Upper East Side."

2. In advertising and direct mail, use ellipses to imply the pace of spoken comments.

If you've ever wanted to live on a tropical island...cruise to the Bahamas...or live in a castle in Spain...you can make your dreams come true with Vacations Extraordinaire.

■ Italics versus Underlining

1. Underlining causes the reader's eye to **fixate**, or stop unnecessarily, thereby interfering with both reading speed and retention. Unless you're typing or handwriting documents, it is preferable to use italics to indicate titles or emphasis:

Calgary Sun

Maclean's

Boom, Bust and Echo 2000

Titles of brochures and pamphlets are put in quotation marks.

2. Italicize words to emphasize them.

Here's a bulletin that gives you, in handy chart form, *workable data* on more than 50 different types of tubing and pipe.

Note: You may alternatively use **bold** to emphasize words.

■ How should I write numbers and dates?

Spell out numbers under 10 and those used at the beginning of sentences.

Spell out numbers from one to nine. Use digits for numbers 10 and over in most cases. Always use digits for amounts of money.

Numbers (for example *19 percent*) should not begin sentences. Spell out any number that appears at the beginning of a sentence. If spelling it out is impractical, revise the sentence so that it does not begin with a number.

Fifty students filled out the survey.

The year 1992 marked the official beginning of the European Economic Community.

When two numbers follow each other, use words for the smaller number and digits for the larger number.

In dates, use digits for the day and year. The month is normally spelled out. Be sure to spell out the month in international business communication. Canadian usage puts the year first: *07/01/10* means *January 10, 2007*. United States usage puts the month first, so *1/10/07* means *January 10, 2007*. European usage puts the day first, so *10/01/07* means *January 10, 2007*.

Modern punctuation uses a comma before the year only when you give both the month and the day of the month:

May 1, 2007

but

Summers 2005–07

August 2005

Fall 2001

No punctuation is needed in military or European usage, which puts the day of the month first: 13 July 2007. Do not use spaces before or after the slash used to separate parts of the date: 5/99–10/01.

Use a hyphen to join inclusive dates.

March-August 2007 (or write out: March to August 2007)

'98–'03

1996–2007

Note that you do not need to repeat the century in the date that follows the hyphen: 2000–02. But do give the century when it changes: 1999–2001.

How do I mark errors I find when proofreading?

Use these standard proofreading symbols.

Use the proofreading symbols in Figure 16.1 to make corrections when you don't have access to a computer. Figure 16.2 shows how the symbols can be used to correct a typed text.

FIGURE 16.1
Proofreading Symbols

ℯ	delete	⌐	move to left
ℓ	insert a letter	⌐	move to right
¶	start a new paragraph here	⌐	move up
stet	stet (leave as it was before the marked change)	⌐	move down
tr ∿	transpose (reverse)	#	leave a space
lc	lowercase (don't capitalize)	⌒	close up
═	capitalize	//	align vertically

FIGURE 16.2
Marked Text

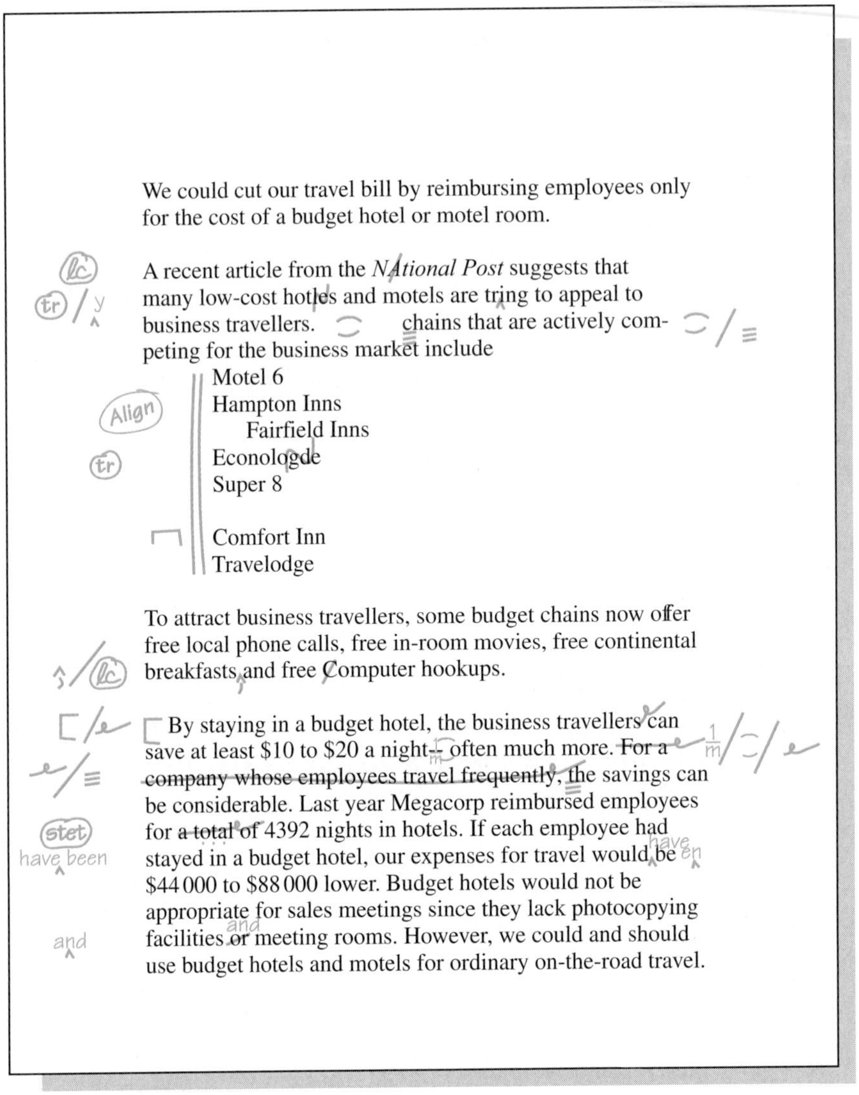

We could cut our travel bill by reimbursing employees only
for the cost of a budget hotel or motel room.

A recent article from the *National Post* suggests that
many low-cost hotles and motels are tring to appeal to
business travellers.   chains that are actively competing for the business market include

Motel 6
Hampton Inns
    Fairfield Inns
Econolodge
Super 8

Comfort Inn
Travelodge

To attract business travellers, some budget chains now offer
free local phone calls, free in-room movies, free continental
breakfasts and free Computer hookups.

By staying in a budget hotel, the business travellers can
save at least $10 to $20 a night—often much more. For a
company whose employees travel frequently, the savings can
be considerable. Last year Megacorp reimbursed employees
for a total of 4392 nights in hotels. If each employee had
stayed in a budget hotel, our expenses for travel would be
$44 000 to $88 000 lower. Budget hotels would not be
appropriate for sales meetings since they lack photocopying
facilities or meeting rooms. However, we could and should
use budget hotels and motels for ordinary on-the-road travel.

Employability Skills 2000+

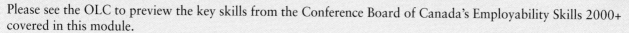

The Conference Board of Canada
Insights You Can Count On

Please see the OLC to preview the key skills from the Conference Board of Canada's Employability Skills 2000+ covered in this module.

Review of Key Points

1. At what stage of the writing process should writers focus on editing?
2. What six grammatical errors should good writers focus on correcting?
3. What eight punctuation marks should writers use correctly?
4. When do writers spell out numbers?
5. What words make clauses subordinate?

Assignments for Module 16

Questions for Critical Thinking

16.1 Consuela sees a lot of errors in the writing of managers at her workplace. If they don't know or don't care about correctness, why should she?

16.2 After surveying readers in her workplace (see problem 16.12), Nikki finds that most of them are not bothered by errors in grammar and punctuation. Does that mean that she doesn't need to fix surface errors?

16.3 Joe knows that his variety of English isn't the privileged variety, but he is afraid that using standard edited English will make him "uppity" to people in his home community. Should he try to use standard grammar and pronunciation? Why or why not?

Exercises and Problems

16.4 Making Subjects and Verbs Agree

Identify and correct the errors in the following sentences.

1. My education and training has prepared me to contribute to your company.
2. I know from my business experience that good communication among people and departments are essential in running a successful corporation.
3. A team of people from marketing, finance, and production are preparing the proposal.
4. The present solutions that has been suggested are not adequate.
5. There has also been suggestions for improving the airflow in the building.

16.5 Using the Right Pronoun

Identify and correct the errors in the following sentences.

1. A new employee should try to read verbal and non-verbal signals to see which aspects of your job are most important.
2. With people like yourself giving gifts, the Habitat for Humanity program will be able to grow.
3. If a group member doesn't complete their assigned work, it slows down the whole project.
4. Todd drew the graphs after him and I discussed the ideas for them.
5. Thank you for the help you gave Joanne Jackson and myself.

16.6   Fixing Dangling and Misplaced Modifiers

Identify and correct the errors in the following sentences.

1. As one of the students in a good program, our company is interested in interviewing you.
2. By making an early reservation, it will give us more time to coordinate our trucks to better serve your needs.
3. Children are referred to the Big Brother or Big Sister program by their school social workers, often from underprivileged homes.
4. At times while typing and editing, the text on your screen may not look correct.
5. All employees are asked to cut back on energy waste by the manager.

16.7   Creating Parallel Structure

Identify and correct the errors in the following sentences.

1. We help clients
   - Manage change
   - Marketing/promotion
   - Developing better billing systems
2. Volunteers need a better orientation to Planned Parenthood as a whole, to the overall clinic function, and to the staff there is also a need to clarify volunteer responsibilities.
3. The benefits of an online catalogue are
   1. We will be able to keep records up-to-date.
   2. Broad access to the catalogue system from any networked terminal on campus.
   3. The consolidation of the main catalogue and the catalogues in the departmental and branch libraries.
   4. Cost savings.
4. You can get a reduced rate on your life insurance if you have an annual medical exam. Another rebate is available to employees who do not use tobacco. Exercising for 30 minutes a day three times a week also entitles employees to an insurance rebate.
5. The ideal job candidate will be able to
   - Create and maintain Web pages.
   - The ability to create PowerPoint™ slides is expected.
   - It would be best if the candidate could speak a second language.

16.8   Correcting Sentence Errors

Identify and correct the errors in the following sentences.

1. Videoconferencing can be frustrating. Simply because little time is available for casual conversation.
2. Not everyone is promoted after six months some people might remain in the training program a year before being moved to a permanent assignment.
3. Pay yourself with the Automatic Savings Account, with this account any amount you choose will be transferred automatically from your chequing account to your savings account each month.
4. You can take advantage of several banking services. Such as automatic withdrawal of a house or car payment and direct deposit of your paycheque.
5. Our group met seven times outside class, we would have met even more if we could have found times when we could all get together.

16.9 Providing Punctuation within Sentences

Provide the necessary punctuation in the following sentences. Note that not every box requires punctuation.

1. The system□s□ user□friendly design□ provides screen displays of work codes□ rates□ and client information.
2. Many other factors also shape the organization□s□ image□ advertising□ brochures□ proposals□ stationery□ calling cards□ and so on.
3. Miss Manners □ author of □Miss Manners□ Book of Modern Manners□□ says□ □Try to mention specifics of the conversation to fix the interview permanently in the interviewer□s□ mind and be sure to mail the letter the same day□ before the hiring decision is made□□
4. What are your room rates and charges for food service□
5. We will need accommodations for 150 people□ five meeting rooms□one large room and four small ones□□coffee served during morning and afternoon breaks□ and lunches and dinners.
6. The Operational Readiness Inspection□ which occurs once every three years□ is a realistic exercise□ that evaluates the □ Royal Canadian Air Cadet □s□ ability to mobilize□ deploy□ and fight.
7. Most computer packages will calculate three different sets of percentages□ row percentages□ column percentages□ and table percentages□
8. In today□s□ economy□ it□s almost impossible for a firm to extend credit beyond it□s□ regular terms.
9. The Ministry of Transportation does not have statutory authority to grant easements□ however□ we do have authority to lease unused areas of highway right□of□way.
10. The program has two goals□ to identify employees with promise□ and to see that they get the training they need to advance.

16.10 Providing Punctuation

Provide the necessary punctuation in the following sentences. Note that not every box requires punctuation.

1. To reduce executive assistants□ overtime hours□ the office should hire part□time secretaries to work from 5:00 to 9:00 P.M.
2. Since memberships can begin at any time during the year□ all member□s□ dues are recognized on a cash basis□ when they are received.
3. I would be interested in working on the committee□ however□ I have decided to do less community work□ so that I have more time to spend with my family.
4. One of the insurance companies□ Allstate Insurance □□ Fredericton □ □NB□ said it hopes to persuade the provincial government to reconsider the rule.
5. The city already has five□ two□ hundred□bed hospitals.
6. Students□ run the whole organization□ and are advised by a board of directors from the community.
7. I suggest putting a bulletin board in the rear hallway with all the interviewer□s□ pictures on it.
8. □Most small businesses just get enough money to open the doors□□ says Mr. Quinn□ adding □that the $10000 or so of savings he used to start up simply wasn□t enough□□
9. Otis Conward Jr□□ who grew up in this area□ now heads the Council for Economic Development.
10. Volunteers also participate in a one□on□one pal program.

16.11 Fixing Errors in Grammar and Punctuation

Identify and correct the errors in the following passages.

a. Company's are finding it to their advantage to cultivate their suppliers. Partnerships between a company and its suppliers can yield hefty payoffs for both company and supplier. One example is Bombardier, a Montreal headquartered company. Bombardier makes airplanes, subway cars and control systems. They treat suppliers almost like departments of their own company. When a Bombardier employee passes a laser scanner over a bins bar code the supplier is instantly alerted to send more parts.

b. Entrepreneur Trip Hawkins appears in Japanese ads for the video game system his company designed. "It plugs into the future! he says in one ad, in a cameo spliced into shots of U.S kids playing the games. Hawkins is one of several U.S. celebrities and business people whom plug products on Japanese TV.

c. Between 1989 and 2004 the number of self-employed grew by more than 40 percent to 2.4 million; but this growth includes a huge increase of one person operations. "The self-employed sector now accounts for more than 16 percent of all workers; an increase from 13 percent in 1989. According to bizSmarts report Self-Employment in Canada, Trend's and Prospect's, over the next ten years, self-employment will become even more dominant in the Canadian labour market

16.12 Identifying Audience Concerns about Grammar

Most readers care passionately about only a few points of grammar. Survey one or more readers (including your boss, if you have a job) to find out which kinds of errors concern them. Use a separate copy of this survey for each reader.

Directions: Each of the following sentences contains an error. Please circle Y if the error bothers you a good bit; S if the error bothers you slightly; and N if you would not be bothered by the error (or perhaps even notice it).

Y S N 1. She brung her secretary with her.

Y S N 2. Him and Richard were the last ones hired.

Y S N 3. Wanted to tell you that the meeting will be November 10.

Y S N 4. Each representative should bring a list of their clients to the meeting.

Y S N 5. A team of people from administration, human services, and animal control are preparing the proposal.

Y S N 6. We cannot predict, how high the number of clients may rise.

Y S N 7. He treats his clients bad.

Y S N 8. She asked Eva and I to give a presentation.

Y S N 9. Update the directory by reviewing each record in the database and note any discrepancies.

Y S N 10. He has went to a lot of trouble to meet our needs.

Y S N 11. She gave the report to Davlic and myself.

Y S N 12. I was unable to complete the report. Because I had a very busy week.

Y S N 13. The benefits of an online directory are
a. We will be able to keep records up-to-date.
b. Access to the directory from any terminal with a modem in the county.
c. Cost savings.

Y S N 14. By making an early reservation, it will give us more time to plan the session to meet your needs.

Y S N 15. She doesn't have no idea how to use the computer.

Y S N 16. The change will not effect our service to customers.

Y S N 17. Confirming our conversation, the truck will leave Monday.

Y S N 18. The sessions will begin January 4 we will pass around a sign-up sheet early in December.

Y S N 19. I will be unable to attend the meeting, however I will send someone else from my office.

Y S N 20. Its too soon to tell how many proposals we will receive.

Compare your responses with those of a small group of students.

- Which errors were most annoying to the largest number of readers?
- How much variation do you find in a single workplace? in a single type of business?

As your instructor directs,

a. Present your findings to the class in a short group report.
b. Present your findings to the class in an oral presentation.

Polishing Your Prose

Using Spell Checkers and Grammar Checkers

Most word processing programs come with spell checkers and grammar checkers. Although these computer tools can be useful, remember that they have limitations.

Spell checkers identify words that don't match their dictionary. If the word is a real word, the spell checker can't tell whether it's the right word for the context (e.g., "their" versus "there," as in "We will review there report when we get their.")

Grammar checkers only suggest possible errors and solutions; you must make the final decision. That is, a grammar checker may tell you that you've used passive voice, but the checker can't tell you whether the passive is appropriate in that particular sentence.

Therefore, use spell checkers and grammar checkers as one of several tools to make your writing better. In addition, keep a dictionary, thesaurus, and stylebook handy. Work to improve your command of spelling and grammar; take a class or work with a college or university writing centre for help.

Exercises

Type the following sentences into your word processor. First, run a spell check on them. Are all the words or constructions that show up as errors really wrong? Are there any errors that don't show up? Then, run a grammar check and answer the same questions.

1. There product is sitting over their.
2. The project will have been completed by next Thursday?
3. Its not really a good idea to have had lunch before the flight.
4. The solution was created in the '90s using a new chemical process.
5. Martika is happy with her purchase; shell order online again.
6. I call your office because were needed in in the mailroom.
7. Les says, "Less is more.
8. Kadji is looking in to buying more property but it won't happen really soon.
9. The Internet is a powerfull research tool—so what?
10. This computers spellchecker did a pretty good job.

Check your answers to the odd-numbered exercises on page 572.

Online Learning Centre

Visit the Online Learning Centre at www.mcgrawhill.ca/olc/locker to access module quizzes, a searchable glossary, résumé and letter templates, additional business writing samples, CBC videos, and other learning and study tools.

■ CBC Video Cases

Visit the Online Learning Centre at www.mcgrawhill.ca/olc/locker to view "A Science Lesson," Unit Four's online CBC Video Case. You'll get a critical view of how companies search for impressive "scientific" terms to promote their products—and find out how the consumer audience reacts to this specialized vocabulary.

■ Cases for Communicators

■ A Hard Lesson in Grammar

Bad grammar or punctuation can make even the best writer appear to be ill-trained, unprofessional, and even unintelligent. Errors in punctuation and grammar can confuse, mislead, and even cause readers to disregard or ignore an otherwise well-written letter. In some cases, such errors can generate a great deal of unwanted attention, with decidedly negative consequences. Consider the case of a class of graduating high school students from Vorobyovo, Russia. In anticipation of their upcoming graduation party, several members of the class sent a one-page, handwritten letter to Russian President Vladimir Putin, inviting him to their celebration and asking him to send a video camera so they could tape the festivities. On receiving the letter, the Kremlin returned it to the local school district with a request that the authors be identified. When the school officials read the missive, they were horrified! Written on a small, dirty piece of paper, the note had several punctuation and grammar mistakes, the most egregious of which was an error in the salutation to President Putin. As one school official noted, "This is not what educated and smart people do."

The embarrassed district officials' response was quick and severe. They ordered the director of the school to write an explanatory note and meet with them about the students' letter, and then they examined the school records of the students involved. Two of the students had just been awarded special silver medals for their exceptional performance on final exams. The school administrators revoked those medals.

Losing that honour in this manner had severe repercussions for the two students, dashing their hopes for an advanced education and a future outside of their small village. Ironically, the Kremlin itself was unfazed by the errors. It responded to the students' letter by sending the video camera just in time for graduation.

Fortunately, grammatical and punctuation errors do not generally carry such a high penalty as loss of lifelong dreams, but these errors can greatly damage others' perception of you as an intelligent, professional business person. As these students learned the hard way, grammar and punctuation can be the most important part of your message!

Source: Michael Wines, "A Letter to the President, a Lesson in Style," *New York Times*, June 23, 2000, http://www.nytimes.com, retrieved August 8, 2002.

Individual Activity

Imagine that you are the principal of the high school where the grammar furor erupted. You know that your students are intelligent, and you pride yourself on the good writing skills that are taught at the school. Unfortunately, as a result of this incident, administrators no longer have the same impression. You need to take action or your job may be in jeopardy!

Write a letter to the superintendent of schools discussing the recent events and describing your philosophy about good grammar and writing skills. To illustrate that you recognize the importance of mastering these skills, be sure to include at least three specific points describing how poor grammar and punctuation can affect the perception of both the writer and an otherwise well-written document.

The school's curriculum is complete and well crafted. You believe it was merely haste and a resulting failure to adequately polish the offending letter, rather than ignorance of good grammar and punctuation, that created the embarrassing situation. Therefore, you believe that the academic medals should be returned to your students.

Before you begin writing your letter, ask yourself the following question: What do I really mean?

After you've written your first draft, read it out loud. Then, think about these questions as you polish your letter:

- Did I use active verbs most of the time?
- Did I use verbs to carry the weight of my sentences?
- Did I include any words that mean nothing?
- Can I make my writing more concise by combining sentences or using gerunds and infinitives?
- Did I vary sentence length and structure?
- Did I use parallel structure?
- Did I begin most paragraphs with strong topic sentences?
- Did I use transitions to link ideas?

Given the current situation, the superintendent will have no tolerance for errors, so be sure to carefully review your letter for typographical and grammatical errors.

Group Activity

(Note: To prepare for this group activity, print out a new version of your draft, omitting all punctuation and formatting. The end result should be one large block of text without any clear sentence or paragraph structure. Next, break the members of the group into pairs.)

You want to share your draft with the school's teachers. Unfortunately, as you prepare to print out copies for them, your unreliable laptop computer crashes! The only version you can recover is complete but lacks punctuation and formatting. You only have one copy of the final letter, so since you are pressed for time, you decide to distribute this "raw" version.

Exchange unformatted drafts with your partner. Carefully read through the letter. Then go back through it and, using the correct proofreading marks, note where the punctuation and paragraph breaks should go.

Unit 5

Interpersonal Communication

Interpersonal Communication

"My communication skills have enabled me to travel and work all over the world, and to find employment opportunities beyond the limits of my formal education," says entrepreneur Clayton Peters, who credits family and friendships as formative influences:

"My father was an extremely articulate man, with a formidable command of the English language. He was quick to correct my brother (comedian Russell Peters) and me on any mispronunciation or grammatical errors. I also grew up in Toronto and Brampton, Ontario, with friends from Jamaica, Trinidad, India, China, the Philippines, Pakistan, Italy, and the British Isles. This multi-cultural environment taught me to be sensitive to other people's values, and allowed me to respect the differences of the people I dealt with in business, whether I was in North Africa, China or Russia.

I was also fortunate enough to travel to Europe, India, and the United States, as a child and into my teens, with my parents."

Clayton claims to have been a bored, unfocused high school student. Nevertheless, his career choices demonstrate the self-reliance, ambition, and sense of responsibility typical of both entrepreneurs and second-generation immigrants. He has worked in retail management, transportation management, industrial manufacturing, distribution, and marketing, product management, and the services industry—both nationally and internationally.

Meanwhile, he has continued his formal education, taking night school courses in distribution management, marketing, logistics, and small business management.

Founder and president of CPI Management Services Ltd., Clayton now manages the careers of actors and comedians based in Toronto and Los Angeles, including the career of his brother, Russell Peters.

"The variety of my work experiences and work environments allowed me to hone my communication, analytical and team building skills. All of these skills have been critical to creating my own support networks in the entertainment/business management field.

I have always been independent and self-reliant and didn't see myself as a 'team player.' However, upon reflection I realize that throughout my career I have had to build teams of people to achieve organizational and interpersonal goals. These teams became a series of alliances offering collective and individual member benefits. For example, I allied myself with people from whom I could learn, or whose skills compensated for my limitations. I also had to learn to network with individuals outside of my immediate workplace—customers, competitors, distributors, and vendors—at trade shows, exhibitions, and company events.

Today I recognize the value of this networking experience. I have built a team of people in this industry whom I trust and to whom I can go for advice and counsel. This team is the key to my own current level of success, and that of my clients."

P A I B O C

Analysis

1. According to Clayton, what are the **benefits** of working as part of a team?

2. Who are the different **audiences** to whom Clayton must represent his clients?

3. What current **contextual** factors might impact Clayton's management of Canadian talent?

MODULE

17 Listening

Module Outline

- What do good listeners do?
- What is active listening?
- How do I show people that I'm listening to them?
- Can I use these techniques if I really disagree with someone?

Review of Key Points

Assignments for Module 17

Polishing Your Prose: Combining Sentences

LEARNING OBJECTIVES

After reading and applying the information in Module 17, you'll be able to demonstrate

Knowledge of
- The fundamentals of good listening practice
- Active listening as a core communication competency

Skills to
- Listen actively
- Continue to learn how to build goodwill

The Conference Board of Canada
Insights You Can Count On

Please see the OLC to preview the key skills from the Conference Board of Canada's Employability Skills 2000+ covered in this module.

FYI

A recent survey by Select Appointments North America found that 80 percent of responding executives rated listening as the most important skill in the workforce. Soft skills such as listening and problem solving ranked far higher than technical skills. However, listening skills were also rated by 28 percent of executives as the most lacking in the workforce.

Source: "Why All This Fuss About Listening ?" http://www.accelteam.co/communications/busComms_02.html, retrieved August 23, 2006.

Despite the universal "You weren't listening!" lament of friends, lovers, parents, teachers, co-workers, and employers, we rarely receive formal training in this key skill. In fact, active listening is an acquired skill that takes a lifetime of practice, and requires an enormous amount of energy.

As Module 2 explains (◀▷ pp. 27–28), to receive a message, the receiver must first perceive the message, then decode it (that is, translate the symbols into meaning), and then interpret it. In interpersonal communication, **hearing** denotes perceiving sounds. **Listening,** however, means decoding and interpreting them correctly.

What do good listeners do?

They consciously follow four practices.

Good listeners pay attention, focus on the other speaker(s) in a generous way, avoid making assumptions, and listen for feelings as well as for facts.

1. Pay Attention

Good listening requires energy. You have to resist distractions and tune out noise (◀▷ Module 2), whether it's another conversation nearby or your worry about your parking meter expiring.

You can do several things to avoid listening errors caused by not paying attention:

- Before the conversation, anticipate the answers you need. Make a mental or paper list of your questions. When is the project due? What resources do you have? What is the most important aspect of this project from the other person's point of view? During a conversation, listen for answers to your questions.
- At the end of the conversation, check your understanding with the other person. Especially check who does what next.
- During or after the conversation, write down key points that affect deadlines or work assessment.

2. Focus on the Other Speaker(s) in a Generous Way

Most of us half hear while we listen to our own internal monologues. We focus on factors incidental to the topic, or look for flaws: "What an ugly tie." "She sounds like a little girl." "There's a typo in that slide." Often we listen only for the pause that signifies it's our turn to speak, or, as if the discussion were a competition, collect weapons to attack the other speaker. "Ah hah! You're wrong about *that*!"

Polish your listening skills. You'll need them on the job as well as in your personal life.

Good listeners, in contrast, are more generous. They realize that people who are not polished speakers may nevertheless have something to say. Rather than pouncing on the first error they hear and tuning out the speaker while they wait impatiently for their own turn to speak, good listeners weigh all the evidence before they make a judgment. They realize that they can learn something even from people they do not like, or do not agree with.

You have several ways to avoid listening errors caused by self-absorption:

- Focus on the content: on what the speaker says, not his or her appearance or delivery.
- Spend your time evaluating what the speaker says, not just planning your rebuttal.
- Consciously work to learn something from every speaker.

■ 3. Avoid Making Assumptions

Many listening errors come from making faulty assumptions, assumptions based on a natural tendency to focus on our own ego needs, and to interpret the speaker's meaning according to our own experiences. However, each of us brings our own unique experiences to the meaning-making process. Furthermore, we perceive experience through our own cultural biases. We are socialized to communicate the way we do. People from different cultures speak and listen very differently. (◀▶ to Modules 2 and 3) The most adept listeners, therefore, strive to listen for understanding without making assumptions.[1]

Active listeners ask questions to elicit and clarify information. Superb salespeople listen closely to client questions and objections, to better identify and respond to the sticking points of a sale. Magazine advertising account representative Beverly Jameson received a phone call from an ad agency saying that a client wanted to cancel the space it had bought. Jameson saw the problem as an opportunity: "Instead of hearing 'cancel,' I heard, 'There's a problem here—let's get to the root of it and figure out how to make the client happy.'" Jameson met with the client, asked questions, and discovered that the client wanted more flexibility. She changed some of the markets, kept the business, and turned the client into a repeat customer.[2]

You can avoid listening errors caused by faulty assumptions:

- Focus on the other person's background and experiences. Why is this point important to the speaker? What might he or she mean by it? How can its importance to the speaker benefit you?
- Query instructions you think are unnecessary. Before you do something else, check with the order giver to see whether there is a reason for the instruction.
- Paraphrase what the speaker has said, giving him or her a chance to correct your understanding.

■ 4. Listen for Feelings as Well as Facts

Sometimes, someone just needs to blow off steam, to vent (◀▶ p. 331). Sometimes, people just want to have a chance to fully express themselves; "winning" or "losing" may not matter. Sometimes, people may have objections that they can't quite put into words.

You can learn to avoid listening errors caused by focusing solely on facts by:

- Consciously listening for feelings
- Paying attention to tone of voice, facial expression, and body language (◀▶ p. 52)
- Paraphrasing what the speaker has said, and acknowledging the feelings you are observing
- Not assuming that silence means consent. Invite the other person to speak.

What is active listening?

Active listening involves feeding back the literal meaning, or the emotional content, or both.

In **active listening**, receivers actively demonstrate that they've heard and understood by feeding back to the speaker either the literal meaning or the emotional content, or both. Other techniques in active listening are asking for more information and stating your own feelings.

Five strategies create active responses:

1. Paraphrase the content. Feed back the meaning, as you understand it, in your own words.
2. Mirror the speaker's feelings. Identify the feelings you think you hear.
3. State your own feelings. This strategy works especially well when you are angry.
4. Ask for information or clarification.
5. Ask how you can help.

Instead of mirroring what the other person says, many of us respond to our own needs by attempting to analyze, solve, or dismiss the problem. People with problems need to know above all that we hear that they're having a rough time. Table 17.1 lists some of the responses that block communication. Ordering and interrogating tell the speaker that the listener doesn't want to hear what he or she has to say.

Preaching attacks the other person. Minimizing the problem suggests that the other person's concern is misplaced. Even advising shuts off discussion. Giving a quick answer minimizes what the person feels and puts him or her down for not seeing (what is to us, because it's not our problem) the obvious answer. Even if it is a good answer from an objective point

TABLE 17.1
Blocking Responses versus Active Listening

Blocking Response	Possible Active Response
Ordering, threatening	**Paraphrasing content**
"I don't care how you do it. Just get that report on my desk by Friday."	"You're saying that you don't have time to finish the report by Friday."
Preaching, criticizing	**Mirroring feelings**
"You should know better than to air the department's problems in a general meeting."	"It sounds like the department's problems really bother you."
Interrogating	**Stating one's own feelings**
"Why didn't you tell me that you didn't understand the instructions?"	"I'm frustrated that the job isn't completed yet, and I'm worried about getting it done on time."
Minimizing the problem	**Asking for information or clarification**
"You think that's bad. You should see what I have to do this week."	"What parts of the problem seem most difficult to solve?"
Advising	**Offering to help solve the problem together**
"Well, why don't you try listing everything you have to do and seeing which items are most important?"	"What can I do to help?"

Source: The five responses that block communication are based on a list of 12 in Thomas Gordon and Judith Gordon Sands, *P.E.T. in Action* (New York: Wyden, 1976), 117–18.

of view, the other person may not be ready to hear it. And sometimes, the off-the-top-of-the-head solution doesn't address the real problem.

Active listening takes time and energy. Even people who are skilled active listeners can't do it all the time, because the listener's feelings interfere with open reception. Furthermore, as experts have pointed out, active listening works only if you genuinely accept the other person's ideas and feelings. Active listening can reduce the conflict that results from miscommunication, but it alone cannot reduce the conflict that comes when two people want apparently inconsistent things or when one person wants to change someone else.[3]

How do I show people that I'm listening to them?

Acknowledge their comments in words, in non-verbal symbols, and in actions.

Active listening is a good way to show people that you are listening. Referring to another person's comment is another way: "I agree with Diana that..."

Acknowledgement responses or **conversation regulators**—nods, uh huh's, smiles, frowns—also help carry the message that you're listening. Remember, however, that listening responses vary from culture to culture.

European Canadians indicate attention and involvement by making eye contact, leaning forward, and making acknowledgement responses. However, as Module 3 shows (◄|▷ p. 53), some cultures show respect by looking down. In a multicultural workforce, you won't always know whether a colleague who listens silently agrees with what you say or disagrees violently but is too polite to say so. The best thing to do is to observe the behaviour, without assigning a meaning to it: "You aren't saying much." Then let the other person speak.

Of course, if you go through the motions of active listening but then act with disrespect, people will feel that you have not heard them. Acting on what people say is necessary for people to feel completely heard.

Can I use these techniques if I really disagree with someone?

Yes!

Most of us do our worst listening when we are in highly charged emotional situations, such as talking with someone with whom we really disagree, getting bad news, or being criticized. Certainly you don't need to listen to a radio talk show host whose views you deplore. But at work, you do need to listen, even to people with whom you have major conflicts.

At a minimum, good listening enables you to find out why your opponent objects to the programs or ideas you support. Understanding the objections to your ideas is essential if you are to create a persuasive campaign to overcome those objections.

Good listening is crucial when you are being criticized, especially by your boss. You need to know which areas are most important and exactly what kind of improvement counts. Otherwise, you might spend your time and energy changing your behaviour but changing it in a way not valued by your organization.

Listening can do even more. Listening to people is an indication that you're taking them seriously. If you really listen to the people you disagree with, you show that you respect them. And taking that step may enable them to respect you and listen to you.

EXPANDING A CRITICAL SKILL

Leading by Listening

Enormous energy, stamina, and curiosity characterize the best managers. And they draw on these resources ceaselessly, since at least 90 percent of their day is spent communicating. Canadian, American, British, and Swedish managers demonstrate a marked preference for gathering information by word of mouth, and through conversations, telephone calls, and meetings, rather than by reading documents. These managers lead by putting themselves in the centre of the organization's information flow. Listening to "soft" data, including opinions and gossip, allows them to recognize problems and opportunities, make decisions, motivate and negotiate. To accumulate and disseminate the information necessary to do their job, these leaders spend most of their day listening.

In fact, experts and practitioners agree that the most effective leaders apply sophisticated interpersonal skills, not management theory, to manage people. Major-General Lewis MacKenzie, former chief of staff of the United Nations Protection force in Yugoslavia, espouses leadership tenets he learned first-hand. Significantly, MacKenzie believes that learning to listen became one of his most powerful leadership techniques.

According to an article in *the training report*, "MacKenzie said that early in his career he always thought that he knew more than the person talking to him, and often didn't hear what they were saying to him because he was constructing his response midway through their sentence. It was a slap in the face when he finally realized that half the people who worked for him knew more than he did. But then he learned that if he listened to a subordinate's idea, implemented it, and gave that person credit,..." he'd look just as good, the subordinate would gain in recognition and morale and the organization would be improved. To get people talking, MacKenzie also had to listen: "...he found out what their passions were and used those interests as a threshold to open communication."

Peacekeeper MacKenzie "commanded a multinational force that spoke 16 different languages and hailed from 31 different countries." Despite the obvious communication difficulties, "MacKenzie and his troops opened the airport in Sarajevo in 1992, sidestepping normal channels and allowing for the daily delivery of 250 to 300 tons of desperately needed food and medicine."

The key to active listening is preparedness. Being prepared and receptive listeners can transform our lives.

In 1996, out-of-work stagehand Sam Holman, who had a disability from a chronic knee injury and was ineligible for disability insurance, was casually talking baseball with friend Bill MacKenzie in The Mayflower, an Ottawa pub. MacKenzie, a baseball scout for more than 20 years, commented on the number of bats that major leaguers broke each season. Then he suggested that Holman use his carpentry skills to do something about the problem: "Why don't you start making bats?" Hundreds of hours of research later, Holman carved the prototype Sam Bat, the first maple bat in the history of baseball. Although its original price didn't cover production costs, by August 1977 the Sam Bat had attracted important converts: the Blue Jays' Joe Carter loved the bat and began to lobby the league to approve it. In 1998, the Sam Bat received approval—the first maple bat in major-league history to do so. Meanwhile heavy hitters on all the major league teams began ordering Holman's bats, which many credited for their improved batting averages. By 1999, not only the majors, but college, little league, Taiwanese, and Mexican teams, were also ordering Sam Bats. Today Holman custom-makes 200 different bat models while overseeing the four employees of the Original Maple Bat Corporation.

Sources: Henry Mintzberg, "The Manager's Job: Folklore and Fact," http://www.uu.edu/personal/bnance/318/mintz.html, retrieved August 14, 2006; "Lessons in Leadership," *the training report*, May/June 2001; Alex Gillis, "Batman," *National Post Business*, October 1999, 60–69.

Employability Skills 2000+

The Conference Board of Canada
Insights You Can Count On

Please see the OLC to preview the key skills from the Conference Board of Canada's Employability Skills 2000+ covered in this module.

Review of Key Points

1. What's the difference between hearing and listening?
2. What are the four key behaviours of good listeners?
3. What can you do to reduce listening errors caused by self-absorption?
4. What can you do to reduce listening errors caused by misinterpretation?
5. What can you do to avoid listening errors caused by focusing only on facts?
6. How can you demonstrate active listening?

Assignments for Module 17

Questions for Critical Thinking

17.1 Why is listening such hard work?
17.2 How do you show someone that you are listening?
17.3 Who are the people and what are the circumstances in your life when you find it most difficult to listen? Why do you find it difficult?

17.4 Think of a time when you really felt that the other person listened to you and a time when you felt unheard. Describe the verbal and non-verbal content in each situation. How did you know the other person was listening? What behaviours and words caused you to feel unheard? Now describe your feelings in each situation. What was different in each situation?

Exercises and Problems

17.5 Identifying Responses That Show Active Listening

Which of the following responses show active listening? Which block communication?

1. Comment: Whenever I say something, the group ignores me.
   Responses:
   a. That's because your ideas aren't very good. Do more planning before group meetings.
   b. Nobody listens to me, either.
   c. You're saying that nobody builds on your ideas.

2. Comment: I've done more than my share of work on this project. But the people who have been freeloading are going to get the same grade I worked so hard to earn.
   Responses:
   a. Yes, we're all going to get the same grade.
   b. Are you afraid we won't do well on the assignment?
   c. It sounds as if you feel resentful.

3. Comment: My parents are going to kill me if I don't have a job lined up at the end of this term.
   Responses:
   a. You know they're exaggerating. They won't really kill you.

b. Can you blame them? I mean, you've been in school for six years. Surely you've learned something to make you employable!

c. If you act the way in interviews that you do in our class, I'm not surprised. Companies want people with good attitudes and good work ethics.

17.6 Practising Active Listening

Do this exercise as a class. Let each student complain about something (large or small) that really bothers him or her. Then the next student(s) will

a. Check his or her understanding of what the speaker said.

b. Paraphrase the statement.

c. Check for feelings that might lie behind the statement.

d. Ask questions to better identify the problem.

17.7 Interviewing Workers about Listening

Interview someone about his or her on-the-job listening. Possible questions to ask include the following:

- Whom do you listen to as part of your job? your superior? subordinates? (How many levels down?) customers or clients? who else?
- How much time a day do you spend listening?
- What people do you talk to as part of your job? Do you feel they hear what you say? How do you tell whether or not they're listening?
- Do you know of any problems that came up because someone didn't listen? What happened?

- What do you think prevents people from listening effectively? What advice would you have for someone on how to listen more accurately?

As your instructor directs,

a. Share your information with a small group of students in your class.

b. Present your findings orally to the class.

c. Present your findings in a memo to your instructor.

d. Join with other students to present your findings in a group report or presentation.

17.8 Reflecting on Your Own Listening

Keep a listening log for a week. Record for how long you listened, what barriers you encountered, and what strategies you used to listen more actively and more effectively. What situations were easiest? Which were most difficult? What cultural assumptions affected how and when you listened? What discourse communities have influenced your listening habits? Which parts of listening do you need to work hardest on?

As your instructor directs,

a. Share your information with a small group of students in your class.

b. Present your findings orally to the class.

c. Present your findings in a memo to your instructor.

d. Join with other students to present your findings in a group report or presentation.

17.9 Reflecting on Others' Listening Behaviours

Observe four different cross-cultural conversations (for example, between a man and a woman, an urban and rural dweller, a member of a collectivist and an individualistic culture, and a member of a high-context and a member of a low-context culture (◀▮▶ Module 3). Note the talking and listening behaviours. For your analysis, use the following questions as a guide:

Who speaks more? What does that person talk about? Who listens more? What are the differences in tone? What are the differences in pauses, interruptions, questions, and nonverbal cues and clues?

As your instructor directs,

a. Share your information with a small group of students in the class.
b. Present your findings orally to the class.
c. Present your findings in a memo to your teacher.
d. Join with other students to present your findings in a group report or presentation.

17.10 Reflecting on Acknowledgement Responses

Try to be part of at least three conversations involving people from more than one culture. What acknowledgement responses do you observe? Which seem to yield the most positive results? If possible, talk to the other participants about what verbal and non-verbal cues show attentive listening in their cultures.

As your instructor directs,

a. Share your information with a small group of students in your class.
b. Present your findings orally to the class.
c. Present your findings in a memo to your instructor.
d. Join with other students to present your findings in a group report or presentation.

Polishing Your Prose

Combining Sentences

Combining sentences is a powerful tool to make your writing more concise and more forceful.

When too many sentences in a passage have fewer than 10 words and follow the same basic pattern, prose is *choppy*. Choppy prose seems less unified and either robot-like or frenzied in tone. Combining short sentences to create longer flowing ones can eliminate this problem.

Choppy: I went to the office supply store. I purchased a computer, a fax machine, and a laser printer. I went to my office. I installed the equipment. I am more efficient.

Better: At the office supply store, I purchased a computer, a fax machine, and a laser printer. After installing the equipment in my office, I am more efficient.

There are several ways to combine sentences.

1. Use **transitions**: words and phrases that signal connections between ideas. Common transitions are *first, second, third, finally, in addition, likewise, for example, however, on the other hand, nevertheless, because, therefore, before, after, while,* and *in conclusion.*

Choppy: Neil drove the truck to the warehouse. Charlie loaded it with cement. Phil supervised the work.

Better: First, Neil drove the truck to the warehouse. Then Charlie loaded it with cement, while Phil supervised the work.

2. Rewrite sentences using **subordinate clauses**. A clause with one of the following words will be subordinate: *after, although, though, because,* or *since.*

Better: After Neil drove the truck to the warehouse, Charlie loaded it with cement. Phil supervised the work.

3. Join simple sentences together with *coordinating conjunctions,* like *and, but,* or *or.* These conjunctions can also function as transitional words. Be sure to use the comma

before the conjunction when combining two independent clauses.

Better: Neil drove the truck to the warehouse, Charlie loaded it with cement, and Phil supervised the work.

4. Create a list using commas and coordinating conjunctions.

Choppy: Sam put our old files in the storeroom. Sam placed extra copies of the company telephone directory in the storeroom. Sam put boxes of three-ring binders in the storeroom.

Better: Sam put old files, extra copies of the telephone directory, and boxes of three-ring binders in the storeroom.

Exercises

Combine the following sentences to make them easier to read.

1. You can get promoted quickly at our company. Being organized and on time will help. Not meeting deadlines will not help.

2. There are many reasons to choose Canadian Human Resource Planners as your human resources consulting firm. Our organization has more than 20 years in the business. We have regional offices in Calgary and Toronto. Canadian Human Resource Planners has an international membership of members from industry, government, non-profit groups, educational institutions, and consulting firms.

3. Changing the toner cartridge on the photocopier is simple. Open the front panel. Find the green tabs. Depress the green tabs with your thumbs. Pull the black toner cartridge out. Put the toner cartridge in the recycling box. Slide a new toner cartridge into the compartment. The green tabs will snap back into place. Close the panel.

4. The development team members took a plane to Victoria. That was on Friday. They attended a conference. That was on Saturday. They came home. That was on Sunday. On Friday it rained. The team members used umbrellas. The other two days it did not rain. They did not need umbrellas on those days.

5. The tornado plan for our building has five parts. One part is to go to your designated shelter area in the basement of the building. One part is to listen for the tornado alert siren. One part is to sit down on the floor. One part is to take the stairs and not the elevator. One part is to cover your head with your arms.

Check your answers to the odd-numbered exercises on page 572.

▇ Online Learning Centre

Visit the Online Learning Centre at www.mcgrawhill.ca/olc/locker to access module quizzes, a searchable glossary, résumé and letter templates, additional business writing samples, CBC videos, and other learning and study tools.

18 Working and Writing in Teams

Module Outline

- What kinds of communication happen in groups?
- What roles do people play in groups?
- How should we handle conflict?
- How can we create the best co-authored documents?

Review of Key Points

Assignments for Module 18

Polishing Your Prose: Delivering Criticism

LEARNING OBJECTIVES

After reading and applying the information in Module 18, you'll be able to demonstrate

Knowledge of

- The ground rules for working well with others
- Roles people play in groups
- The characteristics of successful work teams

Skills to

- Work effectively in a team
- Lead productively
- Resolve conflicts constructively
- Write collaborative documents

The Conference Board of Canada
Insights You Can Count On

Working in teams is fundamental to doing business today. People work in teams to create new products, streamline processes, hire employees, identify and solve problems, and to brainstorm and articulate strategic organizational objectives.

The most effective teams agree on and adopt explicit ground rules. Table 18.1 lists some of the most common ground rules used by workplace teams.

What kinds of communication happen in groups?

Different messages occur at different points in a group's development.

Group messages fall into three categories: information and procedural messages relate to getting the task done; interpersonal messages focus on maintaining group norms and fostering group cohesion.

1. **Informational messages** focus on content: the problem or challenge, data, and possible solutions.
2. **Procedural messages** focus on method and process. How will the group make decisions? Who will do what? When will assignments be due?
3. **Interpersonal messages** focus on people, promoting friendliness, cooperation, and group loyalty.

Dr Bruce Tuckman's "Forming, Storming, Norming, Performing" model[1] identifies four behavioural stages in a team's development. Different kinds of communication typify the various stages. During the **orientation** (**forming**) stage, when members meet to begin to define the task, team members struggle to develop some sort of social cohesiveness, and to agree on procedures for meeting and acting. Interpersonal and procedural communications reduce tension and begin building the trust necessary for teamwork. Insistence on information in this first stage can hurt the group's long-term productivity.

During **formation** (**storming**), conflicts almost always arise when the group chooses a leader and defines the problem. Successful leaders make the procedure clear so that each member knows what he or she is supposed to do. Interpersonal communication is needed to articulate

TABLE 18.1
Possible Group Ground Rules

- Start on time; end on time.
- Come to the meeting prepared.
- Focus comments on the issues.
- Avoid personal attacks.
- Listen to and respect members' opinions.
- Practise NOSTUESO (No One Speaks Twice Until Everybody Speaks Once).

- If you have a problem with another person, tell that person, not everyone else.
- Everyone must be 70 percent comfortable with the decision and 100 percent committed to implementing it.
- If you agree to do something, do it.
- Communicate immediately if you think you may not be able to fulfill an agreement.

Sources: Nancy Schullery and Beth Hoger, "Business Advocacy for Students in Small Groups," Association for Business Communication Annual Convention, San Antonio, November 9–11, 1998; "An Antidote to Chronic Cantankerousness," *Fast Company*, February/March 1998, 176; John Grossmann, "We've Got to Start Meeting Like This," *Inc.*, April 1998, 70; Gary Dessler, "Winning Commitment," quoted in *Team Management Briefings*, preview issue (September 1998), 5; and 3M Meeting Network, "Groundrules and Agreements," http://www.3M.com/meetingnetwork/readingroom/meetingguide_grndrules.html, retrieved October 25, 2006.

and resolve the conflict that surfaces during this phase. Successful groups define, analyze, and agree on the problem carefully before they begin to search for solutions.

Coordination (norming), is the longest phase, during which most of the group's work is done. Procedural and interpersonal communication maintain the trust necessary to gather and focus on the task information. Good information is essential to good decisions. Creative conflict reoccurs as the group debates alternate solutions.

Eagle's Flight® is a leader in experiential training for the business community. Here, participants investigate a realistic crime scene, an environment designed to teach the critical elements of effective communication through sharing, evaluation, and organization of information.

In **formalization (performing)**, the group seeks consensus. The success of this phase determines how well the group's decision will be implemented. In this stage, the group tries to forget earlier conflicts.

SEE THE OLC!

Bruce Tuckman's Team Development Model

In our diverse workplace, European Canadians' assumptions about teamwork and task orientation don't agree with the values and norms of high-context cultures. Collective cultures focus much more strongly on relationship building (the storming and norming stages) to ensure mutual understanding and respect among team members. Establishing and fostering this respect are vital processes for team development and future productivity.

Not surprisingly, businesses that incorporate the group dynamics of collective cultures enjoy higher employee retention and productivity rates. The "network group" adapts "… Aboriginal community-building concepts such as talking circles, collective decision-making, holistic approaches to life, cooperation, and respect for others and respect of self" to retain valuable Aboriginal employees. In our increasingly diverse and complex workplace, building relationships must be the first order of team business.[2]

■ What roles do people play in groups?

People play both maintenance and task roles, and every role can be positive or negative.

Positive *maintenance* roles and actions that help the group build loyalty, resolve conflicts, and function smoothly to achieve task goals include the following:

- **Listening actively:** Showing group members that they have been heard and that their ideas are being taken seriously (◀▷ Module 17)
- **Encouraging participation:** Demonstrating openness and acceptance, recognizing the contributions of members, calling on quieter group members
- **Relieving tensions:** Joking and suggesting breaks and activities
- **Checking feelings:** Asking members how they feel about group activities and sharing one's own feelings with others
- **Solving interpersonal problems:** Opening discussion of interpersonal problems in the group and suggesting ways to solve them

Positive roles and actions that help the group achieve its **task** goals include the following:[3]

- **Seeking information and opinions:** Asking questions, identifying gaps in the group's knowledge
- **Giving information and opinions:** Answering questions, providing relevant information
- **Summarizing:** Restating major points, pulling ideas together, summarizing decisions
- **Evaluating:** Comparing group processes and products to standards and goals
- **Coordinating:** Planning work, giving directions, and fitting together contributions of group members

Negative roles and actions that hurt the group's products and processes include the following:

- **Blocking:** Disagreeing with everything that is proposed
- **Dominating:** Trying to run the group by ordering, shutting out others, and insisting on one's own way
- **Clowning:** Making unproductive jokes and diverting the group from the task
- **Withdrawing:** Being silent in meetings, not contributing, not helping with the work, not attending meetings

Criticizing ideas is necessary if the group is to produce the best solution, but criticizing every single idea without suggesting possible solutions blocks a group. Jokes can defuse tension and make the group more creative, but too many jokes or inappropriate jokes can frustrate or offend team members, or impede progress.

Leadership in Groups

You may have noted that "leader" was not one of the roles listed above. Leadership is based on communication and interpersonal effectiveness. Being a leader does not mean doing all the work yourself. Indeed, someone who implies that he or she has the best ideas and can do the best work is likely playing the negative roles of blocking and dominating.

Effective groups balance three kinds of leadership, which parallel the three group development dimensions:

1. **Informational leaders** generate and evaluate ideas and text.
2. **Interpersonal leaders** monitor the group's process, check people's feelings, and resolve conflicts.
3. **Procedural leaders** set the agenda, make sure that everyone knows what's due for the next meeting, communicate with absent group members, and check to be sure that assignments are carried out.

Although it's possible for one person to take on all these responsibilities, in many groups, three (or more) different people take on the three kinds of leadership. Some groups formally or informally rotate or share these responsibilities, so that everyone—and no one—is a leader.

Several studies have shown that people who talk a lot, listen effectively, and respond non-verbally to other members in the group are considered leaders.[4]

Characteristics of Successful Student Groups

A case study of six student groups completing class projects found that students in successful groups were not necessarily more skilled or more experienced than students in less successful groups. Instead, successful and less successful groups communicated differently in three ways.[5]

EXPANDING A CRITICAL SKILL

Leading with Integrity

According to Harvard Business School professor Amy Edmondson, teams fail because 1) some members don't believe their knowledge is interesting or relevant, 2) people are oblivious to others members' opposing interests, and 3) some members deliberately withhold information.[6] Conversely, people who work together well tend to consult one another openly, honestly, and frequently. Members of successful teams act with integrity: they take responsibility for both task and maintenance functions; they tend to share power; and as team leaders or members, they act on the assumption that every person has a valuable contribution to make to the team.

In their book *Integrity Works*, authors Adrian Telford and Dana Gostick identify 10 behaviours that characterize leaders with integrity:

- You know the little things count.
- You find the white when others see the grey.
- In a situation you mess up, you fess up.
- You create a culture of trust.
- You keep your word.
- You care about the greater good.
- You're honest but modest.
- You act like you're being watched.
- You hire integrity.
- You stay the course.

You can begin to lead your team with integrity by putting some of these behaviours into action:

- **Smile.** Get to know the other members of your group as individuals. Invite members to say something about themselves, perhaps what job they're hoping to get and one fact about their lives outside school.
- **Share.** Tell people about your own work style and obligations, and ask others to share their styles and obligations. Savvy group members play to each other's strengths and devise strategies for dealing with differences. The earlier you know what those differences are, the easier it will be to deal with them.
- **Suggest.** "Could we talk about what we see as our purposes in this presentation?" "One of the things we need to do is...." "One idea I had for a project is...." Presenting your ideas as suggestions gets the group started without suggesting that you expect your views to prevail.
- **Think.** Leaders look at the goal and identify the steps needed to get there. "Our proposal is due in two weeks. Let's list the tasks we need to do in order to write a rough draft."
- **Volunteer.** Volunteer to take notes, to gather some of the data the group will need, or to prepare the charts after the data are in. Volunteer not just for the interesting parts of the job (such as surfing the Web to find visuals for your PowerPoint™ presentation) but also for some of the dull but essential work, such as proofreading.
- **Ask.** Bring other people into the conversation. Learn about their knowledge, interests, and skills so that you'll have as much as possible to draw on as you complete your group projects.

Sources: Jared Sandberg, "Teamwork: When It's a Bad Idea," *The Globe and Mail*, October 1, 2004, C7; Harvey Schachter, "Where Integrity Leads, and Where It Lags," *The Globe and Mail*, June 15, 2005, C3.

1. In the successful groups, the leader set clear deadlines, scheduled frequent meetings, and dealt directly with conflict that emerged in the group. In less successful groups, members had to ask the leader what they were supposed to be doing. The less successful groups met less often, and they tried to pretend that conflicts didn't exist.
2. The successful groups listened to criticism and made important decisions together. Perhaps as a result, everyone in the group could articulate the group's goals. In the less successful groups, a subgroup made decisions and told other members what had been decided.
3. The successful groups had a higher proportion of members who worked actively on the project. The successful groups even found ways to use members who didn't like working in groups. For example, one student who didn't want to be a "team player" functioned as a "freelancer" for her group, completing assignments by herself and giving them to the leader. The less successful groups had a much smaller percentage of active members and each had some members who did very little on the final project.

Student groups produce better documents when they openly disagree over substantive issues of content and document design. The disagreement does not need to be angry: a group member can simply say, "Yes, and here's another way we could do it." Deciding between two (or more) alternative options forces the group member to explain the rationale for an idea. Even when the group adopts the original idea, considering alternatives rather than quickly accepting the first idea produces better writing.[6]

Writer Kimberly Freeman found that the students who spent the most time meeting with their groups had the highest grades—on individual as well as on group assignments.[7]

Peer Pressure and Groupthink

Groups that never express conflict may be experiencing groupthink. **Groupthink** is the tendency for groups to put such a high premium on agreement that they directly or indirectly punish dissent.

Groups that "go along with the crowd" and suppress conflict ignore the full range of alternatives, seek only information that supports the positions they already favour, and fail to prepare contingency plans to cope with foreseeable setbacks. A business suffering from groupthink may launch a new product that senior executives support but for which there is no demand. Student groups suffering from groupthink turn in inferior documents.

The best correctives to groupthink are the following:

- Brainstorm for additional alternatives.
- Test assumptions against those of a range of other people.
- Encourage disagreement, perhaps even assigning someone to be "devil's advocate."
- Protect the right of people in a group to disagree.

How should we handle conflict?

Get at the real issue, and repair bad feelings.

FYI

Using electronic communications like voicemail, email, and text messaging to solve conflicts or repair damaged relationships can escalate the problem, according to employee surveys. Confrontations, sensitive negotiations, and conflict resolution all require face-to-face communications.

Source: Staff, "Tech Worse than Talk in Resolving Conflicts," *The Globe and Mail*, July 29, 2005, C1.

Conflicts will arise in any group of intelligent people who care about the task. Yet many of us feel so uncomfortable with conflict that we pretend it doesn't exist. However, unacknowledged conflicts rarely go away: they fester, impeding progress and productivity.

Try the following ways to reduce the number of conflicts in a group:

- Make responsibilities and ground rules clear at the beginning.
- Acknowledge verbal and non-verbal messages of discomfort, anger, or hostility.
- Discuss problems as they arise, rather than letting them fester until people explode.
- Realize that group members are not responsible for each others' feelings.

Table 18.2 suggests several possible solutions to frequent sources of group conflict. Often the symptom arises from a feeling of not being respected or appreciated by the group. Problems can be averted if people advocate for their ideas in a positive way. The best time to advocate for an idea is when the group has not yet identified all possible options, seems dominated by one view, or seems unable to choose among solutions. A tactful way to advocate for the position you favour is to recognize the contributions others have made, to summarize, and then to hypothesize: "What if...? "Let's look six months down the road." "Let's think about this."[8]

TABLE 18.2

Troubleshooting Group Problems

Behaviour	Possible Solutions
We can't find a time to meet that works for all of us.	*a.* Find out why people can't meet at certain times. Some reasons suggest their own solutions. For example, if someone has to stay home with small children, perhaps the group could meet at that person's home. *b.* Assign out-of-class work to "committees" to work on parts of the project. *c.* Use electronic communications to share, discuss, and revise drafts.
One person isn't doing his or her fair share.	*a.* Ask for information. Is the person overcommitted? Does he or she feel unappreciated? Those are different problems you'd solve in different ways. *b.* Early on, do things to build group loyalty. Get to know each other as writers and as people. Sometimes, do something interesting together. *c.* Encourage the person to contribute. "Maria, what do you think?" "Savio, which part of this would you like to draft?" Then find something to praise in the work. "Thanks for getting us started." *d.* If someone misses a meeting, assign someone else to bring the person up to speed. People who miss meetings for legitimate reasons (job interviews, illness) but don't find out what happened may become less committed to the group. *e.* Consider whether strict equality is the most important criterion. On a given project, some people may have more knowledge or time than others. Sometimes the best group product results from letting people do different amounts of "work." *f.* Even if you divide up the work, make all decisions as a group: what to write about, which evidence to include, what graphs to use, what revisions to make. People excluded from decisions become less committed to the group.
I seem to be the only one in the group who cares about quality.	*a.* Find out why other members "don't care." If they received low grades on early assignments, stress that good ideas and attention to detail can raise grades. Perhaps the group should meet with the instructor to discuss what kinds of work will pay the highest dividends. *b.* Volunteer to do extra work. Sometimes people settle for something that's just OK because they don't have the time or resources to do excellent work. They might be happy for the work to be done—if they didn't have to do it. *c.* Be sure that you're respecting what each person can contribute. Group members sometimes withdraw when one person dominates and suggests that he or she is "better" than other members.
People in the group don't seem willing to disagree. We end up going with the first idea suggested.	*a.* Appoint someone to be a "devil's advocate." *b.* Brainstorm so you have several possibilities to consider. *c.* After an idea is suggested, have each person in the group suggest a way it could be improved. *d.* Have each person in the group write a draft. It's likely the drafts will be different, and you'll have several options to mix and match. *e.* Talk about ways to offer positive and constructive feedback. Sometimes people don't disagree because they're afraid that other group members won't tolerate disagreement.
One person just criticizes everything.	*a.* Ask the person to follow up the criticism with a suggestion for improvement. *b.* Talk about ways to express criticism tactfully. "I think we need to think about x" is more tactful than "You're wrong." *c.* If the criticism is about ideas and writing (not about people), value it. Ideas and documents need criticism to improve them.

■ Steps in Conflict Resolution

Dealing successfully with conflict requires attention to both the issues and to people's feelings. This five-step procedure will help you resolve conflicts constructively.

1. Make Sure That the People Involved Really Disagree

Sometimes someone who's under a lot of pressure may appear upset. But the speaker may just be **venting** anger and frustration; he or she may not in fact be angry at the person who receives the explosion. One way to find out whether a person is just venting is to ask, "Is there something you'd like me to do?"

2. Check to See That Everyone's Information Is Correct

Sometimes different conversational styles (◀▷ p. 56) or cultural differences (◀▷ p. 53) create apparent conflicts when no real disagreement exists. Similarly, misunderstanding can arise from faulty assumptions. Clarify what the obstacle is.

3. Discover the Needs Each Person Is Trying to Meet

Sometimes identifying the real need makes it possible to see a new solution. The **presenting problem** that surfaces as the subject of dissension may or may not be the real problem. For example, a worker who complains about the hours he's putting in may in fact be complaining not about the hours themselves but about not feeling appreciated. A supervisor who complains that the other supervisors don't invite her to meetings may really feel that the other managers don't accept her as a peer. Sometimes people have trouble seeing beyond the problem because they've been taught to suppress their anger, especially toward powerful people. One way to tell whether the presenting problem is the real problem is to ask, "If this were solved, would I be satisfied?" If the answer is no, then the problem that presents itself is not, in fact, the real problem. Solving the presenting problem won't solve the conflict. Keep probing until you get to the real conflict.

4. Search for Alternatives

Sometimes people get into conflict because they see too few alternatives. Indeed, people often see only two polarized choices—known as the *either-or logical fallacy*.

Creative people train themselves to think in terms of possibilities—the more the better. This technique, known as brainstorming, is an essential part of every step in the problem-solving process!

5. Repair Bad Feelings

Conflict can emerge without anger and without escalating the disagreement, as the next section shows. But if people's feelings have been hurt, the group needs to deal with those feelings to resolve the conflict constructively. Only when people feel respected and taken seriously can they take the next step of trusting others in the group.

SEE
THE
OLC!

The Creative Process
Logical Fallacies

■ Responding to Criticism

Conflict is particularly difficult to resolve when someone else criticizes or attacks us directly. When we are criticized, our natural reaction is to defend ourselves—perhaps by counterattacking. The counterattack prompts the critic to defend himself or herself. The conflict escalates; feelings are hurt; and issues become muddied and more difficult to resolve.

Just as resolving conflict depends on identifying the needs each person is trying to meet, dealing with criticism depends on understanding the real concern of the critic. Constructive ways to respond to criticism and get closer to the real concern include the following:

- Paraphrasing
- Checking for feelings
- Checking for inferences
- Buying time with limited agreement

Paraphrasing

SEE THE OLC!

Edward De Bono: Creative or Lateral Thinking

To **paraphrase**, repeat in your own words the verbal content of the critic's message. The purposes of paraphrasing are (1) to be sure that you have heard the critic accurately, (2) to let the critic know what his or her statement means to you, and (3) to communicate the feeling that you are taking the critic and his or her feelings seriously.

Criticism:	You guys are stonewalling my requests for information.
Paraphrase:	You think that we don't give you the information you need quickly enough.

Checking for Feelings

When you check the critic's feelings, you identify the emotions that the critic seems to be expressing verbally or non-verbally. The purposes of checking feelings are to try to understand (1) the critic's emotions, (2) the importance of the criticism for the critic, and (3) the unspoken ideas and feelings that may actually be more important than the voiced criticism.

Criticism:	You guys are stonewalling my requests for information.
Feeling check:	You sound pretty angry.

Always *ask* the other person if you are right in your perception. Even the best reader of non-verbal cues is sometimes wrong.

Checking for Inferences

When you check the inferences you draw from criticism, you identify the implied meaning of the verbal and non-verbal content of the criticism, taking the statement a step further than the words of the critic to try to understand why the critic is bothered by the action or attitude under discussion. The purposes of checking inferences are (1) to identify the real (as opposed to the presenting) problem and (2) to communicate the feeling that you care about resolving the conflict.

Criticism:	You guys are stonewalling my requests for information.
Inference:	Are you saying that you need more information from our group?

Inferences can be faulty. In the above interchange, the critic might respond, "I don't need more information. I just think you should give it to me without my having to file three forms in triplicate every time I want some data."

Buying Time with Limited Agreement

Buying time is a useful strategy for dealing with criticisms that really sting. When you buy time with limited agreement, you avoid escalating the conflict (as an angry statement might do) but also avoid yielding to the critic's point of view. To buy time, restate the part of the criticism that you agree is true. (This is often a fact, rather than the interpretation or evaluation the critic has made of that fact.) *Then let the critic respond, before you say anything else.* The purposes of buying time are (1) to allow you time to think when a criticism really hits home and threatens you, so that you can respond to the criticism rather than simply reacting defensively, and (2) to suggest to the critic that you are genuinely listening to what he or she is saying.

Criticism:	You guys are stonewalling my requests for information.
Limited agreement:	It's true that the cost projections you asked for last week still aren't ready.

Do *not* go on to justify or explain. A "Yes, but..." statement is not a time-buyer.

■ You-Attitude in Conflict Resolution

You-attitude (◀▷ p. 107) means looking at things from the audience's point of view, respecting the audience, and protecting the audience's ego. The *you* statements that many people use when they're angry attack the audience; they do not illustrate you-attitude. Instead, substitute statements about your own feelings. In conflict, *I* statements show good you-attitude!

Lacks you-attitude:	You never do your share of the work.
You-attitude:	I feel that I'm doing more than my share of the work on this project.
Lacks you-attitude:	Even you should be able to run the report through a spell checker.
You-attitude:	I'm not willing to have my name on a report with so many spelling errors. I did lots of the writing, and I don't think I should have to do the proofreading and spell-checking, too.

■ How can we create the best co-authored documents?

Talk about your purposes and audiences.

■ Discussing Drafts and Revisions

Whatever your career, it is likely that some of the documents you produce will be written with a group. Indeed, 87 percent of the 700 professionals in seven fields who were

SEE THE OLC!

Effective Teams

surveyed responded that they sometimes wrote as members of a team or a group.[9] Collaboration is often prompted by one of the following situations:

- The task is too big or the time is too short for one person to do all the work.
- No one person has all the knowledge required to do the task.
- A group representing different perspectives must reach a consensus.
- The stakes for the task are so high that the organization wants the best efforts of as many people as possible; no one person wants the sole responsibility for the success or failure of the document.

Collaborative writing can be done by two people or by a much larger group. The group can be democratic or run by a leader who makes decisions alone. The group may share or divide responsibility for each of the eight stages in the writing process (◀|▷ Module 4).

Research in collaborative writing is beginning to tell us about the strategies that produce the best writing. Rebecca Burnett found that student groups that voiced disagreements as they analyzed, planned, and wrote a document produced significantly better documents than those that suppressed disagreement, going along with whatever was first proposed.[10] A case study of two collaborative writing teams in an agency found that the successful group distributed power equally, worked to soothe hurt feelings, and was careful to involve all group members. In terms of writing process, the successful group understood the task as a response to a rhetorical situation, planned revisions as a group, saw supervisors' comments as legitimate, and had a positive attitude toward revision.[11]

Professors Ede and Lunsford's detailed case studies of collaborative teams in business, government, and science create an "emerging profile of effective collaborative writers." The profile reflects those interpersonal competency skills so sought after by employers: "They are flexible; respectful of others; attentive and analytical listeners; able to speak and write clearly and articulately; dependable and able to meet deadlines; able to designate and share responsibility, to lead and to follow; open to criticism but confident in their own abilities; ready to engage in creative conflict."[12]

■ Planning the Work and the Document

Collaborative writing is most successful when the group articulates its understanding of the document's purposes and audiences and explicitly discusses the best way to achieve these rhetorical goals. Businesses schedule formal planning sessions for large projects to set up a time line specifying intermediate and final due dates, meeting dates, who will attend each meeting, and who will do what. Putting the plan in writing reduces misunderstandings during the project.

When you plan a collaborative writing project, follow these guidelines:

- Make your analysis of the problem, the audience, and your purposes explicit so you know where you agree and where you disagree.
- Plan and agree on the organization, format, and style of the document before anyone begins to write, to make it easier to blend sections written by different authors.
- Consider your work styles and other commitments. A writer working alone can stay up all night to finish a single-authored document. But members of a group need to work together to accommodate each other's styles and to enable members to meet other commitments.
- Build in project-management time lines.
- Build some leeway into your deadlines. It's harder for a group to finish a document when one person's part is missing than it is for a single writer to finish the last section of a document on which he or she has done all the work.

Brainstorming

Composing the Drafts

Most writers find that composing alone is faster than composing in a group. However, composing together may reduce revision time later, since the group examines every choice as it is made.

Two things can help when you draft a collaborative writing project:

- Use word processing to make it easier to produce the many drafts necessary in a collaborative document.
- Have the best writer(s) draft the document after everyone has gathered the necessary information.

Revising the Document

Revising a collaborative document requires attention to content, organization, and style. The following guidelines can make the revision process more effective:

- Evaluate the content and discuss possible revisions as a group. Brainstorm ways to improve each section so the person doing the revisions has some guidance.
- Recognize that different people favour different writing styles. If the style satisfies the demands of standard English and the conventions of business writing, accept it even if you wouldn't say it that way.
- When the group is satisfied with the content of the document, one person—probably the best writer—should make any changes necessary to make the writing style consistent throughout.

Editing and Proofreading the Document

Since writers' mastery of standard English varies, a group report needs careful editing and proofreading.

- Have at least one person read the whole document for consistency of appearance and tone (e.g., formatting, numbering).
- Have another group member check the whole document for correct grammar, spelling, and usage.
- Use a spellchecker.
- Have all group members proofread the document one last time, because spellcheckers cannot think, and therefore cannot catch out-of-context misspellings (e.g., "there," "their," and "they're").

Making the Group Process Work

A co-authored document requires special attention:

- Allow plenty of time to discuss problems and find solutions. Students writing group reports spend six to seven hours a week outside class in group meetings—not counting the time they spend gathering information and writing their drafts.[13]
- Take the time to get to know group members and to build group loyalty. Group members will work harder and the final document will be better if the group is important to members.

FYI

Men and women do communicate differently. Researchers in a joint British-American study found that "[w]omen are more assertive, more likely to take risks and more empathetic than their male counterparts." Moreover, women executives, "...more flexible and [with] better interpersonal skills...are more likely to listen to subordinates and co-workers than their male colleagues [are]."

Source: adapted from New York Times Service, "Women More Assertive, Empathetic, Study Shows," *The Globe and Mail*, May 25, 2005, C5.

- Be a responsible group member. Attend all the meetings; do what you've committed to do, and plan so you will meet deadlines.
- Be aware that people have different ways of experiencing reality and of expressing themselves.
- Because talking is "looser" than writing, people in a group can think they agree when they don't. Don't assume that because the discussion went smoothly, a draft written by one person will necessarily be acceptable.

Employability Skills 2000+

The Conference Board of Canada
Insights You Can Count On

Please see the OLC to preview the key skills from the Conference Board of Canada's Employability Skills 2000+ covered in this module.

Review of Key Points

1. What are the three kinds of group leadership?
2. What are the behaviours of productive groups?
3. What is groupthink, and how can team members correct groupthink?
4. What ten behaviours characterize ethical leaders?
5. How can you deal with conflict positively?
6. How can you respond to criticism constructively?

Assignments for Module 18

Questions for Critical Thinking

18.1 Why are so many people so afraid of conflict in groups? What can a group do to avoid groupthink?

18.2 Why is it better for groups to deal with conflicts, rather than just trying to ignore them?

18.3 What is the most successful group or team you've been part of? What made it effective?

Exercises and Problems

18.4 Identifying and Analyzing Group Dynamics

Observe your behaviours and the behaviours of others in the group to identify and analyze team roles and interpersonal leadership qualities.

a. Each group member writes his/her answers to the following questions after each group meeting.
b. Each member shares his/her perceptions with the group.
c. Each member identifies one leadership or positive team role he/she has demonstrated.
d. Each member identifies one leadership or positive team role he/she wants to develop.

Group Process Analysis

1. How do you help others in the group talk and give their opinions? How do other members encourage your opinions? What could group members do to encourage greater participation?
2. Describe your active listening techniques. Describe how other group members demonstrate they are listening. What could other members do to improve their listening techniques? What could you do?
3. What kinds of questions are you asking each other: open-ended? Encouraging? Paraphrasing? Interested? Closed? Who asks the most questions? Who asks the least?
4. How does the group keep track of discussions and tasks to be done? Who takes notes? How was that person chosen? What happens to those notes?
5. Describe how the group reaches agreement. Describe what happens when members disagree.

Describe how you usually deal with conflict. Describe how every other member deals with conflict. Assess how well these strategies work. In exercises 18.5 through 18.8, assume that your group has been asked to recommend a solution.

As your instructor directs,

a. Send email messages to group members identifying your initial point of view on the issue and discussing the various options.

b. Meet as a group to come to a consensus.

c. As a group, answer the message.

d. Write a memo to your instructor telling how satisfied you are with

   • The decision your group reached
   • The process you used to reach it

e. Write a memo describing your group's dynamics (18.11).

18.5   Recommending a Fair Way to Assign Work around the Holidays

You are on the labour-management committee. This email arrives from the general manager:

Subject: Allocating Holiday Hours

As you know, lots of people want to take extra time off around holidays to turn three-day weekends into longer trips. But we do need to stay open. Right now, there are allegations that some supervisors give the time off to their friends. But even "fair" systems, such as giving more senior workers first choice at time off, or requiring that workers with crucial skills work, also create problems. And possibly we need a different system in December, when many people want to take off a week or more, than we do for other holidays, when most people take only an extra day or two.

Please recommend an equitable way to decide how to assign hours.

Write a group response recommending the best way to assign hours.

Hint:

Agree on an office, factory, store, hospital, or other workplace to use for this problem.

18.6   Recommending an Internet Use Policy

You're on the information technology integration committee. You get this message from your manager.

Subject: Need Internet Use Policy

We have no policy on Internet use. Is it OK for people to play games or surf the Web during work hours? Should we block access to certain Web sites?

The biggest problem may be responses to email lists and comments on electronic bulletin boards. There's no problem when people log on from home. But if they post responses from their workstations here, people might think the comment represents the official organizational stance on the issue—and it doesn't.

Write a group response recommending a policy.

Hint:

Agree on an office, factory, store, hospital, or other workplace to use for this problem.

18.7   Recommending Ways to Retain Workers

You are on the recruitment and retention committee.
This email arrives from the vice president, Human
Resources:

Subject: Retaining Workers

As you know, it's a challenge to find employees with the skills we want. To limit the need to hire new people, we want to reduce turnover. What could we do to keep people happy? Please divide your recommendations into low-cost and high-cost solutions.

Write a group response recommending ways to retain
workers.

Hint:

Agree on an office, factory, store, hospital, or other
workplace to use for this problem.

18.8   Judging Suggestions

You're on the suggestion committee. Employees submit
suggestions that will save money or improve quality,
procedures, or morale. Your committee must decide
whether to accept, partially accept, or reject each
suggestion.

Write a message to each suggester, informing him or
her of your decision.

1.   From: Ewelena Kusznirewicz, Human Resources

   Subject: Suggestion to Change Sick-Leave Policy

   Right now, employees can "cash in" their unused sick-leave days each year and many people do that. The trouble is that people have too few days left if they need to have major surgery or chemotherapy. I recommend that we change the policy to allow people to "cash in" unused sick-leave days only when they retire or leave their jobs.

2.   From: Ivan Lin, Call Centre

   Subject: Suggestion—Open Corporate Store

   We should have a store. I visited a friend whose company had a store with company-logo clothing, toys, and sundries (mugs, mouse pads, etc.) as well as greeting cards, snacks, and so forth.

3.   From: Mohammed Chaar, Accounts Receivable

   Subject: Suggestion: Allow Pets at Work

   We should let people bring pets to work. Pets reduce stress and blood pressure. People like Justin's seeing-eye dog.

18.9   Planning a Game*

Many companies are using games and contests to solve
problems in an enjoyable way. One company promised to
give everyone $30 a month extra if they reduced the error
rate below 0.5 percent. The rate improved immediately.
After several successful months, the incentive went to $40
a month for getting it under 0.3 percent and finally to
$50 a month for getting it under 0.2 percent. Another
company offered workers two "well hours" if they got in
by 7 A.M. every day for a month. An accounting and
financial-services company divided its employees into two

teams. The one that got the most referrals and new accounts received a meal prepared and served by the losing team (the firm paid for the food). Games are best when the people who will play them create them. Games need to make business sense and give rewards to many people, not just a few. Rewards should be small.

Think of a game or contest that could improve productivity or quality in your classroom, on campus, or in a workplace you know well.

As your instructor directs,

a. Write a message to persuade your instructor, boss, or other decision maker to authorize the game or contest.

b. Write a message announcing the game and persuading people to participate in it.

Based on John Case, The Open-Book Experience: Lessons from Over 100 Companies Who Successfully Transformed Themselves (Reading, MA: Addison-Wesley, 1998), 129–201.

18.10 Creating Brochures

In a collaborative group, create a series of brochures for an organization and present your design and copy to the class in a group oral presentation. Your brochures should work well as a series but also be capable of standing alone if a reader picks up just one. They should share a common visual design and be appropriate for your purposes and audience. You may use sketches rather than photos or finished drawings. Text, however, should be as it will appear in the final copy.

As you prepare your series, talk to a knowledgeable person in the organization. For this assignment,

although the person is knowledgeable, he or she does not have to have the power to approve the brochures.

In a manila folder, turn in

1. Two copies of each brochure
2. A copy of your approved proposal (◁|▷ Module 22)
3. A narrative explaining (a) how you responded to the wishes of the person in the organization who was your contact and (b) five of the choices you made in terms of content, visuals, and design, and the reasons that you made these choices

18.11 Analyzing the Dynamics of a Group

Analyze the dynamics of a group of which you are or were a member. Answer the following questions:

1. Who was the group's leader? How did the leader emerge? Were there any changes in or challenges to the original leader?
2. Describe the contribution each member made to the group and the roles each person played.
3. Did any members of the group officially or unofficially drop out? Did anyone join after the group had begun working? How did you deal with the loss or addition of a group member, both in terms of getting the work done and in terms of helping people work together?
4. What planning did your group do at the start of the project? Did you stick to the plan or revise it? How did the group decide that revision was necessary?

5. How did your group make decisions? Did you vote? reach decisions by consensus?
6. What problems or conflicts arose? Did the group deal with them openly? To what extent did conflicts interfere with the group's task?
7. Evaluate your group both in terms of its task and in terms of the satisfaction members felt. How did this group compare with other groups you've been part of? What made it better or worse?

As you answer the questions,

- Be honest. You won't lose points for reporting that your group had problems or did something "wrong."
- Show your knowledge of good group dynamics. That is, if your group did something wrong, show that you know what should have been done. Similarly, if your group worked well, show that you know why it worked well.
- Be specific. Give examples or anecdotes to support your claims.

As your instructor directs,

a. Discuss these questions with the other group members.
b. Present your findings orally to the class.
c. Present your findings in an individual memo to your instructor.
d. Join with the other group members to write a collaborative memo to your instructor.

Polishing Your Prose

Delivering Criticism

No one likes to be told that his or her work isn't good. But criticism is necessary if people and documents are to improve.

Depending on the situation, you may be able to use one of these strategies:

1. Notice what's good as well as what needs work.
   The charts are great. We need to make the text as good as they are.
   I really like the ideas you've used in the slides. We need to edit the bulleted points so they're parallel.

2. Ask questions.
   Were you able to find any books and articles, in addition to sources on the Internet?
   What do you see as the most important revisions to make for the next draft?

3. Refer to the textbook or another authority.
   The module on design says that italic type is hard to read.
   Our instructor told us that presentations should have just three main points.

4. Make statements about your own reaction.
   I'm not sure what you're getting at in this section.
   I wouldn't be convinced by the arguments here.

5. Criticize what's wrong, without making global attacks on the whole document or on the writer as a person.

There are a lot of typos in this draft.
You begin almost every sentence with *um*.

Exercises

Rewrite each criticism to make it less hurtful. You may add or omit information as needed.

1. This is the worst report I've ever seen.
2. My 10-year-old can spell better than you do.
3. I can't believe that you didn't go to the library to get any sources.
4. You've used four different fonts in this report. Didn't you read the book? Don't you know that we're not supposed to use more than two?
5. This design is really lame. It looks like every other brochure I've ever seen.
6. There's no way we'll get a passing grade if we turn this in.
7. Were you asleep? Didn't you hear our instructor say that we had to use at least five sources?
8. This is really creative. You've written the perfect illustration for "How to Fail This Course."
9. This proposal makes no sense.
10. This clip art is sexist. There's no way we should use it.

Check your answers to the odd-numbered exercises on page 573.

■ Online Learning Centre

Visit the Online Learning Centre at www.mcgrawhill.ca/olc/locker to access module quizzes, a searchable glossary, résumé and letter templates, additional business writing samples, CBC videos, and other learning and study tools.

Module Outline

- What planning should precede a meeting?

- When I'm in charge, how do I keep the meeting on track?

- What decision-making strategies work well in meetings?

- How can I be an effective meeting participant?

- What should be in meeting minutes?

- How can I use informal meetings with my boss to advance my career?

- Do virtual meetings require special consideration?

Review of Key Points

Assignments for Module 19

Polishing Your Prose: Hyphens and Dashes

LEARNING OBJECTIVES

After reading and applying the information in Module 19, you'll be able to demonstrate

Knowledge of
- Meeting management
- Networking opportunities

Skills to
- Plan a meeting
- Lead a meeting
- Participate in meetings
- Take good meeting minutes
- Network effectively

The Conference Board of Canada
Insights You Can Count On

Please see the OLC to preview the key skills from the Conference Board of Canada's Employability Skills 2000+ covered in this module.

People spend more time in meetings today than ever before. Although meetings have always made up the largest proportion of the average manager's day, emphasis on teamwork means that meeting time for all employees will continue to grow. However, according to "... the first international scientific study ...on the effects of meeting time on employee well-being...," when people perceive their meetings as organized, with productive results, they feel their time has been well spent.[1]

On average, employees attend three meetings a week; as people rise in the organization, they attend many more meetings. Ipsos-Reid's May 2001 survey indicated that, because sharing information with co-workers had become so important, Canadian office workers spent an average of 5.2 hours per week in meetings. In larger organizations with 500 or more employees, people averaged almost seven hours per week in meetings.[2]

People in organizations attend several types of meetings:

Robert's Rules of Order

- **Informal, one-on-one,** or **hall meetings** are the most significant meetings; people see them as an opportunity to exchange meaningful information. Employees talk by the photocopier or the refrigerator. One person walks into a colleague's office or cubicle to ask a question. A supervisor stops to chat with an employee, to ask how things are going and thereby "manage by walking around." These informal meetings create or reinforce company culture, support networking, and facilitate advancement.

  Indeed, according to experts, informal meetings that include gossip serve as vital organizational arteries; gossip "...can be a powerful way to spread information, boost bonding and morale, and release stress.... [G]ossip in the office, over the Internet or on the phone...causes us to relax...and tell[s] [us] something about the underlying..." organizational culture.[3]

- **Team meetings** bring people together to manage projects, solve problems, and collaborate on documents. (◀|▷ Module 18) Recorded agendas and minutes formalize these meetings.

- **Regular staff meetings** are held to disseminate information, announce new policies and products, answer questions, share ideas, and motivate people. Recorded agendas and minutes formalize these meetings.

  Other frequent organizational meetings include **sales meetings, staff training sessions, conventions,** and **retreats.** These sessions allow people to develop themselves professionally, to team build, and/or to do long-range planning.

- **Parliamentary proceedings** are the most formal types of meetings, run according to strict rules, like the rules of parliamentary procedure summarized in *Robert's Rules of Order.* These meetings are common only for boards of directors and legislative bodies.

Meetings today are usually supported by technology. For example, some organizations display proceedings for all the participants to see. "People literally see themselves being heard. Related comments are identified, linked, and edited on screen. The digressions and tangents quickly become apparent." The resulting document can be posted on the company intranet for further discussion and comments.[4]

Other organizations use group support software. Each person sits at a workstation. Participants key in their own brainstorming ideas and comments. People can vote by ranking items on a 1-to-10 scale; the software calculates the averages.[5]

Because of political uncertainty and increasing fuel costs, organizations continue to seek alternatives to their employees travelling to meetings. Speakerphones and conference calls allow people in different locations to participate in the same conversation. Online meetings, such as those hosted by WebEx <http://www.webex.com>, allow you to bring together five other participants for a simultaneous email conversation in your own private chat room. Many computer systems support video as well as data or audio transmissions. Videoconferences provide high-quality video and audio transmissions. And now blogging allows a "chairperson" to initiate the worldwide cyber-meeting, and air his or her opinion without interruption.

Many important meetings are informal.

Despite these choices, employees still express a distinct preference for face-to-face meetings. Many factors affect the outcome of meetings: the organizational culture, the people who attend, the length and purposes of the meeting, and the use of resources.

■ What planning should precede a meeting?

Identify the purposes and create an agenda.

Meetings can have at least six purposes:

1. To share information
2. To brainstorm ideas
3. To evaluate ideas
4. To make decisions
5. To create a document
6. To motivate members

When meetings combine two or more purposes, it's useful to make the purposes explicit. For example, in the meeting of a university student government or a company's board of directors, some items are presented for information. Discussion is possible, but the group will not be asked to make a decision. Other items are presented for action; the group will be asked to vote. A business meeting might specify that the first half-hour will allotted for brainstorming, with the second half-hour devoted to evaluation.

Most companies recognize four different decision-making processes:

- Authoritative (the leader makes the decision alone)
- Consultative (the leader hears group comments but then makes the decision alone)
- Voting (the majority wins)
- Consensual (discussion continues until everyone can "buy into" the decision)

Telling participants how their input will be used clarifies expectations and focuses the conversation.

Once you've identified your purposes, think about how you can make them happen. Usually, participants need to receive and read materials before the meeting. Perhaps people should bring drafts to the meeting so that creating a document can go more quickly.

For team meetings called on short notice, the first item of business is to create an agenda. This kind of agenda can be informal, simply listing the topics or goals.

SEE THE OLC!

3M's Meeting Network

For meetings with more lead time, distribute an agenda several days before the meeting. (*Agenda* is Latin for "to be done.") If possible, give participants a chance to comment, and revise the agenda in response to those comments. A good agenda answers five questions:

- Where and when: time and place of the meeting
- What: agenda items
- Why: each item flagged for purpose—information, discussion, or decision
- Who: participants and individuals sponsoring or introducing each item
- How: meeting duration and time allotted for each item

Figure 19.1 shows an example of a meeting agenda.

Many groups deal first with routine items on which agreement will be easy. If there's a long list of routine items, save them until the end or, in a parliamentary meeting, dispense with them in an omnibus motion. An **omnibus motion** allows a group to approve many items together rather than voting on each separately. A single omnibus motion might cover multiple changes to operational guidelines, or a whole slate of candidates for various offices, or various budget recommendations.

FIGURE 19.1
Sample Meeting Agenda

SEE THE OLC!

Start Your Own Blog

Distribute agenda early

Marketing Program Advisory Committee Meeting
October 15, 2007
5 P.M.
President's Board Room

5:00	1. Approve last meeting's minutes	Everyone
5:15	2. Marketing Co-op Program Updates (For information)	Fiona
5:30	3. Awards report (For information)	Giosa
5:45	4. Report from Mobile Subcommittee (For decision: choose one of three alternatives)	Doug
6:15	5. Report from Diversity Committee (For decision: approve recruitment plan)	Zainab
6:30	6. Supper	
7:00	7. Report from Curriculum Review Committee (For review and discussion on new course)	Doug
7:30	8. New business	Everyone
8:00	9. Adjourn	

People don't vote on information items

Realistic time estimates help keep a meeting on track

Decisions will be made during the meeting

People can bring new ideas to the table

Schedule controversial items early in the meeting, when people's energy levels are high and to allow enough time for full discussion. Giving a controversial item only half an hour at the end of the meeting leads people to suspect that the leaders are trying to manipulate them.

The best meetings encourage participation, creativity, and fun. Networking and socializing are vital to participants' perceptions of the value of the meeting. For meetings that will last longer than an hour—conferences or training sessions, for example—plan

- Short breaks every two hours
- Longer breaks twice a day so participants can chat informally with each other and
- Social functions

Finally, you may want to leave five minutes at the end of the meeting to evaluate it. What went well? What could be better? What do you want to change next time?

When I'm in charge, how do I keep the meeting on track?

Pay attention both to task and to process.

The chair's role is to clarify the meeting's significance and goals, and to encourage participation in a timely and comprehensive way. When the issues are simple and clear-cut, you may only need to introduce the speaker on each issue, recognize people who want to speak, and remind the group of its progress. "We're a bit behind schedule. Let's try to get through the committee reports quickly." When the issues are complex, or when members have major disagreements, you may need to acknowledge and negotiate conflict, shape the discussion or summarize issues: "We're really talking about two things: whether the change would save money and whether our customers would like it. Does it make sense to keep those two together, or could we talk about customer reaction first, and then deal with the financial issues?"

As chair, you may want to make ground rules explicit. Based on the corporate culture, ground rules vary considerably from company to company and sometimes even within organizations (◀▶ Module 2). In some meetings, participants are expected to stay for the entire session, even if not all agenda items are relevant to them. In others, people are free to attend just part of the meeting. In some cultures, participants are expected to give their full attention to the discussion. In others, it may be acceptable to check one's email or even work on other projects during the meeting. Some organizations ask senior people to wait to speak until after junior people have spoken; others may expect senior people to speak first. If the issue is contentious, the chair may ask that speakers for and against a motion alternate. If no one remains on one side, then the discussion can stop.

SEE THE OLC!

Team Dynamics

A good chairperson attends to both the **task** and **maintenance functions** of the meeting. **Task functions** include all communications (stating objectives, clarifying topics, questioning, summarizing, tracking time) devoted to the meeting task or purpose.

Paying attention to people and process—the maintenance of the participants' emotional engagement—is equally important for success. At informal meetings, a good leader observes non-verbal feedback and invites everyone to participate. If conflict seems to be getting out

EXPANDING A CRITICAL SKILL

Networking

Build your interpersonal relationships because networking continues to be the most successful way to get a job.

Getting to know people within and beyond your own organization builds contacts of colleagues and friends.

Get to know people in your own organization:

- Most days, have lunch with other people in your organization. At least once a month (more often is better) invite someone whom you don't know well. You can go someplace inexpensive or even bring brown-bag lunches. But don't work through lunch more than twice a week. Use the time to widen your circle of acquaintances at the place where you work.
- At a meeting, sit by someone you don't know well. Introduce yourself, and find out something about the other person.

Get to know other business people in your community:

- Participate in your community: Canadians value community involvement. Canvass for charity; coach little league; join your neighbourhood ratepayers' association or your town's business association, arts council, Toastmaster's, Lion's Club, Knights of Columbus, Big Brother/Sister organization, chamber of commerce, or board of trade. You can start your own book club or become a member of local bookstores' clubs. Every person you meet knows a minimum of three other people, so every volunteer activity, association, and club membership expands your network.
- At events, sit with people you don't yet know. For example, if your company buys a table of 10 seats at a charity luncheon, ask the organizers to put two of you at each of five tables, so that you can use the lunch to network.

- Attend meetings of the trade association for your industry and meetings of businesspeople specifically designed to network or to share ideas.

Join an email list to get to know other people in your field. To find the appropriate group, visit http://www.topica.com, with links to many business email groups.

Consider everyone a customer. Prepare for every networking opportunity. Read widely and pay attention to local news of interest. When you meet new people, express interest: ask what they and their companies do. And listen ([◀][▶] Module 17)! When you know someone's specialty, ask his or her opinion about challenges or events in that industry. After you find out about the other person, give a short, 60-second description of your work and your company. Then probe more deeply into the other person's experience and ideas. Find out what his or her position is. Exchange business cards. And ask for the names of other people in that organization whom you should talk to, depending on your own interests and your job.

Nurture your contacts. Some businesspeople like to send a short follow-up message right after the first meeting. In some cases, you may want to set up occasional lunches with people—in your own or in other organizations—who are particularly interesting. The very best follow-up is to send something the other person can truly use—information about a book or article, a URL, the address for an email group you find useful. Think of networking not only as a way to meet people who can be useful to you, but also as a way to be more useful and visible in your own organization and in the community in which you live and work.

Sources: Robert Sheppard, "We Are Canadian," *Maclean's,* December/January, 2001, 26–32; Marc Kramer, *Power Networking: Using the Contacts You Didn't Even Know You Have to Succeed in the Job You Want* (Lincolnwood, IL: VGM Career Horizons, 1998).

of hand, a leader may want to focus attention on the group process and ways that it could deal with conflict ([◀][▶] Module 18), before getting back to the content issues.

If the group doesn't formally vote, summarize the group's agreement after each point so that it is clear to everyone what decision has been made and who is responsible for implementing or following up on each item.

Meetings depend on social interaction as well as a good agenda.

Source: FOR BETTER OR WORSE reprinted by permission of United Feature Syndicate, Inc.

■ What decision-making strategies work well in meetings?

Try the standard agenda or dot planning.

Probably the least effective decision-making strategy is to let the person who talks first, last, loudest, or most determine the decision. Voting is quick but may leave people in the minority unhappy with and uncommitted to the majority's plan.

Coming to consensus takes time but results in speedier implementation of ideas. Two strategies that are often useful in organizational groups are the standard agenda and dot planning.

The **standard agenda** is a seven-step decision-making process for solving problems.

1. Clarify and reach agreement on the task: what the group has to deliver, in what form, by what due date. Identify available resources.
2. Identify and reach agreement on the problem or the situation: What question is the group trying to answer? What exactly is the issue?
3. Gather information, share it with all group members, and examine it critically.
4. Establish criteria: What would the ideal solution include? Which elements of that solution would be part of a less-than-ideal but still acceptable solution? What legal, financial, moral, or other limitations might keep a solution from being implemented?
5. Generate alternative solutions: Brainstorm and record ideas for the next step.
6. Measure the alternatives against the criteria.
7. Choose the best solution.[6]

Dot planning offers a way for large groups to choose priorities quickly. First, the group brainstorms ideas, recording each on pages that are put on the wall. Then each individual gets three to five adhesive dots in two colours. One colour represents high priority, the other lower priority. People then walk up to the pages and affix dots beside the points they care most about. Some groups allow only one dot from one person on any one item; others allow someone who is really passionate about an idea to put all of his or her dots on it. As Figure 19.2 shows, the dots make it easy to see which items the group believes are most important.

FIGURE 19.2

Dot Planning Allows Groups to Set Priorities Quickly

Here, green dots mean "high priority;" blue dots mean "low priority." Group members can see at a glance which items have widespread support, which are controversial, and which are low priority.

Directory of Resources	Marketing materials
Group Health Plan	Develop two rep tracks: independent & franchise
Have all reps use FAFN name	Directory of reps & specialties
One-page social analysis	Reps pay nominal costs for specialized materials
Conference: 5 minutes for each rep to talk	Having more rep-only sessions at conference
Increase fee account compensation	Write product manuals
System of compensating mentors	Handbook on how to set up fee business
Free basic brochure to reps	Increased insurance production
Create rep advisory council	New product R&D

Source: "The Color-Coded Priority Setter," *Inc.*, June 1995, 70–71; http://www.inc.com/magazine/19950601/2300.html, retrieved August 15, 2006.

How can I be an effective meeting participant?

Be prepared.

Take the time to prepare for meetings. Read the materials distributed before the meeting and think about the issues to be discussed. Bring those materials to the meeting, along with something to write on and with, even if you're not the secretary.

In a small meeting, you'll probably get several chances to speak. Research indicates that the most influential people in a meeting are those who say something in the first five minutes of the meeting (even just to ask a question), who talk most often, and who talk at greatest length.[7]

In a large meeting, you may get just one chance to speak. Make notes of what you want to say so that you can be concise, fluent, and complete.

It's frustrating to speak in a meeting and have people ignore what you say. Here are some tips for being taken seriously.[8]

- Show that you've done your homework. Laura Sloate, who is blind, establishes authority by making sure her first question is highly technical: "In footnote three of the 10K, you indicate...."
- Link your comment to the comment of a powerful person. Even if logic suffers a bit, present your comment as an addition, not a challenge. For example, say, "John is saying that we should focus on excellence, AND I think we can become stronger by encouraging diversity."
- Find an ally in the organization and agree ahead of time to acknowledge each other's contributions to the meeting, whether you agree or disagree with the point being made. Explicit disagreement signals that the comment is worth taking seriously: "Peter has pointed out..., but I think that...."

What should be in meeting minutes?

Minutes should include topics discussed, decisions reached, and lists of who does what next.

Meeting expert Michael Begeman suggests recording three kinds of information:

1. Decisions reached
2. Action items, where someone needs to implement or follow up on something
3. Open issues—issues raised but not resolved[9]

Minutes of formal meetings include who was present and absent, the wording of motions and amendments, and the votes. Committee reports are often attached for later reference. For less formal meetings, brief minutes are fine. The most important items are the decisions and action assignments. Long minutes are most helpful when assignments are set off visually from the narrative.

> We discussed whether we should switch from road to rail shipment.
> Action: Laya will get the figures on costs for the next meeting.
> Action: Jaffer will conduct an online survey of current customers to ask their opinions.

How can I use informal meetings with my boss to advance my career?

Plan scripts to present yourself positively.

You see your supervisor several times a week. Some of these meetings will be accidental: you'll meet by the coffee pot or ride the elevator together. Some of them will be deliberately initiated: your boss will stop by your area, or you'll go to your boss's area to ask for something.

You can take advantage of these meetings by planning for them. These informal meetings are often short. An elevator ride, for example, may last about three minutes. So plan 90-second scripts that you can use to give your boss a brief report on what you're doing, ask for something you need, or lay the groundwork for an important issue.

Planning scripts is especially important if your boss doesn't give you much feedback or mentoring. You need to take the initiative. Make statements that show the boss you're thinking about ways to work smarter. Show that you're interested in learning more so that you can be more valuable to the organization.

■ Do virtual meetings require special consideration?

Yes. Watch interpersonal communication.

For important projects, build in some real meetings as well as some virtual ones.

When you meet technologically rather than in person, you lose the informal interactions of going to lunch or chatting during a break. Those interactions not only create bonds, so that people are more willing to work together, but also give people a chance to work out dozens of small issues. Listening (◀▶ Module 17), working positively together and constructively resolving conflicts (◀▶ Module 18) become even more crucial.

Be aware of the limitations of your channel. When you are limited to email, you lose both tone of voice and body language. In addition, email messages are often more brusque than comments in person (◀▶ Module 10). Audio messages provide tone of voice but not the non-verbal signals that tell you whether someone wants to make a comment or understands what you're saying. Even videoconferencing gives you only the picture in the camera's lens. With any of these technologies, you'll need to attend specifically to interpersonal skills.

For an important project, North Americans continue to rely on telephone and in-person meetings. Tom Vassos, innovation executive with IBM Canada and M.B.A. instructor and ebusiness stream director at the University of Toronto, prefers the telephone to virtual meetings using Web-conferencing software. Because of our preference for a human voice, Web-based conferencing software has, so far, had a negligible business impact.[10]

Employability Skills 2000+

The Conference Board of Canada
Insights You Can Count On

Please see the OLC to preview the key skills from the Conference Board of Canada's Employability Skills 2000+ covered in this module.

Review of Key Points

1. What should go into a meeting agenda?
2. What five ways of communicating can you use to make meetings more effective?
3. What are the seven problem-solving steps you can use in meetings?
4. When would dot planning be most effective?
5. What should be in meeting minutes?
6. How can you prepare to contribute to a meeting?

Assignments for Module 19

Questions for Critical Thinking

19.1 What opportunities do you have to network?
19.2 List three ways you can immediately begin to increase your networking activities.
19.3 In the groups of which you're a member (at school, at work, and in volunteer organizations), what kinds of comments are most valued in meetings?
19.4 What is the best meeting you ever attended? What made it so effective?

Exercises and Problems

19.5   Writing an Agenda

Write an agenda for your next collaborative group meeting.

As your instructor directs,

a. Write a memo to your instructor, explaining the choices you made.

b. Share your agenda with the ones developed by others in your group. Use the agendas as drafts to help you create the best possible agenda.
c. Present your best agenda to the rest of the class in a group oral presentation.

19.6   Taking Minutes

As your instructor directs,

Have two or more people take minutes of each class or collaborative group meeting for a week. Compare the accounts of the same meeting.

- To what extent do they agree on what happened?
- Does one contain information missing in other accounts?

- Do any accounts disagree on a specific fact?
- How do you account for the differences you find?

19.7 Writing a Meeting Manual*

Create a procedures manual for students next term, describing how to have effective meetings as they work on collaborative projects.

*Adapted from Miles McCall, Beth Stewart, and Timothy Clipson, "Teaching Communication Skills for Meeting Management," 1998 Refereed Proceedings, Association for Business Communication Southwestern United States, ed. Marsha L. Bayless (Nacogdoches, TX), p. 68.

19.8 Planning Scripts for Three-Minute Meetings

Create a script for a 90-second statement to your boss for each of the following:

1. Describe the progress on a project you're working on.
2. Provide an update on a problem the boss already knows about.
3. Tell about a success or achievement.
4. Tell about a problem and ask approval for the action you recommend.
5. Ask for resources you need for a project.
6. Ask for training you'd like to receive.
7. Lay the groundwork for a major request you need to make.

As your instructor directs,

a. Discuss your scripts with a small group of students.
b. Present your script to the class.
c. Write a memo to your instructor explaining the choices you have made in terms of content, arrangement, and word choice.

Polishing Your Prose

Hyphens and Dashes

Hyphens and dashes are forms of punctuation used within sentences. Use a hyphen to do the following:

1. Indicate that a word has been divided between two lines.

   Correct: Our biggest competitor announced plans to introduce new models of computers into the European market.

Divide words only at syllable breaks. If you aren't sure where the syllables break, look up the word in a dictionary. When a word has several syllables, divide it after a vowel or between two consonants.

Although many word-processing programs automatically hyphenate for you, knowing where and when to divide words is important for words the program may not recognize or for special cases. For instance, don't divide words of one syllable (e.g., *used*), and don't divide a two-syllable word if one of the syllables is only one letter long (e.g., *acre*).

2. Join two or more words used as a single adjective.

   Correct: After a flurry of requests, we are marketing new lines of specialty dinners for Asian- and Jamaican-Canadian customers.

             Order five 10- or 12-m lengths.

Here, hyphens prevent misreading. Without the hyphen, readers might interpret *Asian-Canadian* incorrectly as Asian. (Typically, compound adjectives such as *Asian-Canadian* and *Jamaican-Canadian* are not hyphenated when used as nouns.) In the second sentence, five lengths are needed, not lengths of 5, 10, or 12m.

3. Use a dash to emphasize a break in thought.

   Correct: Despite our best efforts—which included sending a design team to Paris and increasing our promotional budget—sales are lagging.

Create a dash by typing the hyphen key twice. With some word processors, this double hyphen will automatically be replaced with a longer, single dash (called an "em-dash"), which is used in type-setting.

Exercises

Supply necessary dashes or hyphens in the follow-ing sentences. If no punctuation is needed—if a space is correct—leave the parentheses blank.

1. Our biggest competitors( )including those in the Asian and European markets( )intro( )duced more product models during the fourth quarter.
2. Our cutting( )edge fashions sell best in French( )Canadian cities like Montreal.
3. Please pick up three( )2( )by( )4 posts at the lumberyard.
4. Next Monday, *The Aboriginal Times*( ) magazine will do a cover story on a thriving new business created by native( )Canadians.
5. Painters from the building( )services department plan to give Tarik's office two( )coats of paint.
6. Our gift certificates come in 5( ), 10( ), and 15( )dollar denominations.
7. The latest weather reports suggest that travel over South( )and Latin( )America may be interrupted by storms.
8. We need to work on more cost( )effective versions of our best( )selling software( ) programs.
9. You can email the results to my office in the early( )morning.
10. Katrina gave us four( )options during the sales( )meeting on Friday afternoon.

Check your answers to the odd-numbered exercises on page 573.

Online Learning Centre

Visit the Online Learning Centre at www.mcgrawhill.ca/olc/locker to access module quizzes, a searchable glossary, résumé and letter templates, additional business writing samples, CBC videos, and other learning and study tools.

20 Making Oral Presentations

Module Outline

- What decisions do I need to make as I plan a presentation?
- How should I organize a presentation?
- How can I create a strong opening and close?
- What are the keys to delivering an effective presentation?
- How should I handle questions from the audience?
- What are the guidelines for group presentations?

Review of Key Points

Assignments for Module 20

Polishing Your Prose: Choosing Levels of Formality

LEARNING OBJECTIVES

After reading and applying the information in Module 20, you'll be able to demonstrate

Knowledge of

- The differences between written and oral messages
- Types of presentations
- The criteria for effective presentations

Skills to

- Reframe written material into an oral presentation
- Plan and deliver oral presentations
- Develop a good speaking voice
- Prepare and deliver group presentations

The Conference Board of Canada
Insights You Can Count On

Please see the OLC to preview the key skills from the Conference Board of Canada's Employability Skills 2000+ covered in this module.

FIGURE 20.1

P A I B O C

Questions for Analysis

P What is the **purpose** of your presentation? What do you want to happen as a result of your speaking? What do you want the audience to think, feel, say, and do?

A Who is your **audience?** What do they already know? What do they need to know? What's in it for them? What do they care about? What will motivate them? How do members of your audience differ? What do you have to say that is relevant to them?

How can you grab the audience's attention?

I What **information** do you want the audience to take away? What information must your message include? What information is most relevant to your audience?

Presenters have less than 90 seconds to make that first—and lasting—impression. Powerful speakers know how to make that 90 seconds work for them.

People make presentations to inform, persuade, and build goodwill. Most presentations serve more than one purpose, and every presentation contains an element of persuasion. If you're not persuasive, it's unlikely the audience will pay attention to you or your message.

Oral presentations inform, persuade, and build goodwill. And like written messages, most oral presentations serve more than one purpose.

Informative presentations inform or teach the audience. For example, health and safety training sessions are primarily informative. Secondary purposes may be to conform to legislation, to meet ISO standards, to persuade employees to follow organizational procedures rather than doing something their own way, and to acculturate new employees (◀▷ Module 2).

Persuasive presentations motivate the audience to act or to believe. Giving information and evidence persuades through appeals to credibility and reason (◀▷ Module 12). Moreover, the speaker must build goodwill by appearing to be credible and sympathetic to the audience's needs. The goal of most presentations is to get to *yes*. In business presentations, speakers want to persuade the audience to buy their product, proposal, or idea. Sometimes the goal is to change attitudes and behaviours, or to reinforce existing attitudes. Thus, a speaker at a workers' compensation and benefits information meeting may stress the importance of following safety procedures; a speaker at a city council meeting will talk about the problem of homelessness in the community to try to build support for homeless shelters.

Goodwill presentations entertain and validate the audience. In an after-dinner speech, the audience wants to be entertained. Presentations at sales meetings may be designed to stroke the audience's egos and to validate their commitment to organizational goals.

Regardless of the type of presentation, the best orators

- Begin by identifying their audience
- Introduce themselves and their message, appropriately
- Are themselves
- Use the word "you"
- Tell stories
- Are creative
- Encourage feedback[1]

■ What decisions do I need to make as I plan a presentation?

Use PAIBOC: Identify your purpose as specifically as possible. Then reframe your purpose into a benefit for your audience.

An oral presentation needs to be simpler than a written message to the same audience. For one thing, people can listen almost twice as fast as speakers talk; therefore, good presenters compensate for this *listening lag* by reinforcing their ideas through clarity, repetition, and emphasis.

Identify the one idea you want the audience to take away. Once you've determined this idea, phrase it so that it offers a specific benefit to the audience.

SEE THE OLC!

Tips for Successful Presentations

**FIGURE 20.1
(Continued)**

What information is most relevant to your purpose(s)? How long is your presentation? What can you leave out? What information can you convey in your visuals? What information should you include in a handout?

B What reader benefits and reasons will appeal to your audience?

O What objections will your audience members have? What information do you have to overcome those objections? What are the negative aspects of your message? How can you de-emphasize, compensate for, or overcome these negatives?

C What is the context of your presentation? How will audiences perceive your presentation? What time of day is your presentation? Where is your presentation? In what kind of room? How can you make your presentation interactive and stimulating? What multimedia can you use?

Weak:	The purpose of my presentation is to discuss saving for retirement.
Better:	The purpose of my presentation is to persuade my audience to put their retirement funds in stocks and bonds, not in money market accounts and CDs.
or:	The purpose of my presentation is to explain how to calculate how much money someone needs to save in order to maintain a specific lifestyle after retirement.

Note: Your purpose is *not* the introduction of your talk; it is the principle that guides your decisions as you plan your presentation.

Simplify your supporting detail so it's easy to follow. Simplify visuals so they can be taken in at a glance. Simplify your words and sentences so they're easy to understand.

Analyze your audience for an oral presentation just as you do for a written message. If you'll be speaking to co-workers, talk to them about your topic or proposal to find out what questions or objections they have. For audiences inside the organization, the biggest questions are often practical ones: Will it work? How much will it cost? How long will it take?[2] And what's in it for me?

Before you begin planning your presentation, you need to know *for how long*, *where*, and *when* you will be speaking. Your time and the audience's expectations determine both the content and the kind of presentation you will give. The size and comfort of the room will affect the success of your presentation, as will the time of day. What size is the room? What equipment will be available? Will the audience be tired at the end of a long day of listening? sleepy after a big meal? Will the group be large or small? The more you know about your audience and your environment, the better you can adapt your presentation for maximum persuasive impact.

■ Choosing the Kind of Presentation

When you have identified your *purpose*, including the results you want to achieve, analyzed your audience's needs, and considered your time, you can decide on the kind of presentation you will give. Table 20.1 identifies the speaker's role in three kinds of presentations: monologue, guided discussion, and sales.

In a **monologue presentation**, the speaker functions as an expert, speaks without interruption and solicits questions at the end of the presentation. The speaker plans the presentation in advance and delivers it without deviation. This kind of presentation may represent the most common educational situation, but it's often boring for the audience. Good delivery skills are crucial, since the audience is comparatively uninvolved.

Guided discussions offer a better way to present material and encourage an audience to really engage. In a guided discussion, the speaker presents the questions or issues that both speaker and audience agree on. Rather than functioning as an expert with all the answers, the speaker serves as a facilitator to help the audience tap its own knowledge. This kind of presentation works well

Michael Goldman is president and senior consultant of Facilitation First, a professional consulting firm specializing in expert meeting facilitation and training. Michael has edited several leading books on facilitation and team interventions. He also acts as a contributing editor for the *training report* and the Banff Centre of Management's *Leadership Compass*. You can email him at ⟨goldman@facilitationfirst.com⟩ or visit his Web site: ⟨http://www.facilitationfirst.com⟩.

Three Purposes of Presentations

- **Informative presentations** inform or teach the audience.
- **Persuasive presentations** motivate the audience to act or to believe.
- **Goodwill presentations** entertain and validate the audience.

Most oral presentations have more than one purpose.

TABLE 20.1
Michael Goldman's Guidelines for Choosing Your Presentation Role

Chair when you want to	Facilitate when you want to
Exchange information	Increase participation
Get informal feedback	Deal with group dynamics
Hear members report back	Have members problem solve
Overview the current agenda	Have members make decisions
Set the parameters of the discussion	Have members create action plans
Review meeting objectives with members	Shift ownership and commitment levels

Source: Michael Goldman, "To Chair or to Facilitate, That is the Question," *the training report*, Jan/Feb 2001, page 13.

for adult training and for presenting the results of consulting projects, when the speaker has specialized knowledge, but the audience must implement the solution if it is to succeed. Guided discussions need more time than monologue presentations but produce *more audience response, more responses involving analysis*, and *more commitment to the result*.[3]

A **sales presentation** is a *conversation*, even if the salesperson stands up in front of a group and uses charts and overheads. The sales representative uses questions to determine the buyer's needs, probe objections, and gain temporary and then final commitment to the purchase. Even in a memorized sales presentation, the buyer will talk at least 30 percent of the time. In a problem-solving sales presentation, the buyer may talk 70 percent of the time.

How should I organize a presentation?

Start with the main point. Often, one of five standard patterns will work.

Most presentations use a direct pattern of organization, even when the goal is to persuade a reluctant audience. In a business setting, the audience members are in a hurry and know that you want to persuade them. Be honest about your goals, but prepare your opening to demonstrate that your goal meets the audience's needs too.

Overviews and Signposts

Immediately after your opener, provide an overview of the main points you will make. Offer a clear **signpost** as you come to each new point. A signpost is an explicit statement of the point you have reached.

In a persuasive presentation, start with your strongest point, your best reason. If time permits, give other reasons as well and respond to possible objections. Put your weakest point in the middle so that you can end on a strong note.

Often, one of five standard patterns of organization will work.

1. **Chronological.** Start with the past, move to the present, and end by looking ahead.
2. **Problem-causes-solution.** Explain the symptoms of the problem, identify its causes, and suggest a solution. This pattern works best when the audience will find your solution easy to accept.
3. **Exclude alternatives.** Explain the symptoms of the problem. Explain the obvious solutions first and show why they won't solve the problem. End by discussing a solution that will work. This pattern may be necessary when the audience will find the solution hard to accept.

4. **Pro-con.** Give all the reasons in favour of something, then those against it. This pattern works well when you want the audience to see the weaknesses in its position.

5. **1-2-3.** Discuss three aspects of a topic. This pattern works well to organize short informative briefings. "Today I'll review our sales, production, and profits for the last quarter."

Early in your talk—perhaps immediately after your opener—provide an agenda or overview of the main points you will make.

> First, I'd like to talk about who the homeless in Vancouver are. Second, I'll talk about the services the Open Shelter provides. Finally, I'll talk about what you—either individually or as a group—can do to help.

An overview provides a mental peg that hearers can hang each point on. It can also prevent someone missing what you are saying because he or she wonders why you aren't covering a major point that you've saved for later.[4]

Offer a clear signpost as you come to each new point. A **signpost** is an explicit statement of the point you have reached. Choose wording that fits your style. The following statements are four different ways that a speaker could use to introduce the last of three points:

> Now we come to the third point: what you can do as a group or as individuals to help homeless people in Vancouver.

> So much for what we're doing. Now let's talk about what you can do to help.

> You may be wondering, what can I do to help?

> As you can see, the Shelter is trying to do many things. We could do more things with your help.

SEE THE OLC!

Toastmasters International

How Can I Adapt My Ideas to the Audience?

Remember that *people can take in only so much information before they shut down*! Measure the message you'd like to send against where your audience is now. If your audience is indifferent, skeptical, or hostile, focus on the part of your message the audience will find most interesting and easiest to accept.

Don't seek a major opinion change in a single oral presentation. If your audience has already decided to hire a financial advisor, a strong presentation can convince them that you are the one to hire. However, if you're talking to a prospect who is not convinced that he/she needs investment advice, limit your purpose. You may simply strive to prove that expert advice can make the investor more money and free up his/her precious time for other activities. Only *after* the audience is receptive would you make the second sales presentation to prove that your investor should hire you rather than the competition.

Make your ideas relevant to your audience by linking what you have to say to the audience's experiences, interests, and needs. Showing your audience members that the topic affects them directly is the most effective strategy. When you can't do that, at least link the topic to some everyday experience.

When was the last time you were hungry? Maybe you remember being hungry while you were on a diet, or maybe you had to work late at a lab and didn't get back to the dorm in time for dinner.

Speech about world hunger to an audience of college students.

How can I create a strong opening and close?

Use your introduction and your conclusion as points of emphasis.

The beginning and end of a presentation, like the beginning and end of a written document, are positions of emphasis. Use those key positions to interest the audience and emphasize your key point. You'll sound more natural and more effective if you write out your opener and close in advance and memorize them. (They'll be short: just a sentence or two.)

Your introduction is particularly important. To catch and hold audience attention, try these strategies

- Stand still.
- Focus on your audience.
- Attract their interest with a **dramatic statement**, **story**, **question** or **quotation**.
- Make the hook or grabber relevant to them.

The more you can do to personalize your opener for your audience, the better. Recent events are better than things that happened long ago; local events are better than events at a distance; people they know are better than people who are only names.

Dramatic Statement

Twelve of our customers have cancelled orders in the past month.

This presentation to a company's executive committee went on to show that the company's distribution system was inadequate and to recommend a third warehouse located in the west.

Story

A mother was having difficulty getting her son up for school. He pulled the covers over his head.
"I'm not going to school," he said. "I'm not ever going again."
"Are you sick?" his mother asked.
"No," he answered. "I'm sick of school. They hate me. They call me names. They make fun of me. Why should I go?"
"I can give you two good reasons," the mother replied. "The first is that you're 42 years old. And the second is you're the school principal."[5]

This speech given at a seminar for educators went on to discuss "the three knottiest problems in education today." Educators had to face those problems; they couldn't hide under the covers.

Question

> Are you going to have enough money to do the things you want to when you retire?

This presentation to a group of potential clients discusses the value of using the services of a professional financial planner to achieve retirement goals.

Quotation

> According to Towers Perrin, the profits of Fortune 100 companies would be 25 percent lower—they'd go down $17 billion—if their earnings statements listed the future costs companies are obligated to pay for retirees' health care.

This presentation on options for health care for retired employees urges executives to start now to investigate options to cut the future cost.

Your opener must interest the audience and establish rapport. Some speakers use humour to achieve those goals. However, an inappropriate joke can turn the audience against the speaker. Never use humour that's directed against the audience. In contrast, speakers who make fun of themselves almost always succeed:

> It's both a privilege and a pressure to be here.[6]

Humour isn't the only way to set an audience at ease and establish a positive emotional connection. Smile at your audience before you begin; let them see that you're a real person and a pleasant one.

The end of your presentation should be as strong as the opener. For your close, do one or more of the following:

- Restate your main point.
- Refer to your opener to create a frame for your presentation.
- End with a vivid, positive picture.
- Tell the audience exactly what to do to solve the problem you've discussed.

The following close from a fundraising speech combines a restatement of the main point with a call for action, telling the audience what to do.

> Plain and simple, we need money to run the foundation, just like you need money to develop new products. We need money to make this work. We need money from you. Pick up that pledge card. Fill it out. Turn it in at the door as you leave. Make it a statement about your commitment...make it a big statement.[7]

When you write out your opener and close, remember that listeners can take in only so much information; then they disengage and tune out. When preparing your presentation, apply the *KISS formula: keep it short and simple*. As you can see in the example close just shown, speaking style uses shorter sentences and shorter, simpler words than writing does. Oral style can even sound a bit choppy when it is read. Oral style uses more personal pronouns, a less varied vocabulary, and much more repetition.

EXPANDING A CRITICAL SKILL

Finding Your Best Voice

Paralanguage—how we say what we say—accounts for more than 30 percent of the meaning in our messages. Next to your face, therefore, your voice is your most important presentation aid! Effective speakers use their voices to support and enhance content. Your best voice will manipulate pitch, intonation, tempo, and volume to express energy and enthusiasm.

Pitch

Pitch measures whether a voice uses sounds that are low (like the bass notes on a piano) or high. Low-pitched voices project more credibility than do high-pitched voices. Low-pitched presenters are perceived as being more authoritative, and more pleasant to listen to. Most voices go up in pitch when the speaker is angry or excited; some people raise pitch when they increase volume. People whose normal speaking voices are high may need to practise projecting their voices to avoid becoming shrill when they speak to large groups.

To find your best pitch, try humming. The pitch where the hum sounds loudest and most resonant is your best voice.

Intonation

Intonation marks variation in pitch, stress, or tone. Speakers who use many changes in pitch, stress, and tone usually seem more enthusiastic; often they also seem more energetic and more intelligent. Someone who speaks in a monotone may seem apathetic or unintelligent. Non- native speakers whose first language does not use tone, pitch, and stress to convey meaning and attitude may need to practise varying these voice qualities.

Avoid raising your voice at the end of a sentence, since in English a rising intonation signals a question. Therefore, speakers who end sentences on a questioning or high tones—known as *uptalk*—sound immature or uncertain of what they're saying.

Tempo

Tempo is a measure of speed. In a conversation, match your tempo to the other speaker's to build rapport. In a formal presentation, vary your tempo. Speakers who speak quickly and who vary their volume during the talk are more likely to be perceived as competent.

Volume

Volume is a measure of loudness or softness. Very soft voices, especially if they are also breathy and high-pitched, give the impression of youth and inexperience. People who do a lot of speaking to large groups need to practise projecting their voices so they can increase their volume without shouting.

Sources: George B. Ray, "Vocally Cued Personality Prototypes: An Implicit Personality Theory Approach," *Communication Monographs* 53, no. 3 (1986): 266–76; and Jacklyn Boice, "Verbal Impressions," *Selling Power*, March 2000, 69.

How should I use visuals?

Be selective and specific.

People understand and retain information better when they both *see* and *hear* the facts; they understand and remember best when they *see*, *hear*, and *do*. However, your topic or your time allotment may preclude having your audience practise what you're preaching.

North American audiences expect business presentations to be supported by attractive visuals. Moreover, visuals can give your presentation a professional image (◄|▷ Module 5). One study found that presenters using overhead transparencies were perceived as "better prepared, more professional, more persuasive, more credible, and more interesting" than speakers who did not use visuals. They were also more likely to persuade a group to adopt their recommendations. Coloured overhead transparencies were most effective in persuading people to act.[8]

However, be warned: audiences and experts agree that PowerPoint slides—once unusual attention-grabbers—are now misused and overused in presentations.[9]

Well-designed visuals can serve as an outline for your talk (see Figure 20.1), eliminating the need for additional notes. Plan at most one visual for every minute of your talk, plus two visuals to serve as title and conclusion. Don't try to put your whole talk on visuals. *Visuals should highlight your main points, not give every detail.*

To create effective presentation visuals, use these guidelines:

SEE THE OLC!

PowerPoint™ Tips

- Use a sans serif font (Ariel, Helvetica, Technical) to maximize text readability.
- Use a minimum 24-point type to maximize readability (◀▶ Module 5, Figure 5.4 re. fonts).
- Keep it simple.
- Replace text with illustrations—charts, graphs, tables, clipart—whenever possible.
- Make only one point with each visual. Break a complicated point down into several visuals.
- Give each visual a title that makes a point connected to your presentation's main point.
- Limit the amount of text: no more than five lines per slide or five words per line.

To present your visuals effectively, use these guidelines:

- Use a friend/colleague to manage the visuals for you, so you can concentrate on your ideas and your delivery.
- Use your visuals as enhancement, not competition.
- Use no more than one visual or slide per minute.
- Put up your visual (or have your friend/colleague put up the visual) when you are ready to talk about it.
- Leave the visual up until your next point.

See ◀▶ Module 25 for information on how to present numerical data through visuals.

Visuals work only if the technology they depend on works. When you give presentations in your own office, check the equipment in advance. When you make a presentation in another location or for another organization, arrive early so that you'll have time not only to check the equipment but also to track down a service worker if the equipment isn't working. Be prepared with a backup plan if you're unable to show your slides or videotape.

Remember too that because PowerPoint™ presentations have become commonplace, you must engage your audience in a variety of other ways:

- Students presenting on intercultural business communications demonstrated the way Chinese, Japanese, and Canadians exchange business cards by asking audience members to role-play the differences.
- Another student discussing the need for low-salt products brought in a container of salt, a measuring cup, a measuring spoon, and two plates. As he discussed the body's need for salt, he measured out three teaspoons onto one plate: the amount the body needs in a month. As he discussed the amount of salt the average diet provides, he continued to measure out salt onto the other plate, stopping only when he had 500 g of salt—the amount in the average North American diet. The demonstration made the discrepancy clear in a way words or even a chart could not have done.[10]

Some presenters use quizzes and games formats—like *Family Feud* or *Who Wants to be a Millionaire?*—to encourage audience members to share their expertise with others.

FIGURE 20.2
PowerPoint™ Slides for an Informative Presentation

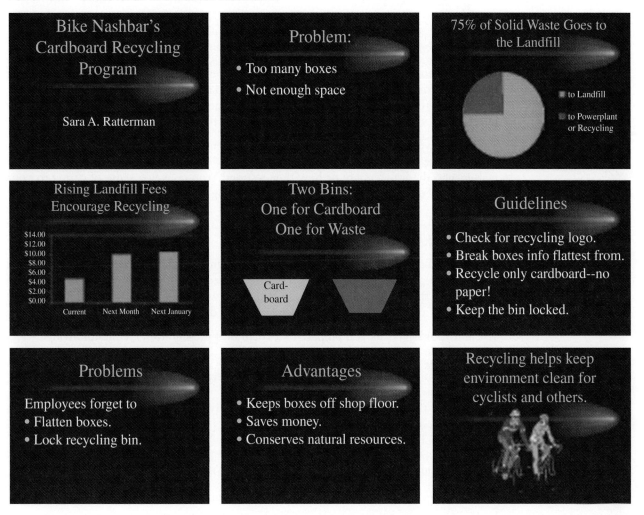

- To make sure that his employees understood where money went, the CEO of a specialty printing shop printed up $2 million in play money and handed out big cards to employees marked *Labour, Depreciation, Interest,* and so forth. Then he asked each "category" to come up and take its share of the revenues. The action was more dramatic than a colour pie chart could ever have been.[11]
- Another speaker who was trying to raise funds used the simple act of asking people to stand to involve them, to create emotional appeal, and to make a statistic vivid:

> [A speaker] was talking to a luncheon club about contributing to the relief of an area that had been hit by a tsunami. The news report said that 70 percent of the people had been killed or disabled. The room was set up with ten people at each round table. He asked three persons at each table to stand. Then he said, "…You people sitting are dead or disabled. You three standing have to take care of the mess. You'd need help, wouldn't you?"[12]

What are the keys to delivering an effective presentation?

Turn your fear into energy, look at the audience, and use natural gestures.

Audience members want you to succeed in your presentation out of a vested self-interest: they don't want to feel uncomfortable for you. They also want the sense that you're talking directly to them, that you've taken the time and trouble to prepare, that you're interested in your subject and that you care about their interest.

They'll forgive you if you get tangled up in a sentence and end it ungrammatically. They won't forgive you if you seem to have a "canned" talk that you're going to deliver no matter who the listeners are or how they respond. You convey a sense of caring to your audience by making direct eye contact and by using a conversational style.

Using Fear

The best and most experienced speakers get butterflies. Even great actors have attested to experiencing paralytic fear before every performance. Feeling nervous is normal. But you can harness that nervous energy to do your best work. As one student said, you don't need to get rid of your butterflies. All you need to do is make them fly in formation.

To calm your nerves as you prepare to give an oral presentation try the following:

SEE THE OLC!

Handling Stage Fright

- Be prepared: Analyze your audience, organize your thoughts, prepare visual aids, practise your opener and close, check out the arrangements.
- Practise, practise, practise.
- Use only the amount of caffeine you normally use. More or less may make you jumpy.
- Avoid alcoholic beverages.
- Relabel what you're feeling. Instead of saying, "I'm scared," try saying, "My adrenaline is high." Adrenaline sharpens our reflexes and helps us do our best.

Just before your presentation, use relaxation techniques:

- Consciously contract and then relax your muscles, starting with your feet and calves and going up to your shoulders, arms, and hands.
- Take several deep breaths from your diaphragm.

During your presentation, be sure to do the following:

- Pause and look at the audience before you begin speaking.
- Concentrate on communicating well.
- Channel your body energy into emphatic gestures and movement.

Using Eye Contact

Look directly at the people you're talking to. Speakers who looked the most at the audience during a seven-minute informative speech were judged to be better informed, more experienced, more honest, and friendlier than speakers who delivered the same information with less eye contact.[13] An earlier study found that speakers judged sincere looked at the audience 63 percent of the time, while those judged insincere looked at the audience only 21 percent of the time.[14]

The point in making eye contact is to establish one-on-one contact with the individual members of your audience. People want to feel that you're talking to them. Looking directly at individuals also enables you to be more conscious of feedback from the audience, so that you can modify your approach if necessary.

■ Standing and Gesturing

Stand with your feet far enough apart for good balance, with your knees flexed. Unless the presentation is very formal or you're on camera, you can walk if you want to. Some speakers like to come out from the lectern to remove that barrier between themselves and the audience.

Build on your natural style for gestures. Gestures usually work best when they're big and confident.

■ Using Notes and Visuals

Unless you're giving a very short presentation, you'll probably want to use notes. Even experts use notes. The more you know about the subject, the greater the temptation to add relevant points that occur to you as you talk. Adding an occasional point can help to clarify something for the audience, but adding too many points will overwhelm the audience, destroy your outline, and put you over the time limit.

Put your notes on cards or on sturdy pieces of paper. Most speakers like to use 10 × 15 cm or 12 × 17 cm cards because they hold more information. Your notes need to be complete enough to help you if you go blank, so use long phrases or complete sentences. Under each main point, jot down the evidence or illustration you'll use. Indicate where you'll refer to visuals.

Look at your notes infrequently. Direct your eyes to members of the audience. Hold your notes high enough so that your head doesn't bob up and down like a yo-yo as you look from the audience to your notes and back again.

If you have lots of visuals and know your topic well, you won't need notes. If possible, put the screen to the side so that you won't block it. *Face the audience, not the screen.* With transparencies, you can use colour marking pens to call attention to your points as you talk. Show the entire visual at once: don't cover up part of it. If you don't want the audience to read ahead, prepare several visuals that build up. In your overview, for example, the first visual could list your first point, the second could list the first and second points, and the third could list all three points.

Keep the room lights on if possible; turning them off makes it easier for people to fall asleep and harder for them to concentrate on you.

■ How should I handle questions from the audience?

Anticipate questions that might be asked. Be honest. Rephrase biased or hostile questions.

Prepare for questions by listing every fact or opinion you can think of that challenges your position. Treat each objection seriously and try to think of a way to deal with it. If you're talking about a controversial issue, you may want to save one point for the question period, rather than making it during the presentation. Speakers who have visuals to answer questions seem especially well prepared.

During your presentation, tell the audience how you'll handle questions. If you have a choice, save questions for the end. In your talk, answer the questions or objections that you expect your audience to have.

During the question period, acknowledge questions by looking directly at the questioner. As you answer the question, expand your focus to take in the entire group.

If the audience may not have heard the question or if you want more time to think, repeat the question before you answer it. Link your answers to the points you made in your presentation. Keep the purpose of your presentation in mind, and select information that advances your goals.

If a question is hostile or biased, rephrase it before you answer it. "You're asking whether...." Or suggest an alternative question: "I think there are problems with both the positions you describe. It seems to me that a third possibility is...."

Sometimes people will ask a question really designed to state the their own position. Respond to the question if you want to. Another option is to say, "I'm not sure what you're asking," or "That's a clear statement of your position. Let's move to the next question now." If someone asks about something that you already explained in your presentation, simply answer the question without embarrassing the questioner. Even when actively participating, audiences remember only about 70 percent of what you say.

If you don't know the answer to a question, say so and promise to get the information and respond as soon as possible. Write down the question so that you can look up the answer before the next session. You may want to refer the question to your audience, which both involves and flatters them. If it's a question to which you think there is no answer, ask whether anyone in the room knows. When no one does, your "ignorance" is vindicated.

At the end of the question period, take two minutes to summarize your main point once more. (This can be a restatement of your close.) Questions may or may not focus on the key point of your talk. Take advantage of having the floor to repeat your message briefly and forcefully.

What are the guidelines for group presentations?

In the best presentations, voices take turns within each point.

Plan carefully to involve as many members of the group as possible in speaking roles. The easiest way to make a group presentation is to outline the presentation and then divide the topics, giving one to each group member. Another member can be responsible for the opener and the close. During the question period, each member answers questions that relate to his or her topic.

In this kind of divided presentation, be sure to do the following:

- Plan transitions.
- Strictly enforce time limits.
- Coordinate your visuals so that the presentation seems a coherent whole.
- Choreograph the presentation: plan each member's movement and seating arrangements as the group transfers from speaker to speaker. Take turns managing the visual support so that each speaker can focus on content and delivery, without worrying about changing slides or transparencies.
- Practise the presentation as a group at least once; more is better.

The best group presentations are even more fully integrated: together, the members of the group complete the important tasks:

- Writing a very detailed outline
- Choosing points and examples
- Creating visuals

Then, *within* each point, speakers take turns. This presentation is most effective because each voice speaks only a minute or two before a new voice comes in. However, it works only when all group members know the subject well and when the group plans carefully and practises extensively.

Whatever form of group presentation you use, introduce each member of the team to the audience at the beginning of the presentation and at each **transition**: use the next person's name when you change speakers: "Now, Jason will explain how we evaluated the Web pages."

As a team member, pay close attention to your fellow speaker; don't ever have sidebar conversations with others in the group. If other members of the team seem uninterested in the speaker, the audience gets the sense that that speaker isn't worth listening to.

Employability Skills 2000+

Please see the OLC to preview the key skills from the Conference Board of Canada's Employability Skills 2000+ covered in this module.

Review of Key Points

1. Why do oral presentations have to be made simpler than written messages to the same audience?
2. All presentations share one purpose. What is that purpose?
3. What are the differences among the monologue, guided discussion, and sales presentations?
4. What seven strategies guarantee you will create and deliver a powerful presentation?
5. What strategies can you adopt to help you calm your nerves and relax before a presentation?
6. What strategies make for the very best group presentations?

Assignments for Module 20

Questions for Critical Thinking

20.1 What tips and techniques should you use to create strong visuals?
20.2 What's the most important part of any presentation? Why?
20.3 What are four possible openers, or "hooks"?
20.4 Why should you be careful using humour?
20.5 What are four possible strong closers?

Exercises and Problems

20.6 Making a Short Oral Presentation

As your instructor directs,

Make a short (two- to five-minute) presentation, with three to eight slides, on one of the following topics:

a. Explain how what you've learned in classes, in campus activities, or at work will be useful to the employer who hires you after graduation.
b. Profile someone who is successful in the field you hope to enter and explain what makes him or her successful.
c. Describe a specific situation in an organization in which communication was handled well or badly.
d. Make a short presentation based on another problem in this book, such as the following:

1.8 Discuss three of your strengths.
2.9 Analyze your boss.
11.6 Explain a "best practice" in your organization.
12.5 Tell your boss about a problem in your unit and recommend a solution.
26.7 Explain one of the challenges (e.g., technology, ethics, international competition) that the field you hope to enter is facing.
28.9 Profile a company you would like to work for and explain why you think it would be a good employer.
29.7 Explain your interview strategy.

20.7 Making a Longer Oral Presentation

As your instructor directs,

Make a 5- to 12-minute presentation on one of the following. Use visuals to make your talk effective.

a. Show why your unit is important to the organization and either should be exempt from downsizing or should receive additional resources.
b. Persuade your supervisor to make a change that will benefit the organization.
c. Persuade your organization to make a change that will improve the organization's image in the community.
d. Persuade classmates to donate time or money to a charitable organization (◀|▶ Module 13).
e. Persuade an employer that you are the best person for the job.

f. Use another problem in this book as the basis for your presentation, such as the following:

2.10 Analyze a discourse community.
2.11 Analyze an organization's corporate culture.

11.19 Present a Web page you have designed.
23.7 Summarize the results of a survey you have conducted.
23.8 Summarize the results of your research.

20.8 Making a Group Oral Presentation

As your instructor directs,

Make a 5- to 12-minute presentation using visuals on one of these topics:

3.8 Show how cultural differences can lead to miscommunication.
5.9 Evaluate the design of three Web pages.

13.14 Recommend an investment for your instructor.
18.7 Recommend ways to retain workers.
18.10 Present brochures you have designed to the class.
24.6 Summarize the results of your research.
29.8 Share the advice of students currently in the job market.

20.9 Creating a Presentation Skills Evaluation Matrix

As your instructor directs,

Together with four peers, create an evaluation guide to evaluate your class presentations. Begin by brainstorming the components of a presentation, such as content, delivery, visuals, time, organization,

audience relevance, and so on. Create a table to describe the behaviours you would expect in an excellent presentation.

Be prepared to explain your evaluation guide to the rest of the class.

Polishing Your Prose

Choosing Levels of Formality

Some words are more formal than others. Generally, business messages call for a middle-of-the-road formality, not too formal,but not so casual as to seem sloppy.

Formal and stuffy	Short and simple
ameliorate	improve
commence	begin, start
enumerate	list
finalize	finish, complete
prioritize	rank
utilize	use
viable option	choice

Sloppy	Casual
befuddled	confused
diss	criticize
guess	assume
haggle	negotiate
nosy	curious
wishy-washy	indecisive, flexible

What makes choosing words so challenging is that the level of formality depends on your purposes, the audience, and the situation. What's just right for a written report will be too formal for an oral presentation or an advertisement. The level of formality that works in one discourse community may be inappropriate for another.

Listen to the language that people in your discourse community use. What words seem to have positive connotations? What words persuade? As you identify these terms, use them in your own messages.

Exercises

In each sentence, choose the better word or phrase. Justify your choice.

1. On Monday, I [took a look at/inspected] our [stuff/inventory].
2. [Starting/commencing] at 5 P.M., all qualifying employees may [commence/begin] their [leave times/vacations].

3. Though their [guy/representative] was [firm/stubborn], we eventually [hashed out/negotiated] a settlement.

4. Call to schedule [some time/a meeting] with me to [talk about/deliberate on the issues in] your memo.

5. The manager [postponed making/waited until she had more information before making]a decision.

6. Rick has [done his job/performed] well as [top dog/manager] of our sales department.

7. In my last job, I [ran lots of errands/worked as a gofer] for the marketing manager.

8. Please [contact/communicate with] [me/the undersigned] if you [have questions/desire further information or knowledge].

9. This report [has problems/stinks].

10. In this report, I have [guessed/assumed] that the economy will continue to grow.

Check your answers to the odd-numbered questions on page 573.

Online Learning Centre

Visit the Online Learning Centre at www.mcgrawhill.ca/olc/locker to access module quizzes, a searchable glossary, résumé and letter templates, additional business writing samples, CBC videos, and other learning and study tools.

CBC Video Case

Visit the Online Learning Centre at www.mcgrawhill.ca/olc/locker to view "Small Talk" and "The Trouble with Teams," two online CBC Video Cases that highlight key issues from Unit Five. "Small Talk" looks in as an M.B.A. class is coached on one of the toughest skills for students to master—the art of making conversation in a business setting. And "The Trouble with Teams" explores recent studies indicating that perhaps teamwork—once seen as a surefire way to boost productivity and creativity—is not as successful as previously thought.

Cases for Communicators

WestJet's Team Flies in Formation

Few companies encourage entrepreneurial attitudes to enhance employee performance or to foster teamwork. But the success of Calgary-based WestJet Airlines demonstrates that people thrive in a workplace that emphasizes flexibility and fun as part of its entrepreneurial culture.

Flexibility informs every aspect of the company's business—from recruitment and retention strategies to innovative practices in work time and place. WestJet's respect for its employees includes its hiring practices: people volunteer for the peer selection teams whose members design the interview process. Employees create their work schedules according to

their family, cultural, or religious priorities. High-performing sales agents participate in the "home res" program, working in the company call centre from their homes. And WestJet's profit-sharing and stock-option plans let employees own a piece of the company.

Superior customer service through teamwork is recognized and rewarded. Company communiqués (emails, memos, the intranet, newsletter) recount success stories provided by customers and employees. The corporate Web site holds contests and awards prizes for best practices anecdotes. The value of every individual's contribution to the WestJet team is consistently reinforced.

After only four years in the industry, WestJet could boast of being North America's second most profitable airline. In 2002 it ranked seventh in Ipsos-Reid's survey of Canada's most respected companies, and in 2003, Alberta's Most Respected Corporations' annual survey identified WestJet as the Most Respected Corporation for Innovative Practices. WestJet's story proves that building the team builds the business.

Sources: Susan Pedersen, "Calgary's Ten Best Places to Work," *Calgary Magazine*, http://www.macleoddixon.com/best_places_to_work_v2.pdf, retrieved October 30, 2006; Pino Mancuso, "WestJet's Home Res Program an Innovative Success," *Connections* 4, no. 4, http://www.abcallcentre.com/PDF/Vol%204%20Iss%204.pdf, retrieved September 1, 2003; Gord McLaughlin, "CEO # 4 Clive Beddoe," *National Post*, http://www.nationalpost.com/nationalpostbusiness/story.html?id=%7BAC2207 8C-542D-41D3-B86C-3823F0219A77%7D, retrieved August 10, 2003; WestJet Corporate Web Site, "Student Information," http://c0dsp.westjet.com/internet/sky/about/studentsTemplate.jsp, retrieved August 17, 2003.

Individual Activity

During your interview for the position of WestJet sales agent, your prospective team asks you to create a 15-minute oral presentation on "listening" for them. Topics that you might cover in your presentation include the following:

- What is good listening?
- What is active listening?
- What are blocking responses?
- How do people show that they are listening?

Before you begin writing your presentation, consider the following questions:

- What is the purpose of the presentation? Is it informative, persuasive, or goodwill?
- What type of presentation is this? Is it a monologue, a guided discussion, or a sales presentation?
- How does the type of presentation affect interactions with my audience?
- How can I make my ideas relevant to my audience?
- What is my main point?

Choose an appropriate organization—chronological, problem-causes, solution, exclude alternatives, pro-con, or 1-2-3—and outline your presentation, using enough detail to make the content clear.

Identify possible visuals. Brainstorm at least three different ways you could involve your audience.

Finally, craft a good, short opener for your presentation, using one of the four primary opener types: startling statement, narration or anecdote, question, or quotation.

Now you are ready to take a deep breath, find your best voice, and go for it!

Group Activity

Your group has been asked to write a 500-word essay on what makes a good leader. You must create and polish this document as a team.

Plan the work and the document as a team. In this process, discuss the following questions:

- What is the purpose of this document?
- Who is the audience?
- What organization, format, and style should the essay take?

Once the planning is done, begin drafting the essay as a group.

Next, evaluate the content and discuss possible revisions as a group. Remember that business writing can embrace many different styles; keep this point in mind if your revision discussions stall over questions of style.

With a solid revision in hand, you are ready to edit and proofread the document. This stage may be even more important for group writing projects because of the myriad writing styles and levels of expertise involved. In addition to running a spell check, therefore, be sure to have at least one person check the whole document for grammar, mechanics, accuracy, and completeness.

After you have completed the document, discuss the following questions as a team:

- Did the majority of team members work actively on the project?
- Can you identify the positive roles and actions demonstrated during the writing process? (For example, did anyone encourage participation?)
- Can you identify any negative roles and actions demonstrated during the writing process? (For example, did a group member clown or attempt to dominate the group?)
- Can you identify an informational leader, interpersonal leader, and procedural leader in your group?

Finally, reflect as a group on the issue of conflict. Did conflict arise during this group project? If so, did you work as a team to identify the source and type of conflict and then follow the appropriate steps to resolve the issue?

Unit 6

Research, Reports, and Visuals

"The Internet has allowed me to turn my passion into a livelihood," says Mark DeWolf, who, with his partner Adelle Lyon, writes for the trailblazing magazine, *Appellation America* (http://www.appellationamerica.com/). *Appellation America*, an online resource for wine hobbyists and enthusiasts, focuses on Canadian and American appellation regions (viticulture grape-producing areas). The magazine's mission is to promote North America's burgeoning wine industry.

Each of the magazine's four writers is responsible for researching and writing about a specific North American wine region—which may contain as many as 700 wineries in 70 areas. Adelle's territory includes Ontario, Washington, and the southern United States: Florida, Georgia and Mississippi. Mark covers appellations, areas, and wineries in the Atlantic Provinces, California, Oregon, and the Virginias. Mark and Adelle write thumbnail sketches (about 200 words) on every appellation in their respective territories. They also write feature articles on their wineries, and descriptors for every grape grown in North America.

Grape growing is a scientific topic, factual and analytical, dealing with climates, wind currents, and soils. Making the subject user-friendly for the wine hobbyist *and* appealing to the wine connoisseur is the challenge.

For their primary research, the writers interview wine growers and oenologists in person and via email. They consult wine experts in the Midwestern U.S. and at Brock University in Guelph, Ontario, which offers a BSc in Enology—the science of producing wine.

Because our wine industry is so young, secondary research is sparse, says Adelle, and includes digging through tourist bureau information, wineries' web sites, and documents produced by national grape growers' associations. Eventually, however, the *Appellation America* website, with its comprehensive wine-producing coverage and cutting-edge graphics, will become *the* major resource on the Canadian—and U.S.—wine industries.

How did Economics majors (Mark has a BSc in Economics from Dalhousie University and Adelle a BSc from Trent University, and an MSc from the London School of Economics) become wine researchers and writers? After graduation, both began working in Halifax's hospitality service industry. To move into management, they enrolled in a nationally certified sommelier program, where they did so well that the magazine's founder—a Nova Scotia wine pioneer—recruited them.

"I use my education to research and write: my transferable skills contribute to a ground-breaking publication," says Adelle.

Mark concurs, "You have to find what your passion in life is. I fell in love with food and became a maitre d' and sommelier in one of Canada's best restaurants. We started waiting tables and asked ourselves, 'What do we have to do to be the best in this business?' We're lucky: the Internet and our passion have allowed us to find our way."

P A I B O C

Analysis

1. Who are the **audiences** for *Appellation America*?

2. What **information** would these readers value?

3. What **benefits** does the publication provide its readers?

MODULE

21 Finding, Analyzing, and Documenting Information

Module Outline

- How do I begin my research?
- How can I find information online and in print?
- How do I decide whom to survey or interview?
- How do I write questions for surveys and interviews?
- How should I analyze the information I've collected?
- How should I document sources?
- Why should I document my sources?

Review of Key Points

Assignments for Module 21

Polishing Your Prose: Using MLA and APA Style

LEARNING OBJECTIVES

After reading and applying the information in Module 21, you'll be able to demonstrate

Knowledge of

- How and where to get information
- What quantitative and qualitative information are
- How to begin to analyze information
- How to avoid unintentional plagiarism

Skills to

- Identify primary and secondary sources
- Find electronic and print information
- Use the Internet for research
- Write questions for surveys and interviews
- Analyze sources
- Cite and document sources correctly and ethically

The Conference Board of Canada
Insights You Can Count On

Please see the OLC to preview the key skills from the Conference Board of Canada's Employability Skills 2000+ covered in this module.

In our knowledge-based global village, you need to know

- Where to find information
- How to evaluate and use the information you find, and
- How to use that information professionally and ethically

Researchers today can access more information than ever before. Indeed, because of technology, no matter how much information you find, every second of every day there's more! More, however, isn't necessarily better. To paraphrase Mark Twain, researchers today can also find more lies, damned lies, and statistics than ever before.

Therefore, knowledge workers must know not only what information they need, and where to find it, but also how to evaluate the data they find, and how to use it ethically.

How do I begin my research?

Focus your search: identify your objective, or working thesis.

To narrow your search for relevant information, identify your objective: what are you looking for, and why? Use the PAIBOC analysis to focus on your purpose. Write down your **hypothesis**, or working thesis: I am going to prove that...

- we need to hire more salespeople to handle customer orders
- engineering is a hot job
- China's economy depends on investing heavily in our energy
- Ontario's manufacturing sector is still doing well

Now you can begin to consider where best to find information that can serve your purposes by proving your hypothesis. There are two types of research: primary and secondary. **Primary research** methods gather new information. Surveys, focus groups, interviews, and observations are common information-gathering methods in business. Documenting policies or procedures in your workplace, and printing monthly sales figures for a report are also examples of primary research. **Secondary research** retrieves information others have gathered: library, newspapers, magazines, and online article searches are examples of secondary research.

Web Search Strategies Tutorial

How can I find information online and in print?

Learn what credible resources are available, and how to use them.

A visual and auditory introduction to the Internet

Libraries (literary/hard copy) and the Internet (electronic) offer a wealth of secondary resources for information seekers. In fact, most information, including magazines and newspapers, is freely available online at your local library and through your university or college library. Use a computer to search for print as well as online sources, and include print sources in your research. Information in most periodicals is checked before it goes to print; papers in scholarly journals are reviewed by peer experts before being accepted. Therefore, print resources are often more credible and more reliable than Web pages, which anyone can publish.

How to do keyword searches

Figure 21.1 and Tables 21.1, 21.2 and 21.3 list some of the many resources available.

FIGURE 21.1

Some Examples of Online Resources available through Sheridan Institute's Library

---

INDEXES AND FULL TEXT DATABASES

❑ AccessScience

Online encyclopedia of science and technology containing essay topics and a scientific dictionary.

❑ Academic Search Premier (EB500)

More than 3,900 magazines, journals, newspapers and trade publications are available in full-text, covering nearly every area of academic study.

❑ Books 24×7

ReferenceWare for Professionals: ITPro, Office Essentials, BusinessPro, FinancePro

❑ Canadian Business and Current Affairs (CBCA) (Proquest)

Indexing and full text for 140 Canadian business and trade publications.

❑ Canadian Centre for Occupational Health and Safety

Login Access:
User ID = SHERCOLL
Password = SEP2004
CCOHS databases:
— MSDS Material Safety Data Sheets
— CHEMINFO Health and safety information on chemicals
— HSELINE, NIOSHTIC Summaries and citations to international documents on health & safety
— RTECS Toxicology exposure limits and regulatory information on chemical substances

❑ Canadian Newsstand (Proquest)

Canadian Newsstand offers unparalleled access to the full text of Canadian newspapers.

❑ Corporate Retriever (replacement for CanCorp Financials)

❑ E-STAT

Statistical and demographic data about Canada from Statistics Canada.
Login Access:
User ID = shercollege
Password = estat

❑ Electric Library (Proquest)

Features a wide variety of general information resources, some of which are Canadian. The completely fulltext database is composed of over 550 magazines, 100+ reference books, 200+ newspapers from around the world, a selection of U.S. TV and radio transcripts, and picture and map libraries.

❑ Euromonitor (Global Market Information Database)

GMID is an excellent resource for all types of project work such as market research, international business case studies, developing business plans and comparative analysis. Information sources included country statistics, lifestyle indicators, lifestyle analysis, market data, country profiles, company profiles, market shares and performance indicators and market reports.

❑ Financial Post

❑ Grove Dictionary of Art Online

Grove Art Online presents the entire text of The Dictionary of Art (published in 1996), updated and fully-indexed, searchable and browsable.

❑ Net Library

NetLibrary provides access to your library's collection of eContent. eContent can be digital versions of printed material such as books or journals, databases or any digital content. All available twenty-four hours a day, seven days a week.

❑ WestLaw Online Legal Research

❑ Wilson Applied Science & Technology Abstracts (Proquest)
Full text & images for periodicals covering computers, engineering, physics, telecommunications & transportation.

❑ Wilson Art Full-Text

Ask your teacher or the reference librarian about the free resources available in your library.

TABLE 21.1
Sources for Electronic Research

These CD-ROM databases are available in many university and college libraries:	
ABI/Inform (indexes and abstracts for 800 journals in management and business)	*ERIC* (research on education and teaching practices in Canada and other countries)
Biological and Agricultural Index	*Foreign Trade and Economic Abstracts*
Canadian Government Sources:	International Film Archive
Canadian Federal Government	*LEXIS/NEXIS Services*
Canadian Government Information (National Library of Canada)	*McGraw-Hill Encyclopedia of Science*
Canadian Government Information on the Internet	*Newspaper Abstracts*
Government of Canada Web site	*PAIS International—Public Affairs Information Service*
Parliament of Canada	*Peterson's College Database*
Industry Canada's Strategis: The Information Site that Means Business	*Social Sciences Index*
Government of Canada Depository Services Program	*Wilson Business Abstracts*
CINAHL (nursing and allied health)	*Women's Resources International*
ComIndex (indexes and abstracts of journals in communication)	

TABLE 21.2
Sources for Web Research

Subject Matter Directories	News Sites
SmartPros Accounting http://accounting.smartpros.com	AJR NewsLink (links Canadian, U.S., and international newspapers, magazines, and resources online) http://newslink.org/menu.html
Canada Business Service Centres http://www.cbsc.org	*Business Week* online http://www.businessweek.com
Canada's Business and Consumer Site http://www.strategis.ic.gc.ca	*Canadian Business* online http://www.canadianbusiness.com
FINWeb http://www.finweb.com	CBC http://cbc.ca/newsworld
International business sources on the WWW http://globaledge.msu.edu/ibrd/ibrd.asp	CNN/CNNFN http://www.cnn.com (news) http://money.cnn.com
Marketing, Research, Advertising, Selling, Promotion & More http://www.knowthis.com	The *Manchester Guardian* online http://www.guardian.co.uk
Technical Dictionaries for ebusiness and technology terms http://www.globetechnology.com/site/tech_encyclopedia.html	*The Globe and Mail* online http://www.globeandmail.com
The Webopedia dictionary http://www.pcwebopaedia.com	*Maclean's* online http://www.macleans.ca
The Computer User High Tech Dictionary http://www.computeruser.com/resources/dictionary/dictionary.html	The *National Post* online http://www.nationalpost.com
The WWW Virtual Library http://www.vlib.org	*The New York Times* on the Web http://www.nyt.com
Free Satellite Mapping Software http://earth.google.com	*The Wall Street Journal* Interactive Edition http://www.wsj.com

TABLE 21.2
Sources for Web Research (continued)

Canadian Government Information

Statistics Canada
http://www.statcan.ca

Most recent five years of data, constantly updated
http://www40.statcan.ca/ol/esto1/

The Daily News, with analytical summaries of current StatsCan info
http://www.statcan.ca/menu-en.htm

Profile of Canadian Communities: tables for more than 5000 Canadian communities from most recent census, with the ability to create local base maps
http://www12.statcan.ca/english/census01/home/index.cfm

Download more than 100 publications free
http://www.statcan.ca/cgi-bin/downpub/freepub.cgi

Canadian historical statistics
http://www.statcan.ca/bsolc/english/bsolc?catno=11-516-X&CHROPG=1

Canada's online homepage
http://www.canadaspace.com/canadian-media.html

CBC Radio
http://cbc.ca/programguide/

Reference Collections

Britannica Online
http://www.eb.com

CEO Express
http://www.ceoexpress.com

Hoover's Online (information on more than 13 000 public and private companies worldwide)
http://www.hoovers.com/free/

Topica (mailing lists)
http://www.topica.com

Reference Desk
http://www.refdesk.com

Web directory, business resource and reference dictionary
http://www.reference.com/

Web addresses may change. For links to the current URLs, see the Web site for this book at http://www.mcgrawhill.ca/olc/locker.

TABLE 21.3
Print Sources for Research

Indexes:
    Accountants' Index
    Business Periodicals Index
    Canadian Business Index
    Hospital Literature Index
    Personnel Management Abstracts

Facts, figures, and forecasts (also check the Web):
    Canada Year Book
    Almanac of Business and Industrial Financial Ratios

Moody's Manuals
The Statistical Abstract of the U.S.

Canadian Census reports (also available on the Web):
    Census of Manufacturers
    Census of Retail Trade

International business and government:
    Dun and Bradstreet's Principal International Businesses
    European Marketing Data and Statistics
    Statistical Yearbook of the United Nations

■ How do I write questions for surveys and interviews?

Test your questions to make sure they're clear and neutral.

SEE THE OLC!

Quebec English Schools Network: Web Scavenger Hunts

A **survey** questions a large group of people, called **respondents** or **subjects**. The easiest way to ask many questions is to create a **questionnaire**, a written list of questions that people respond to. Page 415 ◀▶ Module 22 shows an example of a questionnaire. An **interview** is a structured conversation with someone who is able to give you useful information. However, surveys and interviews are useful only if the questions are well designed.

SEE THE OLC!

Evaluating Internet Information

Although survey and interview queries are based on your ideas and a theory—or *working thesis*—it's important to phrase questions in a way that won't lead the respondent to the answer you want, or bias the response. Remember that people tend to answer only the questions they are asked. Poor questions yield poor data.

Phrase questions clearly. Use words that mean the same thing to your respondents as they do to you. Whenever you can, use concrete, quantitative, measurable language. Words like *important* and *often* are open to anyone's interpretation.

> **Vague:** Do you use the Web often?

> **Better:** How many hours a week do you spend on the Web?

Avoid questions that make assumptions about your subjects, unless you are seeking to qualify your respondents. The question "Does your spouse have a job outside the home?" assumes that the respondent is married.

Closed questions—those questions to which people can answer only *yes* or *no*—limit information. **Open questions**—the journalism or "W" questions (*what, who, why, where, when, how*)—encourage information and do not lock the subject into any sort of response. Figure 21.2 gives examples of closed and open questions. Closed questions are faster for

FIGURE 21.2
Closed and Open Questions

Closed Questions

Are you satisfied with the city bus service? (yes/no)

How good is the city bus service?
    Excellent   5   4   3   2   1   Terrible

Indicate whether you agree or disagree with each of the following statements about city bus service:

    A   D   The schedule is convenient for me.

    A   D   The routes are convenient for me.

    A   D   The drivers are courteous.

    A   D   The buses are clean.

Rate each of the following improvements in the order of their importance to you (1 = most important, 6 = least important)

_____ Buy new buses.

_____ Increase non-rush-hour service on weekdays.

_____ Increase service on weekdays.

_____ Provide earlier and later service on weekdays.

_____ Buy more buses with wheelchair access.

_____ Provide unlimited free transfers.

Open Questions

How do you feel about the city bus service?

Tell me about the city bus service.

Why do you ride the bus? (or, Why don't you ride the bus?)

What do you like and dislike about the city bus service?

How could the city bus service be improved?

subjects to answer and easier for researchers to score. However, since all answers must fit into chosen categories, closed questions cannot probe the complexities of a subject. You can improve the quality of closed questions by conducting a pretest with open questions to find categories that matter to respondents.

When you use multiple-choice questions, make sure that only one answer fits in any one category. In the following example of overlapping categories, a person who worked for a company with exactly 25 employees could check either *a* or *b*. The resulting data would be unreliable.

Overlapping categories:	Indicate the number of full-time employees in your company on **May 16:**

        __a. 0–25
        __b. 25–100
        __c. 100–500
        __d. more than 500

Discrete categories:	Indicate the number of full-time employees in your company on **May 16:**

        __a. 0–25
        __b. 26–100
        __c. 101–500
        __d. more than 500

Branching questions direct different respondents to different parts of the questionnaire based on their answers to earlier questions.

10. Have you talked to an academic advisor this year?
    yes _____ no _____
    (if "no," skip to question 14.)

Use closed, multiple-choice questions for potentially embarrassing topics (for example: Formal education: (a) high school, (b) college diploma, (c) university undergraduate degree, (d) graduate degree). Seeing their own situation listed as one response can help respondents feel that it is acceptable. However, very sensitive issues are perhaps better asked in an

Poor questions yield poor data.

Source: Tribune Media Services, Inc. All rights reserved. Printed with Permission.

EXPANDING A CRITICAL SKILL

Using the Internet for Research

Most research projects today include the Internet. However, don't rely solely on the Internet for research. Powerful as it is, the Internet is just one tool. Your public or school library, experts in your company, journals and newspapers, and even information in your files are other tools that you can use.

Finding Web Pages

Use root words to find variations. A root word such as stock followed by the plus sign (*stock+*) will yield *stock*, *stocks*, *stockmarket*, and so forth.

Use quotation marks for exact terms. If you want only sites that use the term "business communication," put quotes around the term.

Uncapitalize words. Capitalizing words limits your search to sites where the word itself is capitalized; if the word doesn't have to be capitalized, don't.

Some search engines group related sites based on keywords. Look for these links at the top of your search engine.

If you get a broken or dead link, try shortening the URL. For example, if http://www.mirror.com/newinfo/index.html no longer exists, try http://www.mirror.com. Then check the site map to see whether it has the page you want.

Evaluating Web Pages

Anyone can post a Web site, and no one checks the information for accuracy or truthfulness. By contrast, many print sources, especially academic journals, have an editorial board that reviews manuscripts for accuracy and truthfulness. The review process helps ensure that information meets high standards.

For a list of Web sites about evaluating information, see http://www.vuw.ac.nz/staff/alastair_smith/evaln/evaln.htm.

Use reputable sources. Start with sites produced by universities and established companies or organizations. Be aware, however, that such organizations are not going to post information that makes them look bad. To get the other side of the story, you may need to monitor bulletin boards and email lists or access pages critical of the organization. (Search for "consumer opinion" and the name of the organization.)

Look for an author. Do individuals take "ownership" of the information? What are their credentials? How can you contact them with questions? Remember that ".edu" sites could be from students not yet experts on a subject.

Check the date. How relevant is the information?

Check the source. Is the information adapted from other sources? If so, try to get the original.

Compare the information with other sources. Internet sources should complement print sources. When facts are correct, you'll likely find them recorded elsewhere.

Citing Web Pages

Your professional credibility depends on your giving credit to your sources. To demonstrate your research skills and your professional and ethical worth, you:

Must identify where you got any information that does not belong to you. Internet information may be fast and free, but copyright law covers it. Using facts, figures, words, opinions, commentary, ideas—any concept that is new to you, that is not general knowledge, or that you do not discover for yourself—does not belong to you. Cite it.

Are ethically responsible for crediting others' ideas, facts, figures and words. Failure to do so, even unintentionally, can damage your reputation.

Are legally liable for giving credit. All universities and colleges articulate their policies on plagiarism. Most include expulsion for the offence. In business, you can be sued for damages and revenue, as Research in Motion's court battles illustrated. (Find out more about citing and document sources at http://library.ucalgary.ca/subjectpages/science&engineering/science&technology-general/citingsources.php).

interview, where interviewers can build trust and reveal information about themselves to encourage the interviewee to answer.

Put questions that will be easy to answer (like gender or program of study) early in the questionnaire. Put questions that are harder to answer, or that people may be less willing to answer (e.g., age and income) near the end of the questionnaire. Even if people choose not to answer such questions, you'll still have the rest of the survey filled out. (◁▮▶ Module 22, page 415.)

Pay careful attention to the physical design of the document. Use indentations and white space effectively; make it easy to mark and score the answers. Include a brief statement of purpose if you (or someone else) will not be available to explain the questionnaire, or answer questions. Pretest the questionnaire to make sure the directions are clear. One researcher handed out a double-sided questionnaire without testing it and fifty percent of respondents answered only the questions on the first side.[1]

■ How do I decide whom to survey or interview?

Use a random sample for surveys, if time and money permit.
Use a judgment sample for interviews.

The **population** is the group you want to make statements about. Depending on the purpose of your research, your population might be all *Report on Business* Top 1000 companies, all business students at your college or university, or all consumers.

Defining your population correctly is crucial to getting useful information. For example, Microscan wanted its sales force to interview "customer defectors." At first, salespeople assumed that a "defector" was a former customer who no longer bought anything at all. By that definition, very few defectors existed. But then the term was redefined as customers who had stopped buying *some* products and services. By this definition, quite a few defectors existed. And the fact that each of them had turned to a competitor for some of what they used to buy from Microscan showed that improvements—and improved profits—were possible.[2]

FYI

Canadians now spend 12.7 hours a week online, more time than they spend listening to the radio. Young Canadians between the ages of 18 and 34 now spend more time online than they do watching television.

Source: Simon Avery, "Calling and Clicking Like Never Before," *The Globe and Mail*, August 10, 2005, A1 and A7.

Because it is not feasible to survey everyone, you select a **sample**. If you take a true random sample, you can generalize your findings to the whole population from which your sample comes. In a **random sample**, each person in the population theoretically has an equal chance of being chosen. When people say they did something *randomly* they often mean *without conscious bias*. However, unconscious bias always exists. Someone passing out surveys in front of the library will be more likely to approach people who seem friendly, and less likely to ask people who seem intimidating, in a hurry, much older or younger, or of a different race, class, or sex. True random samples rely on random digit tables generated by computers and published in statistics texts and books such as *A Million Random Digits*.

A **convenience sample** is a group of respondents who are easy to reach: students who walk through the student centre, people at a shopping mall, workers in your own unit. Convenience samples are useful for a rough pretest of a questionnaire. However, you cannot generalize from a convenience sample to a larger group.

A **judgment sample** is a group of people whose views seem useful. Someone interested in surveying the kinds of writing done on campus might ask each department for the name of a faculty member who cares about writing, and then send surveys to those people. Judgment samples are often good for interviews, where your purpose is to talk to someone whose views are worth hearing.

How should I analyze the information I've collected?

Look for answers to your research questions, patterns, and emerging stories.

As you analyze your data, look for answers to your research questions and for interesting nuggets that may not have been part of your original questions but that emerge from the data. Such stories can be more convincing in reports and oral presentations than pages of computer printouts.

Understanding the Source of the Data

SEE THE OLC!

The bookmarks manager service that gives you access to your favourites from anywhere, and links you with others' bookmarks

If your report is based on secondary data from library and online research, look at the sample, the sample size, and the exact wording of questions to see what the data actually measure. Some studies bias results by limiting the alternatives. In one survey, 90 percent of students surveyed by Levi Strauss & Co. said Levi's 501 jeans would be the most popular clothes that year. But Levi's was the only brand of jeans on the list of choices.[3]

Identify the assumptions used in analyzing the data. When studies contradict each other, the explanation sometimes lies in the assumptions. For example, a study finding disposable diapers better for the environment than cloth diapers assumed that a cloth diaper lasted for 92.5 uses. Further research found that cloth diapers lasted for 167 uses.[4]

SEE THE OLC!

A Beginner's Guide to assessing online resources

Evaluating online sources, especially Web pages, is absolutely vital, since anyone can post pages on the Web, or contribute comments to chat rooms. Check the identity of the writer: is he or she considered an expert? Can you find at least one source printed in a credible newspaper or journal that agrees with the Web page? If a comment appeared in chat rooms, did others in the room support the claim? Does the chat room include people who could be expected to be unbiased and knowledgeable? To expand your critical thinking and bolster your research, evaluate your sources and seek alternative views.

Analyzing Quantitative Data

Many reports analyze numbers—either numbers from databases and sources or numbers from a survey you have conducted.

If you've conducted a survey, your first step is to transfer the responses on the survey form into numbers. For some categories, you'll assign numbers arbitrarily. For example, you might record men as "1" and women as "2"—or vice versa. Such assignments don't matter, as long as you're consistent throughout your project. In these cases, you can report the number and percentage of men and women who responded to your survey, but you can't do anything else with the numbers.

When you have numbers for salaries or other figures, start by figuring the average, or mean, the median, and the range. The **average** or **mean** is calculated by adding up all the figures and dividing by the number of samples. The **median** is the number that is exactly in the middle. When you have an odd number of observations, the median will be the middle number. When you have an even number, the median will be the average of the two numbers in the centre. The **range** is the high and low figures for that variable.

Finding the average takes a few more steps when you have different kinds of data. For example, it's common to ask respondents whether they find a feature "very important," "somewhat

SEE THE OLC!

A checklist for evaluating sources

important," or "not important." You might code "very important" as "3," "somewhat important" as "2," and "not important" as "1." To find the average in this kind of data,

1. Multiply the code for each response by the number of people who gave that response.
2. Add up the figures.
3. Divide by the total number of people responding to the question.

For example, suppose you have surveyed 50 people about the features they want in a proposed apartment complex.

The average gives an easy way to compare various features. If a party room averages 2.3 while extra parking for guests is 2.5, you know that your respondents would find extra parking more important than a party room. You can now arrange the factors in order of importance:

"How Important Is Each Factor to You in Choosing an Apartment?"

$n = 50$; 3 = "Very Important"

Extra parking for guests	2.5
Party room	2.3
Pool	2.2
Convenient to bus line	2.0

Often it's useful to simplify numerical data: round it off and combine similar elements. Then you can see that one number is about 2.5 times another. Charting can also help you see patterns in your data. Look at the raw data as well as at percentages. For example, a 50 percent increase in shoplifting incidents sounds alarming—but an increase from two to three shoplifting incidents sounds well within normal variation.

INSTANT REPLAY

Analyzing Numbers

The **average** or **mean** is calculated by adding up all the figures and dividing by the number of samples. The **median** is the number that is exactly in the middle. The **range** is the high and low figures for that variable.

■ Analyzing Qualitative Data

If your data include words, try to find out what the words mean to the people who said them. Respondents to Whirlpool's survey of 180 000 households said that they wanted "clean refrigerators." After asking more questions, Whirlpool found that what people really wanted were refrigerators that looked clean, so the company developed models with textured fronts and sides to hide fingerprints.[5] Also, try to measure words against numbers. When he researched possible investments, Peter Lynch found that people in mature industries were pessimistic. People in immature industries were optimistic, even when the numbers weren't great.[6]

Look for patterns. If you have library sources, on which points do experts agree? Which disagreements can be explained by early theories or numbers that have now changed? by different interpretations of the same data? by different values and criteria? In your interviews and surveys, what patterns do you see?

- Have things changed over time?
- Does geography account for differences?
- What similarities do you see?
- What differences do you see?
- What confirms your hunches?
- What surprises you?

SEE THE OLC!

Logic and Analytical Thinking Skills

■ Checking Your Logic

Don't confuse causation with correlation. **Causation** means that one thing causes or produces another. **Correlation** means that two things happen at the same time. One might cause the other, but both might be caused by a third.

For example, suppose that you're considering whether to buy cellphones for everyone in your company, and suppose that your surveys show that the people who currently have cellphones are, in general, more productive than people who don't use cellphones. Does having a cellphone lead to higher productivity? Perhaps. But perhaps productive people are more likely to push to get cellphones from company funds, while less productive people are more passive. Perhaps productive people earn more and are more likely to be able to buy their own cellphones if the organization doesn't provide them.

Consciously search for at least three possible causes for each phenomenon you've observed and at least three possible solutions for each problem. The more possibilities you brainstorm, the more likely you are to find good options. In your report, mention all the possibilities; discuss in detail only those that will occur to readers and that you think are the real reasons and the best solutions.

When you have identified patterns that seem to represent the causes of the problem or the best solutions, check these ideas against reality. Can you find support in the quotes or in the numbers? Can you answer counterclaims? If you can, you will be able to present evidence for your argument in a convincing way.

If you can't prove the claim you originally hoped to make, you will need to revisit your working thesis or modify your conclusions to fit your data. Even when your market test is a failure, you can still write a useful report.

- Identify changes that might yield a different result (for example, selling the product at a lower price might enable the company to sell enough units).
- Discuss circumstances that may have affected the results.
- Summarize your negative findings in progress reports to let readers down gradually and to give them a chance to modify the research design.
- Remember that negative results aren't always disappointing to the audience. For example, the people who commissioned a feasibility report may be relieved to have an impartial outsider confirm their suspicions that a project isn't feasible.[7]

How should I document sources?

Business documents use MLA or APA style.

SEE THE OLC!

APA and MLA Documentation

The two most widely used formats for endnotes and bibliographies in reports are those of the American Psychological Association (APA) and the Modern Language Association (MLA). Figures 21.3 and 21.4 show the MLA and APA formats for books, government documents, journal and newspaper articles, online sources, and interviews.

Formatting styles, like language itself, constantly evolve; you can find MLA and APA updates on their respective home pages. User-friendly Web site http://www.easybib.com/ offers free automatic MLA formatting. Users can get the same APA formatting style service for a small fee.

Why should I document my sources?

Citing your sources of information demonstrates your honesty, enhances your credibility, and protects you from charges of plagiarism.

Citation means attributing an idea or fact to its source *in the body of the report.* "According to the 2006 Census..." "Jane Bryant Quinn argues that...." **Documentation**

FIGURE 21.3
MLA Format for Documenting Sources

MLA Format

MLA internal documentation gives the author's last name and page number in parentheses in the text for facts as well as for quotations (Gilsdorf and Leonard 470). If the author's name is used in the sentence, only the page number is given in parentheses. A list of Works Cited gives the full bibliographic citation, arranging the entries alphabetically by the first author's last name.

Works Cited

Web Site
When referencing an entire Web site in MLA style, begin with the name of the author or corporate author and the name of the site in italics.

American Express. *Creating an Effective Business Plan*. 2001. 20 Dec. 2001.
<http://home3.americanexpress.com/smallbusiness/tool/biz_plan/index.asp>. *Put web address in angle brackets. End entry with a period.*

Government Document

Business Development Bank of Canada. *Financing a Small Business*: *A Guide for Women Entrepreneurs*. Ottawa: Industry Canada, 1999.
Omit province or state when city is well known.

Book or Pamphlet with a Corporate Author *Put in square brackets information known to you but not printed in source.*

Citibank. *Indonesia: An Investment Guide*. [Jakarta:] Citibank, 2006. *Date after city and publisher*

Book

Cross, Geoffrey A. *Forming the Collective Mind: A Contextual Exploration of Large-Scale Collaborative Writing in Industry*. Creskill, NJ: Hampton Press, 2001.

Email Message *day month*

DiDomenico, Jennifer. "Comments on Modules 21–30." Email to Kathryn Braun. 8 July 2003. *year*

Posting to an Electronic Mailing List *Date of posting.*

Dietrich, Dan. "Re: Course on Report and Proposal Writing." Online posting. 31 Aug. 2002.
BizCom Discussion Group. 23 Dec. 2001 <bizcom@ebbs.English.vt.edu>. *If discussion group has a Web archive, give the Web address.*

Interview Conducted by the Researcher *Date you accessed posting* *If it doesn't have a Web page, give the email address of the list.*

Drysdale, Andrew. Telephone interview. 12 Apr. 1999.

Article in a Journal *Comma First name first for second author Put quotation marks around title of article.*

Capitalize all major words in titles of articles, books, journals, magazines, and newspapers. Gilsdorf, Jeanette, and Don Leonard. "Big Stuff, Little Stuff: A Decennial Measurement of Executives' and Academics' Reactions to Questionable Usage Elements." *The Journal of Business Communication* 38 (2001): 448–75. *Omit "4" in "475."* *Italicize title of journal, magazine, or newspaper.* *Volume number*

Article from a Publication on the Web

Greengard, Samuel. "Scoring Web Wins." *Business Finance Magazine*. May 2001. 12 July 2001. <http://www.businessfinancemag.com/archives/appfiles/Article.cfm?IssueID=348&ArticleID=13750>. *Don't add any extra hyphens when you break a long Web address.*

Article from an Edited Book

Give authors', editors' names as printed in the source. Killingsworth, M. Jimmie, and Martin Jacobsen. "The Rhetorical Construction of Environmental Risk Narratives in Government and Activist Websites: A Critique." *Narrative and Professional Communication*. Ed. Jane M. Perkins and Nancy Blyler. Stamford, CT: Ablex. 167–77. *Spell out editors' names. Join with "and."*
Give state or province when city is not well known.

Article in a Periodical

McCartney, Scott. "Why a Baseball Superstar's Megacontract Can Be Less Than It Seems." *The Wall Street Journal*, 27 Dec. 2000: B1+. *Use a "plus" when pages are discontinuous*

Government Document Available on the Web from the GPO Access Database

United States. General Accounting Office. *Aviation Security: Terrorist Acts Demonstrate Urgent Need to Improve Security at the Nation's Airports*. Testimony before the Committee on Commerce, Science, and Transportation, U.S. Senate (GAO-01-1162T). 20 Sept. 2001. 20 Dec. 2001 <http://www.gao.gov/new.items/d011162t.pdf>.

FIGURE 21.4
APA Format for Documenting Sources

APA Format

APA internal documentation gives the author's last name and the date of the work in parentheses in the text. A comma separates the author's name from the date (Gilsdorf & Leonard, 2001). The page number is given only for direct quotations (Cross, 2001, p. 74). If the author's name is used in the sentence, only the date is given in parentheses. A list of References gives the full bibliographic citation, arranging the entries alphabetically by the first author's last name.

References

Web Site
Year (period outside parenthesis).
    American Express. (2001). Creating an effective business plan. Retrieved August 31, 2002, from the World Wide Web:http://home3.americanexpress.com/smallbusiness/tool/biz_plan/index.asp
No punctuation after URL

Government Document
    Business Development Bank of Canada. (1999). *Financing a small business: A guide for women entrepreneurs*. Ottawa: Industry Canada.

Book or Pamphlet with a Corporate Author
Put in square brackets information known to you but not printed in document.
    Citibank. (1994). *Indonesia: An investment guide*. [Jakarta:] Author.
Initials only
Indicates that the organization authoring document also published it
Italicize title of book.

Book
    Cross, G. A. (2001). *Forming the collective mind: A contextual exploration of large-scale collaborative writing in industry*. Creskill, NJ: Hampton Press.

comma
last name first
No quotes around title of article

Article in a Periodical
    Gilsdorf, J., & Leonard, D. (2001). Big stuff, little stuff: A decennial measurement of executives' and academics' reactions to questionable usage elements. *Journal of Business Communication, 38*, 439–475.
In titles of articles and books capitalize only
(1)first word,
(2)first word of subtitle,
(3)proper nouns.
Italicize volume.
no "pp." when journal has a volume number
Capitalize all major words in title of journal, magazine, or newspaper.

Article from a Publication on the Web
    Greengard, S. (2001, May). Scoring web wins. *Business Finance Magazine*. p. 37. Retrieved July 12, 2001, from http://www.businessfinancemag.com/archives/appfiles/Article.cfm?IssueID=348&ArticleID=13750

Article in an Edited Book
Ampersands join names of co-authors, co-editors.
    Killingsworth, M. J., & Jacobsen, M. (1999). The rhetorical construction of environmental risk narratives in government and activist websites: A critique. In J. M. Perkins & N. Blyler (Eds.), *Narrative and professional communication* (pp. 167–177). Stamford, CT: Ablex.
Editors before book title
Editors' names have last names last.
Repeat "1" in 177.

Article in a Periodical
    McCartney, S. (2000, December 27). Why a baseball superstar's megacontract can be less than it seems. *The Wall Street Journal*, p. B1, B3.
Give state or province when city is not well known.
Separate discontinuous pages with comma and space.

Government Document Available on the Web from the GPO Access Database
    U.S. General Accounting Office. (2001, September 20.) Aviation security: Terrorist acts demonstrate urgent need to improve security at the nation's airports. Testimony before the Committee on Commerce, Science, and Transportation, U.S. Senate (GAO-01-1162T). Retrieved December 20, 2001, from General Accounting Office Reports Online via GPO Access: http://www.gao.gov/new.items/d011162t.pdf

Email Message
    [Identify email messages in the text as personal communications. Give name of author and as specific a date as possible. Do not list in References.]

Interview Conducted by the Researcher
    [Identify interviews in the text as personal communications. Give name of interviewee and as specific a date as possible. Do not list in References.]

Posting to an Electronic Mailing List
    [Identify messages on electronic mailing lists to which one must subscribe in the text as personal communications. Give name of author and as specific a date as possible. Do not list in References.]

---

means providing the information readers would need to find the original source. Note that citation and documentation are used in addition to quotation marks. If you use the source's exact words, you'll use the name of the person you're citing and quotation marks in the body of the report; you'll indicate the source in parentheses and in a list of *References* or *Works Cited*. If you put the source's idea into your own words, or if you condense or synthesize information, you don't need quotation marks, but you *still need to tell whose idea it is and where you found it.*

Indent long quotations on the left and right to set them off from your text. Indented quotations do not need quotation marks; the indentation shows the reader that the passage is a quotation. Since many readers skip quotations, always summarize the main point of the quotation in a single sentence before the quotation. If the last sentence before the quotation is a complete sentence, end the sentence with a colon, not a period, since it introduces the quotation.

Interrupt a quotation to analyze, clarify, or question it. Use square brackets around words you add or change to clarify the quotation or make it fit the grammar of your sentence. Omit any words in the original source that are not essential for your purposes. Use ellipses (spaced dots) to indicate omissions. Careful observation of these rules shows your ethical and intellectual professionalism.

Employability Skills 2000+

The Conference Board of Canada
Insights You Can Count On

Please see the OLC to preview the key skills from the Conference Board of Canada's Employability Skills 2000+ covered in this module.

Review of Key Points

1. What criteria should you use when deciding to use a Web source?
2. Identify three primary sources of research.
3. Define open and closed questions. Which should you use, when, and why?
4. What are the differences among random, convenience, and judgment samples?

5. What's the difference between causation and correlation?
6. Define citation versus documentation. Give an example of each.

Assignments for Module 21

Questions for Critical Thinking

21.1 Why do you need to know the exact way a question was phrased before using results from the study as evidence?
21.2 How do you decide whether a Web site is an acceptable source for a report?

21.3 Why should you test a questionnaire with a small group of people before you distribute it?
21.4 Why should you look for alternative explanations for your findings?

Exercises and Problems

21.5   Evaluating Survey Questions

Evaluate each of the following questions. Are they acceptable as they stand? If not, how can they be improved?

a. Questionnaire on grocery purchases.
   1. Do you usually shop at the same grocery store?
       a. Yes
       b. No
   2. How much is your average grocery bill?
       a. Under $25
       b. $25-50
       c. $50-100
       d. $100-150
       e. more than $150

b. Survey on technology
   1. Would you generally welcome any technological advancement that allowed information to be sent and received more quickly and in greater quantities than ever before?
   2. Do you think that all people should have free access to all information, or do you think that information should somehow be regulated and monitored?

c. Survey on job skills

How important are the following skills for getting and keeping a professional-level job in Canadian business and industry today?

	Low				High
Ability to communicate	1	2	3	4	5
Leadership ability	1	2	3	4	5
Public presentation skills	1	2	3	4	5
Selling ability	1	2	3	4	5
Teamwork capability	1	2	3	4	5
Writing ability	1	2	3	4	5

21.6   Evaluating Web Sites

Evaluate seven Web sites related to the topic of your report. For each, consider

- Author(s)
- Objectivity
- Information
- Revision date

Based on these criteria, which sites are best for your report? Which are unacceptable? Why?

As your instructor directs,

a. Share your results with a small group of students.
b. Present your results in a memo to your instructor.
c. Present your results to the class in an oral presentation.

21.7   Designing Questions for an Interview or Survey

Submit either a one- to three-page questionnaire or questions for a 20- to 30-minute interview *and* the information listed below for the method you choose.

Questionnaire
1. Purpose(s), goal(s)
2. Subjects (who, why, how many)
3. How and where to be distributed
4. Rationale for order of questions, kinds of questions, wording of questions

Interview
1. Purpose(s), goal(s)
2. Subject (who and why)
3. Proposed site, length of interview
4. Rationale for order of questions, kinds of questions, wording of questions, choice of branching or follow up questions

As your instructor directs,

a. Create questions for a survey on one of the following topics:
- Survey students on your campus about their knowledge of and interest in the programs and activities sponsored by a student organization.
- Survey students about their knowledge and use of campus services, like the counselling, health, career, or tutoring centres.
- Survey workers at a company about what they like and dislike about their jobs.
- Survey people in your community about their willingness to pay more to buy products that use recycled materials and to buy products that are packaged with a minimum of waste.
- Survey students and faculty on your campus about whether adequate parking exists.
- Survey two groups on a topic that interests you.

b. Create questions for an interview on one of the following topics:
- Interview an international student about the form of greetings and farewells, topics of small talk, forms of politeness, festivals and holidays, meals at home, size of families, and roles of family members in his or her county.
- Interview the owner of a small business about the problems the business has, the strategies the owner has already used to increase sales and profits and the success of these strategies, and

the owner's attitudes toward possible changes in product line, decor, marketing, hiring, advertising, and money management.

- Interview someone who has information you need for a report you're writing.

21.8. Reporting your Survey Results*

Together with three of your peers.

- Form a research team and decide on a relevant investigation topic.
- Choose a topic related to your audience's interests and which will elicit interesting and varied responses (tuition fees, transportation to school part-time work, dating trends, career plans, hobbies, gender miscommunication post-secondary choices, quality of teaching)
- Create a survey questionnaire (minimum five questions: see exercise question 21.7) to interview people (20) who would have the information or opinions you seek
- Use closed, open and probe question to provide you with enough data for analysis

As your instructor directs,

a. Using your findings, prepare a short oral report for the class, with headings and topic sentences; arrange your information to reflect the way you want your readers to think about the data. *Introduction: topic/purpose, scope, method (number of people interviewed, who)*
b. Create PowerPoint slides to summarize your qualitative data.
c. Draw conclusions based on your information. *You might want to use your questions as headings throughout the report.* *Conclusion: What did you discover? Why might your audience care?*
d. Use APA in-text citations and end with a Reference page indicating your sources.

*Thanks to Professor Kathryn Voltan, University of Toronto, for adding this exercise.

Polishing Your Prose

Using MLA and APA Style

Persuasion begins with your *credibility*: your audience pays attention to your message when you and your information appear trustworthy. It's vital, therefore, to research thoroughly and cite your sources correctly. Referencing your sources also prevents plagiarism —the conscious or unconscious theft of others' work.

As you research, document your sources immediately; this habit will save you hours of time and labour when you are composing your final copy.

When citing sources, whether using MLA or APA style, attend to the order of the words and the punctuation. For example, when you use a short quotation (39 words or fewer), the sentence period goes outside the parentheses with the page number. In a long indented quotation (40 words or more), the parentheses and the page number follow the period at the end of the sentence.

For details on how to use MLA and APA style, see Figures 21.3 and 21.4 and <http://owl.english. purdue.edu/handouts/research/index.html> and <http://library.concordia.ca/services/citations.html>.

Exercises

Identify and correct the errors in MLA format in the following Works Cited items.

1. Aparita Bhandari, "Workers Bring Culture to their Cubicle," *The Globe and Mail*, p. C1.
2. G. McGovern and Rob Norton, *Content Critical* (FT Prentice Hall: London, 2002).
3. Locker, K. O., Kaczmarek, S. K., and Braun, K. Business Communication: Building Critical Skills. 3nd Canadian ed. McGraw-Hill Ryerson. 2007.
4. Mark Cox, "Business Courtesy Declining, Many Executives Say," Human Resources Professionals Association of Ontario (2004):

http://www.hrpao.org/HRPAO/HRResource
Centre/KnowledgeCentre/newscluster2/
Business+Courtesy+Declining.htm,
retrieved August 30, 2006.

Identify and correct the errors in APA format in the following References items.

5. Catherine Schryer. "Walking a fine line: writing negative letters in an insurance company," Journal of Business and Technical Communication 14 (October 2000): 445-97

6. McClelland S. (2003 July 21) Sugar And Spice No More. Maclean's p. 44-45.

7. Chidley, Joe. Spam-a-lama-ding-dong. Retrieved July 20, 2003 from the world wide web (page 6) http://www.canadianbusiness. com/columns/article.jsp?content!E20030707_5 4772_54772 July 7, 21, 2003. Volume 76 Issue 13.

8. Morgan, G. (1997). Images of Organizations. London, UK. Sage Publications.

9. http://www.scotiabank.com/ScotiaLine for Students. Retrieved July 20, 2005.

10. John Loomis, telephone conversation with author, June 20, 2005.

Check your answers to the odd-numbered exercises on page 573.

Online Learning Centre

Visit the Online Learning Centre at www.mcgrawhill.ca/olc/locker to access module quizzes, a searchable glossary, résumé and letter templates, additional business writing samples, CBC videos, and other learning and study tools.

22 Proposals and Progress Reports

Module Outline

- What is a "report"?

- How do I identify a problem or situation to study?

- What should go into a proposal?

- What should go into a progress report?

Review of Key Points

Assignments for Module 22

**Polishing Your Prose:
Who/Whom and I/Me**

LEARNING OBJECTIVES

After reading and applying the information in Module 22, you'll be able to demonstrate

Knowledge of

- Types of reports
- Sales proposals

Skills to

- Identify relevant problems or situations to study
- Analyze your report's purpose(s) and audience(s)
- Apply appropriate report formats
- Begin to write persuasive and informative reports

The Conference Board of Canada
Insights You Can Count On

Please see the OLC to preview the key skills from the Conference Board of Canada's Employability Skills 2000+ covered in this module.

Reports provide the information that people in organizations need to communicate, plan, and problem solve.

The report-writing process includes several stages:

- Identifying the problem and gathering information
- Analyzing the information and defining or redefining the problem
- Organizing the information
- Writing parts and drafts of the report
- Writing and revising the final copy of the report

For most writers, this process is seldom straightforward: after you've gathered, analyzed, and organized your information, you may need to redefine the problem. Your initial problem definition, or working thesis (◀▶ Module 21), may change as a result of your research findings and analysis.

This module reviews the most common types of reports. ◀▶ Modules 23 and 24 focus on report organization.

What is a "report"?

Any kind of document can be a report.

In some organizations, a report is a long document or a document that contains numerical data. In others, one- and two-page memos are called reports. A proposal to your supervisor in memo format or to a client in letter format is an example of a report. **Formal reports** contain formal elements such as a title page, a transmittal, a table of contents, and a list of illustrations. **Informal reports** may be letters and memos, or even computer printouts of production or sales figures.

Reports can provide information, provide information and analyze it, or provide information and analysis to support a recommendation (see Table 22.1 on page 406). Reports can be called **information reports** if they collect data for the reader, **analytical reports** if they interpret data but do not recommend action, and **recommendation reports** if they recommend action or a solution. Regardless of their purpose, reports should be as concise as possible, to satisfy readers' demands for clarity and brevity.

How do I identify a problem or situation to study?

Pick something real, important, and specific.

Good report problems grow out of real situations: incongruence between reality and the ideal vision, lack of information to make an informed decision, the need to make a choice. When you write a report as part of your job, your role or your supervisor defines the topic. To identify a problem for a class or course report, pick a topic that's important and relevant to you. Consider organizational or communication problems at work. Identify the challenges that the following institutions face: your college or university, campus housing, social, religious, and professional groups on campus and in your city, local businesses, or municipal, city, provincial, or federal governments and their agencies. Read your campus and local papers and newsmagazines, watch the news on TV, or listen to it on the CBC or your local radio station.

FYI

Students who regularly read the newspaper—online or hard copy—expand their grammar, usage, and vocabulary skills while connecting classroom learning to real-world applications. These readers also do better in school.

Source: J.D.M. Stewart, "A Newspaper a Day Keeps Bad Grades at Bay," (September 15, 2005). http://www.workopolis.com/ servlet/Content/fasttrack/ 20050915/COSTEWART15? section=Education, retrieved August 16, 2006.

FIGURE 22.1

TABLE 22.1
Levels of Reports

Reports Can Provide
Information only
• **Incident reports** (health & safety transgressions)
• **Sales reports** (sales figures for the week or month)
• **Quarterly reports** (figures showing a plant's productivity and profits for the quarter)
Information plus analysis
• **Annual reports** (financial data and an organization's accomplishments during the past year)
• **Audit reports** (interpretations of the facts revealed during an audit)
• **Make-good or pay-back reports** (calculations of the point at which a new capital investment will pay for itself)
• **Technical reports** (descriptions of scientific/technical processes)
Information plus analysis plus a recommendation
• **Feasibility reports** evaluate two or more alternatives and recommend which alternative the organization should choose
• **Justification reports** justify the need for a purchase, an investment, a new personnel line, or a change in procedure
• **Problem-solving reports** identify the causes of an organizational problem and recommend a solution

A good report presents a situation or problem that is significant to its writer and audience, and provides evidence to support the analysis, conclusions, and recommendations about that situation.

1. The situation or problem is
   • Real
   • Important
   • Specific
2. The audience for the report is
   • Real
   • Interested in and affected by the information
   • Able to implement recommended action
3. The data, evidence, and facts are
   • Sufficient to document the severity of the problem
   • Sufficient to support the recommendation that will solve the problem
   • Available to *you*
   • Comprehensible to *you*

Often you need to narrow your problem perspective. For example, the topic "improving the college or university experiences of international students studying in Canada" is far too broad. Instead, use the following example to narrow the perspective and find your purpose:

- Choose one college or university.
- Identify the specific situation or problem: what do you want the report to accomplish?
- Identify the specific audience with a vested interest in the situation, or the power to implement your recommendations.

Your purpose statement might then be "Niagara College can attract more international students by increasing the language, housing, cultural, and social choices on campus." Your audience might be the academic vice-president, the Office of International Studies, or a service organization on campus or in town.

Pick a problem you can solve in the time available. Six months of full-time (and overtime) work and a team of colleagues might allow you to look at all the ways to make a store more profitable. If you're producing a report in six to twelve weeks for a class that is only one of your responsibilities, limit the topic. Depending on your interests and knowledge, you could examine the store prices and product styles, its inventory procedures, its overhead costs, its layout and decor, or its advertising budget.

Remember the key tenet of the decision-making process: *How you define the problem shapes the solutions you find.* For example, suppose that a manufacturer of frozen foods isn't making money. If the researcher defines the situation as a marketing problem, he or she may analyze the product's price, image, advertising, and position in the market. But perhaps the real problem is that overhead costs are too high due to poor inventory management, or that an inadequate distribution system does not get the product to its target market. *Defining the problem accurately is essential to finding an effective solution.*

Once you've defined your problem, you're ready to write a purpose statement. The purpose statement—or thesis—goes in both your proposal and your final report. A good **purpose statement** clearly articulates three things:

- The situation, problem, or conflict
- The specific information that must be explored or questions that must be answered to solve the problem or resolve the situation
- The purpose(s) of the report, *expressed as benefits to the audience*

The following purpose statement has all three elements. The report's audience is the Parks Canada Agency, which is responsible for Alberta's Elk Island National Park.

> Current management methods keep the elk population within the carrying capacity of the habitat but require frequent human intervention. Both wildlife conservation specialists and the public would prefer methods that controlled the elk population naturally. This report will compare the current short-term management techniques (hunting, trapping and transporting, and winter-feeding) with two long-term management techniques, habitat modification and the reintroduction of predators. The purpose of this report is to recommend which techniques or combination of techniques would best satisfy the needs of conservationists, hunters, and the public.

To write a good purpose statement, you must identify and analyze the problem and, based on your experience, observation, and research, have some idea of the questions that your report will answer. Note, however, that you can (and should) write a working purpose statement before researching the specific alternatives the report will discuss.

SEE THE OLC!

How to write a funding proposal

▨ What should go into a proposal?

What you're going to do, why, how and when you'll do it, and evidence that you'll do it well should all appear in the proposal.

Proposals suggest a method for finding information or solving a problem.[1] (See Table 22.2.)

TABLE 22.2
Relationship among Situation, Proposal, and Final Report

Company's Current Situation	The Proposal Offers to	The Final Report Will Provide
We don't know whether we should change.	Assess whether change is a good idea.	Insight, recommending whether change is desirable.
We need to/want to change, but we don't know exactly what we need to do.	Develop a plan to achieve the desired goal.	A plan for achieving the desired change.
We need to/want to change, and we know what to do, but we need help doing it.	Implement the plan, increase (or decrease) measurable outcomes.	A record of the implementation and evaluation process.

Source: Adapted from Richard C. Freed, Shervin Freed, and Joseph D. Romano, *Writing Winning Proposals: Your Guide to Landing the Client, Making the Sale, Persuading the Boss* (New York: McGraw-Hill, 1995), p. 21.

Proposals have two goals: to get the project accepted and to get you accepted to do the job. Proposals must stress reader benefits and provide specific supporting details. Attention to details—including good visual impact and proofreading—helps establish your professional image and suggests that you'd give the same care to the project if your proposal were accepted. (See Figure 22.2.)

To write a good proposal, you need to have a clear view of the problem you hope to solve and the kind of research or other action needed to solve it. A proposal must answer the following questions convincingly:

- What problem are you going to solve?
- How are you going to solve it?
- What exactly will you provide?
- How can you deliver what you promise?
- What benefits can you offer?
- When will you complete the work?
- How much will you charge?

Government agencies and companies often issue **requests for proposals,** known as **RFPs.** Follow the RFP exactly when you respond to a proposal. Competitive proposals are often scored by giving points in each category. Evaluators look only under the heads specified in the RFP. If information isn't there, the proposal gets no points in that category.

▨ Proposals for Class Research Projects

A proposal for a student report usually has the following sections:

1. **Controlling statement or summary.** In your first paragraph (no heading), summarize in a sentence or two the topic and purposes of your report.

INSTANT REPLAY

Purpose Statements

A good **purpose statement** makes three things clear:

- The organizational problem or conflict
- The specific technical questions that must be answered to solve the problem
- The rhetorical purpose the report is designed to achieve

FIGURE 22.2
Sample Proposal Letter

commun*icore* inc

242 Balsam Drive Oakville, ON L6J 3X6 905.845.5414
communicore1@cogeco.ca, http://www.communicore.on.ca

February 1, 2006

Sen Lee Chang
President
Tele-Direct Systems
1011 Bloor Street East
Oshawa, ON L1H 7K6

Dear Sen Lee Chang:
Re: **Customer Service Strategies** employee training

Thank you for considering **commun*icore* inc** for your training needs. Based on our conversation last Friday, I am pleased to propose this preliminary outline of the customer service workshop, and to suggest ways to maximize your investment of time and money.

Workshop Overview
The two-day **Customer Service Strategies** workshop focuses on defining and refining the criteria for superb customer service. During the professional development days that you are offering on March 4 and March 5, participants will

❑ Begin with self-assessment and goal-setting exercises
❑ Role-play active listening, strategic questioning and positive feedback techniques
❑ Identify and apply conflict-reducing strategies
❑ Define excellence in customer service attitudes and behaviours
❑ Articulate best practices' attitudes and behaviours as the organizational standard.

Depending on your preference, we can begin at 8:00 or 8:30 am and finish at 3:30 pm, with an hour for lunch.

Methods
Using a variety of interactive exercises—including case analysis, recorded role-play, facilitator and peer performance feedback, and peer and self-assessment—participants apply organizational criteria for excellence, and identify strategies for continuous improvement.

Since customized content maximizes learning transfer, I should like an opportunity to visit your office to observe your service representatives for a few hours before the training dates. This complimentary needs assessment will allow me to gather information about current service practices, and to view your training facilities.

Resources
As we discussed, your employees will need uninterrupted time to review and apply customer service techniques. Because people will be working together, and moving around, we'll need group seating, four to a table, and enough room to comfortable accommodate 16 people.

FIGURE 22.2
Sample Proposal Letter (continued)

You mentioned that the room is equipped with an LCD projector and laptop. Participants will need writing materials. We will also be using the whiteboard, and four flipcharts.

Qualifications
Our facilitators offer over 20 years' training experience, and expertise and accreditation in adult education, business and interpersonal communications, and service training. Please visit our web site http://www.communicore.on.ca for details.

Costs
Regardless of the time involved, the needs assessment is free. The cost for training, including tailoring the materials to participants' experiences, printing and binding of all materials, two-day interactive training facilitation, workshop evaluation, and best practices procedures specific to your organization, is $6000.00 plus GST.

Again, thank you for your interest and consideration. Please call or email me about your proposed employee professional development training, at your convenience.

Sincerely,

Kathryn Hughes
Kathryn Hughes
President

Knowledge workers depend on proposals to sell their ideas and services.

2. **Problem.** What product/service problem exists? What needs to change? What needs to improve? Who needs information? Why? What background is relevant?
3. **Feasibility.** Can a solution be found, given the available resources? How do you know?
4. **Audience.** Who in the organization has the power to implement your recommendation? What secondary audiences might be asked to evaluate your report? What audiences would be affected by your recommendation? Will anyone serve as a gatekeeper, determining whether your report is sent to decision makers? What watchdog audiences might read the report? (◀▶ Module 2.)

For each of these audiences and for your initial audience (your instructor), give the person's name, job title, and business address and answer the following questions:

- What is the audience's major concern or priority?
- What will the audience see as the advantages of your proposal?
- What objections, if any, is the reader likely to have?
- How interested is the audience in the topic of your report?
- How much does the audience know about the topic of your report?
- List any terms, concepts, equations, or assumptions that one or more of your audiences may need to have explained. Briefly identify ways in which your audiences may affect the content, organization, or style of the report.

5. **Topics to investigate.** List the questions and subquestions you will answer in your report, the topics or concepts you will explain, and the aspects of the problem you will discuss. Indicate how deeply you will examine each aspect you plan to treat. Explain your rationale for choosing to discuss some aspects of the problem and not others.
6. **Methods or procedure.** How will you get answers to your questions? Whom will you interview or survey? What published sources will you use? What Web sites will you

consult? (◀▮▶ Module 21). Give the full bibliographic references. Your methods section should clearly indicate where and how you will get the information you need to answer the questions in the topics to investigate section.

7. **Qualifications, facilities, resources.** What attitudes, knowledge, and skills qualify you to conduct this study? Do you work in the organization? Do you have a contact or source for information? What's your professional or personal interest? How has your education prepared you for the investigation? Do you have access to the resources you will need to conduct your research (computer, books, etc.)? Where will you turn for help if you hit an unexpected snag? You'll be more convincing if you have already scheduled an interview, checked out books, or perused online sources.

8. **Work schedule.** List both the total time you plan to spend on and the date when you expect to finish each of the following activities:

   - Gathering information
   - Analyzing information
   - Preparing the progress report
   - Organizing information
   - Writing the draft
   - Revising the draft
   - Preparing the visuals
   - Editing the draft
   - Proofreading the report

   Answer these questions either in a chart or in a calendar. A good schedule provides realistic estimates for each activity, allows time for unexpected snags, and indicates that you can manage a project and complete the work on time.

9. **Close or call to action.** In your final paragraph, indicate that you'd welcome any suggestions your instructor may have for improving the research plan. Ask your instructor to approve your proposal so that you can begin work on your report. Provide a contact number or email address for confirmation.

Figure 22.3, starting on the next page, shows a student proposal for a long report using online, library, and survey research.

▮ Sales Proposals

Sales proposals are the most common type of business reports, since writers use them to sell ideas, goods, or services. Because proposals contain a persuasive component, you must convey you-attitude (◀▮▶ Module 6) and demonstrate reader benefits (◀▮▶ Module 8) for everything you offer. Consider using psychological description (p. 139) to make the benefits vivid.

Use language appropriate for your audience. Even if the buyers want a state-of-the-art system, they may not want the level of detail that your staff could provide; they may not understand or appreciate technical jargon (◀▮▶ Module 15).

With long proposals, provide a one-page cover letter. Organize the cover letter in this way:

1. Catch the reader's attention and summarize up to three major benefits you offer.
2. Discuss each of the major benefits in the order in which you mention them in the first paragraph.
3. Deal with any objections or concerns the reader may have.
4. Mention other benefits briefly.
5. Ask the reader to approve your proposal and provide a reason for acting promptly.

SEE THE OLC!

Royal Bank: Tips on Writing a Business Plan

FIGURE 22.3

Proposal for a Student Report Using Online, Library, and Survey Research

October 15, 2007

To: Kathryn Braun

From: Natalie M. Rogal *NMR*

Subject: Proposal to Write a Report Recommending the Best Summer Co-op Program for FFI Health
           Services

In subject line ① indicate that this is a proposal ② specify the kind of report ③ specify the topic

Summarize topic and purposes of report. Many companies use summer co-op programs to recruit and "try out" students who will eventually become permanent employees. FFI Health Services does not have such a program. It is interested in creating a program that will attract quality applicants. Using survey data, materials available on campus and on the Web, and my own experience, I will design a co-op program that will meet FFI's needs.

Background on FFI Health Services   *Background gives your reader information needed to understand the problem.*

FFI Health Services is a small prescription benefit management company based in Edmonton, Alberta. Started five years ago with only two employees, it has experienced explosive growth. It now has 43 employees in the Edmonton office and seven in Surrey, British Columbia. Gross profits this year will be approximately $60 million. One of the founders, Mr. Paul Wutz, sees the company as a sort of "niche player" in the private health care industry. He describes his company as no longer simply providing traditional prescription benefits but rather as being an entrepreneurial marketing company working with pharmacy retailers and manufacturers.

Background on Summer Co-op Programs   *Not all proposals need background sections.*

Student advisors strongly encourage students to pursue co-ops and internships for a variety of reasons, including developing career interests and establishing career goals. The best students aggressively seek co-ops and use their summer experiences to narrow the field of possible employers. Without a co-op program, a company is cutting itself off from some of the most determined and well-rounded undergraduates. Companies can use co-op programs to screen permanent hires. Watching a person for three months gives much more information about a person's work ethic and his or her ability to interact with customers or clients than can any interview. Student workers have proven an excellent resource for filling temporary or special needs. They are positively motivated because the work relates to their educational objectives and career interests.

Current FFI Co-op Situation   *Some problems may need several paragraphs of explanation.*

FFI Health Services does not have a co-op program that would help it attract high-potential undergraduate students. Currently the company conducts national searches for managerial positions and runs classified ads in local papers for lower-level jobs. A co-op program would enable the company to "grow" its own managers.

If "Problem" section is detailed and well-written, you may be able to use it unchanged in your report.

FIGURE 22.3

Proposal for a Student Report Using Online, Library, and Survey Research (continued)

Proposal to Write a Recommendation Report on Co-op Programs
October 15, 2007
Page 2

Feasibility *Convince your instructor that you have a backup plan if your original proposal proves unworkable.*

I expect that my research will enable me to recommend a program for FFI. However, if FFI is unable to fund the kind of program necessary, or if none of the models I can find will work for FFI, I will recommend that the company delay implementing a program until circumstances change.

Audiences *Identify the kinds of audiences and the major concerns or priority of each.*

All of my audiences are at least somewhat interested in the topic of my report. None of them is hostile to it, so I will be able to present information straightforwardly. The topic is not particularly technical, so everyone should be able to understand my report easily.

My primary audience is Mr. Paul Wutz, partner of FFI Health Services, Edmonton, Alberta. He has the power to approve my plan. He describes himself as the Human Resources Department director and is concerned about the time that would be needed for current staff to train and supervise co-op students. Still, he is open to the idea and currently views a co-op program as a kind of philanthropic effort. He also appreciates the fact that I am acting as an outside consultant at no charge to conduct this study for his company.

You are my initial audience. You've told me that you understand co-op programs and are interested in them.

Secondary audiences for my report include the workers at FFI who would train and supervise co-op students, the students who might apply for co-ops, and the campus placement offices who help students find co-op placements. Most of these people would welcome additional co-op programs.

Topics to Investigate *Indicate what you'll discuss briefly and what you'll discuss in more detail. This list should match your audience's concerns.*

I will investigate the following topics in detail:

1. What do students want from the co-op experience?
   - How do students view co-ops? (a chance to get experience? build a résumé? make connections? a way to get a permanent job?)
   - What do interns want from a summer experience?
   - How willing would out-of-province students be to accept co-ops at FFI? (interest in managed health care as a field, willingness to spend the summer in Edmonton)

All items in list must be grammatically parallel. Here, all are questions.

2. What kinds of co-op experiences can the company offer?
   - What resources are available to train, mentor, and supervise students?
   - What interesting, meaningful assignments could the company have them do?
3. What models of co-ops are available?
   - What do co-op students typically do?
   - What features should a program have?
   - What are common problems and how can FFI avoid them?

If it is well-written, "Topics to Investigate" section will become the "Scope" section of the report —with minor revisions.

I will briefly discuss the advantages to students and the company of summer co-ops and how students and co-op programs can be evaluated.

FIGURE 22.3

Proposal for a Student Report Using Online, Library, and Survey Research (continued)

Proposal to Write a Recommendation Report on Co-op Programs
October 15, 2007
Page 3

Indicate any topics relevant to your report that you choose not to discuss.

I do not plan to discuss how the co-op program should be publicized or at what schools the company should focus its recruiting efforts.

Methods

If you're writing a report based on library research, list 10–15 sources that look relevant. Give full bibliographic citations.

If you'll administer a survey or conduct interviews, tell how many subjects you'll have, how you'll choose them, and what you'll ask them.

I expect to get data from three sources: (1) a survey of Athabasca students to learn what features are important to them in a co-op programs; (2) interviews with Mr. Wutz and other workers at FFI to discover the company's needs and resources; and (3) material on co-op programs from the Athabasca Business Placement Office, the Web, and my own experience coordinating a co-op program last summer.

A draft of my survey questions is attached. Ideally, I would like to get a list of business students and send the survey to a random sample of about 200 students (hoping for at least 100 responses). If that is not possible, I will need to use a convenience sample.

Qualifications

Cite knowledge and skills from other classes, jobs, and activities that will will enable you to conduct the research and interpret your data.

As a student in Rhetoric and Composition at Athabasca University with a focus in business writing, I have done much research and writing. I am also employed by a large international law firm for which I do administrative and analytical work. Last summer I coordinated and evaluated the summer co-op program. I am familiar with strategies involved in organizing and maintaining a co-op program.

Work Schedule

The following schedule will enable me to complete the report by the due date.

Activity	Total Time	Completion Date
Gathering information	25 hours	Nov. 12
Analyzing information	10 hours	Nov. 19
Preparing the progress report	3 hours	Oct. 26
Organizing information	5 hours	Nov. 21
Writing the draft/Drafting visuals	15 hours	Nov. 29
Revising draft and visuals	12 hours	Dec. 5
Editing	7 hours	Dec. 8
Proofreading	3 hours	Dec. 10

Time needed will depend on the length and topic of the report, your knowledge of the topic, and your writing skills.

Allow plenty of time! Good

Final paragraph signals close and makes it easy for the reader to contact the writer

Good reports need good revision, editing, and proofreading as well as good research.

Could we set up a conference to discuss my proposal and survey draft? I would welcome any suggestions you may have for improving the research plan or making the report better. Please email me (rogaln@athabascau.ca) to let me know if you approve this proposal so that I can begin work on my report.

It's tactful to indicate you'll accept suggestions. End on a positive note.

FIGURE 22.3

Proposal for a Student Report Using Online, Library, and Survey Research (continued)

In your introductory paragraph,
① tell how to return the survey   **Survey on Co-op Programs**
② tell how the information will be used

Please answer the following questions and return the completed survey to the person who gave it to you. All information will be confidential and used only for a class project examining the feasibility of establishing a co-op program for a particular business.

1. Major/Program _____

2. Rank: First year _____
          Second year _____
          Third year _____
          Fourth year _____ .

Start with easy-to-answer questions

3. How important it is to you to have one or more co-op placements before you graduate?
   ___ Very important
   ___ Somewhat important
   ___ Not important

Put directions in parentheses to separate them from the question itself.

Branch questions allow readers to skip questions.

4. Did you have a co-op placement last summer?
   ___ Yes   ___ No (Skip to Question 6.)

5. What were the most beneficial aspects of your co-op? (Check all that apply.)
   ___ Work related to my major
   ___ Likely to get a job offer/got a job offer
   ___ Chance to explore my interests
   ___ Made connections
   ___ Worked with clients
   ___ Looks good on my résumé
   ___ Other (Please explain.)

6. How much money did you make last summer? (Approximate hourly rate, before taxes.)

Give readers information _____ they need to understand your question.

   ❏ Check here if you did not make any money last summer.

7. For next summer, could you afford to take an unpaid co-op placement?
   ___ Yes   ___ No

8. For next summer, could you afford to take a co-op placement paying only the minimum wage?
   ___ Yes   ___ No

9. How important is each of the following criteria in choosing whether to accept a specific co-op?

These abbreviations are OK when you survey skilled readers

	Very impt.	Some impt.	Not impt.
a. Money	❏	❏	❏
b. Prestige of company	❏	❏	❏
c. Location near where you live now	❏	❏	❏
d. Quality of mentoring	❏	❏	❏
e. Building connections	❏	❏	❏
f. Chance of getting a job with that company	❏	❏	❏
g. Gaining experience	❏	❏	❏

Make sure to break up the lines. Leaving an extra space makes it more likely that the respondent will check the right line.

10. How interested are you in a career in managed care?
   ___ Very interested
   ___ Somewhat interested
   ___ Not interested

11. Could you take a job in Edmonton next summer?
   ___ Definitely
   ___ Maybe
   ___ No

12. Have you heard of FFI Health Services?
   ___ Yes
   ___ No

13. I invite any other comments you would like to make regarding co-op placments.

Using columns gets the survey on one side, saving money in copying and eliminating the problem of people missing questions on the back. But it leaves almost no room to write in comments.

Thank you for taking the time to answer this survey. Please return to the person who gave it to you.

Repeat where to turn in or mail completed surveys.

Identifying "Hot Buttons"

When planning your documents and presentations, it's crucial to identify your audience's "hot buttons." Hot buttons are the issues that evoke a strong emotional response in your audience. It's a mistake to assume that people will be motivated by the same arguments that would convince you, or that people will embrace change because the change would improve their lives. Hot buttons cause people to make decisions that appear illogical or irrational, unless you understand the decision-makers' real priorities.

For example, a phone company lost a $36-million sale to a university because it did not investigate the university's priorities. The company assumed the university's priority would be cost. However, because the university wanted a state-of-the-art system, it accepted a competitor's higher bid.

Meeting people's emotional needs is more compelling than providing logical evidence. When electricity was introduced in a Cape Breton village in the 1930's, it was a non-starter. People were not motivated to pay for something they didn't need to change. They had always done chores by hand and kept warm with firewood. "The electricity lines languished at the entrance to the village and people's lives went on as before."

However, the lure of radio technology changed attitudes overnight. Radio brought entertainment, company, and important weather information. The need to own a radio, and the status such ownership conferred, converted Cape Bretoners to electricity.

Status and power remain hot buttons for many. How else to explain the continued popularity of gas-guzzling SUVs and Hummers? However, today's compelling hot button issues include Canadian culture, alternative energy sources, ethical decision-making, boards' and individuals' accountability, sustainable development, and eco-friendly products and services. These hot buttons spark positive press and economic support, as the launch of The University of Toronto's BikeChain proves. The U of T's Sustainability Office venture, "a free, self-help bike repair shop and resource centre on campus," is modelled on the University of British Columbia's program. Expert student mechanics "...will be on standby every weekday afternoon...[to] fix flat tires, change brake pads, clean chains and make minor alignment adjustments." The venture's co-coordinator Carlene Thatcher-Martin's goal is to promote bike riding over car driving, thereby reducing traffic and improving city air quality. The initiative is funded "by a three-year grant of $250,000 from the Toronto Atmospheric Fund, along with additional support from the Eco-Action Project, Environment Canada, Ontario's Ministry of the Environment, and offices and departments within U of T...." University of Toronto's Sustainability Office, with an annual budget of $150,000, joins "...Laval, UBC, Harvard and the University of Michigan," as the only universities "...with environmental watchdog offices..."

Sources: Madelaine Drohan, "Hands Up Those Who Want $100-a-Barrel Oil," *The Globe and Mail*, May 23, 2005, A13; Clive Doucet, "Cultural Lag, A Lethal Drag," *The Globe and Mail*, May 23, 2005, A13; John Gray, "A Higher Calling," *Canadian Business*, August 15–28, pp. 41–43; Carlene Thatcher-Martin, U of T Sustainability Office to Launch Bike Repair Facility in September, September 12, 2005, http://www.environment.utoronto.ca/NewsandEvents/OtherEnviroNews/OtherNewsFolder/BikeChain, retrieved August 16, 2006; Unnati Gandhi, "New Environmental Office Offers Repair Shop, Mechanics to Encourage Cycling," *The Globe and Mail*, A17.

■ Proposals for Funding

If you need money for a new or continuing public service project, you may want to submit a proposal for funding to a foundation, a corporation, a government agency, or a religious agency. In a proposal for funding, stress the needs your project will meet and show how your project helps fulfill the goals of the organization you are asking to fund it. Every funding source has certain priorities; most post lists of the projects they have funded in the past.

◼ Figuring the Budget

A good budget is crucial to making the winning bid. Ask for everything you need to do a quality job. Asking for too little may backfire, leading the funder to think that you don't understand the scope of the project.

Read the RFP to find out what is and isn't fundable. Talk to the program officer and read successful past proposals to find out three things:

- What size projects will the organization fund in theory?
- Does the funder prefer making a few big grants or many smaller grants?
- Does the funder expect you to provide in-kind or matching funds from other sources?

Think about exactly what will be done and who will do it. What will it cost to get that person? What supplies or materials will he or she need? Also think about indirect costs for using office space, about retirement and health benefits and salaries; and about office supplies, administration, and infrastructure.

Detail the specifics of your estimates.

> **Weak:** 75 hours of transcribing interviews $1500
>
> **Better:** 25 hours of interviews; a skilled transcriber can complete an hour of interviews in 3 hours; 75 hours @ $20/hour $1500

Without inflating your costs, give yourself a cushion. For example, if the going rate for skilled transcribers is $20 an hour, but you think you might be able to train someone and pay only $17 an hour, use the higher figure. Then, even if your grant is cut, you'll still be able to do the project well.

◼ What should go into a progress report?

Include what you've done, why it's important, and what you will do next in your progress report.

When you're assigned to a single project that will take a month or more, you'll probably be asked to file one or more progress reports. A progress report assures the funding agency or employer that you're making progress, and allows you and the agency or employer to resolve problems as they arise. Different readers may have different concerns. An instructor may want to know whether you'll have your report in by the due date. A client may be more interested in what you're learning about the problem. Adapt your progress report to meet the needs of the audience.

You can use progress reports to do more than just report progress:

- **Enhance your image.** Provide details about the number of documents you've read, people you've surveyed, or experiments you've conducted to create a picture of a hard-working person doing a thorough job.
- **Float trial balloons.** Explain, "I could continue to do X [what you approved]; I could do Y instead [what I'd like to do now]." The detail in the progress report can help back up your claim. Even if the idea is rejected, you don't lose face because you haven't made a separate issue of the alternative.

SEE THE OLC!

Progress Reports

- **Minimize potential problems.** As you do the work, it may become clear that implementing your recommendations will be difficult. In your regular progress reports, you can alert your boss or the funding agency to the challenges that lie ahead, enabling your audience to prepare psychologically and physically to act on your recommendations.

A study of the progress reports in a large research and development organization found that poor writers tended to focus on what they had done and said very little about the value of their work. Good writers, in contrast, spent less space writing about the details of what they'd done but much more space explaining the value of their work for the organization.[2]

Subject lines for progress reports are straightforward. Specify the project on which you are reporting your progress.

> Subject: Progress on Developing a Marketing Plan for TCBY
>
> Subject: Progress on Group Survey on Campus Parking

If you are submitting weekly or monthly progress reports on a long project, number your progress reports or include the time period in your subject line. Include dates for the work completed since the last report and to be completed before the next report.

Report as positively as you honestly can. You'll build a better image of yourself if you show that you can take minor problems in stride and that you're confident of your own abilities.

Negative:	I have not deviated markedly from my schedule, and I feel that I will have very little trouble completing this report by the due date.
Positive:	I am back on schedule and expect to complete my report by the due date.

Progress reports can be organized in three ways: by chronology, by task, and to support a recommendation.

◼ Chronological Progress Reports

The following pattern of organization focuses on what you have done and what work remains (see Figure 22.4):

1. **Summarize your progress in terms of your goals and your original schedule.** Use measurable statements.

Poor:	My progress has been slow.
Better:	The research for my report is about one-third complete.

2. **Under the heading Work Completed, describe what you have already done.** Be specific, both to support your claims in the first paragraph, and to allow the reader to appreciate your hard work. Acknowledge the people who have helped you. Describe any serious obstacles you've encountered and tell how you've dealt with them.

Poor:	I have found many articles about Procter & Gamble on the Web. I have had a few problems finding how the company keeps employees safe from chemical fumes.
Better:	On the Web, I found Procter & Gamble's home page, its annual report, and mission statement. No one whom I interviewed could tell me about safety

FIGURE 22.4
A Student Chronological Progress Report

October 29, 2007

To: Kitty O. Locker

From: David G. Bunnel *DGB*

Subject: Progress on CAD/CAM Software Feasibility Study for the Architecture Firm, Patrick
         and Associates, Inc.

¶ 1:
*Summarize
results in
terms of
purpose,
schedule.*

I have obtained most of the information necessary to recommend whether CADAM or CATIA is
better for Patrick and Associates, Inc. (P&A). I am currently analyzing and organizing this
information and am on schedule.

Work Completed *Underline Headings
or Bold.*

*Be very
specific
about
what
you've
done.*

To learn how computer literate P&A employees are, I interviewed a judgment sample of five
employees. My interview with Bruce Ratekin, the director of P&A's Computer-Aided Design
(CAD) Department on October 15 enabled me to determine the architectural drafting needs of
the firm. Mr. Ratekin also gave me a basic drawing of a building showing both two- and
three-dimensional views so that I could replicate the drawing with both software packages.

*Show how
you've
overcome
minor
problems.*

I obtained tutorials for both packages to use as a reference while making the drawings. First I
drew the building using CADAM, the package designed primarily for two-dimensional architectural drawings. I encountered problems with the isometric drawing because there was a mistake
in the manual I was using; I fixed the problem by trying alternatives and finally getting help from
another CADAM user. Next, I used CATIA, the package whose strength is three-dimensional
drawings, to construct the drawing. I am in the process of comparing the two packages based
on these criteria: quality of drawing, ease of data entry (lines, points, surfaces, etc.) for
computer experts and novices, and ease of making changes in the completed drawings. Based
on my experience with the packages, I have analyzed the training people with and without
experience in CAD would need to learn to use each package.

*Indicate changes in purpose, scope, or recommendations.
Progress report is a low-risk way to bring the readers on board.*

Work to Be Completed

Making the drawings has shown that neither package can do everything that P&A needs.
Therefore, I want to investigate the feasibility of P&A's buying both packages.

*Specify
the work
that
remains.*

As soon as he is back at work after recovering from an unexpected illness that has kept him out
of the office, I will meet with Tom Sasaki, the CAD systems programmer for Georgian College,
to learn about software expansion flexibility for both packages as well as about the costs for
initial purchase, installation, maintenance, and software updates. After this meeting, I will be
ready to begin the first draft of my report.

Whether I am able to meet my deadline will depend on when I am able to meet with Mr. Sasaki.
Right now, I am on schedule and plan to submit my report by the December 10 deadline.

End on a positive note.

programs specifically at P&G. I have found seven articles about ways to protect workers against pollution in factories, but none mentions P&G.

3. **Under the heading Work to Be Completed, describe the work that remains.** If you're more than three days late (for school projects) or two weeks late (for business projects) submit a new schedule, showing how you will be able to meet the original deadline. You may want to discuss "Observations" or "Preliminary Conclusions" if you want feedback before writing the final report, or if your reader has asked for substantive interim reports.

4. **Either express your confidence in having the report ready by the due date or request a conference to discuss extending the due date or limiting the project.** If you are behind your original schedule, show why you think you can still finish the project on time.

Task Progress Reports

In a task progress report, organize information under the various tasks you have worked on during the period. For example, a task progress report for a group report project might use the following headings:

> Finding Background Information on the Web and in Print
> Analyzing Our Survey Data
> Working on the Introduction of the Report and the Appendices

Under each heading, the group could discuss the tasks it has completed and those that remain.

Recommendation Progress Reports

Recommendation progress reports recommend action: increasing the funding for a project, changing its direction, cancelling a project that isn't working out. When the recommendation will be easy for the reader to accept, use the direct request pattern of organization from Module 13 (◀▶). If the recommendation is likely to meet strong resistance, the problem-solving pattern (◀▶ Module 13) may be more effective.

Employability Skills 2000+

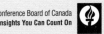

The Conference Board of Canada
Insights You Can Count On

Please see the OLC to preview the key skills from the Conference Board of Canada's Employability Skills 2000+ covered in this module.

Review of Key Points

1. What is the purpose of the information report? The analytical report? The recommendation report?
2. What three elements does a strong purpose statement contain?
3. What six questions does a proposal answer for the reader?
4. What organizational pattern should you follow for a sales proposal?
5. What is an RFP?
6. How does the RFP relate to the organization of the proposal?

Assignments for Module 22

Questions for Critical Thinking

22.1 How can you find your audience's hot buttons?
22.2 What should you do if you have information you want to put in a proposal that the RFP doesn't call for?
22.3 In the budget for a proposal, why isn't it to your advantage to try to ask for the smallest amount of money possible?
22.4 How do you decide whether to write a chronological, task, or recommendation progress report?

Exercises and Problems

22.5 Writing a Proposal for a Student Report

Write a proposal to your instructor to do the research for a formal or informal report. (See Problems 23.5, 23.6, 23.7, 23.8, 24.4, and 24.7.)

The headings and the questions in the section titled "Proposals for Class Research Projects" are your RFP; be sure to answer every question and to use the headings exactly as stated in the RFP. Exception: Where alternative heads are listed, you may choose one, combine the two ("Qualifications and Facilities"), or treat them as separate headings in separate categories.

22.6 Writing a Chronological Progress Report

Write a memo summarizing your progress on your report.

In the introductory paragraph, summarize your progress in terms of your schedule and your goals. Under a heading titled "Work Completed," list what you have already done. (This is a chance to toot your own horn: If you have solved problems creatively, say so! You can also describe obstacles you've encountered that you have not yet solved.) Under "Work to Be Completed," list what you still have to do. If you are more than two days behind the schedule you submitted with your proposal, include a revised schedule, listing the completion dates for the activities that remain.

In your last paragraph, either indicate your confidence in completing the report by the due date or ask for a conference to resolve the problems you are encountering.

As your instructor directs,

Send the email or paper progress report to

a.   The other members of your group
b.   Your instructor

22.7   Writing a Task Progress Report

Write a memo summarizing your progress on your report in terms of its tasks.

As your instructor directs,

Send the email or paper progress report to

a.   The other members of your group
b.   Your instructor

22.8   Writing a Chronological Progress Report for a Group Report

Write a memo to your instructor summarizing your group's progress.

In the introductory paragraph, summarize the group's progress in terms of its goals and its schedule, your own progress on the tasks for which you are responsible, and your feelings about the group's work thus far.

Under a heading titled "Work Completed," list what has already been done. Be most specific about what you have done. Describe briefly the chronology of group activities: number, time, and length of meetings; topics discussed and decisions made at meetings.

If you have solved problems creatively, say so! You can also describe obstacles you've encountered that you

have not yet solved. In this section, you can also comment on problems that the group has faced and whether or not they've been solved. You can comment on things that have gone well and have contributed to the smooth functioning of the group.

Under "Work to be Completed," list what you personally and other group members still have to do. Indicate the schedule for completing the work.

In your last paragraph, either indicate your confidence in completing the report by the due date or ask for a conference to resolve the problems you are encountering.

Polishing Your Prose

Who/Whom and I/Me

Even established writers sometimes get confused about when to use *who* versus *whom* and *I* versus *me*. These pronouns serve different functions in a sentence or part of a sentence.

Use *who* or *I* as the subject of a sentence or clause.

Correct: Who put the file on my desk?
(*Who* did the action, *put*.)

Correct: Keisha and I gave the presentation at our annual meeting.
(Both *Keisha* and *I* did the action, *gave*.)

Correct: Ai-Lan, who just received a Ph.D. in management science, was promoted to vice president.
(*Who* is the subject of the clause "who just received a Ph.D. in management science.")

Use *whom* and *me* as the object of a verb or a preposition.

Correct: Whom did you write the report for?
(*Whom* is the object of the preposition *for*.)

Correct: She recommended Thuy and me for promotions.
(*Me* is an object of the verb *recommended*.)

Though some print sources may use *who* and *whom* interchangeably, stick to the rules until this practice becomes widely acceptable.

If you're not sure whether a pronoun is being used as a subject or object, try substituting *he* or *him*. If *he* would work, the pronoun is a subject. If *him* sounds right, the pronoun is an object.

Correct: He wrote the report.

Correct: I wrote the report for him.

Exercises

Choose the correct word in each set of brackets.

1. Karen and [I/me] visited St. Francis Xavier University last week.

2. For [who/whom] is this letter intended?
3. Dr. Jacobsen, [who/whom] serves on the board of directors, is retiring.
4. Take it from Les and [I/me]: it pays to be prepared in business.
5. [Who/Whom] is the most experienced person on your staff?
6. There was only about an hour for Kelly, Maria, and [I/me] to get to the airport.
7. My supervisor told me the committee will decide [who/whom] gets the promotion.
8. It is the customer for [who/whom] we make our product.
9. Three people at the firm [who/whom] can speak a second language are Van, Chang, and [I/me].
10. Trust [I/me]: it's not a good idea to begin a letter with "To [who/whom] it may concern," even if people frequently do.

Check your answers to the odd-numbered exercises on page 573.

■ Online Learning Centre

Visit the Online Learning Centre at www.mcgrawhill.ca/olc/locker to access module quizzes, a searchable glossary, résumé and letter templates, additional business writing samples, CBC videos, and other learning and study tools.

23 More Short Reports

Module Outline

- How should I organize my report?

- What are the basic strategies for organizing information?

- Should I use the same style for reports as for other business documents?

Review of Key Points

Assignments for Module 23

Polishing Your Prose: Being Concise

LEARNING OBJECTIVES

After reading and applying the information in Module 23, you'll be able to demonstrate

Knowledge of
- Strategies for organizing information
- The criteria for a specific report pattern

Skills to
- Organize information in reports
- Create a good writing style for reports
- Ask good questions on the job

The Conference Board of Canada
Insights You Can Count On

Please see the OLC to preview the key skills from the Conference Board of Canada's Employability Skills 2000+ covered in this module.

P A I B O C

Questions for Analysis

Use the PAIBOC questions to analyze your report's organization and format.

P What are your **purposes** in writing?

A Who is your **audience?** How do members of your audience differ? What audience characteristics are relevant to this particular message?

I What **information** must your message include?

B What reasons or reader **benefits** can you use to support your position?

O What **objections** can you expect your readers to have? What negative elements of your message must you de-emphasize or overcome?

C How will the **context** affect the reader's response? Think about your relationship to the reader, the morale in the organization, the economy, the time of year, and any special circumstances.

Whenever you have a choice, write a short report rather than a long one. Choose to use only the information that your reader needs to make a decision. In today's information-saturated world, every extra word costs you—in credibility and goodwill.

Email has had the most significant impact on why, how, and when we write. Before email, most people's jobs didn't require writing. Now more of us have to write to communicate, and computers have reshaped writing style. Our declining attention spans demand brevity and conciseness. Twenty years ago, the average sentence length in a novel was 20 words; today, sentences consist of seven to 14 words. One-sentence paragraphs, once sparingly used for dramatic effect, are common. And bullet-point writing, a function of Internet communication, telegraphs compact information based on parallelism, a quality that used to characterize poetry. Cyberlanguage isn't just a new vocabulary; it's an intellectual and cultural shift.[1]

Short reports normally use letter or memo format, depending on whether they are written to an external audience or to a reader in your organization.

How should I organize my report?

Identify and assess your purpose for writing—what results do you want?—and the expectations of your readers.

Successful reports are organized according to readers' expectations for that kind of report.

Informative and Closure Reports

An **informative** or **closure report** summarizes completed work or research that does not result in action or recommendation.

Informative reports often include the following elements:

- An *introductory paragraph* summarizing the problems or successes of the project
- A *chronological account* of problem identification, actions, and results
- A *concluding paragraph* with suggestions for later action. In a recommendation report, the recommendations would be based on proof. In contrast, the suggestions in a closure or recommendation report are not proved in detail.

Figure 23.1 on the next page presents this kind of informative report.

Feasibility Reports

Feasibility reports evaluate several alternatives and recommend one of them. (Doing nothing or delaying action can be one of the alternatives.)

Feasibility reports normally open by explaining the decision to be made, listing the alternatives, and explaining the criteria. The body of the report evaluates each alternative according to the criteria. Discussing each alternative separately is better when one alternative is clearly superior, when the criteria interact, and when each alternative is indivisible. If the choice depends on the weight given to each criterion, you may want to discuss each alternative under each criterion.

FIGURE 23.1
An Informative Memo Report

March 27, 2007

To: Kathryn Hughes

From: Sheema Khan

Subject: Self-Evaluation, Group Presentation Performance

First paragraph summarizes completed work

Last Thursday, my team members and I delivered our first multimedia presentation, "Bikes: More Than Just a Ride in the Park." Anthony, Thomas, Ajay, and I worked well together, as was evident by the class reaction to our presentation.

When I had the opportunity to view my performance on video, I was impressed with how much I've improved over last year. Watching the video, however, allowed me to see specific speaking habits I would like to change.

Identifies purpose and scope of the report

Overview of the Team's Success

Chronological background: what was done, by whom, why

Our team chose this topic because it was of interest to all of us, especially Thomas. He rides mountain bikes competitively in the summer and is now president of a board organizing a summer bike-riding camp in memory of his friend Mahon. We all agreed that the topic was relevant to the class because everyone has owned or ridden a bike at least once and could, therefore, find some useful information in our presentation.

Overall our presentation worked well. Of course there were some flaws, but we look forward to refining it and having the chance to present it again at the end of the semester. In general, our group worked well together, our attitudes meshed, and no one tried to dominate or slack off. I felt that each of us brought an important ability to the group presentation:

- ❑ Thomas is very knowledgeable about mountain bike riding and very enthusiastic about sharing that knowledge. You could see it in his delivery: his eye contact, smile, positive manner, and so on.
- ❑ Anthony is very good at organizing information and kept us to predetermined objectives and time lines.
- ❑ Ajay's good ideas and sense of humour inspired us.
- ❑ I contributed the technical and design aspects of the PowerPoint™ presentation.

My Presentation Contribution

Specific details of writer's role in the project

My strengths included taking responsibility for the PowerPoint™ slide show. I took this on because I have confidence in my technical knowledge and design abilities; I knew that I could create a slide show that would include all the other team members' ideas.

FIGURE 23.1
An Informative Memo Report (continued)

As I watched the video of our presentation, I noticed a number of other positives about my performance:

- ❏ I knew the information inside and out. I made sure that before I got up in front of the class and you, I knew every detail in my part. In fact, that's the only way I can feel comfortable presenting: I have to know what I am explaining and why the information is relevant.
- ❏ While watching the video, I also noticed that my eye contact has improved. I made eye contact with members of the audience throughout the room. This was actually the first presentation I have done without holding papers or cue cards in front of my face, or using a lecturn. I wanted to discover if I could relax enough to present to an audience without a sheet of paper to depend on.
- ❏ I also thought my voice modulation had improved. Obviously it's something I can work on, but I felt that my enthusiasm came across in my voice.

Plans for Continuous Improvement

Although my performance was much better than in the past, I need to improve in specific areas, as was evident when I viewed the video:

- ❏ I kept using "umm…" In fact, saying "umm" once or twice is too much, but I think I say it because I get nervous. Or maybe I just say it out of habit. When I watched the video, I noticed that I repeated "umm" two or three times; I was not aware that I had this habit until I watched myself on camera. *Information on problems discovered*
- ❏ Another area I intend to work on is my ability to use my voice for emphasis. I need to make my content more interesting for the listener by varying my volume and rate of speaking.

Plan for subsequent action
I've developed two strategies for change: first, I've asked family members and friends to give me immediate feedback if and when I use vocal interferences—"umm" or "like," for example—in my conversation; secondly, I've begun to record myself reading aloud, trying different tonal inflections. Both these strategies will make me conscious of these habits and enable me to develop a more powerful speaking style.

Summary repeats project's success
In summary, I was pleased with our team effort and with the presentation organization and delivery. By next month, when we have an opportunity to present formally again, my group members and I will be practiced enough to take advantage of our speaking strengths and to eliminate the weaknesses. Although it felt a bit weird to watch myself on video, I learned a great deal about my skills and the areas that I need to build on.

Whether recommendations should come at the beginning or the end of the report depends on the reader. Most readers want the "bottom line" up front. However, if your solution will cost time or money, provide all your evidence before giving the recommendation.

◼ Justification or Analytical Reports

Justification or **analytical reports** recommend or justify a purchase, investment, hire, or change in policy. If your organization has a standard format for justification reports, follow that format. If you can choose your headings and organization, use the *direct*,

Model Formal Reports

FYI

English, with about 500 000 words, has the largest vocabulary of any language. Yet, even educated people use only about 20 000 words in speech and in writing.

Source: http://hypertextbook.com/facts/2001/JohnnyLing.shtml, retrieved August 18, 2006.

How to Write a Business Plan

deductive, or good news pattern (◀▶ Module 13) when your recommendation is easy for your reader to accept:

1. **Indicate what you're asking for and why it's needed.** Since the reader has not asked for the report, you must link your request to organizational goals.
2. **Briefly give the background of the problem or need.**
3. **Explain each of the possible solutions.** For each, give the cost and the advantages and disadvantages.
4. **Summarize the action needed to implement your recommendation.** If several people will be involved, indicate who will do what, and how long each step will take.
5. **Ask for the action you want.**

When the reader is reluctant to grant your request because action will cost time or money, use the *indirect, inductive, or bad news* variation of the problem-solving pattern described in ◀▶ Modules 12 and 13:

1. **Describe the organizational problem (which your request will solve).** Provide specific examples (results) to demonstrate the seriousness of the problem.
2. **Prove that easier or less expensive solutions will not solve the problem.**
3. **Present your solution impersonally.**
4. **Show that the disadvantages of your solution are outweighed by the advantages.**
5. **Summarize the action needed to implement your recommendation.** If several people will be involved, indicate who will do what and how long each step will take.
6. **Ask for the action you want.**

The detail you need to give in a justification report depends on your reader's knowledge of and attitude toward your recommendation and on the corporate culture. Many organizations expect justification reports to be short—only one or two pages. Other organizations may expect longer reports with much more detailed budgets and a full discussion of the problem and each possible solution.

■ What are the basic strategies for organizing information?

Try one of these seven patterns.

Any of these patterns can be used to organize all or part of a report.

1. General to particular or particular to general
2. Comparison or contrast
3. Problem-solution
4. Elimination of alternatives
5. Geographic or spatial
6. Functional
7. Chronological

■ 1. General to Particular or Particular to General

General to particular starts with the problem as it affects the organization, or as it manifests itself in general, and then moves to a discussion of the parts of the problem and solutions to each of these parts. Particular to general starts with the problem as the audience defines it and moves to larger issues of which the problem is a part. Both are useful patterns when you need to redefine the reader's perception of the problem to solve it effectively.

INSTANT REPLAY

Seven Ways to Organize Information

1. General to particular or particular to general
2. Comparison/contrast
3. Problem-solution
4. Elimination of alternatives
5. Geographic or spatial
6. Functional
7. Chronological

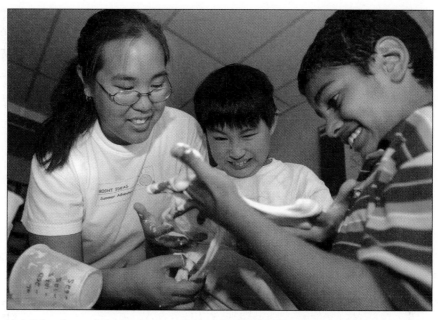

York University psychology major Susan Ngo, 22, launched her successful summer business, Bright Ideas Summer Adventure Camp, with an initial $1500 grant from the Ministry of Economic Development and Trade.

Source: Emily Chung, "Entrepreneurs of Summer," *The Toronto Star*, August 2, 2005, C1.

2. Comparison or Contrast

Comparison or contrast examines each alternative in turn, discussing strengths and weaknesses. Feasibility studies usually use this pattern.

A variation of the divided pattern is the **pro-con pattern**. In this pattern, under each specific heading, give the arguments for and against that alternative.

Whatever information comes second will carry more psychological weight. This pattern is least effective when you want to de-emphasize the disadvantages of a proposed solution, for it does not permit you to bury the disadvantages between neutral or positive material.

3. Problem-Solution

Identify the problem; explain its background or history; discuss its extent and seriousness; identify its causes. Discuss the factors (criteria) that affect the decision. Analyze the advantages and disadvantages of possible solutions. Conclusions and recommendations can go either first or last, depending on the preferences of your reader. This pattern works well when the reader is neutral.

4. Elimination of Alternatives

After discussing the problem and its causes, discuss the impractical solutions first, showing why they will not work. End with the most practical solution. This pattern works well when the solutions the reader is likely to favour will not work, while the solution you recommend is likely to be perceived as expensive, intrusive, or radical.

5. Geographic or Spatial

In a geographic or spatial pattern, you discuss problems and solutions in units by their physical arrangement. Move from office to office, building to building, factory to factory, province to province, region to region, and so on.

A sales report uses a geographic pattern of organization:

> Sales Have Risen in the European Economic Community
> Sales Have Fallen Slightly in Asia
> Sales Are Steady in North America

6. Functional

Functional patterns discuss the problems and solutions of each functional unit. For example, a report on a new plant might divide data into sections on the costs of land and building, on the availability of personnel, on the convenience of raw materials, and so on. A government report might divide data into the different functions an office performed, taking each in turn.

7. Chronological

A chronological report records events in the order in which they happened or are planned to happen. Many progress reports are organized chronologically.

Should I use the same style for reports as for other business documents?

Yes, use the same style with some modifications.

INSTANT REPLAY

Report Style

Reports use the same style as other business documents, with three exceptions:

1. Reports use a more formal style than do many letters and memos.
2. Reports rarely use the word *you*.
3. Reports should be all-inclusive.

The advice about style in ◀▶ Modules 14 and 15 also applies to reports, with these modifications:

1. **Use a more formal style.** Letters and memos are more informal than reports. More formal language follows the rules of grammar closely and generally avoids usages such as parenthetical statements and contractions.
2. **Use the third person; avoid the word** *you***.** In a document to multiple audiences, it will not be clear who *you* is. Instead, use the third person ("first-year accounting students," "nursing graduates," "employees," "managers," "waste management services").
3. **Include in the report all the definitions and documents needed to understand the recommendations.** The multiple audiences for reports include readers who may consult the document months or years from now. Explain acronyms and abbreviations the first time they appear. Explain the history or background of the problem. Add as appendices previous documents on which you have built.

The following points apply to any kind of writing, but they are particularly important in reports:

1. Say what you mean.
2. Keep your writing concise.
3. Use blueprints, transitions, topic sentences, and headings to make your organization clear to your reader.

Let's look at each of these principles as they apply to reports.

1. Say What You Mean

Right word choices result in successful reports, often skimmed by readers who are looking for the bottom line, or who know very little about the subject. Putting the meaning of your sentence in the verbs will help you say what you mean.

Vague: My report revolves around the checkout lines and the methods used to get price checks when the need arises.

Better: My report shows how price checks slow checkout lines and recommends ways to reduce the number of price checks needed.

The right word can give the sentence maximum impact.

Incorrect: The first problem with the incentive program is that middle managers do not use good interpersonal skills in implementing it. For example, the hotel chef openly ridicules the program. As a result, the kitchen staff fear being mocked if they participate in the program.

Better: The first problem with the incentive program is that some middle managers undercut it. For example, the hotel chef openly ridicules the program. As a result, the kitchen staff fear being mocked if they participate in the program.

2. Keep Your Writing Concise

FYI

North Americans' dread of conversational pauses marks our speech patterns. Vocal interferences—"like," "you know," and the all-Canadian "eh?"— and filler words like "basically" create a deadly impression on listeners.

Eliminate unnecessary words, use gerunds and infinitives, combine sentences, and reword sentences to cut the number of words.

Wordy: Campus Jewellers's main objective is to increase sales. Specifically, the objective is to double sales in the next five years by becoming a more successful business.

Better: Campus Jewellers's objective is to double sales in the next five years.

3. Use Blueprints, Transitions, Topic Sentences, and Headings

Blueprints are overviews or forecasts that tell the reader what you will discuss in a section or in the entire report. Make your blueprint easy to read by telling readers how many points they'll be reading, and by numbering them. In the following example, the first sentence in the revised paragraph tells the reader to look for four points; the numbers separate the four points clearly. This overview paragraph also establishes readers' expectations; they now expect to read about tax benefits first and employee benefits last.

Paragraph without numbers: Employee Stock Ownership Programs (ESOPs) have several advantages. They provide tax benefits for the company. ESOPs also create tax benefits for employees and for lenders. They provide a defence against takeovers. In some organizations, productivity increases because workers now have a financial stake in the company's profits. ESOPs are an attractive employee benefit and help the company hire and retain good employees.

Revised paragraph with numbers: Employee Stock Ownership Programs (ESOPs) provide four benefits. First, ESOPs provide tax benefits for the company, its employees, and lenders to the plan. Second, ESOPs help create a defence against takeovers. Third, ESOPs may increase productivity by giving workers a financial stake in the company's profits. Fourth, as an attractive employee benefit, ESOPs help the company hire and retain good employees.

Transition words, phrases, or sentences signal that the discussion is continuing on the same point or shifting points.

There are economic advantages, too.
(Tells the reader that we are still discussing advantages but that we have now moved to economic advantages.)

An alternative to this plan is…
(Tells reader that a second option follows.)

These advantages, however, are found only in A, not in B or C.
(Prepares reader for a shift from A to B and C.)

A **topic sentence** introduces or summarizes the main idea of a paragraph. Readers follow your ideas more easily when each paragraph begins with a topic sentence.

Hard to read (no topic sentence):	Another main use of ice is to keep the fish fresh. Each of the seven kinds of fish served at the restaurant requires 3.78 L twice a day, for a total of 52.9 L. An additional 22.7 L a day are required for the salad bar.
Better (begins with topic sentence):	Seventy-six litres of ice a day are needed to keep food fresh. Of this, the biggest portion (52.9 L) is used to keep the fish fresh. Each of the seven kinds of fish served at the restaurant requires 3.78 L twice a day ($7 \times 7.56 = 52.9$ L). An additional 22.7 L a day are required for the salad bar.

Headings are single words, short phrases, or complete sentences that indicate the topic in each section. The best writers use headings as signposts to the reader, signalling the topics or sections that are coming up next. A heading must cover all the material under it until the next heading. For example, *Cost of Tuition* cannot include the cost of books or of room and board. You can have just one paragraph or several pages under a heading. When you have several pages between headings, consider using subheadings, particularly when you have two or more divisions within a main heading.

Topic headings focus on the structure of the report. As you can see from the following example, topic headings give very little information.

Recommendation
Problem
    Situation 1
    Situation 2
Causes of the Problem
    Background
    Cause 1
    Cause 2
Recommended Solution

EXPANDING A CRITICAL SKILL

Asking Specific and Polite Questions

Learning to ask the right question the right way is a critical skill in both business and interpersonal communications. *Because people tend to answer only the questions we ask*, it's crucial to ask the right questions. Good business communicators use specificity and politeness.

Specificity

Vague questions generate vague or rambling answers. Therefore, make sure you ask the right question for the kind of answer you want. To get a short answer,

- Ask closed questions (◀▶ Module 21):
  Do you prefer flex hours?
- Give simple choices:
  When you work extra hours, would you prefer overtime pay or comp time (the same number of hours off)?
- Ask the real question:
  Not: When do you want to meet?
  But: Which day is best for you to meet?
- Ask for a quantifiable or measurable response, such as facts, dates, statistics, and so forth:
  What percentage of our customers are repeat business?

When you want longer, more qualitative answers, make your question specific enough for your audience to understand what you're asking:

- Use one of the six Ws or journalism questions: *Who*, *what*, *where*, *when*, *why*, or *way* (*how*):
  How would your telecommuting contribute to our bottom line?
- Add concrete language that invites a qualified response:
  What reservations do you have about my proposal? Why do you want to work for this firm?

Politeness

Courtesy is a matter of timing, tone, language, and culture (◀▶ Module 3). Remember that when and how you ask the question is as important as the question itself. To increase your chances of creating goodwill and getting the information you need,

- Time your queries. Pay attention to others' emotional space: people respond to psychological as well as physical space. Don't assault people with questions the moment they arrive or get up to leave. If someone is upset, give him or her time to calm down. Avoid questions when it's obvious someone doesn't want them.
- Keep questions to a minimum. Review all the resources at your disposal first to see whether the answers are there.
- Avoid embarrassing or provocative questions. Even if you are comfortable discussing such issues, don't assume other people are.
- Avoid language that implies doubt, criticism, or suspicion.
  Rude: You don't really think you can handle this project, do you?
  Polite: How do you feel about managing this project?
- Use you-attitude and empathy. Try to look at situations from the other person's point of view, particularly if a conflict is involved.

Because culture affects the rules of politeness—and because culture changes—keep on top of what is and isn't acceptable in society. Remember that different cultures have different concepts of politeness.

Informative or **talking heads**, in contrast, tell the reader what to expect. Informative heads, like those in the examples in this chapter, provide an overview of each section and of the entire report:

Recommended Reformulation for Vibe Bleach
Problems in Maintaining Vibe's Granular Structure
    Solidification during Storage and Transportation
    Customer Complaints about "Blocks" of Vibe in Boxes
Reasons Why Vibe Bleach "Cakes"
    Vibe's Formula
    The Manufacturing Process
    The Chemical Process of Solidification
Modifications Needed to Keep Vibe Flowing Freely

Headings must have **parallel structure** (◀▶ Module 14): they must use the same grammatical structure. Subheads must be parallel to each other but do not necessarily have to be parallel to subheads under other headings.

Employability Skills 2000+

The Conference Board of Canada
Insights You Can Count On

Please see the OLC to preview the key skills from the Conference Board of Canada's Employability Skills 2000+ covered in this module.

Review of Key Points

1. What seven possible patterns of organization can report writers use?
2. What factors influence writers' organizational choices?
3. What are informative or talking headings?

4. What are transitions?
5. What is the indirect variation of the problem-solving report?
6. When would writers use the indirect pattern?

Assignments for Module 23

Questions for Critical Thinking

23.1 Why shouldn't you put all the information you have into a report?
23.2 Why do reports often use a more formal style than other business documents?

23.3 Why should you avoid *you* in reports?
23.4 Why are topic sentences especially useful in reports?

Exercises and Problems

23.5 Explaining "Best Practices"

Write a report describing the "best practices" of a unit or team where you work. Convince your reader that these practices could be adopted by other units in your organization.

23.6 Recommending Action

Write a report recommending an action that your unit or organization should take. Address your report to the person who has the power to approve your recommendation. Possibilities include

- Hiring an additional worker for your department
- Making your organization more employee-friendly

- Making a change that will make the organization more efficient
- Making changes to improve accessibility for customers or employees with disabilities

23.7 Writing up a Survey

Survey two groups of people on a topic that interests you. Possible groups are men and women, people in business and in English programs, younger and older students, students and non-students. Non-random samples are acceptable.

As your instructor directs,

a. Survey 40 to 50 people.
b. Team up with your classmates. Survey 50 to 80 people if your group has two members, 75 to

120 people if it has three members, 100 to 150 people if it has four members, and 125 to 200 people if it has five members.
c. Keep a journal during your group meetings and submit it to your instructor.
d. Write a memo to your instructor. (◀ ▶ Module 18 on working and writing in groups.)

As you conduct your survey, make careful notes about what you do so that you can use this information when you write your report. If you work with a group, record who does what. Use a memo format. Your subject line should be clear. Omit unnecessary words such as "Survey of." Your first paragraph serves as an introduction, but it needs no heading. The rest of the body of your memo could be divided into four sections with the following headings: Purpose, Procedure, Results, and Discussion. Alternatively, make your survey report more interesting by using talking headings.

In your first paragraph, briefly summarize (not necessarily in this order) who conducted the experiment or survey, when it was conducted, where it was conducted, who the subjects were, what your purpose was, and what you found out.

In your **Purpose** section, explain why you conducted the survey. What were you trying to learn? Why did this subject seem interesting or important?

In your **Procedure** section, describe in detail exactly what you did.

In your **Results** section, first tell whether your results supported your hypothesis. Use both visuals and words to explain what your numbers show. (◁|▷ See Module 25 on how to design visuals.) Process your raw data in a way that will be useful to your reader.

In your **Discussion** section, evaluate your survey and discuss the implications of your results. Consider these questions:

1. Do you think a scientifically valid survey would have produced the same results? Why or why not?
2. Were there any sources of bias either in the way the questions were phrased or in the way the subjects were chosen? If you were running the survey again, what changes would you make to eliminate or reduce these sources of bias?
3. Do you think your subjects answered honestly and completely? What factors may have intruded? Is the fact that you did or didn't know them, or that they were or weren't of the same sex, relevant?
4. What causes the phenomenon your results reveal? If several causes together account for the phenomenon, or if it is impossible to be sure of the cause, admit this. Identify possible causes and assess the likelihood of each.
5. What action should the reader take?

The discussion section gives you the opportunity to analyze the significance of your survey. Its insight and originality lift the otherwise well-written memo from the ranks of the merely satisfactory to the ranks of the above average and the excellent.

23.8 Writing a Report Based on Your Knowledge and Experience

Write a report on one of the following topics.

1. What should Canadian managers know about dealing with workers from _____ [you fill in the country or culture]? What factors do and do not motivate people in this group? How do they show respect and deference? Are they used to a strong hierarchy or to an egalitarian setting? Do they normally do one thing at once or many things? How important is clock time and being on time? What factors lead them to respect someone? age? experience? education? technical knowledge? wealth? or what? What conflicts or miscommunications may arise between workers from this culture and other workers due to cultural differences? What cultural norms specific to these workers are similar to English-speaking Canadians? What cultural variation could the organization learn and benefit from?

2. Describe an ethical dilemma encountered by workers in a specific organization. What is the background of the situation? What competing loyalties exist? In the past, how have workers responded? How has the organization responded? Have "whistle-blowers" been rewarded or punished? What could the organization do to foster ethical behaviour?

3. Describe a problem or challenge encountered by an organization where you've worked. Explain why it needed to be solved, who did what to try to solve it, and how successful the efforts were. Possibilities include

   - How the organization is implementing work teams, downsizing, or a change in organizational culture

- How the organization uses email or voicemail, statistical process control, or telecommuting
- How managers deal with stress, make ethical choices, or evaluate subordinates
- How the organization is responding to changing Canadian demographics, the Charter

of Rights and Freedoms' equality guarantee and employees with disabilities, international competition and opportunities, or challenges from dot.com companies

Polishing Your Prose

Being Concise

Being concise in business writing means using only necessary words to make your point, without sacrificing politeness or clarity. Wordy sentences may confuse or slow readers:

Wordy: All of our employees at Haddenfield and Dunne should make themselves available for a seminar meeting on the 5th of August 2007, at 10 o'clock in the morning. Please make sure you come to the conference room on the 2nd Floor of the Main Complex.

Concise: Please plan to attend a seminar at 10 A.M., August 5, 2007, in the Main Complex 2nd Floor conference room.

Being concise does not mean eliminating necessary information. Sometimes you'll have to write longer sentences to be clear.

Nor does being concise mean using short, choppy sentences.

Choppy: We have a new copier. It is in the supply room. Use it during regular hours. After 5 P.M., it will be shut down.

Concise: A new copier is available in the supply room for use before 5 P.M.

Use Concrete Words.
Instead of vague nouns and verbs with strings of modifiers, use specifics.

Vague: The person who drops off packages talked about the subject of how much to charge.

Concrete: The delivery person discussed fees.

Avoid Vague or Empty Modifiers.
Words like *very*, *some*, *many*, *few*, *much*, *kind of/ sort of*, and so forth, usually can be cut.

Cut Redundant Words or Phrases.
Don't say the same thing twice. *Cease* and *desist*, *first* and *foremost*, the *newest* and *latest*, *official company* policy, 24 *storeys tall*, *said out loud*, and *return* the form *back* to me are all redundant.

Avoid Unnecessarily Complex Constructions.
Instead of *the bid that won the contract*, use *the winning bid*.

Stick to Simple Verb Tenses.
Standard edited English prefers them. Instead of "I *have been attending* Royal Roads University" use "I *attend* Royal Roads University." Instead of "By 2007, I *will have completed* my degree" use "I *will graduate* by 2007."

Exercises

Rewrite the following sentences to make them concise.

1. It would be in your best interest to return the order form to us as quickly as possible.
2. Our official records show that you are a very responsible person.
3. The automobile that is blue belongs to the woman in charge of legal affairs.
4. The mainframe computer is located in our subterranean basement.
5. Call us on the telephone if you want to confirm your order.
6. We faxed a reproduced copy of the application on the fax machine.
7. Enclosed along with the rest of this job application letter is a list of references who can talk about my job qualifications because I used to work for them.

8. I enjoyed the presentation very much.
9. To begin with, let me start by telling you some stories about our guest of honour.
10. The guy that runs our advertising department yelled loudly across the parking lot that a delivery truck had left its two headlights on.

Check your answers to the odd-numbered exercises on page 573.

Online Learning Centre

Visit the Online Learning Centre at www.mcgrawhill.ca/olc/locker to access module quizzes, a searchable glossary, résumé and letter templates, additional business writing samples, CBC videos, and other learning and study tools.

MODULE

24 Formal Reports

Module Outline

- What does a formal report look like?
- How should I organize my time?
- How do I create the report?

Review of Key Points

Assignments for Module 24

Polishing Your Prose: Improving Paragraphs

LEARNING OBJECTIVES

After reading and applying the information in Module 24, you'll be able to demonstrate

Knowledge of
- The parts of a formal report

Skills to
- Put together a formal report
- Write an Executive Summary
- Project a professional attitude

The Conference Board of Canada
Insights You Can Count On

Please see the OLC to preview the key skills from the Conference Board of Canada's Employability Skills 2000+ covered in this module.

FIGURE 24.1

P A I B O C

Questions for Analysis

Use the PAIBOC (pronounced "payback") questions to analyze business communication problems:

P What are your **purposes** in writing?

A Who is your **audience?** How do members of your audience differ? What audience characteristics are relevant to this particular message?

I What **information** must your message include?

B What reasons or reader **benefits** can you use to support your position?

O What **objections** can you expect your readers to have? What negative elements of your message must you de-emphasize or overcome?

C How will the **context** affect the reader's response? Think about your relationship to the reader, the morale in the organization, the economy, the time of year, and any special circumstances.

Formal reports are distinguished from informal letter and memo reports by their length, and layout, their additional parts. Because of the "time is money" attitude of North American business, today's report writers write shorter, more informal documents, particularly proposals, rather than formal reports. Although government and scientific discourse communities expect longer, more formal reports, most organizations produce an annual formal report only for shareholders.

What does a formal report look like?

Formal reports are longer, often written in more formal language with illustrations, and begin with an Executive Summary.

A full formal report *may* contain the following components:

- Cover
- Letter or Memo of Transmittal
- Title Page
- Table of Contents
- List of Illustrations
- Executive Summary
- Report Body
  - Introduction (May include subheadings for Purpose and Scope; may also have Limitations, Assumptions, and Methods.)
  - Background/History of the Problem (Serves as a record for later readers of the report.)
  - Body (Presents and interprets data in words and visuals. Analyzes causes of the problem and evaluates possible solutions. Specific headings will depend on the topic of the report.)
  - Conclusion (Summarizes main points of report.)
- Recommendations (Recommends actions to solve the problem. May be combined with Conclusion; may be put before body rather than at the end.)
- Appendices (Provide additional materials that the careful reader may want: transcript of an interview, copies of questionnaires, tallies of all the questions, computer printouts, previous reports.)
- References or Works Cited (Sources of information used in the report.)

I've never written a long document. How should I organize my time?

Swiss-cheese the project: break your research and writing into manageable bites.

To use your time efficiently, think about the parts of the report before you begin writing. Much of the introduction comes from your proposal with only minor revisions: purpose, scope, assumptions, and methods.

The bibliography from your proposal can form the first draft of your references. Save a copy of your questionnaire or interview questions to use as an appendix. As you tally and analyze the data, prepare an appendix summarizing all the responses to your questionnaire, your figures and tables, and a complete list of references.

You can write the title page and the transmittal as soon as you know what your recommendations will be.

Report Writing Resources

Sample Scientific Formal Reports

After you've analyzed your information, write the body and the conclusions and recommendations. Prepare a draft of the table of contents and the list of illustrations. Write the executive summary last. The summary sums up the whole report in brief and goes first in your final copy.

When you write a long report, list all the sections (headings) that your report will have. Mark those that are most important to your reader and your proof, and spend most of your time on them. Write the important sections early. That way, you won't spend all your time on the background or history of the problem. Instead, you'll get to the meat of your report.

How do I create each part of a formal report?

Follow the sections laid out below.

As you read each section below, you may want to turn to the corresponding pages of the long report in Figure 24.2, starting on page 446, to see how the component is set up and how it relates to the total report.

FYI

In addition to annual financial reports, 35 percent of the world's largest corporations also issue environmental reports. "Green reporting" builds good PR, attracts talented employees, and identifies areas for cost savings.

Source: Ann Kolk, "Green Reporting," *Harvard Business Review*, January–February 2000, 15.

Title Page

The title page of a report contains four items: the title of the report, for whom the report is prepared, by whom it is prepared, and the release date.

The title of the report should be as informative as possible.

Poor title: New Office Site

Better title: Why St. John's is the Best Site for the New Info.com Office

In many cases, the title will state the recommendation in the report: "Improving Productivity at Cambridge International: Updating Communications Policies." However, the title should omit the recommendation when the following are true:

- The reader will find the recommendations hard to accept.
- Putting all the recommendations in the title would make it too long.
- The report does not offer recommendations.

If the title does not contain the recommendation, it usually indicates what problem the report tries to solve.

Letter or Memo of Transmittal

Canadian Government Organizations' Reports

Use a *memo* of transmittal if you are a regular employee of the organization for which you prepare the report; use a *letter* if you are not. The transmittal has several purposes: to transmit the report, to orient the reader to the report, and to build a good image of the report and of the writer.

Organize the transmittal in this way:

1. Tell when and by whom the report was authorized and the purpose it was to fulfill.
2. Summarize your conclusions and recommendations.
3. Indicate minor problems you encountered in your investigation and show how you surmounted them. Thank people who helped you.

4. Point out additional research that was necessary, if any.
5. Thank the reader for the opportunity to do the work and offer to answer questions. Even if the report has not been enjoyable to do, expressing satisfaction in doing the project is expected.

■ Table of Contents

In the table of contents, list the headings exactly as they appear in the body of the report. If the report is shorter than 25 pages, list all the headings. In a very long report, list the two or three highest levels of headings.

■ List of Illustrations

Report visuals comprise both tables and figures. **Tables** are words or numbers arranged in rows and columns. **Figures** are everything else: bar graphs, pie graphs, maps, drawings, photographs, computer printouts, and so forth. Tables and figures are numbered independently, so you may have both a "Table 1" and a "Figure 1." In a report with maps and graphs but no other visuals, the visuals are sometimes called "Map 1" and "Graph 1." Whatever you call the illustrations, list them in the order in which they appear in the report; give the name of each visual as well as its number.

See ◀▮▶ Module 25 for information about how to design and label visuals.

■ Executive Summary

An **executive summary** provides an overview of the whole report, including a summary of the recommendations. If your report ends with conclusions, provide the conclusions section in the executive summary. If your report ends with recommendations, put these in the summary.

INSTANT REPLAY

Report Titles
Normally, the title of the report should give the recommendation. Omit the recommendation in three cases:

- The reader will find the recommendations hard to accept.
- Putting all the recommendations in the title would make it too long.
- The report does not offer recommendations.

If the title does not contain the recommendation, it normally indicates what problem the report tries to solve.

> To market life insurance to mid-40s urban professionals, Great North Insurance should advertise in upscale publications and use direct mail.
>
> Network TV and radio are not cost-efficient for reaching this market. This group comprises a small percentage of the prime-time network TV audience and a minority of most radio station listeners. They tend to discard newspapers and general-interest magazines quickly, but many of them keep upscale periodicals for months. Magazines with high percentages of readers in this group include *Architectural Digest*, *Bon Appétit*, *Canadian Home*, *Canadian Gardening*, *Golf Digest*, and *Smithsonian*. Most urban professionals in their mid-40s already shop by mail and respond positively to well-conceived and well-executed direct mail appeals.
>
> Any advertising campaign needs to overcome this group's feeling that they already have the insurance they need. One way to do this would be to encourage them to check the coverage their employers provide and to calculate the cost of their children's expenses through college or university graduation. Insurance plans that provide savings and tax benefits as well as death benefits would also appeal to this target market.

EXPANDING A CRITICAL SKILL

Projecting Professional Attitude

As more Canadians use clothing to reflect their personalities and/or ethnicities, organizations are adopting more flexible dress codes.

Even on dress-down or casual Fridays, however, organizations still expect employees to take care of business. Attention to detail, organization, accuracy, economy, and courtesy are the norm. According to Max Messruer, chairman of Accountemps and author of the best-selling *Job Hunting For Dummies*® (IDG Books Worldwide), what you wear determines others' perceptions of you, and directly affects your career advancement.

On casual days, wear clothes in good condition that are one or two "notches" below what you'd wear on other days. If suits are the norm, choose blazers and slacks or skirts. If blazers and slacks or skirts are the norm, choose sweaters or knit sport shirts; khakis, simple skirts, or dressier jeans; or simple dresses. Wear good shoes and always be well groomed. Avoid anything that's ill-fitting or revealing.

Other symbols also convey professionalism. Your work area, for instance, says a lot about you. If your organization allows employees to personalize their desks or offices with photographs, knickknacks, and posters, don't display so much that you seem frivolous. And never display offensive photos or slogans, even in an attempt to be funny. The same caution goes for screen savers and radio stations. It isn't professional to play a morning "shock jock" who uses coarse language and offensive stereotypes.

If your organization allows employees to listen to music, keep the volume at a reasonable level. If your organization allows, consider wearing headphones.

Avoid playing computer games, surfing the Web inappropriately, or ordering personal items on company time.

These activities are fine on your own clock, but unethical, and in some cases illegal, on the organization's clock. You can be fired for browsing for inappropriate material online.

Keep your voicemail message succinct and professional— find out what co-workers say in theirs.

Keep your desk organized. File papers; keep stacks to a minimum. Throw away anything you don't need. Don't store food in your office. Clean periodically. Water your plants.

The volume of your voice can also disturb others. Although most people wouldn't shout across an office, many of us don't realize how loud our voices can be when we're excited or happy. Keep personal conversations to a minimum, in person and on the phone.

Learn the culture of your organization and fit into it as much as you can. When in doubt, follow the lead of someone the organization respects.

Source: Aparita Bhanadari, "Workers Bring Culture to Their Cubicle," *The Globe and Mail*, September 28, 2005, and Pat Boer, "Business Casual: The New Dress Code," (2005), http://wlb.monster.com/articles/newcode/, retrieved August 18, 2006.

■ Introduction

SEE THE OLC!

A Guide to Writing Technical Formal Reports

The **introduction** of the report contains a statement of purpose and scope, and may include all the following:
- **Purpose.** Identify the organizational problem the report addresses, the technical investigations it summarizes, and the rhetorical purpose (to explain, to recommend).
- **Scope.** Identify the topics the report covers. For example, Company XYZ is losing money on its line of radios. Does the report investigate the quality of the radios? the advertising campaign? the cost of manufacturing? the demand for radios? If the report was authorized to examine only advertising, then readers cannot fault the report for not considering other factors.

- **Limitations.** Limitations make the recommendations less valid or valid only under certain conditions. Limitations usually arise because time or money constraints haven't permitted full research. For example, a campus pizza restaurant considering expanding its menu may not have enough money to take a random sample of students and non-students. Without a random sample, the writer cannot generalize from the sample to the larger population. Many recommendations are valid only for a limited time. For example, a store wants to know what kinds of clothing will appeal to college men. The recommendations will remain in force only for a short time: a year from now, styles and tastes may change.
- **Assumptions.** Assumptions are statements whose truth you assume and that you use to support your conclusions and recommendations. If they are wrong, the conclusion will be wrong too. For example, recommendations about what cars appeal to drivers aged 18 to 34 would be based on assumptions both about gas prices and about the economy. If gas prices radically rose or fell, the kinds of cars young adults wanted would change. If there were a major recession, many people wouldn't be able to buy new cars.
- **Methods.** Tell how you chose the people for a survey, focus groups, or interviews and how, when, and where they were interviewed. Omit methods if your report is based solely on library and online research. Instead, simply cite your sources in the text and document them in the references or works cited section. See ◀▐▷ Module 21 on how to cite and document sources.

Background or History

Although the current audience for the report probably knows the situation, reports are filed and then consulted years later. These later audiences will probably not know the background, although it may be crucial for understanding the options that are possible.

In some cases, the history section may cover many years. For example, a report recommending that a Quebec consortium purchase an Ontario superhighway will probably provide the history of the highway ownership from its construction date, several years before. In other cases, the background or history is much briefer, covering just the immediate situation.

Conclusions and Recommendations

The **conclusions** section sums up the key ideas proven by the facts presented in the body of the report. Present these concluding *insights* as they relate to the report's purpose and audience relevance.

Recommendations identify action items that would solve or partially solve the problem. The way you organize and present the relevant facts in the body of the report should lead the reader to your conclusions and recommendations.

Be sure to number the recommendations to make them easy to discuss. If your readers will find your recommendations expensive, difficult, or controversial, give a brief rationale paragraph after each recommendation. If your recommendations are easy for the audience to accept, simply list them without comments or reasons. The recommendations will also be in the executive summary and perhaps in the title and the transmittal.

FIGURE 24.2
A Long Report

*You may also design
a letterhead for yourself,
especially if you're assuming
that you are doing the report
as a consultant.*

*This letter uses
block format (see Figure 9.2).
Modified block format is
also acceptable.*

1470 Highland Street
Calgary, AB T2G 5N2
December 10, 2007

Mr. Paul Wutz
Vice President
FFI Health Services
127 Street Northwest
Edmonton, AB T5M 1H7

Dear Mr. Wutz:

*In paragraph 1, release the report.
Note when and by whom the report
was authorized. Note the report's purpose.*

Here is the report you authorized in October exploring the kind of co-op
program that might be best for FFI.

FFI Health Services can benefit from establishing a co-op program while providing a
valuable service to students. To establish a co-op program, you should do the following:

*Give
recommendations
or thesis.*

- Use the guidelines suggested by Athabasca University's Professional Experience
  Program.
- Pilot the program, focusing on finance and computer science majors the first
  summer.
- Set co-op salaries at $9–$10 an hour for all majors except computer science.
  Start computer science majors at $15 an hour.
- Survey your staff to find out which employees would like to supervise and
  mentor co-op students.
- Publicize the program on the Web as well as in Athabasca's Career Services
  Centre. Conduct further research on the best way to reach computer science
  majors.
- Conduct further research to identify other colleges and universities that would also
  be good sources of co-op students.

The information for this report came from online and print sources, a survey of 150
Athabasca University's students, and an interview with Mindy Kannard of Career Services at
the Athabasca Faculty of Business. I especially appreciate the guidance of Ms. Kannard and
others involved in the Professional Experience Program.

*Thank
people
who
helped
you.*

Thank the reader for the opportunity to do the research.

Thank you for the opportunity to conduct this research. I appreciate the chance to apply my
experience helping to run a co-op program last summer. If you have any questions about the
material in this report, please call me at 403-555-2443.

Sincerely,

*Offer to answer questions about the report.
Answers would be included in your fee—no extra charge!*

Natalie Rogal

Natalie Rogal

FIGURE 24.2
A Long Report (continued)

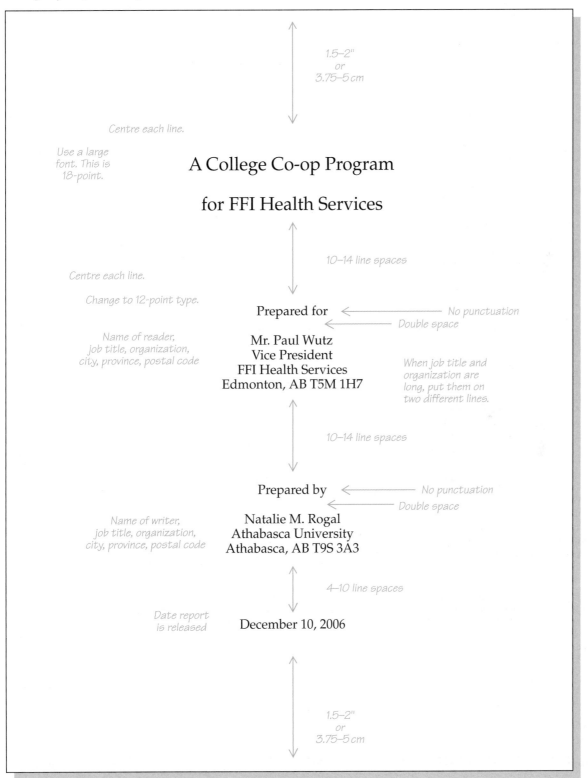

1.5–2"
or
3.75–5 cm

Centre each line.

Use a large
font. This is
18-point.

A College Co-op Program

for FFI Health Services

10–14 line spaces

Centre each line.

Change to 12-point type.

Prepared for ← No punctuation
← Double space

Name of reader,
job title, organization,
city, province, postal code

Mr. Paul Wutz
Vice President
FFI Health Services
Edmonton, AB T5M 1H7

When job title and
organization are
long, put them on
two different lines.

10–14 line spaces

Prepared by ← No punctuation
← Double space

Name of writer,
job title, organization,
city, province, postal code

Natalie M. Rogal
Athabasca University
Athabasca, AB T9S 3A3

4–10 line spaces

Date report
is released

December 10, 2006

1.5–2"
or
3.75–5 cm

FIGURE 24.2
A Long Report (continued)

Table of Contents

Table of Contents does not list itself.

Use lower-case Roman numerals for front matter.

Executive Summary... i

Introduction... 1
  Purpose... 1
  Scope... 1
  Assumptions... 1
  Methodology... 2
  Limitations... 2
  Criteria.. 2

Indent subheads.

Intro begins on page "1".

Background on FFI Health Services.. 2

General Benefits of University Co-op Programs...................................... 3

A Model Co-op Program... 3
  Co-op Duties.. 3
  Program Features.. 4
    Supervising Students.. 5
    Evaluating Students... 5
    Setting Salary.. 5
  Common Problems... 5

Capitalize first letter of each major word in headings.

Making Co-ops Attractive to Athabasca Students.................................... 6
  Providing Good Experience... 6
  Providing Competitive Pay... 7
  Finding a Niche for FFI Co-op Placements.. 7

Conclusions and Recommendations... 8
  1. Choosing Positions for Co-op Students.. 8
  2. Setting Salaries... 8
  3. Choosing Supervisors and Mentors... 8
  4. Publicizing the Program.. 8
  5. Recruiting Students.. 9

Some reports have separate sections for "Conclusions" and "Recommendations"

Appendix A: Raw Survey Data... 10

Appendix B: Responses to Open-Ended Question...................................... 11

References.. 12

Line up at right margin (justify).

Headings or subheadings must be parallel within a section. Here, headings are nouns and noun (gerund) phrases. Questions and complete sentences can also be used.

Add a "List of Illustrations" at the bottom of the Table of Contents or on a separate page if the report has graphs and other visuals. Omit "List of Illustrations" if you have only tables.

FIGURE 24.2
A Long Report (continued)

**A University Co-op Program
for FFI Health Services**

*Report
title*

Executive Summary

Start with recommendations or thesis.

FFI Health Services should create a university co-op program following the model outlined in Athabasca University's Professional Experience Program. Following this program will cover the basics of a sound co-op program and will enable FFI to hire co-op students from Athabasca University.

*Provide
brief
support
for each
recom-
mendation.*

FFI can eventually offer co-ops in eight areas: accounting, computer science, finance, human resources, marketing, social services, transportation logistics, and Web maintenance. FFI does work in each of these areas and could benefit both from the projects that co-op students might complete and from the opportunity to make permanent hires in these areas. In its first year, however, the co-op program should focus on two or three main areas of employment to pilot the program. Finance and computer science are FFI's areas of greatest need.

Since the best students have several options, FFI should offer co-op students a competitive wage. The average co-op student earned between $8 and $10 last summer, so FFI Health Services should set co-op pay at $9–$16 an hour for all majors except computer science. To hire the best computer science majors will require starting salaries of at least $18 an hour. Providing housing would make the co-ops more attractive and would enlarge the pool of applicants.

At least two full-time FFI employees should supervise the students, even during the first summer when there may be only two or three co-op students. FFI will need to conduct internal research to determine how potential supervisors and mentors feel about working closely with co-op students. Acting as a mentor should be a voluntary position to ensure active and enthusiastic guidance for the student.

Participating in the Professional Experience Program will mean that FFI's job descriptions will be available to students who come to Athabasca's Career Services Centre looking for co-ops. However, other kinds of publicity are also desirable so that FFI can have the widest pool of applicants from which to choose. Announcing the co-ops on FFI's Web site is an obvious step and would bring up FFI's co-ops when students do Web searches for "co-ops." Many other companies already give information about co-ops on Web sites. If computer majors remain in such high demand, FFI will need to do something special to attract them. Further research will be needed to determine what kind of niche FFI can develop.

FFI may want to recruit at other postsecondary institutions. More research needs to be done to determine the optimal places for FFI Health Services to recruit students. Since students may not be able to relocate for the summer or may only move if given a substantial pay incentive, recruiting at other Alberta universities may make sense. In addition, it would be useful to identify any university that offers majors in managed care. Such a university would be a good source of students who would be interested in the kind of work FFI does.

*Language in Executive Summary
can come from report. Make sure
any repeated language is well-
written!*

*The Executive Summary
contains the logical skeleton of
the report: the recommendation(s)
and evidence supporting them.*

(i)

FIGURE 24.2
A Long Report (continued)

A running header is optional.
A University Co-op Program for FFI Health Services

*Here, the running head and page numbers
are one point size smaller than the text
used for the body of the report.*

Start with the introduction.

Introduction

*Centre first-level heads. This author
uses bold (one point larger than body).*

Many companies use co-op programs to recruit and "try out" students who will eventually become permanent employees. Co-op placements are so popular that they have increased 37 percent in the last five years (Ferguson, 1998). FFI Health Services is interested in creating a co-op program that will attract quality applicants.

Purpose

Rhetorical purpose

The purpose of this report is to recommend a postsecondary co-op program that will meet FFI's needs.

*Tell what you discuss and how thoroughly you discuss each topic. Scope section
should match report. This section has changed a bit from the proposal because
of the available information.*

Scope

This report focuses on three topics: models of co-ops, Athabasca students' co-op needs, and the kinds of co-op experiences FFI Health Services can offer. Information about models for co-op placements comes largely from Athabasca's Professional Experience Program (PEP). PEP suggests activities for co-op placements and outlines the features for a co-op program. The report also uses anecdotal evidence about common co-op problems and describe how FFI can avoid them.

The report discusses what Athabasca students want from the co-op experience based on a survey of 150 students. The report also covers how students view co-op placements, what students want from a summer experience, and their willingness to accept co-ops at FFI. Finally, based on interviews with staff members, especially Paul Wutz, the report discuss the kinds of co-op experiences FFI can offer.

*Give
topics
in the
order
in which
you'll
discuss
them.*

The report also briefly presents the general advantages of co-op placements and describes how the co-op program could be publicized.

List relevant topics that you will not discuss.

The report does not discuss the financial feasibility of the program or the schools where the company should focus its recruiting efforts.

Assumptions

*Assumptions cannot be proven. But if they are wrong,
the report's recommendation may no longer be valid.*

Report recommendations are based on three assumptions:

*These
ideas could
be
presented in
a paragraph.
But the
list provides
visual variety
and makes
it easier for
the reader
to skim the page.*

- The job market will remain tight, making it difficult to find qualified applicants. The tight job market makes a co-op program especially desirable. If the job market changes so that there are many more applicants than jobs, FFI might be able to hire managers more easily without needed to "grow" its own managers.

- FFI's central office will remain in Edmonton, making it desirable to recruit students from the universities of Edmonton, Calgary, and Lethbridge, as well as Athabasca. If the central office moved, students from other universities might be more desirable than Alberta students as co-op students.

- Athabasca students' preferences regarding co-op placements are typical of students at other universities.

FIGURE 24.2
A Long Report (continued)

If you use only library and online sources, you do not need a "Methodology" section. Instead, briefly describe your sources in a paragraph under "Purpose."

A University Co-op Program for FFI Health Services   Page 2

Even if it focuses on Athabasca's students, FFI will hire co-op students from other universities as well and should investigate preferences at other universities.

Methodology

If you collected original data (surveys, interviews, or observations), tell how you chose whom to study, what kind of a sample you used, and on what date(s) you collected the information.

Information for this report comes from print and online sources, interviews, and a survey of 150 Athabasca University students. on November 20, 2005, at the Student Union during a Career Fair.

Summarize the demographic information about your respondents.

The students who responded represent a wide variety of majors and interests. Two-thirds of the students in the sample were third-year and fourth-year; 32 percent had a co-op placement last summer. (See Appendix A for all the raw data from the survey.) *Refer to your Appendices in the text of your report.*

Limitations

If your report has limitations, state them. Giving the number makes it easier for the reader to read the paragraph.

The report's research has four limitations. First, only students at Athabasca University were surveyed, and FFI will probably want to recruit from other universities as well. Second, at Athabasca, FFI is probably most interested in students from the Colleges of Business and of Engineering, where Computer Science is housed. However, the sample covers a wide variety of colleges and has no engineering students at all. Third, because the survey is based on a convenience sample, we cannot generalize from the survey to all postsecondary students. Indeed, respondents' demographics show that the students surveyed are not representative. The College of Social and Behavioural Sciences has the most undergraduate majors at Athabasca, yet it is not the college with the most students in the sample. Fourth, the survey may have interviewer error, which results from the interviewer answering questions differently for different people. Some respondents asked for clarification on some questions while others did not. Wording was open to interpretation and may have affected the responses. This source of error probably did not significantly affect the accuracy.

Criteria

Triple-space (2 empty line spaces) before the new head. Double-line space after head before paragraph.

According to Paul Wutz, the two most important criteria for a co-op program are that (1) supervising students take as little time as possible and (2) the program yield permanent promotable workers. A less important criterion is that co-op students be able to complete some of the projects that full-time FFI personnel have not had time to do.

FIGURE 24.2
A Long Report (continued)

A University Co-op Program for FFI Health Services *Major head of body needs to start a new page* Page 3

Background on FFI Health Services

FFI Health Services contracts with companies to manage prescription benefits. FFI enables employers to give employees prescription coverage at a very reasonable price. Employees can order deeply discounted prescription drugs on FFI's Web site.

The company is five years old and started with two employees. FFI Health Services has experienced explosive growth. It now employs 50 people in two offices, one in Edmonton, Alberta, and the other in Surrey, British Columbia. Hiring qualified personnel is a challenge. Current hiring procedures include running classified advertisements or conducting nationwide searches depending on the type of position to be filled. Some specialized positions such as computer programmers are in such high demand that FFI Health Services does not always feel it is getting the best candidates.

Use talking heads. Note how much more informative this is than "Advantages."

General Benefits of University Co-op Programs

Begin most paragraphs with topic sentences.

Businesses benefit enormously from hiring co-op students. Students are good, productive employees who are positively inclined toward work that is related to their career interests. They can serve as temporary staff or provide assistance for ongoing or special projects. Hiring students also increases access for hiring women and minorities. Students cost less to hire than regular permanent employees and improve morale in the workplace. Furthermore, student employees bring new ideas and technology to the work site ("Internships," 2002).

Other benefits include recruiting opportunities. When co-op students become full-time employees, they need less training and orientation into the company. "Research shows that the turnover rate of employees who have had co-op/internship experience with the organization is significantly less than that for those who did not have this type of job-related opportunity" (Aetna, 2004, "Criteria and Guidelines"). *APA format calls for page numbers when you quote a source. This Web source doesn't have page numbers, but the student gives the subpage from which the quote was taken.*

A Model Co-op Program

When starting a new co-op program, a company can benefit by following a model. The Director of the Professional Experience Program (PEP) at Athabasca works with employers to design co-ops that benefit both the company and the student. The PEP Employer Handbook offers extensive, specific guidelines for employers. In addition, several articles suggest general guidelines for successful co-ops.

Spell out term the first time you use it, with the abbreviation in parentheses. Then you can use the abbreviation by itself.

Co-op Duties

When author's name is in the sentence, use only year and page number in parentheses.

Appropriate job duties are at the heart of a successful co-op program. Admitting that gofer and grunt work are "ubiquitous" in co-op programs, Martha Stone argues that the best programs provide "planned, hands-on" tasks in the field of the student's major (2002, p. 8). Some companies ask interns to do small projects that no one in the organization has time for but that the organization wants to have done.

Another option is to give co-op students the same kinds of jobs that entry-level employees would have. Allegiance Healthcare (Watson, 2004), Micron Technology (King, 2001), and Aetna are three of the many companies that take this approach. Aetna's actuarial co-op students analyze data, improve processes, and "mak[e] things happen" (1999, "Qualifications and Rewards"). One student reports, *Use square brackets for your changes in quoted text.*

Quote when the source is especially credible for the point you want to make.

> As an Aetna actuarial intern, I worked closely with the other actuaries in my area. I helped to develop a reserving system and price a new contract. I began contributing to the area on my first day, which really surprised me. I worked side-by-side with the other actuaries in the area, as well as the other non-financial areas. What I did really made a difference. My technical, communication, and analytical skills were appreciated and demanded. (2004, On the Job with Aetna Actuarial Interns)

This quotation comes from the Web and has no page number. Title of subpage makes it easy for reader to find page on which quote appears.

FIGURE 24.2
A Long Report (continued)

A University Co-op Program for FFI Health Services   Page 4

The Professional Experience Program requires that the employer submit a one-page job description. Examples of job duties in past co-ops include the following:

Accounting
- Perform inventory costing and cost accounting
- Prepare monthly and year-end close-outs
- Prepare and produce financial statements for reports
- Implement and audit programs to verify accuracy
- Coordinate procurement and transmittal records for audit
- Use Excel, Lotus 1-2-3, and other business software

Periods could be used to end each line. But because this is part of a quotation, give text exactly as it appears in the source.

Finance
- Prepare program management cost estimates for projects
- Perform capital investment analysis—analyze the net present value and internal rate of return
- Gather financial and accounting data for financial planning and analysis purposes
- Prepare cost of capital estimates
- Prepare monthly cash budgets

This line could be tightened—"Analyze capital investments." But because this is part of a quotation, give it exactly as in the source. If you make changes, put them in square brackets [ ].

Human Resources
- Train employees on writing and supervisory skills
- Redesign clerical salary structures
- Evaluate and track recruiting efforts
- Develop a guide for cooperative education
- Assist with targeted selection recruiting plan
- Conduct grievance and disciplinary interviews (Athabasca Faculty of Business, 2004, Job Descriptions)

Other duties are also possible. For example, the Professional Experience Program guidelines suggest that employers may want to ask students to present their projects to other managers or to employees within the department, both to inform other employees and to enhance students' communication skills.

As these job descriptions suggest, students can be assigned the same work that might be given to entry-level employees. One question that a company might have is whether students who have not yet graduated can really do the work normally assigned to graduates. Anecdotal evidence suggests that they can. According to Mindy Kannard, Director of Athabasca's Professional Experience Program, "We have very few problems" (personal communication, November 1, 2004). Testimonials from companies that have hired co-op students are even more positive. According to Heidi A. Willis, Co-op Coordinator

When the source is in the paragraph, the parentheses come before the period at the end of the sentence.

Long quotations are indented; no quotation marks necessary.

> Implementing a successful co-op program was effortless with the help of the Career Services staff. Students from the Faculty of Business selected to join our co-op team have an elevated level of maturity, a hearty appetite for success, and an active desire to convert learned theories into working ideas. (Athabasca Faculty of Business, 2000, Testimonials)

Note that the source parenthesis goes after the period at the end of the sentence in indented quotations.

Program Features

Employers who work with Athabasca's Professional Experience Program must supervise and evaluate co-op students. Setting appropriate salaries is also important.

FIGURE 24.2
A Long Report (continued)

Indent third-level headings to make them distinct

Third-level headings have periods even when they are not complete sentences.

Quote when you can't think of any better words than those in the source.

Supervising Students. Co-op students must receive supervision that is "on-going, consistent and positive" (Athabasca Faculty of Business, 2004, "Criteria & Guidelines.") At the beginning of the assignment, orientation should include identifying the "key players," the chain of command, office policy (for example, time sheets, overtime, and sick leave), and the corporate culture (including appropriate dress). Ideally, the supervisor or someone else should mentor the student, not merely give an assignment and disappear. Students benefit from learning not only what is needed, but also why it's needed—how it fits into the larger picture of the company's goals. Identifying specific learning goals can help co-op students budget their time and also makes evaluation easier.

Mr. Wutz has assumed that since FFI does not have a Human Resources department, he would have to do all the work of supervising and evaluating students. However, this work could be done by people in the areas in which the co-op students are working. Because the mentor provides guidance and acts as a "go-to" person for addressing concerns and questions, a mentor working in the same area as the student is ideal. It is important that each student be matched with an enthusiastic mentor who will take an active role in guiding the student's development and providing career advice.

Evaluating Students. Co-op students should be evaluated midway through the work period and again at the end. The evaluation should be based on specific goals established earlier. Areas for evaluation might include quality of work, enthusiasm toward assignments, comprehension and knowledge, organizational skills, and judgment. Objectives set forth at the onset of the co-op program should be reiterated at the placement evaluation and discussed again before the student returns to school. The supervisor should discuss the evaluation with the student and provide constructive criticism and encouragement.

The Professional Experience Program provides a sample form that the employer can use (www.cob.athabascau.edu/careers/pep/EmpEvual.htm). Employers can also use another evaluation instrument but must turn in some form of written evaluation to the Faculty of Business Career Services Centre.

Setting Salary. The Professional Experience Program at Athabasca gives useful suggestions for setting co-op students' salaries. Although the initial salary should be high enough to attract quality applicants, it should be low enough so that wages can be raised commensurate with increased responsibilities should the student be hired again for another placement or hired as a permanent employee.

Second-level heads are flush with the left margin and bolded. Triple-space before new head; double-space after.

Common Problems

Some of the possible problems, such as not giving co-op students substantive work assignments, can be prevented by following the guidelines for the Professional Experience Program. Professor Dawn Kalmuth, who teaches a class for co-op students, reports that most students experience situations in which they feel uncertain. Discussions among co-op students are helpful in understanding situations, brainstorming alternatives, and developing strategies for implementing the preferred alternative. Some students find that their supervisors are not in fact very knowledgeable and that they need to seek information from more active (but busier) people. Some co-op students have been given huge assignments that require massive overtime. Other co-op students are asked to pick up a project started by a former student without adequate documentation about what has been done and why. Still other co-op students experience problems that might be encountered by full-time employees, including sexual harassment (Dawn Kalmuth, personal communication, November 12, 2004). Telling the student about company channels for dealing with problems and emphasizing good communication between the co-op student and his or her mentor or supervisor are essential.

APA format for phone calls, conversations, and other sources that the reader cannot check

FIGURE 24.2
A Long Report (continued)

*Heading must cover everything under that
heading until the next head or
subhead at that level.*

Making Co-op Placements Attractive to Athabasca Students

Only 15 percent of those surveyed had heard of FFI Managed Care. Companies with strong co-op programs are "overwhelmed with applications" ("Internships," 2002, p. 102), but it will be a while before FFI commands that kind of interest. To get off to a good start, FFI's co-op program should be attractive to Athabasca's students.

*When an article has no author,
use the first word of the title to
identify it.*

Providing Good Experience

The students surveyed ranked experience as the most important factor in accepting a specific co-op placement, as Table 1 shows.   *Refer to Tables in your text.*

Table 1. How Important Are Various Criteria in Accepting a Specific Placement?

Rank	Criterion	Average; $N = 150$ (3 = Very impt., 2 = Somewhat impt., 1 = Not impt.)
1	Gaining experience	2.99
2	Quality of mentoring	2.92
3	Building connections	2.73
4	Chance of getting a job with that company	2.57
5	Prestige of company	2.43
6	Location where you live now	2.36
7	Money	2.22

*Compare Table 1 with
the raw data for Question 9
in Appendix A (p. 10 of report).
Here, the items have been
re-arranged to go from the
highest to the lowest score.*

This emphasis on gaining experience is consistent with the reports of people who had placements last summer. The top four benefits of their placements, according to the people who had them last summer, were "looks good on my résumé, work related to my major, chance to explore my interests," and "made connections." (See Table 2.) If FFI provides co-op placements that give students experience related to their majors, it can attract students even though it is not yet well known.

Table 2. What Were the Most Beneficial Aspects of Your Co-op Placement?

Rank	Aspect	$N = 48$ n	%
1	Looks good on my résumé	42	86%
2	Work related to my major	41	85%
3	Chance to explore my interests	35	73%
4	Made connections	34	71%
5	Worked with clients	22	46%
6	Likely to get a job offer/got a job offer	15	31%

*"N" is the total number of
people responding to the
question; "n" is the number
of people giving a particular
response. Giving percentages
makes it easier for readers
to understand data.*

Surprisingly, as Table 1 shows, "chance of getting a job with that company" ranked only fourth out of seven criteria. Fewer than a third of the students who had co-op placements got or expected to get a job offer from that company (Table 2). This emphasis on experience rather than employment will work to FFI's benefit. Only 13 percent of the students I surveyed were "very interested" in a career in managed care, with a full 47 percent "not interested." But since students do not necessarily expect to work permanently at the site of their co-op placements, they probably will be

*Quote to give the exact wording of survey questions, so reader can
interpret data accurately.*

FIGURE 24.2
A Long Report (continued)

willing to accept any placement that gives them good experience. Then, a good co-op experience can convince students that FFI is a good employer.

Part of providing good experience is assigning students to a good mentor. Some companies assign students to otherwise unproductive people (Dawn Kalmuth, personal communication, November 12, 2004). However, this is a mistake. FFI should assign its most effective people as mentors, so that students have the best co-op experience possible.

FFI's greatest needs are computer personnel, including a Web weaver, and finance personnel (Paul Wutz, personal communication, November 18, 2004). The company also could offer co-op placements in accounting, human resources, marketing, social services, and transportation logistics. Each of these areas could offer solid experience to students while meeting FFI's needs.

Providing Competitive Pay

Begin most paragraphs with topic sentences. Numbering your points helps the reader.

Survey results indicate three points in regards to pay. First, students who did not have placements last summer made an average of $8.00 per hour. The average wage for students with co-ops was $14.00. The highest-paid placements seem to be those majoring in Management Information Sciences (MIS): One respondent reported that computer science co-op student received $2500 a month plus a bonus. Second, the survey demonstrates that only 20 percent of the respondents could afford to take an unpaid co-op next summer. However, 49 percent could afford to take a co-op paying only the minimum wage next summer. Third, although money is the least important of the seven criteria in choosing whether to accept a specific placement, it is at least "somewhat important" to most students. Therefore, FFI should offer competitive wages to attract the best students.

Here published, online, and survey data are combined.

Some co-op programs provide more than just an hourly wage. Micron Technology provides corporate housing (King, 2001). Aetna provides not only housing but also round-trip travel to and from its corporate headquarters (Aetna, 2004). Only 15 percent of the students surveyed said they could definitely take a job in Edmonton next summer. These may well be students who live in Calgary. Providing housing and round-trip transportation could win over many of the students who say they "could not" take a job in Edmonton.

Vary paragraph lengths to provide good visual impact.

Not every idea needs a source. Use your knowledge of people and of business.

Finding a Niche for FFI Co-op Placements

Don't need author's name in parentheses if name is used in the sentence.

Simply announcing the placements may not be enough to get high-demand students such as MIS majors. If FFI develops an image or "niche" it will stand a better chance of attracting the strongest students. Natalie Engler (2003) shows the lengths to which some companies go. Sapient Corporation conducts "Super Saturdays" eight times a year. These team-based exercises are designed not only to test students' skills but, more important, to develop a good impression of Sapient. In one exercise, teams of six were asked to design and build a gift made out of Legos for a book-writing marine biologist. Sapient has used these Super Saturdays to attract employees. The company has added 300 people in the last year and has a very low rate of turnover.

Vary sentence length and sentence structure.

What sets Allegiance Healthcare's program apart is its on-campus "virtual internship" program. Allegiance installed workstations on campus, which students used to complete Allegiance projects throughout the school year (Watson, 2004). Thus, Allegiance's location was immaterial; students did not need to relocate. An added benefit to Allegiance was that the students' work could continue year-round.

Since most students don't know about FFI and don't come to the hiring process interested in managed care, it would be useful for FFI to develop some strategy that could set it apart in students' minds.

FIGURE 24.2
A Long Report (continued)

Conclusions repeat points made in the report.
Recommendations are actions the readers should take.

12 pt. **Conclusions and Recommendations**

11 pt. FFI Health Services should establish a co-op program following the model outlined in the Professional Experience Program. Following this program will cover the basics of a sound co-op program and will enable FFI to hire students at Athabasca University. Decisions to be made include choosing which positions to offer *List in* students, deciding how much to pay them, identifying supervisors and mentors within each department, and *the order* determining how to publicize the program and at which universities to recruit. *in which you'll discuss them.*

Some companies ask for Conclusions and
1. Choosing Positions for Co-op Students *Recommendations at the beginning of reports.*

FFI should eventually offer co-op placements in eight areas: accounting, computer science, finance, human resources, marketing, social services, transportation logistics, and Web maintenance. FFI does work in each of these areas and could benefit both from the projects that students might complete and from the opportunity to make permanent hires in these areas.

In its first year, the co-op program should focus on two or three main areas of employment. For instance, hiring only finance and computer science majors will give FFI Health Services the opportunity to pilot the program. This strategy will help to ensure that each student gets the necessary attention and career-related experience. Also, FFI Health Services can detect and correct any flaws in the initial program.

2. Setting Salaries

According to survey results, only 20 percent of students can afford to take an unpaid co-op, and 51 percent are not be able to work for minimum wage. Since the best students have several options, FFI should offer co-op students a competitive wage. Because the average student earned between $8 and $10 last summer, I recommend that FFI Health Services set co-op pay at $15–$16 an hour for all majors except computer science. Hiring the best computer science majors requires starting salaries of at least $18 an hour. Providing housing would make the co-op placements more attractive and would enlarge the pool of applicants.

Numbering the issues makes it easy
3. Choosing Supervisors and Mentors *for readers to discuss them.*

One person should not attempt to supervise all the co-op placements, even during the first summer when there may be only two or three students. We should conduct internal research to determine how potential supervisors and mentors feel about working closely with students. Acting as a mentor should be a voluntary position to ensure active and enthusiastic guidance for the student. Supervisors should become familiar with assignment and evaluation procedures and should feel comfortable with their role in the co-op program. Willing and dedicated supervisors and mentors will make for a more effective program.

4. Publicizing the Program

Participating in the Professional Experience Program will mean that FFI's job descriptions will be available to students who come to the Faculty of Business Career Services Centre looking for co-op placements. However, other kinds of publicity are also desirable so that FFI can have the widest pool of applicants from which to choose.

FIGURE 24.2
A Long Report (continued)

Announcing the co-op placements on FFI's Web site is an obvious step and would bring up FFI's co-ops when students do Web searches for "co-ops." Many other companies already give information about co-ops on Web sites. If computer majors remain in such high demand, FFI will need to do something special to attract them. Further research will be needed to determine what kind of niche FFI can develop.

5. Recruiting Students

Although this research focuses on Athabasca students, FFI may want to recruit at other schools. More research needs to be done to determine the optimal places for FFI Health Services to recruit students. Since students may not be able to relocate for the summer or may only move if given a substantial pay incentive, recruiting at universities in Alberta and in British Columbia may make sense. In addition, it would be useful to identify any postsecondary institutions that offer majors in managed care. Such universities and colleges would be a good source of students who would be interested in the kind of work FFI does.

Because many readers turn to the "Recommendations"
first, provide a brief rationale for each. The ideas in
this section must be logical extensions of the points
made and supported in the body of the report.

FIGURE 24.2
A Long Report (continued)

A University Co-op Program for FFI Health Services   Page 10

Tell how many people responded.

Appendix A: Raw Survey Data

N = 150. Percentages sometimes total more than 100% due to rounding.

1. Major (Grouped by University)
    Agriculture *Also give* 7 (5%)
    Arts *percentages.* 11 (7%)
    Business 35 (23%)
    Human Ecology 15 (10%)
    Humanities 41 (27%)
    Math & Physical Sciences 23 (15%)
    Social & Behav. Sciences 18 (12%)

2. Rank: First year 15 (10%)
          Second year 34 (23%)
          Third year 47 (31%)
          Fourth year 54 (36%)

3. How important is it to you to have one or more co-op placements before you graduate?
    80 (53%) Very important
    57 (38%) Somewhat important
    14 (9%) Not important

4. Did you have a placement last summer?
    48 (32%) Yes
    103 (68%) No (skip to Question 6)

5. What were the most beneficial aspects of your placement? (Check all that apply.)
    41 (85%) Work related to my major
    15 (31%) Likely to get a job offer/ got a job offer
    35 (73%) Chance to explore my interests
    34 (71%) Made connections
    22 (46%) Worked with clients
    42 (86%) Looks good on my résumé

6. How much money did you make last summer? (Approximate hourly rate, before taxes)
    Co-op student: average $8.20/hr
    Non-co-op student: average $7.67/hr

    ☐ Check here if you did not make any money last summer.
    3 co-op students; 9 non-co-op students

7. For next summer, could you afford to take an unpaid co-op placement?
    30 (20%) Yes   120 (80%) No

8. For next summer, could you afford to take a co-op paying only minimum wage?
    73 (49%) Yes   76 (51%) No

9. How important is each of the following criteria in choosing whether to accept a specific co-op placement?

	Very impt. (3)	Some impt. (2)	Not impt. (1)	Average
a. Money				2.22
b. Prestige of company				2.43
c. Location near where you live now				2.36
d. Quality of mentoring				2.92
e. Building connections				2.73
f. Chance of getting a job with that company				2.57
g. Gaining experience				2.99

10. How interested are you in a career in health services?
    19 (13%) Very interested
    63 (42%) Somewhat interested
    71 (47%) Not interested

11. Could you take a job in Alberta next summer?
    22 (15%) Definitely
    70 (47%) Maybe
    58 (39%) No

12. Have you heard of FFI Health Services?
    23 (15%) Yes
    122 (81%) No

Include a copy of your survey with the raw data. Here, the format is changed a bit to make room for the data.

FIGURE 24.2
A Long Report (continued)

Appendix B: Responses to Open-Ended Question

"Whether or not I could take an unpaid internship or one paying minimum wage would depend on the type of co-op and how relevant the experience would be."

"I wish co-ops would pay."

"I might sacrifice money for one summer if the co-op was worth it in terms of gaining experience."

"Just as long as it dealt with my career field, I would be interested in taking a co-op placement."

"It was told to me that co-ops are as important as some classes. Yet students who work themselves through college or university cannot afford some of these do to pay. Companies need to start making it worth the while for the working student."

Give responses verbatim, errors and all!

"Another important factor in deciding whether or not to accept a specific co-op would be how enjoyable and comfortable the atmosphere is."

"I'll only work where it is warm!"

"Everyone should have a co-op placement at least one quarter."

"I feel co-ops are *extremely* important!"

"MIS majors can make $33 000 or $2500 + bonus a month for co-op placements."

"Philosophy students don't do co-ops, too much like work."

"I think co-ops are very important."

"Co-op placements give you a taste for what your career will be like and what it's like to work in the 'real world.'"

Provide the text of survey comments so readers get a sense of the flavour of responses.

FIGURE 24.2
A Long Report (continued)

A University Co-op Program for FFI Health Services   Page 12

Treat short Web   *APA Format*
pages like journal articles.   **References**

Aetna. (2004). *Actuarial internships.* Retrieved November 4, 2005, from   *When you use two sets of*
    http://www.aetna.com/working/interns.htm   *pages that are part of one Web site,*
    combine them in a single entry.

Athabasca Faculty of Business. (1998). *The professional experience program: Employer handbook.* Retrieved
    November 4, 2004, from http://www.cob.athabasca.edu/careers/pep/

Engler, N. (2003, March 23). We want you! (Please?!?) *Computerworld,* pp. 72–73.

Ferguson, L. H. (2003, April). Guidelines for a safety internship program in industry. *Professional Safety,*
    43(no. 4), 22–25.

Give the page
number(s) Internships identify promising future employees among college students. (2002, April). *HRMagazine,*
without   42(4), 102.   *Start with the title of the article when no author is given.*
"p." when
you give King, J. (2001, February 17). Companies use co-op students as hiring pool. *Computerworld,* pp. 63, 65.
the volume
and issue   *Use "pp." when you don't have volume and issue number.*
number. Stone, M. L. (2002, June). How to offer successful co-op placements. *Advertising Age's Business Marketing,* p. 8.

Watson, S. (2004, September 21). Changing perceptions. *Computerworld,* pp. C2–C4.
    Month or date of   *Underline titles of magazines,*
    issue goes after year.   *journals, and books if you don't have*
    italics.

List all the printed and online
sources cited in your report. Do not
list sources you used for background
but did not cite. Do not list interviews,
phone calls, or other information to which
the reader has no access.

Employability Skills 2000+

The Conference Board of Canada
Insights You Can Count On

Please see the OLC to preview the key skills from the Conference Board of Canada's Employability Skills 2000+ covered in this module.

Review of Key Points

1. What additional sections and/or documents are in a formal report?
2. When do you write a memo of transmittal versus a letter of transmittal?
3. What is the transmittal's purpose? How should it be organized?
4. Why is there so much repetition in a longer report?
5. What information goes into the executive summary? How should you organize the executive summary?
6. What information goes into the conclusion section?
7. When does a report include a recommendations section?

Assignments for Module 24

Questions for Critical Thinking

24.1 How do you decide what headings to use in the body of the report?
24.2 How do you decide how much background information to provide in a report?

24.3 How much evidence do you need to provide for each recommendation you make?

Exercises and Problems

As your instructor directs,

Turn in the following documents for Problems 24.4 through 24.7:

a. The approved proposal
b. Two copies of the report, including

    Cover
    Letter or Memo of Transmittal
    Title Page
    Table of Contents

    List of Illustrations
    Executive Summary
    Body (Introduction, all information, recommendations). Your instructor may specify a minimum length, a minimum number or kind of sources, and a minimum number of visuals.
    Appendixes, if useful or relevant
    References or Works Cited

c. Your notes and rough drafts

24.4   Writing a Feasibility Study

Write an individual or group report evaluating the feasibility of two or more alternatives. Explain your criteria clearly, evaluate each alternative, and recommend the best course of action. Possible topics include the following:

1. Is it feasible for a local restaurant to open another branch? Where should it be?
2. Is it feasible to create a program to mentor women and traditionally underrepresented groups in your organization?

3. Is it feasible to create or enlarge a daycare centre for the children of students?
4. Is it feasible to start a monthly newsletter for students in your program?

5. With your instructor's permission, choose your own topic.

24.5   Analyzing a Feasibility Study

Analyze and evaluate one of the model feasibility studies on the OLC.

As your instructor directs,

1. Form a group with two or three other students.
2. Using the information in Module 24, and your own experience, brainstorm criteria for an excellent feasibility study (use PAIBOC analysis and Module 24 headings to get you started).

3. Agree on and write down your criteria for the ideal feasibility report.
4. Choose one model report and evaluate according to your criteria. Be specific.
5. Present your findings in a memo to your teacher.

Present your findings orally to your class.

24.6   Writing a Library Research Report

Write an individual or group library research report. Possible topics include your province's health care policies, your city's strategies for providing homeless shelters, Canadian copyright or defamation legislation related to Internet material, your province's small business support resources or your province's welfare strategies. Or, with your professor's permission, choose your own topic.

Start the project by finding the most current information available online or in print.

24.7   Writing a Recommendation Report

Write an individual or group recommendation report. Possible topics include the following:

1. **Recommending courses.** What skills are in demand in your community? What courses at what levels should the local college or university offer? What accreditation courses should graduates in your programs pursue to increase their marketability and salaries?
2. **Improving sales and profits.** Recommend ways a small business in your community can increase sales and profits. Focus on one or more of the following: the products or services it offers, its advertising, its decor, its location, its accounting methods, its cash management, or any other aspect that may be keeping the company from achieving its potential. Address your report to the owner of the business.
3. **Increasing student involvement.** How could an organization on campus persuade more of the students who are eligible to join or to become active in its programs? Do students know that it

exists? Is it offering programs that interest students? Is it retaining current members? What changes should the organization make? Address your report to the officers of the organization.
4. **Evaluating a potential employer.** What training is available to new employees? How soon is the average entry-level person promoted? How much travel and weekend work are expected? Is there a "busy season," or is the workload consistent year-round? What fringe benefits are offered? What is the corporate culture? Is the climate non-racist and non-sexist? How strong is the company economically? How is it likely to be affected by current economic, demographic, and political trends? Address your report to a college or university placement office; recommend whether it should encourage students to work at this company.
5. With your instructor's permission, choose your own topic.

24.8 Writing Parts of the Formal Report

Write an Executive Summary and a Conclusion for the model draft on the OLC.

As your instructor directs,

1. Form a team with two other students.
2. Read and discuss your versions of the Executive Summary and the Conclusion.
3. Together, rewrite and revise to create your team's version of the Executive Summary and Conclusion.
4. Hand in for grading.

Polishing Your Prose

Improving Paragraphs

Good paragraphs demonstrate unity, detail, and variety.

The following paragraph from a sales letter illustrates these three qualities:

> The best reason to consider a Schroen Heat Pump is its low cost. Schroen Heat Pumps cost 25 percent less than the cheapest competitor's. Moreover, unlike the competition, the Schroen Heat Pump will pay for itself in less than a year in energy savings. That's just 12 months. All this value comes with a 10-year unlimited warranty—if anything goes wrong, we'll repair or replace the pump at no cost to you. That means no expensive repair bills and no dollars out of your pocket.

A paragraph is **unified** when all its sentences focus on a single central idea. As long as a paragraph is about just one idea, a topic sentence expressing that idea is not required. However, using a topic sentence makes it easier for the reader to skim the document. (Essays use a *thesis statement* for the central idea of the entire document.) Sentences throughout the paragraph should support the topic sentence or offer relevant examples.

Transitions connect ideas from one point to another. Common transitions are *and, also, first, second, third, in addition, likewise, similarly, for example (e.g.), for instance, indeed, to illustrate, namely, specifically, in contrast,* and *on the other hand.*

Detail makes your points clearer and more vivid. Good details express clearly and completely what you mean. Use concrete words, especially strong nouns, verbs, adjectives, and adverbs that paint a picture in the reader's mind and say what you mean. Avoid unnecessary repetition.

Variety is expressed first in sentence length and patterns and second in the number of sentences in each paragraph. Most sentences in business writing should be 16 to 20 words, but an occasional longer or very short sentence gives punch to your writing.

The basic pattern for sentences is subject-verb-object (SVO): *Our building supervisor sent the forms.* Vary the SVO pattern by changing the order, using transitions and clauses, and combining sentences.

Also vary paragraph length. First and last paragraphs can be quite short. Body paragraphs will be longer. Whenever a paragraph runs eight typed lines or more, think about dividing it into two paragraphs.

Exercises

Rewrite the following paragraphs to improve unity, detail, and variety.

1. I used to work for McCandless Realty as a receptionist. My many experiences in the accounting field make me an ideal candidate for a position as senior administrative assistant with Graham, Chang, and Associates.

I answered phones at McCandless. I typed there. I worked at Dufresne Plastics as a secretary. At McCandless, I also handled payroll. There are a lot of reasons why I liked Dufresne. These included the opportunity for training in data entry and Microsoft Word. I learned to type 70 WPM with no mistakes.

2. Mr. Walter Pruitt visited our business communication class yesterday. He spoke about the importance of co-op placements. Mr. Pruitt works for Global Energy. Global Energy provides network and service management to companies around the world. Mr. Pruitt, who works for Global Energy, told us he got his first job because of a co-op. A co-op is an opportunity for students to work with a company for a period of time to get business experience. Mr. Pruitt went to university and worked at a co-op placement for Global Energy. At first, Global Energy only wanted him to work for 10 weeks. Mr. Pruitt did such a good job, they kept him on another 10 weeks and another. Mr. Pruitt was offered a job by Global Energy when he graduated.

Check your answer to the odd-numbered exercise on page 573.

Online Learning Centre

Visit the Online Learning Centre at www.mcgrawhill.ca/olc/locker to access module quizzes, a searchable glossary, résumé and letter templates, additional business writing samples, CBC videos, and other learning and study tools.

MODULE

25 Using Visuals

Module Outline

- Why should I use visuals?
- What are stories, and how do I find them?
- Does it matter what kind of visual I use?
- What design conventions should I follow?
- Can I use colour and clip art?
- What else do I need to check for?
- Can I use the same visual in my document and in my presentation?

Review of Key Points

Assignments for Module 25

Polishing Your Prose: Writing Subject Lines and Headings

LEARNING OBJECTIVES

After reading and applying the information in Module 25, you'll be able to demonstrate

Knowledge of
- How visuals tell stories
- How to choose appropriate visuals

Skills to
- Choose visuals to tell a story
- Match the visual to your story
- Design visuals
- Choose ethical visuals
- Use visuals in your documents and presentations

The Conference Board of Canada
Insights You Can Count On

Please see the OLC to preview the key skills from the Conference Board of Canada's Employability Skills 2000+ covered in this module.

FIGURE 25.1

P A I B O C

Questions for Analysis

Use the PAIBOC questions to analyze what visuals you should use and where you should place them.

P What are your purposes in writing or presenting?

A Who is your audience? What do they know? What do they need to know? What illustrations would appeal to them and why? What visuals would make it easier for them to understand and agree with your message?

I What information must your message include? What information includes numerical or quantitative data? What information would work better in a visual? What visual would best convey that information?

B What reasons or reader benefits can you offer your audience? What illustration/visual would emphasize these benefits?

O What about your message would your audience object to? What objections can you anticipate?

Because the Internet enables everyone to publish, we are inundated with information. Information overload has escalated our expectations of immediacy while reducing our patience with written text. Thus, the adage "a picture is worth 1000 words" has never been truer.

Why should I use visuals?

Appropriate, attractive visuals tell your story immediately: they are faster and easier to understand, and more memorable.

Visuals—illustrations, charts, and graphs—readily convey and clarify information; therefore, visuals are a reader-friendly way to communicate your points. This module shows you how to turn data into charts and graphs. See ◀▶ Module 5 for a discussion of designing slides for oral presentations and ◀▶ Module 20 for a discussion of other aspects of good oral presentations.

In your rough draft, use visuals

- **To see that ideas are presented completely.** A table, for example, can show you whether you've included all the items in a comparison.
- **To find relationships.** For example, charting sales on a map may show that the sales representatives who made their quotas all have territories on the west coast or in the Atlantic provinces. Is the product one that appeals to coastal lifestyles? Is advertising reaching the coasts but not the Prairie provinces, Ontario, or Quebec? Even if you don't use the visual in your final document, creating the map may lead you to questions you wouldn't otherwise ask.

In the final presentation or document, use visuals

- **To make points vivid.** Readers skim memos and reports; a visual catches the eye. The brain processes visuals immediately. Understanding words—written or oral—takes more time.
- **To emphasize material** that might be skipped if it were buried in a paragraph.
- **To present material more compactly and with less repetition** than words alone can.

The number and type of visuals you need depend on your purposes, your information, and the audience. You'll use more visuals when you want to show relationships and to persuade, when the information is complex or contains extensive numerical data, and when the audience values visuals.

Your chart is only as good as the underlying data. Check to be sure that your data come from a reliable source (◀▶ Module 21).

What are stories, and how do I find them?

A story is something that is happening, according to the data. To find stories, look for relationships and changes.

Every visual should tell a story. Stories can be expressed in complete sentences that describe something that happens or changes. The sentence can also serve as the title of the visual.

FIGURE 25.1
(continued)

How could you use visuals to deemphasize or overcome audience objections?

C How will the **context** impact your message? How long is your message? What time of day is your presentation? How will people be affected by your message? By using visuals, what parts of your message can you make more interesting and accessible?

Not a story: Canadian Exports, 2002–2007

Possible stories: China is the New Economic Lion
                        Alberta's Oil Riches Pay Out
                        Canada's Young Entrepreneurs Rank Worldwide
                        Energy Costs Continue to Climb

Stories that tell us what we already know are rarely interesting. Instead, good stories do at least one of several things:

- Support a hunch you have
- Surprise or challenge so-called common knowledge
- Show trends or changes you didn't know existed
- Have commercial or social significance
- Provide information needed for action
- Have personal relevance to you and the audience

You can find stories in three ways:

1. **Focus on a topic** (starting salaries, alternative music demographics, and so forth).
2. **Simplify the data** on that topic and convert the numbers to simple, easy-to-understand units.
3. **Look for relationships and changes.** For example, compare two or more groups: do men and women have the same attitudes? Look for changes over time. Look for items that can be seen as part of the same group. For example, to find stories about TV ads, you might group ads in the same product category—ads for cars, for food, for beverages.

When you think you have a story, test it against all the data to be sure it's accurate.

Some stories are simple straight lines: "Average workweek," as illustrated in Figure 25.2. But other stories are more complex, with exceptions or outlying cases. Such stories will need more nuanced titles to do justice to the story. Sometimes the best story arises from the juxtaposition of two or more stories. In Table 25.1 on the next page, *Canadian Business* magazine uses a **matrix table** to make a graphic comparison. The matrix provides a snapshot of English-speaking Canadians' satisfaction with certain industries.

FYI

Using visuals as well as words more than quadruples the audience's retention rate and makes the audience twice as likely to agree with the speaker's recommendations.

Source: Epson's corporate Web site, "The Numbers on Why You Need Visuals," http://www.presenterson line.com/basics/visuals/ needvisuals.shtml, retrieved August 23, 2006.

FIGURE 25.2
Average Workweek

France's lower house of parliament approved a government proposal to end the 35-hour workweek and boost employment and income.

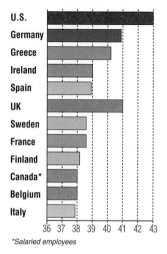

*Salaried employees

Source: Eurostat, Statistics Canada, Bureau of Labor Statistics.

Your audience should be able to see what the visual says:

> Does the chart support the title, and does the title reinforce the chart? So if I say in my title that "sales have increased significantly" I want to see a trend moving up at a sharp angle. If not, if the trend parallels the baseline, it's an instant clue that the chart needs more thinking.[1]

For optimum audience impact, use the "tell, show, tell" rule: first, *tell* your readers or listeners what they are about to see; next, *show* your audience what you promised to show them; finally, *tell* them the significance of the visual. And, of course, the visual must depict exactly what you said it would.

The Six Components of Every Visual

1. A title that tells the story that the visual shows
2. A clear indication of what the data are
3. Clearly labelled units
4. Labels or legends identifying axes, colours, symbols, and so forth
5. The source of the data, if you created the visual from data someone else gathered and compiled
6. The source of the visual, if you reproduce a visual someone else created

TABLE 25.1

A Matrix Table Tells a Complete Story

Sector/company	% Satisfied	% Just OK	% Unsatisfied
CUSTOMER SATISFACTION RATINGS			
Airlines	**32**	**30**	**38**
Air Canada	16	35	49
WestJet Airlines	89	9	1
Other	50	28	21
Banks	**46**	**30**	**25**
Bank of Montreal	38	36	26
Bank of Nova Scotia	42	37	21
Canadian Imperial Bank of Commerce	39	27	33
Credit unions	82	9	9
Royal Bank	41	35	25
TD Canada Trust	47	30	23
Other	54	21	24
Telephone companies	**53**	**31**	**16**
AT&T Canada	46	41	14
Bell Canada	54	30	16
Telus	49	33	18
Other	60	28	13
Wireless providers	**51**	**30**	**19**
Bell Mobility	57	29	14
Fido	53	31	16
Rogers AT&T Wireless	45	31	23
Telus Mobility	49	31	21
Other	60	18	21
Consultancies	**67**	**21**	**12**
Canada Customs and Revenue Agency	**37**	**35**	**28**
PERFORMANCE OVER LAST YEAR			
Airlines	19	33	48
Banks	23	50	27
Canada Customs and Revenue Agency	22	62	16
Consultancies	32	55	13
Telephone companies	25	62	13
Wireless providers	24	61	15
WILL YOU CONTINUE TO PURCHASE?			
Airlines	57	26	17
Banks	57	23	20
Consultancies	60	28	12
Telephone companies	70	21	9
Wireless providers	62	23	15

Methodology: *Canadian Business* and General Content Corp. surveyed *Canadian Business's* online readers last spring about their experiences with service providers in the banking, airline, telecom, consulting, and wireless industries. The survey received 926 valid responses, the overwhelming majority from English-speaking Canada. With a sample of this size, the results are considered accurate 19 times out of 20 within ±3.7 to ±4.5 percentage points, depending on the sector (except consultancies, which has an error margin of 8.9 points). Respondents tended to be executives or managers, with 80% of them working at businesses with fewer than 100 employees. And 74% of all respondents are involved in purchasing decisions.

Source: Todd Korol, "Satisfaction Guaranteed," General Content Corp., October 28, 2002, 78.

Almost every data set allows you to tell several stories. You must choose the story you want to tell. Dumps of uninterpreted data confuse and frustrate your audience; uninterpreted data undercut the credibility and goodwill you want to create.

Does it matter what kind of visual I use?

Yes! The visual must match the kind of story.

Visuals are not interchangeable. Choose the visual that best matches the purpose of presenting the data.

- Use **tables** when the reader needs to be able to identify exact values (see Figure 25.3a)
- Use a chart or graph when you want the reader to focus on relationships[2]
- To compare a part to the whole, use a **pie graph** (see Figure 25.3b)
- To compare one item to another item, or items over time, use a **bar graph** or a line graph (see Figures 25.3c and 25.3d)

FIGURE 25.3

Choose the Visual to Fit the Story

Canadian sales reach $44.5 million.			
	Millions of dollars		
	2000	2003	2005
British Columbia	10.2	10.8	11.3
Ontario & Quebec	7.6	8.5	10.4
Prarie Provinces	8.3	6.8	9.3
Atlantic Provinces	11.3	12.1	13.5
Totals	37.4	38.2	44.5

a. Tables show exact values.

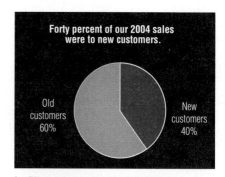

b. Pie graphs compare a component to the whole.

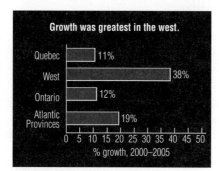

c. Bar graphs compare items or show distribution or correlation.

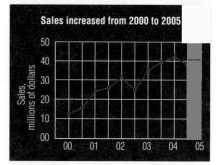

d. Line charts compare items over time or show distribution or correlation.

What design conventions should I follow?

Check your visuals against the lists that follow.

Every visual should contain six components:

1. A title that tells the story that the visual shows
2. A clear indication of what the data are
3. Clearly labelled units
4. Labels or legends identifying axes, colours, symbols, and so forth
5. The source of the data, if you created the visual from data someone else gathered and compiled
6. The source of the visual, if you reproduce a visual that someone else created

Formal visuals are divided into tables and figures. **Tables** are numbers or words arranged in rows and columns; **figures** are everything else. In a document, formal visuals have both numbers and titles, such as "Figure 1. The Falling Cost of Computer Memory, 1994–2004." In an oral presentation, the title is usually used without the number: "The Falling Cost of Computer Memory, 1994–2004." The title should tell the story so that the audience knows what to look for in the visual and why it is important. Informal or spot visuals are inserted directly into the text; they do not have numbers or titles.

Tables

Use tables only when you want the audience to focus on specific numbers. Graphs convey less specific information but are always more memorable.

- Round off to simplify the data (e.g., 35 percent rather than 35.27 percent; 34 000 rather than 33 942)
- Provide column and row totals or averages when they're relevant
- Put the items you want readers to compare in columns rather than in rows to facilitate mental subtraction and division
- When you have many rows, screen alternate entries or double space after every five entries to help readers line up items accurately

Pie Graphs

Pie graphs force the audience to measure area. Research shows that people can judge position or length (which a bar graph uses) much more accurately than they can judge area. The data in any pie graph can be put in a bar graph.[3] Therefore, use a pie graph only when you are comparing one segment to the whole. When you are comparing one segment to another segment, use a bar graph, a line graph, or a map—even though the data may be expressed in percentages.

- Start at 12 o'clock with the largest percentage or the percentage you want to focus on. Go clockwise to each smaller percentage or to each percentage in some other logical order.
- Make the graph chart a perfect circle. Perspective circles distort the data.
- Limit the number of segments to five or seven. If your data have more divisions, combine the smallest or the least important into a single "miscellaneous" or "other" category.
- Label the segments outside the circle. Internal labels are hard to read.

Bar Graphs

Bar graphs are easy to interpret because they ask people to compare distance along a common scale, which most people judge accurately. Bar graphs are useful in a variety of situations: to compare one item to another, to compare items over time, and to show correlations. Use horizontal bars when your labels are long; when the labels are short, either horizontal or vertical bars will work.

- Order the bars in a logical or chronological order.
- Put the bars close enough together to make comparisons easy.
- Label both horizontal and vertical axes.
- Put all labels inside the bars or outside them. When some labels are inside and some are outside, the labels carry the visual weight of longer bars, distorting the data.
- Make all the bars the same width.
- Use different colours for different bars only when their meanings are different: estimates as opposed to known numbers, negative as opposed to positive numbers.
- Avoid using perspective. Perspective makes the values harder to read and can make comparison difficult.

Several varieties of bar graphs exist. See Figures 25.4 and 25.5 for examples.

FIGURE 25.4

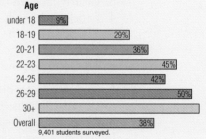

Going to the Bank

Frustrated with the government loan system, a growing number of post secondary students are turning to private lines of credit from their local financial institutions.

Personal line of credit
The percentage of students by age, who say they have a personal line of credit from a financial institution:

Age
- under 18: 9%
- 18-19: 29%
- 20-21: 36%
- 22-23: 45%
- 24-25: 42%
- 26-29: 50%
- 30+
- Overall: 38%

9,401 students surveyed.

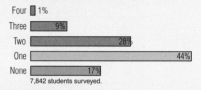

Types of debt
A large percentage of students say they have more than one source of debt. The number of types of debt:

- Four: 1%
- Three: 9%
- Two: 28%
- One: 44%
- None: 17%

7,842 students surveyed.

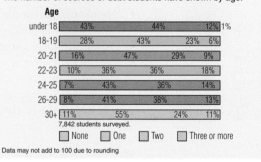

Sources of debt
The number of sources of debt students have shown by age:

Age
Age	None	One	Two	Three or more
under 18	43%	44%	12%	1%
18-19	28%	43%	23%	6%
20-21	16%	47%	29%	9%
22-23	10%	36%	36%	18%
24-25	7%	43%	36%	14%
26-29	8%	41%	38%	13%
30+	11%	55%	24%	11%

7,842 students surveyed.

☐ None ☐ One ☐ Two ☐ Three or more

Data may not add to 100 due to rounding

Source: *Canada Millennium Scholarship Foundation*, www.millenniumscholarships.ca. Paul Kittmer/*The Globe and Mail.*

- **Grouped bar graphs** allow you to compare several aspects of each item or several items over time.
- **Segmented, subdivided, or stacked bars** sum the components of an item. It's hard to identify the values in specific segments; grouped bar charts are almost always easier to use.
- **Deviation bar graphs** identify positive and negative values, or winners and losers.
- **Paired bar graphs** show the correlation between two items.
- **Histograms or pictographs** use images to create the bars.

Line Graphs

Line graphs are also easy to interpret. Use line graphs to compare items over time, to show frequency or distribution, and to show correlations.

FIGURE 25.5
Varieties of Bar Graphs

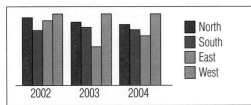

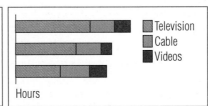

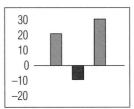

a. Grouped bar graphs compare several aspects of each item, or several items over time.

b. Segmented, subdivided, or **stacked bars** sum the components of an item.

c. Deviation bar graphs identify positive and negative values.

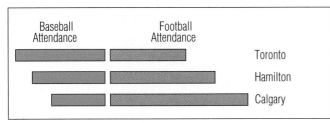

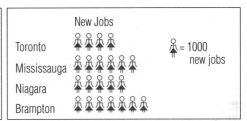

d. Paired bar graphs show the correlation between two items.

e. Histograms or **pictographs** use images to create the bars.

- Label both horizontal and vertical axes.
- When time is a variable, put it on the horizontal axis.
- Avoid using more than three different lines on one graph. Even three lines may be too many if they cross each other.
- Avoid using perspective. Perspective makes the values harder to read and can make comparison difficult.

■ Can I use colour and clip art?

Use colour carefully. Avoid decorative clip art in memos and reports.

Colour makes visuals more dramatic, but it creates at least two problems. First, readers try to interpret colour, an interpretation that may not be appropriate. Second, meanings assigned to colours differ depending on the audience's culture and profession.

Connotations for colour vary from culture to culture and within cultures (◀▶ Module 3). Blue suggests masculinity in North America, criminality in France, strength or fertility in Egypt, and villainy in Japan. Red is sometimes used to suggest danger or stop in North American culture; it means go in China and is associated with festivities. Yellow suggests caution or cowardice in North America, prosperity in Egypt, grace in Japan, and femininity in many parts of the world.[4]

Corporate, national, or professional associations may supersede these general cultural associations. Some people associate blue with IBM or Hewlett-Packard and red with Coca-Cola, communism, or Japan. People in specific professions learn other meanings for colours. Blue suggests *reliability* to financial managers, *water* or coldness to engineers, and *death* to health care professionals. Red means *losing money* to financial managers,

EXPANDING A CRITICAL SKILL

Integrating Visuals into Your Text

Refer to every visual in your text. Normally give the table or figure number in the text but not the title. Put the visual as soon after your reference as space and page design permit. If the visual must go on another page, tell the reader where to find it:

> As Figure 3 shows (p. 10),...
> (See Table 2 on page 3.)

Summarize the main point of a visual before you present the visual itself. Then when readers get to it, they'll see it as confirmation of your point.

Weak: Listed below are the results.

Better: As Figure 4 shows, sales doubled in the last decade.

How much discussion a visual needs depends on the audience, the complexity of the visual, and the importance of the point it makes. If the material is new to the audience, you'll need a fuller explanation than if similar material is presented to this audience every week or month. Help the reader find key data points in complex visuals. If the point is important, discuss its implications in some detail. In contrast, one sentence about a visual may be enough when the audience is already familiar with the topic and the data, when the visual is simple and well designed, and when the information in the visual is a minor part of your proof.

When you discuss visuals, spell out numbers that fall at the beginning of a sentence. If spelling out the number or year is cumbersome, revise the sentence so that it does not begin with a number.

Correct: Forty-five percent of the cost goes to pay wages and salaries.

Correct: The year 1992 marked the official beginning of the European Economic Community.

---

danger to engineers, but *healthy* to health care professionals. Green usually means *safe* to engineers, but *infected* to health care professionals.[5]

These various associations suggest that colour is safest with a homogenous audience that you know well. In an increasingly multicultural workforce, colour may send signals you do not intend.

When you do use colour in visuals, experts suggest the following guidelines:[6]

- Use no more than five colours when colours have meanings.
- Use glossy paper to make colours more vivid.
- Be aware that colours on a computer screen always look brighter than the same colours on paper because the screen sends out light.

In any visual, use as little shading and as few lines as are necessary for clarity. Don't clutter up the visual with extra marks. When you design black and white graphs, use shades of grey rather than stripes, wavy lines, and checks to indicate different segments or items.

In memos and reports, resist the temptation to make your visual "artistic" by turning it into a picture or adding clip art. **Clip art** is predrawn images that you can import into your newsletter, sign, or graph. A small drawing of a car in the corner of a line graph showing the number of kilometres driven is acceptable in an oral presentation or a newsletter, but depending on your audience, may be out of place in a written report.

Chartjunk impedes readability and detracts from your credibility.[7] Turning a line graph into a highway to show kilometres driven makes it harder to read: it's hard to separate the data line from lines that are merely decorative. If you use clip art, you must be sensitive to your audience's pluralistic interpretations: be sure that the images of people show a good mix of both sexes, various races and ages, and various physical conditions (◄|▷ Module 3).

What else do I need to check for?

Be sure that the visual is accurate and ethical.

Always double-check your visuals to be sure that the information is accurate. Be aware, however, that many visuals have accurate labels but misleading visual shapes. Visuals communicate quickly; audiences remember the shape, not the labels. If the reader has to study the labels to get the right picture, the visual is unethical even if the labels are accurate.

Figure 25.6 is distorted by chartjunk and dimensionality. In an effort to make the visual interesting, the artist used a picture of a young man (presumably an engineer) rather than simple bars. By using a photograph rather than a bar, the graph implies that all engineers are young, nerdy-looking white men. Women, people of colour, and men with other appearances are excluded. The photograph also makes it difficult to compare the numbers. The number represented by the tallest figure is not quite five times as great as the number represented by the shortest figure, yet the tallest figure takes up 12 times as much space and appears even bigger than that. Two-dimensional figures distort data by multiplying the apparent value by the width as well as by the height—four times for every doubling in value. Perspective graphs are especially hard for readers to interpret and should be avoided.[8]

FIGURE 25.6
Chartjunk and Dimensions Distort Data

$5.6 million

How much is that engineer in the window?

Here's how much an employee in Silicon Valley was worth over the past year, determined by dividing the value of a sample acquisition by the number of employees acquired.

$1.9 million

$1.3 million

GETTY IMAGES (3)

Nov. 2000   July 2001   Nov. 2001

Even simple bar and line graphs may be misleading if part of the **scale** is missing, or **truncated**. Truncated graphs are most acceptable when the audience knows the basic data set well. For example, graphs of the stock market almost never start at zero; they are routinely truncated. This omission is acceptable for audiences who follow the market closely.

Data can also be distorted when the context is omitted. For example, a drop may be part of a regular cycle, a correction after an atypical increase, or a permanent drop to a new, lower plateau.

You can do several things to make your visuals more accurate:

- Differentiate between actual and estimated or projected values.
- When you must truncate a scale, do so clearly with a break in the bars or in the background.
- Avoid perspective and three-dimensional graphs.
- Avoid combining graphs with different scales.
- Use images of people carefully in histograms to avoid sexist, racist, or other exclusionary visual statements.

■ Can I use the same visual in my document and in my presentation?

Use it in both only if the table or graph is simple.

For presentations, simplify paper visuals. To simplify a complex table, cut some information, round off the data even more, or present the material in a chart rather than in a table.

Visuals for presentations should have titles but don't need figure numbers. Know where each visual is so that you can return to one if someone asks about it during the question period. Decorative clip art is acceptable in oral presentations as long as it does not obscure the story you're telling with the visual.

Employability Skills 2000+

The Conference Board of Canada
Insights You Can Count On

Please see the OLC to preview the key skills from the Conference Board of Canada's Employability Skills 2000+ covered in this module.

Review of Key Points

1. Why use visuals in your reports?
2. How can a writer find stories to illustrate?
3. What is the difference between a table and a figure?
4. What ethical decisions must writers make when using visuals?

5. What culturally sensitive decisions should writers make when using visuals?
6. How do you decide how much discussion your visual needs?

Assignments for Module 25

Questions for Critical Thinking

25.1 Why does each visual need to tell a story?
25.2 Why are charts more memorable than tables?
25.3 When is chartjunk most likely to be acceptable? Why?

25.4 When is a truncated scale most likely to be acceptable?

Exercises and Problems

25.5   Identifying Stories

Of the following, which are stories?

1. Computer Use
2. Computer Sales Fall
3. More Single Parents Buy Computers Than Do Any Other Group

4. Where Your Tax Dollars Go
5. Sixty Percent of Tax Dollars Pay Entitlements, Interest

25.6   Matching Visuals with Stories

What visual(s) would make it easiest to see each of the following stories?

1. Canada buys 35 percent of U.S. exports.
2. Undergraduate enrolment rises, but graduate enrolment declines.

3. Population growth will be greatest in southwestern Ontario, in Montreal and its suburbs, and in Mahone Bay, Nova Scotia.
4. Companies with fewer than 200 employees created a larger percentage of new jobs than did companies with more than 5000 employees.
5. Canada's population is aging.

25.7   Evaluating Visuals

Evaluate each of the following visuals.

1.

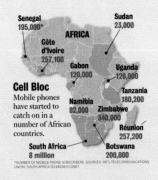

Source: *Newsweek*, August 27, 2001.

2.

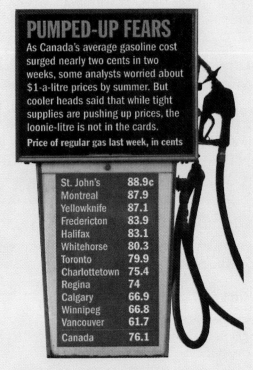

Source: *Maclean's*, May 14, 2001, 21. Reprinted with permission.

3.

How My Time Will Be Used

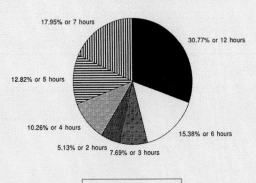

4.

Transparency & Corruption

Here are the 2005 Corruption Perception Index (CPI) rankings by country. Scores range from 10 for clean and zero for corrupt.

Iceland	9.7
Finland	9.6
New Zealand	9.6
Denmark	9.5
Singapore	9.4
Sweden	9.2
Switzerland	9.1
Norway	8.9
Australia	8.8
Austria	8.7
Netherlands	8.6
United Kingdom	8.6
Luxembourg	8.5
Canada	8.4
Hong Kong	8.3
Germany	8.2
United States	7.6

Source: Transparency International.
Richard Johnson/*The Globe and Mail*.

5.
Higher Learning
Young Canadians—especially women—are among the world's best educated.

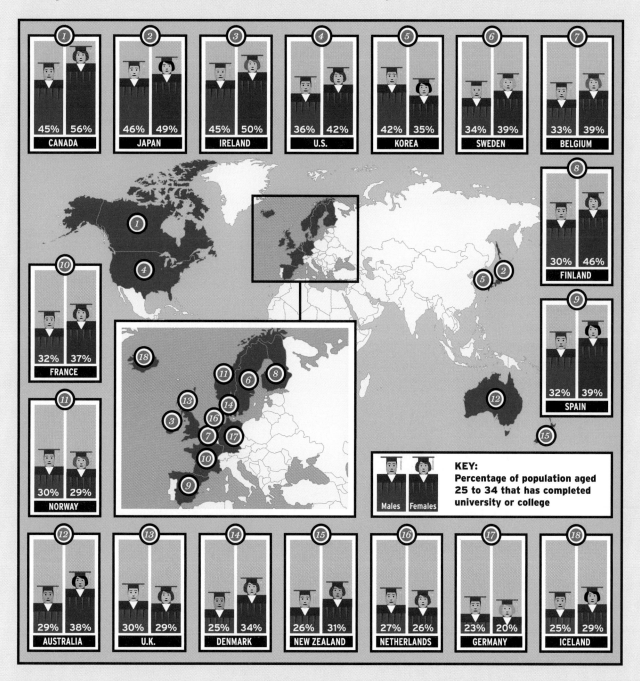

1 CANADA 45% 56%
2 JAPAN 46% 49%
3 IRELAND 45% 50%
4 U.S. 36% 42%
5 KOREA 42% 35%
6 SWEDEN 34% 39%
7 BELGIUM 33% 39%
8 FINLAND 30% 46%
9 SPAIN 32% 39%
10 FRANCE 32% 37%
11 NORWAY 30% 29%
12 AUSTRALIA 29% 38%
13 U.K. 30% 29%
14 DENMARK 25% 34%
15 NEW ZEALAND 26% 31%
16 NETHERLANDS 27% 26%
17 GERMANY 23% 20%
18 ICELAND 25% 29%

KEY:
Males Females
Percentage of population aged 25 to 34 that has completed university or college

EDUCATION LEVELS According to a recent OECD study, Canada now has the developed world's highest percentage of women graduates: 56% of Canadian women between the ages of 25 and 34 have completed a university degree or college program. That compares to 45% for Canadian men, who tie with Ireland for the No. 2 rank (Japan is No. 1 at 46%). Post-secondary education levels have been rising steadily in OECD countries for decades—but this is the first generation in which women across the developed world are more educated than men.
Source: "Higher Learning," *National Post*, January 2003, p. 74. Graphic by Kagan Mcleod; Based on *Education at a Glance: OECD Indicators 2002*, OECD.

- Is the visual's message clear?
- Is it the right visual for the story?
- Is the visual designed appropriately? Is colour, if any, used appropriately?

- Is the visual free from *chartjunk?*
- Does the visual distort data or mislead the reader in any way?

25.8 Interpreting Data

As your instructor directs,

a. Identify at least seven stories in one or more of the following data sets.
b. Create visuals for three of the stories.
c. Write a memo to your instructor explaining why you chose these stories and why you chose these visuals to display them.

d. Write a memo to some group that might be interested in your findings, presenting your visuals as part of a short report. Possible groups include career counsellors, financial advisors, radio stations, advertising agencies, and local restaurants.
e. Brainstorm additional stories you could tell with additional data. Specify the kind of data you would need.

1. **Consumer Price Index, alcoholic beverages and tobacco products, by province (monthly)**

	August 2004	July 2005	August 2005	July 2005 to August 2005	August 2004 to August 2005
		1992 = 100		% change	
Saskatchewan					
All items	**129.5**	**132.4**	**132.9**	**0.4**	**2.6**
Alcoholic beverages and tobacco products	161.1	162.8	**163.1**	0.2	1.2
Alcoholic beverages	127.8	128.5	**129.5**	0.8	1.3
Served alcoholic beverages	133.8	131.0	**133.9**	2.2	0.1
Alcoholic beverages purchased from stores	123.8	126.4	**126.5**	0.1	2.2
Tobacco products and smokers' supplies	184.8	187.4	**187.0**	−0.2	1.2
Alberta					
All items	**131.9**	**135.0**	**135.0**	**0.0**	**2.4**
Alcoholic beverages and tobacco products	162.1	163.5	**164.1**	0.4	1.2
Alcoholic beverages	135.9	136.4	**137.7**	1.0	1.3
Served alcoholic beverages	131.7	131.3	**133.9**	2.0	1.7
Alcoholic beverages purchased from stores	139.3	140.7	**140.8**	0.1	1.1
Tobacco products and smokers' supplies	177.2	179.3	**179.3**	0.0	1.2

Source : Statistics Canada, CANSIM, table (for fee) 326-0001 and Catalogue nos. 62-001-X and 62-010-X.
Last modified: 2005-09-26.

2. **Consumer Price Index, alcoholic beverages and tobacco products, by province (monthly)**

	August 2004	July 2005	August 2005	July 2005 to August 2005	August 2004 to August 2005
		1992 = 100		% change	
Canada					
All items	**124.8**	**127.5**	**128.0**	**0.4**	**2.6**
Alcoholic beverages and tobacco products	144.7	147.7	**148.0**	0.2	2.3
Alcoholic beverages	125.7	127.4	**128.1**	0.5	1.9
Served alcoholic beverages	126.3	128.7	**129.8**	0.9	2.8
Alcoholic beverages purchased from stores	125.3	126.6	**127.0**	0.3	1.4
Tobacco products and smokers' supplies	144.6	148.5	**148.3**	−0.1	2.6
Newfoundland and Labrador					
All items	**123.6**	**126.6**	**126.7**	**0.1**	**2.5**
Alcoholic beverages and tobacco products	143.1	147.2	**147.4**	0.1	3.0
Alcoholic beverages	123.3	127.4	**127.7**	0.2	3.6
Served alcoholic beverages	128.8	136.8	**137.6**	0.6	6.8
Alcoholic beverages purchased from stores	121.3	123.9	**124.1**	0.2	2.3
Tobacco products and smokers' supplies	156.9	161.0	**161.0**	0.0	2.6

Source : Statistics Canada, CANSIM, table (for fee) 326-0001 and Catalogue nos. 62-001-X and 62-010-X.
Last modified: 2005-09-26.

3. Rating Life on Campus

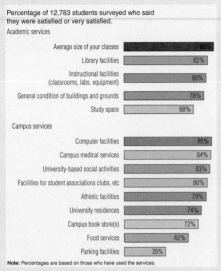

Percentage of 12,783 students surveyed who said they were satisfied or very satisfied.

Academic services

Average size of your classes	88%
Library facilities	82%
Instructional facilities (classrooms, labs, equipment)	80%
General condition of buildings and grounds	78%
Study space	68%

Campus services

Computer facilities	85%
Campus medical services	84%
University-based social activities	83%
Facilities for student associations clubs, etc	80%
Athletic facilities	79%
University residences	74%
Campus book store(s)	72%
Food services	62%
Parking facilities	39%

Note: Percentages are based on those who have used the services.

Source: *Canada Millennium Scholarship Foundation*, www.millenniumscholarships.ca. Bernard Bennell/ *The Globe and Mail*.

4. Population Urban and Rural, by Province and Territory (Canada)

	Total Population	Urban	Rural	Urban	Rural
		number		% of total population	
Canada					
1851	2 436 297	318 079	2 118 218	13	87
1861	3 229 633	527 220	2 702 413	16	84
1871	3 737 257	722 343	3 014 914	19	81
1881	4 381 256	1 109 507	3 271 749	25	75
1891	4 932 206	1 537 098	3 395 108	31	69
1901	5 418 663	2 023 364	3 395 299	37	63
1911	7 221 662	3 276 812	3 944 850	45	55
1921	8 800 249	4 353 428	4 446 821	49	51
1931	10 376 379	5 572 058	4 804 321	54	46
1941	11 506 655	6 252 416	5 254 239	54	46
1951	14 009 429	8 628 253	5 381 176	62	38
1956	16 080 791	10 714 855	5 365 936	67	33
1961	18 238 247	12 700 390	5 537 857	70	30
1966	20 014 880	14 726 759	5 288 121	74	26
1971	21 568 305	16 410 785	5 157 520	76	24
1976	22 992 595	17 366 970	5 625 625	76	24
1981	24 343 177	18 435 923	5 907 254	76	24
1986	25 309 330	19 352 080	5 957 250	76	24
1991	27 296 856	20 906 872	6 389 984	77	23
1996	28 846 758	22 461 207	6 385 551	78	22
2001	30 007 094	23 908 211	6 098 883	80	20

Note: The rural population for 1981 to 2001 refers to persons living outside centres with a population of 1000 **and** outside areas with 400 persons per square kilometre. Previous to 1981, the definitions differed slightly but consistently referred to populations outside centres of 1000 population.

Source : Statistics Canada, Censuses of Population, 1851–2001. Last modified: 2005-09-01.

25.9 Graphing Data from the Web

Find data on the Web about a topic that interests you. Sites that provide data include

> http://www.canoe.ca
> http://www.statcan.ca
> http://www.findarticles.com
> Graphic, Visualization, & Usability
> Center's WWW surveys: http://www.cc.
> gatech.edu/gvu/user_surveys/

As your instructor directs,

a.   Identify at least seven stories in the data.

b.   Create visuals for three of the stories.
c.   Write a memo to your instructor explaining why you chose these stories and why you chose these visuals to display them.
d.   Write a memo to some group that might be interested in your findings, presenting your visuals as part of a short report.
e.   Print out the data and include it with a copy of your memo or report.

Polishing Your Prose

Writing Subject Lines and Headings

Subject lines are the title of a letter, memo, or email message. Headings within a document tell the reader what information you will discuss in that section.

Good subject lines are specific, concise, and appropriate for your purposes and the response you expect from the reader. Subject lines are required in memos, optional in letters.

- Put in good news if you have it.
- If information is neutral, summarize it.
- Use negative subject lines if the reader may not read the message or needs the information to act, or if the negative is your error.
- In a request that is easy for the reader to grant, put the subject of that request, or a direct question, in the subject line.
- When you must persuade a reluctant reader, use a common ground, a reader benefit, or a directed subject line that makes your stance on the issue clear.

Headings are single words, short phrases, or complete sentences that indicate the topic in a document section. Headings must be parallel—that is, they must use the same grammatical structure—and must cover all the information until the next heading.

The most useful headings are **informative** or **talking heads**, which sum up the content of the section.

Weak:	Problem
	Cause 1
	Cause 2
	Cause 3

Better:	Communication Problems between Air Traffic Controllers and Pilots
	Selective Listening
	Indirect Conversational Style
	Limitations of Short-Term Memory

Exercises

For the situations in 1-5, write a good subject line. Make 6–10 into effective headings using parallel form.

1. I'm your new boss
2. I wanted those annual enrolment forms back from you last week
3. Blood drive
4. Not that it will really affect you, but starting next week there will be an opportunity for non-hourly workers (you're hourly) to also get overtime compensation for extra hours worked
5. We're going to raise your insurance rates!
6. Making the Most of Undergraduate Years; Making the Most of Graduate School; Now What?
7. Research; Logistics: What's in It for Us?
8. Pros of Investing in Short-Term Mutual Funds; Cons of Investing in Short-Term Mutual Funds; The Market
9. Clemente Research Group's Five-Year Goals; What We Want to Accomplish in Ten Years; Our Fifteen-Year Goals
10. Overview; Budget; the Problem of Avondale Expanding into Europe

Check your answers to the odd-numbered exercises on page 573.

■ Online Learning Centre

Visit the Online Learning Centre at www.mcgrawhill.ca/olc/locker to access module quizzes, a searchable glossary, résumé and letter templates, additional business writing samples, CBC videos, and other learning and study tools.

■ CBC Video Case

CBC Visit the Online Learning Centre at www.mcgrawhill.ca/olc/locker to view "Small Talk" and "The Trouble with Teams," two online CBC Video Cases that highlight key issues from Unit Five. "Small Talk" looks in as an M.B.A. class is coached on one of the toughest skills for students to master—the art of making conversation in a business setting. And "The Trouble with Teams" explores recent studies indicating that perhaps teamwork—once seen as a surefire way to boost productivity and creativity—is not as successful as previously thought.

■ Cases for Communicators

■ Wash the Dishes, Save a Duck

Supported by reputable wildlife organizations, Procter and Gamble uses emotional appeal to market Dawn, its dishwashing liquid.

Dawn, it seems, is highly effective at cleaning the feathers of birds caught in oil spills. In fact, the product has been used in the cleanup of environmental disasters for more than 20 years, most notably in the aftermath of the Exxon Valdez spill.

In its new Dawn campaign, the company communicates its concern for community and environment through touching television and print ads. The television ads, for example, show an oil-covered duck being cleaned, an image that is sure to tug at the heartstrings of even the most stoical consumer.

Although it is clearly crafted to elicit strong emotions, the campaign is also designed to promote action. Procter & Gamble has committed to donating 10¢ for each bottle of Dawn redeemed in its "Save-A-Duck" program, to a total of $50 000. The donations will be divided between two wildlife rescue groups.... To participate in the program, consumers just need to input the UPC number from their bottle of Dawn on the Save-A-Duck Web site (http://www.saveaduck.com); in return, they will receive a certificate of appreciation for each purchase they register.

If successful, this campaign will strike a chord with environmentally aware consumers, creating an emotional connection with Dawn that they will, either consciously or unconsciously, take with them the next time they go to the store. Only time will tell if the Save-A-Duck campaign has cut through Dawn's competitors as well as Dawn cuts through oil!

Source: Jay Holcomb, "Dawn Comes to the Rescue—Again" (2005), http://www.ibrrc.org/save_a_duck.html, retrieved August 30, 2006.

Individual Activity

Imagine that you work in the market research department at Procter & Gamble Canada. The redemption program on the Save-A-Duck Web site presents your group with a fantastic opportunity to gather additional information from active, engaged consumers. Write an online questionnaire that will elicit critical data about customer demographics and purchase habits from these respondents.

The questionnaire, which will be put on the Save-A-Duck Web site, will appear immediately after visitors input the UPC number from their Dawn purchase and before they receive their certificate of appreciation. Customers will have the opportunity to opt out of filling out the questionnaire, but they will continue to see it on return visits until they fill it out. Return customers who have completed the questionnaire will not see it a second time.

Your manager has created a list of 10 general questions for the questionnaire:

1. Have these customers seen any of the Save-A-Duck advertisements? If so, which ones (print or television)?
2. How did they learn about the Save-A-Duck Web site?
3. Did the Save-A-Duck campaign convince them to buy Dawn?
4. How many of these people are new Dawn users?
5. How many use Dawn already?
6. If they are new users, which dishwashing liquid do they typically buy?
7. If they are regular Dawn users, how often do they buy the product?
8. Is this campaign hitting the market of a specific competitor?
9. How old are these individuals?
10. Is the campaign more effective with men or women?

Before you begin writing the questionnaire, consider these points:

- What type of questions should I write—open or closed?
- Who is the population for this questionnaire?
- Is my sample a random sample, a convenience sample, or a judgment sample?
- How does the sample type affect my ability to generalize my findings?

As you write the questionnaire, ask yourself the following questions:

- Are my questions phrased in such a way as to be neutral and clear?
- Have I made any inappropriate assumptions in my questions?
- Am I using branching questions where appropriate?
- Have I structured the questionnaire so that easier questions come before harder questions?
- Do my questions cover the necessary points as outlined by my manager?
- Have I used indentations and white space effectively?

Make the questionnaire clear, concise, and easy to tabulate.

Group Activity

The Save-A-Duck campaign—comprising print ads, television ads, and a Web site—is nearing completion, and discussions have already begun about its future. Some marketing executives believe that the campaign should be ended, while others think it should be extend indefinitely as part of the overall advertising approach for Dawn.

You and your colleagues in the marketing department have been asked to present a recommendation report to marketing executives on this very issue. You know that the campaign was successful in meeting its donation goals—in fact, the $50 000 was raised much more quickly than anyone anticipated—but you are not sure if it generated enough additional product sales to warrant its continuation.

With other members of your group, brainstorm the questions to which you'd like to get answers in order to write a report. For each question, brainstorm one or more possible stories the data might tell and which kind of visual would best tell that story.

Unit 7

Job Hunting

Because of his interpersonal and communication skills, Michael Moore enjoys an unusual degree of personal and professional freedom. His talents have enabled him to change careers and to work internationally while building an impressive repertoire of employability experience.

After receiving his Bachelor of Commerce from Mount Allison University, Michael interviewed with a number of large Ontario-based corporations and accepted a position with London Life as an investment advisor. Michael then moved to Scotiabank as a personal banking officer, but he found his place in the marketing side of the operation. Realizing he did not want a career in banking, Michael enrolled in a post-degree corporate communications program. He secured a summer internship at Fleishman-Hillard—one of the top communications agencies in the world—after three rounds of interviews. Fleishman-Hillard ultimately hired Michael full-time—before he had even completed the program.

In 2005, the Toronto investor relations firm Equicom Group recruited Michael to build relationships with American investment bankers and analysts.

Michael's advice to job seekers is to "network, have informal interviews to make more connections, and always follow up. When looking for employment, start with friends and former colleagues. Never burn a bridge and never forget those you've built. Those bridges can reach many destinations.

"When you write a cover letter, use four basic paragraphs. In the first, briefly introduce yourself and your purpose. In the second, describe your experience specifically. In the third, again using specifics, very briefly describe how your experience will benefit the employer. Finally, thank them for their time and finish with a call to action or a plan of action such as 'I look forward to meeting you and will call your office next week to discuss when we can meet.'"

As for the résumé format and content, Michael says that "if you lack experience but have good skills (a situation most recent graduates face), use the skills résumé setup to accentuate what you can offer a potential employer. Use bullets! No one wants to read a novel about your abilities.

"To secure that interview, follow up with telephone calls. Know the organization as completely as possible, and use the interview to demonstrate that knowledge. Do your homework: spend a few hours before the interview researching the company's Web site and recent press releases. Then, during the interview, use every opportunity to show what you know. Mention initiatives and objectives the company is working on, and explain how you may be able to contribute.

"After the interview, follow up again with an email to thank the interviewers for their time. Mention what a pleasure it was to meet them and express the hope of meeting with them again soon."

Michael also has experience vetting résumés and sitting on hiring teams. What three skills do the companies he's worked for value in a potential employee?

"Personal skills, writing skills, and flexibility," says Michael. "And you can demonstrate these traits throughout the whole process. For example, when you apply for an interview, be persistent. HR isn't always going to call you back. That doesn't necessarily mean that you don't deserve an interview; they're busy people and things slip through the cracks. Follow up! And network. Most jobs aren't found in the want ads. Get to know people...and get people to know you. That's the secret to getting the interview—and to getting the job."

P A I B O C

Analysis

1. According to Michael, what skills offer the most **benefits** to prospective employees?

2. What **information** is vital to a successful interview?

3. From the prospect's viewpoint, what is the primary **purpose** of the interview?

MODULE

26 Researching Jobs

Module Outline

- What do I need to know about myself to job hunt?

- What do I need to know about companies that might hire me?

- What is the information interview?

- What is the "hidden job market"? How do I tap into it?

- How do I present my non-traditional experiences?

Review of Key Points

Assignments for Module 26

Polishing Your Prose: Using Details

LEARNING OBJECTIVES

After reading and applying the information in Module 26, you'll be able to demonstrate

Knowledge of

- Job search techniques
- Job search strategies
- Information interviews
- The hidden job market
- New job interview practices

Skills to

- Self-assess realistically
- Find information about employers
- Use the Internet in your job search
- Find posted jobs and explore the hidden job market
- Present your non-traditional experience positively
- Prepare for job interviews

The Conference Board of Canada
Insights You Can Count On

Please see the OLC to preview the key skills from the Conference Board of Canada's Employability Skills 2000+ covered in this module.

Perhaps you already have a job waiting for you; perhaps your skills are in such demand that employers will seek you out. If, however, you're not sure how to secure your ideal job, the modules in this unit will help you find your way.

The first step in any job search is to think about your own interests and needs. Indeed, Richard Bolles, author of the classic job-hunter's guide *What Color Is Your Parachute?* claims that the most successful job hunting method hasn't changed:

> Do thorough homework on yourself. Know your best skills, in order of priority. Know the fields in which you want to use those skills. Talk to people who have those kinds of jobs. Find out whether they're happy, and how they found their jobs. Then choose the places where you want to work, rather than just those places that have advertised openings. Thoroughly research these organizations before approaching them. Seek out the person who actually has the power to hire you for the job that you want. Demonstrate to that person how you can help the company with its problems. Cut no corners; take no shortcuts. That method has an 86 percent success rate.[1]

What do I need to know about myself to job hunt?

Your need to realistically self-assess: identify your knowledge, skills, abilities, interests, and values.

SEE THE OLC!

Employability Tips

SEE THE OLC!

Use workopolis.com resources to assess yourself and find your career

Each person could happily do several jobs. Personality and aptitude tests can tell you what your strengths are, but they won't say, "You should be a _____." In preparation for the job search, and for the interview, you need to answer specific questions like these:

- What achievements have given you the most satisfaction? Why did you enjoy them?
- Would you rather have firm deadlines or a flexible schedule? Do you prefer working alone or with other people? Do you prefer specific instructions and standards for evaluation or freedom and uncertainty? How comfortable are you with pressure? How do you manage multiple deadlines? How much challenge do you want?
- Are you willing to take work home? Are you prepared to travel? How important is recognition to you? How important is money compared to having time to spend with family and friends?
- Where do you want to live? What features in terms of weather, geography, and cultural and social life do you see as ideal?
- What do you want from your work? Do you work to achieve certain purposes or values, or is work "just a way to make a living"? Are the organization's culture and ethical standards important to you?

Once you have identified in writing what is most important to you, look at the job market to see where you can find what you want. For example, your greatest interest is athletics, but you aren't good enough for the pros. Your job market analysis might suggest several alternatives. You could teach sports and physical fitness as a high school coach or a corporate fitness director. You could cover sports for a newspaper, a magazine, a TV station, or the Web. You could go into management or sales for a professional sports team, a health club, or a company that sells sports equipment. You could create or manage a sports Web page.

What do I need to know about companies that might hire me?

You need to know as much as you can.

Organizations hire people who demonstrate motivation, energy, and critical thinking. Preparation through research demonstrates all these skills. Moreover, to adapt your letter and résumé to a specific organization and to shine at the interview, you need information both about the employer and about the job itself. You'll need to know

- **What the job itself involves.** Start your research at the college or university career centre. Notebooks at campus placement offices often have fuller job descriptions than appear in ads. Talk to friends who have graduated recently to learn what their jobs involve. Request information interviews to learn more about opportunities that interest you.
- **The name and address of the person who should receive the letter.** To get this information, check the ad or the organization's Web site, or call the company. An advantage of calling is that you can find out whether your contact prefers a courtesy title (*Mr.*, *Ms.*, or *Mrs.*).
- **What the organization does and at least four or five facts about it.** Knowing the organization's larger goals enables you to describe how your specific work will help the company meet its goals. Useful facts include the following:
  - Market share
  - Competitive position
  - New products, services, or promotions
  - Technology or manufacturing equipment applications
  - Plans for growth or downsizing
  - Challenges the organization faces
  - The corporate culture (◀|▷ Module 2)

The directories listed in Table 26.1 provide information ranging from net worth, market share, and principal products to the names of officers and directors. Ask your librarian to identify additional directories. To get specific financial data (and to see how the organization presents itself to the public), get the company's annual report on the Web. (Note: only companies whose stock is publicly traded are required to issue annual reports. In this day of mergers and buyouts, many companies are owned by other companies. The parent company may be the only one to issue an annual report.) Many company Web sites provide information about training programs and career paths for new hires. To learn about new products, plans for growth, or solutions to industry challenges, read business newspapers such as the *National Post*, *The Globe and Mail*, *The Wall Street Journal*, or the *Financial Post*; business magazines such as *Report on Business*, *Canadian Business*, *Strategy Magazine*, *Fortune*, *Business Week*, and *Forbes*; and trade

The world is our workplace, as this photo of a Canadian working abroad illustrates. The adventuresome find that personal and career benefits far exceed any temporary cultural discomfort.

Source: Wallace Immen, *The Globe and Mail*, February 22, 2006, C1.

SEE THE OLC!

Finding Information on Canadian Businesses

TABLE 26.1
Where to Get Addresses and Facts about Companies

General Directories	Dun and Bradstreet
Directory of Corporate Affiliations	Franchise Annual: Directory
Dun's Million Dollar Directory	Hoover's Handbook of American Business
Standard & Poor's Register of Corporations, Directors, and Executives	O'Dwyer's Directory of Public Relations Firms
	The Rand McNally Bankers' Directory
Thomas Register of American Manufacturers	Scott's Business Directory
Specialized Directories and Resource Books	Standard Directory of Advertisers ("Red Book")
Accounting Firms and Practitioners	Television Factbook
Directory of Hotel and Motel Systems	Traders

TABLE 26.2
Examples of Trade Journals and Magazines

Advertising Age	Computer Dealer News	HR Focus
Business to Business Magazine	Computing Canada	Information Highways
	Direction Informatique	Medical Post
CAmagazine	Essense (Canadian Federation of Chefs & Cooks)	Northern Miner (mining news)
Canada Employment Weekly		
Canadian Auto World	Farm & Country (Ontario commercial farmer trade)	The Western Producer (Saskatoon)
Canadian Business		
The Canadian Firefighter	Financial Analysts Journal	
Canadian Musician	Graphic Arts Monthly	

journals. Each of these has indexes listing which companies are discussed in a specific issue. A few of the trade journals available are listed in Table 26.2.

The Internet has much of this information, including information about corporate culture and even anonymous statements from employees. Check blogs, professional electronic mailing lists and electronic bulletin boards. Employers sometimes post specialized jobs on them: they're always a good way to get information about the industry you hope to enter.

■ What is the information interview?

Information interviews are a sophisticated form of networking. They're crucial if you're not sure what you want to do.

In an **information interview,** you talk to someone who works in the area you hope to enter. The interview allows you to find out what the day-to-day work involves and how you can best prepare to enter that field. However, if you're prepared, you can use the

EXPANDING A CRITICAL SKILL

Selling Yourself in the New Work World

In the new world of work, non-traditional employment has replaced the cradle-to-grave job security of your parents and grandparents. "Almost 40 per cent of Canadians are earning a living as temps, part-timers, contract workers or self-employed consultants, and their numbers are growing."

Although small and medium-sized businesses offer the best employment opportunities for today's job-seekers, all employers, regardless of company size, seek people who are well prepared, can think on their feet, and who demonstrate values that match those of the organization.

To better insure that match, hiring processes are also evolving. Because the traditional employment interview has proven inadequate, employers are trying other methods, including multiple interviews, team interviews, behavioural interviews, and psychological testing. Aspiring candidates should prepare thoroughly to answer the "key question in the mind of potential employers...: 'How will hiring this person make my life easier?'"

- Research the organization, "...[the] industry[,]and [current] challenges..."

- Know the corporate culture, and be prepared to describe specifically how your skills and values fit that culture
- Prepare to answer behavioural questions, such as "Describe a situation in which you diffused a potential conflict;" "Describe a situation in which you demonstrated leadership skills;" "Why did you apply for this job?...Give ...an 'example of a difficult situation you were in with people and how you handled it'"
- Prepare for expert recruiters who will dig for unrehearsed answers (and character insights) with such queries as "'When is it okay to lie? How far would you go to close a deal? What does independence mean to you?'"

Astute interviewees understand that even the deceptively simple, kick-off question, "Tell me about yourself," translates as "Tell me specifically why I should hire you." Savvy employment searchers come prepared with specific examples to answer that question.

Source: Ron McGowan, "Forget a Job: Grads Must Sell Selves to New World of Work," *The Globe and Mail*, May 4, 2004, C1; Wallace Immen, "Thinking on Your Feet Gets a Foot in the Door," *The Globe and Mail*, September 16, 2005, C.3; Andy Holloway, "Recruit Right: A Guide to Finding the Best Fit," *Canadian Business*, October 10–23, 2005, p.123; and Arlen H. Hirsch, "'Tell Me About Yourself' Response is Trickier than You Might Think," *The Globe and Mail*, November 10, 2004, C9.

information interview to self-recruit ("I want to work for you!") and to make a positive impression.

SEE THE OLC!

Canadian Career Resources on the Web

An information interview can tell you several things:

- It can let you know whether you'd like the job.
- It can give you specific information that you can use to present yourself effectively in your résumé and application letter.
- It can create a good image of you in the mind of the interviewer, so that he or she thinks of you when openings arise.

In an information interview, you might ask the following questions:

- What are you working on right now?
- How do you spend your typical day?
- How does what you do make or save the organization time or money?
- How have your duties changed since you first started working here?
- What do you like best about your job? What do you like least?

To reach your career goals, define them clearly, understand your strengths, and find information about employers.

- What do you think the future holds for this kind of work?
- How did you get this job?
- What courses, activities, or jobs would you recommend to someone who wanted to do this kind of work?

To set up an information interview, phone, or write a letter like the one in Figure 26.1 on the next page. If you write, phone the following week to set up a specific time.

What is the "hidden job market"? How do I tap into it?

The "hidden market," comprising jobs that are never advertised, is accessible to those who know how to use networking techniques. Referral interviews and prospecting letters can help you find it.

Most great jobs are never advertised—and the number rises the higher up the job ladder you go. More than 60 percent of all new jobs come not from responding to an ad but from networking with personal contacts.[2] Some of these jobs are created especially for a specific person. These unadvertised jobs are called the **hidden job market**; creating your own opportunities to meet and work with others informally—through *volunteer community involvement*, for example—is the optimum method of tapping into this market. (For tips on finding volunteer community involvement, see (◀▮▶ Module 19.)

Referral interviews, an organized method of networking, offer another way to tap into these jobs. Schedule referral interviews to learn about current job opportunities in your field. Sometimes an interview that starts out as an information interview turns into a referral interview.

A referral interview gives you information about current opportunities available in the area you're interested in, refers you to other people who can tell you about job opportunities, and enables the interviewer to see that you could make a contribution to his or her organization. Therefore, the goal of a referral interview is to put you face-to-face with someone who has the power to hire you: the owner of a small company, the division vice president or branch manager of a big company, or the director of the local office of a provincial or federal agency.

FIGURE 26.1
Letter Requesting an Information Interview

774 Sherbrooke Street East
Montreal, PQ H8S 1H1

April 18, 2007

Kam Yuricich
Clary Communications
1420 Sherbrooke Street East
Montreal, PQ H3G 1K9

Dear Mr. Yuricich:

You-attitude focuses on the reader's importance.

Your talk to McGill's PRSSA Chapter last week about the differences between working for a PR firm and being a PR staff person within an organization, really interested me. Your advice would be invaluable to me as I find my niche in the workforce. *Emotional appeal flatters the reader.*

Information establishes the writer's credibility.

Last summer I had a co-op placement with Management Horizons. Although some of my assignments were gofer jobs, my supervisor, Jason Correila, gave me the chance to work on several brochures and to draft two speeches for managers. I enjoyed this variety and would like to learn more about the possibility of working in a PR firm. Could I schedule an information interview with you to learn more about how public relations consultants work with their clients? *The specific request makes a logical appeal.*

Emphasizes the reader's expertise.

Perhaps we could discuss the courses you think would best prepare me for PR work. I have a year and a half left before graduation and would like to choose electives that would make me most employable.

Tells the reader the limits of the request.

When convenient for you, I would greatly appreciate 30 minutes of your time. I'll call you early next week to set up an appointment. *Makes it easy for the reader*

Sincerely,

Lee Tan
Lee Tan

INSTANT REPLAY

Information Interviews

In an **information interview** you talk to someone who works in the area you hope to enter, to find out what the day-to-day work involves and how you can best prepare to enter that field.

Start by scheduling interviews with people you know who may know something about that field—professors, co-workers, neighbours, friends. Call your alumni office to get the names and phone numbers of alumni who now work where you would like to work. Your (purported) purpose in talking to them is to get advice about improving your résumé and about general job-hunting strategies. Your real intention: to become a known commodity and thereby get referrals to other people. In fact, go into the interview with the names of people you'd like to talk to. If the interviewee doesn't suggest anyone, say, "Do you think it would be a good idea for me to talk to _____ ?"

Then, armed with a referral from someone you know, call the former and say, "So-and-so suggested I talk with you about job-hunting strategy." If the person says, "We aren't hiring," you say, "Oh, I'm not asking you for a job. I'd just like some advice from a knowledgeable person about the opportunities in banking [or desktop publishing, or whatever] in this city." If this person does not have the power to create a position, ask for more referrals at the end of this interview. (You can also polish your résumé, if you get good suggestions.)

Even when you talk to the person who could create a job for you, you *do not ask for a job*. To give you advice about your résumé, however, the person has to look at it. When a powerful person focuses on your skills, he or she will naturally think about the problems and needs in that organization. When there's a match between what you can do and what the organization needs, that person may be able to create a position for you.

Remember the two truisms of job hunting: **self-recruitment is still the number one way to get hired,** and **people hire people they know.** Although the idea of cold calling may seem daunting, you'll find most people receptive. You are likely to get the interview when you mention a familiar name ("So-and-so suggested I talk with you.") and sound enthusiastic. Prepare as carefully for these interviews as you would for a job interview. Think of good questions in advance; know something about the general field or industry; learn as much as you can about the specific company.

Always follow up information and referral interviews with personal thank-you letters. Use specifics to show that you paid attention during the interview, and enclose a copy of your revised résumé.

■ How do I present my non-traditional experiences?

Address the employer's potential concerns positively.

Today, people bring a variety of non-traditional experiences to the job search. These experiences often build the transferable skills that savvy employers search for. In a world where the ability to learn is recognized as the key to employability, your communication skills will determine whether you get the job.

This section gives advice on presenting your previous experience positively.

■ "All My Experience Is in My Family's Business"

In your résumé, simply list the company you worked for. For a reference, instead of a family member, list a supervisor, client, or vendor who can talk about your work. Since the reader may wonder whether "Jim Clarke" is any relation to "Clarke Construction Company," be ready to answer interview questions about why you're looking at other companies. Prepare an answer that stresses the broader opportunities you seek but doesn't criticize your family or the family business.

◼ "I've Been out of the Job Market for a While"

You need to prove to a potential employer that you're up-to-date and motivated:

- Research changes in your field to identify prospective employers' priorities. When you can demonstrate that you can make an immediate contribution, you'll have a much easier sell. To do that, however, you need to know what the employer needs: what skills are employers looking for?
- Be active in professional organizations. Attend meetings; read magazines, newspapers, and trade journals.
- Learn the computer programs that professionals in your field use.
- Show how your at-home experience relates directly to the workplace. Multi-tasking, organizing food bank drives, managing projects, chairing PTA meetings, dealing with unpredictable situations, building consensus, listening, raising money, and making presentations are all transferable skills.
- Create a portfolio of your work—even if it's for imaginary clients—to demonstrate your expertise.[3] Most of Canada's provinces and territories offer prior learning assessment and recognition (PLAR) to adults with work experience. Based on a demonstration of the requisite knowledge and skills, you can get credit for postsecondary courses. Most high-level courses require that candidates prepare a proposal and a portfolio of work to demonstrate subject knowledge and skills.

SEE THE OLC!

PLAR (Prior Learning Assessment and Recognition)

◼ "I Want to Change Fields"

Learn about the skills needed in the job you want. Learn the language of the industry. Then you can identify a good reason (from the prospective employer's point of view) for choosing to explore a new field. "I want a change" or "I need to get out of a bad situation" will not convince an employer that you know what you're doing.

Think about how your experience relates to the job you want. Jack is an older-than-average student who wants to be a pharmaceutical sales representative. He has sold woodstoves, served subpoenas, and worked on an oil rig. A chronological résumé makes his work history look directionless. But a skills résumé (◀▶ Module 27) could focus on persuasive ability (selling stoves), initiative and persistence (serving subpoenas), and technical knowledge (courses in biology and chemistry).[4]

◼ "I Was Fired"

First, deal with the emotional baggage. You need to reduce negative feelings to a manageable level before you're ready to job hunt.

Second, try to learn from the experience. You'll be a much more attractive job candidate if you can show that you've learned from the experience—whether your lesson is improved work habits or the need to choose a job where you can do work you're proud of.

Third, suggests Phil Elder, an interviewer for an insurance company, call the person who fired you and say something like this: "Look, I know you weren't pleased with the job I did at _____ . I'm applying for a job at _____ now and the personnel director may call you to ask about me. Would you be willing to give me the chance to get this job so that I can try to do things right this time?" All but the hardest of heart, says Elder, will give you one more chance. You won't get a glowing reference, but neither will the statement be so damning that no one is willing to hire you.[5]

INSTANT REPLAY

The Hidden Job Market and Referral Interviews

Unadvertised jobs are called the **hidden job market**. Referral interviews, an organized method of networking, offer the most systematic way to tap into these jobs. Schedule **referral interviews** to learn about current job opportunities in your field.

■ "I Don't Have Any Experience"

You can get experience in several ways:

- Take a fast-food job—and keep it. If you do well, you may be promoted to a supervisor within a year. Use every opportunity to learn about the management and financial aspects of the business.
- Volunteer. Coach a community little-league team, join the PTA, help out at your local food bank, canvass for charity. If you work hard, you'll quickly get an opportunity to do more: manage a budget, write fundraising materials, and supervise other volunteers.
- Freelance. Design brochures, create Web pages, do tax returns for small businesses. Use your skills—for free, if you have to at first.
- Write. Create a portfolio of ads, instructions, or whatever documents are relevant for the field you want to enter. Ask a professional—an instructor, a local businessperson, someone from a professional organization—to critique them. Volunteer your services to local fundraising organizations and small businesses.

Pick something where you interact with other people, so that you can show that you can work well in an organization.

If you're in the job market now, think carefully about what you've really done. Write sentences using the action verbs in ◀▮▶ Table 27.1 on pages 512–513. Think about your experiences and skills development in courses, in volunteer work, in unpaid activities. Focus especially on your communications skills: problem solving, critical thinking, managing projects, working as part of a team, persuasive speaking, and writing. Solving a problem for a hypothetical firm in an accounting class, thinking critically about a report problem in business communication, working with a group in a marketing class, and communicating with people at the senior centre where you volunteer are all valuable experiences, even if no one paid you.

If you're not actually looking for a job but just need to create a résumé for this course, ask your instructor whether you may assume that you're graduating and add the things you hope to do between now and that time.

■ "I'm a Lot Older Than They Want"

Even before the recent dot.com backlash, more mature workers were in demand for their sophisticated interpersonal and communications abilities. Uninformed employers are concerned that older people won't be flexible, up-to-date, or willing to be supervised by someone younger. You can counter these fears:

- Keep up-to-date. Read trade journals; attend professional meetings.
- Learn the computer programs your field uses. Refer to technology in the résumé, job letter, and interview: "Yes, I saw the specifications for your new product on your Web site."
- Work with younger people, in classroom teams, in volunteer work, or on the job. Be able to cite specific cases where you've learned from young people and worked well with them.
- Use positive emphasis (◀▮▶ Module 7). Talk about your ability to relate to older customers (who have so much disposable income), the valuable perspective you bring. Focus on fairly recent events, not ones from 20 years ago.
- Show energy and enthusiasm to counter the stereotype that older people are tired and ill.

On a final note, the most successful job hunters are prepared: they seek opportunities to impress others positively and they understand that everyone they meet is both a potential employer and a potential customer.

Employability Skills 2000+

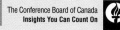

The Conference Board of Canada
Insights You Can Count On

Please see the OLC to preview the key skills from the Conference Board of Canada's Employability Skills 2000+ covered in this module.

Review of Key Points

1. Identify six sources where you can find specific information about employers and jobs.
2. What is the hidden job market, and how can you find out about "hidden" jobs?
3. How can an information interview help job seekers?
4. What should you know about yourself before applying for a job?
5. Why is it important to research the companies and industries in which you want to work?
6. What is your biggest weakness as you prepare to job hunt? How can you compensate for, or minimize, this weakness?

Assignments for Module 26

Questions for Critical Thinking

26.1 Why is it desirable to start thinking about jobs months—even years—before you'll actually be on the market?

26.2 What primary sources can you use to begin your company research?

26.3 What secondary print and electronic resources can you use to begin your research?

Exercises and Problems

26.4   Beginning Your Self-Inventory

Initiate the job-hunting process on the nextSteps.org Job Search site (http://www.nextsteps.org/jobsearch/) by completing the inventory questionnaire. Note the results as part of the process of knowing yourself.

26.5   Evaluating Career Web Sites*

Evaluate three or more Web sites for job hunters, considering the following questions:

- Is the site easy to navigate?
- Is it visually attractive?
- Are any ads unobtrusive?
- Does it contain good advice?

- Does it let job hunters specify who may not see their posted résumés (e.g., the current employer)?
- Does it have any features that you don't find in other career Web sites?

*Inspired by a problem written by Gary Kohut, University of North Carolina at Charlotte.

26.6   Networking

Write to a friend who is already in the workforce, asking about one or more of the following topics:

- Are any jobs in your field available in your friend's organization? If so, what?
- If a job is available, can your friend provide information beyond the job listing that will help

you write a more detailed, persuasive letter? (Specify the kind of information you'd like to have.)
- Can your friend suggest people in other organizations who might be useful to you in your job search? (Specify any organizations in which you're especially interested.)

26.7   Gathering Information about an Industry

Use six recent issues of a trade journal to report on three to five trends, developments, or issues that are important in an industry.

As your instructor directs,

a.   Share your findings with a small group of students.

b.   Summarize your findings in a memo to your instructor.

c.   Present your findings to the class.

d.   Email your findings to the other members of the class.

e.   Join with a small group of other students to write a report summarizing the results of this research.

26.8   Gathering Information about a Specific Organization

Gather printed information about a specific organization, using several of the following methods:

- Use the most current edition of *The Career Directory.*
- Check the company's Web site.
- Read the company's annual report.
- Talk to someone who works there.
- Pick up relevant information at your local board of trade or chamber of commerce.
- Read articles in trade publications and *The Globe and Mail,* the *National Post, The Wall Street Journal,* or the *Financial Post* that mention the organization (check the indexes).

- Get the names and addresses of its officers (from a directory or from the Web).
- Read recruiting literature provided by the company.

As your instructor directs,

a.   Share your findings with a small group of students.

b.   Summarize your findings in a memo to your instructor.

c.   Present your findings orally to the class.

d.   Email your findings to the other members of the class.

e.   Join with a small group of other students to write a report summarizing the results of this research.

26.9   Conducting an Information Interview

Interview someone working in a field you're interested in. Use the questions listed in the module or the shorter list here:

- How did you get started in this field?
- What do you like about your job?
- What do you dislike about your job?
- Who are three other people who could give me additional information about this job?

As your instructor directs,

a.   Share the results of your interview with a small group of students.

b.   Write up your interview in a memo to your instructor.

c.   Present the results of your interview orally to the class.

d.   Email a summary of your interview to other members of your class.

e.   Write to the interviewee thanking him or her for taking the time to talk to you.

Polishing Your Prose

Using Details

Details are especially important in reader benefits (◀I▶ Module 8), reports, résumés, job application, and sales letters. Customers or potential employers look for specific details to help them make decisions, such as what makes your product better than the competition's or how your experience would help the reader. Here's an example:

> I can offer you more than ten years of advertising experience, including five years of broadcast sales in Ottawa, where I generated more than $19 million in revenue, as well as three years with J. Walter Thompson, Toronto's leading advertising company. For the first four years of my career, I also wrote advertising copy, including hundreds of local and regional radio spots for such diverse products as cookies, cat food, fishing tackle, and children's toys. I also wrote print pieces, including the entire 15-month campaign for Vancouver-based "Uncle Bill's Electronic Bazaar," which increased sales by nearly 37 percent during that period.

Reader Benefits

What features or experiences make your product or service unique? useful? cost-effective?

Weak: With the Stereobooster, your car will sound great.

Better: The Stereobooster safely gives your car audio system a full 30 watts per channel of sheer sound excitement, double that of other systems on the market—all for under $50.

The Five Senses

Describe sight, sound, taste, touch, and smell. Some sensations are so powerful that they immediately conjure up thoughts or emotions—the smell of fresh coffee, the sound of ocean waves, the feeling of sunlight against the skin.

Concrete Nouns and Verbs

Concrete nouns and verbs are better than more general nouns and verbs combined with adjectives and adverbs. For instance, *manager* and *15 months* are more concrete than *the person in charge* or *a while*. Concrete words make meaning clear and vivid:

Weak: At my last job, I typed stuff.

Better: As a clerk typist II for Hughes and Associates, I typed hundreds of memos, letters, and reports.

Increase your vocabulary by reading a variety of materials. Keep a dictionary and thesaurus handy. Do crossword puzzles or computer word games to practise what you know.

Adjectives and Adverbs That Count

Omit or replace vague or overused adjectives and adverbs: *basically, some, very, many, a lot, kind/sort of, partly, eventually.* Increasingly, novice writers are using *so* as an adjective, as in "He was so happy about the promotion." Exactly how happy is this?

Conversational English, Not Jargon or Obscure Words

In general, choose the more conversational option over jargon or obscure words: *exit, typical,* or *second to last* rather than *egress, quintessential,* or *penultimate.*

Exercises

Add details to the following sentences.

1. I work for a company.
2. The person in charge of our department wants some files.
3. Sometime in the future I will get a job in my field.
4. It's been a while since I went there.
5. Our product will help you.
6. There are lots of reasons why you should hire me.
7. This product is so much better than its competitors.
8. We will have a meeting in the afternoon.
9. My experience makes me a good candidate for this job.
10. We plan to travel to a couple of provinces sometime next month.

Check your answers to the odd-numbered exercises on page 573.

Online Learning Centre

Visit the Online Learning Centre at www.mcgrawhill.ca/olc/locker to access module quizzes, a searchable glossary, résumé and letter templates, additional business writing samples, CBC videos, and other learning and study tools.

27 Creating Persuasive Résumés

Module Outline

- How can I encourage the employer to pay attention to my résumé?

- What kind of résumé should I use?

- How do résumé formats differ?

- What parts of résumé formats are the same?

- What should I do if the standard categories don't fit?

- When should I limit my résumé to just one page?

- How do I create a scannable résumé?

Review of Key Points

Assignments for Module 27

Polishing Your Prose: Proofreading

LEARNING OBJECTIVES

After reading and applying the information in Module 27, you'll be able to demonstrate

Knowledge of

- Current résumé-writing practices

Skills to

- Create the résumé that best showcases your qualifications
- Make your experience relevant to employers
- Increase the number of "hits" your résumé receives

The Conference Board of Canada
Insights You Can Count On

Please see the OLC to preview the key skills from the Conference Board of Canada's Employability Skills 2000+ covered in this module.

FIGURE 27.1

P A I B O C

Questions for Analysis

Use the PAIBOC questions to analyze business communication problems:

P What are your purposes in writing?

A Who is your audience? How do members of your audience differ? What audience characteristics are relevant to this particular message?

I What information must your message include?

B What reasons or reader benefits can you use to support your position?

O What objections can you expect your readers to have? What negative elements of your message must you de-emphasize or overcome?

C How will the context affect reader response? Think about your relationship to the reader, the morale in the organization, the economy, the time of year, and any special circumstances.

A résumé summarizes your qualifications so persuasively that you get an interview. When you're in the job market, having a résumé makes you prepared for every opportunity. When you're employed, having a current résumé allows you to assess your continuous improvement; this ongoing inventory makes it easier for you to take advantage of even better job opportunities that come up. Even if you're several years away from job hunting, preparing a résumé now will make you more conscious of what to do in the next two or three years to make yourself an attractive candidate. Writing a résumé is also an ego-building experience: the person who looks so good on paper is *you*!

If your skills are in great demand, you might be able to ignore every résumé-writing guideline and still get a good job. When you must compete against many applicants, however, these guidelines can showcase your employability skills.

Of course, the PAIBOC writing formula (see Figure 27.1) applies to all job communications. Tailor your résumé to your specific audiences and purposes, and to your unique qualifications. Adopt the wording or layout of an example if it's relevant to your own situation, but consider your résumé a lifelong work in progress. Your experiences, the nature of work, the labour market, and the demands of the potential job change constantly; so will your résumé.

■ How can I encourage the employer to pay attention to my résumé?

> *Write your résumé to create the best first impression and to show how your qualifications fit the job and the company.*

Your résumé can be screened in two ways: electronically or by a person. If people do the reading, employers may skim the résumés quickly, dividing the documents into two piles: "reject" and "maybe." In the first round, each résumé may get as little as 2.9 seconds of the reader's attention. Then the reader goes through the "maybe" pile again, weeding out more documents. If there are a lot of résumés (and some companies get 2000 résumés a week), résumés may get only 10 to 30 seconds in this stage. After the initial pile has been culled to one-half or one-hundredth of the initial pile, the remaining documents will be read more carefully to choose the people who are invited for interviews.

Alternatively, your résumé may be electronically scanned into a job-applicant tracking system. Then a computer does the first set of cuts. The employer specifies the keywords from the job description, listing the knowledge, skills, and abilities that the ideal applicant would have. Sometimes personal characteristics (e.g., *hard worker, good writer, willing to travel*) may also be included. The employer receives the résumés that match the keywords, arranged with the most "hits" first. The employer then chooses the interviewees. In the current job market, you need both a paper résumé that's attractive to the human eye, and a scannable résumé that serves your purposes in a job-applicant tracking system. You can do several things to increase the chances that a real human being will attend to your résumé:

- Make your résumé *attractive* and *readable*: use picture-frame placement, plenty of white space, and a serif font (Times New Roman, for example); bold major headings.
- Revise and edit your résumé to ensure it's error-free: grammar and spelling mistakes will cost you the interview.
- Specify how you contributed to the organization. If possible, quantify your contribution: *increased sales 10 percent; saved the company $13 000; supervised five people.*

EXPANDING A CRITICAL SKILL

Use the KISS Checklist to Create Attention-Getting Résumés

Keep your résumé **s**imple and **s**pecific since you have only a few minutes to attract and hold recruiters' attention. Employment experts suggest following these strategies to create a résumé that gets you the job interview:

Pay Attention to Appearance

If submitting a hard copy

- Use a laser printer to print your résumé on high-quality letter-sized paper. White paper is standard for business résumés; cream, pale grey, and parchment colours are also acceptable.
- Use the same font throughout; vary font size, and use bold and italics for emphasis.
- Format the résumé, and use white space to maximize readability.
- Avoid résumé templates; they suggest lack of creativity and interest.

If emailing your résumé

- Attach your résumé as a Word document.
- Save the doc. with your name so the recruiter can easily retrieve it amongst others.

Consider the Content

Employers want to interview eligible candidates. Ensure your résumé emphasizes your eligibility.

- Highlight skills that are relevant to the position and the organization.
- Be specific: reframe experiences into skills; provide facts and numbers.
- Be clear: use short, concrete nouns, and active verbs to describe your skills.
- Be clean. Even if potential employers don't check—and increasingly they do—lies and exaggerations are often glaringly obvious.
- Proofread, and then have someone else proofread for you. Spelling and grammar mistakes immediately turn prospective employers off. They assume that since you cannot be bothered to double-check your own résumé, you probably cannot be bothered to do the job correctly.

Sources: Wendy Mclellan, "Starting Off on an Honest Footing: Résumé Fraud: It Isn't Worth It to Lie—Or to Avoid Checking Up on Job Applicants," (2005), http://www.ceridian.ca/en/news/2005/jul3_2005.html; and Wallace Immen, "How Did You Get to the Top with that Résumé?" *The Globe and Mail*, October 12, 2005, C3.

FYI

The personal qualities employers want most are communication skills and self-motivation, according to a survey by the National Association of Colleges and Employers.

Source: Albert R. Karr, "Work Week," *The Wall Street Journal*, February 8, 2000, A1.

- Emphasize achievements that are relevant to the position for which you're applying.
- Identify your abilities in order of financial worth to the organization. Idea people are worth the most, because creative or innovative notions can make or save companies billions of dollars; cite your strategic/problem-solving accomplishments first. People skills are the next most valuable abilities; refer to your training, supervising, and scheduling responsibilities. "Things" skills—software knowledge, for example—are most easily acquired and immediately obsolete; cite these last, unless these technical skills are key to the job.
- Use the language and terminology of the industry and the organization you want to join.
- Include transferable skills: the ability to write and speak well, to identify and solve problems, to work well independently and with others, to speak a second language, and to use computer programs.
- Design one résumé to appeal to the human eye and the second to be easily processed by an electronic scanner.

The more you tailor your résumé to a specific employer, the greater your chances for securing an interview.

What kind of résumé should I use?

Use the format that makes you look best.

FYI

Researching industry trends and population and labour demographics is key to your job search success. For example, Ontario's Niagara Region, one of Canada's fastest growing economies, has one of the country's oldest populations. The result: 50 000 to 70 000 new jobs—in tourism, engineering, science, architectural management, construction, health care, and education—will be available over the next five years.

Source: Pat Brennan, "Niagara Rises: Jobs are Ripe for the Picking," *Toronto Star*, March 17, 2001, N19.

Depending on their experience and the audience, people use one of three kinds of résumés: **chronological, functional** or **combination, or skills.** The chronological résumé summarizes what you have accomplished, starting with the most recent events and going backward in reverse chronology. It emphasizes degrees, job titles, and dates. Figure 27.2 on the next page shows a chronological résumé. Use a chronological résumé when you have limited relevant work experience and your education and experience show

- A logical preparation for the position for which you're applying
- A steady progression leading to the present

The **functional** or **combination résumé** emphasizes the applicant's most important (to the reader) job titles and responsibilities, or functions, regardless of chronology. Usually, the functional résumé reverts to the **reverse chronology** listing for information not related to paid employment, as reflected in Figure 27.3 on page 507. Use the functional/combination résumé if you meet these criteria:

- Your work experiences match the position responsibilities
- Your skills and expertise match the position requirements
- Your education and experience are not the usual route to the position for which you're applying
- You want to de-emphasize your formal education

The **skills résumé** emphasizes the skills you've acquired through work experience. Figure 27.4 on page 509, shows a skills résumé. Use a skills résumé when you meet these criteria:

- You want to combine experience from paid jobs, activities or volunteer work, and courses to show the extent of your experience in administration, finance, speaking, and so on
- Your education and experience are not the usual route to the position for which you're applying
- You're changing fields
- Your recent work history may create the wrong impression (e.g., it has gaps, shows a demotion, shows job-hopping, etc.)

The best résumés convey relevant details as concisely and attractively as possible. Most résumés use bullet points, omit *I*, and use sentence fragments punctuated as complete sentences. Complete sentences are acceptable, as are *me* and *my*, if they are the briefest way to present information.

FYI

Résumé is a French word meaning *summary*. To create the é (e with an acute accent) in a word-processing program, click Insert and select Symbol. Never use the apostrophe to replace the accent. However, you can write RESUME in full caps or use resume without the accent marks.

How do résumé formats differ?

They showcase you differently, depending on your experiences, your purpose (the job you're applying for), and your audience.

A chronological résumé, like the one in Figure 27.2, focuses on when, then what, and emphasizes academic qualifications. Experience is organized by dates, with the most recent job first. The functional or combination résumé (Figure 27.3) showcases the applicant's qualifications based on relevant job functions, or responsibilities. Extensive experience, not dates or academic degrees, is the focus. Seasoned and highly qualified applicants

FIGURE 27.2
A Chronological Résumé

A vertical line provides visual variety.

Jerry A. Jackson

2105 East Hill Avenue, Saskatoon, SK S7J 3C8

306-555-4108 jjackson@ccw.sk.ca

Vary font sizes. The name is in 18-point, the main headings in 12-point, and the text in 11-point type.

If you have a professional Web page, include its URL.

Education

A.A.S. in Finance, May 2004, Community College of Winnipeg, Winnipeg, SK

B Average

Courses Related to Program:

List not only major courses but also others that will enhance your performance.

Intermediate Accounting I and II	Microeconomics
Business Writing	Presentation Skills
Consumer Finance	Public Speaking
Financial Management	Report and Technical Writing
Interpersonal Communication	Sociology of Marriage and Family
Investments	Statistics

Sports Experience

Intramural Volleyball Team (Champions, Winter 2004)

Two-year Varsity Letterman, Community College of Winnipeg

Men's NCAA Division II Basketball

Experience

Financial Sales Representative, Primerica Company, Winnipeg, SK, February 2004–present. Work with clients to plan investment strategies; recommend specific investments.

Entrepreneur, Winnipeg, SK, and Saskatoon, SK, September 2003–January 2004. Created a saleable product, secured financial backing, found a manufacturer, supervised production, and sold product—12 dozen T-shirts at a $5.25 profit each—to help pay for school expenses.

Landscape Maintenance Supervisor, Saskatoon, SK, Summers 1999–2003. Formed a company to cut lawns, put up fences, fertilize, garden, and paint houses. Hired, fired, trained, motivated, and paid friends to complete jobs.

How to handle self-employment

Collector and Repairman, ACN Inc., Saskatoon, SK, Summer 2001. Collected and counted up to $10 000 a day. Worked with technicians to troubleshoot and repair electronic and coin mechanisms of video and pinball games, cigarette machines, and jukeboxes. Drove company cars and trucks throughout Saskatoon metro area to collect cash and move and repair machines.

Specify large sums of money.

Provide details to interest readers, set you apart from other applicants.

FIGURE 27.3
A Functional or Combination Résumé

Mohammed Shaffer

1803 Albert Road Windsor, ON N8W 3X1 705-555-8998

Fax 705-333-8991 mshaffer@sympatico.com

Attractive design element: text on left for emphasis: reader's eye does not have to travel to middle of page

CAREER HIGHLIGHTS

In order of relevance to reader, not in chronological order

Highlights measurable achievements related to sales management position

- ❑ Recognized as top Ontario salesperson for General Foods Canada, 2002, 2003
- ❑ Co-authored *Marketing for Dummies*, which sold more than 500 000 copies internationally
- ❑ Founded landscape design and build business, generating more than $200 000 business annually
- ❑ Featured in *Canadian Gardens*, Spring 2000
- ❑ Recognized as Windsor's Volunteer of the Year, 2000
- ❑ Computer literate including DOS, Windows, Linux Operating Systems
- ❑ Design using Nextel CAD
- ❑ Fluent in Spanish, Italian, French, and Hindi

WORK EXPERIENCE

Ontario Sales Manager   Nabisco Canada
2003–present   Windsor, Ontario

- ❑ Responsible for all Ontario sales; consistently exceeded sales quotas by 10 percent–15 percent
- ❑ Managed a diverse workforce of 25 salespeople
- ❑ Represented company at international marketing conventions
- ❑ Served as Nabisco's media liaise person, Windsor location

Salesperson   General Foods Canada
2000–2003   Windsor, Ontario

- ❑ Responsible for all southern Ontario sales region
- ❑ Consistently exceeded sales quotas by 25 percent
- ❑ Wrote *Sales Processes and Procedures Manual*, used by company Canada-wide
- ❑ Recruited by Nabisco Canada

Owner/Manager   Decorative Decks LTD
1998–Present   Windsor, Ontario

- ❑ Originated landscape design and build business
- ❑ Manage 4 full-time, 30 seasonal employees   *Current employment less significant to reader*
- ❑ Market services to over 300 clients
- ❑ Acquire 30 new clients annually
- ❑ Write weekly garden and landscape design column for the *Windsor Star*

1

FIGURE 27.3
A Functional or Combination Résumé (continued)

Mohammed Shaffer

1803 Albert Road Windsor, ON N8W 3X1 705-555-8998
Fax 705-333-8991 mshaffer@sympatico.com

VOLUNTEER EXPERIENCE
Indicates community involvement

1997–present   sailing instructor, Windsor Sailing Academy
1994–present   coach, Windsor Soccer Club

PUBLICATIONS

Résumé now identifies relevant experience in reverse chronology

"Gardening in Paradise," the *Windsor Star's* Living section: weekly column,
"Creating a Deck for All Seasons," *Canadian Gardening*, Spring, 2002. Toronto: Southam Press.
Marketing for Dummies. Toronto: McGraw-Hill 1996.

ASSOCIATIONS

2000–present   Editors' Association of Canada   *Indicates professional development*
1990–present   Toastmasters, Canada
1994–present   Canadian Association of Marketing Professionals
1990–1998   Association for Business Communications

EDUCATION

St. Clair College   Business Administration, Marketing   *Perhaps formal education cannot compete with other applicants. De-emphasized through placement*
University of Windsor, Windsor, Ontario   B.A., Commerce, completed Year 2

HONOURS AND AWARDS

Nabisco Canada's Manager of the Year, 2004
Top Salesperson for General Foods Ontario region, 2002, 2003
Valedictorian, St. Clair College Business Administration program, class of 1999

HOBBIES AND INTERESTS

Writing for publication, bridge, backgammon, poker and chess, tennis golf, sailing and skiing: *optional*
downhill and slalom, gourmet cooking

REFERENCES on request   *} optional*

2

FIGURE 27.4
A Skills Résumé

Sagarika Coulombe

210 Steeles Avenue (West), Brampton, Ontario L6Y 2K3
905-555-3828 sagarikacoulombe@rogers.ca

Objective

Excellent philosophy

To find a challenging information technology position where my communication and technical skills would make a valuable and valued contribution to the organization

Profile

Highlights communication and technical skills

- Motivated team player with good organizational, communication, and people skills
- Quick learner and good problem solver
- Detail oriented and analytical
- Able to work independently and under pressure
- Meticulous and adept manager of time-critical projects *Concrete and specific details*
- Trained and experienced in superb customer service skills
- Unix, DOS, Win2000, NT, VMS, VB6, Perl, Java, SQL, Novell Net Ware 5.0
- System Analysis, DataBase Design, Data Communication, and LAN
- Knowledge of quality control procedures and software testing
- Seismic Data processing on VAX/VMS platform

Education

- Systems Analyst Co-operative Program
  2000–2004   Sheridan College, Brampton ON

- Master of Science & Technology in Applied Geophysics
  1991–1995   Indian School Of Mines, Dhanbad, India

- Bachelor of Science (Major in Physics)
  1982–1986   Scottish Church College, Calcutta University, India

Achievements

- A average in all Sheridan Institute courses
- First class with distinction at Masters level (OGPA 4.02/5)
- Class and Residence Prefect college and university levels

1 of 2

FIGURE 27.4
A Skills Résumé (continued)

Sagarika Coulombe

210 Steeles Avenue (West), Brampton, Ontario L6Y 2K3
905-555-3828 sagarikacoulombe@rogers.ca

Computer Skills
- MSDOS, Windows 2000, Unix, VMS, NT, Novell Netware 5.0
- Visual Basic6, Perl, Java, SQL
- MS Office 2000
- Systems Analysis, Design Methodologies & Database Design
- Data communication and LAN
- Email and Internet research
- Data entry, data analysis and processing in VAX/VMS platform
- Knowledge of ODBC, OLE

Scientific and Administrative Skills
- Research, work distribution, and scheduling
- Project documentation and analyses
- Processing of oil exploration data and also data entry and analyses
- Operation of thermal transfer label printers

Client Services
- Good listening, verbal, and written communication skills
- Excellent techno-economic presentation skills
- Excellent negotiating skills

Work History

Teklynx
Software Quality Analyst   2004–present
Creating test plans and test scripts
- Set up/maintain test environment
- Conduct planned and ad hoc testing
- Analyze and document defects and causes of defects

Responsibilities optional
Reverse chronology

India Rainbow Community Services of Peel
Administrative Assistant   Summer, 1999
- General administrative duties, front desk, customer service, filling, preparing documents in MSWord and assisting in the training program on WHMIS

Sagarika includes this because it is so impressive

Computech Ispat Ltd. Calcutta, India
Senior Geophysicist   1995–1999
- Performed seismic data processing on VAX/VMS platform
- PC-based processing using application software from Seismic Image software, Calgary
- Interpreted sub-surface geology in oil exploration

References available on request   *optional*

2 of 2

use this format. A skills résumé, like the one in Figure 27.4, summarizes experience and acquired skills needed for the job. Under each heading, information is listed in order of importance, combining paid and unpaid work (in classes, activities, and community groups). An Employment History section lists job titles (or functions), employers, city, and province.

Chronological Résumés

In a chronological résumé, start with the Education heading. Under Work Experience or Employment History, include employment dates, position or job title, organization, city, province, and other details: seasonal, full- or part-time status, job duties, special responsibilities, and promotions with companies. Include unpaid jobs and self-employment if they provided relevant skills (e.g., supervising people, budgeting, planning, persuading). If you've held co-op or intern placements (very significant to employers), include these under a separate heading like Co-operative Placement Experience.

Normally, go back as far as the summer after high school. Include earlier jobs if you started working someplace before graduating from high school but continued working there after graduation. However, give minimal detail about high school jobs. If you worked full-time after high school, make that clear.

If as an undergraduate you've earned a substantial portion of your college or university expenses, say so, either under Experience or in the Interpersonal or Skills Profile section with which you can begin the résumé. (Graduate students are expected to support themselves.)

> These jobs paid 40 percent of my university expenses.
>
> Paid for 65 percent of expenses with jobs, scholarships, and loans.

Omit information about low-level jobs, unless they illustrate experience important to your reader. Use details when they display your attitudes, abilities, or talents. Tell how many people you trained or supervised, how much money you budgeted or raised. Describe the aspects of the job you did.

Too vague: 2002–2004 Sales Manager, the *Daily Collegian*, Mount Royal College, AB. Supervised staff; promoted ad sales.

Good details: 2002–2004 Sales Manager, the *Daily Collegian*, Mount Royal College, AB. Supervised 22-member sales staff; helped recruit, interview, and select staff; assigned duties and scheduled work; recommended best performer for promotion. Motivated staff to increase paid ad sales 10 percent over previous year's sales.

Verbs or gerunds (the -*ing* form of verbs) always create a more dynamic image than do nouns, so use them on résumés that will be read by people rather than computers. (Rules for scannable résumés to be read by computers come later in this module.) In the revisions below, nouns, verbs, and gerunds are in bold type.

Nouns: 2002–2004 Chair, Income Tax Assistance Committee, Winnipeg, MB. Responsibilities: **recruitment** of volunteers; flyer **design, writing**, and **distribution** for **promotion** of program; **speeches** to various community groups and nursing homes to advertise the service.

Verbs:	2002–2004 Chair, Income Tax Assistance Committee, Winnipeg, MB. Recruited volunteers for the program. Designed, wrote, and distributed a flyer to promote the program; made presentations to various community groups and nursing homes to advertise the service.
Gerunds:	2002–2004 Chair, Income Tax Assistance Committee, Winnipeg, MB. Responsibilities included recruiting volunteers for the program; designing, writing, and distributing a flyer to promote the program; and presenting to various community groups and nursing homes to advertise the service.

Note that the items in the list must be in parallel structure (◀❚▶ Module 16). Table 27.1 lists action verbs that work well in résumés.

TABLE 27.1
Action Verbs for Résumés

accomplished	assessed	combined	cultivated	discharged
achieved	assigned	communicated	customized	discussed
acted	assisted	compiled	debugged	dispensed
adapted	assured	completed	decided	displayed
addressed	attended	composed	decreased	disseminated
acquired	audited	computed	dedicated	documented
activated	authorized	conceived	defined	drafted
adjusted	automated	conducted	delegated	earned
administered	began	concluded	delineated	edited
adopted	billed	condensed	delivered	educated
advised	budgeted	conferred	documented	elected
advanced	built	constructed	demonstrated	eliminated
aided	calculated	consulted	depicted	employed
allocated	calibrated	contracted	derived	engaged
altered	canvassed	contributed	described	engineered
analyzed	carried out	controlled	designed	ensured
announced	categorized	converted	detailed	entertained
answered	caused	cooperated	detected	equipped
appointed	changed	coordinated	determined	estimated
appraised	charted	corresponded	developed	evaluated
approved	clarified	corrected	devised	examined
arranged	classified	costed	diagnosed	exchanged
ascertained	collaborated	counselled	differentiated	expanded
assembled	collected	created	directed	expedited

TABLE 27.1
Action Verbs for Résumés (continued)

experimented	inquired	officiated	recorded	studied
explained	inspected	operated	rectified	strengthened
explored	instituted	orchestrated	reduced	submitted
extracted	instructed	organized	referred	summarized
fabricated	insured	oversaw	refined	supervised
facilitated	integrated	packaged	regulated	supplied
filed	interfaced	paid	related	supported
filled	interpreted	participated	released	surveyed
financed	interviewed	performed	removed	taught
finalized	introduced	persuaded	reorganized	tested
formed	invented	planned	repaired	theorized
forwarded	investigated	positioned	reported	timed
founded	justified	practised	represented	traced
furnished	labelled	precipitated	researched	trained
gathered	licensed	predicted	responded	transferred
generated	located	prepared	restored	transformed
graded	maintained	prescribed	retained	translated
graduated	managed	presented	retrieved	transmitted
granted	manipulated	preserved	reviewed	transported
guarded	manufactured	presided	revised	transposed
guided	mapped	prevented	sampled	treated
handled	marketed	priced	saved	tutored
helped	maximized	printed	scheduled	updated
identified	measured	produced	screened	upgraded
implemented	mechanized	programmed	searched	used
illustrated	mediated	projected	secured	utilized
imported	minimized	protected	selected	validated
improved	mobilized	provided	sold	valued
improvised	modelled	published	served	verified
incorporated	monitored	purchased	set	visited
induced	motivated	questioned	set up	worked
inducted	negotiated	qualified	settled	wrote
influenced	modified	rated	solicited	
informed	observed	received	started	
initiated	obtained	recommended	stimulated	

Good résumés provide accurate details about what you've done, rather than exaggerate.

Source: FOR BETTER OR WORSE reprinted by permission of United Feature Syndicate, Inc.

Functional or Combination Résumés

Functional or Combination and Skills Résumés

Use a **functional** or skills **résumé** in these cases:

- Your education and experience are not the usual route to the position.
- You're changing fields.
- You want to combine experience from paid jobs, activities and volunteer work, and courses.
- Your recent work history may create the wrong impression.

The functional résumé focuses on the *what*; this format provides the flexibility to highlight relevant job responsibilities or functions, and to include disparate experiences. Mature, highly skilled people with the right job credentials use the functional résumé to describe their extensive skills sets.

Begin with Career Achievements or Career Highlights, where you summarize your primary professional accomplishments. The Employment History is most important: describe your work responsibilities and subsequent skills as they relate to the position for which you are applying. Later in the résumé, identify conferences, clubs, and professional associations in reverse chronology to demonstrate your industry currency. Unless applying for job where your education credentials are paramount (like an academic position) and you have those credentials, place Education near the end of this format.

Skills Résumés

Skills résumés use the *skills* or *aspects* of the job you are applying for as headings, rather than the category title or the dates of the jobs you've held (as in a chronological résumé). For entries under each skill, combine experience from paid jobs, unpaid work, classes, activities, and community service.

Use headings that reflect the jargon of the job for which you're applying: *logistics* rather than *planning* for a technical job; *procurement* rather than *purchasing* for a civilian job with the military. Figure 27.5 shows a skills résumé for someone who is changing fields. Marcella suggests that she already knows a lot about the field she hopes to enter by using its jargon for the headings.

You need at least three headings related to the job in a skills résumé; six or seven is not uncommon. Give enough detail to convince the reader that you have developed the requisite skill sets through a variety of experience. Put the most important category—**from the reader's perspective**—first.

FIGURE 27.5
A Skills Résumé for Changing Job Fields

On the first page of a skills résumé, put skills directly related to the job for which you're applying.

The centred format is eye-catching but it can be hard to read. Here, bold headings draw the reader's eye.

Marcella G. Cope

370 Mahon Avenue
Vancouver, BC V7M 3E1
250-555-1997
mcope@postbox.com

Objective

To help create high quality CD-ROM products in Metatec's New Media Solutions Division

Put company's name in objective.

Editing and Proofreading Experience

Edited a textbook published by Simon and Schuster, revising with attention to format, consistency, coherence, document integrity, and document design.
Proofed training and instructor's manuals, policy statements, student essays and research papers, internal documents, and promotional materials.
Worked with authors in a variety of fields including English, communication, business, marketing, economics, education, history, sociology, biology, agriculture, computer science, law, and medicine to revise their prose and improve their writing skills by giving them oral and written feedback.

Writing Experience

Wrote training and instructor's manuals, professional papers, and letters, memos, and reports.
Co-authored the foreword to a forthcoming textbook (Fall 2007) from NCTE press.
Contributed to a textbook forthcoming (Fall 2007) from Bedford Books/St. Martin's Press.

Computer Experience

Centre headings only when you use a large font. Here 14 pt. is used.

Designed a Web page using Microsoft Front Page
(www.cohums.ohio-state.edu/english/People/Bracken.1/Sedgwick/)
Learned and used a variety of programs on both Macintosh and PC platforms:
Word processing and spreadsheets
Microsoft Project
Front Page
Pagemaker
Aspects (a form for online synchronous discussion)
Storyspace (a hypertext writing environment)
PowerPoint
Email

Computer experience is crucial for almost every job. Specify the software and hardware you've worked with.

Other Business and Management Experience

Developed policies, procedures, and vision statements.
Supervised new staff members in a mentoring program.
Coordinated program and individual schedules, planned work and estimated costs, set goals, and evaluated progress and results.
Member of team that directed the nation's largest first-year writing program.

FIGURE 27.5
A Skills Résumé for Changing Job Fields (continued)

Marcella G. Cope

Page 2

Employment History

Graduate Teaching Associate, Department of English, the University of Victoria,
September 2004–Present. Taught Intermediate and First-Year Composition.
Writing Consultant, University Writing Centre, Simon Fraser University, January–April 2003
Program Administrator, First-Year Writing Program, the University of Victoria
September 1998–January 2000

Honours

Phi Kappa Phi Honour Society, inducted 2004. Membership based on performance
in top 10 percent of graduate students nationwide.
Letters of Commendation, 2003. Issued by the Director of
Graduate Studies in recognition of outstanding achievement.
Dean's List

Education

Master of Arts, June 2004, the University of Victoria
Cumulative GPA: 4.0/4.0
Bachelor of Arts, June 2003, Simon Fraser University
Graduated with Honours.

A job description can give you ideas for headings. Possible headings and subheadings for skills résumés include

Administration	Communication
Alternatives or subheadings:	Alternatives or subheadings:
Coordinating	Conducting Meetings
Evaluating	Editing
Implementing	Fundraising
Negotiating	Interviewing
Planning	Speaking
Keeping Records	Negotiating
Scheduling	Persuading
Solving Problems	Proposal Writing
Budgeting	Report Writing
Supervising	

Many jobs require a mix of skills. Include the skills that you know will be needed in the job you want.

In a skills résumé, list your paid jobs under Employment History near the end of the résumé (see Figure 27.4). List only job title, employer, city, province, and dates. Omit details about what you did, since you will have already used them under Experience.

What parts of résumé formats are the same?

Increasingly all résumés begin with an attention-grabbing heading like Communications and Technical Skills, Interpersonal Profile, or Career Achievements.

SEE THE OLC!

Preparing Résumés

Every résumé should have an overview of your communication skills and an Education section. Career Objective, Honours and Awards, and References are optional.

Career Objective

Career objective statements should sound like the job descriptions an employer might use in a job listing. Keep your statement brief—two or three lines at most. Tell what you want to do and what level of responsibility you want to hold.

Ineffective career objective:	To offer a company my excellent academic foundation in hospital technology and my outstanding skills in oral and written communication.
Better career objective:	Selling state-of-the-art Siemens medical equipment.

Including the employer's name in the objective is a nice touch.

As an alternative to writing a Career Objective statement, put the job title or field under your name:

Joan Larson Ooyen	Terence Edward Garvey	David R. Lunde
Marketing	Technical Writer	Corporate Fitness Director

Note that many recruiters consider Career Objective statements irrelevant.

Interpersonal Profile/Communications Skills, Career Achievements

Highlight proficiency in foreign or computer languages and identify your outstanding communication skills, in order of importance to the reader:

- Excellent researching, writing, and presentation skills
- Completely conversant in all software applications
- Speak, read, and write Portuguese
- Internet, Intranet, and LAN proficient

The functional or combination résumé uses career achievements to showcase measurable accomplishments:

- As Western Division Sales Manager, generated revenue of $3.5 million over quota
- Implemented employee mentoring program resulting in a 40 percent retention rate increase
- Created new assembly procedure that cut production costs by 25 percent
- Developed procedures manual now used in every national and international office

■ Education

Education can be your first major category if you've just earned (or are about to earn) a degree, if you have a degree that is essential or desirable for the position you're seeking, or if you lack relevant work experience. Put Education later if you need all of page one to emphasize your skills and experience, or if you lack a degree that other applicants may have.

Include summer school if you took optional courses or extra electives to graduate early. Include study abroad, even if you didn't earn college credits. If you got a certificate for international study, give the name and explain the significance of the certificate.

Professional certifications can be listed under Education, under or after your name, or in a separate category.

Include your GPA only if it's good. Because grade point systems vary, specify what your GPA is based on: "3.4/4.0" means 3.4 on a 4.0 scale. If your GPA is under 3.0 on a 4.0 scale, use words rather than numbers: "B average." If your GPA isn't impressive, calculate your average in your major and your average for your last 60 hours. If these are higher than your overall GPA, consider using them.

List in reverse chronological order (most recent first) each degree earned, field of study, date, school, city, province, or state of any graduate work, short courses and professional certification courses, university, college, community college, or school from which you transferred.

B.S. in personnel management, June 2004, University of Waterloo, Waterloo, ON

A.S. in office management, June 2005, Georgian Community College, Barrie, ON

To fill a page, you can also list selected courses, using short descriptive titles rather than course numbers. Use a subhead such as "Courses Related to Major" or "Courses Related to Financial Management" that will allow you to list all the courses (including psychology, speech, and business communication) that will help you in the job for which you're applying.

Bachelor of Science in management, May 2004, University of Guelph, Guelph, ON

GPA: 3.8/4.0
Courses Related to Management:

Personnel Administration	Business Decision-Making
Finance	International Business
Management I and II	Marketing
Accounting I and II	Legal Environment of Business
Business Report Writing	Business Speaking

Salutatorian, Eastview High School, June 2000, Toronto, ON

A third option is to list the number of hours in various subjects, especially if the combination of courses qualifies you for the position for which you're applying.

B.Sc. in marketing, May 2004, St. Francis Xavier University, Nova Scotia
30 hours in Marketing
15 hours in Spanish
9 hours in Human Resources Management

■ Honours and Awards

The Honours and Awards heading creates a positive impression even when the reader skims the résumé. Include this category for all awards that reflect your drive for achievement and recognition.

Include the following kinds of entries in this category:

- Listings in recognition books (e.g., *Who's Who in Web Design*)
- Academic honour societies (specify the nature of Greek-letter honour societies so the reader understands that these are more than social clubs)
- Fellowships and scholarships
- Awards given by professional societies and community associations
- Major awards given by civic groups
- Music accreditation and awards; varsity letters; selection to provincial or national sports teams; finishes in provincial, national, or Olympic meets (These could also go under Activities but may look more impressive under Honours. Put them under one category or the other—not both.)

Omit honours such as "Miss Congeniality" that work against the professional image you want your résumé to create.

As a new graduate, you should try to put Honours on page one. In a skills and functional or combination résumé, place Honours and Awards on page two or three, depending on the space your Work Experience takes.

References

Including references on a separate page anticipates the employer's needs and removes a potential barrier to your getting the job. You can, however, omit this category on your résumé, since prospective employers now take it for granted that applicants will supply references when required.

When you list references, use three to five. Include at least one professor and at least one employer or advisor—someone who can comment on your work habits and leadership skills.

Always ask the person's permission to list him or her as a reference. Don't say, "May I list you as a reference?" Instead, say, "Can you speak specifically about my work?" Jog the person's mind by taking along copies of work you did for him or her and a copy of your current résumé. Tell the person what points you'd like him or her to stress in a letter. Keep your list of references up to date. If it's been a year or more since you asked someone, ask again—and tell the person about your recent achievements.

References the reader knows are by far the most impressive. In a functional and skills résumé, choose people to recommend you who can testify to your abilities in the most important skills areas.

What should I do if the standard categories don't fit?

Create new ones.

Create headings that match your qualifications: Computer Skills, Military Experience, Foreign Languages, Summer and Part-Time Jobs, Marketing Experience, Publications, Exhibitions, Professional Associations.

Education and Experience (if you use the latter term) always stand as separate categories, even if you have only one item under each head. Combine other headings so that you have at least two long or three short items under each heading. For example, if you're in one honour society, two social clubs, and on one athletic team, combine them all under Activities and Honours.

If you have more than seven items under a heading, consider using subheadings. For example, a student who had a great many activities might divide them into Student Government, Other Campus or Extracurricular Activities, and Community Service.

Put your strongest categories near the top and at the bottom of the first page. If you have impressive work experience, you might want to put that category first after your name, put Education in the middle of the page, and put your address at the bottom.

When should I limit my résumé to just one page?

A one-page résumé is sufficient, but do fill the page. Don't limit the length if you have lots of qualifications.

The average résumé is now two pages, unless you need more space to emphasize your qualifications. Executive search firm founder Michael Stern (Michael Stern Associates, Toronto) says readability always trumps conciseness: "…someone with a lot of experience and expertise is better going to three pages than trying to fit everything on two pages of tiny, hard-to-read type."[1]

If you do use more than one page, the second page should have at least 10 to 12 lines. Use a second sheet and staple it to the first so that readers who skim see the staple and know that there's more. Leave less important information for the second page. Put your name and "Page 2" or "Cont." on the second page. If the pages are separated, you want the reader to know whom the qualifications belong to and that the second page is not your whole résumé.

■ How do I create a scannable résumé?

Take out all your formatting.

Figure 27.6 on the next page is an example of a scannable résumé. Use the following points to increase the chances that the résumé is scanned correctly:

- Use a standard typeface: Helvetica, Futura, Optima, Times Roman, New Century Schoolbook, Courier, Univers, or Bookman.[2]
- Use 12- or 14-point type.
- Use a ragged right margin. Scanners can't always handle the extra spaces between words and letters that full justification creates.
- Don't italicize or underline words—even for titles of books or newspapers that grammatically require such treatment.
- Put the text in bold to make sure letters don't touch each other. Then remove the bold.
- Don't use lines, boxes, script, leader dots, or borders.
- Don't use two-column formats or indented or centred text.
- Put each phone number on a separate line.
- Use plenty of white space.
- Don't fold or staple the pages.
- Don't write anything by hand on your résumé.
- Send a laser copy. Stray marks defeat scanners.

Use the following tips to increase the number of matches or "hits":

- Use a Keywords section under your name, address, and phone. In it, put degrees, job field or title, accomplishments and interpersonal strengths and attitudes: *dependable, skill in time management, leadership, sense of responsibility.*[3]
- Use industry buzzwords and jargon, even if redundant. For example, "Webpage design and HTML coding" will "match" either "Web" or "HTML" as a keyword.
- Use nouns. Some systems don't handle verbs well.
- Use common headings such as Summary of Qualifications, Strengths, Certifications, as well as Education, Experience, and so on.
- Use as many pages as necessary.
- Mention specific software programs (e.g., Lotus Notes) that you've used.
- Be specific and quantifiable. "Managed $2 million building materials account" will generate more hits than "manager" or "managerial experience." Listing Microsoft Front Page as a skill won't help as much as "Used Microsoft Front Page to design an interactive Web page for a national fashion retailer, with links to information about style trends, current store promotions, employment opportunities, and an online video fashion show."

FIGURE 27.6
A Scannable Résumé

Jerry A. Jackson   *Use 12- or 14-point type in a standard typeface. Here, Times Roman is used.*

Keywords: family financial management; financial planning; retirement planning; investment sales; computer modelling; competitive; self-starter; hard worker; responsible; self-managing; collegiate athletics; sales experience
In keywords, use labels and terms that employers might include in job listing.

Campus Address
St. Mary's Road
Winnipeg, SK R2H 1J2
(306) 555-5718
Email address: jjackson@ccw.sk.ca
Created a Web page on saving for life goals, such as a home, children's education, and retirement:
http://hotmail.com/jackson.2495/home.htm

Permanent Address   *Give as much information as you like. The computer doesn't care how long the document is.*
2105 East Hill Avenue
Saskatoon, SK S7J 3C8
(306) 555-4108

Summary of Qualifications
High energy. Played sports during two years of college. Started two businesses.
Sales experience. Sold both clothing and investments successfully.
Presentation skills. In individual and group presentations, spoke to groups ranging from 2 to 75 people. Gave informative, persuasive, and inspirational talks.
Financial experience. Knowledgeable about stocks and bonds, especially energy and telecommunication companies.
Computer experience. Microsoft Word, Excel, SPSS, PowerPoint, and Dreamweaver.
Experience creating Web pages.

Education
A.A.S. in Finance, May 2004, Community College of Winnipeg, Winnipeg, SK
B Grade Point Average
Comprehensive courses related to program provide not only the basics of family financial management but also skills in communication, writing, speaking, small groups, and computer modelling
Intermediate Accounting I and II
Business Writing
Consumer Finance   *Don't use columns. Scanners can't handle them.*
Financial Management
Interpersonal Communication
Investments
Microeconomics
Presentation Skills
Public Speaking
Report and Technical Writing
Sociology of Marriage and Family
Statistics

Sports Experience
Intramural Hockey Team (Champions, Winter 2004)
Two-Year Varsity Letterman, Community College of Winnipeg
Men's NCAA Division II Basketball

FIGURE 27.6
A Scannable Résumé (continued)

Experience
Financial Sales Representative, Primerica Company, Winnipeg, SK, February 2004–present. Work with clients to plan investment strategies; recommend specific investments, including stocks, bonds, mutual funds, and annuities.

Entrepreneur, Winnipeg, SK, and Saskatoon, SK, September 2003–January 2004. Created a saleable product, secured financial backing, found a manufacturer, supervised production, and sold product—12 dozen T-shirts at a $5.25 profit each—to help pay for school expenses.

Landscape Maintenance Supervisor, Saskatoon, SK, Summers 1999–2003. Formed a company to cut lawns, put up fences, fertilize, garden, and paint houses. Hired, fired, trained, motivated, and paid friends to complete jobs. Managerial experience.

Collector and Repairman, ACN Inc., Saskatoon, SK, Summer 2001. Collected and counted up to $10 000 a day. Worked with technicians to troubleshoot and repair electronic and coin mechanisms of video and pinball games, cigarette machines, and jukeboxes. Drove company cars and trucks throughout Saskatoon metro area to collect cash and move and repair machines.

Willing to relocate
Willing to travel
Canadian citizen

Don't justify margins.
Doing so creates extra spaces
that confuse scanners.

SEE THE OLC!

Résumé Posting Sites

- Join honour societies and professional and trade organizations, since they're often used as keywords.[4] Spell out Greek letter societies (the scanner will mangle Greek characters, even if your computer has them): "Pi Sigma Alpha Honour Society." For English words, spell out the organization name; follow it with the abbreviation in parentheses: "College Newspaper Business and Advertising Managers Association (CNBAM)." That way, the résumé will be tagged whether the recruiter searches for the full name or the acronym.
- Put everything in the résumé, rather than "saving" some material for the cover letter. Although some applicant tracking systems can search for keywords in cover letters and other application materials, most only extract information from the résumé, even though they store the other papers. The length of the résumé doesn't matter.

Employability Skills 2000+

The Conference Board of Canada
Insights You Can Count On

Please see the OLC to preview the key skills from the Conference Board of Canada's Employability Skills 2000+ covered in this module.

Review of Key Points

1. Why is it important to create a strong résumé and to update it even when you have a job?
2. Identify five strategies you can use to create an attention-getting résumé that will demonstrate your superiority to other applicants.
3. What are the major differences between the chronological, the functional, and the

skills résumé? How do you decide which one to use?
4. What can you do if you have valuable experience, expertise, and/or skills not covered by traditional résumé headings?
5. Why is it not a good idea to exaggerate on your résumé to make yourself look even better?

Assignments for Module 27

Questions for Critical Thinking

27.1 Is it ethical to omit information that might hurt you, such as a low grade-point average?
27.2 What are the arguments for and against listing references on your résumé?
27.3 Should someone who is having trouble creating a good résumé pay a résumé service to create a document for him or her?

27.4 Suppose that you know that people with your qualifications are in great demand. Is there any reason for you to take the time to write a strong résumé?

Exercises and Problems

27.5 Analyzing Your Accomplishments

List the 10 accomplishments that give you the most personal satisfaction. These could be achievements that other people wouldn't notice. They can be accomplishments you've done recently or things you did years ago.

Answer the following questions for each accomplishment:

1. What skills or knowledge did you use?
2. What personal traits did you exhibit?

3. What about this accomplishment makes it personally satisfying to you?

As your instructor directs,

a. Share your answers with a small group of students.
b. Summarize your answers in a memo to your instructor.
c. Present your answers orally to the class.

27.6   Remembering What You've Done

Use the following list to jog your memory about what you've done. For each, give three or four details as well as a general statement.

Describe a time when you

1. Used facts and figures to gain agreement on an important point
2. Identified a problem faced by a group or organization and developed a plan for solving the problem
3. Made a presentation or a speech to a group
4. Responded to criticism

5. Interested other people in something that was important to you and persuaded them to take the actions you wanted
6. Helped a group deal constructively with conflict
7. Demonstrated creativity

As your instructor directs,

a. Identify which job(s) each detail is relevant for.
b. Identify which details would work well on a résumé.
c. Identify which details, further developed, would work well in a job letter.

27.7   Evaluating Career Objective Statements

None of the following career objective statements is effective. What is wrong with each statement as it stands? Which statements could be revised to be satisfactory? Which should be dropped?

1. To use my acquired knowledge of accounting to eventually own my own business.
2. A progressively responsible position as a MARKETING MANAGER where education and

ability would have valuable application and lead to advancement.
3. To work with people responsibly and creatively, helping them develop personal and professional skills.
4. A position in international marketing that makes use of my specialization in marketing and my knowledge of foreign markets.
5. To design and maintain Web pages.

27.8   Writing a Paper Résumé

Write a résumé on paper that you could mail to an employer or hand to an interviewer at an interview.

As your instructor directs,

a. Write a résumé for the field in which you hope to find a job.

b. Write two different résumés for two different job paths you are interested in pursuing.
c. Adapt your résumé to a specific company you hope to work for.

27.9   Writing a Scannable Résumé

Take the résumé you like best from problem 27.8 and create a scannable version of it.

Polishing Your Prose

Proofreading

Wait until the final draft is complete to edit and proofread. There is no point in proofreading words and passages that might change. (Some writers claim to proofread documents while they're composing; this practice is like trying to mow the lawn and trim the hedges at the same time.)

Editing includes checking for you-attitude and positive emphasis, fixing any sexist or biased language, and correcting grammatical errors.

Proofreading means making sure that the document is free from typos. Check each of the following aspects.

Spelling. Scan for misspelled or misused words that spell checkers don't catch: *not* instead of *now*, *you* instead of *your*, *its* instead of *it's*, *their* instead of *there* or *they're*, *one* instead of *won*, and so forth.

Consistency. Check abbreviations and special terms.

Names. Double-check the reader's name.

Punctuation. Make sure that parentheses and quotation marks come in pairs. Be on the lookout for missing or extra commas and periods.

Format. Look for errors in spacing, margins, and document design, especially if you compose your document on one computer and print it out at another. Use the correct format for citations—MLA, APA, Chicago, and so on.

Numbers and dates. Double-check all numbers to make sure they add up. Make sure page numbers appear where they should and are sequential. Do the same for tables of contents or appendices. Check dates.

How to proofread is as individual as writing style. Try these methods or invent your own:

- **Read the document from last word to first word** to catch spelling errors.
- **Read the document in stages**—first page, second page, third page—with plenty of "rest" in between so you are fresh for each page.
- **Read pages out of sequence** so you can concentrate on the characters on the page rather than the meaning.
- **Read the document aloud,** listening for awkward or incorrect phrasing.
- **Ask a friend to read the document aloud,** voicing punctuation, while you follow along with the original.

Whatever your approach, build time into the composing process for proofreading. If possible, finish the document a day or two before it's due to allow enough time. (If the document is a 100-page report, allow even more time.) If you're in a hurry, use a spell checker, proof the document yourself, and ask a friend or colleague to proof it as well.

Exercises

Proofread the following passages:

1. Ours are a company worth doing business with. Your can count on our promiss to provide not only the best service but, also the finest in materials, fit, and, finish. All of are products our made to exacting specifications meaning that you received the best product for the best prices. If you aren't satisfied for any reason, simply call the toll-free hotline at 1-800-555-1212 to get a promp refund. Or you can right us at: The John Doe Company, 123 Main Street Anytown Canada M6V 2B4. Remember; our moto is "the customers is always's right?

2.

Resumee for Kathy Jones

332 West Long Strt.
Moncton, New Brunswick E4Z 1Z8
614-555-8188

Objection

A management position in fullfilament services where my skills, expereince can be best be used to help your company acheeve it's goals.

Relevent Experience:

2000 to Present Day: Ass. Manager for high-end sports equipment distributor. Responsible for checking new customers out.
1895-1999: Owned and Operated Jones, Inc., a telephone order procesing company for lady's apparel.
1997: Received a plague for Must Promising Executive of the Year" from *Monthly* Magazine.
1998: Delivery address to local high school seniors on why accuracy is important in business.

Special Skills

Type 7 or more words per minute
Studied English all my life. Fluent in French.
Shot at local gun club.

Check your answers to the odd-numbered exercises on page 574.

Online Learning Centre

Visit the Online Learning Centre at www.mcgrawhill.ca/olc/locker to access module quizzes, a searchable glossary, résumé and letter templates, additional business writing samples, CBC videos, and other learning and study tools.

28 Job Application Letters

Module Outline

- What kind of letter should I use?
- How are the two letters different?
- What parts of the two letters are the same?
- How long should my letter be?
- How do I create the right tone?
- The company wants an email application. What should I do?

Review of Key Points

Assignments for Module 28

Polishing Your Prose: Using You and I

LEARNING OBJECTIVES

After reading and applying the information in Module 28, you'll be able to demonstrate

Knowledge of
- The two types of application letter formats

Skills to
- Organize the solicited application letter
- Organize the prospecting application letter
- Catch the reader's interest even when the company isn't planning to hire
- Show that you have the qualifications for the job
- Persuade the employer that you're in the very top group of applicants
- Use information about the company effectively in your letter

The Conference Board of Canada
Insights You Can Count On

Please see the OLC to preview the key skills from the Conference Board of Canada's Employability Skills 2000+ covered in this module.

FIGURE 28.1

Questions for Analysis

Use the PAIBOC questions to analyze business communication problems:

P What are your **purposes** in writing?

A Who is your **audience**? How do members of your audience differ? What audience characteristics are relevant to this particular message?

I What **information** must your message include?

B What reasons or reader **benefits** can you use to support your position?

O What **objections** can you expect your readers to have? What negative elements of your message must you de-emphasize or overcome?

C How will the **context** affect reader response? Think about your relationship to the reader, the morale in the organization, the economy, the time of year, and any special circumstances.

The purpose of a job application letter, together with your résumé, is to get an interview. If you get a job through interviews arranged by a campus placement office or through contacts, you may not need to write a letter. However, you will need a letter if you want to work for an organization that isn't interviewing on campus, or when you change jobs. Writing a letter is also good preparation for a job interview, because the letter is your first step in showing a specific company what you have to offer.

In your letter, focus on these items:

- Key requirements of the job for which you're applying, using the language in the job posting
- Skills and knowledge that separate you from other applicants
- Information that demonstrates your knowledge of the organization
- Qualities that every employer is likely to value: the ability to write and speak effectively, to solve problems, to get along with people

Note that the advice in this book applies to job-hunting in Canada. Conventions, expectations, and criteria differ from culture to culture: different norms apply in different countries. Even within Canada, different discourse communities (◀|▶ Module 2) may have different preferences. For example, letters applying for sales jobs might need to be more aggressive than the examples in this module. Whether you're seeking employment in your home province, nationally, or internationally, however, your PAIBOC analysis (see Figure 28.1) is vital to your success. Well-written job application letters are the most persuasive messages.

Every employer wants businesslike employees who understand professionalism. Follow these guidelines to make your application letter professional:

- Create your letter on a computer. Use a standard serif font (Times Roman) in 12-point type.
- Address your letter to a specific person. If the reader is a woman, call the office to find out whether she prefers a courtesy title (◀|▶ Module 9).
- Use the language of the organization and the industry.
- Use contact or employee names if the reader knows them and thinks well of them, if they think well of you and will say good things about you, and if you have permission to use their names.
- Always connect an experience (coursework, co-op placement, community involvement) with a resultant skill that you know the prospective employer wants.
- Unless you're applying for a creative job, use business stationery and a conservative style: few contractions, no sentence fragments, clichés, or slang.
- Edit the letter carefully and proof it several times to make sure it's perfect.

■ What kind of letter should I use?

It depends on whether the company has asked for applications.

Two different hiring situations call for two different kinds of application letters. Write a **solicited letter** when you know that the company is hiring: you've seen an ad, you've been advised to apply by a professor or friend, or you've read in a trade publication that the company is expanding. Sometimes, however, the advertised positions may not be what you want, or you may want to work for an organization that has not announced that it has openings in your area. Then the situation calls for an **unsolicited** or **prospecting letter**.

Prospecting letters help you tap into the hidden job market (◀▶ Module 26). In some cases, your prospecting letter may arrive at a company that has decided to hire but has not yet announced the job. In other cases, companies create positions to get a good person who is on the market. Even in a hiring freeze, jobs are sometimes created for specific individuals.

How are the two letters different?

They begin and end differently.

SEE THE OLC!

Career Lab

When you know the company is hiring, organize your letter in this way:

1. State that you're applying for the job (phrase the job title as your source phrased it). Tell where you learned about the job (ad, referral, Web). Briefly show that you have the major qualifications required by the ad: a degree, professional certification, job experience, and so forth. Summarize your other qualifications briefly in the same order in which you plan to discuss them in the letter. This **summary sentence** or **paragraph** then covers everything you will talk about, and serves as an organizing device for your letter.

> I have a good background in standard accounting principles and procedures and a working knowledge of some of the special accounting practices of the oil industry. This working knowledge is based on practical experience in the oil fields: I've pumped, tailed rods, and worked as a roustabout.
>
> Let me put my creative eye, artistic ability, and experience to work for McLean Design.

2. Develop your major qualifications in detail. Be specific about what you've done; relate your achievements to the work you'd be doing in this new job. This is not the place for modesty!
3. Develop your other qualifications, even if the ad doesn't ask for them. (If the ad asks for a lot of qualifications, pick the most important three or four.) Show what separates you from the other applicants who will also answer the ad. Demonstrate your knowledge of the organization.
4. Ask for an interview; tell when you'll be available to be interviewed and to begin work. End on a positive, forward-looking note.

FIGURE 28.2
How to Organize a Solicited Job Letter

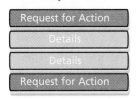

Figure 28.2 presents this pattern of organization visually. Figures 28.3 and 28.4 (pp. 531–532) are examples of a solicited letter.

When you don't have any evidence that the company is hiring, organize your letter this way:

1. Catch the reader's interest.
2. Create a **bridge** between the attention-getter and your qualifications. Focus on what you know and can do. Since the employer is not planning to hire, he or she won't be impressed with the fact that you're graduating. Summarize your qualifications briefly in the same order in which you plan to discuss them in the letter.
3. Develop your strong points in detail. Be specific. Relate what you've done in the past to what you could do for this company. Show that you know something about the company. Identify the specific niche you want to fill.
4. Ask for an interview and tell when you'll be available for interviews. (Don't tell when you can begin work.) End on a positive, forward-looking note.

FIGURE 28.3
A Solicited Letter (1)

880 Middlegate Road
Mississauga, ON L4Y 1M3

Block format is standard in business.

September 5, 2007

Mr. William Chen
Director
The Resources Corporation
2025 Sheppard Avenue East
Toronto, ON M2J 1V7

Paragraph 1 is thesis or controlling paragraph. It repeats language of the ad and identifies the specific qualifications the rest of the letter will demonstrate.

Dear Mr. William Chen:

Please consider my application for the position of **Auditor**, advertised in the *Toronto Star*, September 3, 2007. My education and auditing experience, and my organizational, analytical, and communication skills make me an ideal candidate for the position.

Begins as few sentences as possible with "I"

After graduating in Business Administration, Finance, I received my CA designation in November 2005. My Finance program focused on the Canadian regulatory/securites industry standards and by-laws. Indeed, in my third year at Centennial College, I completed an analytical report about the Canadian regulatory and security market. During my co-operative placement with Tort, Tort, and Tort, I also assisted CA's in their field examinations and in-office desk reviews of regulatory filings of association audit jurisdiction firms. Although we often worked under intense pressure, my organizational and communication skills helped me to graduate with an A+ average; furthermore, based on my performance with the firm, Tort, Tort, and Tort offered me a full-time position upon graduation.

Provides specific auditing experience

Details demonstrate applicant has excellent communication skills.

Shows self-motivation, sales and managerial skills; demonstrates active learner with transferable skills

Instead, I chose to work as a financial sales representative for Templeton Trust. As you know, financial selling is a highly competitive field, but I enjoy competing. While in high school, for example, I created a business, hired a staff, and recruited clients. Subsequently, in my landscaping business, I delegated work and motivated my employees to do the quality jobs that our clients expected. My entrepreneurial experiences taught me the value of hard work, dedication, and accountability, requisite qualities for auditors.

In the last year, as financial sales representatives for Templeton Trust, I've honed my analytical and communication skills while helping clients develop financial plans and investment products tailored to their needs. I welcome the opportunity to contribute my knowledge and skills to the continuing success and superb reputation of The Resources Corporation.

Can we meet to discuss this possibility? Please call me at (416) 555-4415, to arrange an interview time and date at your convenience.

Ask for the interview.

Sincerely,

Jerry Jackson

Jerry Jackson
Enclosure: Résumé

**FIGURE 28.4
A Solicited Letter (2)**

638 Changery Court
Lethbridge, AB T1J 2A5
May 21, 2007

Shelley Aquina
Human Resources Manager
Home Outfitters
425 18 Avenue Northwest
Calgary AB T2N 2G6

*addresses reader
as ad indicates*

Dear Shelly Aquina:
RE: File # 7664566-F

← quotes file number as ad requests

*Repeats
words of
the ad*

Please consider me for the position of sales manager, advertised in the *Calgary Sun*, Saturday, May 20.
I possess the educational background, work experience, and exceptional organizational and
communication skills for which you have advertised.

*The thesis
or controlling
paragraph
tells the
reader
what's going
to be proven
in the letter.*

*Specifics
directly
connect
the exper-
ience with
the resul-
tant skill*

In June I will graduate with a business administration diploma from Mount Royal College, Calgary,
Alberta. Throughout my college career I worked with peers on a variety of projects, including sales
proposals, formal reports, and sales presentations. In my third year I was chosen team captain for our
marketing project, a year-long analysis, and oral and written report of possible marketing initiatives
for a Calgary client, MediaWaves. My responsibilities included identifying time lines, delegating
tasks, negotiating conflicts among group members, reporting to the client and our marketing
professor, and revising and editing the final 30-page report. Our team project not only secured the top
grade in the class, but the client also accepted our recommendations, resulting in an immediate
10 percent sales increase for MediaWaves. Because I'm very aware of the importance of listening
when working with others, I have made a conscious effort to improve this key communication skill.
I believe that part of the success of our project can be attributed to my managing through active
listening.

Since Grade 11 I have worked part-time and summers at Canadian Tire in Lethbridge, Alberta.
Although I started as a stock clerk, I worked my way up to sales associate. My supervisor has
commented on my excellent sales skills, particularly my product knowledge and ability to up-sell.
During my employment with Canadian Tire—a high-energy, fast-paced environment—I learned to
focus calmly on clients' concerns and to communicate confidently. As a result of my performance I
was promoted to assistant manager, a job I held while finishing college. While working part-time,
attending school, and participating in varsity basketball, I learned to juggle multiple priorities, to
manage my time, and to problem solve.

*Jargon
of the
marketing
industry*

*These skills
would have
been
identified
in the ad as
necessary
for the
position.*

*Demonstrates
research
and industry
awareness*

Enclosed please find my résumé with further details.

The market for home decorations and furnishings has become increasingly competitive, and, with the
entry of American big box stores like Heritage Homes, it promises to become even more so. I would
like an opportunity to increase your market share while developing my own marketing career. Please
call me at 403–555-4339 to arrange an interview time and date at your convenience.

*Asks for
the interview*

Sincerely,

Carlos DeLeon
ENC: résumé

Figure 28.5 presents this pattern visually. Figure 28.6 shows an example of a prospecting letter.

■ The First Paragraph of a Solicited Letter

When you know that the firm is hiring, refer to the specific position in your first sentence. Your letter can then be routed to the appropriate person, thus speeding up consideration of your application. Identify where you learned about the job: "the position of junior accountant announced in Sunday's *Vancouver Sun*," "Kadji Kado, our placement director, told me that you are looking for...."

Note how the following paragraph picks up several of the characteristics of the ad:

Ad: Business Education Instructor at University of New Brunswick. Candidate must possess a bachelor's degree in Business Education. Will be responsible for providing in-house training to business and government leaders.... Candidate should have at least six months' office experience. Prior teaching experience not required.

Letter: Please consider me for the position of **Business Education Instructor**, advertised in Monday's *Telegraph-Journal*. My Business Education degree, knowledge of adult education principles, and previous office experience make me the ideal candidate for the position.

Good word choices can help set your letter apart from the hundreds of letters the company is likely to get in response to an ad. The following first paragraph of a letter in response to an ad by Allstate Insurance Company shows a knowledge of the firm's advertising slogan and sets itself apart from the dozens of letters that start with "I would like to apply for...."

> The Allstate Insurance Company is famous for its "Good Hands Policy." I would like to lend a helping hand to many Canadians as a financial analyst for Allstate, as advertised in yesterday's *National Post*. I have an Accounting Co-op diploma from Georgian College and I have worked with figures, computers, and people.

Note that the last sentence forecasts the organization of the letter, preparing for paragraphs about the student's academic background and (in this order) experience with "figures, computers, and people."

■ First Paragraphs of Prospecting Letters

In a prospecting letter, asking for a job in the first paragraph is dangerous; unless the company plans to hire but has not yet announced openings, the reader is likely to throw the letter away. Instead, catch the reader's interest. Then in the second paragraph shift the focus to your skills and experience, showing how they can be useful to the employer.

Here is an effective first paragraph and the second paragraph of a letter applying to be a computer programmer for an insurance company:

SEE THE OLC!

Truly terrible cover letters

http://www.killian advertising.com/ coverletters.html

SEE THE OLC!

The Quintessential Careers and Job-Hunting Guide offers free advice on every part of the job search process, including how to write dynamic application letters.

FIGURE 28.5

How to Organize a Prospecting Letter

FIGURE 28.6
A Prospecting Letter

Kristine Manalili
2 Inverary Court
Porters Lake, Nova Scotia B3E 1M8
902-555-6488 kmanalili@hotmail.com

Kristine creates a boxed "letterhead"

2007-06-25

Mr. John Harrobin
HealthRhab Inc.
2653 Dublin Street
Halifax, NS B3K 3J7

In an unsolicited or prospecting letter, open with a sentence that
① will create reader interest
② provides an natural bridge to talking about yourself

Dear Mr. Harrobin:

Providing an athlete with physiotherapy can assist with a debilitating injury in the short term but may not provide the long-term product and therapy information necessary for complete recovery. It can be a real challenge finding employees who are conversant with the latest injury-management modalities, who are familiar with the most current injury-management support equipment, and who also work well with rehabilitating clients. However, you will see from my enclosed résumé that I have this useful combination of skills.

Refers to her enclosed résumé

Refers to mutual acquaintance *Shows knowledge of the company*

Rita Haralabidis tells me that HealthRhab needs people to identify injury-management therapy and equipment for your clients. My education and work experience have provided me with the injury evaluation and product knowledge that you require. While studying at Nunavut Arctic College's Sports Injury Management program, for example, I provided more than 200 hours of successful client care at the college clinic.

Moreover, I was able to apply the most current therapy modalities and to learn about sophisticated sports injury products and equipment while serving my four-month co-op term at Wu's Sports Clinic in Victoria, British Columbia. Wu's Clinic is renowned for its progressive therapy options. My co-op placement provided me with practical experience in injury prevention and treatment. Equally important, I learned about the latest equipment, products, and techniques available to maximize client rehabilitation and recovery.

Demonstrates skill sets she promised in first paragraph

Relates what she's done to what she could do for this company

My communication skills and product knowledge would enable me to adapt immediately to clients' specific needs and to develop programs for your clients. I am flexible, a quick study, and committed to proactive health care. I will call you next week to arrange a mutually convenient time when we can discuss putting my talents to work for HealthRhab.

Promises action

Sincerely,

Kristine Manalili
Enclosed: Résumé

Computers alone aren't the answer to demands for higher productivity in the competitive insurance business. Merging a poorly written letter with a database of customers just sends out bad letters more quickly. But you know how hard it is to find people who can both program computers and write well.

My education and training have given me this useful combination of skills. I'd like to put my associate's degree in computer technology and my business experience writing to customers to work in Sun Canada's service approach to insurance.

Last Paragraphs

FYI

Alberta has Canada's lowest unemployment rate, and the most significant job growth in the natural resources sector, and in "...professional, scientific[,] and technical services.

Source: Labour Force Survey, *The Daily*, October 7 2005, http://www.statcan.ca/Daily/English/051007/d051007a.htm, retrieved August 24, 2006.

In the last paragraph, indicate when you'd be available for an interview. If you're free any time, say so. But it's likely that you have responsibilities in class and work. If you'd have to go out of town, there may be only certain days of the week or certain weeks that you could leave town for several days. Use a sentence that fits your situation.

I could come to Thunder Bay for an interview anytime between March 17 and 21.

Please call me at 519-555-4229, for an interview time and date at your convenience.

Should you wait for the employer to call you, or should you call the employer to request an interview? In a solicited letter, it's safe to wait to be contacted: you know the employer wants to hire someone, and if your letter and résumé show that you're one of the top applicants, you'll get an interview. However, for sales jobs, say that you'll call the employer—and do it! In a prospecting letter, also call the employer. Because the employer is not planning to hire, you'll get a higher percentage of interviews if you're assertive. Don't, however, be rude. No one owes you a response. And when you do call, be polite to the person who answers the phone.

If you're writing a prospecting letter to a firm that's more than a few hours away by car, say that you'll be in the area the week of such-and-such and could stop by for an interview. Some companies pay for follow-up visits, but not for first interviews. A company may be reluctant to ask you to make an expensive trip when it isn't yet sure it wants to hire you.

End the letter on a positive note that suggests you look forward to the interview and that you see yourself as a person who has something to contribute, not as someone who just needs a job.

On Wednesday, April 25, I will call you between 9:00 and 9:30 A.M. to schedule a time when we can talk.

I look forward to discussing with you ways in which I could contribute to Blackberry's continued growth.

What parts of the two letters are the same?

The body paragraphs discussing your qualifications are the same.

In both solicited and prospecting letters you should follow these guidelines:

- Address the letter to a specific person.
- Indicate the specific position for which you're applying.

FYI

College/university career days provide genuine opportunities to impress recruiters. Experts recommend these strategies:

- Dress for success— tailored and conservative: men should wear wool or wool-blend suits (navy, grey), long-sleeved shirt with tie, and "lace-up Oxford shoes or classic loafers..."; women should wear a suit or pantsuit "...with a silk blouse, closed-toe pumps with 11/2-inch heels and a medium-sized purse."
- Shine those shoes.
- Shake hands firmly.
- Ask for the recruiter's business card, and, as a mark of interest and respect, look at it closely when you receive it.
- Be prepared: research the organization beforehand.
- Be prepared for "Tell me about yourself," with a practised, concise response that highlights your qualifications.
- Be prepared: to ask the recruiter questions that demonstrate your interest in, and research of, the company and the industry.

Source: Richard Bloom, "Career-day Checklist: Suit, Spiel, Dry Palm," *The Globe and Mail*, September 30, 2005, C2.

- Be specific about your qualifications.
- Show what separates you from other applicants.
- Demonstrate a knowledge of the company and the position.
- Refer to your résumé (which you would enclose with the letter).
- Ask for an interview.

Showing a Knowledge of the Position and the Company

If you can substitute another inside address and salutation and send out the letter without any further changes, it isn't specific enough. Use your knowledge of the position and the company to choose relevant evidence from what you've done to support your claims that you could help the company. (See Figures 28.4 and 28.6.)

One or two specific details are usually enough to demonstrate your knowledge. Be sure to use the knowledge, not just repeat it. Never present the information as though it will be news to the reader. After all, the reader works for the company and presumably knows much more about it than you do.

Separating Yourself from Other Applicants

Your knowledge of the company separates you from other applicants. You can also use course work, an understanding of the field, and experience in jobs and extracurricular events to show that you're unique.

- This student example uses summer jobs and course work to set herself apart from other applicants:

> A company as diverse as Monsanto requires extensive record keeping as well as numerous internal and external communications. Both my summer jobs and my course work have prepared me for these responsibilities. As office manager for Safety Express Limited, I was in charge of most of the bookkeeping and letter writing for the company. I kept accurate records for each workday, and I often entered more than 100 transactions in a single day. In business and technical writing I learned how to write persuasive letters and memos and how to present extensive data in clear and concise reports.

How long should my letter be?

Highlight the fit between the position and your qualifications clearly and concisely.

Your cover letter and résumé may be one of hundreds under review. The more readable your application letter, the more likely you will attract the favourable attention of those responsible for deciding whom to interview. Keep your letter as concise and clear as possible. Write one page or less.

Without eliminating content, make each sentence concise (◀▏▶ Module 14) to be sure that you're using space as efficiently as possible. If your letter is still slightly over a page, use smaller margins, a type size that's one point smaller, or justified proportional type to get more on the page.

If you need more than a page, use it. The extra space gives you room to be more specific about what you've done and to add details about your experience that separate you from

EXPANDING A CRITICAL SKILL

Targeting a Specific Company in Your Letter

If your combination of skills is in high demand, a one-size-fits-all letter may get you an interview. But when you must compete against dozens—perhaps hundreds or even thousands—of applicants for an interview slot, you need to target your letter to the specific company. Targeting a specific company also helps you prepare for the job interview.

The Web makes it easy to find information about a company. The example below shows how applicants could use information posted on the Sleeman Breweries Limited Web site at <http://www.sleeman.com/>.

Check for Facts about the Company.

Like most corporate Web sites, Sleeman offers dozens of facts about the company. A computer network administrator might talk about helping to keep the 3500 LANS working well. A Web weaver could talk about supporting a new investor relations site, or about developing even more interactive content for both national and international potential investors. Someone in corporate communication, advertising, marketing, or multimedia programs might write a prospecting letter about Sleemans' recent media campaign. An interviewee with experience in international business might pitch the company on the know-how necessary to do business in Boston, Germany, and South Africa. And someone in human resources management could talk about the electronic processing of HR data benefits for the thousands of employees joining this expanding company, or about current recruitment and retention strategies for the company CIBC World Markets Inc., reports is "...a well-managed, creative company."

Check News Releases and Speeches.

Recent press releases have covered everything from the company's national expansion—across the Maritimes, into Quebec, and Western Canada—to its international partnerships with U.S., German, and South African breweries. Anyone in international business could talk about helping Sleeman expand its base into China—and beyond.

An April 3, 2001, press release announced the launch of the company's second annual Writer's Craft Award, $10 000 for the best short-story collection published by an Ontario writer. Students about to complete marketing, finance, and management programs could show how their course work and experience prepare them to market this and similar community-focused programs; or students could offer technical or managerial expertise on the best way for Sleeman Breweries to adopt ebusiness strategies for their continuing growth.

Check the Corporate Culture.

In his media interviews, President John Sleeman emphasizes that his family-owned business produces a quality product based on his great-great-grandfather's recipe. The company's Web site material also refers to the family beer-making tradition and the site's design reinforces this commitment to traditional values. These promotional strategies appeal to the mature consumers who buy Sleeman beers. Yet Sleeman's partnership arrangements and media advertisements indicate the company's enthusiasm for creativity and flexibility. Prospective job applicants would do well to stress their creative abilities and their support of community arts activities.

Source: Michael Van Aelst as quoted by Oliver Bertin, "Sleeman Brew Balance of Risk and Caution," *The Globe and Mail*, June 20, 2001, M1.

---

other applicants. Employers don't want longer letters, but they will read them *if* the letter is well written and *if* the applicant establishes early in the letter that he or she has the credentials the company needs.

■ How do I create the right tone?

Use you-attitude and positive emphasis.

You-attitude and positive emphasis help you sound assertive without being arrogant.

What Job Letters Must Do

- Address the letter to a specific person.
- Indicate the specific position for which you're applying.
- Be specific about your qualifications.
- Show what separates you from other applicants.
- Show a knowledge of the company and the position.
- Refer to your résumé (which you would enclose with the letter).
- Ask for an interview.

You-Attitude

Unsupported claims may sound overconfident, selfish, or arrogant. Create you-attitude (◀▶ Module 6) by describing exactly what you have done and by showing how that relates to what you could do for this employer.

Lacks you-attitude:	An inventive and improvising individual like me is a necessity in your business.
You-attitude:	Building a summer house-painting business gave me the opportunity to find creative solutions to challenges.

Remember that the word *you* refers to your reader. Using you when *you* really mean yourself or "all people" can insult your reader by implying that he or she still has a lot to learn about business.

Since you're talking about yourself, you'll use *I* in your letter. Do so sparingly. Reduce the number of *I*'s by revising some sentences to use *me* or *my*.

> Under my presidency, the Agronomy Club…
>
> Courses in media and advertising management gave me a chance to…
>
> My responsibilities as a co-op student included…

In particular, avoid beginning every paragraph with I. Begin sentences with adverbs (presently, currently), prepositional phrases, or introductory clauses.

Positive Emphasis

Be positive. Don't plead ("Please give me a chance") or apologize ("I cannot promise that I am substantially different from everyone else").

Avoid word choices with negative connotations (◀▶ Module 7). Note how the following revisions make the writer sound more confident.

Negative:	I have learned an excessive amount about writing through courses in journalism and advertising.
Positive:	Courses in journalism and advertising have taught me to recognize and to write good copy. My profile of a professor was published in the campus newspaper; I earned an "A" on my direct mail campaign for the Canadian Dental Association to persuade young adults to see their dentist more often.

Excessive suggests that you think the courses covered too much—hardly an opinion likely to endear you to an employer.

The company wants an email application. What should I do?

Compose a document using a word-processing program. Then attach it to a courteous email message.

When you submit an email letter (see Figure 28.7 on page 539) with an attached résumé, you need to follow a few rules:

- Tell in what word-processing program your scannable résumé is saved.
- Put the job number or title for which you're applying in your subject line and in the first paragraph.

- Prepare your letter in a word-processing program with a spell checker to make it easier to edit and proof the document.
- Don't send anything in all capital letters.
- Don't use smiley faces or other emoticons.
- Put your name and email address at the end of the message. Most email programs send along the "sender" information on the screen, but a few don't, and you want the employer to know whose letter this is!

FIGURE 28.7

An Email Application Letter

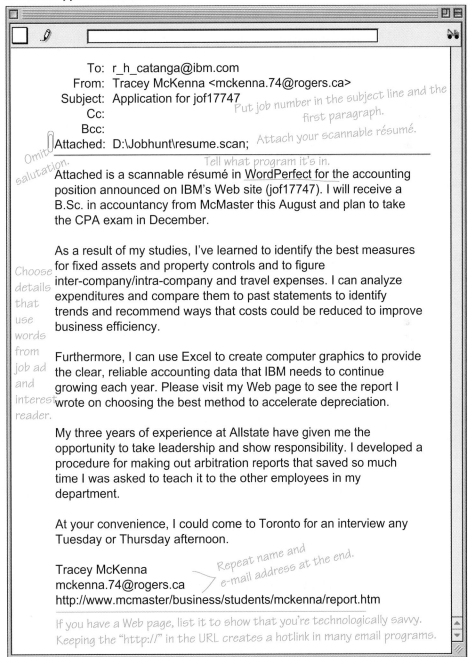

Employability Skills 2000+

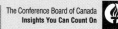

The Conference Board of Canada
Insights You Can Count On

Please see the OLC to preview the key skills from the Conference Board of Canada's Employability Skills 2000+ covered in this module.

Review of Key Points

1. When should you choose to write a prospecting job letter?
2. How should you organize a solicited letter?
3. How should you organize a prospecting letter?
4. What strategies can you use to make your letter more persuasive?

5. If you are not a good writer, is it ethical for you to hire someone to write the letter for you?
6. Where can you get information about the organization to include in your letter?

Assignments for Module 28

Questions for Critical Thinking

28.1 Why is it important for you to separate yourself from other applicants?
28.2 Why should you not ask for a job in the first paragraph of a prospecting letter?
28.3 Why is a good writing style particularly important in a job application letter?

28.4 Is it ethical for someone who isn't a good writer to hire someone to write the letter for him or her?
28.5 Suppose that people with your qualifications are in great demand. Why should you take the time to write a strong letter?

Exercises and Problems

28.6   Analyzing First Paragraphs of Prospecting Letters

The following are first paragraphs in prospecting letters written by new graduates. Evaluate the paragraphs on these criteria:

- Is the paragraph likely to interest the reader and motivate him or her to read the rest of the letter?
- Does the paragraph have some content that the student can use to create a transition to talking about his or her qualifications?
- Does the paragraph avoid asking for a job?
  1. Ann Gibbs suggested that I contact you.
  2. Each year, the holiday shopping rush makes more work for everyone at Zellers, especially for the Credit Department. While working for Zellers Credit Department for three holiday

seasons and summer vacations, I became aware of many credit situations.

3. Whether to plate a five-centimetre eyebolt with cadmium for a tough, brilliant shine or with zinc for a rust-resistant, less expensive finish is a tough question. But similar questions must be answered daily by your salespeople. With my experience in the electroplating industry, I can contribute greatly to your constant need of getting customers.
4. Prudential Insurance Company did much to help my university career, as the sponsor of my National Merit Scholarship. Now I think I can give something back to Prudential. I'd like to put my education, including a degree in finance

from _____ University, to work in your investment department.

5. Since the beginning of Delta Electric Construction Co. in 1997, the size and profits have grown steadily. My father, being a stockholder and vice president, often discusses company dealings with me. Although the company has prospered, I understand there have been a few problems of mismanagement. I feel with my present and future qualifications, I could help ease these problems.

28.7 Improving You-Attitude and Positive Emphasis in Job Letters

Revise each of these sentences to improve you-attitude and positive emphasis. You may need to add information.

1. I understand that your company has had problems due to the mistranslation of documents during international ad campaigns.
2. Included in my résumé are the courses in finance that earned me a fairly attractive grade average.
3. I am looking for a position that gives me a chance to advance quickly.
4. Although short on experience, I am long on effort and enthusiasm.
5. I have been with the company from its beginning to its present unfortunate state of bankruptcy.

28.8 Writing a Solicited Letter

Write a letter of application in response to an announced opening for a full-time job that a new graduate could hold.

Turn in a copy of the listing. If you use option (a), (b), or (d) below, your listing will be a copy. If you choose option (c), you will write the listing and can design your ideal job.

a. Respond to an ad in a newspaper, in a professional journal, in the placement office, or on the Web. Use an ad that specifies the company, not a blind ad. Be sure that you are fully qualified for the job.
b. Take a job description and assume that it represents a current opening. Use a directory to get the name of the person to whom the letter should be addressed.
c. If you have already worked somewhere, assume that your employer is asking you to apply for full-time work after graduation. Be sure to write a fully persuasive letter.
d. Respond to one of the listings below. Use a directory or the Web to get the name and address of the person to whom you should write.
   1. Cotts Beverages is hiring an **assistant auditor**. Minimum 12 hours of accounting experience. Work includes analysis and evaluation of operating and financial controls and requires contact with many levels of company management. Extensive travel (50 percent of job hours) required through the Canadian West, along with some international work. Effective written and oral communication skills a must, along with sound decision-making abilities. Locations: Edmonton, Toronto, Halifax, New York, Los Angeles, Dallas, Atlanta, Philadelphia, Denver, Chicago. Refer to job FA-2534.
   2. Roxy Systems (Roxy.com) seeks **Internet marketing coordinators** to analyze online campaigns and put together detailed reports, covering ad impressions and click-through rates. Must have basic understanding of marketing; be organized, creative, and detail-oriented; know Microsoft Excel; have excellent communication skills; and be familiar with the Internet. Send letter and résumé to mike@roxy.com.
   3. Bose Corporation seeks **public relations/communications administrative associate** (Job Code 117BD). Write, edit, and produce the in-house newsletter using desktop publishing software. Represent the company to external contacts (including the press). Provide administrative support to the manager of PR by scheduling meetings, preparing presentations, tabulating and analyzing surveys, and processing financial requests. Excellent organizational, interpersonal, and communication skills (both written and oral) required. Must be proficient in MS Office and Filemaker Pro.

4. The Gap is hiring **executive development program trainees**. After completing 10-week training programs, trainees will become assistant buyers. Prefer people with strong interest and experience in retailing. Apply directly to the store for which you want to work.

5. A local non-profit seeks a **coordinator of volunteer services**. Responsibilities for this full-time position include coordinating volunteers' schedules, recruiting and training new volunteers, and evaluating existing programs. Excellent listening and communication skills required.

28.9   Writing a Prospecting Letter

Pick a company you'd like to work for and apply for a specific position. The position can be one that already exists or one that you would create, if you could, to match your unique blend of talents. Give your instructor a copy of the job description with your letter.

Address your letter to the president of a small company, or the area vice president or branch manager of a large company. Use directories or the Web to get the name and address of the person with the power to create a job for you.

Polishing Your Prose

Using You and I

You-attitude (◀|▷ Module 6) means that you'll use lots of *you's* in business messages. However, use *you* only when it refers to your reader. When you mean "people in general," use another term.

Incorrect: When I visited your office, I learned that you need to find a way to manage your email.

Correct: When I visited your office, I saw the importance of managing one's email.

Incorrect: Older customers may not like it if you call them by their first names.

Correct: Older customers may prefer being called by courtesy titles and their last names.

Omit *you* when it criticizes or attacks the reader.

Not you-attitude: You didn't turn your expense report in by the deadline.

You-attitude: Expense reports are due by the fifth of each month. We have no record of receiving your report.

When you talk about what you've done, use *I*.

Correct: In the past month, I have completed three audits.

In general, keep *I's* to a minimum. They make you sound less confident and more self-centred.

Weak: I think that we would save money if we bought a copier instead of leasing it.

Better: We would save money by buying a copier instead of leasing it.

Weak: I want to be sure that I understand how I will be affected by this project.

Better: How will this project affect our unit?

When you write a document that focuses on you (such as a progress report or a job application letter), vary sentence structure so that you don't begin every sentence with *I*.

Correct: This job gave me the opportunity to...

Correct: As an intern, I...

Correct: Working with a team, I...

When you use a first-person pronoun as part of a compound subject or object, put the first-person pronoun last.

Correct: She asked you and me to make the presentation.

Correct: You, Mohammed, and I will have a chance to talk to members of the audience before the dinner.

Be sure to use the right case. Omit the other part(s) of the compound to see the case you should use:

She asked me.

I will have a chance.

Use the same form when you restore the other words.

Exercises

Revise the following sentences to eliminate errors and improve the use of *you* and *I*.

1. I worked with a team to create a class Web page. I was responsible for much of the initial design and some of the HTML coding. I also tested the page with three people to see how easily they could navigate it. I and the other team members presented the page to a committee of local businesspeople.
2. I have taken a lot of time and trouble to get a copy of *Using Excel* for each of you.
3. If you offend someone in the team, you need to resolve the conflict you have created.
4. Please return the draft to me and Mehtap.
5. I think that it would be a good idea for us to distribute an agenda before the meeting.
6. I have asked each department head if he or she had information to announce at the meeting, collated the responses, and arranged the topics to cover in an agenda. I have indicated how much time each topic will take. I am herewith distributing the agenda for Friday's meeting.
7. You haven't made the Web page accessible to users with impaired vision.
8. My last job showed me that you have to be able to solve problems quickly.
9. I observed department meetings during my co-op. I also sat in on client meetings. I designed PowerPoint™ slides for client presentations. I participated in strategy sessions. Finally, I drafted brochures.
10. The client asked me and my supervisor to explain our strategy more fully.

Check your answers to the odd-numbered exercises on page 574.

■ Online Learning Centre

Visit the Online Learning Centre at www.mcgrawhill.ca/olc/locker to access module quizzes, a searchable glossary, résumé and letter templates, additional business writing samples, CBC videos, and other learning and study tools.

Preparing for Job Interviews

Module Outline

- Why do I need an interview strategy?
- What details should I think about?
- Should I practise before the interview?
- How should I answer traditional interview questions?
- How can I prepare for behavioural, situational, and stress interviews?
- How can I prepare for phone or video interviews?

Review of Key Points

Assignments for Module 29

Polishing Your Prose: Matters on Which Experts Disagree

LEARNING OBJECTIVES

After reading and applying the information in Module 29, you'll be able to demonstrate

Knowledge of

- Job interview best practices

Skills to

- Be your best self at a job interview
- Plan and practise for the interview
- Answer traditional interview questions
- Shine in behavioural, situational, and stress interviews
- Participate in phone or video interviews
- Negotiate salary and benefits

The Conference Board of Canada
Insights You Can Count On

Please see the OLC to preview the key skills from the Conference Board of Canada's Employability Skills 2000+ covered in this module.

Even when you've prepared thoroughly, job interviews are scary: you know what you want, but you don't feel in control of the situation. When you are prepared, however, you can harness the adrenaline to work for you so that you make the best possible impression to get the job you want.

Today many employers expect job candidates to do the following:

Successful job applicants prepare an interview strategy tailored to their audience.

- Be assertive. One employer deliberately tells the company receptionist to brush off callers who ask about advertised openings. He interviews only those who keep calling and offer the receptionist reasons why they should be interviewed. However, if you're rejected even after giving reasons, accept the rejection gracefully.
- Follow instructions to the letter. The owner of a delivery company tells candidates to phone at a precise hour. Failing to do so means that the person couldn't be trusted to deliver packages on time.[1]
- Participate in many interviews, including the panel or group interview. In these interview situations, several people in the organization are present throughout the interview. Each person is assigned a question to ask the candidate, and the whole team assesses the applicant's interview performance.
- Have one or more interviews by phone, computer, or video.
- Take one or more tests, including psychological/personality assessments, aptitude tests, computer simulations, and essay exams where you're asked to explain what you'd do in a specific situation.
- Be approved by the team you'll be joining. In companies with self-managed work teams, the team has a say in who is hired.
- Provide—at the interview or right after it—a sample of the work you're applying to do. You may be asked to write a memo or a proposal, calculate a budget on a spreadsheet, make a presentation, or do a mini-teach.

Be courteous to the receptionists, secretaries, and assistants you speak to. Find out the person's name on your first call, and use it on subsequent calls. "Thank you for being so patient. Can you tell me when a better time might be to try to reach Mr. or Ms. X? I'll try again on [date]." Sometimes, if you call after 5 P.M., executives answer their own phones since clerical staff members have gone home.

If you get voicemail, leave a concise message with your name and phone number. (Note: your own voicemail message should be professional!) Even if you've called 10 times, keep your voice pleasant. If you get voicemail repeatedly, call the main company number to speak with a receptionist. Ask whether the person you're trying to reach is in the building. If he or she is on the road, ask when the person is due in.

Why do I need an interview strategy?

You need a strategy so that you can do everything possible to get what you want!

Develop an overall strategy based on your answers to these three questions:

1. **What do you want the interviewer to know about you?** Pick two to five points that represent your strengths for that particular job. These facts may be achievements,

FYI

Experts agree on the interview behaviours that can keep you out of the running. Avoid:

- looking sloppy
- appearing arrogant or lacking in self-confidence
- knowing nothing about the organization
- being unprepared with questions that demonstrate you have researched the organization thoroughly
- focusing on salary and benefits
- not listening
- canned and unfocused responses
- criticizing previous employers, and
- not being personable.

Peter Kua, "How to Screw-up Your Interview," May 2006, RadicalHop.com, http://radicalhop.com/blog/2006/05/21/how-to-screw-up-your-interview/, retrieved August 29, 2006.

character traits (such as enthusiasm, attention to detail, creativity), experiences that qualify you for the job and separate you from other applicants, your passion for working for this company, and so on. For each strength, identify and write down a specific action or accomplishment to support it. For example, be ready to give an example to prove that you're "hard working." Show how you have saved money, served customers better, or led the team in other organizations where you've worked. Then at the interview, listen to every question to see how you

In Nelvana's creative environment, employees are hired because they possess both the skills to do the job and the creativity to imagine original ideas. Applicants' portfolios are expected to contain evidence of both.

can make one of your key points part of your answer. If the questions don't allow you to make your points, bring them up at the end of the interview.

2. **What disadvantages or weaknesses do you need to minimize?** Expect that you may be asked to explain apparent weaknesses in your record: lack of experience, so-so grades, or gaps in your record.

3. **What do you need to know about the job and the organization to decide whether to accept this job if it is offered to you?**

Do primary research to ensure the organization is the right fit for you. Analyze the company Web site: its language, colours, and navigation can tell you plenty about organizational values. Network: use information interviews (◀|▶ Module 26) as opportunities to scope out the reception area, the way visitors are greeted and treated, the congruence between mission statement and morale. Talk to as many employees and friends of employees as you can.

What details should I think about?

Decide what you'll wear, what you'll take with you, and how to get there.

Wearing inappropriate clothing or being late can cost you a job. Put enough time into planning details so that you can focus on content planning.

What to Wear

Your interview clothing should be at least as formal as the clothing of the person likely to interview you. When the interview is scheduled, ask the person who invites you whether the company has a dress policy. If the dress is "casual," wear a button-up shirt and a good-quality skirt or pants, not jeans.

If you're interviewing for a management or office job, wear a business suit. What kind of suit? If you've got good taste and a good eye for colour, follow your instincts. If fashion isn't your strong point, read John Molloy's *New Dress for Success* (men's clothes) and *New Woman's Dress for Success*. Perhaps the best suggestion in the books is his advice to visit expensive stores, noting details—the exact shade of blue in a suit, the number of buttons on the sleeve, the placement of pockets, the width of lapels—and then go to stores in your price range and buy a suit that has the details found on more expensive clothing. You can find quality clothes at bargain prices in second-hand and vintage clothing shops in your town or city.

INSTANT REPLAY

Interview Strategy

Plan an interview strategy based on these three questions:

1. What two to five facts about yourself do you want the interviewer to know?

2. What disadvantages or weaknesses do you need to overcome or minimize?

3. What do you need to know about the job and the organization to decide whether you want to accept this job if it is offered to you?

If you're interviewing for a position that involves working, visiting, or supervising muddy or dirty sites, wear sturdy clothes that suggest you're willing to get dirty.[2] In this case, looking "good" is less important than looking businesslike.

Consider the corporate culture. A woman interviewing for a job at the Gap wore a matching linen skirt and blouse that were similar to Gap clothing. Her clothing was evidence that she'd researched the job.[3]

Choose comfortable shoes. The last thing you want to be thinking about during an important interview is how much your feet hurt! You may also do a fair amount of walking during the office visit or plant trip.

Take care of all the details. Check your heels to make sure they aren't run down; make sure your shoes are shined. Have your hair cut or styled conservatively. Jewellery and makeup should be understated. Personal hygiene must be impeccable. If you wear cologne or perfume, keep it to a minimum.

What to Bring to the Interview

Interview Success

Bring extra copies of your résumé. If your campus placement office has already given the interviewer a data sheet, present the résumé at the beginning of the interview: "I thought you might like a little more information about me."

Bring something to write on, something to write with, and a small notepad with the questions you want to ask on it.

Bring copies of your work or a portfolio: an engineering design, a copy of a report you wrote on a job or in a business writing class, an article you wrote for the campus paper. You don't need to present these unless the interview calls for them, but they can be very effective.

Bring the names, addresses, and phone numbers of your references if you haven't already provided them. Bring complete details about your work history and education, including dates and street addresses, in case you're asked to fill out an application form.

If you can afford it, buy a briefcase to carry these items. An inexpensive briefcase is acceptable.

Note-Taking

During or immediately after the interview, write down the details:

- The name of the interviewer (or all the people you talked to, if it's a group interview or an office visit)
- The traits/facts the interviewer seemed to like best about you
- Any negative points or concerns that came up that you need to counter in your follow-up letter or phone calls
- Answers to your questions about the company
- The date you'll hear from the company

The easiest way to get the interviewer's name is to ask for his or her card.

How to Get There

If you're going to a place you haven't been before, do a practice run at the same time of day your interview is scheduled for. Check out bus transfers or parking fees. On the day of the interview, leave early enough so that you'll get to the interview 15 minutes early.

SEE
THE
OLC!

**University of Waterloo:
Career Development
Manual**

Use the extra time to check your appearance in the restroom mirror and to look through the company publications in the waiting room. If an accident does delay you, call to say you'll be late.

Should I practise before the interview?

Absolutely!

Your interviewing skills will improve with practice. Rehearse everything you can: put on the clothes you'll wear and practise entering a room, shaking hands, sitting down, and answering questions. Ask a friend to interview you. Saying answers out loud is surprisingly harder than saying them in your head.

Some campuses have digital videotaping facilities so that you can watch your own sample interview. Videotaping is more valuable if you can do it at least twice, so you can modify behaviour the second time and check to see whether the modification works.

How to Act

Should you "be yourself"? There's no point in assuming a radically different persona. If you do, you run the risk of getting into a job that you'll hate (though the persona you assumed might have loved it). On the other hand, we all have several selves: we can be lazy, insensitive, bored, slow-witted, and tongue-tied, but we can also be energetic, perceptive, interested, intelligent, and articulate. Be your best self at the interview.

Interviews can make you feel vulnerable and defensive; to counter this, review your productive personality traits and accomplishments—the things you're especially proud of having done—in writing. You'll make a better impression if you have a firm sense of your own self-worth.

Every interviewer repeats the advice that parents often give: sit up straight, don't mumble, look at people when you talk. It's good advice for interviews. Be aware that many people respond negatively to smoking.

Office visits that involve meals and semi-social occasions call for sensible choices. When you order, choose something that's easy and not messy to eat. Watch your table manners. Eat a light lunch, with no alcohol, so that you'll be alert during the afternoon. At dinner or an evening party, decline alcohol if you don't drink, or are underage. If you do drink, accept just one drink—you're still being evaluated. Be aware that some people respond negatively to applicants who drink hard liquor.

Parts of the Interview

Every interview has an opening, a body, and a close.

In the **opening** (two to five minutes), good interviewers will try to set you at ease. Some interviewers will open with easy questions about your major or interests. Others open by telling you about the job or the company. If this happens, listen so you can answer later questions to show that you can do the job, or contribute to the company that's being described.

The **body** of the interview (10 minutes to an hour) is an all-too-brief time for you to highlight your qualifications and find out what you need to know to decide if you want to accept a second interview. Expect questions that allow you to showcase your strong points, and questions that probe any weaknesses evident from your résumé. (You were neither in school nor working last fall. What were you doing?) Normally the interviewer will also try to sell you on the company and give you an opportunity to raise questions.

Be aware of time so that you can make sure to get in your key points and questions: "We haven't covered it yet, but I want you to know that I...." "I'm aware that it's almost 10:30. I do have some more questions that I'd like to ask about the company."

In the **close** of the interview (two to five minutes), the interviewer will usually tell you what happens next: "We'll be bringing our top candidates to the office in February. You should hear from us in three weeks." One interviewer reports that he gives applicants his card and tells them to call him. "It's a test to see if they are committed, how long it takes for them to call, and whether they even call at all."[4]

Close with an assertive statement. Depending on the circumstances, you could say: "I've certainly enjoyed learning more about ITracks." "I hope I get a chance to visit your office. I'd really like to see the new system you talked about." "This job seems to be a good match between what you're looking for and what I'd like to do."

■ How should I answer traditional interview questions?

Choose answers that fit your qualifications and your interview strategy.

As Table 29.1 on page 550 shows, successful applicants use different communication behaviours than do unsuccessful applicants. Successful applicants are more likely to use the company name during the interview, support their claims with specific details, and ask specific questions about the company and the industry. In addition to practising the content of questions, try to incorporate these tactics.

The following questions are frequently asked during interviews. Do some thinking on paper before the interview so that you'll be able to come up with answers that are responsive, honest, and paint a good picture of you. Choose answers that fit your qualifications and your interview strategy.

1. **Tell me about yourself.**

   Don't launch into an autobiography. Instead, talk about your achievements as they relate to the organization's culture and goals. Give specific examples to prove each of your strengths.

2. **What makes you think you're qualified to work for this company? Or, I'm interviewing 120 people for two jobs. Why should I hire you?**

   This question may feel like an attack. Use it as an opportunity to state your strong points: your qualifications for the job, the skills, knowledge, and character traits that separate you from other applicants.

3. **What two or three accomplishments have given you the greatest satisfaction?**

   Pick accomplishments that you're proud of, that create the image you want to project, and that enable you to share one of the things you want the interviewer to know about you. Focus not just on the end result, but on the transferable skills—teamwork, problem solving, and critical thinking—that made the achievement possible.

TABLE 29.1
The Communication Behaviours of Successful Interviewees

Behaviour	Unsuccessful Interviewees	Successful Interviewees
Statements about the position	Had only vague ideas of what they wanted to do; changed "ideal job" up to six times during the interview.	Were specific and consistent about the position they wanted; were able to tell why they wanted the position.
Use of company name	Rarely used the company name.	Referred to the company by name four times as often as unsuccessful interviewees.
Knowledge about company and position	Made it clear that they were using the interview to learn about the company and what it offered.	Made it clear that they had researched the company; referred to specific brochures, journals, or people who had given them information.
Level of interest, enthusiasm	Responded neutrally to interviewer's statements: "OK," "I see." Indicated reservations about company or location.	Expressed approval of information provided by the interviewer non-verbally and verbally; "That's great!" Explicitly indicated desire to work for this particular company.
Non-verbal behaviour	Made little eye contact; smiled infrequently.	Made eye contact often; smiled.
Picking up on interviewer's cues	Gave vague or negative answers even when a positive answer was clearly desired ("How are your math skills?").	Answered positively and confidently—and backed up the claim with a specific example of "problem solving" or "toughness."
Response to topic shift by interviewer	Resisted topic shift.	Accepted topic shift.
Use of industry terms and technical jargon	Used almost no technical jargon.	Used technical jargon: "point of purchase display," "NCR charge," "two-column approach," "direct mail," "big pharma."
Use of specifics in answers	Gave short answers—10 words or fewer, sometimes only one word; did not elaborate. Gave general responses: "fairly well."	Supported claims with specific personal experiences, comparisons, statistics, statements of teachers and employers.
Questions asked by interviewee	Asked a small number of general questions.	Asked specific questions based on knowledge of the industry and the company. Personalized questions: "What would my duties be?"
Control of time and topics	Interviewee talked 37 percent of the interview time; initiated 36 percent of the comments.	Interviewee talked 55 percent of the total time, initiated subjects 56 percent of the time.

Source: Based on research reported by Lois J. Einhorn, "An Inner View of the Job Interview: An Investigation of Successful Communicative Behaviors," *Communication Education* 30 (July 1981), 217–28; and Robert W. Elder and Michael M. Harris, eds., *The Employment Interview Handbook* (Thousand Oaks, CA: Sage, 1999), 300, 303, 327–28.

4. **Why do you want to work for us? What is your ideal job?**

Even if you're interviewing just for practice, make sure you have a good answer—preferably two or three reasons you'd like to work for that company. Do your homework; know everything possible about the company and the job. If you don't seem to be taking the interview seriously, the interviewer won't take you seriously, and you won't even get good practice.

5. **What college or university courses did you like best and least? Why?**

This question may be an icebreaker; it may be designed to discover the kind of applicant the organization is looking for. If your favourite class was something outside your program, prepare an answer that shows that you have qualities that can help you in the job you're applying for: "My favourite class was Canadian Literature. We got a chance to think on our own, rather than just regurgitate facts; we made presentations to the class every week. I found I really like sharing my ideas with other people and presenting reasons for my conclusions about something."

6. **Why are your grades so low?**

If possible, show that the cause of low grades has now been solved or isn't relevant to the job you're applying for: "My father almost died last year, and my schoolwork really suffered." "When I started, I didn't have any firm goals. Since I discovered the program that is right for me, my grades have all been B's or better." "I'm not good at multiple-choice tests. But you need someone who can work with people, not someone who can take tests."

7. **What have you read recently? What movies have you seen recently?**

These questions may be icebreakers; they may be designed to probe your intellectual depth. Be prepared: read at least one book or magazine (regularly) and see at least one movie that you could discuss at an interview.

8. **Show me some samples of your writing.**

The year you're interviewing, go through your old papers and select the best ones, retyping them if necessary, so that you'll have samples if you're asked for them. Show interviewers essays, reports, or business documents, not poetry or song lyrics.

If you don't have samples at the interview, mail them to the interviewer immediately after the interview.

9. **Where do you see yourself in five years?**

Employers ask this question to find out whether you are a self-starter or if you passively respond to what happens. You may want to have several scenarios for five years from now to use in different kinds of interviews. Or you may want to say, "Well, my goals may change as opportunities arise. But right now, I want to...."

10. **What are your interests outside work? What campus or community activities have you been involved in?**

Although it's desirable to be well-rounded, naming 10 interests may work against you: the interviewer may wonder when you'll have time to work. If you mention your fiancé, spouse, or children in response to this question ("Well, my fiancé and I like to go sailing"), it is perfectly legal for the interviewer to ask follow-up questions ("What would you do if your spouse got a job offer in another town?"), even though the same question would be illegal if the interviewer brought up the subject first.

11. **What have you done to learn about this company?**

An employer may ask this to see what you already know about the company (if you've read the recruiting literature, the interviewer doesn't need to repeat it). This question may also be used to see how active a role you're taking in the job search and how interested you are in this job.

12. **What adjectives would you use to describe yourself?**

Use only positive ones. Be ready to illustrate each with a specific example of something you've done.

13. **What is your greatest strength?**

Employers ask this question to give you a chance to sell yourself and to learn something about your values. Pick a strength related to work, school, or activities: "I'm good at working with people." "I can really sell things." "I'm good at solving problems." "I learn quickly." "I'm reliable. When I say I'll do something, I do it." Be ready to illustrate each with a specific example of something you've done.

14. **What is your greatest weakness?**

Use a work-related negative, even if something in your personal life is really your greatest weakness. Interviewers won't let you get away with a "weakness" like being a workaholic or just not having any experience yet. Instead, use one of the following three strategies:

a. Discuss a weakness that is not related to the job you're being considered for and that will not be needed even when you're promoted. End your answer with a positive that is related to the job:
[For a creative job in advertising:] I don't like accounting. I know it's important, but I don't like it. I even hire someone to do my taxes. I'm much more interested in being creative and working with people, which is why I find this position interesting.
[For a job in administration:] I don't like selling products. I hated selling cookies when I was a Girl Guide. I'd much rather work with ideas—and I really like selling the ideas that I believe in.

b. Discuss a weakness that you are working to improve:
In the past, I wasn't a good writer. But last term I took a course in business writing that taught me how to organize my ideas and how to revise. Now I'm a lot more confident that I can write effective reports and memos.

c. Discuss a work-related weakness:
Sometimes I procrastinate. Fortunately, I work well under pressure, but a couple of times I've really put myself in a bind.

15. **Why are you looking for another job?**

Stress what you're looking for in a new job, not why you want to get away from your old one.
If you were fired, say so. There are four acceptable ways to explain why you were fired:

a. You lost your job, along with many others, when the company downsized for economic reasons.

b. It wasn't a good match. Add what you now know you need in a job, and ask what the employer can offer in this area.

c. You and your supervisor had a personality conflict. Make sure you show that this was an isolated incident and that you normally get along well with people.

d. You made mistakes, but you've learned from them and are now ready to work well. Be ready to offer a specific anecdote proving that you have indeed changed.

16. **What questions do you have?**

This gives you a chance to cover things the interviewer hasn't brought up; it also gives the interviewer a sense of your priorities and values. Don't focus on salary or fringe benefits. Instead, ask specific questions:

- What would I be doing on a day-to-day basis?
- What kind of training program do you have? If, as I'm rotating among departments, I find that I prefer one area, can I specialize in it when the training program is over?
- How do you evaluate employees? How often do you review them? Where would you expect a new trainee (banker, staff accountant) to be three years from now?
- What happened to the last person who had this job?
- How are interest rates (a new product from competitors, imports, demographic trends, government regulation, etc.) affecting your company?
- How would you describe the company's culture?
- This sounds like a great job. What are the drawbacks?

Increasingly, candidates are asking about work-life balance and about the control they'll have over their own work:

- Do people who work for you have a life off the job?
- If my job requires too much travel, can I change jobs without doing serious damage to my career?
- Do you offer flextime?
- How much pressure do you have to achieve your projects? How much freedom is there to extend a deadline?[5]

You won't be able to anticipate every question you may get. (One interviewer asked applicants, "What vegetable would you like to be?" Another asked, "If you were a cookie, what kind of cookie would you be?"[6]) Check with other people who have interviewed recently to find out what questions are being asked in your field.

How can I prepare for behavioural, situational, and stress interviews?

Think about skills you've used that could transfer to other jobs.

Learn as much as you can about the culture of the company you hope to join.

Many companies are now using behavioural or situational interviews. **Behavioural interviews** ask the applicant to describe actual behaviours, rather than plans or general principles. Thus, instead of asking, "How would you motivate people?" the interviewer might ask, "Tell me what happened the last time you wanted to get other people to do something." Follow-up questions might include, "What exactly did you do to handle the situation? How did you feel about the results? How did the other people feel? How did your superior feel about the results?" Since behavioural questions require applicants to tell what they actually did—rather than to say what ought to be done—interviewers feel they offer better insight into how someone will actually function as an employee. Problem 29.8 on page 558 lists common behavioural questions.

Situational interviews put you in a situation that allows the interviewer to see whether you have the qualities the company is seeking.

Situational interviews may also be conducted using traditional questions but evaluating behaviours other than the answers. Greyhound hired applicants for its customer-assistance centre who made eye contact with the interviewer and smiled at least five times during a 15-minute interview.[7]

Stress Interviews

A **stress interview** deliberately puts the applicant under stress. If the stress is physical (for example, you're given a chair where the light is in your eyes), be assertive: move to another chair or tell the interviewer that the behaviour bothers you.

Usually the stress is psychological. A group of interviewers fire rapid questions. A single interviewer probes every weak spot in the applicant's record and asks questions that elicit negatives. If you get questions that put you on the defensive, *rephrase* them in less inflammatory terms, if necessary, and then *treat them as requests for information.*

> Q: Why did you major in physical education? That sounds like a pretty Mickey Mouse major.
>
> A: You're asking whether I have the academic preparation for this job. I started out in physical education because I've always loved sports. I learned that I couldn't graduate on time if I officially switched to business administration, because the requirements were different in the two programs. But I do have 21 hours in business administration and 9 hours in accounting. And my sports experience gives me practical training in teamwork, motivating people, and management.

Respond assertively. The candidates who survive are those who stand up for themselves and who explain why they are indeed worth hiring.

Silence can also create stress. One woman walked into her scheduled interview to find a male interviewer with his feet up on the desk. He said, "It's been a long day. I'm tired and I want to go home. You have five minutes to sell yourself." Since she had planned the points she wanted to be sure interviewers knew, she was able to do this. "Your recruiting brochure said that you're looking for someone with a major in accounting and a minor in finance. As you may remember from my résumé, I'm majoring in accounting and have had 12 hours in finance. I've also served as treasurer of a local campaign committee and have worked as a volunteer tax preparer through the Accounting Club." When she finished, the interviewer told her it was a test: "I wanted to see how you'd handle it."

Increasingly common is the variety of stress interview that asks you to do—on the spot—the kind of thing the job would require. An interviewer for a sales job handed applicants a ball-point pen and said, "Sell me this pen." (It's OK to ask who the target market is and whether this is a repeat or a new customer.) Candidates who make it through the first two rounds of interviews for sales jobs at Dataflex are invited to participate in a week's worth of sales meetings, which start at 7 A.M. four times a week. The people who participate—not merely attend—are the people who get hired.[8] More frequent interview stress requests include asking applicants to participate in role-plays, to make presentations, or to lead meetings.

EXPANDING A CRITICAL SKILL

Negotiating Salary and Benefits

The best time to negotiate for salary and benefits is after you have the job offer. Try to delay discussing salary early in the interview process, when you're still competing against other applicants. In 2006, attraction and retention concerns will mean cash for Canadian employees, particularly in high-demand and hot-job sectors like skilled trades, engineers, and health care and IT professionals. A 2005 Hewitt Associates survey of 400 Canadian organizations indicated that potential high-achievers will get signing bonuses and top performers will receive cash rewards.

Prepare for salary negotiations by finding out what the going rate is for the kind of work you hope to do. Cultivate friends who are now in the workforce to find out what they're making. If your campus has a placement office, ask what last year's graduates got. Check Web sites (such as http://www.shrc.ca/lmi/reports/pdf/salaries_report_Mar17_2006.pdf) and trade journals for salaries, often segmented into entry-level, median, and high salaries and even by city. Specialized books can also help (◀▶ Module 21, Table 21.3) such as the annual *Direct Marketing and Telemarketing Guide* or the *Robert Half and Accountemps Salary Guide*.

If the interviewer asks you about your salary requirements before a job offer has been made, try this response: "I'm sure your firm can pay me what I'm worth." Then either ask about pay ranges or go back to your qualifications for the job. If the interviewer demands a response, give a range using specific increments based on your research: "I'd expect to make between $37 300 and $41 900." As you say this, watch the interviewer. If he or she has that blank look we use to hide dismay, you may have asked for much more than the company was planning to offer. Quickly continue, "...depending, of course, on fringe benefits and how quickly I could be promoted. However, salary isn't the most important criterion for me in choosing a job, and I won't necessarily accept the highest offer I get. I'm interested in going somewhere where I can get good experience and use my talents to make a real contribution."

The best way to get more money is to convince the employer that you're worth it. During the interview process, show what you can do that the competition can't. Work to redefine the position in the employer's eyes from a low-level, anybody-could-do-it job to a complex combination of duties that only someone with your particular mix of talents could do.

After you have the offer, begin negotiating salary and benefits. You're in the strongest position when (1) you've done your homework and know what the usual salary and benefits are and (2) you can walk away from this offer if it doesn't meet your needs. Again, avoid naming a specific salary. Don't say you can't accept less. Instead, Kate Wendleton suggests, say you "would find it difficult to accept the offer" under the terms first offered.

Remember that you're negotiating a package, not just a starting salary. A company that truly can't pay any more money now might be able to review you for promotion sooner than usual, or pay your moving costs, or give you a better job title. Some companies offer fringe benefits that may compensate for lower taxable income: use of a company car, reimbursements for education, child care or eldercare subsidies, or help in finding a job for your spouse or partner. And think about your career, not just the initial salary. Sometimes a low-paying job at a company that will provide superb experience will do more for your career (and your long-term earning prospects) than a high salary now with no room to grow.

Work toward a win-win solution. You want the employer to be happy that you're coming on board and to feel that you've behaved maturely and professionally.

Sources: Kate Wendleton, *Through the Brick Wall: How to Job-Hunt in a Tight Market* (New York: Villard Books, 1992), 278; and Jack Griffin, *How to Say It at Work: Putting Yourself Across with Power Words, Body Language, and Communication Secrets* (Priamus, NJ: Prentice Hall, 1998), 69; and Virginia Galt, "Pay for Performance on the Upswing: Study," *The Globe and Mail*, September 16, 2005, C2.

▪ How can I prepare for phone or video interviews?

Practise short answers. Retape until you look good.

Try to schedule phone interviews for home, not work, and for a time when things will be quiet. If a company wants to interview you on the spot, accept only if the timing is good.

If it isn't, say so: "We just sat down to dinner. Could you call back in 30 minutes?" Then get your information about the company, ask the kids to be quiet, and get your thoughts in order.

Two strategies are important when preparing for a phone interview:

- Tape yourself so you can make any adjustments in pronunciation and voice qualities.
- Practise short answers to questions. After giving a short answer in the interview, say, "Would you like more information?" Without a visual channel, you can't see the body language that tells you someone else wants to speak.

Two kinds of video interviews exist. The first kind is a live interview using videoconferencing equipment. For this kind of interview, use the same guidelines as for a phone interview. In the second kind, the company sends a list of questions, asking the applicant to tape the responses.

If you're asked to prepare a videotape, you can do three things to help you succeed:

- Practise your answers.
- Tape the interview as many times as necessary to get a tape that presents you at your best.
- Be specific. Since the employer can't ask follow-up questions, you need to be detailed about how your credentials could help the employer.

For both kinds of interviews, smile when you talk to put more energy into your voice.

Employability Skills 2000+

The Conference Board of Canada
Insights You Can Count On

Please see the OLC to preview the key skills from the Conference Board of Canada's Employability Skills 2000+ covered in this module.

Review of Key Points

1. How can you develop an overall interview strategy? What three questions should you thoroughly answer before the interview?
2. What should you bring to the interview?
3. What main points should you note during and after the interview?
4. What are seven interview habits of highly successful job applicants?
5. Define stress, behavioural, and situational interviews. How should you prepare for each of these?
6. What can you do if you believe you are being asked an illegal interview question?

Assignments for Module 29

Questions for Critical Thinking

29.1 What are your greatest strengths? How can you demonstrate them during an interview?
29.2 What are your weaknesses? How will you deal with them if they come up during an interview?
29.3 What are your options if you are asked what you believe is an illegal interview question? Which option seems best to you? Why?
29.4 Is it unethical to practise answering interview questions, so that you come across as very poised at an interview?

Exercises and Problems

29.5 Interviewing Job Hunters

Talk to students at your school who are interviewing for jobs this term. Possible questions to ask them include the following:

- What field are you in? How good is the job market in that field this year?
- What questions have you been asked at job interviews? Were you asked any stress or sexist questions? any really oddball questions?
- What answers seemed to go over well? What answers bombed?
- Were you asked to take any tests (skills, physical, drugs)?
- How long did you have to wait after a first interview to learn whether you were being invited for an office visit? How long after an office visit did it take to learn whether you were being offered a job? How much time did the company give you to decide?
- What advice would you have for someone who will be interviewing next term or next year?

As your instructor directs,

a. Summarize your findings in a memo to your instructor.
b. Report your findings orally to the class.
c. Join with a small group of students to write a group report describing the results of your survey.

29.6   Interviewing an Interviewer

Talk to someone who regularly interviews candidates for entry-level jobs. Possible questions to ask include the following:

- How long have you been interviewing for your organization? Does everyone on the management ladder at your company do some interviewing, or do people specialize in it?
- Do you follow a set structure for interviews? What are some of the standard questions you ask?
- What are you looking for? How important are (1) good grades, (2) leadership roles in extracurricular groups, or (3) relevant work experience? What advice would you give to someone who doesn't have one or more of these?
- What behaviours do students exhibit that create a poor impression? Think about the worst candidate you've interviewed. What did he or she do (or not do) to create such a negative impression?
- What behaviours make a good impression? Recall the best student you've ever interviewed. Why did he or she impress you so much?
- How does your employer evaluate and reward your success as an interviewer?
- What advice would you give to someone who still has a year or so before the job hunt begins?

As your instructor directs,

a. Summarize your findings in a memo to your instructor.
b. Report your findings orally to the class.
c. Join with a small group of students to write a group report describing the results of your survey.
d. Write to the interviewer thanking him or her for taking the time to talk to you.

29.7   Preparing an Interview Strategy

Based on your analysis for Problems 27.5 and 27.6, prepare an interview strategy.

1. List two to five things about yourself that you want the interviewer to know before you leave the interview.
2. Identify any weaknesses or apparent weaknesses in your record and plan ways to explain them or minimize them.

3. List the points you need to learn about an employer to decide whether to accept an office visit or plant trip.

As your instructor directs,

a. Share your strategy with a small group of students.
b. Describe your strategy in a memo to your instructor.
c. Present your strategy orally to the class.

29.8   Preparing Answers to Behavioural Interview Questions

Tell about a time when you

1. Worked effectively under pressure
2. Handled a difficult situation with a co-worker
3. Made an unpopular decision
4. Tolerated an opinion that differed from yours
5. Were unable to complete a project on time
6. Overcame a major obstacle
7. Adapted to a difficult situation

As your instructor directs,

a. Share your answers with a small group of students.
b. Present your answers in a memo to your instructor, and explain why you've chosen the examples you describe.
c. Present your answers orally to the class.

29.9   Preparing Questions to Ask Employers

Prepare a list of questions to ask at job interviews.

1. Prepare a list of three to five general questions that apply to most employers in your field.

2. Prepare two to five specific questions for each of the three companies you are most interested in.

As your instructor directs,

a. Share the questions with a small group of students.
b. List the questions in a memo to your instructor.

c. Present your questions orally to the class.

Polishing Your Prose

Matters on Which Experts Disagree

Any living language changes. New usages appear first in speaking. Here are five issues on which experts currently disagree:

1. Plural pronouns to refer to *everybody*, *everyone*, and *each*. Standard grammar says these words require singular pronouns: *his* or *her* rather than *their*.
2. Split infinitives. An infinitive is the form of a verb that contains *to*: to understand. An infinitive is **split** when another word separates the *to* from the rest of an infinitive: *to easily understand, to boldly go*. The most recent edition of the *Oxford English Dictionary* allows split infinitives. Purists disagree.
3. *Hopefully* to mean *I hope that*. *Hopefully* means "in a hopeful manner." However, a speaker who says "Hopefully, the rain will stop" is talking about the speaker's hope, not the rain's.
4. *Verbal* to mean *oral*. *Verbal* means "using words." Therefore, both writing and speaking are verbal communication. Non-verbal communication (for example, body language) does not use words.
5. Comma before *and* (the serial or series comma). In a series of three or more items, some experts require a comma after the next to last item (the item before the *and*); others don't.

Ask your instructor and your boss whether they are willing to accept the less formal usage. When you write to someone you don't know, use standard grammar and usage.

Exercises

Each of the following sentences illustrates informal usage. (a) Which would your instructor or your boss accept? (b) Rewrite each of the sentences using standard grammar and usage.

1. Everyone should bring their laptops to the sales meeting.
2. The schedule includes new product information, role-plays with common selling situations and awards to the top salespeople.
3. To really take advantage of the meeting, you need to bring all of your new product info.
4. Prepare to make a brief verbal report on a challenging sales situation.
5. Think of a time when it was hard to even get in the door to see a potential customer.
6. Hopefully, we will have time to work through many of these situations in our role-plays.
7. Awards include best rookie sales representative, the most improved region, everyone who beat their quota and sales representative of the year.
8. We'll feature verbal quotes from customers in our radio ads.
9. Our Web page will let people listen to each customer summarizing verbally what they like best about our products.
10. Hopefully, the Web page will be live so that we can access it during the meeting.

Check your answers to the odd-numbered exercises on page 574.

■ Online Learning Centre

Visit the Online Learning Centre at www.mcgrawhill.ca/olc/locker to access module quizzes, a searchable glossary, résumé and letter templates, additional business writing samples, CBC videos, and other learning and study tools.

30

Following the Interview: Follow-up Letters and Emails, and Job Offers

Module Outline

- What should I say in a follow-up email or letter?

- What do I do if my first offer isn't for the job I most want?

Review of Key Points

Assignments for Module 30

Polishing Your Prose: Using Standard English

LEARNING OBJECTIVES

After reading and applying the information in Module 30, you'll be able to demonstrate

Knowledge of

- The attitudes and behaviours employers seek

Skills to

- Make a good impression in follow-up letters and emails
- Choose a job that will give you what you want
- Express your enthusiasm to employers

The Conference Board of Canada
Insights You Can Count On

Please see the OLC to preview the key skills from the Conference Board of Canada's Employability Skills 2000+ covered in this module.

FIGURE 30.1

P A I B O C

Questions for Analysis

Use the PAIBOC questions to analyze business communication problems:

P What are your **purposes** in writing?

A Who is your **audience**? How do members of your audience differ? What audience characteristics are relevant to this particular message?

I What **information** must your message include?

B What reasons or reader **benefits** can you use to support your position?

O What **objections** can you expect your readers to have? What negative elements of your message must you de-emphasize or overcome?

C How will the **context** affect reader response? Think about your relationship to the reader, the morale in the organization, the economy, the time of year, and any special circumstances.

SEE THE OLC!

Interview Follow-up Letters

What you do after the interview may determine whether you get the job. One woman wanted to switch from banking, where she was working in corporate relations, to advertising. The ad agency interviewer expressed doubts about her qualifications. Immediately after leaving the agency, she tracked down a particular book the interviewer had mentioned he was looking for but had been unable to find. She presented it to him—and was hired.[1]

Xerox expects applicants for sales and repair positions to follow up within 10 days. If they don't, the company assumes that the person wouldn't follow up with clients.[2]

If the employer sends you an email query, answer it promptly. You're being judged not only on what you say, but also on how quickly you respond.

What should I say in a follow-up email or letter?

Reinforce positives and overcome any negatives.

After a first interview, follow-up with an email or a letter to reinforce positives from the first interview, to overcome any negatives, and to get information you can use to persuade the interviewer to hire you (see Figure 30.2). Career coach Kate Weldon suggests asking the following questions:

- "What additional information can I give you?"
- "I've been giving a lot of thought to your project and have some new ideas. Can we meet to go over them?"
- "Where do I stand? How does my work compare with the work others presented?"[3]

A letter (whether a hard copy or an email attachment) is a more formal follow-up message than an email. Base your decision on which to send on your audience analysis. A letter thanking your hosts is essential, however, when your interview includes an office visit or other forms of hospitality. A well-written letter can be the deciding factor that gets you the job.[4] In your letter be sure to do the following:

- Thank the interviewer for his or her time and hospitality.
- Reinforce the interviewer's positive impressions.
- Counter any negative impressions that may have come up at the interview.
- Use the jargon of the company and refer to specific things you learned during your interview or saw during your visit.
- Be enthusiastic.
- Refer to the next step: whether you'll wait to hear from the employer or whether you want to call to learn about the status of your application.

Be sure that the letter is well written and error-free. One employer reports,

> I often interviewed people whom I liked,...but their follow-up letters were filled with misspelled words and names and other inaccuracies. They blew their chance with the follow-up letter.[5]

Use your PAIBOC analysis (Figure 30.1) to compose your interview follow-up message. Figures 30.2 and 30.3 offer examples of follow-up messages.

FIGURE 30.2
A Follow-up Email

From: Ahmed Dhanray <adhanray@rogers.ca>
To: dland@wilson.ca
Sent: Monday, August 11, 2007, 5:45 PM
Subject: Thank you

Dear Delmarie Land:

Acknowledges hospitality and reinforces interest in the position

Thank you for your hospitality during my interview last Thursday. After visiting Wilson International and speaking with you and your team, I am convinced that a career in logistics is the right choice for me.

Seeing Kelly, Gene, and Leah work together to coordinate an international client's shipment gave me a sense of the deadlines you have to meet and of the collaboration required for customer service success. As we discussed, I learned to meet deadlines and work collaboratively during my summer co-op placement with Crowley Logistics. As I mentioned during the interview, my team at Crowley suggested a computerized warehouse system that saved the company more than $30 000 in its first year of implementation. I welcome the opportunity to make a similar contribution at Wilson.

Reminds the reader of strengths

Follow-up makes it easy for the reader

Please call me at 416-555-4567 if you have additional questions or if I can provide you with more information.

Sincerely,
Ahmed Dhanray

INSTANT REPLAY

Follow-Up Letters

A letter after an office visit should

- Remind the interviewer of what he or she liked in you.
- Counter any negative impressions.
- Use the jargon of the company and refer to specifics from the visit.
- Be enthusiastic.
- Refer to the next move.

■ What do I do if my first offer isn't for the job I most want?

Phone your first-choice employer to find out where you are on that list.

Some employers offer jobs at the end of the office visit. In other cases, you may wait for weeks or even months to hear. Employers almost always offer jobs orally. You must say something in response immediately, so plan some strategies.

If your first offer is not from your first choice, express your pleasure at being offered the job, but do not accept it on the phone. "That's great! May I let you know?" Some companies offer "exploding" job offers that expire in one week or less,[6] but most firms will give you a week to decide.

Then call the other companies you're interested in. Explain, "I've just gotten a job offer, but I'd rather work for you. Can you tell me what the status of my application is?" Nobody will

FIGURE 30.3
A Follow-up Letter

71 Autumn Ridge Road
Kitchener, ON N2P 2J6

March 23, 2007

Mr. Gino Focasio
Human Resources Department
Mueller Canada
8069 Lawson Road
Milton, ON L9T 5C4

Dear Mr. Focasio:

Thank you for interviewing me for the industrial engineering technician position, available in
your Milton plant. I appreciate the time that Ms. Rossiter, Mr. Alverez, Mr. Storino, and you gave
me.

*Refers to
important
items he
saw and
heard
during the
interview*

My expertise in jig and fixture design, and in auto-cad software, would contribute to your
commitment to continuous improvement, as described by Mr. Storino during the interview.
Seeing your machining and assembly processes assured me that I would be able to apply my
CNC programming experience to benefit the company.

*Reminds
interviewer
of his
strong
points*

Again, thank you for your time and for the plant tour. I am very excited at the prospect of
working with Mueller Canada. Please call me at 519-555-5912, or email me at zhang@hotmail.com
if you have any additional questions.

*Provides
positive
confirmation
of interest
in the
position*

*Makes
it easy
for the
reader
to respond*

Sincerely,

Zhang Huang
Zhang Huang

put that information in writing, but almost everyone will tell you over the phone. With this
information, you're in a better position to decide whether to accept the original offer.

Make your acceptance contingent on a written job offer confirming the terms. That letter
should spell out not only salary but also fringe benefits and any special provisions you
have negotiated. If something is missing, call the interviewer for clarification: "We agreed
that I'd be reviewed for a promotion and higher salary in six months, but I don't see that
in the letter." You have more power to resolve misunderstandings now than you will after
six months or a year on the job.

FYI

January 2006 employee hourly wage statistics indicate that applied and natural science professionals earn the most, with people in social science, education, and government service, and those in health occupations close behind (at average hourly wages of $27.70, $25.74, and 22.60 respectively); trades people and transport and equipment operators earn more ($19.39) than both those in business, finance and administrative occupations ($18.65), and sales and service ($12.93).

Source: Average hourly wages of employees by selected characteristics and profession, unadjusted data, by province (monthly) http://www40.statcan.ca/l01/cst01/labr69a.htm?sdi=average%20hourly%20wages%20employees%20selected, retrieved August 18, 2006.

The skilled trades continue to be underemployed, despite their multiple attractions: excellent remuneration, numerous opportunities, and work flexibility. York Region's Apprenticeship project, supported by the Ontario Youth Apprenticeship Program, offers high school students a semester of technical apprenticeship, under the tutelage of skilled co-op teachers like Phil MacDonald, pictured here with a student. Licensed skilled trades workers, including plumbers, electricians, and construction workers, can make over

$100,000.00 annually. Yet a recent Manpower Inc. survey found that "...66 percent of the 1000 Canadian firms surveyed were having difficulty filling positions, including those in the skilled construction trades."

Source: Anthony Reinhart, "Learning a New Way to Build a Future," *The Globe and Mail*, March 2, 2006, A17.

When you've accepted one job, let the other places you visited know that you're no longer interested. Then they can go to their second choices. If you're second on someone else's list, you'll appreciate other candidates' removing themselves so the way is clear for you. Because the world is a small place, because everyone is the customer, and because you may someday want to work for the company you're currently turning down, follow the *KISS formula: keep it short and simple.*

> Dear Jackson Phillips:
>
> Thank you for offering me the sales position in your electronics division. Allied Signal enjoys an international reputation for innovative quality products; I'm pleased to be considered part of the Allied team.
>
> After a great deal of thought, however, I have decided to look for employment opportunities closer to home while investigating courses for an advanced degree. I must, therefore, decline your offer.
>
> Again, thank you for your consideration.
>
> Sincerely,

SEE THE OLC!

Thank-You Letters

Employability Skills 2000+

The Conference Board of Canada
Insights You Can Count On

Please see the OLC to preview the key skills from the Conference Board of Canada's Employability Skills 2000+ covered in this module.

Review of Key Points

1. Why send a follow-up memo or letter?
2. When should you send your follow-up letter or memo?
3. What should you put in the follow-up document?
4. What should you do if your first offer is not from your first-choice employer?
5. Is it ethical for a quiet, reserved person to try to appear more enthusiastic?
6. Is it ethical to ask the company making you an offer to wait for your response while you try to find out your status from your first-choice employer?

Assignments for Module 30

Questions for Critical Thinking

30.1 Why is "mirroring" an interviewer's communication style a good interview tactic? Is it ethical?

30.2 Why is it important to get a job offer in writing before you accept it officially?

Exercises and Problems

30.3 Writing a Follow-up Letter after an Office Visit or Plant Trip

Write a follow-up email message or letter after an office visit or plant trip. Thank your hosts for their hospitality; relate your strong points to things you learned about the company during the visit; overcome any negatives that may remain; be enthusiastic about the company; and submit receipts for your expenses so you can be reimbursed.

30.4 Clarifying the Terms of a Job Offer

Last week, you got a job offer from your first-choice company, and you accepted it over the phone. Today, the written confirmation arrived. The letter specifies the starting salary and fringe benefits you had negotiated. However, during the office visit, you were promised a 5 percent raise after six months on the job. The job offer says nothing about the raise. You do want the job, but you want it on the terms you thought you had negotiated.

Write to your contact at the company, Damon Winters.

Polishing Your Prose

Using Standard English

Many speakers use a dialect of English. Dialects are logical and clear to the group that developed and uses the dialect. Often, dialects illustrate considerable creativity. However, in Canadian business, it's easier to get hired and promoted if you use standard edited English.

Most speakers learn that they're speaking (and perhaps writing) a dialect only when someone else tells them that their words don't sound "right." Dialects are distinguished from each other first by pronunciation. (Does pick rhyme with creek?) In addition, some dialects use different idioms than does standard English; some handle verbs or negation differently. Many assign different meanings to words than does standard English.

Dialect:	I thought youse was going.
Standard:	I thought you were going.
Dialect:	Don't give us no dead computers.
Standard:	Don't give us any computers that don't work.
or:	Give us only computers that work.
Dialect:	I be takin' night classes to get my degree.
Standard:	I am taking night classes to get my degree.
Dialect:	This Web site is bad!
Standard:	This Web site is good.

Exercises

Revise the following sentences to create standard English.

1. Did youse get the equipment?
2. I will ax her if she be surfing the Web.
3. Don't gimme no excuses, eh?
4. Them that can't use no computer ain't gonna get ahead.
5. Me, I think we oughtta reconsider.
6. So I'm like, where we gonna find workers? You know?
7. He don't know how good he's got it.
8. I decide to go to college to get my diploma.
9. I asked what the problem is and she goes, "Nothin!"
10. If I would have seen the report I would would have faxed it right away.

Check your answers to the odd-numbered exercises on page 574.

■ Online Learning Centre

Visit the Online Learning Centre at www.mcgrawhill.ca/olc/locker to access module quizzes, a searchable glossary, résumé and letter templates, additional business writing samples, CBC videos, and other learning and study tools.

■ CBC Video Case

Visit the Online Learning Centre at www.mcgrawhill.ca/olc/locker to view "Résumés," an online CBC Video Case for Unit 7 featuring advice from experts on how to put your résumé together. What comes first? What do you include? These questions and more are answered.

Cases for Communicators

Getting Résumé Recognition

The average online job applicant can be invisible to potential employers, hidden among the résumés crowding their databases and in-boxes.

Online job boards have greatly increased organizations' pool of potential applicants. However, technology has also resulted in an exponential increase in the number of résumés flooding human resources departments. In response, many companies now use special software programs that filter out all but those résumés containing specific key words. Other companies now include questionnaires as part of the online application process; these questionnaires are designed to assess the "fit" of the candidate. Still other companies have stopped using the general job boards, and rely instead on niche job boards (like iHireNursing.com, Retailjobs.com, and Accountants.com) that focus on special skills or career areas.

Tailoring your résumé to match specific jobs is critical today, especially when applying for a position online. You need to research your potential position carefully so that you can include relevant details and keywords. General-purpose boards may provide an overview of employment opportunities, but you're more likely to find a job on niche boards and employment sites operated by organizations, colleges and universities, and professional organizations.

Indisputably, however, the best way to stand amongst other applicants—and to learn about jobs in the hidden job market—is to know someone within the company. Networking continues to be the most effective job search strategy. And today's technology helps you to make and maintain those connections by taking advantage of blogs, personal Web sites, pod casting, and email.

Sources: T. Shawn Taylor, "With So Many Resumes on the Internet, Many End up Cyber-Trashed," *Chicago Tribune*, January 30, 2002, http://www.chicagotribune.com, retrieved August 16, 2002; http://content.monster.ca/6759_en-CA_p1.asp, retrieved October 30, 2006; http://www.ivc.ca/jobs/findingemployment.html, retrieved October 30, 2006; http://www.workopolis.ca/servlet/Content/fasttrack/20050205/RCOACH05?section=HomePage, retrieved October 30, 2006.

Individual Activity

Imagine that you are a consultant at an employment services company. In this position, you offer job seekers advice and expertise on targeted job searches, résumés, cover letters, and interviewing.

The company has an extensive database of employment resources, but you and your colleagues must constantly work to keep the information complete and accurate. In addition to your consulting schedule, you must identify one career path per week and do an exhaustive search of placement and informational resources in that field.

Your task is to think of a career in which you are interested and create a list of resources that you could use to find job leads, get information, and identify networking possibilities. Use all information options available to you, including the local library, school resources, and the Internet, among others.

Before you being your search, consider the following questions:

- What general directories or resource books could I use?
- What specialized directories or resource books should I investigate?
- What trade journals could I explore?
- Have I identified general online search sites?
- What niche sites could I explore?
- Which professional organizations would have information or resources?
- What major companies in the field should I investigate?
- What are their competitors?
- What additional career information could I find in my campus placement office?
- Do I know anyone who is already in the field?
- How can I access alumni networks or placement services?
- Have I reviewed local and national papers for job leads?
- What professional electronic mailing lists or electronic bulletin boards would be relevant?
- What other resources could I explore to find out more about opportunities in this field?

Group Activity

(Note: To prepare for this group activity, find at least three job postings that include detailed descriptions of the position, required skills, and hiring company. These types of postings are relatively easy to find on online job search engines such as Monster.ca. Copy these postings and distribute them to each member of the group.)

As a consultant at an employment services company, you meet regularly with your colleagues to review the quality of the company's offerings and to hone your skills through group training. Last week, in a discussion about client needs, you realized that, as a result of the upswing of employment opportunities in the area, your company has seen an increased number of clients who need help targeting their cover letters and résumés for specific positions.

Review the first job posting. As you read, consider the following:

- What are the key words in this posting?
- What specific information, if any, does the posting highlight about the company, its industry, or its products or services?

- What are the specific skills required for the position?

As a group, discuss the advice that you might give to someone applying for this position. What advice could you give to this client on targeting a cover letter or résumé?

Answer the following questions:

- What are the key words you would expect this employer to look for in a résumé?
- What active words should your client try to use in a résumé or cover letter?
- What skills or types of skills should your client emphasize?
- What details about the company could or should the client include in this solicited letter?

Review each job posting. How do you think this type of exercise might benefit you as you prepare your own résumé and cover letters, and begin to interview for positions?

Credits

FIGURES/TABLES

Employability Skills 2000+ Brochure E/F: Employability Skills 2000+ reproduced by permission of The Conference Board of Canada, Ottawa. Subsequent end of module features containing excerpts from the Employability Skills 2000+ list also reproduced with permission.

Figure 1.1, page 6: reprinted with permission of the author.

Figure 2.2, page 26: based on Vincent J. Brown, "Facing Multiple Audiences in Engineering and R&D Writing: The Social Context of a Technical Report," Journal of Technical Writing and Communication 24, no. 1 (1994): 67–75.

Table 2.2, page 33: Based on Isabel Briggs Myers, "Effects of Each Preference in Work Situations," *Introduction to Type*, Consulting Psychologists Press, 1962, 1980.

FYI Box, page 39: Reprinted with permission from *Canadian Business*.

FYI Box, page 48: Data is adapted in part from Statistics Canada publication "The Daily", *2002 Ethnic Diversity Survey*, Catalogue 11-001, Released September 29, 2003, pages 3 and 4; URL: http://www.statcan.ca/Daily/English/020929/td030929.htm.

Table 3.1, page 49: Adapted from Table 5.1, p 148 of *International Business Communication* by David A. Victor. Copyright 1992 by HarperCollins Publishers Inc. Reprinted by permission of Addison-Wesley Educational Publishers, Inc.

Table 3.2, page 51: Reproduced by permission. From *Multicultural Management 2000*. Copyright © 1998, Gulf Publishing Company, Houston, Texas, 800-231-6275. All rights reserved.

Table 3.3, page 56: Adapted from Farid Elashmawi and Philip R. Harris, *Multicultural Management 200: Essential Cultural Insights for Global Business Success* (Huston: Gulf, 1998), p 169.

Table 3.4, page 58: Adapted from Farid Elashmawi and Philip R. Harris, *Multicultural Management 200: Essential Cultural Insights for Global Business Success* (Huston: Gulf, 1998), p 169.

Figure 4.4, page 77: Email and proposal based on Fred Reynolds, "What Adult Work-World Writers have Taught Me About Adult Work-World Writing," Professional Writing in Context: Lesson from Teaching and Consulting in Worlds of Work (Hillsdale, NJ: Lawrence Erlbaum Associates, 1995), pp 18, 20.

Table 4.2, page 80: Tom McArthur, ed., The Oxford Companion to the English Language (Oxford: Oxford University Press, 1992), p 407.

Cases for Communicators, page 102: Reprinted with permission—Torstar Syndication Services.

You-Attitude, page 107: Reprinted with permission from *The Globe and Mail*.

Figure 6.1, page 108: Courtesy of The Salvation Army, Ontario Central Division. Reprinted with permission.

FYI Box, page 135: Reprinted with permission from *The Globe and Mail*.

Feature/Benefit, page 139; Reprinted with permission from *The Globe and Mail*.

FYI Box, page 140: Data is adapted in part from Statistics Canada publication "The Daily", *Survey of Household Spending*, Catalogue 11-001, Released December 13, 2004; URL: http://www.statcan.ca/Daily/English/041213/d041213b.htm.

Figure 14.1, page 264: Courtesy of McPherson Associates Inc.

Table 17.1, page 325: The S responses that block communication are based on a list of 12 in Thomas Gordon and Judith Gordon Sands, P.E.T. in Action (New York: Wyden 1976) 117–18.

Figure 19.2, page 605: From *Inc.: The Magazine for Growing Companies*. © 1995 by Business Innovator Group Resources, Inc. Reproduced with permission of Business Innovator Group Resources, Inc. via Copyright Clearance Center.

Table 20.1, page 367: Courtesy of Michael Goldman and *The Training Report*.

Expanding a Critical Skill, page 371: George B. Ray, "Vocally Cued Personality Prototypes: An Implicit Personality Theory Approach," Communication Monographs 53, no. 2 (1986) 266–67; and Jacklyn Boice, "Verbal Impressions," Selling Power, March 2000, 69.

Figure 21.1, page 387: Reprinted with permission of Sheridan College Institute of Technology and Advanced Learning.

Table 22.2, page 408: Adapted from Richard C. Freed, Shevin Freed, and Joseph D. Romano, Writing Winning Proposals: Your Guide to Landing the Client, Making the Sale, Persuading the Boss (New York: McGraw-Hill, 1995), p 121.

Figure 25.4, page 472: Reprinted with permission from *The Globe and Mail*.

Figure 25.6, page 475: Reprinted with permission of Getty Images.

Exercise 25.7, page 478–479: Evaluating Visuals: Cell Bloc—from *Newsweek*, August 27, 2001. © 2001 Newsweek, Inc. all rights reserved;

Evaluating Visuals: Pumped-Up Fears—reprinted with permission of *Maclean's Magazine*; Evaluating Visuals: Transparency & Corruption —Reprinted with permission from *The Globe and Mail*;

Evaluating Visuals: Higher Learning—"Higher Learning," *National Post*, January 2003, p 74. Graphic by Kagan Mcleod; Based on *Education at a Glance: OECD Indicators 2002*, OECD.

Exercise 25.8, page 481–482: Interpreting Data—Consumer Price Index: (Saskatchewan, Alberta) Adapted from Statistics Canada Web site: http://www40.statcan.ca/101/cst01/cpis15e.htm; (Newfoundland and Labrador) Adapted from Statistics Canada Web site http://www40.statcan.ca/101/cst01/cpis15a.htm;

Interpreting Data: Rating Student Satisfaction—Reprinted with permission from *The Globe and Mail*; Interpreting Data: Population Urban and Rural—Adapted from Statistics Canada Web site: http://www40.statcan.ca/101/cst01/demo62a.htm.

FYI Box, page 489: from Statistics Canada publication "The Daily", Labour Force Survey, September 2005, Catalogue 11-001, Released October 7, 2005, URL: http://www.statcan.ca/Daily/English/051007/d051007a.htm.

FYI Box, page 535: from Statistics Canada publication "The Daily", Labour Force Survey, September 2005, Catalogue 11-001, Released October 7, 2005, http://www.statcan.ca/Daily/English/051007/d051007a.htm.

FYI Box, page 536: Reprinted with permission from *The Globe and Mail*.

FYI Box, page 549: Reprinted with permission from *The Globe and Mail*.

PHOTOS

Polishing Your Prose

Shown here in green are possible solutions to the odd-numbered exercises. Check with your instructor on any other solutions you propose.

Module 1: Sentence Fragments

1. Our retail sales division posted record sales for November.
3. Ms. Singh began the meeting a few minutes late because the computer crashed.
5. Although the car ran fine, we were late to the meeting because of traffic.
7. Terrell announced a plan to introduce our latest computer model to retail electronics stores.
9. The Accounting Department recently received several awards for excellence.

Module 2: Comma Splices

1. The conference call came at 1 p.m., and we took it immediately.
3. Janelle drafted her problem-solving report and sent a copy to each committee member for review.
5. When Katya called the hotel in Montreal for a reservation, the desk staff booked a room for her immediately.
7. I'll have Tina call the main office; you ask Brian to set up an appointment for the four of us tomorrow.
9. I like to make oral presentations because they're fun.

Module 3: Using Idioms

1. Race the clock = Work quickly to meet a deadline.
3. Juggle a schedule = Make significant changes to a busy schedule.
5. Punch the clock = Begin or end the workday.
7. Cold call a customer = Make an unsolicited telephone sales call.
9. Open up new markets = Increase sales in a new market.

Module 4: Commas in Lists

1. Please send the "fruit of the month" in April, May, June, and July. (Last comma is optional).
3. The special parts division is opening offices in Brampton, Ontario; Fredericton, New Brunswick; and Big Salmon, Yukon.
5. I need to telephone Mary, Frank, and Paul, to finish my report, and mail copies of it to Ted, Sam, and Latanya. (While semi-colons could be used after Paul and report, commas are acceptable because the groupings of listed items are understandable with commas.)

7. The weather affects our offices in Montreal, New York City, and Philadelphia.
9. Elizabeth, Tyrone, Mark, and Sara presented the team's recommendations.

Module 5: Active and Passive Voice

1. Unless the context of the sentence is negative, change to active voice. The vice president of finance signed the contract.
3. The visitors' arrival is more important than who is expecting them. Therefore, use passive voice.
5. Changing this sentence to active voice would cast blame. Therefore, use passive voice.
7. The human resources administrator returned phone calls.
9. Return phone calls within 24 hours.

Module 6: It's/Its

1. It's too bad that the team hasn't finished its presentation.
3. It's going to require overtime because the data centre needs its reports quickly.
5. The company will announce its new name at a press conference.
7. It's a good idea to keep your travel receipts in a separate file.
9. The Saskatoon office will share its findings with the other branch offices.

Module 7: Singular and Plural Possessives

1. We design products based on our customers' needs.
3. Canadians' views of the economy reflect their confidence in the stock market.
5. We meet the local, provincial, and federal governments' standards for quality control.
7. The committee's duties will be completed after it announces its decision.
9. We'll decide whether to have more computer training sessions based on employees' feedback.

Module 8: Plurals and Possessives

1. Canadian companies are competing effectively in the global market.
3. The manager's ability to listen is just as important as his or her technical knowledge.
5. Social workers should tell clients about services available in the community.
7. Information about the new community makes the family's move easier.
9. Memos are sent to other workers in the same organization.

Module 9: Making Subjects and Verbs Agree

1. Each of us is entitled to company health care benefits.
3. The price of our stocks is increasing.
5. We order a dozen new toner cartridges each month.
7. Ms. Schiff and her assistant are attending the conference in Halifax.
9. Professor Beauparlant, Mr. Kincaid, and Ms. Carolla are on the guest list and plan to sit at the same table.

Module 10: Dangling Modifiers

1. After working a year, you will be covered by dental insurance.
3. I bought my daughter her first share of stock when she was 10.
5. By calling ahead of time, you can make reservations efficiently.
7. As I told you on the phone, your order was shipped on April 1.
9. If you share files with our legal department, our attorneys can work better with you.

Module 11: Parallel Structure

1. Last week, Alain and Rochelle flew to Toronto, Montreal, Québec City, and Lansing.
3. To ship a package:
   1. Fill out an address form.
   2. Specify on the form how the package should be sent.
   3. Have your supervisor initial the appropriate box on the address form if you want the package shipped by overnight mail.
5. Appointments can be scheduled in 5-minute, 10-minute, 15-minute, or 20-minute intervals.
7. This report discusses
   Why We Should Upgrade Capital Equipment
   Why We Should Increase Staff by 25 percent
   Why We Should Decrease Employee Turnover
   Why We Should Identify New Product Markets
9. Use the telephone to answer customer questions, email to send order confirmations, and our Web page to take orders.

Module 12: Narrative Voice

1. This voice sounds authoritative, perhaps even threatening due to the constant use of will commands and all caps in no exception.
3. Phrases like superlative and most relevant and the wordiness make this voice overly contrived.
5. Teenagers often interrupt speech with like and you know and end what should be declarative statements with questions. This statement sounds like a classic Valley Girl/Boy.
7. Most readers would find this voice acceptable in business.
9. Because of the large amount of jargon, this voice sounds cold and technical.

Module 13: Making Nouns and Pronouns Agree

1. Correct.
3. The company announces its quarterly profits today.
5. A CEO's pay is often based on the performance of his or her company.
7. In my first month of work, I learned to check my email at least three times a day.
9. Correct.

Module 14: Using Spell and Grammar Checkers

1. Their product is sitting over there.
3. It's not really a good idea to have lunch before the flight.
5. Martika is happy with her purchase; she'll order online again. (Online is generally not hyphenated.)
7. Les says, "Less is more."
9. The Internet is a powerful research tool—so what? (Internet is a proper term; most word processors will automatically make two hyphens into a dash, though two hyphens are acceptable.)

Module 15: Run-on Sentences

1. The marketing department ordered new, four-colour brochures. They are really nice.
3. Let's schedule a meeting next week. We'll talk about your promotion so you can transition easily into the new job.
5. Employees may request benefits changes during the annual enrolment period. Supervisors should pass out the required forms, and employees should have them completed by the deadline on the form.
7. Mohammed should make sure he specifies 20-lb. rather than 15-lb. paper stock, Jenna should call the print shop and ask whether the employees need anything, and Bruce should tell Ms. Winans we appreciate her letting us know we originally ordered the wrong stock.
9. A few customers are concerned about the shipping date, but the mailroom is sure we can ship overnight. I think there's no reason to be concerned.

Module 16: End Punctuation

1. Where is the file on the Richman proposal?
3. Ms. Amarotti will arrive by plane tomorrow.
5. Take a moment to read the instructions before completing the form.
7. Congratulations on your recent promotion to line manager. (If you know this person well or the message is informal, then using an exclamation point may also be acceptable.)
9. Remember, when we turn on the break-room lights, everyone is to yell, "Happy Birthday, Susharita!"

Module 17: Combining Sentences

1. To get promoted quickly at our company, be organized, be on time, and meet deadlines.

3. Changing the toner cartridge on the photocopier is simple. To begin, open the front panel. Find the green tabs and depress them with your thumbs. Next, pull the black toner cartridge out and put it in the recycling box. Slide a new toner cartridge into the compartment until the green tabs snap back into place. Finally, close the panel.

5. The tornado plan for our building has five parts: first, listen for the tornado alert siren; second, go to your designated shelter area in the basement of the building; third, be sure to take the stairs and not the elevator; fourth, sit down on the floor; fifth, cover your head with your arms.

Module 18: Delivering Criticism

1. We need to make this report meet our company's standards.
3. This assignment must have library resources.
5. The information in this brochure is terrific. Let's work on making the design match the content.
7. Our instructor said that we have to use at least five sources.
9. Would you help me to better understand this proposal?

Module 19: Hyphens and Dashes

1. Our biggest competitors—including those in the Asian and European markets—introduced more product models during the fourth quarter.
3. Please pick up three 2-by-4 posts at the lumberyard.
5. Painters from the building services department plan to give Tarik's office two coats of paint.
7. The latest weather reports suggest that travel over South and Latin America may be interrupted by storms.
9. You can email the results to my office in the early morning.

Module 20: Choosing Levels of Formality

1. On Monday, I inspected our inventory.
3. Though the representative was firm, we eventually negotiated a settlement.
5. The manager postponed making a decision.
7. In my last job, I worked as a gofer for the Marketing manager.
9. This report has problems.

Module 21: Using MLA and APA Style

1. Bhandari, Aparita. "Workers Bring Culture to their Cubicle." *The Globe and Mail*: C1.
3. Locker, K. O., Stephan Kyo Kaczmarek, and Kathryn Braun. *Business Communication: Building Critical Skills*. 2nd Canadian ed. Toronto, ON: Mc-Graw-Hill Ryerson, 2004.
5. Wellner, Alison Stein. "The National Headcount." *American Demographics*, March 2001: S12.
7. Chidley, J. (2003, July 7, 21). Spam-a-lama-ding-dong. *Canadian Business*. 76 (13) 6. Retrieved July 20, 2003,

from http://www.canadianbusiness.com/columns/ article.jsp?content=20030707_54772_54772
9. Scotiabank. (2003). ScotiaLine for Students. Retrieved July 20, 2003, from http://www. scotiabank. com/ScotiaLine for students

Identify telephone call in text as personal communication. Give name of caller and specific date. Do not list in References.

Module 22: Who/Whom and I/Me

1. Karen and I visited Shawnee Community College last week.
3. Dr. Jacobsen, who serves on the Board of Directors, is retiring.
5. Who is the most experienced person on your staff?
7. My supervisor told me the committee will decide who gets the promotion.
9. Three people at the firm who can speak a second language are Phillip, Stacy, and I.

Module 23: Being Concise

1. Please return the order form ASAP.
3. The blue car is the legal affairs director's.
5. Call to confirm your order.
7. The enclosed references can discuss my job qualifications further.
9. Let me start by sharing stories about our guest of honour.

Module 24: Improving Paragraphs

1. My experience in the secretarial field makes me an ideal candidate for a position as senior administrative assistant with Graham, Chang, and Associates. As a receptionist at McCandless Realty, I typed, answered phones, and handled payroll. Then, as a secretary at Dufresne Plastics, I took training courses in data entry and Microsoft Word and learned to type 70 WPM with no mistakes.

Module 25: Writing Subject Lines and Headings

1. An Introduction from the New Customer Service Department Supervisor. (Better with actual name.)
3. Your donation of blood on Tuesday can save a life.
5. Insurance Rates Will Increase July 31.
7. Research; Logistics; Profit
9. Clemente Research Group's Five-Year Goals; Clemente Research Group's Ten-Year Goals; Clemente Research Group's Fifteen-Year Goals

Module 26: Using Details

1. I am the Webmaster for the Jessica London Company.
3. In June, I plan to graduate from Seneca Community College and start my career in respiratory therapy at St. Ann's Hospital.

5. Fortified with antioxidants and Vitamins D and K, EnVigorate Power Drink will make you feel healthy and energetic all day long.
7. The new Mark VII pool filter is 33 percent more energy efficient than competitors' filters and features a 10-year warranty, the best on the market.
9. More than 17 years of experience and $7.9 million in real estate sales make me the ideal candidate for district sales manager.

Module 27: Proofreading

1. Ours is a company worth doing business with. You can count on our promise to provide not only the best service but also the finest in materials, fit, and finish. All of our products are made to exacting specifications, meaning that you receive the best product for the best prices. If you aren't satisfied for any reason, simply call the toll-free hotline at 1-800-555-1212 to get a prompt refund. Or you can write us at The John Doe Company, 123 Main Street, Anytown, Canada M6V 2B4. Remember, our motto is "The customer is always right."

Module 28: Using You and I

1. Our team created a class Web page. I was responsible for much of the initial design and some of the HTML coding. Four of us tested the page to see how easily we could navigate it. We presented the page to a committee of local businesspeople.
3. Team members should resolve any conflicts they have created with other team members.

5. Please distribute an agenda before the meeting.
7. Make the Web page accessible to users with impaired vision.
9. During my co-op placement, I observed department meetings, sat in on client meetings, designed PowerPoint™ slides for client presentations, participated in strategy sessions, and drafted brochures.

Module 29: Matters on Which Experts Disagree

1. Everyone should bring his or her laptop to the sales meeting.
3. To take advantage of the meeting fully, you need to bring all of your new product information.
5. Think of a time when it was hard even to get in the door to see a potential customer.
7. Awards include best rookie sales representative, the most improved region, everyone who beat his or her sales quota, and sales representative of the year.
9. Our Web page will let people listen to each customer summarizing orally what he or she likes best about our products.

Module 30: Using Standard English

1. Did you get the equipment?
3. Don't give me any excuses.
5. I think we ought to reconsider.
7. He doesn't know how good he has it.
9. I asked her what the problem was and she answered, "Nothing!"

Notes

Module 1

Unit One Opener: Source: Helena Katz, Summer 2003. Word power. Homemakers, p. 110. Heather Andrews Miller (2003). Kahnawake teen knows how to get the job done. *Windspeaker*. Retrieved November 5, 2005, from http://www.ammsa.com/windspeaker/topnews-Feb-2003.html#anchor374139. Ed Kromer (2003). MBAs help plan Kahnawake Library. *McGillReporter*. May 8, 2003, Volume 35, Number 15. Retrieved November 5, 2005, from http://www.mcgill.ca/reporter/35/15/kahnawake/.

1. "Technical Training Ain't All It's Cracked Up to Be," *The Training Report*, January/February 2000, 8.
2. Ann Kerr, "Hard Lessons in Soft Skills," *The Globe and Mail*, Globe Careers, Friday, February 21, C1.
3. Henry Mintzberg, *The Nature of Managerial Work* (New York: Harper & Row, 1973), 32, 65.
4. Elaine Vets, "Voice Mail Converts Boss into a Secretary," *The Columbus Dispatch*, August 10, 1995, 3E; Rochelle Sharpe, "Work Week," *The Wall Street Journal*, September 26, 1995, A1.
5. Heather Sokoloff, "Engineers Forced to Learn How to Write," *National Post*, May 28, 2003, A6.
6. http://search3.workopolis.com/jobshome/db/work.job_posting?pi_job_id=7630586&pi_search_id=616018147&pi_sort=POST_DATE&pi_curjob=12&pi_maxjob=500.
7. http://www.leader-values.com/Content/detail.asp?ContentDetailID=883, retrieved July 26, 2006.
8. Claudia MonPere McIsaac and Mary Ann Aschauer, "Proposal Writing at Atherton Jordan, Inc.: An Ethnographic Study," *Management Communication Quarterly* 3 (1990): 535.
9. Elizabeth Allen, "Excellence in Public Relations & Communication Management," IABC/Dayton Awards Banquet, Dayton, OH, July 12, 1990.

Module 2

1. Audiences 1, 3, and 4 are based on J.C. Mathes and Dwight Stevenson, *Designing Technical Reports: Writing for Audiences in Organizations*, 2nd ed. (New York: Macmillan, 1991), 40. The fifth audience is suggested by Vincent J. Brown, "Facing Multiple Audiences in Engineering and R&D Writing: The Social Context of a Technical Report," *Journal of Technical Writing and Communication* 24, no. 1 (1994): 67–75.
2. http://www.peterursbender.com/quiz/index.html, retrieved July 26, 2006.
3. Isabel Briggs Myers, Introduction to Type (Palo Alto, CA: Consulting Psychologists Press, 1980).
4. Isabel Briggs Myers and Mary H. McCaulley, *Manual: A Guide to the Development and Use of the Myers-Briggs Type Indicator* (Palo Alta, CA: Consulting Psychologists Press, 1985), pp. 251, 248, respectively.
5. Keith McArthur, The Globe and Mail, Monday, June 6, 2005, http://www.theglobeandmail.com/servlet/story/RTGAM.20050606.wxrbrand06/BNStory/Business/, retrieved July 26, 2006.
6. "Ford's Model E," Forbes.com, July 2000, 30–34.
7. Erin Anderssen, "They Know When You are Sleeping, They Know When You're Awake and Whether You Like Sushi," Globe Focus, *The Globe and Mail*, Saturday, December 18, 2004, F1 and F8 and http://www.theglobeandmail.com/servlet/story/RTGAM.20041220.gtcover20/BNStory/einsider/?pageRequested=all, retrieved July 26, 2006; and http://www.tetrad.com/pricing/can/prizmce.html, retrieved July 26, 2006.
8. TD-Canada Trust Web site, http://www.tdcanadatrust.com, and Royal Bank Web site, http://www.royalbank.com, both retrieved August 25, 2006.
9. Matt Siegel, "The Perils of Culture Conflict," *Fortune*, November 9, 1998, 258.
10. Linda Driskill, "Negotiating Differences among Readers and Writers," presented at the Conference on College Composition and Communication, San Diego, CA, March 31–April 3, 1993.

Module 3

1. "Teamwork Differs for Men and Women," *University of Toronto Magazine*, Autumn, 2005, 10.
2. http://www.pch.gc.ca/progs/multi/respect_e.cfm, retrieved July 26, 2006.
3. Erin Anderssen, "People Deficit Gives Workers Upper Hand," *The Globe and Mail*, January 22, 2003, A6.
4. ibid.
5. http://www.pch.gc.ca/progs/multi/respect_e.cfm, retrieved July 26, 2006.
6. David A. Victor, *International Business Communication* (New York: HarperCollins, 1992), 148–60.
7. John Webb and Michael Keene, "The Impact of Discourse Communities on International Professional Communication," in *Exploring the Rhetoric of International Professional Communication: An Agenda for Teachers and Researchers*, ed. Carl R. Lovitt with Dixie Coswami (Amityville, NY: Baywood, 1999), 81–109.
8. Christina Haas and Jeffrey L. Funk, "'Shared Information:' Some Observations of Communication in Japanese Technical Settings," *Technical Communication* 36, no. 4 (November 1989): 365.

9. Laray M. Barna, "Stumbling Blocks in Intercultural Communication," in *Intercultural Communication*, ed. Larry A. Samovar and Richard E. Porter (Belmont, CA: Wadsworth, 1985), 331.

10. Marjorie Fink Vargas, *Louder than Words* (Ames: Iowa State University Press, 1986), 47.

11. Michael Argyle, *Bodily Communication* (New York: International University Press, 1975), 89.

12. Jerrold J. Merchant, "Korean Interpersonal Patterns: Implications for Korean/American Intercultural Communication," *Communication* 9 (October 1980): 65.

13. Ray L. Birdwhistell, *Kinesics and Context: Essays on Body Motion Communication* (Philadelphia: University of Philadelphia Press, 1970), 81.

14. Paul Ekman, Wallace V. Friesen, and John Bear, "The International Language of Gestures," *Psychology Today* 18, no. 5 (May 1984): 64.

15. Carmen Judith Nine-Curt, "Hispanic-Anglo Conflicts in Nonverbal Communication," in *Perspectivas Pedagogicas*, ed. I. Abino et al. (San Juan: Universidad de Puerto Rico, 1983), 235.

16. Brenda Major, "Gender Patterns in Touching Behavior," in *Gender and Nonverbal Behavior*, ed. Clara Mayo and Nancy M. Henley (New York: Springer-Verlag, 1981), 26, 28.

17. "Minor Memos," *The Wall Street Journal*, February 12, 1988, 1.

18. Natalie Porter and Florence Gies, "Women and Nonverbal Leadership Cues: When Seeing Is Not Believing," in *Gender and Nonverbal Behavior*, ed. Clara Mayo and Nancy M. Henley (New York: Springer-Verlag, 1981), 48–49.

19. Lawrence B. Nadler, Marjorie Keeshan Nadler, and Benjamin J. Broome, "Culture and the Management of Conflict Situations," in *Communication, Culture, and Organizational Processes*, ed. William B. Gudykunst, Lea P. Stewart, and Stella Ting-Toomey (Beverly Hills, CA: Sage, 1985), 103.

20. Argyle, *Bodily Communication*, 90.

21. Mary Ritchie Key, *Paralanguage and Kinesics* (Metuchen, NJ: Scarecrow, 1975), 23.

22. Fred Hitzhusen, conversation with Kitty Locker, January 31, 1998.

23. Lisa Davis, "The Height Report: A Look at Stature and Status," *Columbus Dispatch*, January 19, 1988, E1, New York Times Special Features.

24. Deborah Tannen, *That's Not What I Meant!* (New York: William Morrow, 1986).

25. Karen Ritchie, "Marketing to Generation X," *American Demographics*, April 1995, 34–36.

26. Daniel N. Maltz and Ruth A. Borker, "A Cultural Approach to Male-Female Miscommunication," in *Language and Social Identity*, ed. John J. Gumperz (Cambridge: Cambridge University Press, 1982), 202.

27. Vincent O'Neill, "Training the Multi-Cultural Manager," Sixth Annual EMU Conference on Languages and Communication for World Business and the Professions, Ann Arbor, MI, May 7–9, 1987.

28. Akihisa Kumayama, comment during discussion, Sixth Annual EMU Conference on Languages and Communication for World Business and the Professions, Ann Arbor, MI, May 7–9, 1987.

29. Brad Edmondson, "What Do You Call a Dark-Skinned Person?" *American Demographics*, October 1993, 9.

30. Lisa Tyler, "Communicating about People with Disabilities: Does the Language We Use Make a Difference?" *Bulletin of the Association for Business Communications* 53, no. 3 (September 1990): 65.

Module 4

1. Adapted from *Lawyer as Writer—Notes from Peter Elbow, Writing Without Teachers* (New York: Oxford University Press, 1973), http://www.wvu.edu/~lawfac/jelkins/writeshop/elbow.html, retrieved October 24, 2006.

2. Leslie Butler, personal communication, November 26, 2005.

3. Elizabeth Braun, personal communication, November 26, 2005.

4. See especially Linda Flower and John R. Hayes, "The Cognition of Discovery: Defining a Rhetorical Problem," *College Composition and Communication* 31 (February 1980): 21–32; and the essays in two collections: Charles R. Cooper and Lee Odell, *Research on Composing: Points of Departure* (Urbana, IL: National Council of Teachers of English, 1978), and Mike Rose, ed., *When a Writer Can't Write: Studies in Writer's Block and Other Composing-Process Problems* (New York: Guilford Press, 1985).

5. Rebecca E. Burnett, "Content and Commas: How Attitudes Shape a Communication-Across-the-Curriculum Program," Association for Business Communication Convention, Orlando, FL, November 1–4, 1995.

6. Peter Elbow, *Writing with Power: Techniques for Mastering the Writing Process* (New York: Oxford University Press, 1981), 15–20.

7. See Gabriela Lusser Rico, *Writing the Natural Way* (Los Angeles: J.P. Tarcher, 1983), 10.

8. Rachel Spilka, "Orality and Literacy in the Workplace: Process- and Text-based Strategies for Multiple Audience Adaptation," *Journal of Business and Technical Communication* 4, no. 1 (January 1990): 44–67.

9. Fred Reynolds, "What Adult Work-World Writers Have Taught Me About Adult Work-World Writing," *Professional Writing in Context: Lessons from Teaching and Consulting in Worlds of Work* (Hillsdale, NJ: Lawrence Erlbaum Associates, 1995), 18–21.

10. Raymond W. Beswick, "Communicating in the Automated Office," American Business Communication Association International Convention, New Orleans, LA, October 20, 1982.

11. This three-step process is modelled on the one suggested by Barbara L. Shwom and Penny L. Hirsch, "Managing the Drafting Process: Creating a New Model for the Workplace," *Bulletin of the Association for Business Communication* 57, no. 2 (June 1994): 10.

12. Glenn J. Broadhead and Richard C. Freed, "The Variables of Composition: Process and Product in a Business Setting," Conference on College Composition and Communication Studies in Writing and Rhetoric (Carbondale, IL: Southern Illinois University Press, 1986), 57.

13. Students, 1976–2005, Participants' Writing Workshops, 1982–2005, Personal communications with author.

Module 5

1. Linda Reynolds, "The Legibility of Printed Scientific and Technical Information," *Information Design*, ed. Ronald Easterby and Harm Zwaga (New York: Wiley, 1984), 187–208.

2. Robin Williams. (1994). *The Non-Designer's Design Book*, http://www.amazon.com/gp/product/0321193857/sr=8-1/qid=1155051585/ref=pd_bbs_1/104-1775709-7119129?ie=UTF8, retrieved August 8th, 2006.

3. Once we know how to read English, the brain first looks to see whether an array of letters follows the rules of spelling. If it does, the brain then treats the array as a word (even if it isn't one, such as *tweal*). The shape is processed in individual letters only when the shape is not enough to suggest meaning. Jerry E. Bishop, "Word Processing: Research on Stroke Victims Yields Clues to the Brain's Capacity to Create Language," *The Wall Street Journal*, October 12, 1993, A6.

4. Jakob Neilsen, "Top Ten Mistakes in Web Design," May 1996, http://www.useit.com/alertbox/9605.html, retrieved October 24, 2006.

5. Nicholas Keung, "Wanted: Minorities," *Toronto Star*, March 18, 2006, B1 and B3.

Module 6

1. Lima Paul, "An On-line Concierge Service's Ticket to Success," *The Globe and Mail*, Technology, Small & Medium Business, July 14, 2005, B8.

2. Artwork produced in the Enrichment Program at The Salvation Army's Broadview Village, an adult residential program. Residents attend school, a day program, or work placement training in the Toronto area.

Module 7

1. Charles E. McCabe, edited and updated by Ryan P. Allis, 2004, "Motivating and Retaining Employees," http://www.zeromillion.com/business/employee-motivate.html, retrieved August 8, 2006.

2. Jill Lambert, "The Economics of Happiness," *Canadian Business*, Summer 2005, 184–187.

3. Mayo Clinic, *Mayo Clinic Study Finds Optimistic People Live Longer*, February 8, 2000, http://www.mayoclinic.org/news2000-rst/603.html, retrieved August 8, 2006.

4. The Business Link, "The Makeup of a Successful Entrepreneur," 2005, http://www.cbsc.org/alberta/newsletter/February2005_1.html, retrieved August 8, 2006.

5. Jim Sutherland, "Cold Warrior," Report on (Small) Business, *The Globe and Mail*, Fall 2005, http://www.theglobeandmail.com/servlet/ArticleNews/TPStory/LAC/20051006/SB10SHAN//?query=royal+bank, retrieved August 8, 2006.

6. Annette N. Shelby and N. Lamar Reinsch, Jr. "Positive Emphasis and You-Attitude: An Empirical Study," *Journal of Business Communication* 32, no. 4 (October 1995): 303–327.

7. Mark A. Sherman, "Adjectival Negation and the Comprehension of Multiply Negated Sentences," *Journal of Verbal Learning and Verbal Behavior* 15 (1976): 143–57.

8. Margaret Baker Graham and Carol David, "Power and Politeness: Administrative Writing in an 'Organized Anarchy,'" *Journal of Business and Technical Communication* 10.1 (January 1996): 5–27.

9. John Hagge and Charles Kostelnick, "Linguistic Politeness in Professional Prose: A Discourse Analysis of Auditors' Suggestion Letters, with Implications for Business Communication Pedagogy," *Written Communication* 6, no. 3 (July 1989): 312–39.

Module 8

1. See Tove Helland Hammer and H. Peter Dachler, "A Test of Some Assumptions Underlying the Path-Goal Model of Supervision: Some Suggested Conceptual Modifications," *Organizational Behavior and Human Performance* 14 (1975): 73.

2. Edward E. Lawler, III, *Motivation in Work Organizations* (Monterey, CA: Brooks/Cole, 1973), 59. Lawler also notes a third obstacle: people may settle for performance and rewards that are just OK. Offering reader benefits, however, does nothing to affect this obstacle.

3. Abraham H. Maslow, *Motivation and Personality* (New York: Harper & Row, 1954).

4. Domini Clark, "Saved by the Call!" *The Globe and Mail*, July 16, 2005, L3.

5. John J. Weger reports Herzberg's research in *Motivating Supervisors* (New York: American Management Association, 1971), 53–54.

6. Diane L. Coutu, "Human Resources: The Wages of Stress," *Harvard Business Review*, November–December 1998, 21–24; and Charles Fishman, "Sanity, Inc.," *Fast Company*, January 1999, 85–99.

7. Susan Greco, "Hire the Best," *Inc.*, June 1999, 32–52.
8. Kevin Leo, "Effective Copy and Graphics," DADM/DMEF Direct Marketing Institute for Professors, Northbrook, IL, May 31–June 3, 1983.

Module 10

1. Heinz Tschabitscher, "The First Email Message," 2005, http://email.about.com/cs/emailhistory/a/first_email.htm, retrieved August 8, 2006.
2. Heather Lotherington, "How to Chat in English and Chinese: Emerging Digital Language Conventions," (2004), http://www.yorku.ca/foe/People/Faculty/ProfilesFac/file_Lothering_Xu_2004.pdf, retrieved August 8, 2006; and Heather Lotherington, "The Internet is Changing the Way We Spell, Talk and Communicate," http://callforhelptv.com/callforhelp/guests/0148A.shtml, retrieved August 8, 2006.
3. Sinclair Stewart and Richard Bloom, "BlackBerry Battle Chills Bay St. Gossips," July 7, 2005, http://www.theglobeandmail.com/servlet/ArticleNews/TPStory/LAC/20050107/BLACKBERRY07/TPNational/TopStories, retrieved August 8, 2006; and Javad Heydary, "Is Your Boss Monitoring Your BlackBerry?" *E-Commerce Times*, May 26, 2005, http://www.ecommercetimes.com/story/43376.html, retrieved August 8, 2006.
4. Lizette Alvarez, "Got Two Extra Hours for Your Email?" *The Globe and Mail*, November 12, 2005, L10.
5. Sara Kiesler, Jane Siegel, and Timothy W. McGuire, "Social Psychological Aspects of Computer-Mediated Communication," *American Psychologist* 39, no. 10 (October 1984): 1129. People still find it easier to be negative in email than on paper or person; see John Affleck, "You've Got Bad News," Associated Press, June 19, 1999.
6. I. John Harvey, "Time To Come Clean," *Toronto Star*, March 24, 2005, J1; Lizette Alvarez, "Got Two Extra Hours for Your Email?" *The Globe and Mail*, November 12, 2005, L10; Judith Timson, "Love It or Hate It, More Work is Here to Stay," *The Globe and Mail*, May 11, 2005, C3.
7. Bettina A. Bair, "Teaching Technology," email to Kitty Locker, October 22, 1999.

Module 11

1. In a study of 483 subject lines written by managers and M.B.A. students, Priscilla S. Rogers found that the average subject line was five words; only 10 percent of the subject lines used 10 or more words ("A Taxonomy for Memorandum Subject Lines," *Journal of Business and Technical Communication* 4, no. 2, September 1990: 28–29).
2. Richard C. Whitely, *The Customer-Driven Company* (Reading, MA: Addison-Wesley, 1991), 39–40.
3. Deborah Tannen, *That's Not What I Meant: How Conversational Style Makes or Breaks Your Relations with Others* (New York: Morrow, 1986), 108.

Module 12

1. Jack W. Brehm, *A Theory of Psychological Reactance* (New York: Academic Press, 1966).
2. John D. Pettit, "An Analysis of the Effects of Various Message Presentations on Communicatee Responses," Ph.D. dissertation, Louisiana State University, 1969; and Jack D. Eure, "Applicability of American Written Business Communication Principles Across Cultural Boundaries in Mexico," *Journal of Business Communication* 14 (1976): 51–63.
3. Lillian H. Chaney and Jeanette S. Martin, *Intercultural Business Communication* (Englewood Cliffs, NJ: Prentice Hall Career and Technology, 1995), 185; and Larry A. Samovar and Richard E. Porter, *Communication Between Cultures* (Belmont, CA: Wadsworth Publishing, 1990), 234–44.
4. Gabriella Stern, "Companies Discover That Some Firings Backfire into Costly Defamation Suits," *The Wall Street Journal*, May 5, 1993, B1.
5. An earlier version of this problem, the sample solutions, and the discussion appeared in Francis W. Weeks and Kitty O. Locker, *Business Writing Cases and Problems* (Champaign, IL: Stipes, 1980), 40–44.

Module 13

1. For a discussion of sales and fund-raising letters, see Kitty O. Locker, *Business and Administrative Communication*, 5th ed. (Burr Ridge: Irwin/McGraw-Hill, 2000), 276–301.
2. Karen Lowry Miller and David Woodruff, "The Man Who's Selling Japan on Jeeps," *Business Week*, July 19, 1993, 56–57.
3. Min-Sun Kim and Steven R. Wilson, "A Cross-Cultural Comparison of Implicit Theories of Requesting," *Communicating Monographics* 61, no. 3 (September 1994): 210–35.
4. J. C. Mathes and Dwight W. Stevenson, *Designing Technical Reports: Writing for Audiences in Organizations* (Indianapolis: Bobbs-Merrill, 1979), 18–19.
5. Daniel J. O'Keefe, *Persuasion* (Newbury Park, CA: Sage, 1990), 168: Joanne Martin and Melanie E. Powers, "Truth or Corporate Propaganda," *Organizational Symbolism*, ed. Louis R. Pondy, Thomas C. Dandridge, Gareth Morgan, and Peter J. Frost (Greenwich, CT: JAI Press 1983), 97–107; and Dean C. Kazoleas, "A Comparison of the Persuasive Effectiveness of Qualitative versus Quantitative Evidence: A Test of Explanatory Hypotheses," *Communication Quarterly* 41, no. 1 (Winter 1993): 40–50.
6. "Phoning Slow Payers Pays Off," *Inc.*, July 1996, 95.
7. An earlier draft of this problem and analysis appeared in Francis W. Weeks and Kitty O. Locker, *Business Writing Problems and Cases* (Champaign, IL: Stipes, 1980), 78–81.

Module 14

1. Robert L. Brown, Jr., and Carl G. Herndl, "An Ethnographic Study of Corporal Writing:

Job Status as Reflected in Written Text," *Functional Approaches to Writing: A Research Perspective*, ed. Barbara Couture (Norwood, NJ: Ablex, 1986), 16–19, 22–23.

2. Linda Flower, *Problem-Solving Strategies for Writing* (New York: Harcourt Brace Jovanovich, 1981), 39.

3. Harris B. Savin and Ellen Perchonock, "Grammatical Structure and the Immediate Recall of English Sentences," *Journal of Verbal Learning and Verbal Behavior* 4 (1965): 348–53; Pamela Layton and Adrian J. Simpson, "Deep Structure in Sentence Comprehension," *Journal of Verbal Learning and Verbal Behavior* 14 (1975): 658–64.

4. Arn Tibbetts, "Ten Rules for Writing Readably," *Journal of Business Communication* 18, no. 4 (Fall 1981): 55–59.

5. Thomas N. Huckin, "A Cognitive Approach to Readability," *New Essays in Technical and Scientific Communication: Research, Theory, Practice*, ed. Paul V. Anderson, R. John Brockmann, and Carolyn R. Miller (Farmingdale, NY: Baywood, 1983), 93–98.

Module 15

1. Richard C. Anderson, "Concretization and Sentence Learning," *Journal of Educational Psychology* 66, no. 2 (1974): 179–83.

2. Based on Lynn Ashby, "7, 8 Facilitate," *Houston Post*, February 17, 1978.

Module 17

1. Adapted from Building Collaborative Solutions Inc., "Communicating Across Cultures," (2004), http://www.bcsolutions.org/olccommacrosscultures.html, retrieved August 14, 2006; and Chadwick Fleck,"Understanding Cheating in Nepal," (2000), http://www.eastern.edu/publications/emme/2000spring/fleck.html, retrieved August 14, 2006.

2. "Listen Up and Sell," *Selling Power*, July/August 1999, 34.

3. Thomas Gordon with Judith Gordon Sands, *P.E.T. in Action* (New York: Wyden, 1976), 83.

Module 18

1. Adapted from Bruce Tuckman's 1965 original concept, and Alan Chapman 1995–2005 review and code, http://www.businessballs.com/tuckmanformingstorming normingperforming.htm, Worcester Polytechnic Institute. (2002), retrieved August 14, 2006; http://www.cs.wpi.edu/~dcb/courses/CS3041/Group-info2.html, retrieved August 14, 2006.

2. Adapted from D.M. Zinni, Barry Wright, and Mark Julien, "Research Forum: Want to Retain Employees? Try a Networking Group," *HRProfessional*, July/August 2005, http://www.yorku.ca/hrresall/frm2005~08.htm, retrieved August 14, 2006.

3. For a fuller listing of roles in groups, see David W. Johnson and Frank P. Johnson, *Joining Together: Group Theory and Group Skills* (Englewood Cliffs, NJ: Prentice Hall, 1975), 26–27.

4. Beatrice Schultz, "Argumentativeness: Its Effects in Group Decision-Making and Its Role in Leadership Perception," *Communication Quarterly* 30, no. 4 (Fall 1982): 374–75; Dennis S. Gouran and B. Aubrey Fisher, "The Functions of Human Communication in the Formation, Maintenance, and Performance of Small Groups," in *Handbook of Rhetorical and Communication Theory*, ed. Carroll C. Arnold and John Waite Bowers (Boston: Allyn and Bacon, 1984), 640; and Curt Bechler and Scott D. Johnson, "Leadership and Listening: A Study of Member Perceptions," *Small Group Research* 26, no. 1 (February 1995): 77–85.

5. Nance L. Harper and Lawrence R. Askling, "Group Communication and Quality of Task Solution in a Media Production Organization," *Communication Monographs* 47, no. 2 (June 1980): 77–100.

6. Rebecca E. Burnett, "Conflict in Collaborative Decision-Making," in *Professional Communication: The Social Perspective*, ed. Nancy Roundy Blyler and Charlotte Thralls (Newbury Park, CA: Sage, 1993), 144–62.

7. Kimberly A. Freeman, "Attitudes Toward Work in Project Groups as Predictors of Academic Performance," *Small Group Research* 27, no. 2 (May 1996): 265–82.

8. Nancy Schullery and Beth Hoger, "Business Advocacy for Students in Small Groups," Association for Business Communication Annual Convention, San Antonia, TX, November 9–11, 1998.

9. Lisa Ede and Andrea Lunsford, *Singular Texts/Plural Authors: Perspectives on Collaborative Writing* (Carbondale, IL: Southern Illinois Press, 1990), 60.

10. Rebecca Burnett, "Characterizing Conflict in Collaborative Relationships: The Nature of Decision-Making During Coauthoring," Ph.D. dissertation, Carnegie-Mellon University, Pittsburgh, PA, 1991.

11. Kitty O. Locker, "What Makes a Collaborative Writing Team Successful? A Case Study of Lawyers and Social Service Workers in a State Agency," in *New Visions in Collaborative Writing*, ed. Janis Forman (Portsmouth, NJ: Boynton, 1991), 37–52.

12. Ede and Lunsford, 66.

13. Meg Morgan, Nancy Allen, Teresa Moore, Dianne Atkinson, and Craig Snow, "Collaborative Writing in the Classroom," *Bulletin of the Association for Business Communication* 50.3 (September 1987): 22.

Module 19

1. "Scientific Study Finds Meetings At Work Decrease Employee Well-being, But Not For Everyone," *ScienceDaily*, February 2006, http://www.sciencedaily.com/releases/2006/02/060224192947.htm, retrieved August 24, 2006.

2. "Urban Canadian Office Workers Say That Sharing Information and Collaboration At Work is Becoming More Important," Ipsos-Reid Press Release, May 31, 2001, http://www.ipsos-na.com/news/pressrelease.cfm?id=1238, retrieved October 30, 2006.

3. Kevin Voight, "Don't Mind Your Own Business at Work," *The Globe and Mail*, January 26, 2005, C10.

4. Michael Schrage, "Meetings Don't Have to be Dull," *The Wall Street Journal*, April 29, 1996, A12.

5. Eric Matson, "The Seven Deadly Sins of Meetings," *Fast Company Handbook of the Business Revolution*, 1997, 29.

6. H. Lloyd Goodall, Jr., *Small Group Communications in Organizations* (Dubuque, IA: William C. Brown, 1985), 39–40.

7. Roger K. Mosvick and Robert B. Nelson, *We've Got to Start Meeting Like This: A Guide to Successful Meeting Management*, rev. ed. (Indianapolis: Park Avenue, 1996), 177.

8. Cynthia Crossen, "Spotting Value Takes Smarts, Not Sight, Laura Sloate Shows," *The Wall Street Journal*, December 10, 1987, A1, A14; and Joan E. Rigdon, "Managing Your Career," *The Wall Street Journal*, December 1, 1993, B1.

9. Gina Imperator, "You Have to Start Meeting Like This," *Fast Company*, April 1999, 204–???.

10. Rick Spence, "The Future of Meetings," *Canadian Business Online*, November 10, 2005, retrieved August 22, 2006.

Module 20

1. Rick Spence, "Better Communication Crucial—But Tough," *The Globe and Mail*, November 5, 2004, C3.

2. Carol Hymowitz, "When You Tell the Boss, Plain Talk Counts," *The Wall Street Journal*, June 16, 1989, B1.

3. Linda Driskill, "How the Language of Presentations Can Encourage or Discourage Audience Participation," paper presented at the Conference on College Composition and Communication, Cincinnati, OH, March 18–21, 1992.

4. Some studies have shown that previews and reviews increase comprehension; other studies have found no effect. For a summary of the research see Kenneth D. Frandsen and Donald R. Clement, "The Functions of Human Communication in Informing: Communicating and Processing Information," *Handbook of Rhetorical and Communication Theory*, ed. Carroll C. Arnold and John Waite Bowers (Boston: Allyn and Bacon, 1984), 340–41.

5. Ray Alexander, *Power Speech: Why It's Vital to You* (New York: AMACOM, 1986), 156. "A Study of the Effects of the Use of Overhead Transparencies on Business Meetings," Wharton Applied Research Center, reported in Martha Jewett and Rita Margolies, eds., *How to Run Better Business Meetings: A Reference Guide for Managers* (New York: McGraw-Hill, 1987), 109–110, 115.

6. Robert S. Mills, conversation with Kitty O. Locker, March 10, 1988.

7. Phil Thiebert, "Speechwriters of the World, Get Lost!" *The Wall Street Journal*, August 2, 1993, A10.

8. Tad Simons, "Multimedia or Bust?" *Presentations*, February 2000, 44, 49–50.

9. Virginia Galt, "Glazed Eyes A Major Peril of Using PowerPoint," *The Globe and Mail*, June 4, 2005, B10.

10. Stephen E. Lucas, *The Art of Public Speaking*, 2nd ed. (New York: Random House, 1986), 248.

11. John Case, "A Company of Businesspeople," *Inc.*, April 1993, 90.

12. Edward J. Hegarty, *Humor and Eloquence in Public Speaking* (West Nyack, NY: Packer, 1976), 204.

13. S.A. Beebe, "Eye Contact: A Nonverbal Determinant of Speaker Credibility," *Speech Teacher* 23 (1974): 21–25; cited in Marjorie Fink Vargas, *Louder than Words* (Ames, IA: Iowa State University Press, 1986), 61–62.

14. J. Wills, "An Empirical Study of the Behavioral Characteristics of Sincere and Insincere Speakers" Ph.D. dissertation, University of Southern California, 1961; cited in Marjorie Fink Vargas, *Louder than Words* (Ames, IA: Iowa State University Press, 1986), 62.

Module 21

1. Janice M. Lauer and J. William Asher, *Composition Research: Empirical Designs* (New York: Oxford University Press, 1986), 66.

2. Frederick F. Reichheld, "Learning from Customer Defects," *Harvard Business Review*, March–April 1996, 56–69.

3. Cynthia Crossen, "Margin of Error: Studies Galore Support Products and Positions, But Are They Reliable?" *The Wall Street Journal*, November 14, 1991, A1, A7.

4. Cynthia Crossen, "Diaper Debate: A Case Study of Tactical Research," *The Wall Street Journal*, May 27, 1994, B8.

5. "Whirlpool: How to Listen to Consumers," *Fortune*, January 11, 1993, 77.

6. Peter Lynch with John Rothchild, *One Up on Wall Street: How to Use What You Already Know to Make Money in the Market* (New York: Simon and Schuster, 1989), 187.

7. Patricia Sullivan, "Reporting Negative Research Results," and Kitty O. Locker to Pat Sullivan, June 8, 1990.

Module 22

1. For a useful taxonomy of proposals, see Richard C. Freed and David D. Roberts, "The Nature, Classification, and Generic Structure of Proposals," *Journal of Technical Writing and Communication* 19, no. 4 (1989): 317–51.

2. Christine Peterson Barabas, *Technical Writing in a Corporate Culture: A Study of the Nature of Information* (Norwood, NJ: Ablex Publishing, 1990), 327.

Module 23

1. Stephanie Nolen, "Dot-com this!" *The Globe and Mail*, August 28, 2000, R1.

Module 25

1. Gene Zelazny, *Say It with Charts: The Executive's Guide to Successful Presentations*, 2nd ed. (Burr Ridge, IL: IPRO, 1981), 52.
2. Most of these guidelines are given by Zelazny, *Say It with Charts: The Executive's Guide to Successful Presentations*.
3. W.S. Cleveland and R. McGill, "Graphical Perception: Theory, Experiments, and Application to the Development of Graphic Methods," *Journal of the American Statistical Association* 79, no. 3 & 7 (1984): 531–53; cited in Jeffry K. Cochran, Sheri A. Albrecht, and Yvonne A. Greene, "Guidelines for Evaluating Graphical Designs: A Framework Based on Human Perception Skills," *Technical Communication* 36, no. 1 (February 1989): 27.
4. L.G. Thorell and W.J. Smith, *Using Computer Color Effectively: An Illustrated Reference* (Englewood Cliffs, NJ: Prentice Hall, 1990), 12–13; William Horton, "The Almost Universal Language: Graphics for International Documents," *Technical Communication* 40, no. 4 (1993): 687; and Thyra Rauch, "IBM Visual Interface Design," *STC Usability PIC Newsletter*, January 1996, 3.
5. Thorell and Smith, 13.
6. Ibid., 49–51, 214–15.
7. Edward R. Tufte, *The Visual Display of Quantitative Information* (Cheshire, CT: Graphics Press, 1983), 113.
8. Thophilus Addo, "The Effects of Dimensionality in Computer Graphics," *Journal of Business Communication* 31, no. 4 (October 1994): 253–65.

Module 26

1. Richard Bolle, "Here's How to Pack Your Parachute," *Fast Company*, September 1999, 242.
2. Walter Kiechel III, "Preparing for Your Outplacement," *Fortune*, November 30, 1992, 153.
3. Carl Quintanilla, "Coming Back," *The Wall Street Journal*, February 22, 1996, R10; Megan Malugani, "How to Re-Enter the Health-Care Job Market," *Columbus Dispatch*, March 22, 2000, 13.
4. LeAne Rutherford, "Five Fatal Résumé Mistakes," *Business Week's Guide to Careers* 4, no. 3 (Spring/Summer 1986): 60–62.
5. Phil Elder, "The Trade Secrets of Employment Interviews," Association for Business Communication Midwest Convention, Kansas City, MO, May 2, 1987.

Module 27

1. Wallace Immen, "How did You Get to the Top with That Résumé?" *The Globe and Mail*, October 12, 2005, C3.
2. Beverly H. Nelson, William P. Gallé, and Donna W. Luse, "Electronic Job Search and Placement," Association for Business Communication Convention, Orlando FL, November 1–4, 1995.
3. Rebecca Smith, *Electronic Résumés & Online Networking: How to Use the Internet to Do a Better Job Search, Including a Complete, Up-to-Date Resource Guide* (Franklin Lakes, NJ: Career Press, 1999), 191–96.
4. Taunee Besson, *The Wall Street Journal National Employment Business Weekly: Résumés* (New York: John Wiley and Sons, 1994), 245.

Module 29

1. Thomas Petzinger, Jr., "Lewis Roland's Knack for Finding Truckers Keeps Firm Rolling," *The Wall Street Journal*, December 1, 1995, B1.
2. Judith A. Swartley to Kitty Locker, March 20, 1989.
3. Sherri Eng, "Company Culture Dictates Attire for Interviews," *Columbus Dispatch*, August 25, 1996, 33J.
4. The Catalyst Staff, *Marketing Yourself* (New York: G. P. Putnam's Sons, 1980), 179.
5. Sue Shellenbarger, "New Job Hunters Ask Recruiters, 'Is There Life After Work?'" *The Wall Street Journal*, January 29, 1996, B1; and Sue Shellenbarger, "What Job Candidates Really Want to Know: Will I Have a Life?" *The Wall Street Journal*, November 17, 1999, B1.
6. Donna Stine Kienzler, letter to Ann Granacki, April 6, 1988.
7. Christopher Conte, "Labor Letter," *The Wall Street Journal*, October 19, 1993, A1.
8. Richard C. Rose and Echo Montgomery Garrett, "Guerrilla Interviewing," *Inc.*, December, 1992, 145–47.

Module 30

1. The Catalyst Staff, *Marketing Yourself* (New York: G. P. Putnam's Sons, 1980), 101.
2. Claud Dotson, comment at the Association for Business Communication Western Regional Conference, Boise, ID, April 13, 1996.
3. Kate Weldon, Through *the Brick Wall: How to Job-Hunt in a Tight Market* (New York: Villard Books, 1992), 244.
4. Carol A. Hacker, *Job Hunting in the 21st Century: Exploding the Myths, Exploring the Realities* (Boca Raton: St. Lucie Press, 1999), 154.
5. Ray Robinson, quoted by Dick Friedman, "The Interview as Mating Ritual," *Working Woman*, April 1987, 107.
6. Albert R. Karr, "Work Week," *The Wall Street Journal*, November 16, 1999, A1.

Index

A

Accountemps, 444
accurate messages, 11
acknowledgement responses, 326
acronyms, 31
active
    listening, 323, 325–326
    verbs, 261–265
    voice, 101
active listening, 5
adjectives, 500
adjustments, 189
Adurhman, Ilias, 50
adverbs, 500
ageism, 61–62
agendas, 352–353, 356–357
Aliant Inc., 302
Allen, Robert, 6
alternatives, 211
    elimination of, 429
although, 21
American spelling, 297
Amiskwaciy Academy, 50
analytical proposal, 162, 164
analytical reports, 405, 406, 427–428
Anderson, Cameron, 47
annual reports, 406, 427–428, 441
APA format, 395, 401–402, 526
apologies, 129
apostrophe, 304–305
Appellation America, 383
Arbelaez, Brenda, 58
Aristotle, 227
arrogant tone, 235
assessment, 72
Association for Canadian Studies, 51
assumptions, 324
ATI Technologies, 123
attachments, and viruses, 177
audience, 3, 13
    analysis, use of, 36–37
    business messages, 28–29
    communication process, 25–28
    critical thinking, 29
    demographic factors, 31
    different needs, 37–38
    empathy, 29
    external, 7, 8
    gatekeeper, 25–26
    group members as, 29–30
    identification of, 13, 25
    importance of, 25
    individuals, 29–30
    initial, 25–26
    internal, 7, 8
    knowledge of, 29
    large, 38–39
    letters, 151
    memos, 151
    PAIBOC questions, 28–29
    past behaviour, 34
    personality, 32
    primary, 25–26
    prior knowledge, 30
    psychographic characteristics, 32
    questions from, 376
    reaching your audience, 38–39
    reaction, analysis of, 34
    reader benefits, matching, 140
    secondary, 25–26
    subgroups, 138
    talking to, as planning, 74–77
audience subgroups, 138
audit reports, 406
average, 393

B

background, 445
bad news messages.
    see negative messages
bar chart, 470, 472
Barnes, Skawenniio, 3
because, 21
behavioural interviews, 553
behavioural styles, assessment of, 55
beliefs, 32, 49–51
Bender, Peter Urs, 32
benefits, 13
benefits to readers. see reader benefits
Berdahl, Jennifer, 47
Best Buy, 38
better writing, benefits of, 11
bias-free language
    definition, 59
    negative terms, 62–63
    nonagist language, 61–62
    nonracist language, 61–62
    nonsexist language, 59–63

Birdwhistell, 53
Bisaillion, Ted, 12
black Canadians, 50
blind copies, 157
block format, 151, 161
blocking responses, 325
blueprints, 431
body clocks, 54
body language, 52
Boice, Jacklyn, 371
boilerplate, 82
Bolles, Richard, 489
Bolt, Kathryn, 236
brainstorming, 74, 135, 339, 351, 352
Braun, Liz, 71–72
Brehm, Jack W., 211
Broker, Ruth A., 56
Brown, Vincent J., 26
budgets, 417
buffer, 205–208
    effective, 208
bullets, 88
Burnett, Rebecca, 342
business communication
    analysis of situations, 12–14
    culture, 48–49
    intercultural. see culture; diversity
    purpose, 7, 10
business image, 155
business jargon, 283
business plan, writing, 428
business slang, 283
Business Writer's Free Library, 214
businessese, 283
    eliminating, 284
Butler, Leslie, 71–72
buying time, 341
bypassing, 279

C

Canadian Charter of Rights and
    Freedoms, 48
Canadian government organizations
    Web site, 442
Canadian Human Rights Act, 48
Canadian identity, 47–48
Canadian Oxford Dictionary, 283
Canadian provinces, postal
    abbreviations, 159

Canadian spelling, 297
Canadian values, 47, 49
Canwest Insurance, 192–194
carbon copy, 157
career achievements, 517–518
career objective, 517
Caribbean and African Canadian
   Chamber of Commerce, 50
case, 299–300
causation, 394–395
CBC, 405
CD-ROM databases, 387
chair's role in meetings, 354
channel
   communication process, 27
   large audiences, 38–39
   multiple, 38–39
   overload, 27
chartjunk, 474
Chatman, Jennifer, 36
choice
   details of, 37–38
   forced, 562
   information of, 27
choppy prose, 331
chronological
   oral presentations, 367
   progress reports, 418–420
   resumes, 505, 506, 511–513
   short report, 430
Chrysler, 231
CIBC, 169, 210
CIBC World Markets Inc., 537
citation, 395
claim letter, sample, 154
clarity, 11
class, 50
clauses
   dependent, 302
   essential, 306
   independent, 302
   main, 302
   nonessential, 306
   subject, 300
   subordinate, 21, 302, 331
clip art, 474
closed body positions, 52
closure reports, 425
clothing, 444, 546–547
clustering, 74
co-authored documents
   audience, 341
   drafts, 341–342
   editing, 343
   group process, 343–344
   planning, 342–343

proofreading, 343
purposes, 341
revisions, 341–343
Coast Capital Savings, 239
Coca-Cola, 473
collaborative writing, 342
collaborative writing projects. see co-
authored documents
collection letter
   definition, 237
   early letters, 237
   late letters, 238
   legal action, threat of, 238
   middle letters, 238
   sample, 152
colon, 305
colour, use of, 473–474
comma
   fault, 44–45, 302–303, 304
   general use, 305–306
   lists, 85
   lists, in, 331
   placement, 304
   serial, 559
   splice, 304
   splices, 44–45, 302–303
"Commercial ethnography", 34
communication
   context, 38–39
   interpersonal, 8
   non-verbal. see non-verbal
      communication
   oral. see oral communication
   purpose of, 5
   written, 8
communication process
   channel overload, 27
   feedback, 27
   frames of reference, 28
   information overload, 27–28
   noise, 27
   simplified model, 25–28
communications skills, 5, 517–518
company Web sites, 36
comparison/contrast pattern, 429
complete messages, 11
complex constructions, 437
complex sentences, 268
complimentary closes, 151, 157
compliments, 57
compound sentences, 268
compound-complex sentences, 268
comprehensive messages, 11
compromises, 211
computer copy, 157
concise messages, 11, 175, 437

conclusion, 445
concrete words, 437
Conference Board of Canada, 6,
   141, 332
confirmations, 188
conflict resolution, 337–341
   buying time, 341
   criticism, 340–341
   either-or logical fallacy, 339
   feelings, checking, 340
congratulatory notes, 189
conjunctions, 331
connotations, 279–280
   colour, 473–474
content, 37–38, 112
context
   communication, 38–39
   format and, 151
   message, 14, 29
   subject lines, 183
continuation heading, 152
contractions, 118
control, 14
convenience sample, 393
conventions, 351
conversation regulators, 326
   conversational English, 500
   conversational style, 55–56
   coordinating conjunctions, 331
   coordination, 334
   corporate culture. see
      organizational culture
   correlation, 394–395
   correspondence, costs of, 10
   courtesy titles, 127, 158–161
   cover letters, 493, 530
   creative processes, 339
   creative thinking, 12
   credibility, 227, 234
conversational English, 500
conversational style, 55–56
coordinating conjunctions, 331
coordination, 334
Corel, 12
corporate culture, 35
   see also organizational culture
correlation, 394–395
correspondence, costs of, 10
courtesy titles, 127, 158–161
cover letters, 493, 530
creative paradox, 12
creative processes, 339
creative thinking, 12, 340
credibility, 227, 234
critical skills
   computer-created design, 94

critical thinking, 281
discrimination, dealing with, 50–51
goodwill ending, 194
hot buttons, 416
integrity, 336
job assessment, 492
leading by listening, 327
legal implications, 209
networking, 355
online research, 391
performance appraisals,
    preparation for, 236
point of view, others', 111
positive emphasis, ethical use of,
    125
professional image, 155, 298, 444
questions, 433
reader benefits and audience,
    matching, 140
resumes, computer layout and
    design, 504
revisions after feedback, 81
salary and benefits negotiation, 555
targeting specific companies, 537
time management, 176
tone, 260
visuals, integration into text, 474
voice, 371
workplace rules, 29
critical thinking, 29, 281
criticism, 340–341, 349
cultural discrimination, 50
cultural expectations, 48–49
cultural identity, 47, 50–51
culture, 35, 47
    see also diversity
    beliefs, 49–51
    body language, 52
    business communication, 48–49
    compliments, 57
    courtesy, 127
    definition, 47, 48
    exaggeration, 56–57
    eye contact, 52, 326
    gestures, 53
    high-context, 48–49, 53
    idioms, 68
    international audiences. see
        international audience
    job hunting conventions, 529
    low-context, 48–49, 53
    misunderstandings, 52
    monochronic, 55
    motivation, 51
    non-verbal communication, 52
    non-verbal symbols, 55

    oral communication, 55–57
    personal space, 53
    persuasive strategy and, 228
    polychronic, 55
    practices, 49–51
    preferred terms, 62
    religion, influences of, 51
    silence, 57
    spatial arrangements, 54
    time, perception of, 55
    touch, 53–54
    understatement, 56–57
    values, 49–51
Curling, Alvin, 50
customer relations management
 (CRM), 109
customer satisfaction, 189
CV Technologies, 121
cycling, 10, 80–81

D

dangling modifiers, 203, 300
dashes, 307, 361
Dataflex, 554
dates, 310–311
de Bono, Edward, 340
deadwood terms, 283
deaf culture, 62–63
decision makers, 37–38
decision-making strategies, 356–357
decode, 27
deductive request pattern, 228
defensive body positions, 52
definitions, 31
Dell Computer, 12
demographic factors, 31, 238
denotation, 279
dependent clause, 302
descriptive dictionary, 282
descriptors, 385
design
    bullets, 88
    computers, using, 94
    fonts, 91
    form follows function, 151
    full capitals, use of, 89–91
    headings, 88
    justification of margins, 92
    letters, 94
    memos, 94
    multiple fonts, 91
    paper pages, 87
    parallelism, 88
    persuasion, 95
    presentation slides, 92–93

    testing, 95
    visual impact, 89–91
    visuals, 471–473
    Web pages, 93
    white space, 87–88
Desjardins, Gabriel, 9
details, 500
deviation bar graphs, 472
DeWolf, Mark, 383
dialects, 566
dialogue, 282
dictionaries, 282
direct requests, 229
    checklist, 246
    pattern, 228, 229–230
directed subject lines, 241–242
disabilities, 62–63
disagreement and active listening
 strategies, 326
disciplinary notices, 214
discourse communities, 34–36
discourse community, 281
discrimination
    ageism, 61–62
    bias-free language, 59
    bias-free photos and
        illustrations, 63
    Canada, 50–51
    cultural, 50
    dealing with, 50–51
    disabilities, 62–63
    nonagist language, 61–62
    nonracist language, 61–62
    people-first language, 62–63
    racism, 50, 61–62
discussion, 282
diversity. see also culture
    bias-free language, 59
    bias-free photos and illustrations, 63
    disabilities, 63–63
    discrimination in Canada, 50–51
    education, 50–51
    legal recognition, 48
    media misrepresentation, 50
    nonagist language, 61–62
    nonracist language, 61–62
    nonsexist language, 59–63
    people-first language, 62–63
    workplace, in the, 48
document design, 36–37
    see also design
documentation of sources, 395–398
documents
    costs of, 10
    cycle, 10
dot planning, 356–357

double negatives, 125
dress code, 155, 444
Drozdov, Liza, 149

E

editing
after revision, 79
co-authored documents, 343
definition, 72, 77, 526
grammar checker, 79
punctuation rules, 79
readability, 79
Edmondson, Amy, 336
education
diversity, 50–51
resume heading, 518–519
Education and Technology Revolution
(Allen), 6
effective messages
criteria, 11, 12
multiple channels, 38–39
either-or logical fallacy, 339
Elbow, Peter, 71, 82
Elements of Style online, 268
ellipses, 309–310
email communities, 175–177
email messages
acronyms, 175
Canadian use of email, 174
conciseness, 175
content, 170–172
etiquette, 175–177
finding addresses, 175
formats, 170–172
frequency of, 9
guidelines, 169
informative, 173, 175
job application letters, 538–539
legal implications, 209
limitations, 169
negative, 175
PAIBOC analysis, 169–172
persuasive, 175
positive, 173, 175, 176
proofreading, 169
subject lines, 174
templates, 170–172
tone, 172
viruses, 177
when to avoid, 175–177
emotional appeal, 234–235
empathy, 29
Employability Skills 2001+, 6, 15–17
audience, adaptation of
message to, 40

design, 96
email messages, 178
follow-up letters/phone calls, 565
format for letters and memos, 165
grammar and punctuation
editing, 313
informative messages, 196
intercultural communication
checklist, 64
job application letters, 540
job interviews, 557
job offers, 565
job research checklist, 498
listening, 328
long reports, 426
meetings, 360
negative messages, 221
oral presentations, 378
paragraph revision, 274
persuasive messages, 247
planning, writing and revising, 83
positive emphasis, 130
positive messages, 196
progress reports, 421
proposals, 421
reader benefits, 144
research and documentation, 399
resumes, 524
sentence revision, 274
short reports, 435
team work and writing, 345
visuals, 477
word choice, 291
you-attitude, 116
Employment Equity Act, 48
enclosures, 157
encoding, 27
enthusiasm, 563
Environics Analytics, 33
Environics Research Group, 33
Environics social values online
survey, 33
Equicom Group, 487
Eservus.com Online Services Ltd., 107
essential clause, 306
ethics
positive emphasis, 125
visuals, use of, 475–476
ethos, 227
etymological origins of words,
282–283
exaggeration, 56–57
exclamation points, 277
Executive Summary, 443
expectancy theory, 135
external audience, 7, 8

external motivation, 227
extrinsic benefits, 140–141
extrovert, 32
eye contact, 52, 326, 375

F

fairness, 49
faulty logic, 394–395
feasibility reports, 406, 425
FedEx, 87
feedback
communication process, 27
cycling, 80–81
definition, 72
obtaining, 80–81
feeling types, 32
feelings
conflict resolution, 340
listening for, 324
figures, 443, 470, 473
firings, 215
fixed fonts, 91
flaming, 173
Fleischman-Hillard, 487
Flesch Reading Ease score, 79–80
Flesch-Kincaid Grade Level,
79–80
flexibility, and international
audience, 58
fonts, 91
forced choice, 562
Ford Motor Company, 33
form letters, 9, 81–82
formal reports, 405, 441
formal words, 281
formality, 259, 379
formalization, 334
format
APA, 395, 401–402, 526
block, 151, 161
context, 151
email messages, 169–172
full block, 151
letter. *see* letter format
memo. *see* memo format
MLA, 395–396, 401–402, 526
modified block, 151
resumes, 511–520
short reports, 428
formation, 334
frames of reference, 28
freewrite, 74
full block format, 151
full justification, 92
functional pattern, 430

functional/combination resumes, 505, 507–508, 514
funding proposals, 416
Future Shop, 38

G

gatekeeper, 25–26, 37–38
gathering, 72
gender
  bias-free photos and illustrations, 63
  female police officers in Canada, 48
  nonsexist language, 59–63
  professors' titles, 261
  unknown, letter recipient, 160
general slang, 283
general to particular pattern, 428
Generation X, 56
Genuity Capital Markets Technology, 169
geodemographic data, 33
geographic pattern, 430
gerunds, 266
gestures, 53
globalization, 48
Goldman, Michael, 366–367
good new message. *see* positive messages
good news. *see* positive messages
good style, 259–260
goodwill, 8, 112, 121, 184
  apologies, 129
  building, through effective messages, 11
  ending, 184, 194
  highlighting in subject line, 190
  positive emphasis. *see* positive emphasis
  presentations, 365
  reader benefits. *see* reader benefits
  sample letter, 157
  you-attitude. *see* you-attitude
Gostick, Dana, 336
Graddol, David, 52
grammar
  adjectives, 500
  adverbs, 500
  case, 299–300
  checker, 79, 317
  clauses. *see* clauses
  conjunctions, 331
  coordinating conjunctions, 331
  dangling modifiers, 203, 300
  disagreement among experts, 559
  errors, 297–302

formal usage, 559
gerunds, 266
guidelines, 261
independent clause, 302
infinitives, 266
main clause, 302
misplaced modifiers, 301
modifiers, 300
noun-pronoun agreement, 181, 298–299
nouns, concrete, 500
parallelism. *see* parallelism
predication errors, 301–302
"rules", 261
run-on sentences, 294–295, 303
sentence fragments, 21, 303–304
sentences, 302
split infinitives, 559
subject-verb agreement, 166, 297–299
verbs. *see* verbs
Grant, David, 50
grapevine, 8
Grocery Gateway, 36
group presentations, 376–377
grouped bar graphs, 472
groups, 339
  see also teams,
  co-authored documents, 341–343
  conflict in, 337
  conflict resolution. *see* conflict resolution
  coordination, 334
  formalization, 334
  formation, 334
  groupthink, 337
  inferences, 340
  leadership in, 335, 339
  limited agreement, 341
  messages, 333–334
  negative roles, 335
  orientation, 333–334
  paraphrase, 340
  peer pressure, 337
  positive roles, 334–335
  presenting problem, 339
  roles played in, 334–335
  student groups, successful, 335–337
  troubleshooting problems, 338
  venting, 339
  you-attitude, 341
groupthink, 337
guided discussions, 366
Gunning Fog Index, 79

H

Hagge, John, 128
hall meetings, 351
Hall, Edward T., 48, 55
Hall, John, 111
Hallmark Cards, 12
headings
  definition, 88
  design, 88
  effective, 483
  informative, 434, 483
  parallelism, 434
  planning, 76
  resumes, 520
  short reports, 432
  talking heads, 434, 483
  topic, 432
hearing, *vs.* listening, 323
Henry, Frances, 50
here, 297
Hertzberg study, 140
Herzberg, Frederick, 140
Hewlett-Packard, 473
hidden job market, 493–495, 496
hidden negatives, 123, 125
high-context culture, 48–49, 53
histograms, 472
history, 445
Holiturn Winery and Distillery Corporation, 111
Holman, Sam, 327
Holmes, Mike, 149
Home Depot, 149
honours and awards heading, 519
hopefully, 559
hot buttons, 416
Hudson's Bay Company, 141
hyphen, 307, 361

I

I, 542–543
I/me, 422–423
IBM Canada, 12, 141, 359, 4773
idioms, 68
if, 21
illustrations, 63, 443
impersonal constructions, 110, 111
impressions, 300
inattention, 32
independent clause, 302
indirect pattern, 228
individualism, 51
inductive pattern, 228
inferences, 340
infinitives, 266

informal meetings, 351
informal reports, 405
information, 13
  audience, 28
  compact presentation, 126
  gathering, 72
  interviews, 491–493, 494–495
  negative. *see* negative messages
  organization strategies, 428–430
  overload, 27–28
  reports, 405
informational leader, 335
informational messages, 333
informative headings, 434, 483
informative messages, 135
  adjustments, 189
  checklist, 191
  confirmations, 188
  definition, 183
  email, 173, 175
  intrinsic benefits, 186
  organization, 183–184
  PAIBOC formula, 192–193
  primary purposes, 183
  reader benefits, 186
  responses to complaints, 189
  sales promotion in, 186
  sample letter, 156
  secondary purposes, 183
  subject line, 183
  summaries, 188
  transmittals, 186–188
  types of, 186–190
informative presentations, 365
informative reports, 425
informing readers, 8, 13
initial audience, 25–26
internal audiences, 7, 8
International Association of Business
  Communicators, 10
international audience
  bias-free language, 59
  bias-free photos and
    illustrations, 63
  disabilities, 62–63
  flexibility, 58
  negative messages, 57–58
  nonagist language, 61–62
  nonracist language, 61–62
  nonsexist language, 59–63
  organization patterns, 57–58
  people-first language, 62–63
  requests, 57–58
  sensitivity, 58
Internet
  Canadian usage statistics, 193, 392

  evaluation of information on, 391
  job hunting, 492, 493
  news sites, 387
  online research, 385–387, 391
  resumes, scannable, 521–523
interpersonal communication, 33
  definition, 333
  importance of, 8
  listening. *see* listening
  virtual meetings, and, 359
interpersonal leader, 335
interpersonal messages, 333
interpersonal profile, 517–518
interpretation, 27
interviews
  behavioural, 553
  job. *see* job interviews
  phone, 555
  questions, 388–392, 549
  stress, 533–554
  video, 556
intonation, 371
intrinsic benefits, 140–141, 186
introduction, 444–445
introvert, 32
intuitive types, 32
Ipsos-Reid survey, 351
it, 299
it's/its, 118, 133
italics, 310

J

Jamaican culture, 50
Japanese culture, 48–49, 54, 55
jargon, 283, 500
Jedwab, Jack, 51
job application letters
  bridge, 530
  email, 538–539
  knowledge of position/company,
    536
  length, 536–537
  prospecting letter. *see* prospecting
    letter
  purpose, 529
  separation from other applicants,
    535–536
  solicited letter. *see* solicited letter
  summary paragraph, 530
  summary sentence, 530
  targeting specific companies, 537
  types of, 529–530
  unsolicited letter. *see* prospecting
    letter
  you-attitude, 538

job assessment, 492
job descriptions, 490
job functions, 505
job hunting
  cover letters, 493
  follow-up phone call/letter, 561
  hidden job market, 493–495
  information interviews, 491–493,
    494–495
  interviews. *see* job interviews
  job application letter. *see* job
    application letters
  lack of experience, 497
  mature workers, 497
  non-traditional experiences,
    495–497
  offers. *see* job offers
  online information, 492, 493
  referral interviews, 493
  referrals, 4959
  researching companies, 490–491
  resumes. *see* resumes
  self-assessment, 489
  targeting specific companies, 537
  volunteer community
    involvement, 493
job interviews
  behavioural interviews, 553
  body, 548–549
  close, 549
  clothing, 546–547
  enthusiasm, 563
  expectations, 545
  follow-up phone call/letter, 561
  how to act, 548
  note-taking, 547
  offers. *see* job offers
  opening, 548
  parts of interview, 548–549
  phone interviews, 556
  practice, 548
  questions, dealing with, 549–553
  salary and benefits
    negotiation, 555
  situational interviews, 553
  strategy, 545–546
  stress interview, 553–554
  timeliness, 547
  traditional interview questions,
    549–553
  video interviews, 556
  what to bring, 547
job offers
  contingent acceptances, 563
  forced choice, 562
  second-choice jobs, 562

thank you letters, 564
turning down, 564
job titles, 59
judging types, 32
judgment samples, 392
justification of margins, 92
justification reports, 406, 427–428

K

Kahnawake, 3
Kanwal, Preeti, 257
Keene, Michael, 49
keep it short and simple (KISS), 73,
    504, 564
keywords, 385
KISS formula, 73, 504, 564
Kittling Ridge Estate Wines and
    Spirits, 111
Klauser, Henriette Anne, 71
knowledge workers, motivation of,
    351
Kostelnick, Charles, 128

L

Landers, Debbie, 141
language
    bias-free, 59
    boilerplate, 82
    level, 38
    nonagist, 61–62
    nonracist, 61–62
    nonsexist, 59–63
    people-first, 62–63
    standard English, 566
lateral thinking, 340
layoffs, 215
Layton, Kirk, 107
leadership
    groups, in, 335, 339
    integrity, 336
    listening, by, 327
"Leadership from Within", 32
legal implications, 209
letter format
    blind copies, 157
    block, 151
    bolded attention/subject lines, 161
    complimentary closes, 151
    copies, 157
    courtesy titles, 158–161
    "dear", use of, 158
    enclosures, 157
    gender unknown, 160
    mixed punctuation, 151

modified block, 151
    name unknown, 160
    open punctuation, 151
    parallel courtesy titles, 160
    reference line, 155
    salutation, 151, 155
    subject line, 155
    two-point punctuation, 151
letterhead, 153, 161
letters
    audience for, 151
    design, 94
    format. *see* letter format
    job application. *see* job application
        letters
    vs. memo, 151
    organizational pattern, 76
    recommendation, 153, 239
    sample. *see* sample letters
    thank you, 564
    transmittal, of, 442
Levi Strauss, 12, 393
limited agreement, 341
line graph, 470, 472
listening
    acknowledgement responses, 326
    acquired skill, 323
    active, 323, 324–326
    blocking responses, 325
    conversation regulators, 326
    disagreement, and, 326
    faulty assumptions, 324
    feelings, for, 324
    focus, 323–324
    good habits, 326
    vs. hearing, 323
    importance of, 8
    inattention, 323
    internal monologues, 323–324
    lag, 365
    leading by, 327
    preaching, 325
    self-absorption, 323–324
lists
    commas in, 85
    parallelism, 88
logic, 142
logical fallacies, 339
logos, 227
London Life, 487
long reports
    background, 445
    conclusion, 445
    Executive Summary, 443
    figures, 443
    history, 445

illustrations, list of, 443
    introduction, 444–445
    letter/memo of transmittal, 442
    recommendations, 445
    sample, 446–461
    table of contents, 443
    tables, 443
    time management, 441–442
    title page, 442
    titles, 442
Lotherington, Heather, 169, 172
low-context culture, 48–49, 53
loyalty cards, 135
Lynch, Peter, 394
Lyon, Adelle, 383

M

MacKenzie, Bill, 327
MacKenzie, Gordon, 12
MacKenzie, Lewis (Major-General),
    327
main clause, 302
maintenance-related messages, 333
make-good reports, 406
making meaning, 5
Maltz, Daniel N., 56
margin justification, 92
Martin, Roger, 238
Maslow's hierarchy, 135, 205
Maslow, Abraham H., 135
matrix table, 468–469
McCain Foods, 36
McCord, Elizabeth, 209
me/I, 422–423
mean, 393
meaning, 5, 205
Media Matrix Canada survey, 193
media misrepresentation, 50
median, 393
meetings, 5
    agendas, 352–353, 356–357
    career planning, and, 358–359
    chair's role, 354
    computer-supported, 351
    controversial items, 354
    decision-making strategies for,
        356–357
    dot planning, 356–357
    hall, 351
    informal, 351, 358–359
    maintenance functions, 354
    minutes, 351, 358
    one-on-one, 351
    online, 351
    parliamentary, 351

participation, effective, 357–358
pre-meeting planning, 352
purpose, 351
regular staff, 351
standard agenda, 356
task functions, 354
team, 351
team productivity, 351
types of, 351
virtual, 359
memo format
    block format, 161
    letterhead, 161
    standard format, 161
memos
    audience for, 151
    design, 94
    format. *see* memo format
    organizational pattern, 76
    sample informative report,
        426–427
    samples, 162
    transmittal, of, 442
    vs. letters, 151
Messruer, Max, 444
Microscan, 392
Microsoft, 12
Microsystems, 141
Mintzberg, Henry, 7
minutes, 351, 358
misplaced modifiers, 301
mixed punctuation, 151, 157
MLA format, 395–396,
    401–402, 526
Modahl, Mary, 32
modified block format, 151
modifiers
    dangling, 203, 300
    definition, 300
    empty, 437
    misplaced, 301
    vague, 437
monochronic culture, 55
monologue presentation, 366
Moore, Michael, 487
motivation
    culture, 51
    external, 227
    knowledge workers, 351
    performance appraisals, 239
    reader benefits, 135–136
Mowatt, Dave, 121
multi-tasking, 55
multicultural perspective, 47–48,
    241–242
Multiculturalism Act, 48

multitasking, 72
Myers-Briggs Type Indicator, 32

N

names
    courtesy titles. *see* courtesy titles
    gender unknown, 160
    parallel forms, 160
    unknown, 160
narrative voice, 254
Native Canadians, 50–51
negative connotations, 280
negative messages, 135
    alternatives, 211
    bad news pattern, 228
    buffer, 205–208
    burial of, 126–127
    checklist, 220
    common types, 214–214
    compact presentation, 126–127
    compromises, 211
    disciplinary notices, 214
    email, 175–177
    endings, 211–212
    explanation, 209–210
    firings, 215
    hedging your statements, 128
    international audience, 57–58
    justification of, 126–127
    layoffs, 215
    legal implications, 209
    negative performance appraisals, 214
    omission of, 126–127
    organizational pattern, 205–208
    PAIBOC formula, 215–220
    passive verbs, 263
    peers, to, 212–213
    primary purposes, 205
    reasons, 208–209
    refusals, 210, 214
    rejections, 214
    sample letter, 206–207
    sample memo to subordinates, 213
    sample refusal, 207
    secondary purposes, 205
    subject line, 215
    subject lines, 205
    subordinates, to, 212–213
    superiors, to, 212
negative performance appraisals, 215
negative terms
    bias-free language, 62–63
    double negatives, 125
    hidden negatives, 123, 125
    necessity of, 122

reverse psychology, 122
    words to avoid, 122–124
netiquette, 175–176
network groups, 334
networking, 8, 355, 493, 496
"Neuromarketing", 34
Nielsen, Jakob, 93
noise, 27
nominative pronouns, 299
nomos, 227
non-traditional job experiences,
    495–497
non-verbal communication
    body language, 52
    communication symbols, 5
    definition, 51
    eye contact, 52, 326
    gestures, 53
    misunderstanding, 52
    personal space, 53
    spatial arrangements, 54
    symbols, 52, 55
    time, perception of, 55
    touch, 53–54
nonagist language, 61–62
nonessential clause, 306
nonracist language, 61–62
nonsexist language
    job titles, 59
    phrases, 59
    pronouns, 59–63
    vs. you-attitude, 160
    words, 59
norming, 334
North American Free Trade Act
    (NAFTA), 49
noun-pronoun agreement, 181,
    298–299
nouns, concrete, 500
numbers, 310–311, 393–394

O

objections, 14, 28–29, 231–234
objective pronouns, 299
objects of verbs/prepositions, 300
Official Languages Act, 48
omission, 126
omnibus motion, 352
one's, 300
one-on-one meetings, 351
online news sites, 387
online research, 385–387, 391
open body positions, 52
open punctuation, 151, 157
oral communication

compliments, 57
conversational style, 55–56
culture, 55–57
exaggeration, 56–57
Generation X, 56
PowerPoint, 92–93
presentation slides, design of, 92–93
silence, 57
understatement, 56–57
oral presentations
alternatives, excluding, 367
audience, questions from, 376
chronological, 367
close, 369–371
effective delivery, 374–376
eye contact, 375
fear, 374–375
gesturing, 375
goodwill presentations, 365
group, 376–377
guided discussions, 366
idea adaptation, 367
informative presentations, 365
kind of, 366–367
listening lag, 365
location of, 366
monologue presentation, 366
notes, 375
one-two-three, 368
opener, 369–371
organizational patterns, 367
overview, 368
persuasive presentations, 365
planning, 365–366
PowerPoint, 372–374
presentation slides, 92–93
pro-con, 368
problem-causes-solution, 367
purpose, 366
sales presentation, 367
signpost, 368
simplification, 371
standing, 375
storyboard, 76
time of, 366
visuals, 371–374, 375, 476
voice, 371
orders, 237
organization, 112
organizational culture, 34–36, 38, 228, 272–273
organizational pattern
audience analysis, 36, 38
direct requests, 229–230
informative messages, 183–184

negative messages, 205–208
oral presentations, 367
persuasive messages, 229–230
positive messages, 183–184
problem-solving message, 230–231, 234
short reports, 425
subject lines, 190
orientation, 333–334
overview of presentation, 368
Oxford Encyclopedic English Dictionary, 282

P

PAIBOC
audience, 3
audience analysis, 28–29
audience focus, 25
business communications, email, 169–172
channels, 38–39
communications context, 38–39
compared to Maslow's hierarchy, 135
email messages, 169–172
follow-up letter, 561
job application letter, 529
job communication, 503
job offers, 561
key questions, 12–14
negative messages, 215–220
persuasive messages, 242–245
planning, 72
positive messages, 192–193
presentations, 365–366
problem analysis, 151, 192–193
purposes, 3
reports, 406
resume, 503
paired bar graphs, 472
Pang, Peter, 121
paragraph revision
topic sentences, 271–272
transitions, 272
unity, 271
paragraphs
detail, 464
improvement of, 464–465
revision. *see* paragraph revision
summary, 530
transitions, 464
unified, 464
variety, 464
paralanguage, 371
parallelism
courtesy titles, 160

forms for names, 160
general use, 301
headings, 434
lists, 88
structure, 224–225, 270
paraphrase, 340
parental tone, 235
parentheses, 307–308
Parks Canada Agency, 407
parliamentary meetings, 351
particular to general pattern, 428
passive verbs, 110, 261–265
passive voice, 101
past behaviour, 34
pathos, 227
Pay Equity Act, 48
pay-back reports, 406
peer pressure, 337
people-first language, 62–63
perception, 25, 27
perceptive types, 32
performance appraisals
motivational, 239
negative, 214
preparation for, 236, 239
purposes of, 238
sample, 240
specifics, 239
performing, 334
period, 308
personal space, 53
personality, 32
persuasion, 8
best strategy, 228
design, 95
direct request pattern, 228
four significant appeals, 228
indirect pattern, 228
strategy, 228
persuasive messages, 135
collection letter. *see* collection letter, common types, 237–241
credibility, 234
definition, 227
direct requests, 229–230
directed subject lines, 241–242
email, 175
emotional appeal, 234–235
job application letters. *see* job application letters
letters of recommendation, 239
objections, identification and overcoming, 231–234
orders, 237
organizational pattern, 229–230
PAIBOC formula, 242–245

performance appraisals, 239, 240
primary purposes, 227
problem-solving pattern, 229–230, 231
prompt action, reasons for, 235
rational appeal, 234
secondary purposes, 228
subject lines, 241–242
tone, 235
vested interest, 231–234
persuasive presentations, 365
Peters, Clayton, 321
phone interviews, 556
photocopy, 157
photographs, 37, 63
pictograms, 472
pie chart, 470, 471
pitch, 371
planning
audience, talking to, 74–77
brainstorm, 74
career, 358–359
clustering, 74
co-authored documents, 342–343
definition, 72
dot, 356–357
freewrite, 74
guide, 76–77
headings, 76
oral presentations, 365–366
pre-meeting, 352
pre-writing, 74–77
storyboard, 76
time spent on, 74
PLAR (Prior Learning Assessment and Recognition) Web site, 496
plural possessives, 133
plural pronouns, 559
plurals, 146
point of view, others', 111
politeness, 127–128, 433
polychronic culture, 55
poor writing, 10
population, 392
positive connotations, 280
positive emphasis
apologies, 129
burial of negative information, 126–127
compact presentation of negatives, 126–127
creation of, 122
definition, 122
ethical use of, 125
hidden negatives, 123, 125
job application letters, 538

negative information, justification of, 126–127
negative words to avoid, 122–124
omission, 126
point of, 121
politeness, 127–128
power implications, 127–128
reader's ability, emphasis on, 125
tone, 127–128
unnecessary negatives, 126–127
words with negative connotations, 122–124
you-attitude, checking for, 126
positive messages
adjustments, 189
congratulatory notes, 189
definition, 183
email, 173, 175
good news request pattern, 228
intrinsic benefits, 186
organization, 183–184
PAIBOC formula, 192–193
primary purposes, 183
reader benefits, 186
responses to complaints, 189
sales promotion in, 186
sample memo, 163, 185
secondary purposes, 183
subject line, 183
thank-you notes, 189
transmittals, 186–188
types of, 186–190
possessive nouns, 133, 146
possessive pronouns, 118, 133, 299, 300
positive messages (checklist), 191
power implications, 127–128
PowerPoint, 92–93, 372–374
practices, 49–51
pre-meeting planning, 352
preaching, 325
preachy tone, 235
predication errors, 301–302
prejudice, 50–51
    see also discrimination
prepositions, objects of, 300
prescriptive dictionary, 282
presentation slides, 92–93
presentations. see oral presentations
presenting problem, 339
primary audience, 25–26
primary purposes
informative messages, 183
negative messages, 205
persuasive messages, 227
positive messages, 183

primary research, 385
print sources for research, 385–387
prior learning assessment and recognition (PLAR), 496
pro and con pattern, 429
problem-solution, 429
problem-solving pattern, 228, 229–230, 246
problem-solving reports, 406
procedural leader, 335
procedural messages, 333
professional image, 155, 298, 444
progress reports
chronological, 418–420
contents, 417–418
positive, 417–418
recommendation, 420
subject lines, 418
task, 420
pronouns
nominative, 299
nonsexist, 59–63
nouns, agreement with, 181
objective, 299
plural, 559
possessive, 118, 299, 300
reflexive, 300
singular, 559
proofreading, 72
co-authored documents, 343
definition, 77, 526
email messages, 169
methods of, 526
need for, 79–80
spell checking, 78–80
standard symbols, 311–312
proportional fonts, 91
proposals
budgets, 417
business plans, 416
class research projects, 408–411
content, 408
for funding, 416
goals of, 408
hot buttons, 416
RFPs (Requests for Proposals), 408, 417
sales, 411
sample, for student report, 412–415
prospecting letter
body paragraphs, 535
first paragraph, 533–535
last paragraph, 535
organization, 533–535
sample, 534
when to use, 530

psychographic characteristics, 32
psychological reactance, 211
punctuation, 526
    apostrophe, 304–305
    clarification, 300
    colon, 305–306
    comma. *see* comma
    dashes, 307, 361
    ellipses, 309–310
    end, 277
    exclamation points, 277
    hyphen, 307, 361
    mixed, 151
    open, 151
    parentheses, 307–308
    period, 308
    quotation marks, 309
    rules, 79
    semicolon, 308
    serial comma, 559
    square brackets, 309
    two-point, 151
purposes, 3, 13
    business communication, 7, 9
    co-authored documents, 342
    communication, 5
    job application letters, 529
    meeting, 351
    oral presentations, 366
    performance appraisals, 238
    primary. *see* primary purposes
    reader benefits, 135
    secondary. *see* secondary purposes
    statement, 407
    word choice, 279
    writing, 28
    writing, of, 12

Q

quarterly reports, 406
questionnaires, 388–392
questions, 433
Quinn, Jane Bryant, 395
quotation marks, 309
quotes
    documentation, 395
    ellipses, 309–310
    quotation marks, 309
    square brackets, 309

R

racism, 50, 61–62
    see also discrimination
ragged right margins, 92

random sample, 392
range, 393
rational appeal, 234
Ray, George B., 371
readability, 79, 304
reader benefits, 13, 28
    appeal of, 135
    brainstorm, 135
    choice of, 140
    definition, 138
    detailed, 138–140
    details, 500
    expectancy theory, 135
    extrinsic benefits, 140–141
    features of product/policy, 137–138
    full development, 142
    identification, 135–138
    informative messages, 186
    intrinsic benefits, 140–141, 186
    motivation, 135–136
    multiple audiences, 140
    positive messages, 186
    psychological description, 139–140
    purpose, 135
    when to use, 186
    you-attitude check, 143
reader's ability, emphasis on, 125
reading, 5
reasons
    for prompt action, 235
    negative message, 208–209
recommendation reports, 406, 420
recommendations, 445
Red Hat Inc., 12
reference line, 155
references, 520
referral interviews, 493, 496
referrals, 496
reflexive pronouns, 300
refusals, 207, 210, 214
regular staff meetings, 351
rejections, 214
relaxation techniques, 374–375
relevant facts, 30
religion, influences of, 51
Report on Business, 392
reports. *see also* short reports
    analytical, 405, 427–428
    annual, 441
    bad news, 428
    closure, 425
    deductive pattern, 427–428
    definition, 405
    direct pattern, 427–428
    documentation of sources, 395
    feasibility, 425

formal, 405, 441
good news pattern, 427–428
indirect, 428
inductive, 428
informal, 405
information, 405
informative, 425
justification, 427–428
long. *see* long reports
problem, identification of, 405–406
progress. *see* progress reports
purpose statement, 407
recommendation, 406
short. *see* short reports
writing process, 405
writing techniques Web site, 442
requests, 8, 57–58
research
    analysis of data, 393
    branching questions, 390
    causation, 394–395
    CD-ROM databases, 387
    closed questions, 389, 390
    companies, for job search, 490–491
    convenience sample, 392
    correlation, 394–395
    data source, 393
    definition, 385
    documentation of sources, 395–398
    faulty logic, 394–395
    interview questions, 388–392
    judgment samples, 392
    multiple-choice questions, 390
    news Web sites, 387
    numbers analysis, 393–394
    online sources, 385–387
    open questions, 389, 390
    population, 392
    primary, 385
    print sources, 385–387
    random sample, 392
    sample, 392
    secondary, 385
    subject matter directories, 385
    survey questions, 388–392
respondents, 388
responses to complaints, 189
resumes
    action verbs, 512–513
    attention-getting resumes, 503
    career achievements, 517–518
    career objective, 517
    chronological, 505, 506, 511–513
    communications skills, 517–518
    computer layout and design, 504

definition, 503
education, 518–519
formats, 511–520
functional/combination, 505,
    507–508, 514
honours and awards, 519
interpersonal profile, 517–518
kinds of, 505–520
length, 520–521
new headings, creation of, 520
references, 520
scannable, 521–523
skills, 505, 509–510, 514–517
Web sites, 517
retreats, 351
reverse chronological resume, 511
reverse chronology listing, 505
reverse psychology, 122
revision
    after feedback, 81
    checklist, 78
    co-authored documents, 341–343
    definition, 72, 77
    light, 78
    paragraph. *see* paragraph revision
    sentences. *see* sentence revision
    time for, 74, 81
revisions after, 81
RFPs (Requests for Proposals), 408,
    417
right word. *see* word choice
Robert Half International Inc., 236
Robert's Rules of Order, 351
Rogers Communications, 302
Royal Bank, 35–36, 411
Royal Roads University, 137
rudeness, costs of, 107
rules, 261
run-on sentences, 294–295, 303
Russell, Worrick, 50

S

salary and benefits negotiation, 555
sales
    presentation, 367
    promotion, 186
    proposals, 411
    reports, 406
salutation, 151, 155
sample, 392
sample letters
    block format, 152, 156
    claim letter, 154
    collection letter, 152
    goodwill letter, 157

informative letter, 156, 157
job application, 531–532, 534
letter of recommendation, 153
mixed punctuation, 152, 153, 156
modified block format, 153,
    154, 157
negative, 206–207
open punctuation, 154
two-page letter, 156, 157
two-point punctuation, 156, 157
sample memos
    analytical proposal, 162, 164
    informative report, 426–427
    negative, to subordinates, 213
    positive, 163
    positive message, 185
    short report, 162, 164
    subordinates, to, 213
    two-page, 164
sans serif fonts, 91
Sato, Mitsuru, 231–234
Saville-Troike, Muriel, 57
scale, 476
Scotiabank, 487
Scott, Lee, 28
secondary audience, 25–26
secondary purposes
    informative messages, 183
    negative messages, 205
    persuasive messages, 228
    positive messages, 183
secondary research, 385
"Secrets of Powerful Presentations",
    32
segmented bar graphs, 472
Select Appointments North America
    survey, 323
selection of information, 27
self-absorption, 323–324
self-recruitment, 495
semicolon, 308
sensing types, 32
sensitivity, and international
    audience, 58
sentence fragments, 21, 303–304
sentence revision
    active verbs, 261–265
    combining sentences, 267
    complex sentences, 268
    compound sentences, 268
    compound-complex sentences, 268
    gerunds, 266
    grouping into chunks, 269
    infinitives, 266
    long sentences, 269
    parallel structure, 270

readers in sentence, 271
repetition, reduction of, 269
sentence length, 268–270
sentence structure, 268–270
simple sentences, 268
strong action verbs, 263–265
subject, 267
subject/verb closeness, 269–270
tight writing, 265–267
verbs, 267
weight of sentence, 263–265
wordy phrases, elimination of,
    265–267
sentences
    basic pattern, 464
    combining, 267, 331–332
    complex, 268
    compound, 268
    compound-complex, 268
    definition, 302
    length, 268–270
    long, 269
    numbers at beginning of, 310–311
    revision. *see* sentence revision
    run-on, 294–295, 303
    short, 267
    simple, 268
    smooth, 267
    structure, 268–270
    summary, 530
    topic, 271–272, 432
    wordy, 437
serial comma, 559
serif fonts, 91
Shan, Jacqueline, 121
Shoppers Drug Mart, 12
short reports
    analytical reports, 427–428
    blueprints, 431
    closure reports, 425
    feasibility reports, 425
    format, 428
    headings, 432
    information organization strategies,
        428–430
    informative headings, 434
    informative reports, 425
    justification reports, 427–428
    organizational pattern, 425
    paragraph without numbers, 431
    revised paragraph without
        numbers, 431–432
    sample informative memo report,
        426–427
    sample memo, 162, 164
    style, 430–434

talking heads, 434
tight writing, 431
topic headings, 432
topic sentences, 432
transitions, 432
word choices, 431
short words, 280
signpost, 368
silence, 57
simple sentences, 268
singular possessives, 133, 146
situational interviews, 553
skills resumes, 505, 509–510, 514–517
slang, 283
Sleeman Breweries Limited, 36, 537
Sleeman, John, 537
Sleep Country, 142
SMART goals, 176
social distance, 260
social styles, 32
solicited letter
  body paragraphs, 535
  first paragraph, 533
  last paragraph, 535
  organization, 533
  sample, 531–532
  when to use, 529
sources, documentation of, 395–398
spatial arrangements, 54
spatial pattern, 430
speaking, 12
speaking, importance of, 8
specificity, 433
spell checking, 79–80, 317
spelling, 526
spelling differences, 297
Spilka, Rachel, 74
split infinitives, 559
square brackets, 309
stacked bar graphs, 472
standard agenda, 356
standard English, 566
Statistics Canada, 31, 392
stories, 467–470
storyboard, 76
strategy, 36
stress interview, 553–554
Strunk and White online, 268
stuffy tone, 235
style, 37, 259–260
  see also writing style
subject lines
  bolded, 161
  context, 183
  directed, 241–242

effective, 483
email messages, 174
goodwill, highlighting, 190
informative email messages, 174
informative messages, 183–184
letters, 155
negative email messages, 175
negative message, 214
negative messages, 205
organizational pattern, 190
persuasive email messages, 175
persuasive messages, 241–242
positive email messages, 174
progress reports, 418
short, 175
subject matter directories, 385
subject of clause, 300
subject-verb agreement, 166, 297–299
subjects, 388
subordinate clauses, 21, 302, 331
summaries, 188
summary paragraph, 530
summary sentence, 530
survey questions, 388–392

T

table of contents, 443
tables, 443, 470, 471, 473
talking heads, 434, 483
Tannen, Deborah, 47, 55
TD-Canada Trust, 35
teams. *see also* groups
  dynamics, 354
  ground rules for, 333
  meetings, 351
  productivity, and meetings, 351
technical terms, 38, 283
Telford, Adrian, 336
tempo, 371
testing designs, 95
thank-you notes, 189
that, 299
theory, use of, 38
there, 297
thinking types, 32
this, 300
Tim Hortons, 32
Timberjack Corporation, 12
time
  cultural perception of, 55
  management, 176, 441–442
Time is money, 54
title page, 442
Toastmasters International, 368
Tomlinson, Ray, 169

tone, 127–128, 235, 260, 538
topic headings, 432
topic sentences, 271–272, 432
Torvalds, Linus, 12
touch, 53–54
Townsend, Burt, 105
Toyota, 105, 233
transitions, 272, 331, 432, 464
transmission of message, 27
transmittals, 186–188
truncated graphs, 476
Turczyniak, Michael, 141
two-point punctuation, 151, 157

U

U.S. Secretary's Commission on Achieving Necessary Skills (SCANS), 5
U.S. states, postal abbreviations, 159
underlining, 310
understatement, 56–57
United Nations, 327
unity, 271
unsolicited letter. *see* prospecting letter

V

values, 32, 49–51
Vancity Credit Union, 121
Vassos, Tom, 359
venting, 339
verbal, 559
verbs
  action, for resumes, 512–513
  active, 261–265
  concrete, 500
  objects, 300
  passive, 110, 261–265
  simple tenses, 437
  strong, 261, 263–265
  tenses, 437
vested interest, 231–234
Victor, David, 48–49
video interviews, 556
Vietnamese Canadians, 50
virtual meetings, 359
viruses, 177
visuals
  accuracy, 475–476
  audience analysis, 37
  bar chart, 470, 472
  chartjunk, 474
  clip art, 47
  colour, use of, 473
  definition, 467

design, 471–473
ethical, 475–476
figures, 470
final presentation/document, 467
histograms, 472
integration into text, 474
line graph, 470, 472
matrix table, 468–469
oral presentations, 372–374, 375, 476
pictograms, 472
pie chart, 470, 471
rough drafts, 467
stories, 467–470
tables, 470, 471
truncated graphs, 476
types of, 470
vocal interferences, 431
voice
active, 101
narrative, 254
oral presentations, 371
passive, 101
use of your, 371
volume, 371
volunteer community involvement, 493

W

Wall Data, 121
watchdog, 25–26
watchdog audience, 25–26
we, 110
Web page design, 93
Webb, John, 49
WebEx, 352
Weldon, Kate, 561
What Color Is Your Parachute?
(Bolles), 489
which, 300
white space, 87–88
who, 300, 422–423
whom, 300, 422–423
Wong, Milton, 123

word choice
business jargon, 283
bypassing, 279
confusing, 284–290
connotation, 279–280
denotation, 279
formality, 379
jargon, 283
meaning, 279
purpose, 279
response, 279–280
slang, 283
spell checkers, 284–290
technical jargon, 283
wordiness, 265–267
words
concrete, 437
etymological origins, 282–283
formal, 281
meanings of, 282–283
negative, 122–124
negative connotations, 122–124, 280
nonsexist, 59
obscure, 500
positive connotations, 280
power implications of, 127
redundant, 437
short, 280
work in progress, 72
working thesis, 389
workopolis, 489
workplace writing, top problems, 186
writer's block, 82
writing, 5
definition, 72
multitasking, 72
need for, 9
tight, 265–267
you-attitude, 107
"Writing on Both Sides of the Brain", 71
writing process
activities in, 72–73

described, 71–72
different processes, 72–73
recursive nature, 72
reports, 405
time lines, 75
writing style
good style, 259–260
improvement of, 261
organizational culture, 272–273
"rule", 261
short reports, 430–434
written communication, importance of, 8

X

Xerox, 561

Y

you, 542–543
you-attitude
checking for, 126
checklist, 115
conflict resolution, 341
creation of, 107–111
definition, 107, 109
emotions, 109
feelings, 109
impersonal constructions, 110, 111
job application letters, 538
in negative situations, 110–111
vs. nonsexist language, 160
passive verbs, 110, 111
in positive situations, 110
reader benefit, 143
reader, focus on, 109–111
readers' needs, 111–112
we, 110
words to use, 111–112

Z

Zellers, 141